New Perspectives on the Divide Between National and International Law

New Perspectives on the Divide Between National and International Law

Edited by

JANNE NIJMAN AND ANDRÉ NOLLKAEMPER

OXFORD

UNIVERSITY PRESS

UNIVERSITY PRESS

Great Clarendon Street, Oxford, OX2 6DP,
United Kingdom

Oxford University Press is a department of the University of Oxford.
It furthers the University's objective of excellence in research, scholarship,
and education by publishing worldwide. Oxford is a registered trade mark of
Oxford University Press in the UK and in certain other countries

Published in the United States of America by Oxford University Press
198 Madison Avenue, New York, NY 10016, United States of America

British Library Cataloguing in Publication Data
Data available

Library of Congress Cataloging in Publication Data
Data available

ISBN 978–0–19–923194–2

Preface

This book is one of the results of the research program *Interactions between International and National Law*, funded by the Netherlands Organisation for Scientific Research under its 'Pioneer Programme' that was carried out between 2000 and 2007 at the Amsterdam Center for International Law, University of Amsterdam under the leadership of André Nollkaemper. A large part of the program was focused on developments in positive international law that reflect and cause the ever increasing and complex continuities and discontinuities between international law and domestic law. This resulted in several PhDs and academic publications by members of the research group (see <http://www.jur.uva.nl/aciluk/home.cfm>).

The research on interactions between international and domestic law as a matter of positive law was embedded in, and at the same time gave impetus to, theoretical reflections on these interactions. A series of seminars was organized to discuss the theoretical aspects of the interactions between international and domestic law. These seminars culminated in a larger conference in June 2004. Most of the chapters in the book are substantially developed versions of papers presented originally during these events. Not all participants in the seminars and conference could contribute to this book. However, their intellectual contribution is reflected in several of the chapters in this book. We thank in particular Armin von Bogdandy, Ellen Hey, David Kennedy, Benedict Kingsbury, Harold Hongju Koh, Martti Koskenniemi, and Susan Marks for their contributions.

This book has been made possible by the input and energy of the members of the 'Pionier team' into the research program as a whole, and to the project leading to this book in particular: Ward Ferdinandusse, Hege Kjos, Jann Kleffner, Nikos Lavranos, Geranne Lautenbach, Fabian Raimondo, and Erika de Wet. Thanks also to the other members of the Department of International Law and the Amsterdam Center for International Law in which the research was embedded. Financially, the research leading to this book was supported by the Netherlands Organisation for Scientific Research, and (for the June 2004 Conference) the Royal Academy of Sciences. We thank the student assistants Laura Groeneveld, Cassandra Steer and Linde Wolters for their editorial work

Janne Nijman and André Nollkaemper
January 2007

Contents

Contents

Table of Cases

INTERNATIONAL COURTS

International Criminal Tribunal for the Former Yugoslavia

Permanent Court of Arbitration

Permanent Court of International Justice

DOMESTIC COURTS

Argentina

Australia

Austria

Belgium

Bosnia and Herzegovina

Botswana

Canada

Table of Legislation

List of Contributors

Gaetano Arangio-Ruiz Chairman of Chamber Three of the Iran-US Claims Tribunal

Phillip Allott Professor of International Public Law, University of Cambridge

Catherine Brölmann Associate Professor, Amsterdam Center for International Law, Universiteit van Amsterdam

Giorgio Gaja Professor of International Law, University of Florence

William Burke-White Assistant Professor of Law, University of Pennsylvania School of Law

Christine Chinkin Professor of International Law, London School of Economics

Janne Nijman Assistant Professor, Amsterdam Center for International Law, Universiteit van Amsterdam

André Nollkaemper Professor of Public International Law, Amsterdam Center for International Law, Universiteit van Amsterdam

Mayo Moran Associate Professor and Dean, Faculty of Law, University of Toronto

Andreas Paulus Professor of International Law, University of Göttingen

Anne Peters Professor Dr iur, LLM (Harvard), University of Basel Switzerland

Lourens du Plessis Professor of Public Law, University of Stellenbosch

Anne-Marie Slaughter Dean, Woodrow Wilson School of Public and International Affairs, Princeton University

Christian Walter Professor of Public Law, including International and European Law, University of Münster

Introduction

Janne Nijman and André Nollkaemper

1. Aim of the book

This book aims to contribute to our understanding of one of the most pressing issues of modern international law: the disconnection, or 'divide', between the international legal order, on the one hand, and the legal orders of over 190 sovereign states on the other. The book contains 12 chapters that offer alternative perspectives on the relationship between the international and the domestic domain. These chapters address questions such as whether the traditionally dominant perspective of the separation or divide between international and domestic law is still valid in view of developments as globalization, the emergence of common values, and the dispersion of authority over different public and private actors. If not, what perspective can replace it? Has the time come for a (re-)assertion of a monistic perspective, or is our understanding better served by a pluralistic perspective that recognizes the complexities and incompatibilities in legal reality?

The unique nature of this book lies in the fact that the majority of its contributions are of a reflective and theoretical nature. They distance themselves to some degree from positive international law. In the latter area, in recent decades we have seen a substantial number of studies into the relationship between positive international law and national law, for instance, in the fields of human rights law,[1] criminal law,[2] and environmental law.[3] We also have seen studies of how particular states or, on a comparative basis, groupings of states, have dealt with the question of the relationship between international law and domestic law.[4] The OUP online service *International Law in Domestic Courts*[5] further adds to

---

[1] C Heyns, F Viljoen, *The Impact of the United Nations Human Rights Treaties on the Domestic Level* (The Hague: Kluwer Law International, 2002).

[2] WN Ferdinandusse, *Direct Application of International Law in National Courts* (The Hague: TMC Asser Press, 2006).

[3] M Anderson and P Galizi (eds), *International Environmental Law in National Courts* (London: British Institute of International and Comparative Law, 2002).

[4] DB Hollis, MR Blakeslee, and LB Ederington (eds), *National Treaty Law and Practice: Dedicated to the Memory of Monroe Leigh* (Leiden: Nijhoff, 2005); FG Jacobs and S Roberts (eds), *The Effect of Treaties in Domestic Law* (United Kingdom Comparative Law Series, London: Sweet & Maxwell, 1986).

[5] International Law in Domestic Courts database, available at <http://ildc.oxfordlawreports.com/>.

our knowledge of how international and domestic law interact. However, the increasing empirical information on this interaction has not been matched by studies that help us understand at a more fundamental level the directions in which the relationships between domestic legal orders and the international legal order are evolving.

Although theoretical debates on the divide between international law and national law are about as old as the phenomenon of international law itself, [6] in recent years this debate seems to have evaporated. The debates peaked in the time of Anzilotti, Triepel, Scelle, and Kelsen. Still in 1899 Triepel had sighed: 'Die Frage nach dem Verhältnisse des Völkerrechts zum Landesrecht, die auf den folgenden Blätter erhörtert werden soll, gehört zu den stiefmutterlich behandelten kehren der Jurisprudenz'.[7] In the first part of the 20th century, several courses at the Hague Academy were devoted to the topic.[8] However, during the course of the 20th century the debate came to an end. Every textbook on international law still uses the concepts of monism and dualism to describe the main perspectives on the relationship between international and national law. However, most textbooks also take the position that these perspectives are of little use in making students understand practice. A common position is that practice is not in conformity with either monism or dualism, and that one should therefore turn to practice. Brownlie noted that an increasing number of jurists wish to escape from the dichotomy between monism and dualism, holding that the logical consequences of both theories conflict with the way in which international and national organs behave.[9] In that vein, other textbooks also take the position that the dogmatic dispute on issues of monism and dualism is now irrelevant, that international law has nothing to say on the matter except for the rule that a State cannot invoke national law to justify non-compliance with international law, and that otherwise one simply has to turn to national law.[10] On the whole, modern scholarship has become pragmatic, inductive, and largely anti-theoretical. It fits in the broader trend away from abstract theories in favour of technical and practical descriptions of how things work.[11] Perhaps the silence of modern scholarship is also inspired

---

[6] See, eg on the 17th century emergence of the sovereign State as 'a precondition to the dualism between the international and internal legal orders that became central to the modern law of nations', R Lesaffer, 'Peace treaties from Lodi to Westphalia' in R Lesaffer (ed), *Peace Treaties and International Law in European History* (Cambridge: CUP, 2004) 13–14.

[7] H Triepel, *Völkerrecht und Landesrecht* (Leipzig: CL Hirschfeld, 1899) 1.

[8] H Kelsen, 'Les Rapports de Système entre le Droit Interne et le Droit International Public' (1926) 14 Recueil des Cours de L'Académie de Droit International 227; H Triepel, 'Les Rapports entre le Droit Interne et le Droit International' (1923) 1 Recueil des Cours 77.

[9] I Brownlie, *Principles of Public International Law* (5th edn, Oxford: OUP, 1998) 33–34.

[10] P Malanzcuk (ed), *Akehurst's Modern Introduction to International Law* (7th rev edn, London: Routledge, 1997) 63–64.

[11] M Koskenniemi, *From Apology to Utopia. The Structure of International Legal Argument* (2nd edn, Cambridge: CUP, 2006) 3, 187–88.

by a fear of grand theories; by a post-modern scepticism of total theories that would unify our understanding of the grand issues of international law.[12]

The pragmatic approach has come at a cost. Whatever the pitfalls of the theoretical conceptions of monism and dualism, at least they provided observers with a perspective on how to understand the relationship between international and national law and, in their normative dimensions, with a view on the direction in which that relationship should evolve. The dominant pragmatic position is lacking in this respect. On this point at least, international legal scholarship has turned apologetic—there is no other perspective for understanding what is happening in practice other than what States do. Sir Percy Spender wrote that 'it is competent for a State party to any treaty or convention to pass a law binding on its own authorities to the effect that, notwithstanding anything in the treaty or convention, certain provisions thereof binding on that State shall not apply, or to legislate in terms clearly inconsistent with, and intended to override, the terms of an existing treaty'.[13] That certainly is a view that corresponds in large part to practice in most States, including the United States (with its later in time rule), the United Kingdom (with its ruling doctrine of parliamentary supremacy) and the Netherlands (with its limiting doctrine of direct effect). But is it necessarily the case that what States do—in this situation a persistent violation of the law—in itself generates a norm (or rather, a liberty) of public international law? Does the *fact* that states retain the competence under their national law to enact laws inconsistent with their international obligations mean that we have to accept an international legal liberty to do so?

By providing little guidance on our thinking regarding possible normative development, international legal scholarship also fails its primary task of educating new international lawyers. Responsible teaching of international law does not confine what we teach our students to a pragmatic approach that has nothing to say about the choices that students, once they become practitioners, can make and thereby help shape development.

It is the aim of this book to increase our understanding and thus contribute to leading international law theory away from current pragmatism towards a new perspective which is grounded in practice yet reaches beyond mere pragmatism, recognizing the importance of more conceptual and normative perspectives on the evolution of the relationship between national and international law. Aiming for a contribution to international law theory, it will ultimately direct us beyond this particular phenomenon to confront the idea of a changing global society and the changing role of international law in that society.

---

[12] JE Nijman, *The concept of international legal personality. An inquiry into the history and theory of international law* (The Hague: TMC Asser Press, 2004) 397.

[13] Separate opinion to the judgment of the International Court of Justice in the *Guardianship of Infants Case (Netherlands v Sweden)* 1958 ICJ Rep, paras 125–26.

As a prelude to the chapters containing alternative perspectives on the relationship between international and national law, this introduction serves four purposes. First, we will clarify the 'theoretical' nature of the perspectives contained in the book (section 2). Second, we briefly review the classic positions of monism and dualism. Understanding the context of the emergence of monism in response to 19th century dualism will provide an essential yardstick for assessing modern perspectives on the divide between international and domestic law (section 3). Third, we will briefly review current legal developments, which challenge the discipline of international law to rethink these old theories (section 4). Finally, this introduction will provide a roadmap and indicate how these challenges are addressed by the various contributions to this book (section 5).

2. Legal doctrine, theory, and philosophy

Most of the contributions to this book abstract from questions of positive international law. Though most chapters do refer to developments in positive law, they aim to enhance, at a more general level, our insight and understanding of the relationship between international and domestic law. As a whole, the book represents a mix of legal doctrine, legal philosophy, and legal theory.

Legal doctrine is about rationalization and systematization for the short-term, to meet particular—more technical—legal problems. As noted by Cotterrell, 'Legal doctrine is to be organised, systematized and generalized just sufficiently to meet the needs of the moment. Concepts are used pragmatically and not necessarily with concern for broader consistency of meaning.'[14] Legal doctrine is relevant for inquiries into the relationship between international and domestic law. It can deal with such questions as the status and meaning of the principle of supremacy of international law or the principle that States cannot rely on domestic law to justify non-compliance with obligations under international law. Some of the contributions to this book are largely of a doctrinal nature.[15]

Legal philosophy encompasses philosophical speculation on matters of law or related to law.[16] Like legal doctrine, legal philosophy can encompass inquiries into the relationship between international and domestic law. It can address such questions as whether international law (in contrast to national law) is really law and whether a unity between international and domestic law properly reflects the unity of mankind. Some of the chapters of this book contain elements that can be properly characterized as legal philosophy.[17]

Legal theory is positioned between legal doctrine and legal philosophy. It is neither merely systematizing nor contemplating particular practices, nor does it solely

---

[14] R Cotterrell, *The Politics of Jurisprudence: A Critical Introduction to Legal Philosophy* (Philadelphia: University of Pennsylvania Press, 1989) 6.   [15] eg, Anne Peters, ch 10.
[16] Cotterell (n 14 above) 2.   [17] eg, Phillip Allott, ch 3.

address conceptual and normative questions. It is rooted in actual practice which illustrates or evidences a particular phenomenon—yet when explaining this phenomenon, it includes external, conceptual, normative elements and ideas in order to analyse the phenomenon in a broader and more general context and to understand the more general and fundamental implications of the phenomenon for the system as a whole. Legal theory thus is ambivalent: it is both rooted in practice and speculative in nature. It captures in a way a dialectic movement between philosophical speculation about possible legal futures and current (legal) developments in practice.[18]

In this volume we are indeed seeking to postulate general legal theoretical findings on the relationship between international and national law that are open to sociological, that is, more empirical input, as well as inclusive of philosophical, that is, more speculative input. Most of the chapters in this book are stirred by, and often also explore, particular current legal developments. However, for the most part they do not confine themselves thereto, but seek to contribute to our understanding at a more general level. They vary in the emphasis put on either the empirical or the normative, speculative 'side' of the slope. Our aim is to present the contributions as an integrated whole, in the sense that each of the chapters forms a building block, with varying degrees of emphasis on doctrinal or philosophical aspects.

The theoretical reflection on how national law relates to international law and vice versa will eventually confront us with questions which lie beyond the positive law level, such as the deformalization of international law, the nature of the international community, and the legitimacy of (international) law. With these questions our conception of international law also comes into play. Reflections developed on the basis of positive international law, judicial decisions, and legal developments thus will re-direct us to a meta-juridical level. We accept this as a task of our discipline. International law scholarship should not pursue a kind of rootless—groundless—approach which may be pragmatic but also disconnected from international law's fundamental purpose. International law scholarship—also when reflecting upon the relationship between national and international law—can not abstain from making its own particular contribution to a problem which has much more than a purely *legal* dimension.

The book does not aim to present one grand or 'total' theory on the relationship between national and international law. However, we can observe that in the theoretical reflections made by the authors, we do find returning elements which indicate more general developments in both legal practice and legal theory. Notably, these include the de-formalization of law, a focus on common fundamental values, a quest for new (sources of) authority, and the constitutionalization of an international community. We will return to these elements in the conclusion of the book.[19]

---

[18] See for a further typology of types of legal theory, Philip Allott, ch 3.   [19] Ch 12.

3. The origins of the debate on the divide between international and national law: the dualism-monism dichotomy

Any attempt to develop new theoretical perspectives on the relationship between international and national law somehow has to build on the legacy of what historically have been the two main theories on the matter: dualism and monism.

Dualism and monism confirm the dual image explained in the previous section, be it to a different degree at various moments in time. On the one hand, both theoretical models intend to describe the legal reality—ie the empirical, practically rooted side of the story—yet being theoretical models they intend to systematize, analyse, and explain legal practice and subsequently extrapolate future developments. The later aim includes a normative element, which brings us outside the positive law realm.

The chapters in this volume will pay ample attention to the question of the extent to which these theories are still useful for understanding present-day legal developments. However, one aspect of these theories that needs to be highlighted in this introduction is that both theoretical models were responses to somewhat time-bound and non-legal (essentially political) problems. The fact that international law scholarship has for a long time, and is arguably still today, engrossed in the monism-dualism dichotomy may well have prevented us from developing new perspectives on the divide between national and international law, and addressing the questions *currently* at stake. In order to accomplish our present intellectual task, we thus need to understand the intellectual task our discipline previously faced and which was at the origin of the early 20th century debate on monism and dualism.

The monism-dualism debate as it took place in the early decades of the 20th century should be understood as the legal manifestation of a broader (juridico-)political debate dominating intellectual, cultural, and political life at the time: the heated discussions on the ('old' concepts of) State and Sovereignty, and the position of the individual within the (organization of the) polity. During these critical decades in the history of Europe, for many the principal concern was the post World War I crisis of democracy and its dangers for individual freedom. The Interbellum crisis of international law should be understood as part of this more comprehensive European crisis. As in other disciplines, great minds took the lead in confronting the crisis and international law scholarship flourished as a consequence. The debate on monism and dualism, which was at a high point during the inter-war years, should be read in this context. That is to say, in general terms, monism may be understood as part of a rejection of old concepts and an attempt to reconstruct international law and theory in a new and modern way, with an eye for the position of the individual (freedom) in international law. This may be read as the discipline's response to the crisis of democracy.[20] The dualist model was also used by the discipline to reconstruct, however from a more restorative perspective: neither a new world order, nor a new international law was the objective. Rather, it focused on the restoration of the old classical tradition of voluntarism and the doctrine of sovereignty as its threshold. The early 20th century monist-dualist controversy was part of this broader scholarly debate which for a significant part, due to the political context, dealt with issues such as the identity of international law, its independent relevance next to morality and politics, State sovereignty, and the protection of the human individual. The monist and dualist models as we tend to use them today have their origins in this scholarly debate and context.

Dualism was predominant in orthodox 19th century international law theory and often inspired by Hegelian Thought.[21] The State was then understood as a *real* metaphysical Being, mystifying the personality of the State and sanctifying its sovereignty. International law was conceived of merely as *external* law of the State.[22] Under this view, international law concerns the external life of the state but it is not above the State since it has its source *in* the State (will). Internal and external public law, international law and municipal law are completely separate orders. The State's sovereignty and power are not limited by international law, on the contrary international law is used as an instrument to exercise them. Rather than be protected against the State, in this view individual freedom can only be realized by self-sacrifice in service of the State, by the individual (will) being submerged into the State (will). The State is understood in mythical terms: 'the march of God in the world'.[23] Hegelian thought marked international law theory significantly because of its glorification of the State and its sovereignty. Hence, the separate, independent existence of international law as truly *law* was often denied, or its identity was defined as nothing more than each State's external law.[24] In Triepel's theory we see clearly how his conception of the State as a real personality leads him to accept dualism as the only possible perspective: 'two spheres that at best adjoin one another but never intersect'.[25]

---

[20] We can see this in the work of both the monist-*positivist* scholar Hans Kelsen and the monist-*natural law* scholar Hersch Lauterpacht. See Nijman (n 12 above) 85 et seq.

[21] Hegel: 'The state in and by itself is the ethical whole, the actualization of freedom; and it is an *absolute* end of reason that freedom should be actual.' TM Knox (ed), *Hegel's Philosophy of Right* (Oxford: OUP, 1967) 279.

[22] GWF Hegel, *Grundlinien der Philosophie des Rechts* ref § 259 and 330. Also, eg A Lasson, *System der Rechtsphilosophie* (Berlin und Leipzig: J Guttentag, 1882), on the '*Fehlender Rechtscharakter*' of international law, at 394–407.   [23] Knox (n 21 above) 279.

[24] Lasson (n 22 above) 389 and 394: 'Zwischen den Staaten als souveränen Wesen is zwar ein eigentlicher Rechtszustand nicht möglich'.

[25] Triepel, *Völkerrecht und Landesrecht* (n 7 above) 111: 'Völkerrecht und Landesrecht sind nicht nur verscheidene Rechtstheile, sonders auch verscheidene Rechtsordnungen...Sie sind zwei Kreise, die sich höchstens berühren, niemals schneiden'.

This origin could open the door to extremes. Viewed as rooted in a Hegelian-marked concept of State and (International) Law, dualism was soon conceived of as going hand in hand with 'the idolatry of the State' as well as favouring absolutist and authoritarian tendencies. Having these philosophical conceptual origins, (statist) dualism—confronted by renewing (often monist) scholars—was set (perceptually) in the corner of absolute sovereignty, nationalist fanaticism, state mysticism, and the sacrifice of the individual to the State.

However, not all scholars who favoured the dualist model worked from a Hegelian State perspective.[26] Those who had left the (orthodox) origins of dualism behind focused more on the confirmation of the legal nature of positive international law. A peaceful international community depends on basic rules of conduct agreed upon by sovereign States who keep away from each others internal affairs. As such, dualism operated as a model to uphold the 'positive law' identity of international law, to reconcile sovereignty and international law by the concept of self-obligation, and recognized the Family of Nations as an inter-State order (only).[27] Yet its presumption of the State as an actual pre- and meta-legal, social phenomenon, or person included a normative dimension of securing sovereign space and independent presence at the international stage. International law did not and should not govern national social relations. But dualism was also increasingly based on more inductive reasoning, as during the 20th century more and more States were recognized as independent members of the international community and the 'dualist' model dominated constitutional arrangements.

Still, it is fair to posit that the rise of monism within (international) legal scholarship was a response to these mainly 19th century theories of State and Law. Not merely in early 20th century German and Austrian scholarship but also in, eg French, British, and Dutch Scholarship we find monism as a feature of a forceful response to Hegelian driven theories of State, Sovereignty, and (International) Law.

Many Interbellum international law scholars responded with total rejection of dualism and adherence to the monist perspective to liberate the individual and its freedom.[28] Scholars such as Kelsen, Scelle, and Brierly aimed at strengthening the position of the individual, democracy, and subjecting power to the universal rule of law by arguing the existence of international law as a law limiting the state's actions. More than being a response to the technical legal argument of (statist)

---

[26] Not all 19th century orthodox theorists were influenced by German philosophy and jurisprudence, John Austin (1790–1859) is of course the other leading jurist behind the triumph of legal positivism in the later 19th century. He conceived of international law as 'no law proper', merely positive morality, and so, international law and domestic law were completely separate. J Austin, *The Province of Jurisprudence Determined* (1832) (Cambridge: CUP, 1995), Lecture V and Lecture VI.

[27] See, eg G Jellinek, *Allgemeine Staatslehre* (Berlin: J Springer, 1929) at 378–79, 387, and 393.

[28] See, eg Brierly's rejection of Hegel's influence on international law as 'devastating', JL Brierly, 'The Basis of Obligation in International Law' in Lauterpacht and Waldock (eds), *The Basis of Obligation in International Law and Other Papers by the late James Leslie Brierly* (Oxford: Clarendon Press, 1958) 29, 36. See for Kelsen's critique, H Kelsen, *Das Problem der Souveränität und die Theorie des Völkerrechts* (Tübingen: Mohr, 1920), 315–18.

dualism on the relationship between national and international law it responded rather to its moral and political implications. Monism was first and foremost an attempt to restrict power of the State and to empower the individual and protect human dignity.

For instance, Scelle, who saw a global society of humankind rather than of States—*la société humaine universelle*—thus conceived international law as normative federalism, monism without disguise.[29] With the French Third Republic going through a political crisis due to parliamentary absolutism, democracy was in jeopardy. In Scelle's perspective, international law defined and constrained domestic (legal and political) competences. He argued the hierarchical superiority of global solidarity and of the universal society and its law. Monism was in essence about the distribution of competences, about constraining (abuse of) power—*détournement de pouvoir*—by law. As such it was a fundamentally juridico-political—ie *Rechtsstaat* values-driven—perspective on international law inseparable from the issues at stake within the domestic political societies. The distribution of competences and its legitimization concerned a *constitutional* matter then as much as it does today. Similarly, Kelsen's monistic perspective was an integral part of a defence of democracy and the individual. He also welds the whole hierarchical universal legal order together with the notion of competence. Kelsen's rejection has been most rigorous, as he eliminated the concept of State sovereignty altogether and argued for the identification of State and legal order.[30]

The heritage of international law theories bequeathed to our disciple in the early 20th century, when confronted with a very different political context, may explain the (Interwar) heydays of international legal theory. The monist *v* dualist model reflected more general lines of opposition: State as Law *v* State as actual Being; Rule of Law *v* State as 'Absolute Power on Earth'; State Will as a purely legal phenomenon *v* State Will as a socio-political phenomenon; Law as distribution of Competence and as defining Power *v* Law as an instrument of Power; Sovereignty of Law *v* Sovereignty of State; the apology of international law *v* the apology of national law; World federalism *v* Nationalism (at a moderate as well as a more extreme rate); Progressive political powers *v* Conservative/political powers; empowerment of the individual *v* empowerment of the nation-State; Democracy *v* Authoritarianism; universal human society *v* society of nation-States and so on and so forth.

The monist and dualist models which emerged from this debate and continued to structure international law thinking, were thus primarily a response to political

[29] G Scelle, 'La Doctrine de Duguit et les Fondements du Droit des Gens' (1932) 1–2 Archives de Philosophie du Droit et de Sociologie Juridique (Sirey Paris) 108.

[30] H Kelsen, *Introduction to the Problems of Legal Theory* (transl of 1934 edition of *Reine Rechtslehre*, transl, B Litschewski Paulson and SL Paulson), (Oxford: Clarendon Press, 1992) 100, 116, 121–24. 'The theoretical dissolution of the dogma of sovereignty, the principal instrument of imperialistic ideology directed against international law, is one of the most substantial achievements of the Pure Theory of Law.'

problems rather than legal ones. They both took up their own conceptual life within international law arguments with fundamental consequences for our perception of the relationship between international and domestic law. Monism came to be understood as a relative denial of a fundamental divide between international and domestic law, connected with universal, cosmopolitan, or even utopian connotations. Dualism tends to be understood as an articulation and appreciation of a solid divide between international and domestic law, connected with a conceptual (apologetic) affirmation of state sovereignty and international law as inter-State law. In this way, the monism-dualism paradigm has come to structure international law scholarship.

However, as the terms are used today, the models are disconnected from their contextual origins and the urgent problem of endangered European democracy with which they actually dealt. What was in origin an intensely political and moral debate became an issue approached rather pragmatically. From being a debate loaded with political and moral elements it became a more 'normal' doctrinal topic although always marked, consciously or subconsciously, by a conviction of either the moral supremacy of international law or the supremacy of the State will. Late 20th century textbooks at the same time increasingly expressed the relative importance of monism and dualism, as in practice both models rarely apply satisfactorily.[31] With the relatively minor importance of both perspectives and the more general withdrawal of philosophical elements, the monism-dualism debate dried up.

4. Reasons for revisiting the issue

The political and social context that inspired the original theories of dualism and monism is a very different one from that of today. The emergence of new non-legal developments, different from those that inspired traditional monism and dualism, call for alternative theoretical approaches that allow us to systematize, explain, and understand changes in the relationship between international and national law and, at the same time, to give direction to the future development of international and national law.

While protection of sovereignty, individual freedom, and rule of law remain relevant external factors, they are now part of more complex processes and interests. Above all, they have been redefined and submerged by the process of globalization. Increasing cross-border flow of services, goods and capital, mobility, and communication have undermined any stable notion of what is national and what is international.[32]

---

[31] Above, text to nn 9–10.
[32] See for references in this volume to developments that may prompt us to change our understanding of the relationship between international and domestic law: Peters, 252–54; Du Plessis, 310–11.

To be sure, these developments are not entirely new. Globalization is an old phenomenon and its current manifestations are certainly not something that is confined to the new millennium. We have long seen claims that the utility of dualism-monism will decline because of intensification of international relations, because of expansion *ratione personae*, *loci* and *materiea* of international law, because of growth of international institutions, because of the increasing opening of national constitutions to international law, etc.[33] Nonetheless, it is the premise underlying this book that the developments which we loosely cover by the label globalization, and which affect the relationship between the domestic and the international domain are sufficiently substantial to justify our exploration of new theories pertaining to the connection between the national and the international legal order.

In our conclusion to this book, we will highlight three developments. The first is the emergence of a set of international values that underlies policies of states, international organizations, and non-governmental organizations, and that straddles the boundaries of the national and the international domain. These values concern, in particular, the rule of law and human rights: values that are often treated as truly universal values that States should ensure, both in the international legal order and within domestic societies. The second development is the dispersion of sources of authority away from the State in both vertical (sharing of sovereign functions) and horizontal directions (involvement of private actors). The boundaries between international and national law become even less relevant when considering the more informal arrangements between private persons, corporations, etc. The third development, partly overlapping with the first two, is deformalization—a process in which the relative role of international law as a formal institution compared to other forms of normativity relevant to governance of international affairs seems to decline.

Neither dualism nor monism in their traditional form are able to capture the diversity of the processes of globalization. The reduction of the factual power of States to control the entry of international law in their domestic legal orders reduces the explanatory power of dualist theory. In an interdependent world, the boundaries of national legal systems are not watertight. Economic and political processes have led to ever stronger pressure on States to adapt domestic laws. Domestic law can no longer be treated in isolation from outside influences, legal or otherwise.[34]

Superficially, it might be thought that the process of globalization would lead to a piercing of the veil between the international and the domestic domain, and to a situation that one might characterize as monistic. Individuals are no longer invisible, shielded by the domestic legal order; the subject matter of national and international law look more and more alike and sources are less and less controlling of

[33] Arrangio-Ruiz, ch 1, 35.
[34] W Twining, *Globalisation and Legal Theory* (London: Butterworths, 2000) 51.

any particular order. However, the reality is more complicated. We also face what can be called a 'new nationalism' that leads to fragmentation rather than a construction of a universal society.[35] Differences between States and regions are such that the explanatory power of monistic theories is very limited. In many States one may be hard-pressed to find evidence of an evaporation of the shield between the national and the international. Indeed, globalization may lead States and communities to protect their national values and identities against undefined and unwanted foreign influences and lead to a reassertion of sovereignty.

Modern developments thus do not point in one direction and are indeed contradictory. It is for that reason that the present volume presents an array of partly overlapping, partly supplementary, but also partly contradictory theoretical propositions and perspectives. It is the aim of this book to take stock and explore alternative approaches that may provide such perspectives for a modern age.

5. Overview of the contributions

In order to address the challenges sketched above, we have selected a number of contributions that provide a broad range of perspectives on the evolving relationship between the international and domestic legal orders.

Since, as indicated above, the development of new perspectives on the relationship between international law and national law has to deal with the legacy of dualism and monism, the book starts with two contributions that reassess the present-day value of dualistic and monistic thought on the relationship between international and national law. **Gaetano Arangio-Ruiz** argues, in **Chapter 1**, that the dualist theory indeed has continued validity. The chapter seeks to correct some misperceptions of dualist theory and adjusts it to modern developments and also contains a powerful rebuttal against some of the claims made in later chapters to the effect that 'modern' development such as the rise of international organizations and the changing position of the individual would have undermined the fundamental validity of dualism. In **Chapter 2, Giorgio Gaja** presents a more cautious approach on the present-day relevance of dualism and underlines the shortcomings of the theory in regard to modern international law.

In **Chapter 3, Philip Allott** presents a perspective that is closer to legal philosophy than legal doctrine. It recognizes that in most States, as a matter of positive law, there is no unity and that international law is not supreme—a position with which a dualist author would not disagree. However, Allott argues that the trends of the internationalizing of the national, the nationalizing of the international, and the universalizing of value underlie the emergence of a universal legal system. His theory of the universal legal system postulates a legal system with international law at the apex, which would embrace the laws of all subordinate societies that

---

[35] This point is made in this volume by Paulus, 248–50, and Du Plessis, 311.

would exist by virtue of and in accordance with international law. This theory thus has decidedly monistic aspects.

The other seven chapters are, in certain respects, less all-encompassing than the ambitions of dualism and monist theory and deal with various aspects of the complex landscape. Rather than seeking grand alternatives to dualism and monism, they disaggregate these grand questions and identify more specific developments in the international legal order and ask us the question how these developments inform our understanding of the relevance or irrelevance of the national law-international law divide.

Chapter 4 by **Catherine Brölmann** examines how the process of deterritorialization of international law, in which territoriality increasingly gives way to functionality as a dominant organizing principle, affects the relationship between international law and national law.

Anne-Marie Slaughter and **Bill Burke-White** argue in **Chapter 5** that the future of international law is predominantly a political one, located at the domestic level. They view international law as an important force to influence domestic politics in addressing global issues, guiding the legislature. In a sense, this approach is one of empowering governments and legislatures through international law.

In **Chapter 6**, **Christine Chinkin** examines the emergence of private authority and what the role of private authority in law-making and law enforcement means for our traditional understanding of self-contained and comprehensive national and international legal orders.

Mayo Moran discusses in **Chapter 7** the emergence and consequences of the notion of the influential authority of international law. She argues that much of our thinking on the relationship between international and domestic legal orders is erroneously based on the bindingness of international law. Whereas that standard account may leave little room for breaking out of an essentially dualistic paradigm, she argues that a more substance-based conception of international law allows for a richer account of the relevance of international norms in domestic settings and indeed makes formal separations between legal orders largely irrelevant.

In **Chapter 8**, **Christian Walter** explores the utility of the concept of constitutionalism as a perspective to study and understand the changing nature of the relationship between international and national law. His main argument is that we have witnessed a shift from actor-centrism to subject matter-orientation in the general structure of international law, with direct consequences for the relationship between international and national law. In the new, subject matter oriented perspective, the boundary between international and national law is much less controlling.

In **Chapter 9, Andreas Paulus** explores the extent to which modern recognition of an 'international community' influences the relationship between international and national law. The traditional picture is based on an opposition between the State and the international community one the one hand, and State and individual, on the other. If one accepts the notion of an international community that is more than a community of States, what does this mean for the separation of the two legal orders? Would then all subjects traditionally part of the national community be part of the international community, and what would be the consequences thereof for the shield of the national legal order?

In **Chapter 10, Anne Peters** explores the hypothesis that national (State) constitutions have to adapt to globalization. She examines how global governance affects and even undermines basic constitutional principles such as the rule of law, democracy, social security, and federalism. She also discusses how State constitutions are being adapted to globalization in terms of structure, both by formal amendments and by dynamic interpretation.

Chapter 11 by **Lourens du Plessis** is of a fundamentally different nature. While domestic approaches inform several of the contributions to the book, the book does not deal with how, as a matter of positive law, States deal with the reception of international law. This chapter is an exception. It addresses the approach to international law taken by the Constitutional Court of South Africa. The chapter is included because it illustrates several of the more theoretical observations made in earlier chapters and at the same time allows us in the final chapter to draw connections between certain theoretical approaches and developments in practice.

In our concluding **Chapter 12**, we will draw together some of the main themes of the chapters and develop a few more general theoretical lines, notably pertaining to the emergence of common values, the dispersion of authority, and the deformalization of (international) law.

1

International Law and Interindividual Law

Gaetano Arangio-Ruiz

1. Introduction

1. According to a widespread view, the 'monism/dualism' debate would only be a remnant of the pre-second (if not first) World War scholarship. The *coup de grâce* to the debate would have come especially from post-second World War developments, including the unprecedented intensification of international relations, the expansion of the *ratione personarum, loci* and *materiae* scope of international law, the proliferation of international and 'supranational' institutions, and the consequent increase in the number of international customary and treaty rules placing upon States obligations extending to all of the fields of human endeavour, including those areas once considered of null or scarce international concern. Factors such as these would have marked at one and the same time a more or less decisive prevalence of monism and the obsolescence of the debate!

I strongly disagree on both counts—and I find comfort in the felicitous choice of the Amsterdam Institute to devote a long-term research project to such a deserving, but frequently ignored topic. The idea of the demise of dualism is not new. As early as 1957 Joseph Kunz criticized an Italian writer for 'start(ing) from the fallacious basis of the "strictest dualist doctrine" accepted even in the often absurd form given to it recently by Arangio-Ruiz. The author is mistaken when he believes and continuously states that the dualist doctrine is the dominant one; quite to the contrary, it is today generally abandoned and has one of its few remaining oases only in the Italian school.'[1]

(a) To begin with the alleged obsolescence of the topic, it should first of all be noted that monism is not just the well-known theory finely worked out by Verdross, Kelsen, Kunz, and other members of the Vienna school. Although not

---

[1] J Kunz 3 51 AJIL (1957) 849. As noted by Santulli, *Le Statut International de L'ordre Juridique étatique* (Paris: Pedone, 2001) 266–67, 556. J Kunz's criticism, although particularly addressed to the present writer (in (1953) 2 47 AJIL 512–13 and (1957) 3 51 AJIL 849; and in the *Österreichische Zeitschrift für öffentliches Recht* (1955) 105–06) was constantly addressed to all the members of the 'Italian School' whose works he reviewed in the AJIL. Kunz was, however—except with regard to dualism—an admirer of the Italian School of international law. See also para 20 below.

unrelated to that doctrine, monism also manifests itself under different scholarly livery. I refer to all the broadly expanding presentations of international law as a public, constitutional (if not supra-constitutional) system overstanding the legal systems of States in a way essentially comparable to the manner in which the fundamental norms of a federal State overstand the member States' (dependent) systems. These 'constitutional' concepts of international law are just different, less abstract, forms of monism.

With regard to both forms of monism, it must of course be recognized that international and municipal law interact whenever a relationship between international persons is also affected by national legal rules; or, vice versa, whenever a relationship between physical or juristic persons of national law is also affected by rules of international law. The monist assertion that international law and municipal law are part of one and the same legal system finds its origin, presumably, in the consideration that whenever such an interaction occurs in practice between international and domestic norms, it manifests itself, at the international or the national level, in terms of a simultaneous impact of international and domestic norms—or, more concretely, in terms of simultaneous impact, upon the parties in a given legal relationship, of international and national legal rights or obligations. The prima facie impression is thus one of coexistence of the two sets of norms (or the two sets of legal rights or obligations) within a single normative context addressing itself directly to individuals as well as States. That the coexistence of the two sets of norms does not imply that they belong to one and the same system inevitably appears, nevertheless, as soon as one is confronted: (i) with any issues of existence or validity of any of the domestic or international rules under consideration; (ii) with a case of conflict between the domestic and international norms involved. The issue then arises as to which norm or set of norms is valid or existing and eventually which norm or set of norms should prevail for the (judicial or administrative) settlement of the matter at the international or domestic level, according to the case. Such an issue, in its turn, splits into two interrelated questions: (i) the question whether the existence or validity of any relevant norm(s) should be considered as a matter of international or domestic law—in other words, whether one should look, before applying any of the concurring norms, at the rules on the sources (Hart's secondary rules) of international or domestic law—surely not at both sets of rules as if they belonged to one and the same system; (ii) the question whether the national or the international norms prevail, namely whether the primacy, on the international or the domestic plane according to the case, belongs to domestic or international law (paras 8 et seq, below).

If, as assumed, the situation or relationship is one in the regulation of which international and domestic law interact, namely, are both directly or indirectly relevant, the legal answer or solution—by an international or a national operator, according to the case—will be the result of a concurrence of international and national norms. It would be superficial, however, to infer, from such a concrete 'piling-up' of international and national norms (or international and national rights/obligations) in regulating the matter, that the concurrent rules must belong to one and the same system. In addition to belonging to different legal systems and stemming from different sources, the concurrent international and domestic norms also perform different functions in the regulation of the matter; and they are frequently subject, as the dualist doctrine shows far better than monist writers, to different procedural treatment: one to be treated, for example, as a *quaestio iuris* and the other as a *quaestio facti*.

Identical considerations apply to the interaction between the internal law of international or 'supranational' bodies, on the one hand, and international law or any national legal system or systems, on the other hand (see paras 15–16, below).

One must add that a proper definition of the relationship between international law and national law is *essential*, as will be shown, for the proper appreciation of the *very nature* of international law and international organizations (para 13, below).

(b) With regard to the merits, the doctrinal positions are difficult to define and classify, mainly because it is generally not clear whether those who deal with the matter refer to the relationship between international and national law—not to mention other coexisting legal systems—from a *juridical* or a *factual* viewpoint. *Grosso modo*, while a fair number of scholars seem to adhere, expressly or implicitly, to a more or less decisive monist approach (not infrequently tainted by a natural law approach to law in general), quite a number seem to take an obscure middle course between monism and dualism. According to some of the latter, the prevalence of monism or dualism would depend upon the areas or subject-matters. Also rather widespread is the facile view—presented at times like a discovery!— that international law and municipal law are 'complementary': a term meaning entirely different things according to whether one refers to a factual-historical complementarity or to a juridical complementarity. Both Triepel and Anzilotti envisaged intense interrelationship and even 'compenetrazione' in a clearly factual sense. As regards the contemporary adherents to the theory of complementarity, they are obviously dualists or monists according to whether they intend complementarity in a factual or in a juridical sense. Be it as it may of the monist and of the middle course positions, the firm dualism formerly distinguishing the German and the Italian schools seems to be in some disarray due to a variety of causes, the main ones of which will hopefully be clarified in the following discourse. Nevertheless, the dualist construction has been, in my view, ever since its century-old formulation, the closest to the reality of international and transnational legal relations.

(c) In the following discourse I leave out, in principle, from Kelsen's monist theory that *variante* that envisages the primacy of national law. As for dualism, it is perhaps not useless to point out that I use that term, like everybody else, just as the simplified version of the *pluralism* existing between international law, on the one hand, and the several (190-odd) national legal systems, on the other hand (not to mention other species of interindividual legal orders). It will be shown that the number of legal systems to be reckoned with is multiplied by the presence, alongside national systems, of the internal legal systems of international and 'supranational' bodies.

2. As a matter of pure speculation, the monistic theory marks a number of points, the main one being surely the natural unity of human kind. Another argument supporting monism is the interindividual nature of law *par excellence*, namely of national legal systems. A third obvious *datum* is the indispensable role played by human beings, through individual or collective actions or omissions, in the creation and the implementation of any rule of international law. Another strong point of the monistic theory—in my view surely the most formidable, particularly in the Kelsenian version—is the theory's perfect congruity with Hans Kelsen's concept of the State as the legal order of a human society.

Theoretically substantial as they are, such merits do not pass the test of realities.

(a) Although the natural unity of human kind may well justify the prediction that there will be, at some time, a legal community of mankind that would mark an integration of international and national law within a more or less centralized political and legal order, the present fragmentation of universal society into a number of separate, relatively exclusive, political communities, indicates that the prodigy of a universal constitutional law is unlikely to come about soon. The few instances of integration at the regional level, hardly recognizable as 'constitutional' themselves, do not significantly alter the situation at the world level.

(b) The unquestionably interindividual nature of the forms of law other than international law is not a valid argument either. For that argument to be valid, one should first demonstrate that international law is either the very same kind of law, or a kind of law much more similar to the law of national societies than it is generally—and rightly—deemed to be. On the contrary, I propose to show that such is not the case. The persistently inorganic structure of general international law, particularly the prevalent inorganic nature of the law-making, law-determining, and law-enforcing processes of international society, seem to show that even if one accepts that the rules operating among States and other independent entities are, despite their shortcomings, *legal* rules in a broad sense, they are not such in the *same* sense as the rules operating within national societies. This might well justify at least some doubt—or a lack of certainty—also with regard to the interindividual nature of international law. The very uncertainty of such a feature might actually explain, as I propose to stress further on, the peculiarities of international law, particularly the lack of an institutionalized sanctions system—an element in which Kelsen rightly envisages the most essential feature of legal orders.

(c) The same should be said about the necessary concurrence of individuals for States to participate in the creation and implementation of international rules. The fact that international persons—namely States and other independent collective entities—can only 'will' and 'act' through 'volitions' and 'acts' of human beings undoubtedly represents, prima facie, a point of analogy between international persons, on the one hand, and the juristic persons of national law, on the other hand. The monists claim that just as the individuals willing and acting on behalf of a juristic person of national law are determined by the internal legal order of the juristic person, the individuals willing or acting for a State as an international person are determined by the internal order of the State. First, however, this is untrue. There is clear evidence in the law of treaties and in the law of international responsibility—despite some widespread ambiguities about the so-called juridical 'imputation' to States of the conduct of individuals—that national law is neither the last nor (except prima facie) the first word in the attribution (or so-called 'imputation') of actions, omissions, or volitions to a State as an international person. Second, while the juristic persons' internal orders are unquestionably—one could say by definition—part and parcel of the incorporating national legal order, the question whether the same can be said about the internal order of the State as an international person—namely that that order is in any sense part of international law—depends precisely on the issue of the relationship between international and national law. Unless one begs that issue, the weight of the argument can only be measured on the strength of *distinct*, independent evidence.

(d) Coming finally to the point I mentioned earlier as the most formidable among the arguments adduced by the monist theory—namely, Hans Kelsen's (in my view correct) identification of the State with its legal order—one faces again, at the present stage of this discourse, a vicious circle. I refer to the circular relationship established by Kelsen between the notion that States are legal orders, on the one hand, and the notion that, the State of international law being the same thing as the State of national law, international law would be bound to be—as inter-State(s) law—the law of the relations among national legal orders. Although I immodestly believe I have already broken that vicious circle 50-odd years ago, I shall return further on to this most crucial and central issue. I refer to paras 6–8, below. For the moment, I confine myself to expressing just perplexity at the notion that a system of rules that seems so obviously to be addressing themselves to entities of the tangible magnitude of independent States really does not deal with such physical entities but rather, according to Kelsen, with their respective legal orders, its only physical addressees being the individuals determined by those orders.

3. To the noted shortcomings of monism one must add a number of ambiguities and oxymorons surrounding the very notions of monism and dualism that confirm the inanity of the former as a description of existing realities. One of the main ambiguities relates to such terms as 'primacy', of international law or national law, according to the case.

No dualists have ever doubted the primacy of international law at the international level, namely, in inter-State relations and before international courts and tribunals or other international bodies. Dualists contest, precisely, that international law is endowed per se with primacy over national law at the national level, namely before political, legislative, administrative, or judicial organs of national law. The dualist view, in other words, is that the *key* to the implementation of international law within the framework of national law is in the hands of national law itself, as impersonated by the constituent, the legislator, or the courts, in the exercise of powers they respectively derive from national law, and (except for natural law, morality, or ethics) just from that law. For the dualist the *key* remains in the hands of national law even where it has already been turned in such a manner as to open the way to international law. It is so even where the opening has taken place in compliance with specific international State obligations to that effect.

Another striking ambiguity—an oxymoron—is the recent trend of labelling national legal systems as 'monistic' or 'dualistic' according to whether they adopt more or less thorough and automatic adaptation mechanisms of national law to international law: as if the adaptation were not a choice obviously made, clearly on the basis of a dualistic premise, by each national system. An ambiguity within the same ambiguity is the notion that monism prevails wherever national courts apply international law in the absence of express constitutional or legislative adaptation mechanisms—as if the courts of a State were organs established by international law instead of just another part of the national order within which they operate.

A non-negligible weakness of the monist theory is the fact, ironically adducible perhaps as evidence of the triumph of monism, that there are not a few signs that, contrary to the general tendency of monist writers to adhere to the primacy of international law, the practice of the administrative and judicial organs of numerous States—most particularly some major powers—reveals a marked inclination of those national establishments to operate, due to ignorance, national convenience, or arrogance, according to the case, on the basis of an even more questionable and surely not 'progressive' doctrine of the primacy of *national law*.

4. Unlike the imaginatively appealing but unrealistic construction of monist scholarship, the dualist theory appears instead to be a perfect portrait of the hard realities of the modern and contemporary condition of mankind. I refer to the patent fragmentation of the human species into separate political communities. As demonstrated by Triepel and Anzilotti, the internal legal systems of each one of those communities was, as it still is, distinct and separate—*despite the most obvious, continuous interaction*—from the internal system of each one of the other and from international law. Regarding particularly each national order, on the one hand, and international law, on the other hand, they were shown to be distinct and juridically separate, both from the viewpoint of the relations they dealt with—namely, from the viewpoint of their *subjects*—and from the viewpoint of their positive *sources*. It followed that in so far as international treaty or customary rules were taken into account in municipal law, they were expressly or implicitly incorporated—either by general written or unwritten constitutional rules or principles or by *ad hoc* legislation or, simply, by court decisions—into municipal law.

Frequently misunderstood or ignored but never seriously challenged, these fundamental tenets of dualism have been confirmed by the practice of States throughout the 20th century and up to the present time. The research directed by Eisemann, with the participation of authorized scholars from a number of countries, confirmed quite recently, together with the clearly persistent dualist approach in all the European countries considered, that the implementation of international law in those countries is effected by national means or procedures even in the not frequent instances where the relevant international instrument envisages the participating States' obligation to adopt given provisions in their respective legal systems. The experience of the EC and EU confirms this essential point. The said findings are further confirmed *ad abundantiam* by the scholarly works devoted to the implementation of international law within national legal orders, notably in the constitutions of the most developed among modern national systems. It seems hardly necessary to recall the numerous monographic works on the subject. An equally dualistic approach can be found in the 1986 *Proceedings of the German-Soviet Colloque on International Law* at Kiel University. The dualistic approach of English Courts emerges unambiguously from Mann's analysis of 1986.

It will be noted—since not many students nowadays read Triepel's and Anzilotti's works—that although the *exposé* of their theory precedes, within their two main monographs, the analysis of the legislative and judicial practice of States, it is clear that the theory was the outcome of an inductive process carried out within the framework of a positive law concept of law. It was not drawn from ideological or philosophical premises. Nor is it correct to blame Triepel's and Anzilotti's theory for an alleged subjection to the concept of law as just the product of the State's will (the so-called *statalismo giuridico*). Although both masters undoubtedly concentrated their analyses mainly on State legislation, they both also took account of customary (national) law, surely not a product of the State's will.

It is to be stressed further that the two masters' theory was significantly worked out, in the part of their monographs dealing with the practice, in such a manner as to show in detail the many ways in which the distinct and separate systems of international law and municipal law are related in a continuous reciprocal interaction. Both authors were thus able to offer a concrete and accurate classification of the various ways in which municipal law is conditioned—although never directly affected—by States' international obligations. Triepel and Anzilotti were so well aware of that interrelationship that they both worked out a refined theory of reciprocal *renvois* from national law to international law and vice versa. Their fundamental distinctions, especially between *rinvio recettizio*, or *materiale*, and *rinvio non recettizio*, or *formale*, have been accepted and finely developed by their disciples; especially, in Italy, by Perassi, Morelli, Ago, Balladore Pallieri, Bernardini, and Quadri. I am using, of course, the Italian terminology, which has been for some time, and remains, the most refined.

Both authors clearly distinguished internationally 'indifferent' and internationally 'relevant' municipal law rules. *Pace* the critics from the monist side, Triepel and Anzilotti were thus both very far—as shown by such decisive evidence—from considering international law and national law as absolutely disconnected as alleged, *inter alios*, by Guggenheim and Marek. At the same time, they both demonstrated that national legal rules are never directly affected by international law, even where they are not in conformity with international law and States' obligations. Contrary to what was (later) arbitrarily asserted by some monist authors, municipal law not in conformity with international law was (as it still is) neither '*annulé*' (Guggenheim, Marek) nor '*abrogé*' (Scelle) by international law. As recognized even by Kelsen, all that international law is able to do is to impose liability for breach upon the wrongdoing State.

There was, of course, no international court at the time when Triepel and Anzilotti wrote their monographs. It is very significant, though, *pace* partisan monistic scholarship, that every time the PCIJ dealt with the issue, it took a dualist stand: a stand on the strength of which it rendered persuasive and generally accepted judgments or opinions; and despite the frequently unfair criticism of the 1920s and 1930s, the Permanent Court's successor has consistently maintained the dualist stand whenever, as in connection with local remedies or domestic jurisdiction, national law came into the picture in a case. Both courts firmly maintained the principle that the relevance of national law in any case before them is that of a mere fact. It is taken into account by the court not as a part of international law as applied by the Court (*quaestio iuris*) under Article 38 of the Statute but as an aspect of a State's conduct (*quaestio facti*).[2]

5. Despite its essential soundness one must acknowledge some important shortcomings in the dualist theory, none of which however, if adequately corrected, is of a nature to disprove it. One shortcoming is an internal fault dating back to Triepel's and Anzilotti's time; the other issue is, so to speak, an external gap.

(a) The internal fault, first pointed out by Hans Kelsen as a fundamental inconsistency not adverted to by Anzilotti and his direct disciples, was the inadequate attention to the concept of the State in the sense of international law.

(b) The second shortcoming is the relatively more problematic definition and systematization, within the structure of the original dualist theory, of the legal phenomena arising from the development of international and 'supranational' organizations—phenomena that were at their inception in Triepel's and Anzilotti's time.

Issue (a) is dealt with in the following paras 6–8 and issue (b) in paras 14 et seq.

2. Main shortcoming of the original formulations of the dualist theory

6. To begin with the internal shortcoming, the founders of dualism failed fully to perceive the inextricable interrelationship of their theory with the concept of the State in the sense of international law. Indeed, Anzilotti and his more direct disciples did realise that their dualist posture implied what some of them called a *vindicatio in libertatem* of international law with regard to legal personality. Significant steps forward were thus taken by them in that respect, one of the most important being the acknowledgement that one thing is the personality of a State under national

---

[2] A detailed criticism of Marek's writing to the contrary (in Revue générale de droit international public of 1962) can be found in G Arangio-Ruiz, 'Dualism Revisited: International Law and Interindividual Law' (2003) Rivista di diritto internazionale Milano, Giuffrè, 932–36.

law—namely, under the law of that State itself or any other national system—
another thing that same State's personality under international law. The former does
not necessarily entail the latter and vice versa. The fact that a State is not endowed
with a distinct 'over all' legal personality within its national system does not preclude that it appear as a single unit of international relations and thus a person
under international law. The dualists also saw pretty well—although perhaps not
quite thoroughly—that for the purposes of both the conclusion of treaties and the
attribution of responsibility, not to mention a host of other matters, international
law did not 'depend'—or did not depend entirely—upon the national law of the
State. It was thus admitted: (i) that a State can be bound by a treaty concluded not
in conformity with the national law rules on treaty-making; (ii) that a State could
be liable for a breach of international law as a consequence of facts of individuals
not belonging to its structure according to its national law.

Nevertheless, although such findings surely implied a *non complete* coincidence
between a State's structure for the purposes of national law and that State's structure for the purposes of international law, it was not felt necessary to verify whether
and possibly to what extent the entity to which personality is attributed by international law is the same entity that is endowed with personality under national
law. The dualists assumed, on the contrary, that the entity was identical both ways,
the only difference consisting in the distinct personalities—national and international—it enjoyed, and the different sources—national law and international
law—of those personalities. Dualists assumed, in other words, that the 'collective'
entity endowed with international personality was just the external face of the State
of national law (*zwei Seiten Theorie*). And since the State was viewed by national
law as a juristic person or an interindividual institution, the State of international
law was also to be so viewed.

It followed that the dualist theory rested, and still rests for most of its adherents,
upon distinctions—a distinction of sources, a distinction of subjects and a distinction
of 'fields of application'—the key element of which is a State concept that is the same
as the State concept in which the monists see the main argument, as noted in para
2(d), above, contradicting the separation of international and municipal law.

Indeed, none of the three basic differences between international and national
law makes much sense within the framework of a *Zwei-Seiten Theorie*.

(a) To begin with the sources, the difference would vanish with regard to custom
as well as treaty. The distinction between the 'will' or the *opinio* of one State as
the source of national law, and the 'will' or the *opinio* of two or more States as a
source of international law fades out. If the State is an interindividual legal institution (or, better, as rightly maintained by Kelsen for national law, a legal order) in
international as well as national law—if, so to speak, the State of international law
is not any more 'factual' and not any less juridical than the State of national law—
a treaty between States A and B cannot be essentially different from a piece of
national legislation of A or B. As well as a collective labour contract or an agreement
between two member States of a federation, the treaty would be a legal act under a

'total' legal order embracing, in a universal 'decentralized' juridical fabric, the subjects and the structures of the contracting States. Equally evanescent, once States were conceived as interindividual institutions, becomes the distinction between international and national customary law. The attitudes, the behaviours, the usages, the opinions and the interests on the basis of which inter-State custom comes into being would be attitudes, behaviours, usages, opinions, and interests of the agents and the members of interindividual institutions, or, simply, the subjects of national law.

(b) It seems hardly necessary to point out how equally evanescent becomes the distinction *ratione personarum*, or, for that matter, that distinction *ratione materiae*—the 'field of application'—which is but a corollary of the distinction *ratione personarum*. Once the State as an international person was conceived as an interindividual institution or a legal order, it would be absurd to doubt, in jurid-ical principle or in theory, the international legal personality of individuals, of private and public juristic persons and of other dependent entities. To any right or obligation of a State under international law would indirectly correspond, through the State's legal order—indirectly but nevertheless automatically and juridically—rights, obligations, legal situations of private individuals, agents or other persons of national law. Only a difference of degree would survive between the manner in which individuals are juridically involved in the international rights and obligations of States, on the one hand, and the manner in which individuals are juridically involved in the rights and obligations of a private corporation or a public State subdivision under national law, on the other hand. Compared with juristic persons or other national subdivisions, the State's legal system—supposedly 'derived' from international law—would be characterized merely by a higher *degree* of 'auton-omy' in choosing the ways and means—and the degree—of the juridical involve-ment of its subjects and agents. There would not be the qualitative *saltus*, or *solution de continuité*, which is rightly maintained by the dualist school.

It seems clear that the *Zwei-Seiten Theorie*'s identification of the State of inter-national law with the State of national law is based upon the notion that on both sides of the medal—on the external *Seite* facing international law and the internal *Seite* facing national law—one is in the presence of a juristic person (*personne morale*). And it is precisely in the light of the proper concept of juristic persons as juridical entities (as opposed to the prevailing rudimental concept of juristic persons as 'col-lective' entities or entities 'other than human beings') that one should determine the nature of States and the other members of the constituency of international law.

7. Confining our discourse to States, the study of juridical realities offers a host of data proving that, although endowed with legal personality under international law, States are in no sense *creations* of that law—not in any sense comparable, surely, to the sense in which juristic persons and other legal subdivisions of national law are *creations* of national law, nor in the sense in which the State of national law itself is a *creation* of the national community's law. Four solid pieces of evidence must be stressed.

(a) Unlike juristic persons and other subdivisions of national law, which come into being as juridical structures (not just 'collective entities') through private or public juridical acts—and unlike the State of national law itself, the establishment of which follows the formation of the community's law or coincides therewith—States as international persons come de facto into being, continue de facto to exist and de facto are eventually modified or dissolved from the viewpoint of international law. Of course, the setting up and other vicissitudes of States are frequently contemplated by international rules setting forth rights and obligations relating to the attitude that States should take with regard to the establishment, the modification or the dissolution of given States. There are even rules binding States to adopt or not—or to maintain or not—a given regime or a given kind of regime. All such rules are intended to favour or hinder—such as by recognition, or, respectively, non-recognition by other States—the creation, the modification, the dismemberment or the dissolution of a given State, or the change or maintenance of a given regime, or kind of regime, in one or more States. The last few decades mark a relatively high degree of (lawful or unlawful) intervention of States in the 'making' and 'un-making' of other States or governments.

Contrary, though, to the prevailing, presumably monistic, understanding of such phenomena—a tendency emerging also from the titles of some scholarly works[3]—the rules in question do not perform any direct juridical function with respect to the relevant constitutional events in national law, either with regard to the setting up, the modification or the dissolution of a State or with regard to the legitimation of a government or government-modification vis-à-vis the State's people (or, for that matter, any other peoples). Surely not in any sense similar to the sense in which the rules of a national order relating to the comparable vicissitudes of juristic persons or other national law subdivisions—not to mention the State itself under national law—do perform a direct normative function vis-à-vis the membership, the agents and/or the beneficiaries of the juristic person of national law or of the State itself of national law. In other words, the international rules in question do not *directly create* interindividual rights and duties legitimizing or de-legitimizing the target State or Government.

(i) It will first be noted, indeed, that, however strictly the relevant international norms may have been complied with by the States involved, a State or government set up or modified in disregard of the applicable international rules may just the same obtain the allegiance of the people. The possible reaction of the interested States bears no *direct* juridical effect at the interindividual national level or levels. Vice versa, a State or government set up or modified in conformity with the applicable international norms may well be lawfully resisted or otherwise opposed, at the national level, by the people and possibly by other peoples. Again, the concerned

---

[3] See, for example K Marek, *Identity and Continuity of States in Public International Law* (2nd edn, Geneva: Libr Droz, 1968) and by J Crawford, first in *The Criteria for Statehood in International Law* (1975) BYIL 95, and later in *The Creation of States in International Law* (Oxford: OUP, 1979; 2nd edn, 2006).

State's possible reaction does not bear a direct interindividual juridical effect at the national level or levels. In other words, no direct effect on peoples—in terms of interindividual, constitutional, legal rights or obligations related to the legitimacy or illegitimacy of the event—derives from the international rules in question or from compliance or non-compliance therewith. For such effects to occur there should come into operation *not just* international—namely, inter-State—legal rules but constitutional *interindividual* rules ascribable to some kind of universal or regional *public law of men and women,* able naturally to perform a direct constitutional legitimation/delegitimation function similar to the function performed by the comparable rules of any national legal system with regard to the creation, modification, or dissolution of juristic persons or subdivisions, or of the State itself, from the standpoint of domestic law. To put it bluntly, the rights and obligations created by the international rules imaginatively labelled—by scholars influenced by scientifically untenable federal analogies—as 'State-making' or 'un-making' and 'government making' or 'un-making' norms, remain an inter-State affair just as well as the rights and obligations deriving from any other rule of international law.

(ii) Second, even at the level of strictly inter-State relations, the relevant events' conformity or non-conformity with the international norms in question is not juridically decisive of the legal condition of the State or government possibly at stake. Much as the target State's or government's establishment or modification may be condemned as unlawful under the relevant norms and eventually opposed by the other States concerned—even including, possibly, the latter's refusal to establish or maintain diplomatic relations, or the refusal of admission to international organizations—the State will nevertheless be a State (from the standpoint of general international law) and the government a government for the purposes of international personality as well as the purposes of the so-called international representation of the State, or for any other aspects of the legally relevant international relations of the State or government concerned.

(iii) It must be acknowledged, in conclusion, that on both counts—from the viewpoint of interindividual as well as inter-State legal relations—the situation differs in quality so radically from the comparable situations involving national juristic persons or subdivisions (or the State itself from the viewpoint of national law) that to speak of 'creation' of States in international law sounds like an oxymoron.[4] The point I am making can be condensed in the following terms. The setting up of legal persons of national law—and of the State itself under national law—is a juridical *event* (or *effect*) with regard to *both* the setting-up of the entity and its elevation to legal personality. The setting up of a State in the sense of international law, is a juridically relevant *fact,* the only juridical *event* (or *effect*) attached thereto by international law being the attribution (to the factual entity) of legal personality, namely, international rights and obligations, or the capacity thereof. The only tenable analogy applicable to the setting up of a State from the viewpoint

---

[4] I refer again to *Dualism Revisited* (n 2 above) 954–56 and n 73.

of international law is thus—*mutatis*, of course, most fundamental *mutandis*— the biological coming into existence of a human being as a juridically relevant fact (*fatto giuridico, fait juridique*) to which (national) law attaches the legal *event* or *effect* consisting in the acquisition by the individual of a legal personality.

(b) A second *datum* proving the weakness of the *Zwei Seiten Theorie* relates to the organization of States from the standpoint of international law. Unlike national legal systems, where (interindividual) rules appoint physical persons empowered to act as agents of a juristic person or a subdivision, or of the State, international law contains no rules appointing individuals empowered to 'will' and 'act' on behalf of the State for such purposes as treaty-making or liability for internationally unlawful acts. A State 'wills' and 'acts' for international legal purposes through any individuals *factually* connected with it and/or *factually* behaving and accepted as that State's organs within the national community. In other words, the will and the action of a State from the viewpoint of international law is an egregious instance of application of those organic theories of the so-called will and action of collective bodies, which is surely inappropriate for juristic persons or subdivisions of national law. The attribution by the observer of individual wills or acts to a State as an international person, is merely a *factual* operation based upon merely *factual* elements, the latter elements *including* any legal provisions of national law. The attempts to 'juridicize' international 'imputation' in general or in some special instances are unconvincing.[5]

(c) A third piece of evidence against the *Zwei Seiten Theorie* relates to the international status of the members of the States' populations. As a matter of positive law it is not proved that individuals and national corporate bodies (private or public) have so far acquired rights and obligations by direct operation of international law. Whenever, as frequently is the case, interests or behaviours of individuals or corporate bodies are the object of international rules contemplating the protection of such interests or the conditioning of such behaviours by legal consequences, the relevant private rights or duties derive not directly from the international rules. They derive either from national legal systems as adapted to the States' obligations under the relevant norms, or from the legal orders of international bodies as established by States under the relevant international instruments (paras 14–15, below). The monist theory contends in vain that private parties nevertheless become subject to international law through States' or international bodies' legal systems, just as they can be subject to rights and duties under national law through the legal orders of juristic persons and other subdivisions of national law. That superficial analogy is contradicted by two capital differences. First, the members of the national community are the basic components of the constituency of the legal system. They are the original members of the legal community and the primary legal subjects of the whole national order *prior* to belonging to a province, a city or a private association or company. Their bond with the national State is supreme. Their

---

[5] Ibid., 984–85.

being subjects under the legal systems of juristic persons or other subdivisions is just a *secondary* phenomenon in national law. Under international law, even according to the most optimistic views, private parties would *only* acquire rights and obligations indirectly, through 'secondary' legal orders. Private parties, in other words, would *only* be 'secondary' persons of international law. Furthermore, for the monists' contention to be persuasive it should be proved that the States' and international bodies' legal systems coming into play are *derivative* or *partial* legal orders within the framework of international law—which obviously would beg the very question of the relationship between international law, on the one hand, and the internal law of States and international bodies, on the other hand.

(d) The *data* collected so far (on the nature of *Staat im Sinne des Völkerrechts*) find their completion in a fourth *datum* encompassing all the previous ones and even more conclusively contradicting the *Zwei Seiten Theorie*. I refer to the quality of independence, as distinguished from autonomy.

The term autonomy, not infrequently used in the international law literature—as a synonym of independence—in order to describe the condition of the State *vis-à-vis* international law, is not the appropriate one. The concept of autonomy is properly used in the area of constitutional and administrative law to designate the sphere of the normative, administrative, or judicial competence attributed to subdivisions and other dependent entities by the law of a national community. Indeed, autonomy consists of two sets of interacting legal elements. On the one hand, there are a set of rights, obligations, powers, *facultés*, attributed by the statute of the subdivision to the physical persons related to the latter as agents, members, beneficiaries or subjects. On the other hand, there is the direct active presence in those very situations, of the legal system of the whole society, such a presence manifesting itself, both in everybody's (members', beneficiaries', and agents') subjection to that whole legal system, and in the legitimation and control, by the latter, of the subdivision's statute. Such a combination of unity and pluralism—and autonomy with control—is afforded by the integrated and thoroughly interindividual nature—despite the exceptions I mention further on (para 17, below)—of the whole society. The main condition is the presence of a sociologically continuous *milieu* and an equally continuous legal system, within which there are no juridical gaps between the rights and obligations of the subdivision as a unit, on the one hand, and the rights and obligations of members, beneficiaries, or agents, on the other hand. Unless one erroneously identified the subdivision (or the corresponding juristic person) with the underlying factual (sociological) entity, it is only by a way of saying that one speaks of 'collective' rights and duties.

Now, the features of autonomous subdivisions seem to be totally absent in States (or, for that matter, in international persons 'other than States') considered from the standpoint of international law. Of course, States as international persons are collective entities, similar to the entities in which one recognizes the *substrata* of juristic persons or other subdivisions of national law. Nevertheless, States do not possess, from the viewpoint of the universal human society—or any regional portions thereof—*any* of the features of the juristic persons or subdivisions of national law.

(e) One must conclude that, unlike juristic persons and subdivisions of national law, characterized by 'autonomy', States as international persons are instead characterized by independence; and independence is a factual condition: a synonym of sovereignty, another name for that very same factual condition from the standpoint of international relations. Unlike the governmental functions of subdivisions, which are attributed by the law of the whole nation, the governmental functions of sovereign States are *not delegated* by international law, although frequently the object of restrictive or other international obligations. In that sense, the governmental functions of States are 'original', in that they only derive from the respective national law. The fallacy of the view that international obligations bring about restrictions of sovereignty has been authoritatively denounced. The relevant references can be found in the cited *Dualism Revisited* (n 2 above).

The 'missing' international legitimation of States at the *interindividual* level, the 'missing' international-*interindividual* structuring of States, the 'missing' *direct* international personality of individuals—each one of such data clarifying and confirming the others and all of them summed up together in the factual nature of independence (= external sovereignty) as opposed to juridical autonomy—prove that unlike juristic persons and other subdivisions of national law, and unlike the State itself in the sense of national law, States as international persons are not—contrary to the current assumption—juristic persons. They are assumed by international law as given, historical collective entities in a sense comparable, *mutatis mutandis*, to the sense in which human beings are assumed by (national) law as given factual entities. In conclusion, the State in the sense of international law does not coincide with the State of national law.

Kelsen's assertion that 'the international legal order, by means of the principle of effectiveness, determines . . . the reason of validity of the national legal orders' is unacceptable as a proposition of positive—namely existing—international law. The truth is clearly expressed by Kelsen himself when, within the same passage, he states: 'The historically first constitution is valid *because the coercive order exerted on its basis is efficacious as a whole*', namely, I add, as a fact from the standpoint of international law. What Kelsen calls the *principle* of effectiveness is not a legal principle. It is just a tautological rule, namely, no (juridical) rule.

8. This state of affairs determines—and is in turn determined by—a situation that is dramatically different, however difficult it may be to make monist scholars acknowledge it, from the situation obtaining, for instance, among the member States of a federal system. Whereas in a federal State one finds *one* interindividual legal system of the whole nation, embracing a number of dependent (equally interindividual) legal systems, in the universal society one must distinguish the situation 'below' and the situation 'around' the 'summits' of the coexisting national communities. 'Below' the level of those 'summits' there are as many systems of interindividual law as there are sovereign States. 'Around' the said 'summits' one

finds, instead of a public law of mankind as an interindividual law, a body of *sui generis* rules the *raison d'être* of which is the regulation of the relations among States as separate, factual collective units. It will be shown further on (paras 14–16, below) which is the impact, on this state of affairs, of the law of international organs and organizations.

(a)   Regarding the nature of this body of rules—the international legal system— the fact that it finds its *raison d'être* in the coexistence of States outside of the framework of a public law of mankind, indicates that it is not, in its turn, that very public law. On the contrary, between a universal public law of men, on the one hand, and international law, on the other hand, there is a relationship of reciprocal exclusion. Furthermore—and this is important in assessing the attempts at a real international organization—a vicious circle has supervened, in the course of the centuries, between the inter-State system, on the one hand, and the chances that it be replaced by the formation of a legal community of mankind, on the other hand. International law remains thus strictly inter-State law even where its rules *deal*—as with increasing frequency they do—with interests or behaviours of individual human beings or other persons of national law. The only right/obligation legal *relationships* directly instituted by such rules are relations between States or similarly independent entities, interindividual interests or behaviours being only their *object*.

I am unable to share the widespread view (Parry, Jennings) that the structure of the international system has altered significantly as a consequence of such phenomena. These only affect the *content* or the *objects* of the international rules: content and objects that have been impressively multiplying especially in the years following the second World War. I do not believe, in particular, that international law formerly *exclusively* inter-State would now be inter-State *'primarily'*. It is precisely in the nature of international persons, in the nature of the 'State in the sense of international law' as I see it, that resides the ultimate, real *cause* of the distinction and separation—namely, the juridical discontinuity—between international law and national law. And it is in the factual nature of the 'State in the sense of international law' as I see it (and described above), that resides the most decisive proof of the separation that the founders of dualism failed, despite their realistic intuition, to achieve.

(b)   It is also necessary to stress that it would be incorrect to understand the fact that international law only creates rights and obligations for States and similarly independent entities as a limitation comparable to the 'conventional' *ratione personarum* delimitations of given rules or sets of rules in any legal system. Such 'conventional' limitations are the result of a choice made by the *'corps social'*, or the legislator, in order to distinguish, among the *potential* addressees of given legal rules, those who shall from those who shall not be subject to the obligations or enjoy the rights deriving from such rules. This can also happen, *mutatis mutandis*, in international law. For instance, international organizations and the Holy See are generally considered to be 'incapable' of participating in certain kinds of international legal relationships or otherwise excluded from the sphere of the addressee of the relevant rules. An entirely different matter is the exclusion of dependent entities—individuals and private and public subdivisions or corporations of municipal law—from the *emprise relationnelle* of international law. This is an inherent limitation deriving from the uniqueness of the kind of relations international law establishes, and is only apt to establish.

Dualism is not confined, though, to the relationship between international law on the one hand, and each one of the coexisting national legal orders, on the other hand. It extends to the relationship between international law and the internal law of international and 'supranational' organs, as well as between the latter, on the one hand, and each one of the co-existing national legal orders, on the other hand. This will be shown further on (paras 14(c)–16).

9. Considering the misunderstandings of which the dualist theory is not infrequently the object, it may be useful to clarify the matter by comparing the present writer's understanding of dualism with a few particularly significant scholarly positions.

(a) Rightly to begin with Kelsen, it is perhaps not entirely superfluous to take note of the fact that that eminent master of monism was originally a dualist. Nevertheless, he presents dualism rather ambiguously when he states that according to dualists 'the two systems regulate different subject matters. National law, it is said, regulates the behaviour of individuals, international law the behaviour of States.[6] This is not a genuine dualist point. For a dualist, international law and national law deal perfectly well, as explained in the preceding paragraph, with the same *materiae*, namely the same 'subject matters'. Nationality is just one egregious example out of many; and uniform private law or private international law conventions are other examples.

The dualist distinction, far subtler than one of just 'subject matter', is one of relationships and *milieux*. International law may well contemplate nationality, as it obviously does, for a number of international legal purposes—namely in order to tell States what they may, may not, or must, do about nationality or nationalities—but only national law is able to endow an individual or a company with a given nationality or revoke it. An international legal rule granting nationality to an individual or a company would make no sense. More correct, of course (in Kelsen's passage quoted in n 6, below), is the distinction based upon the subjects.

Another ambiguity, however, lurks behind the verb 'regulate'. International norms dealing with nationality do not regulate nationality; they regulate the relations among States—and their rights/obligations—relating to nationality, leaving to

---

6 H Kelsen, *The Principles of International Law* (New York: Rhinehart & Company, 1952) 404: 'The mutual independence of international law and national law is often substantiated by the alleged fact that the two systems *regulate* different subject matters. National law, it is said, regulates the behaviour of individuals, international law the behaviour of States. We have already shown that the behaviour of States is reducible to the behaviour of individuals representing [*sic* !] the States. Thus the alleged difference in subject matter [*sic* !] between international and national law cannot be a difference between the kinds of subjects whose behaviour they *regulate*.'

States the task of regulating the matter. Similarly, a convention on the uniform law of sale or on uniform conflicts of laws rules on the bill of exchange does not regulate the sale or the conflicts of laws it contemplates. It regulates simply the participating States' obligations relating to the regulation of the relevant matter.

Of course, *relations* between States are the typical 'subject matters' of international law, while *relations* among individuals or legal persons are the typical 'subject matters' of national law. In a proper dualist view that surely excludes neither: (a) that relations between two States *in the sense of national law*, namely relations between States as legal persons in their respective (national) legal systems are 'governed'—namely established as juridical relations—by the national law of one of them; nor, (b) that international uniform law conventions set forth—as the object of States' international obligations to adopt them in their respective legal systems— rules intended to govern, within the said systems, relations among individuals or legal persons (of national law).

Kelsen's presentation of dualism is also questionable where, in the same quoted passage, he describes as State representatives the individuals that dualists describe as State organs.

10. (b) Fitzmaurice's dualistic position is firmly announced from the beginning of his very interesting pages:

First of all . . . , a radical view of the whole subject may be propounded to the effect that the entire monist-dualist controversy is unreal, artificial and strictly beside the point because it assumes something that has to exist for there to be any controversy at all—and which in fact does not exist—namely a *common field* in which the two legal orders under discussion both simultaneously have their spheres of activity. It is proposed here to state the case for this view. In order that there can be controversy about whether the relations between two orders are relations of *co-ordination* between self-existent independent orders, or relations of *subordination* of the one to the other, or of the other to the one—or again whether they are part of the same order, but both subordinate to a superior order—it is necessary that they should both be purporting to be, and in fact be, applicable in the same field—that is to the same set of relations and transactions.[7]

This clearly dualistic stand, summed up further on in a two-page 'Resulting position'—starting with a footnote showing the author's reluctance to depart from Kelsen[8]—is weakened, in my view, by some ambiguous conceptualisations.

One ambiguity is the presentation of the difference between international law and domestic law in terms of 'fields' of application: a concept, that of 'fields', that might convey—perhaps less easily but not quite unlike Kelsen's presentation of the dualist theory in terms of different 'subject matters'—the notion of a surely inexistent *ratione materiae* separation.[9]

---

[7] G Fitzmaurice, 'The General Principles of International Law Considered from the Standpoint of the Rule of Law' in Recueil des Cours, Vol 2 (The Hague: Hague Academy of International Law, 1957), 71 (emphasis in the original).   [8] Ibid, at 79, n 1.

[9] H Kelsen as quoted in n 6 above. Further critical references in G Arangio-Ruiz, 'Le Domaine Réservé, l'Organisation Internationale et le Rapport entre Droit International et Droit Interne,

A second, even more serious ambiguity is inherent in the author's insistence, in at least two instances, on a questionable equation of the relationship between international law and domestic law with an allegedly identical relationship between two national legal systems, such as the French and the English. In one of those instances one reads that the 'supremacy of international law in [the international] field': 'is, rather, a supremacy of exactly the same order as the supremacy of French law in France, and of English law in England—*i.e.* a supremacy not arising from <u>content</u>, but from the <u>field of operation</u>—not because the law is *French* but because <u>the place, the field, is</u> *France.*'[10]

This passage shows three inconsistencies with regard to dualism proper. First, while international law and domestic law are made radically different by the nature of their respective social *milieux*—the former operating in a *milieu* of factual collective entities and the latter in interindividual communities, domestic legal systems all relate to interindividual communities. This heterogeneity of national law and international law explains not just separation, but a host of qualitative differences accentuating the separation (para 13 et seq., below). With regard to interaction, in particular, while domestic legal systems are so interchangeable as to 'borrow', so to speak, chunks of private law from one another by means of conflicts of laws rules, international law and domestic law are far less interchangeable, their interactions (as particularly explored and classified by dualist scholars) usually involve not direct 'exchanges' of rules but less invasive forms of interaction (para 4, above). Second, the ambiguity inherent in the equation with the relationship between domestic legal systems is emphasized, in the quoted passage, by the yoking of the reference to '*France*' (as the seat of the French legal system) with such terms as 'the place, the field'.[11] Apart from the difficulty of identifying the scope of any domestic legal system by a merely territorial criterion, it is hard to see in what sense international law has a geographical 'place' or 'field' (or 'place, field') distinguishing it from France in a sense comparable to the sense in which the French legal system may be distinguished (for all or given purposes) from England's legal system. Is the scope or 'field' of international law—*qua* inter-State legal system—not simply universal?

Much as they affect, *à la rigueur*, the consistency of the cited author's dualism, the noted ambiguities are somewhat compensated by the thoughts he sets forth within the same context about what he calls the 'difficulties of the view that the State is only an aggregation of individuals'. This paragraph's five pages contain a critique of what Sir Gerald calls the 'artificial', or 'fiction[al]', 'conception' of the State as an 'aggregation of individuals': a keen critique that, although unjustified in my

Cours général de droit international public', 225 Vol 6 Recueil des Cours (The Hague: Hague Academy of International Law, 1990) 225; and also G Arangio-Ruiz, 'The Plea of Domestic Jurisdiction before the ICJ: Substance or Procedure' in *Fifty Years of the ICJ, Essays in Honour of Sir Robert Jennings*, Lowe and Fitzmaurice (eds), (Cambridge: CUP, 1996).

10 Fitzmaurice, 'The General Principles' (n 7 above) 72. Italics are in the original; the underlining is added. 11 Ibid.

view with regard to Kelsen's (correct) conception of the State from the standpoint of domestic law, seems to me appropriate for the State in the sense of international law. Had these pages been available to me in 1949–1951, when I worked on *Staat im Sinne des Völkerrechts*, I would have found therein some support in my search for that factual concept I finally worked out; and had Sir Gerald been able and willing to read, before his 1957 Hague course, my 1951 book's difficult Italian, he might have seen perhaps some reason to push his analysis of the said 'difficulties' far enough to conclude—as I had rightly or wrongly concluded—that the problem did not consist, or not so much, in questioning Kelsen's or anybody else's juridical (or 'fictional', or 'artificial') concept of the State from the standpoint of both national as well as international law, but rather the problem of whether the State of international law was not a different animal from the State of national law, whether, indeed, the State of international law was not a visible corporeal entity passively acknowledged by international law, rather than the legal person *created* by national law.[12]

11. (c) Account must also be taken of the important, moderately undecisive dualism expressed by Jennings and Watts in their 1990 edition of Oppenheim's treatise. According to these authors:

These differences in doctrine [between monists and dualists] are not resolved by the practice of states or by such rules of international law as apply in this situation. International developments, such as the increasing role of individuals as subjects of international law, the stipulation in treaties of uniform internal laws and the appearance of such legal orders as that of the European Communities, have tended to make the distinction between international law and national law less clear and more complex—than was formerly supposed at a time when the field of application of international law could be regarded as solely the relations of states amongst themselves. Moreover, the doctrinal dispute is largely without practical consequences, for the main practical questions which arise—how do states, within the framework of their internal legal order, apply the rules of international law, and how is a conflict between a rule of international law and a national rule of law to be resolved?—are answered not by reference to doctrine but by looking at what the rules of various national laws and of international law prescribe.[13]

---

[12] Fitzmaurice's concurrence is interesting– p 78 n 1 of the cited *General Course* (n 7)—with those who stress that a *common field* exists between international and national law 'because *the State is common to both the national and the international field*, and has obligations and relations *in both*'. My answer is that it is not the same entity in the two fields. In each field there is the State that belongs to it. In national law there is the interindividual institution, the legal order. On the international plane there is the State of international law. Each system 'produces', or, respectively, merely acknowledges the State which, so to speak, becomes it.

It will be noted incidentally that two separate 'fields' are not conceivable for the juristic persons— namely, *personnes morales*—of national law. In the case of juristic persons (in national law) the entity is the same both within and outside of its (partial) order.

That Fitzmaurice (as well as Anzilotti) misses the concept of the State in the sense of international law is noted in Arangio-Ruiz, 'Le Domaire Réservé' (n 9 above) 455. With respect, he also misses, though (as well as Anzilotti), the proper concept of the legal person.

[13] Jennings and Watts (eds), *Oppenheim's International Law*, Vol 1 (9th edn, London: Longmans, 1992) 54.

This passage, significantly different from Oppenheim's frequently quoted thinking of 1905, calls for the following comments: (i) far from not resolving the differences between monists and dualists, the practice of States has been and still is decisive; the differences in doctrine *are* resolved 'by the practice of states and by ... rules of international and national law', as shown by Triepel (in 1899 and 1923), and by Anzilotti (in 1902, 1905, and 1929); (ii) although the evoked 'international developments' make the distinction more 'complex', they do not make it less 'clear'; in particular, the presence of international and even 'supranational' organs—and their internal law—makes the matter more complex, surely, but not less clear (paras 14 et seq, below); (iii) although the so-called humanization of international law has obviously intensified in the course of the last decades, human interests and behaviours have always been, inter alia, among the objects of international law. The increased international legal relevance of the treatment of individuals (including the existence of international bodies open to them) does not make international law less inter-State or more interindividual than it formerly was. One thing is the content of international rules and the object of the obligations placed by them upon States, another thing is the basic *ratione personarum* scope of international relations and law, such scope remaining inter-State; (iv) the question definitely *has*, as explained in para 1, above, 'practical consequences'; (v) the statement that the 'practical questions'—namely 'how is a conflict between a rule of international law and a national rule to be resolved'—are 'answered not by reference to doctrine but looking at what the rules of various national laws and of international law prescribe' is, from my viewpoint, a rather ambiguous proposition. It depends on what one means by doctrine. Triepel's and Anzilotti's was, and I believe still is, legal doctrine and it was based, clearly, on *data* drawn from the practice of States as well as the rules of international and national law. It is not contended, surely, that those scholars worked out their theory from pure speculation (para 4, above); (vi) the fact that the issue is resolved not 'by reference to doctrine' (alone!) does not mean that doctrine should refrain from tackling it, precisely, 'by looking at what the rules of various national laws and of international law prescribe', after which the doctrine may well provide useful data; (vii) that one should look at the rules 'of various national laws' in the first place is already a decisive dualist/pluralist sign.

On the other hand, I fully share the quoted authors' view that: 'It is of importance not to confuse, as many do, the question of the supremacy of international law and of the direct operation of its rules within the municipal sphere. It is possible to deny the latter while fully affirming the former',[14] provided, though, that it be understood that the supremacy of international law is direct only on the international plane, notably before international tribunals. In the domestic sphere national law is supreme, international law prevailing only where national law implicitly or explicitly so provides. It follows that, *à la rigueur*, a 'direct' operation of international law takes place in the national sphere only by way of saying, namely, only where an

---

[14] Ibid., 54, para 19.

international rule is implemented, by the operation of some constitutional, legislative or judicial rule (of national law), which means not really 'direct', and surely not direct by virtue of international law itself (not even where the automatic adaptation of national law were the object of an international obligation).[15]

12. As a persistent dualist I could perhaps be content with the fact that more than a few authoritative scholarly pronouncements acknowledge that the dualist construction is, in essence, pretty close to the relevant realities. That acknowledgement, however, is mostly, in my view, incomplete. According to Partsch, for example, it would be 'premature to state' whether 'the rule of the supremacy of international law has been accepted everywhere in the domestic sphere'.[16] One matter, though, is whether this is true, another matter, clearly, is whether the actual relationship between international law and municipal law is one of supremacy of the former over the latter also within the sphere of national law. The confusion between these two dicta is one of the main sources of obscurity and misunderstanding. Nor does it seem correct to conclude, as the same author does:

Whether a conclusive formula can be given for the actual relationship between international law and municipal law remains in question. It certainly cannot be found in adherence to either of the traditional theoretical approaches. Dualists have had to introduce so many elements from the opposing concept that their position appears weakened. Likewise monists have had to make considerable concessions in the light of State practice, which has deeply affected their initial idealistic concept.[17]

Dualism has surely weakened in the literature of international law, not in world juridical realities. In a vein similar to Partsch's, another scholar states:

Le monisme a certes connu, pour des raisons idéologiques et pratiques, une nette promotion au cours des dernières décennies. Il est pourtant loin de rendre raison de l'état du droit positif. Un fond dualiste subsiste, sans doute de façon irréductible. Le monisme résulte en effet d'un choix, constitutionnel ou jurisprudentiel suivant les cas, de sorte qu'il constitue non seulement une dérive mais à la limite une modalité du dualisme.[18]

I believe that there is far more than just a *'fond dualiste'*. There is just 'dualisme'; and that *'monisme résulte… d'un choix, constitutionnel ou jurisprudentiel'* is an oxymoron. The constitutional or jurisprudential choice occurs manifestly at the national level, namely, as I understand it, on a dualist, not a monist premise.

13. The dualist/pluralist theory is sufficiently grounded in Triepel's and Anzilotti's works and is further invigorated, I immodestly believe, by the data assembled especially in paras 7–8 above, for any further demonstration to be required. It is worth

---

[15] The prevalently dualist approach of the quoted authors does emerge, however, from the comparative overviews of a number of national systems contained in ibid, 54–86.

[16] Partsch, 'International Law and Municipal Law' (1987) 10 EPIL 238.

[17] Ibid, 255. See also: Rambaud, 'International Law and Municipal Law: Conflicts and Their Review by Third States' (1987) 10 EPIL, and Schreuer, 'International Law in Municipal Law: Law and Decisions of International Organizations and Courts' (1987) 10 EPIL 262–68.

[18] Sur, Combacau, and Sur (eds), *Droit International Public* (Paris: Montchrestien, 1977) 178–79.

adding, though, that the soundness of the theory is in perfect accordance with the uniqueness of the features revealed by international law when compared with national legal systems and in its relations and interactions therewith.

(a) This applies, first of all, to the 'horizontal' structure of the system, lacking as it is in that kind of 'secondary' rules which, even in the less advanced national systems, provide for the organized creation, determination, and implementation of the law. Euphemistically described by monists (together with the 'constitution-alists' and 'interindividualists' in general) as a simple matter of 'decentralization' of a universal legal system—presumably as hypothetical as Kelsen's *Grundnorm*—the nature of international relations and international law is such that the only means for developing the necessary rules are in the hands of States as the primary persons; and the only available legal instrument for States to use—reluctant as they are to resort to any revolutionary law-making processes—is the purely inter-State compact. And States are well aware that the inter-State compact is inapt, even where it provides for the setting-up of international bodies and even if the contracting parties refrain from expressing sovereignty-saving clauses, to establish real organization, namely 'secondary' rules (in Hart's sense) subjecting States to authoritative law-making, law-determining, and law-enforcing procedures. All that the inter-State charters establishing international organs bring about, as I will show further (in para 14(b)), are systems of more or less perfect inter-State obliga-tions, the implementation of which remains in the hands of the member States themselves: Kelsen *docet* also here with his admirable theory of collective security. Considering that the formation of international customary rules is just another inter-State (not interindividual) process, it seems unlikely that significant *structural* improvements of the international system could come about through custom.

(b) Just as it dramatically affects the structure of the system, the inter-State nature of the sources of international law affects the contents of its rules: which explains why Philip Allott can say, about international law, that '[a] legal system which does its best to make sense of murder, theft, exploitation, oppression, abuse of power, and injustice perpetrated by public authorities in the public interest, is a perversion of a legal system'.[19]

It is hardly necessary to specify that international law goes so far in 'perversion' as to have tolerated for ages war and the uses of force 'short of war'. Only a 'per-verted' legal system can be so prone—due, *hélas*, to the lack of any effective oppos-ition from the governments of most States—to accepting such manifest *entorses* to the UN Charter as the long-time and current resort to armed reprisals under the untenable pretence of 'self-defence', not to mention the most recently proposed 'doctrine' of 'preventive war'. Only within the framework of a 'perverted' legal sys-tem, and its current practice by the 'strong', may there be room either for Willem Grewe's sublimation of hegemony as an allegedly integral part of international law and for the theorization of alleged or supposed 'shifting foundations' of international

---

[19] P Allott, *Eunomia: New Order for a New World* (2nd edn, Oxford: OUP, 2001) xvii.

law,[20] not to mention such findings as that of the Independent International Commission on Kosovo quoted with dismay by Michael Byers in his *The Shifting Foundations*.[21] Not less shocking, in my view, is the facile dismissal by the ICTY Prosecutor—rightly castigated by Paolo Benvenuti—of the proposed investigation on the NATO bombing campaign against Yugoslavia.[22]

(c) The lack of norms providing for authoritative law-making, law-determining, and law-enforcing—the basic gap of international law—inevitably leaves the bulk of inter-State legal relationships imprisoned, so to speak, within the strait-jacket model of a 'private law writ large' in conformity with Holland's *mot célèbre* confirmed by Sir Hersch Lauterpacht's egregiously collected (although less consistently brought to bear upon his general concept of international law, which seems to me to adhere decidedly to the monistic trend) 'private law sources and analogies'. Examples of this omnipresent pattern of inorganic law—namely, of an essentially contractual, non constitutional law—can be found in all the chapters of any scientifically valuable treatise on international law. The status of territory (and spaces in general) under international law is unique as compared to the status of territory within the framework of the law of a unitary or a federal State. The legal relations among States concerning nationals and aliens remind one, not less clearly, of analogies with the private law of ownership. However great the merits of the development of an international law of human rights, that pattern remains essentially unaltered at the regional as well as the universal level. The exceptions only concern circumscribed integrated and institutionalised systems of human rights protection within the framework of the internal law of the relevant international organs.

(d) Dualist patterns clearly prevail—despite some prima facie evaluations—in the determination of the 'will' and the 'acts' (or omissions) of States. A considerable part of the doctrine likes to see a role of national and/or international law in a supposedly 'legally' conditioned 'imputation' of acts (or omissions) to the State, which is actually based instead upon the merely factual appurtenance of the acts (or omissions) to the State as a factual collective entity, and in their attribution to the same by an essentially factual process. The Law of Treaties Convention articles clearly indicate that not much has changed, except for some presumptions, since Donato Donati explored the differences and interrelationships between constitutional law and international law in the conclusion and the effects of treaties. Articles 4–11 of the ILC project on State responsibility confirm, as well as Articles 5–15 of the 1996 first reading draft, the essentially factual nature of the conditions and the process

---

[20] M Byers (transl, ed), *WG Grewe: The Epochs of International Law* (Berlin: De Gruyter Press, 2000); and M Byers, 'The Shifting Foundations of International Law: A Decade of Forceful Measures against Iraq' (1997) 8 EJIL 21.

[21] Byers, 'The Shifting Foundations' (n 20 above) 36. I refer particularly to the notion that '(o)ne way to analyze the international law status of the NATO campaign is to consider legality a matter of degree'.

[22] P Benvenuti, 'The ICTY's Prosecutor and the Review of the Nato Bombing Campaign against FRY' (2001) 12 3 EJIL 503.

of attribution of an unlawful act to a State for the purposes of liability under international law.

(e) One finds unique features also in the frequently confused treatment of the problem of fault from the viewpoint of international law, quite wrongly neglected, in our view, by the ILC throughout its work on State responsibility. A unique feature of international law is in particular the perfect admissibility of a *mens rea* (namely of *dolus* or wilful intent) on the part of the State in the sense of international law. The extension to the State of the maxim *societas delinquere non potest* is another absurd consequence of the unrealistic concept of the State of international law as a juristic person. The realization that the 'State in the sense of international law' is a factual entity should have done justice of the notion, manifestly contradicted every day by the perpetration by States of the most serious kinds of delinquencies,[23] that States do not commit crimes. This obvious fact was vainly evoked within the ILC by the present writer in order to reduce the unjustified opposition to the inclusion, in the State responsibility articles, of adequate provisions for the determination of State crimes and their consequences.

(f) A dualistically-viewed nature of international law and the perception that international and national law operate in distinct and different *milieux* are also indispensable to understand domestic jurisdiction reservations as set forth in the Covenant, in the Charter and in instruments relating to the Hague Court's jurisdiction. The study of both the practice of League—and UN—bodies and the jurisprudence of the Hague court shows the untenability of the century-old concept of domestic jurisdiction as the area in which the State is not bound by international obligations. The only way to dispose of that concept—a concept sustained by monistic theories and their express or implied federal analogies—is to acknowledge that the domestic jurisdiction reservations relate not to imaginary *ratione materiae* distinctions of international law from national law, but only with the vertical distinction between the domain of (interindividual) national law, on the one hand, and the inter-State function and scope of international law, on the other hand.[24]

3. The second shortcoming of the original formulations of the dualist theory: inadequately accounting for international and 'supranational' organization

14. As noted in para 5 above, the second important shortcoming of dualism's original formulation is its scarce aptitude to offer a plausible systematization for a phenomenon that was only at its inception in 1899 and 1905. I refer to international

---

[23] See, for example, Allott's definition in subpara (b) .

[24] G Arangio-Ruiz, 'Le Domaine Réservé' (n 9 above); 'The Plea of Domestic Jurisdiction before the ICJ: Substance or Procedure' (n 9 above) 440–63.

and 'supranational' organizations. We all miss, as a consequence, the views that Triepel and Anzilotti could have expressed over the impact of the constituent instruments of the League or the United Nations upon the structure of the international system. I guess, though, that they would have been hesitant to accept the construction of international organizations proposed by the monist school.

(a) In studying international organizations, since about 1950, in the light of the above-mentioned factual concept of the State in the sense of international law, I have been led to distinguishing, within the law of international and 'supranational' bodies (including, of course, together with the United Nations and its Specialized Agencies, isolated international organs such as arbitral tribunals and conciliation commissions, as well as the EC and EU), two elements. On the one hand, there are the constitutive treaties; on the other hand, the international organs' internal legal orders. I call this, precisely—*pace*, again, the 'constitutionalists' (para 1(a), above) and monist scholars in general—'a dualist (or, more exactly, pluralist) theory of international organization'.

(b) To begin with the former element—for example, the UN Charter—the constitutive instrument remains within the sphere of ordinary treaty law. Neither the rules setting forth direct obligations and rights for the member States (such as to refrain from war or force, to settle disputes amicably, to respect each other's territorial integrity, or to cooperate in many areas of human endeavour), nor the rules contemplating the establishing and financing of organs, nor even the rules contemplating the acts of the entity's organs and the consequences they bring about for the member States (such as the obligation to pay the dues decided by the General Assembly under Article 17, to adopt the measures decided upon by the Security Council under Article 41, *et similia*) bring about a significant alteration of the inorganic, horizontal structure of the international system. They bring about neither a change of the member States' condition of 'sovereign equality' among themselves (under general international law), nor a relinquishment of their independence or external sovereignty to the organization. They bring about such prodigies neither in the sense of placing the organization 'over and above' the member States, nor in the sense of placing given member States (such as the permanent members of the Security Council) 'over and above' other member States. Similar considerations apply to any international organ or organization.

Whatever its name—Charter, Statute, Constitution, or just Treaty—the constituent instrument creates, in international law, nothing more than the same kind of mutual right/obligations relationships among the member States that are created by a *compromis* entrusting an arbitral tribunal to settle a dispute between two States. Just as such a tribunal is not placed by the *compromis* 'over and above' the contracting States, no other international organ is so placed 'over and above' the participating States by its constituent treaty. To put it bluntly there is, at the level of the relations governed by the constituent instrument, no real organization in the sense of 'hierarchization'.

Regarding in particular the UN Charter, a minor piece of evidence of this state of affairs is the universally-shared opinion of the founders of the UN (and all the subsequently admitted members) that the organization would not be a 'super-State'. A more weighty piece of evidence is the nature of the personality of the UN, at least as the present writer sees it. I explained in English my long-entertained position in this respect in an article on the '*Federal Analogy*', which appeared in the EJIL in 1997. By far the most impressive, though, is the evidence offered by the lack of adequate reaction by the membership to the arrogant treatment that a few national establishments have been systematically inflicting, now for some time, upon the UN: a treatment that seems currently to be reaching such a gravity as to put in serious jeopardy the prestige if not the very survival of the organization.

(c) Turning to the second of the two elements I believe one must consider in the study of international organizations, the mechanisms through which international bodies, large or small, carry out their action are a different thing from the con-stituent treaties. I refer to the interindividual structures composed of the members of the secretariats' staffs, of the delegates to collective bodies, and to any other per-sons involved in the organs' activity. Obviously, the individuals manning those bodies are organized under legal rules; and the rules in question have now for a long time been rightly singled out by scholarship as the internal legal orders of international organs as more or less sharply distinguished from the inter-State rules of the constituent instruments. The size and complexity of these numerous (but very sparse) systems of interindividual law varies, of course, according to the dimensions and the functions of each organization or organ. There is a great dif-ference, for example, between the relatively small number of rules governing the operation of an *ad hoc* arbitral tribunal or claims commission, on the one hand, and the huge fabric of the internal law of the United Nations, of a Specialized Agency or the EC, on the other hand. More important are some functional differences. Where the organ performs strictly inter-State functions—such as addressing deci-sions, judgments, directives, or recommendations to States (namely, international activity *stricto sensu*)—the subjects of the organ's internal order are just the mem-bers of the organ's staff. Where, however, the organ is called by its statute or by *ad hoc* arrangement to carry out the so-called 'operational' activities—namely, what I call 'vicarious State activities'—its legal order's scope extends, beyond the staff, to all the persons involved in the organ's action within the territory of one or more States. Although the most egregious example is the EC's or the EU's legal system, striking examples are the interindividual rules governing the dozens of UN field operations classifiable under the various generations of UN peace-keeping A current impressive example is UNMIK.

15. The relationship of the internal orders in question with international law, on the one hand, and with national legal systems, on the other hand, is a difficult topic not yet adequately investigated by international legal scholarship. The present writer himself devoted some work on the matter, only a long time ago. These are not good

reasons, however, for me to adhere to the wantonly optimistic presentation of the phenomenon offered by monist scholars.

(a) Indeed, monist writers place the whole law of international organization—encompassing both the constituent instrument and the organs' internal law—under the all-embracing, *bon à tout faire*, umbrella of their imaginary universal legal system (of 'natural law'?) undergoing a 'centralizing' process. Regarding particularly the construction of the internal legal orders of international organs, the monist theory seems to take no account of the undeniable signs of diversity and/or discontinuity that mark the relationship between those internal orders, on the one hand, and both, despite their ancillary position, the relevant constitutive treaties (together with general international law), on the one hand, and the participating States' national legal systems, on the other hand.

For my part, I deem such a view untenable. Due, however, to the noted inadequacy of scholarly work on the matter, I can only venture a few very tentative considerations in the light of the previous work of mine.

(b) From the viewpoint of international law, the internal legal orders of international organs might appear, prima facie, to be sufficiently affected by the organ's constituent instrument as to be acknowledged, unlike national legal systems, as 'derivations' of international law. On the other hand, the internal orders in question are direct creations, not so much of the respective constituent instruments themselves, as of the instruments' *implementation* by the participating *States* and by the *individuals manning each mechanism*. Second, the various organs' internal orders address themselves to entities—individuals—whose international personality is not only generally viewed as problematic but is *rightly contested*, in my opinion, by dualist scholars. It is contested even where, as in the instruments relating to human rights and criminal liability, individual rights or liabilities are expressly covered by the relevant constituent instrument (para 2(b) and (c), above). Furthermore, the internal orders of international bodies are characterized by a sufficiently high degree of *hierarchical organization* to appear strikingly different, in structure, from the inorganic, 'horizontally' shaped inter-State system. The legal orders of international bodies are characterized by the presence of all the organised functions that are typical of national legal systems, including legislation, administration, and compulsory adjudication.

Indirect relationship with the constituent instrument, lack of international personality of the addressees and hierarchical structure, seem thus to point to a *high degree of similarity* between the relationship of international organs' legal orders to international law and the relationship of national legal systems to international law. One might thus conclude in the sense that the legal orders in question present a certain degree of autonomy, perhaps even 'originality', vis-à-vis the constituent instrument and general international law. This in turn would seem to afford some basis for that considerable degree of independence enjoyed by the organ in dealing with its external relations, which justifies the organ's assumption as a primary person under general international law.

(c) However, a further exploration in depth and extension is indispensable, in my view, with regard to the problem of the necessary adaptation of international bodies' legal systems to both their respective constituent instruments and to general international law. This is actually the aspect of the matter that I deem to be in the greatest need of more adequate study. One of the main issues in this respect, is how far the international duty of automatic adaptation of the organs' legal orders to the rules of the constituent instrument and general international law—a duty in principle not present, in international law, in the case of national legal systems—is incumbent upon the participating States and how far it incumbs upon the individuals manning the organ's legal order. A difference must probably be acknowledged here from the problem of adaptation of national legal systems.

(d) As regards the status of the organ's legal order vis-à-vis States' legal orders, since the organ is established as a dependent body of the participating States, its legal order might again be seen in principle, prima facie, as a derivated one. Considering, however, that the dependence relationship is established with all the participating States together, the generality of the latter sharing an interest in maintaining the organ's and its legal order's impartiality, the resulting situation seems to be one of distinct, however relative and limited, independence from any one of the several relevant national systems. This seems to indicate, again, a certain degree of 'originality' of the organ's internal order vis-à-vis the participating States and to offer a further basis for that primary personality of the organ under general international law to which I earlier referred.

(e) Be it as it may of its analogies with, and differences from, national legal orders, the internal legal orders of international bodies interact—as well as national law—with both international law, on the one hand, and national legal orders, on the other hand. (They also interact, incidentally, *inter se*: an area that is even less explored and could usefully be singled out as an *ad hoc* section of the Research Project of Professor Nollkaemper's Institute). Although some differences would presumably emerge from further research on the subject, the interactions involving the legal orders of international bodies in either direction (international law and the several national orders) might well not reveal much more unity—or much less distinction and separation—than between national law and international law. I have just evoked above, under subpara (c), the possible peculiarities that the internal orders of international bodies might present in the area of adaptation.

4. Concluding remarks

16. The relatively high degree of distinction of the myriad of international organs' internal legal systems from both their respective constituent treaties, on the one hand, and the national legal systems of the participating States, on the other hand, leads me to believe that the narrow dichotomy between international law, on the one hand, and each one of the 190 odd national legal orders, on the other

hand—namely, the old but quite solid dichotomy originally proposed by the dualist/pluralist school—should be replaced, in order to complete the theory's coverage of international legal realities, by a broader dichotomy. One must distinguish, precisely, international law, on the one hand, and any *species* of interindividual law, on the other hand. The latter *genus* would include both the several national legal systems, on the one hand, and the several internal legal systems of international bodies, on the other hand, the latter systems to be acknowledged, in order to mark their international character, as unassembled bits and pieces of *international-interindividual law*.

Something must be added with regard to those sets or formations of (mostly unwritten) rules of private law that can be ascribed neither to international law proper nor to the private law (and conflicts of law rules or principles) of national legal systems and also seem to belong to the *genus* of international interindividual law. I refer to '*droit privé des peuples*' and *lex mercatoria*. In the same class one might perhaps ascribe the rules applying to the transactions between States and private parties, namely the rules rightly or wrongly classified by some scholars, together, at times, with the law of international organs, as 'transnational law': this to the extent, of course, that sufficient reason cannot be found for such rules to be ascribed to one or more national legal systems. I just received, thanks to the Author's generosity, Charles Leben's very interesting latest edition (the 6th edition, March 2003) of his booklet *Le droit international des affaires* (in the *Que sais-je?* series of Presses Universitaire de France). To the species of international interindividual law—to the extent, here again, that it cannot be ascribed to given national legal systems—seem also to belong many of the rules governing international non-governmental organizations (NGOs).

17. Considering the factual nature of the State in the sense of international law and the above-described features of the international system, I am encouraged to find it not unreasonable—and not irreverent to the majesty of international law— to point out a certain analogy, *mutatis* all the possible *mutandis*, between the relations among States, on the one hand, and the relations among factual groups within modern national societies, on the other hand. Despite the relatively marginal nature of the latter phenomenon, the analogy *saute aux yeux*; and it seems to me more significant than the more frequently evoked analogy with inter-group relations in primitive societies.

Indeed, in modern, developed societies, once political integration is attained, no factual groups are likely to prosper among which one could envisage the existence of relations and possibly of rules of conduct. The groups coexisting within the community are so thoroughly penetrated by the nation's whole legal order that they are normally absorbed within the legal fabrics of juristic persons or similarly legal subdivisions. The groups underlying corporations, for example—or the human aggregations organized into local territorial communities within the State—are so pervasively conditioned by their charters, statutes, or by-laws, all absorbed into the legal order of the whole society, that from the viewpoint of the latter only the artificial entity created by the law comes into the forefront as an actor. However, even in the most cohesive national communities integration is rarely, if ever, so thorough as to exclude totally the presence of factual groups and inter-group relations. A closer observation reveals, however, that there are factual groups escaping the juridical net, so to speak, of the (interindividual) legal system's controls to an extent sufficient for some inter-group relations permanently or occasionally to manifest themselves, with a possible relevance of their own, distinct from the relevance of their members, agents, subjects, or beneficiaries. Examples of groups coexisting as sociological units within national societies are of course, in the first place, the aggregations of human beings constituting the *substrata* of corporations, associations, and personified or non-personified territorial subdivisions of the national community. More important examples for my present purposes are ethnic minorities and majorities, religious groups, personified or non-personified political parties, labour and trade unions.

While normally acting through agents legally vested with a representative capacity by the total community's legal system, each group being thus imperson-ated by a corporation, such entities do operate at times as factual—although fre-quently not illegal—collective bodies. Only a marginal phenomenon in ordinary circumstances, the occurrences of that kind may assume such dimensions, in situ-ations of ethnic, political, or social tension, that inter-group relations manifest themselves with a relatively high degree of intensity. In more dramatic but not rare cases, the coexisting groups may even take postures of such a nature as to prevent the national legal system's normal operation with regard to both their internal and external relations. In even more serious crises some groups appear in such a stance as to be described as 'States within the State'. In extreme circumstances, the exist-ence of powerful, highly cohesive, and organized groups goes so far as to jeopar-dize the very existence of the national legal system.

Despite a number of features that make it unique, the pattern of the relations among States within the universal society resembles the pattern of the intergroup relations I have just cursorily evoked. *Mutatis mutandis*, States coexist within the universal society as relatively 'closed' political units not totally unlike territorial groups within a primitive society or factual groups within a modern, relatively well integrated society.[25] With regard to some instances of particularly pronounced

---

[25] Speaking of intergroup relations one should not fail to recall the scholarly studies dealing with such relations within primitive societies or in the ancient world. Interesting analogies can also be found in the speculative theories of a number of historians of Roman law, a few of whom thought that some legal features of the public and private law of ancient Rome could be explained by the theory that the Roman *civitas* originated from a federal process involving families, *gentes*, or clans, such entities (*gentes* especially) having previously coexisted as separate political units. One spoke of a 'diritto inter-gentilizio', an expression suggesting perhaps some analogy with international law.

Indeed, Pietro Bonfante's and other scholars' theory of 'diritto intergentilizio'—and of a 'federal' origin of the Roman *civitas*—was sharply criticized by Arangio-Ruiz, Vincenzo, *Le Genti e la Città*, Inaugural Lecture, University of Messina, 1914, reprinted in *Scritti di Diritto Romano* (Vol 1, Napoli Jovene, 1974) 521–87. The latter author actually extended to international law his doubt about the reality or the juridical nature of 'diritto intergentilizio'. In his words: '*Da prima la valutazione delle offese e dei mezzi di ritorsione fu nell'arbitrio delle singole genti; ma successivamente si formò fra le genti*

relations among groups of the latter kind, one must actually register more than just an analogy. A typical case is that of political factions or parties aiming at a change of the country's régime. Whenever such groups engage in open violence and civil strife, they assume the posture of an insurgent party and eventually of a general or local *de facto* government, thus becoming participants in international relations and subjects of international law. The conflictual situations in Yugoslavia and Somalia are recent instances. Intra-State inter-group relations appear in such occurrences not just similar to international relations; they simply *turn into international relations proper*. Instances of a reverse process—international relations turning into intergroup relations within a national community—can easily be found.

Be it as it may of such occurrences, inter-State relations do present, on the other hand, unique features in comparison with other forms of inter-group relations. The multi-secular fragmentation of mankind into diverse political communities separately constituted and separately organized into States (the formation of some of which dates back to an impressive number of centuries) is the cause and the effect, at one time, of the lack of political integration and the absence of a universal or regional public law of men. Unlike the inter-group relations marginally present within a national society, the relations among States must not adversely confront themselves with an interindividual legal order 'of a whole'. International relations are thus a far more firmly settled phenomenon.

The fragmentation of mankind is actually deepened by the fact that the factors of universal disintegration have been consolidated by the very consequences of their own operation through the centuries that divide us from the downfall of *Respublica Christianorum*. May I recall the vicious circle I mentioned in para 8(a), above and take up again below. The partial integrative processes that at times have led to the formation of larger political aggregations are more than counterbalanced by disgregative processes resulting in a multiplication of the coexisting separate units. It is hardly necessary to recall the recent dismemberment of the USSR or Yugoslavia.

Despite the striking increase of the interdependence among peoples and despite the development of international communication facilities in the course of the last century, the most perceptive students of international relations seem to be still convinced, unlike a growing number of constitutional and international lawyers, that the inter-State system is as firmly established as ever. And it is precisely the centuries-old firmness of the inter-State system that determines, together with all its other features, the relationship of international law with national law and interindividual law in general.

18. The realistic concept of the State in the sense of international law and the broadening of the dualist/pluralist theory's scope properly to encompass, together

---

una comune opinione, che si può chiamare diritto intergentilizio <u>con la stessa catacresi con cui oggi si parla di diritto internazionale</u> (p 12 of the off-print, p 528 of the cited reprint, underlined emphasis added).

with the dichotomy of international and national law, any formations of inter-individual rules other than those of national legal orders, opens the way to an even deeper insight into the features of international law only a number of which are stressed in para 13, above.

The strengthening and completion of the theory afford in the first place a clearer perception of the unique nature of international law, particularly of its specific function. As a system of rules finding their *raison d'être*, whatever their objects and contents, in the relations among States as factual entities, factually ruling over distinct, separate political communities, international law is not envisageable as the summit of a universal legal system originating from an alleged 'decentralization' of the medieval 'world State' and evolving, by a process of more or less gradual 'centralization', into a universal legal community. Its unique features, mainly the unique composition of its constituency—hardly affected by the superficially alleged demise of the State and State sovereignty (both quite prosperous for good or evil)—assign to international law a more realistic, transitional, and in a sense ancillary function than that of the universal public law of mankind, envisaged as a current reality by the monists.

19. It follows that one cannot expect the international legal system itself to metamorphose from inter-State to interindividual, from inorganic to organic, from 'private law writ large' to the supreme layer of the universal public law, ultimately into the constitution of the legal community of mankind. The international legal system on the one hand and the 'Legal Community of Mankind To Be' on the other hand, are, in principle, reciprocally exclusive. International law should be envisaged not, per se, as an early stage of that community. It is far less. All it seems able to provide—in addition, hopefully, to preserving the peace—are the instruments by which governments, without necessarily renouncing their sovereign prerogatives—notably their mutual independence and equality—should find the ways and means through which the various communities over which they rule could turn into legal subdivisions of the world community and States themselves into the juristic persons within that community's law. The distinction I am stressing presents a certain analogy, *mutatis mutandis*, with Kant's distinction between *Völkerrecht* as a 'law of nature', on the one hand, and 'cosmopolitan law' (as a law of mankind), on the other hand: except, surely, for the fact, inter alia *mutanda*, that the most important among the fragments of the contemporary 'cosmopolitan' law—namely, the internal legal orders of the innumerable international bodies—are being created by inter-State agreements as a part of an international law—the latter viewed by me, not without some hesitation, as something more than just Kant's *ius naturae*.[26]

The main tools for such a development—an inevitably gradual although technically revolutionary process—are obviously the inter-State compacts by which States could set up increasingly effective international peace-keeping, peace-enforcing, and

---

[26] D Alland, 'Droit des Gens et Droit International' in *Dictionnaire de Philosophie Politique* (2nd edn, Paris: Pedone, 1988) 152, 155–56.

possibly law-making and law-determining or adjudicating collective machineries. Foremost among such machineries States should develop those interindividual internal orders of international and 'supranational' bodies able to take not only inter-State action through decisions, directives or recommendations addressed to governments but also those 'vicarious State activities' that attain the peoples themselves. It is especially in the latter kind of activity, possibly carried out in any State, large or small—not just in 'failing' or actual or allegedly 'rogue' States—that rest presumably the less implausible hopes for the progress toward the achievement of a universal legal community of mankind. It is perhaps in that direction that States should use the law-making means available to them with a view to seconding, under the control of general international law, treaty law and the competent international organizations, their own gradual metamorphosis into legal subdivisions and juristic persons within the law of that community of mankind. There are at present, *hélas*, too many signs that such is not the trend that meets the favour of the most weighty among the participants in the relations that international law should govern. The prevailing trend seems to be a diametrically opposite one, and too many among the governments that should and could resist it seem to be very reluctant to do so.

20. But it is time for closing. In the hope that the present writing elicit sooner or later critical, possibly constructive, responses within the framework of the Amsterdam Institute's programme, I deem it useful to add a few words about my dualism (of course, as explained in para 1(c), above: *dualism/pluralism*) repeatedly qualified as 'absurd' by Joseph Kunz in the interesting reviews I mentioned at the outset.[27]

Compared to Triepel's—if I may say so without sounding conceited—'my' dualism (or, better, pluralism) seems to me to be firmer and less *borné* (or more flexible) at the same time.

It is firmer in that international law and national law are viewed not just as separate but as qualitatively different *genera* of law, the latter being interindividual (as a species of the *genus* interindividual law) and the former inter-State (as a species of inter-group law).

It is also flexible, at the same time, in that it leaves room for phenomena—such as international-interindividual law—that, to say the least, are not easy to classify within Triepel's and Anzilotti's kind of dualism. Even there, though, 'my' dualism is strengthened by its firmness and by its insertion within the framework of that

---

[27] According to Kunz's review of *Gli enti Soggetti dell'ordinamento Internazionale* (Giuffrè Milan, 1951), despite the author's 'highly interesting, deep-searching work' that 'repai[d] study', the 'wish to found anew the dualist doctrine must be regarded as frustrated'. The reviewer also acknowledged, though, that 'from the point of view of the critique of positive international law..[the author's theses] contribute[d] to the understanding of the necessary precariousness of merely "international" as distinguished from "supranational" organization' (1953) AJIL 512 at 513. Similar opinions are expressed by Kunz in his joint review of *Rapporti Contrattuali fra Stati e Organizzazione Internazionale* (*Archivio giuridico Filippo Serafini*, 1950), and *Gli enti* in *Oesterreichische Zeitschrift*, mentioned in n 1, above.

broader dichotomy between the 'inter-State' and the 'interindividual', by which I believe it to be indispensable to replace the narrow dichotomy between the 'international' and the 'national'. It is indeed that firmness that helps systematize the 'snips' and 'snippets' of international-interindividual law (notably the internal legal systems of international organs) in such a manner as to escape that facile, deceptive monistic systematization of those important phenomena within the framework of a purely imaginary public law of mankind *avant la lettre*. (The same should be said, incidentally, about the legal rules relating to transnational corporations and the rules governing international non-governmental organizations to the extent that they elude any national law.)

To the pluralism of legal systems, which is attested by the coexistence of international law with the 190-odd co-existing national systems, one must add the pluralism deriving from the existence of an even higher number of internal legal orders of great and small international and 'supranational' bodies, from the United Nations, and the United Nations family agencies, to the EC, the EU, arbitral tribunals, international criminal courts, etc. Within such an additional pluralism—so far, in my view, inadequately studied—one must reckon a host of bilateral dualisms between each national or international interindividual system and each one of the others, on the one hand, and between each one of those systems and international law proper—namely, inter-State law—on the other hand.

It is a maze of dualistic relationships that cannot be ignored by scholars and practicing lawyers—for the elementary reason indicated in para 1(a), above—without getting into utter confusion. It would be simply impossible to deal properly with such interrelationships within the framework of a science-fictional notion of a universal juridical monism.

In addition to being scientifically questionable (for its lack of any positive basis in an international constitutional law worthy of the name) the monist doctrine seems also to be questionable *de lege ferenda*. It is indeed under monist influence that an increasing number of authoritative scholars are not content with enhancing and emphasizing that 'public' law character of international law, which is implied in that doctrine and so hard to detect from a dispassionate observation of inter-State relations. They are also led lately to promote international law from that rank of a 'set' or 'system of norms' that is implied in its current realistic denomination (especially among English-speaking scholars) to the loftier and rather pretentious rank that would be implied in the expression 'ordre juridique international'.[28] Combined with the 'public' (law) connotation implicit in the monist conception, the concept of 'order' seems to me to introduce into the system's identity a questionable proclivity to accommodate—for precisely the sake of order—unilateral initiatives of States and, worse, unilaterally proclaimed and practised doctrines—which a

[28] See, for example, D Alland, 'De l'Ordre Juridique International' in *Droit international Public* (Paris: PUF, 2002) 79–101.

modest set or system of norms would be perhaps more inclined, in principle, to submit to a severe *normative* scrutiny.[29]

21. One ultimate remark is appropriate here about the nature of international law. The notion that the State of international law is not a juristic person, which in my view is at the very root of the dualist/pluralist theory, is not unrelated to the question of the juridical nature of the international system. Indeed, an obvious condition for international law to be viewed as law is the possibility for States to be envisageable as units capable of being effectively addressed and conditioned in their behaviours by norms of conduct worthy of the name of law. An answer could be that the unity that is not ensured by that mechanism of juridical incorporation that is typical of juristic persons (*personnes morales*) is ensured to a sufficient extent, in the case of the State in the sense of international law, by the sociological factors, national law included, cementing, so to speak, each human aggregation and its statehood.

This state of affairs nevertheless has an impact, though, on the aptness of international law to condition effectively the behaviours of its subjects. Indeed, one thing is the aptness of norms to condition the behaviour of a juristic person through agents and members they directly attain as primary persons, another thing is the aptitude of norms to condition a sociological unit upon the constituency of which

---

[29] Ibid, 79–101. After describing the merits of substituting 'Ordre Juridique International' for the less savoury 'Droit International', the author also advocates the extension to international law (and, of course, to the 'international community') of the concepts proposed by Santi Romano in his 'Ordre juridique' (Paris: Dalloz, 1975). Alland refers in particular to para 17 of that very remarkable book that is entitled *Le Concept d'institution et l'Ordre Juridique International*. With great respect for Santi Romano as well as Denis Alland, I dare say that if '*ordre* juridique international' scares me, I find the yoking of that denomination with Romano's 'istituzione' terrifying. Whatever its merits—surely great—in enlightening the relationship of law with society and the society's structuring, Romano moves too far, in my view, from the concept of law as a normative system with regard to any legal system. He gets even farther, though, with regard to international law. It follows that to look at international law through Romano's lenses would open the way to accepting, as part of the very body of international law, much more sociology than the average international legal scholar—who works, hopefully, essentially on the basis of norms—is ready to accept. Indeed, Romano's concept of law or legal order is too rich in pre-, meta-, or extra-juridical elements for its advocated extension to international law and the international community not to open the way to unacceptable, undemonstrated theories, such as Lasswell's and McDougal's concept of international law as 'a process of authoritative decision'. Norms, hopefully, are less difficult to circumvent by such theories, that seem to be conceived for the very purpose of legitimizing unilateral actions and initiatives and unilaterally proclaimed doctrines.

One need hardly recall, in that connection, the questionable sublimation of hegemony as an integral part of international law, made throughout his book by Grewe, *The Epochs of International Law* (n 20 above); and the possibly related considerations set forth by Byers, 'The Shifting Foundations' (n 20 above) 41, particularly with regard to the sources of international law. As well as the 'processes of authoritative decision', hegemony and 'shifting foundations' would fit beautifully, no doubt, within the framework of Romano's 'institutionalized' international 'legal order'. The same would apply, surely, to the alternative to the UN collective security system proposed by Pescatore, *The US-UK Intervention in Iraq, in ASIL Newsletter*, May/July 2003, 1 and 6, not to mention appalling doctrines such as those proposed (with significant references to Lasswell's and McDougal's theories) in the letter addressed to ASIL's President by FS Tipson (a former consultant with the US Senate Foreign Relations Committee) in *ASIL Newsletter*, March/April, 2003, 1, 4, and 14.

they have no direct, positive juridical control. Undoubtedly considerable, such a difference explains that comparatively low degree of effectiveness of international law that is universally perceived by dualists/pluralists as well as monists, although euphemistically presented by the latter as a simple matter of 'decentralization'. The same feature explains the enormous difficulty of establishing really effective international organizations. Even at European level, where a high degree of economic integration has been attained, it appears to be increasingly difficult to move from a system of intergovernmental (inter-State) treaties and arrangements to a real constitution. As well as the study of universal international institutions the study of the EU and the EC confirm the concept of international law as an inter-State 'private law writ large' rather than that of a universal decentralized public law of mankind.

One could not exclude, I am afraid, an even more pessimistic conclusion that some current world affairs might suggest: namely, that the impact of the factual nature of States upon international relations is too overwhelmingly ponderous for any norms worthy of the name of law to be apt to govern such relations effectively. Considering the implied or express opinions of not a few statesmen and scholars, such a pessimistic conclusion seems, regrettably, neither implausible nor disgraceful. Far better men than the present writer have felt obliged to admit, however reluctantly, that most of what we know as international law possesses not the essential features of positive law[30] in a proper sense.

---

[30] A doubt is expressed by Arangio-Ruiz, Vincenzo, in the passage from *Le Genti e la Città,* quoted in n 25 above.

2

Dualism—a Review

Giorgio Gaja

1. Is dualism an Italian disease?

In his remarkable book *Le statut international de l'ordre juridique étatique* Carlo Santulli recalls in a long footnote[1] that for many years Joseph Kunz had reviewed books written by Italian authors for the American Journal of International Law and that he invariably deplored the dualist approach that in his opinion marred their work. Thus, for instance, Kunz noted in one review that 'for generations the whole Italian school of the science of international law has stood firmly as one man on the basis of the dualistic doctrine as shaped by Triepel and Anzilotti'.[2] In a later review he complained that an Italian author had used the 'fallacious basis of the "strictest dualist doctrine", accepted even in the often absurd form given to it recently by Arangio-Ruiz'.[3] When reviewing a book by Mario Giuliano, Kunz wrote: 'although a Marxist and pro-Communist, he is, nevertheless, an Italian and starts from the fallacious basis of the dualistic doctrine which permeates all parts of the book'.[4] And Santulli to conclude: '*Caveat italicus!*'[5]

Supposing that dualism is a disease, is it also infectious? Should one then not reverse Santulli's warning and tell non-Italian international lawyers to beware of Italian dualists?

2. Defining dualism

It is not certain whether dualism is a single conception or a category of conceptions which have one or more elements in common. The main feature of dualism appears to be that international law and municipal laws are viewed as separate legal systems, which may be defined as self-contained, because within each system the only existing rules are those that are part of the system. Rules which are not

---

[1] C Santulli, *Le Statut International de l'Ordre Juridique Etatique* (Paris: Pedone, 1990/2001) 266, n 556. [2] (1953) 47 AJIL 512.
[3] (1957) 51 AJIL 849.   [4] Ibid, 842.   [5] Santulli (n 1 above) 266, n 556.

created within the system may nevertheless be relevant for the system if they are referred to by a rule included in the system.

Given the fact that the systems under consideration are more than two, it would be more appropriate to call the conception 'pluralist' rather than 'dualist'. However, it may be preferable to adopt here the terminology that is more usual in the discussion of the relations between international law and municipal laws. The traditional way of considering the prevailing conceptions refers to dualism and monism. While dualism stresses the element of separation between the legal systems, monism implies that a link between international law and municipal laws necessarily exists. This link sometimes appears to be a formality: for instance, when, according to the normativist approach, it is said to consist only in the circumstance that the basic norm of each municipal legal system is part of international law. The reverse case in which the basic norm of international law is viewed as part of municipal law need not be considered here, because it would not in fact lead to monism but to the existence of as many separate systems as there are municipal laws.

Monism does not necessarily imply the invalidity of the provisions of municipal law that conflict with international law.[6] The logical necessity for the unity of all legal systems that Hans Kelsen invoked in favour of monism, namely that no conflicts may exist between legal systems,[7] would thus not be satisfied. It is any way questionable whether conflicts between legal provisions pertaining to different systems should not be viewed as physiological. One has only to refer to the regrettably frequent case in which individuals find themselves under conflicting provisions because of different rules of conflict of laws and of unharmonized substantive provisions.

Should dualism be defined, as was suggested above, through the self-contained character of international law and municipal laws, the dualist conception would have to be regarded as valid if all the systems were self-contained. Were neither international law nor municipal laws self-contained, dualism would be unacceptable and all the systems would be coordinated according to one or the other form of monism. Dualism would be partly valid if one or more legal systems were self-contained and one or more other systems were not. Thus, one cannot rule out the existence of a 'third way' between dualism and monism, although that way does not rest with the widespread 'pragmatic' approach that tends to ignore the theoretical debate and fails to give a clear answer to the question whether international law and municipal laws are self-contained or not.[8]

---

[6] According to H Kelsen, 'Les Rapports de Système entre le Droit Interne et le Droit International Public' (1926 IV) 14 Recueil des Cours 227, 273, the provision of the lower legal system would be authorized to derogate from the higher system, albeit provisionally and for a limited time (*'l'ordre inférieur délégué est autorisé à déroger, provisoirement et pour un terme limité, à l'ordre supérieur'*).

[7] Ibid, 267–69.

[8] This may be said also of the eloquent attempt made by M Virally, 'Sur un Pont aux Anes: les Rapports entre Droit International et Droits Internes', *Mélanges offerts à Henri Rolin. Problèmes de Droit des Gens* (Paris: Pedone, 1964) 488.

No doubt, the dualist conception presents some further distinctive features. Some features are implications of what has been here defined as the main common element, some other aspects are not strictly related to the self-contained character of international law and municipal laws. They will be considered later. There are also some features of dualism that are attributed to it by opponents to the dualist conception, in order to build arguments in favour of monism. It may suffice to recall the views expressed by Kelsen that the dualist conception implies a denial of the legal nature of international law,[9] and that, should municipal law not provide for the jurisdictional immunity of diplomatic agents, the existence of a limitation to jurisdiction based on international law would be irreconcilable with the dualist theory.[10] These latter features deserve to be considered only to the extent that they are actually implied in the self-contained character of international and municipal laws.

3. Do international law and municipal laws necessarily have different legal addressees?

According to several dualists the reason why international law and municipal laws are separate legal systems lies with the circumstance that the subjects of international law and municipal laws are different, and therefore the legal systems govern different types of relations. International law is viewed as regulating the conduct of States as subjects of international law and thus inter-State relations, while municipal laws apply to the relations between State organs and individuals and between individuals.[11] In other words, international law is considered as the law pertaining to international society, of which individuals are not regarded as members. Individuals could be reached by international law only indirectly, through provisions of municipal laws that States are under an obligation to adopt.

This assumption implies that current propositions of international law concerning human rights and international crimes have to be re-cast in more appropriate legal terms. To write of human rights or individual crimes under international law could only be valid as a shorthand expression. The pertinent rules of international law would have to be understood as imposing on States an obligation to protect human rights or to repress crimes (in the latter case, possibly as enabling States to repress them). Rights and obligations for individuals would exist only on the basis of rules of municipal law that a State adopts in order to comply with its obligations under international law.

---

[9] Kelsen, 'Les Rapports' (n 6 above) 276–77.   [10] Ibid, 279.

[11] H Triepel, *Völkerrecht und Landesrecht* (Leipzig: Hirschfeld, 1899) 20; D Anzilotti, *Il Diritto Internazionale nei Giudizi Interni* (Bologna: Zanichelli, 1905), reprinted in *Scritti di Diritto Internazionale Pubblico* (Padova: CEDAM, 1956) Vol I, 281, 320; G Arangio-Ruiz, 'Le Domaine Réservé. L'Organisation Internationale et le Rapport entre Droit International et Droit Interne' (1990-VI) 225 Recueil des Cours 9, 448.

It is true that many rules of international law have only States as their legal addressees and thus only govern inter-State relations. However, the view that international law cannot reach individuals is somewhat dated.[12] It was stated by the Permanent Court of International Justice in its advisory opinion on the *Jurisdiction of the Courts of Danzig*, when the Court noted that 'according to a well established principle of international law, the *Beamtenabkommen*, being an international agreement, cannot, as such, create direct rights and obligations for private individuals'.[13] In 2001 the existence of individuals' rights under international law was on the contrary endorsed—not just as a shorthand expression—both by the International Court of Justice and the International Law Commission. In its judgment in the *LaGrand* case the Court held that a bilateral treaty over consular matters 'spells out the obligations the receiving State has towards the detained person and the sending States' and 'creates individual rights'.[14] Article 33, paragraph 2, of the ILC Articles on State responsibility, adopted on second reading, says: 'This Part [of the Articles] is without prejudice to any right, arising from the international responsibility of a State, which may accrue directly to any person or entity other than a State'.[15]

Should one accept the view that international law confers rights and obligations on individuals, it seems reasonable to hold that international law may also impose obligations on specific State organs: for instance, require that national courts grant immunity from their jurisdiction to particular categories of persons.[16] This possibility was not acknowledged by the International Tribunal for Former Yugoslavia in the *Blaskić* case, when the Appeals Chamber found that 'customary international law protects the internal organization of each sovereign State to determine its internal structure' and that 'both under general international law and the Statute itself, Judges or Trial Chambers cannot address binding orders to State officials'.[17] However, even this judgment did not argue from a logical impossibility for international law to reach State officials directly, and assumed the existence of 'a few exceptions'.[18] In its order on interim measures in the *LaGrand* case the International Court of Justice stated that 'the Governor of Arizona was

---

[12] G Balladore Pallieri, 'Le Dottrine di Hans Kelsen e il Problema dei Rapporti fra Diritto Interno e Diritto Internazionale' (1935) 27 Rivista di diritto internazionale 24, 74, had already noted that, even if international law did not govern the conduct of individuals, nothing prevented international law from expanding its reach in this regard ('*nulla gli impedirebbe di estendere maggiormente la sua efficacia*').   [13] PCIJ, Publications, Series B, No 15 at 17.
[14] ICJ Reports 2001, 494 (para 77).
[15] UN Doc. A/56/10 at 233; J Crawford (ed), *The International Law Commission's Articles on State Responsibility* (Cambridge: CUP, 2002) 209.
[16] As it was put by HF van Panhuys, 'Relations and Interactions between International and National Scenes of Law' (1964-II) 112 Recueil des Cours 3, 15, national courts, while under a 'mandate' from their respective State, may have to apply international law because of the 'imperative directive' 'addressed to the mandatory in question emanating from outside the legal order to which the mandate belongs'.
[17] Judgment of 29 October 1997, reproduced in (1998) 81 Rivista di diritto internazionale 190, 213 and 215 (paras 41 and 43).   [18] Ibid, 213 (para 41).

under an obligation to act in conformity with the international undertakings of the United States'.[19]

The latter approach seems in line with the idea that, for the purpose of a State complying with its obligations under international law, State organs are necessarily required to act consistently with those obligations. However, one difficulty with this approach is that, when an obligation is regarded as imposed directly on a State organ, this organ is viewed as having a separate legal personality under international law, while it is in fact only an instrument through which the State operates as a subject of international law.

In any case, current international law does not appear to make a distinction between international law and municipal laws on the basis of their respective legal addressees, at least to the effect that international law may also govern the relations between a State and individuals and create rights and obligations for individuals.

4. The continuity between international society and municipal societies and its implications

The assumption underlying the theory that international law cannot reach individuals is that international society and municipal societies are separate.[20] This assumption does not tally with the observation of social data, which emphasize elements of continuity. The position of a State in international society is due to the fact that the State rules a municipal society. It is the same government—in a wide sense—that operates in the municipal society and as a member of the international society.

It is therefore understandable that, for purposes of attribution of wrongful acts or of defining competence to conclude treaties, international law should basically refer to the internal rules of the State and that these rules are generally regarded as decisive in order to establish whether a wrongful act is to be attributed to the State or else whether a State organ is competent to conclude a treaty. However, the relevance of municipal laws is not unlimited. First of all, there may be cases in which internal rules are in fact not applied and hence a reference to these rules would distort the situation occurring within the 'living' legal system of the State concerned. Furthermore, there are cases in which the security of international relations requires international law to depart from extending a full guarantee to the respect of municipal law. Thus, a treaty is valid when the breach of the internal

[19] ICJ Reports 1999, 16 (para 28).

[20] The 'sociological separation' between international and internal societies was stressed by G Arangio-Ruiz, 'L'Etat dans le Sens du Droit des Gens et la Notion du Droit international' (1975) 26 Österreichische Zeitschrift für öffentliches Recht 265, 404 ('*Malgré les interactions évidentes, les deux milieux—le milieu interne-interindividuel et le milieu international-interpuissances—sont sociologiquement séparés du point de vue spécifique des règles relationnelles de conduite*').

rules on competence is not manifest or does not concern a rule of fundamental importance.[21] Similarly, a wrongful act is attributed to a State also when an organ of the State exceeded its authority or contravened instructions.[22] These exceptions do not substantially affect the continuity between international society and municipal societies.

While international society and municipal societies cannot be regarded as separate, it would be artificial to consider, as some monists hold,[23] that the State acts as a ruler in the respective society only on the strength of a delegation or conferral of competence by international law. It is hard to see how States could be granted their authority by anything short of a world government. States are not shaped by international society. International law regulates the formation of States only insofar as the principle of self-determination applies. Many States have come into existence either before the principle of self-determination emerged or else in circumstances in which the principle was not relevant. Rather than delegating powers to States, international law takes them as existent and guarantees their sovereignty especially through the prohibition of the use of force and the principle of non-intervention.

5. The relations between dualism and voluntarism

The dualist conception was developed by Hans Triepel and Dionisio Anzilotti as a corollary to their view that international law is based on the collective or common will of States.[24] Later, Anzilotti retained a voluntarist conception when basing international law on the principle 'pacta sunt servanda'.[25] The emphasis on the States' will conveys the impression that the international legal system suffers limitations and cannot govern certain matters.

However, there does not appear to be a necessary link between dualism and voluntarism. A voluntarist conception does not imply that international law and municipal laws are self-contained and that, for instance, rules of international law, based on the States' will, cannot be applied by national courts in the relations between a State and individuals. On the other hand, dualism may be conceived without voluntarism: even if a rule of international law binds a State irrespective

---

[21] Art 46, para 1 of the Vienna Convention on the Law of Treaties, 1155 UNTS 343.

[22] Art 7 of the ILC Draft Articles on State Responsibility, Doc. A/56/10 at 99; Crawford, *The International Law Commission's Articles on State Responsibility* (n 15 above) 106.

[23] Among them Kelsen, 'Les Rapports' (n 6 above) 280.

[24] Anzilotti, *Il Diritto Internazionale* (n 11 above) 281, 322–23 argued that since norms of international law were formed by the States' collective will in order to govern inter-State relations, their prohibitions or commands could only concern States ('*se le norme giuridiche internazionali sono poste dalla volontà collettiva degli stati per regolare i loro rapporti, ne viene che i comandi o i divieti in essi contenuti riguardino soltanto gli stati, ed a questi soli conferiscano potestà o diritti, impongano limitazioni o doveri*').

[25] D Anzilotti, *Corso di diritto internazionale* (4th edn, Padova: CEDAM, 1955) 66–67.

of its consent, this does not necessarily mean that the international legal system may not be regarded as self-contained.

6. The status of rules of municipal law within the international legal system

The implication of the self-contained character that dualists attribute to the international and municipal legal systems is that, within each system, rules pertaining to a different system are not *per se* relevant. They only become so if a rule that belongs to the system incorporates a foreign rule or gives the foreign rule some other legal effect.

A blunt expression of this concept is to define as a 'fact' a rule that does not pertain to the system and that is neither incorporated nor given any legal effect. This language was used by Anzilotti in 1925 when describing, in a study on conflict of laws, the relations between different municipal laws.[26] The following year the Permanent Court of International Justice made its famous statement in the case concerning *Certain German Interests in Polish Upper Silesia*: 'From the standpoint of International Law and of the Court which is its organ, municipal laws are merely facts which express the will and constitute the activities of States, in the same manner as do legal decisions or administrative measures.'[27]

This language may not seem inappropriate when the question to be considered by an international court or tribunal is whether a State complied with an obligation under international law. The merits of the case may consist in finding out whether a certain conduct is inconsistent with international law and the State's law may be examined as part of that conduct.[28] However, the language does go too far, as it appears to call into question the legal nature of rules pertaining to a different system. It would be even more unacceptable if a municipal court defined international law as a fact, because it would seem to lead to non-compliance with obligations under international law.

The International Court of Justice used a different wording in the *Barcelona Traction* case. However, this was done in a context, concerning the rights of companies and their shareholders, in which international law was considered by the Court to refer to municipal laws: 'It is to rules generally accepted by municipal legal systems which recognize the limited company whose capital is represented by shares, and not to the municipal law of a particular State, that international law refers. In referring to such rules, the Court cannot modify, still less deform them.'[29]

---

[26] D Anzilotti, *Corso di diritto internazionale privato* (Roma: Athenaeum, 1925) 57.

[27] PCIJ, Publications, Series A, No 7, 19. I dealt on the role that Judge Anzilotti probably had over this wording in my essay 'Positivism and Dualism in Dionisio Anzilotti' (1992) 3 EJIL 123, 137.

[28] Thus Anzilotti (n 25 above) 57 ('*come contegno del subietto a cui la valutazione si riferisce*').

[29] ICJ Reports 1970 37 (para 50). In his separate opinion Judge Sir Gerald Fitzmaurice held that in this area international law refers to municipal law 'only to a certain extent' (72, para 13), while

In an order given in the *Blaskić* case before the International Tribunal for Former Yugoslavia President Cassese held:

> municipal law can be looked at by international courts and tribunals *qua* a set of legal standards and consequently applied by those courts and tribunals—in this respect the old and rather artificial doctrine whereby 'from the standpoint of international law and the Court which is its organ, municipal laws are merely facts' (PCIJ, *German Interests in Polish Upper Silesia*, Ser. A, No. 7 (1926), at 19) can no longer be adhered to because, for the international judge as well, national laws may be material both in normative scope and binding force.[30]

While the last part of this statement is not altogether clear,[31] it does not seem to contradict the view that municipal laws are not per se relevant under the perspective of international law and that they cannot be treated by an international court or tribunal as propositions of law unless there is some kind of reference to them by a rule of international law.

This approach is not sufficient to conclude that the international legal system is self-contained. If one accepts that international law prevails over municipal laws, it seems logical to conclude that, whether the international legal system is self-contained or not, the content of municipal laws does not generally affect the application of rules of international law.

From this perspective, the existence of rules of municipal law cannot anyway be regarded as relevant as such.

7. May national courts apply international law?

The key question in the discussion between dualists and monists concerns the status of international law from the perspective of State organs, in particular national courts. According to the monist approach, those rules of international law that intend to govern the conduct of State organs and individuals are directly applicable to their legal addressees irrespective of any intermediary role played by municipal laws.

On the contrary, dualists consider State organs to be sheltered from international law, which becomes relevant in the State organs' perspective only by means of a rule pertaining to the municipal law system.

Judge Gros followed a different approach: 'In the present case, the rules of municipal law are nothing more than facts in evidence, and they deserve the same attention as the other facts, and the same rigour in their interpretation, but no more' (272, para 10).

[30] Decision of 3 April 1996, reproduced in (1996) 79 Rivista di diritto internazionale 460, 462 (para 6). The decision continues with the following sentence: 'Nevertheless, it remains true that unless expressly or implicitly authorized to the contrary by an international legal rule, international judges cannot interpret national laws in lieu of national courts or administrative authorities.' As a general statement, this view is debatable. Anyway, it does not seem applicable when a rule of international law refers to municipal law.

[31] Even if not as 'obscure' as it was considered by Santulli (n 1 above) 280, n 576.

The traditional dualist conception views the intervention of municipal law as having the effect of transforming rules of international law into rules of municipal law: those which are adopted in order for the State to comply with its obligations under international law. For the dualists that consider that international law only governs inter-State relations, this operation is necessary, because State organs and individuals cannot be legal addressees of rules of international law.[32] As Anzilotti put it, enacting a statute that would make a treaty applicable within the municipal legal system would be tantamount to ordering what is impossible.[33]

A different form of intervention on the part of municipal law consists in enabling State organs to apply rules of international law which may not otherwise be applied. Once the enabling rule has been adopted, international law will be applied untransformed.[34]

Whether an intervention by a rule of municipal law is necessary depends on the self-contained character of the relevant municipal law. It is reasonable to assume that the presence or absence of this character depends on each municipal legal system. What is material to this effect is not whether a certain municipal system is or is not self-contained in relation to other systems of municipal law, but only whether it is so in relation to the international legal system. In this regard openness serves the purpose of ensuring compliance with obligations under international law. The circumstance that a particular system intends fully to conform to international law is an indication that the system is not self-contained, while a limited relevance given to international law is an indication to the contrary. However, there is no logical necessity to assume that a municipal legal system that is fully consistent with international law is not self-contained.

The fact that a municipal legal system provides a general reference to international law in order to ensure compliance could be viewed either as declaratory of effects that international law would any way produce or as indicative of international law only becoming relevant because of that reference.[35] Also the application of international law by municipal courts in the absence of any specific provision could be interpreted either as a sign of the fact that the municipal system is not self-contained or as the effect of an unwritten or implied norm of the municipal system that renders international law applicable.

It is important to note that, should a municipal legal system be regarded as self-contained, the application of a rule of international law to State organs or individuals will not be affected from the perspective of the international legal system. It

---

[32] Triepel (n 11 above) 438–39.

[33] Anzilotti, *Il Diritto Internazionale* (n 11 above) 281, 377, n 67.

[34] For this construction, see especially L Condorelli, *Il Giudice Italiano e i Trattati Internazionali* (Milano: Giuffrè, 1974) 141.

[35] This point was made especially by L Ferrari-Bravo, 'International and Municipal Law: The Complementarity of Legal Systems' in RStJ Macdonald and DM Johnston (eds), *The Structure and Process of International Law: Essays in Legal Philosophy Doctrine and Theory* (The Hague: Martinus Nijhoff, 1986) 715, 737.

may well be, for instance, that a rule of international law puts an obligation on a State organ or gives an individual a right, but that from the perspective of the municipal legal system the same obligation is imposed or the same right is conferred only if a rule of municipal law has been adopted to that effect.

8. The issue of supremacy of international law

One of the reasons of the relative success of the monist conception among international lawyers is an ideological factor: the conviction that only monism ensures that international law prevails over municipal laws. Monism implies coordination between international and municipal laws and coordination cannot but imply, at least in principle, supremacy of international law over municipal laws, because otherwise the binding character of international law would be put in jeopardy. A monist approach appears to give a secure basis for the application of international law. Advocates of supremacy of international law are attracted to a monist approach, rather than to a municipal legal system that requires incorporation of norms of international law in a statute or an instrument of secondary legislation before these norms can be applied by municipal courts.

The concept that municipal laws cannot affect the application of international law has found expression in the first sentence of Article 27 of the Vienna Convention on the Law of Treaties: 'A party may not invoke the provisions of its internal law as justification for its failure to perform a treaty.'[36]

The same concept was expressed in Articles 3 and 32 respectively of the ILC Articles on State Responsibility in the following terms: 'The characterization of an act of a State as internationally wrongful . . . is not affected by the characterization of the same act as lawful by internal law.'[37] 'The responsible State may not rely on the provisions of its internal law as justification for failure to comply with its obligations under this Part [Part Two of the Draft Articles, headed 'Content of the International Responsibility of a State'].'[38]

The need that, in order to avoid the breach of obligations under international law, international law should prevail over municipal law is not denied by dualists. However, according to the dualist conception, the non-application of municipal law because of supremacy of international law may only derive from a rule pertaining to the municipal legal system, such as one of the many constitutional provisions that require compliance with international law, either in general or with regard to customary international law or to treaties. As a consequence, supremacy may be achieved only in part, as far as the constitutional provision goes. Moreover, the result could theoretically be reversed by a change in municipal law.

---

[36] Art 27 of the Vienna Convention on the Law of Treaties, 1155 UNTS 339.
[37] UN Doc A/56/10 at 74; J Crawford (ed), *The International Law Commission's Articles on State Responsibility* (n 15 above) 86. [38] Ibid, 207.

Whether one takes the monist or the dualist approach, the enacting of municipal legislation, even if aimed at achieving a result that is inconsistent with an obligation under international law, does not necessarily represent the breach of an obligation, because this may presuppose some further conduct on the part of the State.[39]

When municipal legislation causes a breach of an obligation under international law, it may be necessary to follow some procedure under municipal law in order to ensure full compliance with international law. For the monists, this could occur only if the rule of international law is not directly applicable and thus some implementing measures by municipal law are required.

In some exceptional cases a rule of municipal law could even survive a temporary inconsistency with a norm of international law. The international norm may be modified, although not technically as a direct consequence of the municipal rule, but rather because of circumstances in which this rule plays a significant part. This possibility is not irreconcilable with monism, because it does not assume that a rule of municipal rule prevails over the international norm: it clearly does not when municipal legislation does not *per se* cause a breach of an obligation under international law. A national statute could conceivably cause a legal development similar to the impact created by President Truman's Continental Shelf Proclamation. It has been noted that even the 'relevant officials of the United States (those who addressed their minds to that issue) did not believe that the content of the Proclamation was already international law', but that there was 'the form of a settled conviction as to what the law should be, and would be for the proclaiming State', which had articulated a 'principle that came to be widely accepted'.[40]

9. Final remarks

My tentative conclusion is that there cannot be a general answer to the question whether a certain legal system should be regarded as self-contained or not. The answer to this question with regard to any legal system would depend on features that pertain to the system itself. Thus, some municipal systems may have to be considered as self-contained while others may not. This would lead to a pragmatic solution of a different kind from the one which is often advocated in textbooks and elsewhere, and which consists in leaving the theoretical debate over monism and dualism aside.

---

[39] JA Stoll, *L'Application et l'Interprétation du Droit interne par les Juridictions Internationales* (Bruxelles: Editions de l'Institut de Sociologie de l'Univ. de Bruxelles, 1962) 30 held the contrary view that monists and dualists would set the moment of the breach at a different time.

[40] Thus J Crawford and T Viles, 'International Law on a Given Day' in *Völkerrecht zwischen normativen Anspruch und politischer Realität. Festschrift für Karl Zemanek zum 65. Geburtstag* (Berlin: Duncker and Humblot, 1994) 45, 66–67. Their theory that the Proclamation was 'neither lawful nor unlawful' when it was made seems justified only if one takes into account the fact that the Proclamation did not per se represent a breach of any obligation under international law. This could have occurred only in the event of conduct actually preventing foreign exploitation of the continental shelf.

3

The Emerging Universal Legal System

Philip Allott

A new potentiality in the theory of international law does not lie in any attempt to resolve a false problem implied by the phrase 'the relationship between international law and national law'. It is to be found in integrating the theory of international law in the theory of the universal phenomenon of law, and in integrating the theory of international society in the theory of the universal phenomenon of society. The product of that integration is the idea of a universal legal system.

1. Transcendental theory

To speak of an 'emerging universal legal system' is to speak at the theoretical level. To form a theory of natural or human phenomena, such as the phenomena of law, is to think simultaneously at three levels of *theory*.[1] It is to think at the level of *transcendental theory*—that is to say, at the level of the theory of theory, at the level of the self-consciousness of consciousness, as the mind forms theories of its own functioning, including theories in the fields conventionally known as epistemology, psychology, linguistics. It is, second, to think at the level of *pure theory*—that is to say, at the level at which theoretical concepts are generalized and ordered in such a way that they can be applied to our thinking about particular phenomena. It is, finally, to think at the level of *practical theory*—that is to say, at the level of thinking as action, the level at which theory is actualized in the process of our acting in relation to actual situations.[2]

---

[1] For further discussion of the three levels of theory: P Allott, *Eunomia, New Order for a New World* (Oxford: OUP, 1990/2001) 2.49.

[2] This distinction between pure theory and practical theory is analogous to Aristotle's distinction between speculative reason and practical reason, Artistotle, *Politics* (VII.14) or, as he expresses it in the *Nicomachean Ethics* (I.VII.19), the difference between the thinking of the geometer and the thinking of the carpenter. It is related also to the Hegelian-Marxian concept of *praxis* (Greek and German word for *practice*), that is, practice theoretically conceived.

At all levels from practical action to the theory of theory, there is a constant and inescapable *reciprocal conditioning* of theory, a dialectical conversation[3] in the course of which each may modify the other and may be modified by the other—as practical action calls for a new theory of itself (eg new technologies of production calling for new theories of the productive process or of the economic constitution of society), or as new ideas about the functioning of the mind call for new theories of social action (eg social systems seen as the product of phylogenetic conflicts in the unconscious mind or conscience seen as the internalization of social controls). The functioning of theory is thus highly biologically adaptive, as the human mind is able to assimilate changing needs and opportunities, and to respond efficiently by modifying its action in relation to an ever-changing environment. The mind is constantly re-presenting the world to itself in order constantly to re-make the world to suit its own purposes. To change the way in which we present the world to our minds is to begin to change the world.

1.1 Free thinking

An extraordinary feature of the mind is that we know of no limit to our capacity to form ideas. This may be a Gödel effect—the mind cannot transcend itself to form a theory of its own limits. Whatever view one may have of 'free will' as a moral theory, we certainly have 'free mind' in the sense that we can form ideas *ad libitum*, imagining the possible and the impossible, the past and the future, the rational and the irrational, the true and the untrue, the good and the bad. The freedom of the mind means that there is also no limit to our capacity to present the world to ourselves in consciousness in the form of a specifically *human reality*, and hence, in principle, no limit to our capacity to re-create the world as a specifically *human world* through the application of the theories that we make. The human mind has the capacity to create new worlds.

However, the freedom of the mind is subject to three fundamental systematic constraints—the thinking subject's personality; the thinking subject's unconscious consciousness, and the public mind of society. As a product of our unique physiology and life-experience, we develop unique ways of thinking which are reflections of our personality, that is to say, the totality of our personal self-constituting over time. Whether or not there are species-characteristics of the unconscious mind (as proposed in the Jungian hypothesis), there is evidently part of our mind which is beyond our immediate control, an 'other' within our self, as it were. And, finally, our private mind exists in systematic co-operation with the public minds of the societies to which we belong. Consciousness flows between the two minds, in a process of mutual conditioning, with the public mind being

---

[3] The Ancient Greek noun *dialektos*, with its associated verb-form, meant conversation, reasoned argument.

formed by the private minds which it helps to form. The human mind is free; my mind is free within certain limits. The public mind is free; the public mind of a given society is free within certain limits.

1.2 Right thinking

The process of theory-making is an ordering, in the sense that the mind has an integrating function, no doubt derived from the physiology of the brain, which unceasingly processes its own contents, combining and separating and re-combining them, into patterns which are, or are capable of being, recognized as such by the mind itself. It is a process which has traditionally been called *reason*.[4] It is an ordering which takes place continuously at the unconscious level of consciousness, revealing itself occasionally in the form of dreaming, and in apparently spontaneous or intuitive thought (unconscious cerebration[5]), and in the whole realm of affective thinking. And it takes place at the level of self-aware consciousness, especially in deliberative and evaluative thinking and in the interpersonal communication of the products of deliberative and evaluative thought.[6] What has traditionally been called *rationality* is an evaluative theory of reason, a theory at all three levels—a transcendental theory of its possibility, a theory of its operation (logic, scientific method etc), and a theory applied in everyday discourse as human communications interact fruitfully.

The idea of thinking rightly—including the traditional concept of 'truth'—implies that we are able to judge the products of the self-ordering of consciousness in relation to some set of standards which transcend them. Those standards are themselves a product of the total dialectical process of consciousness and, once again, they are probably a reflection, in some ultimate way, of the physiology of the brain—related, perhaps, to the experience of what we call pleasure and pain and/or of an organic need to reduce tension in the system.[7] But the standards are not unified, at least at the level of practical theory (our judgment of

---

[4] Allott, *Eunomia* (n 1 above) 2.8.

[5] This useful term, referring to an aspect of the unconscious functioning of the brain, is taken from WB Carpenter, *Principles of Mental Physiology, with their Applications to the Training and Discipline of the Mind, and the Study of Its Morbid Conditions* (London: Henry S King, 1874).

[6] Plato has Socrates describe 'the process of thinking' as 'a discourse which the mind carries on with itself about any subject it is considering. You must take this explanation as coming from an ignoramus, but I have a notion that, when the mind is thinking, it is simply talking to itself, asking questions and answering them, and saying yes or no. When it reaches a decision—which may come slowly or in a sudden rush—when doubt is over and the two voices affirm the same thing then we call that its "judgment". So I should describe thinking as discourse, and judgment as a statement pronounced, not aloud to someone else, but silently to oneself.' Plato, 'Theaetetus' (189e–190a) in E Hamilton and H Cairns (eds), *The Collected Dialogues of Plato* (Princeton: Princeton UP, 1961), 895–96.

[7] At various stages of his intellectual development, Sigmund Freud postulated ideas about a fundamental tendency of the psyche to reduce tension and achieve stability, ideas linked to phenomena in other fields, extending even to the Second Law of Thermodynamics (entropy). See FJ Sulloway, *Freud, Biologist of the Mind* (Cambridge, MA: Harvard UP, 1979), 66–67, 404 et seq.

right-thinking in everyday practice), since we determine the rightness of thinking differently in different contexts—philosophical thought, scientific method, religious belief, aesthetic judgment, moral judgment, forensic argument and forensic decision-making, and so on.[8]

1.3 Hypothetical thinking

One strategy of the mind's thinking process has played a major role in empowering the mind in its constant adaptation to the world, natural and human. It is the mind's capacity to construct 'hypotheses' about the world, that is to say, orderly structures of ideas designed to re-present aspects of the world to the mind in a form which may readily take effect within practical theory and hence may readily return to the world to modify it in accordance with the hypothesis. In the case of the physical world, such partial reconstructions of reality may be used to 'explain' everything from the origin of the universe and the origin of animal species to the properties of sub-atomic particles. In the case of the human world, such partial reconstructions of reality lead to the forming of a parallel human world, full of discrete hypothetical mental entities, reminiscent of the mind-produced 'objects' of the physical world—society, law, nation, State, and so on. In both cases, the products of transcendental and pure theory are liable to have far-reaching world-transforming effects through the medium of practical theory—the nuclear weapon destroys a city, the gene is modified, the law is enacted, the state is recognized.

The mind's hypothetical capacity uses the dialectical process of right thinking (discussed above) constantly to re-form a given hypothesis so that it is integrated more and more fully with relevant contexts. Those contexts reflect the co-ordinates of the functioning of the reasoning process as it retrieves its own contents, relates them to each other, and finds new potentialities within those contents.[9] Relevant contexts may include mechanically produced observations of phenomena of the world (especially by methods traditionally labelled as empiricism) or they may be other kinds of mental phenomena—religious, moral, and political ideas, values of all kinds, other hypotheses and so on. By something which may be called, literally or by analogy, regression analysis, the mind can gradually eliminate incompatible and inconsistent ideas so that the hypothesis comes to be accepted as more and more 'true' or 'right' or 'certain' or even 'proved'. *Pragmatism* seeks to discriminate among hypotheses on the basis of their probable or actual effects within

---

[8] The above approach follows in the tradition established by Locke, following Descartes, which recognizes a capacity of the mind (reason) which is an ordering process rather than merely the application of *a priori* rules and principles but which can produce something (rational knowledge, including moral rationality) which is more than a mere report on experience or a conventional construct. It is a capacity which is accompanied by involuntary thinking (intuition, emotion) and which can also produce error and illusion. J Locke, *An Essay concerning Human Understanding* (Book IV, London, 1789) esp. chs III and XVII. The tradition was developed further by Kant and Hegel.

[9] Allott, *Eunomia* (n 1 above) 2.26.

practical theory. It is a secondary and partial procedure within an immeasurably wider context of transcendental and pure theory, even if its practitioners may be unaware of, or may claim to exclude, that wider context. *Idealism* seeks to integrate hypotheses within the widest possible context.

1.4 Value thinking

The *free-thinking* human mind can create the new *human reality* of a new *human world* using its capacities of *right thinking* and *hypothetical thinking*. But all such creative activity involves the process of *choice*, the movement of the mind which leads to an act of willing and hence to practical action.

We owe to ancient Greek philosophy our conventional hypotheses about the *functional structure* of the human mind, especially its radical dualisms—body and soul, mind and brain, reason and desire, the rational and the irrational, conscious and unconscious, pleasure and pain, necessity and chance, virtue and vice. These dialectical dyads—dialectical, because their opposition is fruitful of more complex ideas—suggested the general hypothesis that the overall function of the mind is to act as an integrating mechanism. This in turn suggested three paradigmatic hypotheses of the *systematic functioning* of the mind. (1) Following Plato and Aristotle, we may postulate the *rationality* of what we call 'morality', seeing the mind as having the pursuit of 'happiness' as the overall purpose of its functioning, made possible by a process of mental integration through the rational control of desire.[10] (2) Following David Hume, we may assert the *omnipotence* of the 'passions' and deny that reason can be a cause of willed action, so that the function of reason is merely to suggest appropriate means to achieve an end dictated by emotion or to offer generalized prudential theories based on experience in the satisfying of desire.[11] (3) Following Sigmund Freud, we may see our unconscious mind (*id*) as a sort of 'state of nature' within us. The function of the rational process of the mind (*ego*) is to integrate the imperious dictates of the unconscious with the imperious demands of a form of arbitrary self-government (the *superego*) which is reminiscent of the instinctive self-governing postulated by Hobbes or Locke in their hypothetical pre-societal 'state of nature'.[12] The *practical theories* of our

---

[10] Plato and Aristotle supposed that the mind is the scene of a permanent struggle between reason and appetite, so that the happiness of the individual and the health of society depend on the development of enlightened self-control, above all through education and through law. 'Thought by itself moves nothing, but only thought directed to an end, and dealing with action ... Hence Choice may be called either thought related to desire or desire related to thought; and man, as an originator of action, is a union of desire and intellect.' H Rackham (transl), *Aristotle: Nicomachean Ethics* (Cambridge MA: Harvard UP, 1982) 331.

[11] 'We speak not strictly and philosophically when we talk of the combat of passion and of reason. Reason is, and ought only to be the slave of the passions, and can never pretend to any other office than to serve and obey them.' L Selby-Bigge and P Nidditch (eds), David Hume, *A Treatise on Human Nature* (2nd edn, Oxford: OUP, 1978), 415.

[12] 'On behalf of the id, the ego controls the paths of access to motility, but it interpolates between desire and action the procrastinating factor of thought, during which it makes use of the residues of

personal lives and, indeed, of the societies to which we belong and the legal systems to which we are subject, are determined by one or more, or some combination, of these pure theories of mental functioning.

Value is the language in which we express the struggle of our self-creating through *choice*. Value mediates between ideas and action, between pure theory and practical theory.[13] The language of value is a product of profound and complex processes of conscious and unconscious reasoning and of a profound and complex interaction between the private mind of the human individual and the public mind of society. Value channels the *impulse of life* which we human beings share with all living things, the force which impels our *becoming*, our unceasing self-constituting as individuals and as societies.[14] It expresses the *desire* which impels us to act as a *cause* of our own *becoming*.[15] It is that which distinguishes *motivation* as the cause of our willing and acting as thinking human beings from the *causation* which determines the becoming of the physical world, including our becoming as participants in the physical world.

Naturalism, especially as systematically organized in the human or mind-sciences (*Geisteswissenschaften*), seeks to assimilate theory about human motivation as closely as possible to theory, at all three levels of theory, about causation in the physical world.[16] *Idealism* is the philosophy of the idea and the ideal. It affirms the power of the human mind to make its own reality—the reality of ideas. It affirms the radical separation between the ideas of causation and motivation. It postulates a particular kind of value—the ideal—whose function is not to dictate substantive rules of conduct but to offer to the mind the forming patterns (the good, the true, the beautiful, justice and others) which make value-judgments possible, patterns which are themselves universal (present in all minds at all times and all places), and which cause the mind to desire to actualize the ideal 'as an end in itself' and not 'as a means to something else'.[17] They offer the permanent possibility of human self-perfecting.

experience stored up in memory. In this way it dethrones the pleasure-principle, which exerts undisputed sway over the processes in the id, and substitutes for it the reality-principle, which promises greater security and greater success.' W Sprott (transl), *Sigmund Freud: New Introductory Lectures on Psycho-Analysis* (New York: Norton, 1946) 101.

[13] Allott, *Eunomia* (n 1 above) 3.27.   [14] Ibid, 3.12.   [15] Ibid, 3.13.

[16] On the fallacy of naturalism and the failure of the Enlightenment project, P Allott, *The Health of Nations. Society and Law beyond the State* (Cambridge: CUP, 2002) especially ch 1.

[17] H Rackham (transl), *Aristotle: Nicomachean Ethics* (Cambridge, MA: Harvard UP, 1982) 27. It is possible, perhaps even logically necessary, to recognize an ideal of all ideals, and even to identify it as 'God', so that 'the love of God' refers both to the attractive power of the ideal (God's love of us) and to our desire to actualize the ideal (our love of God). 'What line of conduct, then, is dear to God and a following of him? There is but one and it is summed up in one ancient rule, the rule that "like"—when it is a thing of due measure—"loves its like". For things that have no measure can be loved neither by one another nor by those who have. Now it is God who is, for you and me, of a truth the "measure of all things", much more truly than, as they say, "man"'. Plato, 'Laws' (716.c) in E Hamilton and H Cairns (eds), *The Collected Dialogues of Plato* (Princeton: Princeton UP, 1961) 1307. Aristotle refers to God and the Good as beyond praise because 'they are the standards to which everything else is referred'. H Rackham (transl), Aristotle, *Nicomachean Ethics* (Cambridge, MA: Harvard UP, 1982) 59.

2. Pure theory

To speak of an 'emerging universal legal system' is to speak at the level of the *pure theory* of law. Pure theories about the origin, nature, and function of law are at least as old as recorded human history.[18] Such theories have been universalising in character, relating to the concept of 'law' as a general phenomenon of the human world, rather than about particular laws or legal systems, and leaving *practical theory* to address the phenomenon of law in particular cultures or societies.

The promiscuous diversity of pure theories of law may be rationalized somewhat by ordering them hierarchically in relation to their respective *phenomenal horizons*—offering, perhaps, the groundwork of a pure theory of pure theories of law.

(1) The *internal* perspective. Law as a self-contained system of rationality.[19]
(2) The *systematic* perspective. Law as a distinct social sub-system.[20]
(3) The *social* perspective. Law as an aspect of the self-constituting of a society.[21]
(4) The *metasocial* perspective. Law as a derived system of order.[22]
(5) The *universal* perspective. Law as mediation between the universal and the particular.[23]

Although pure theories of law have conventionally been presented as if they were random proposals in competition with each other in seeking intellectual assent and real-world application through the medium of practical theory, a pure theory of pure theories of law might propose, on the contrary, that they offer a logically exhaustive set of hypotheses of the five structural dimensions of the phenomenon of law. A syncretic pure theory of law might also propose certain universal hypotheses about the nature of law—hypotheses which would be designed to be useful in the forming of practical theory of law at the universal level, that is to say, at the level of the international society of all-humanity, the society of all societies.

Law is an ordering. The notorious opening words of Montesquieu's *Spirit of the Laws*[24] invoke the age-old hypothesis that 'law'—in the narrow sense of a society's legal system—shares in the universal phenomenon of order or ordering without which natural and human reality could not be grasped by the human mind and

---

18 For further discussion, Allott, *The Health of Nations* (n 16 above), ch 12.

19 For example, Kantian/Kelsenian theories, analytical jurisprudence.

20 For example, realist and positivist (in the Comteian sense) and anthropological theories of law.

21 For example, Aristotelian and socialist (especially Marxian) theories, historical jurisprudence, and the present author's social idealism.

22 For example, natural law theories, pure-idealist (especially Hegelian) theories.

23 For example, Platonist and Neo-Platonist theories, religious theories.

24 'Laws, in their most general signification, are the necessary relations arising from the nature of things. In this sense all beings have their laws: the Deity His laws, the material world its laws, the intelligences superior to man their laws, the beast their laws, man his laws.' T Nugent (trans), Baron de Montesquieu, *The Spirit of the Laws* (New York: MacMillan, 1949) 1.

which presumably reflects some aspect of the underlying reality of the universe whose phenomenal aspect we order through the work of the human mind, especially the underlying reality of what we call 'living' things as organized systems of becoming.

Law is dialectical. Law universalizes the particular and particularizes the universal. For the individual human being, as a *choosing* being, a moment of choice is a particular event. The application of the law to that event transforms it into a universal event. Whether or not the human individual in question is conscious of the fact, the applicability of law makes the event into an event whose significance is also a legal significance within a special legal reality with its own theories, its own form of rationality, its own values.[25] And that special significance is shared with all other events to which the law is applicable. Law thus also particularizes the universal in that its significance, which is abstract and impersonal and categorical and hypothetical, is actualized in being applicable to particular and unique real-world events as they occur.

Law is social self-constituting. A human society is a permanent process of self-constituting. Like a living organism, like a human individual, it uses its past in its present to form its future. Law carries the effects of a society's past decision-making (social willing and acting), including social structures and systems, to act as the cause of new effects in society's permanent self-creating. Society's *legal* self-constituting is a dialectical product of society's self-creating in consciousness (the *ideal* constitution) and its self-creating through the willing and acting of actual human beings (the *real* constitution)—dialectical, in the sense that it is itself also the cause of effects in those other two dimensions of social self-constituting.[26]

Law enacts the common interest. Rousseau's notorious intellectual struggle with the meaning of the concept of the 'general will' invoked the age-old idea that law integrates the particular ground of choice ('interest') of the individual with the ground of choice preferred by the law-maker ('common interest').[27] If the choice made in a particular case by a particular human being is in conformity with the law, the resulting action by that person necessarily serves the common interest, whether or not that action is done in order to conform to the law.

Law is a system of legal relations. Law is not a set of legal rules, norms, or commands. The way in which law achieves its remarkable social effect in a given society is by constructing an infinitely complex network of abstract relations

---

[25] For further discussion of *legal reality*, Allott, *The Health of Nations* (n 16 above) 2.1–2.22.

[26] For further discussion of the three dimensions of the constitution, Allott, *Eunomia* (n 1 above) ch 9.

[27] 'But when the whole people decrees for the whole people, it is considering only itself; and if a relation is then formed, it is between two aspects of the entire object, without there being any division of the whole. In that case the matter about which the decree is made is, like the decreeing will, general. This act is what I call law.' J-J Rousseau, 'The Social Contract' in G D H Cole (transl), *The Social Contract & Discourses* (New York: MacMillan, 1973) 192.

between every actual and potential member of society, and between every member of society and society itself. These relations are patterns of ideas which are enacted as pure potentiality and which are capable of being actualized in relation to actual events involving actual persons in the course of a society's self-constituting so that, since they enact the common interest of society, they actualize that common interest if real-world behaviour conforms to them.[28] Legal relations—*right, duty, power, liability* etc—function in particular systematic ways which have, presumably, evolved through human experience and through the theoretical self-consciousness of human experience.[29]

Law is potentially universal. A society's legal constitution is potentially applicable to every person and to every event. It is for each particular society at any particular time to determine the personal and material scope of the legal relations which it creates. This universal potentiality of a legal system is a necessary corollary of the nature of law outlined above. A society's common interest is as wide as it is conceived to be by that society at any particular time. It follows from this that all the legal systems of all the societies in the world are, in principle, overlapping in their potential scope and hence that the network of legal relations applicable, in principle, to any particular person or event at any particular time is the sum total of the legal relations contained in all legal systems at that time.

Law contains an ideal potentiality. It has been suggested elsewhere that an ideal pure theory of law necessarily implies certain substantive principles at the most general level.[30] They may be regarded as logical corollaries of the nature of law considered above. Such generic principles have the status of *ideals* in the sense discussed above. They exercise a forming power over the form of all other legal relations. Given the freedom of the mind, it is possible to deny them or to ignore them, as it is possible to contradict oneself in one's thinking or to imagine the impossible. It is possible for a society, or for public-realm power-holders within a given society, to deny them or ignore them as a matter of practical theory and to violate them in the everyday social practice of the real constitution. But, like all ideals, such principles always remain as an evaluative potentiality, and as a transformatory, even a revolutionary, potentiality. They are a permanent possibility of a society's self-perfecting.

All the above implies also a pure theory of *society*. The law of a society is a complex conceptual hypothesis in which law and society are mutually dependent conceptual hypotheses.

---

[28] For further discussion, Allott, *Eunomia* (n 1 above) 6.68.

[29] For an hypothesis of this systematic functioning in terms of *matrix, heuristic*, and *algorithm*, Allott, *The Health of Nations* (n 16 above) 3.32–34, 10.15–17.

[30] For discussion of the generic principles of a constitution, Allott, *Eunomia* (n 1 above) ch 11. They are there listed as follows. *Law is part of the total social process. Law is dynamic. All legal power is delegated power. All legal power is limited. All social power is under the law. All legal power is power in the social interest. All social power is accountable.*

Society is an aspect of consciousness. Society exists only as an idea, a feature of the human world within the human reality made by human consciousness. The ideal self-constituting of a society takes place in the private minds of society-members and in the public mind of the society itself and in the creative interaction between the two levels of consciousness.[31]

Society is self and other. Society is a 'self' within its own public mind.[32] Society is also an aspect of the 'self' of each society-member and also an 'other' within individual consciousness. The society-member is an aspect of the 'self' of the society and also an 'other' within social consciousness.[33]

Society is one and many. A society's unity is a negation and an affirmation of its multiplicity. Its structures and systems integrate many persons, institutions, ideas, events, and subordinate societies, together with the superordinate societies of which a given society is itself a member.

Society is one will and many wills. The structures and systems of society integrate the willing and acting of individual human beings and subordinate societies so that the willing and acting of society is more than the sum of the individual inputs.[34]

Society is a self-ordering within an order that transcends it. Just as human being are both a self-contained organic system and also an integral part of a natural and human world which transcends them, so a society's internal integration forms part of superordinate forms of integration, up to the integration of the universe.[35]

Society remains as it changes. As with other organic systems, including human beings, human societies are a permanent process of becoming, never the same from one moment to the next. But the presence within consciousness of the idea of change implies an idea of something to which change occurs.[36]

Society contains an ideal potentiality. Law, as conceived in pure theory is clearly very well adapted to play a major part in producing all these characteristics of *society*, each of which presents itself as a dialectical opposition which must be resolved on a continuing basis and from day to day.[37] In its continuous dialectical resolution of the demands and the possibilities generated in social consciousness (ideal constitution) and in social practice (real constitution), law also continually modifies those demands and possibilities in a dynamic cycle of mutual conditioning. The ideal potentiality of law is thus also central to a conception of the *ideal potentiality* of society as *a permanent process of human self-creating, self-sustaining, self-surpassing, and self-perfecting.*

---

[31] Allott, *Eunomia* (n 1 above) chs 2, 3.

[32] 'For a society is not made up merely of the mass of individuals who compose it, the ground which they occupy, the things which they use and the movements which they perform, but above all is the idea which it forms of itself.' JW Swain (transl), E Durkheim, *The Elementary Forms of Religious Life* (2nd edn, London: Routledge, 1976) 422.   [33] Allott, *Eunomia* (n 1 above) ch 4.

[34] Ibid, ch 5.   [35] Ibid.   [36] Ibid, ch 6.

[37] In ibid at 4.10 these creative oppositions are termed *perennial dilemmas of society.*

3. Practical theory—actual

To speak of an 'emerging universal legal system' is to speak at the level of the *practical theory* of the law phenomenon. Since practical theory is the work of transcendental and pure theory taking effect in the real and legal self-constituting of society, that is, in the world of everyday social practice, it follows that to propose an hypothesis as a matter of practical theory is to seek to change the world.

Social power. In the forming of a given society as a presence within consciousness practical theory is a form of *social power*.[38] Societies, in the day-to-day practice of the real constitution, find the ideas that they need.[39] Holders of public-realm power seek to take power over practical theory. Holders of absolute power seek to take advantage of the vertical integration of theory (transcendental, pure, practical) to control directly the formation of ideas even about transcendental matters (for example, the nature of 'truth') and matters of pure theory (for example, the source of their power or the legitimation of property-power), treating them merely as an aspect of practical theory. In the recorded history of the world, abuse of theoretical social power has been as common as abuse of legal or physical social power. The word *ideology* is used in two senses, one of which refers to the integration of a society's practical theory into the structure of social power.[40] Societies produce an institutionalized thinking-class, who see themselves as an elite of purveyors of theory in the public interest, and who may act as instruments of society's self-enlightenment or else as co-conspirators in the social abuse of mental power.[41]

Social identity. In forming the selfhood of a society, a critical task in the use of practical theory is control of social entity-making.[42] The extraordinary multiplicity

---

[38] Ibid, 10.19.

[39] 'The production of ideas, of conceptions, of consciousness, is at first directly interwoven with the material activity and material intercourse of men, the language of real life. Conceiving, thinking, the mental intercourse of men, appear at this stage as the direct efflux of their material behaviour. The same applies to mental production as expressed in the language of politics, laws, morality, religion, metaphysics, etc., of a people. Men are the producers of their conceptions, ideas, etc.—real, active men.' K Marx and F Engels, *The German Ideology* (ch 1) in *Selected Works*, Vol 1 (Moscow: Progress Publishers, 1969) 24–25.

[40] Karl Mannheim draws a distinction between the sociology of knowledge and the idea of ideology, as it had developed since Marx, and which was concerned with the deliberate manipulation of thought by social power-holders. K Mannheim, *Ideology and Utopia. An Introduction to the Sociology of Knowledge* (London: Routledge, 1936) 238. He gives an account of the earlier history of the more scientific concept of 'ideology' (from Destutt de Tracy onwards).

[41] We may think of the scribes of ancient Egypt and the mandarin of ancient China, Plato's guardians, the priest-class of medieval Christendom, Bacon's invisible college of natural scientists, Saint-Simon's spiritual class, Hegel's universal class, Coleridge's clerisy, the later Comte's spiritual elite, Arnold's cultured class, Mosca and Pareto's elite political class, Weber's rationalist bureaucracy, Galbraith's New (managerial/technostructural) Class (not forgetting the Alpha-Plus class of Huxley's Brave New World, the Thought-Police of Orwell's 1984, the Communist Party of the Soviet Union or the priesthood, more and less corrupted, of the modern university).

[42] 'Without questioning the undoubted primacy of infrastructures, I believe that there is always a mediator between *praxis* and practices, namely the conceptual scheme by the operation of which

of social forms which have been generated in the course of recorded human history is testimony to the theory-making energy of those who have exercized exceptional social-theoretical power. The possible categories of *society* within practical theory seem to be unlimited. Four kinds of social entity may be seen as having acquired paradigmatic status—the family, the polity, the corporation, and the nation. The family is the archetype of the *genetic* social entity, its essence rooted in the fact of birth. The polity and the corporation are archetypes of the *generic* social form, their essence being rooted in their form and function. The nation (or tribe) is the archetype of *superordinate* social entity, capable of existing in genetic or generic form.[43]

Social indeterminacy. Because a society is both a metaphysical entity and an organic process, mirroring many of the characteristics of the human beings who have been, are, and will be its members, it is in a state of permanent flux, an ever-changing resolution of its unity-in-multiplicity. The histories of human societies are testimony to the impermanence of all human arrangements as they transform themselves under internal and external pressures. War, revolution, exploration, migration, colonization, conquest, changing flows of trade and capital and labour, technological and intellectual innovation—such things are the human causes of the structural transformation of human societies. And practical theory allows each society to present to itself a continuing idea of itself in a continuous present of self-consciousness, as a specific product of its particular history with specific potentialities. By way of example, we may think of the ancient societies of Egypt, Mesopotamia, India, China, and Rome, and the long and lively history of the making of the social transformations which led to their modern successors. We may think of more modern examples—the ever-changing structural patterns of France, Italy, Germany over a period of the last millennium. We make think of the patterns of economic structures, including the frenzied structural changes caused by the development of capitalism, changes affecting everything from the organization of government, through the organization of industrial and commercial corporations, to the organization of the labour of hand and brain. All our experience teaches us that societies are what they have been and are never what they were.

Social determination. Since the process of social self-constituting is not a random process but a process dominated by willing and acting human beings, it is no surprise that human history (or, at least, historiography) has been dominated by

---

matter and form, neither with any independent existence, are realized as structures, that is as entities which are both empirical and intelligible. It is to this theory of superstructures, scarcely touched upon by Marx, that I hope to make a contribution.' C Lévi-Strauss, *The Savage Mind* (Chicago, IL: The University of Chicago Press, 1966) 130. Cassirer discussed a similar idea under the name of 'objectification'. 'Man has discovered a new mode of expression: symbolic expression. This is the common denominator in all his cultural activities.... In the very act of linguistic expression our perceptions assume a new form...The act of naming does not simply add a mere conventional sign to a ready-made thing—to an object known before. It is rather a pre-requisite of the very conception of objects...even myth has a certain "objective" aspect and a definite objective function.' E Cassirer, *The Myth of the State* (New Haven: Yale UP, 1946) 45.

[43] For discussion of genetic and generic forms of the nation, Allott, *The Health of Nations* (n 16 above) 4.28.

the struggle to organize the collective will of society. Who is to dominate the process of decision-making in the common interest? Who is to dominate the process of the economy, that is, the transformation of the material world through the labour of hand and brain? The struggle of the collective will is a struggle about something, namely, the something which is the structure of the given society as it is presented to that society in practical theory. The struggle may be about the changing of that structure, about constitutional reform or revolution, or it may be about the actualizing of that structure, the functioning of social structures and systems. And it may, of course, be practical and specific, about what to do within those structures and systems, what laws to make, what common-interest decisions to take. In general terms, the struggle takes the form of *politics*. But the politics of each society at any given time is specific to that society. Democracy and capitalism are examples of practical theories which are social products, which are open to an unlimited range of interpretations and applications, which are determinative of day-to-day political and economic life, and which are actualized in a unique way in each society in which they function as practical theory.

Legal self-constituting. It is as generalized inferences from the practical theory present in the actual social process of particular human societies through the course of human history that we have identified the hypotheses of the unlimited capacity of social power-holders to use practical theory as *social power*, the unlimited range of available social entities which form *social identity*, the unlimited potentiality for structural and systematic change of any society manifesting itself as *social indeterminacy*, and the unlimited range of available social choices acting as continuing *social determination*. They are the combined product of the development of available ideas (ideal self-constituting) interacting with practical action (real self-constituting). And this reveals with particular clarity that it is the role of a society's legal self-constituting to resolve this universal process into a particular form which can be highly efficient in adapting a particular society to its needs and opportunities at a particular time. Historical experience shows that legal systems have an apparently unlimited dynamic capacity to apply the social power of practical theory to the self-constituting of a particular society in a particular form at a particular time. It is the law that makes this particular society into a polity or a nation or a corporation with particular legal characteristics, that makes this particular person into a holder of particular legal powers, that makes this particular action into a particular kind of legal transaction.

When the pure theory of law and the practical theory of law are brought into conjunction with each other, law in a given society can be seen as the particularizing of a universal, the actualizing of a potentiality which is both universal (a society is a society, law is law) and particular (each society and each legal system is unique). It is transcendental theory, which is conceived as being intrinsically universal, which makes possible the union of pure theory and practical theory in such a way that every society and every legal system is universal and particular. All societies and all legal systems are the same and all are different. It follows that there are always particular reasons why actual legal systems are as they are, and that legal systems always contain the potentiality of becoming other than they have been. The responsibility for making legal systems as theory and as practice, and hence of re-making legal systems in theory and in practice, is a permanent challenge of social self-constituting. When the legal system in question is the legal system of international society, the legal system of the society of all societies, the legal system of all legal systems, then the responsibility is the limiting case of the challenge of social self-constituting.

Legal systems. The highly abstract character of pure theory of law, as outlined above, reflects not only the capacity of the human mind to transcend in thought the human reality which it has made. It also reflects the extreme diversity and tran-sience of legal phenomena produced by the ideal and real self-constituting of actual human societies throughout the whole of recorded human history and across the whole face of the human world at any given time. However, it is also possible to see in the complexity of our historical experience of legal phenomena certain general phenomena of the practical theory of law.

(1) On a horizontal axis, legal systems of different societies have co-existed in their extreme diversity, supported by practical theories of extreme diversity (for example, theocracy, accreted custom, absolute monarchy, oligarchies of mili-tary power or wealth or caste, constitutional monarchy, popular democracy).[44]

(2) On a vertical axis, legal systems have existed in a superordinate-subordinate relationship, either forming a single overarching legal system, as in some empires and in federations, or as separate systems but with legal rules deter-mining the relationship between the two (for example, the law of the various Greek inter-polity leagues or of the Hanseatic League, the Roman Law of Nations (*ius gentium*) and Roman multinational commercial law (*lex merca-toria*), the Canon Law of the Church of Rome, the legal systems of the Holy Roman Empire and of the European Union).

(3) On a transcendent axis, legal systems have often recognized something which transcends them, in particular divine law, natural law, or the meta-legal ideal of justice.[45]

(4) On the same axis, the vivid tapestry of forms of society and legal system was often accompanied by ideas of one form or another of suprasocietal and metasocietal universality[46] or, at least, of a bi-polar universality.[47]

---

[44] We may recall Aristotle's surveying of 158 different constitutions, of which we have a recon-structed version of his theoretical analysis of the Athenian constitution (written in about 326 BCE), showing the extraordinary peripeteias in the history of Athenian self-constituting, involving repeated episodes of monarchy, tyranny, oligarchy, and many different strains of democracy.

[45] For further discussion, Allott, *The Health of Nations* (n 16 above) ch 12.

[46] Greek and Roman thought, and pre-Reformation Christian thought, had produced many such ideas: *homonoia, kosmopolis, humanitas, humana civilitas, humana universitas, universitas humani generis, civitas maxima, concordia,* the earthly kingdom, the City of Man, Christendom.

[47] We recall the ideas of barbarian, gentile, heathen, and savage used in various cultures to charac-terize the rest of the human world beyond the limits of the given culture.

International society. Practical theory responds to the needs and opportunities of society at any given time. It must follow that actual practical theory about the nature of international society has been produced by the thinking of actual human beings during a particular historical period, using the potentiality of the pure theory which is available during that period, and using the universal and perennial potentiality of transcendental theory. Because of the relationship of practical theory to social power, we may also assume that the practical theory in question has been formed as an effect of the use and abuse of social power by significant holders of social power during the same period, including holders of public-realm power and those who exercise mental power in the public interest (philosophers, lawyers, historians, commentators, teachers).

Two realities. Two moral orders. Two legal orders. A society which thinks that it is an unsociety. This is the familiar worldview which has continued for at least two centuries as the effective practical theory of the human world. It is a worldview based almost entirely on a horizontal axis, with human societies co-existing in spasmodic conflict and co-operation, with no generally accepted theory of their co-existence, and with the bare minimum of a vertical axis of the supra-societal (superordinate) and the meta-societal (transcendent). It is an unusual form of worldview in that it is formed from a series of *negative hypotheses* in the realm of pure theory.

(1) Pure theory had developed complex conceptions of *society* through the whole history of the self-contemplating of human consciousness, that is to say, the whole history of philosophy. In this way, pure theory, taking effect within practical theory, was able to produce societies exceptionally well adapted to securing the common interest of human beings in their collective survival and prospering. International unsociety would be conceived as a stark negation of all such conceptions, with 'diplomacy' and 'war' serving as the only means of social ordering within generally accepted practical theory.[48]

(2) Pure theory had developed complex conceptions of *morality* over long centuries of human self-contemplating, so that, in the form of practical theory, morality might integrate the self-ordering of human beings with the self-ordering of human societies. International unsociety would be conceived as a stark negation of that kind of moral order and, indeed, as being a realm outside the moral responsibility of individual human beings.

(3) Pure theory had developed complex conceptions of *law*, so that, in the form of practical theory, law might serve as a highly efficient aspect of the self-constituting of intensely dynamic societies, as they adapt to the ever-changing and challenging needs and opportunities of their situation. International unsociety would be conceived as a stark negation of that kind of legal order, with the word 'law' serving a marginal and disputed role in the discourse of 'diplomacy'.

[48] Allott, *Eunomia* (n 1 above) 13.96.

However, in this socio-theoretical wasteland, one aspect of generally accepted pure theory flourished and has fundamentally determined the actual practical theory of international unsociety. That aspect is the pure theory of the 'state'. The theory of the state arose as a special formation within the range of paradigm social entities mentioned above—family, polity, corporation, nation (tribe). State would be a strictly *generic* formation, not relying on the subjectivity of family or nation. Its structural-theoretical content would come to be that of a new kind of polity-society. It would be a society seen as a corporate legal entity in which a public-realm is under the control of a 'government' and which is recognized as such by the governments of other states—the 'public realm' being a legal sub-realm in which legal powers are conferred by the law to be exercised by power-holders to serve the public interest, that is, the common interest of society.[49]

The pre-history of this idea of the 'State' is one of intense complexity and controversy and of great intellectual interest, not least in revealing the use and abuse of pure theory in the service of those seeking to acquire or consolidate ultimate social power. Popes and emperors and kings and city-States fought also on the battlefield of pure theory. The medieval universities were arsenals of theoretical weaponry. Out of all the battles about the unity or pluralism of Christendom, about spiritual and temporal jurisdiction, about the source of kingly power, there emerged a new hypothesis formed from old ideas. To the ideas of the king as *lex loquens* and the idea of the king as the embodiment of the 'State'[50] and the idea of the 'State' as a 'partnership in law'[51] could be added the idea that the unity of the 'State' is to be found in the unity of its legal system. From the pure-theory hypothesis of the 'State' as an expression of the unity of society to the hypothesis of the 'State' as a society in its own right, and from the pure-theory hypothesis of the 'sovereign' to the hypothesis of 'sovereignty' as a defining attribute of the 'State',[52]

---

[49] Ibid, 12.61.

[50] It may not be possible to establish that Louis XIV of France said that he was the State, even if he did refer to the government of France as 'my state': P Burke, *The Fabrication of Louis XIV* (New Haven: Yale UP, 1992) 62. It is certainly the case that Cicero (106–43 BCE) said that the chief magistrate 'carries the person' of the republic (*De officiis*, I.34) and that the Roman poet Ovid (48BCE–18CE) said that the Emperor Augustus 'is the republic' (*res est publica Caesar*) (*Tristia*, IV.4).

[51] *Juris societas* Cicero, *De re publica* (I.32).

[52] For Jean Bodin, 'sovereignty' is 'the distinguishing mark of a commonwealth' but 'no jurist or political philosopher has in fact attempted to define it'. J Bodin, *Six Books of the Commonwealth* (1576), in M Tooley (transl), *Six Books of the Commonwealth* (Oxford: Basil Blackwell, 1955) 25. 'The word law signifies the right command of that person, or those persons, who have absolute authority over all the rest without exception, saving only the law-giver himself... To put it in another way, the law is the rightful command of the sovereign touching all his subjects in general, on matters of general application.' Ibid 43. Cf T Hobbes: '[Sovereigns] make the things they command just, by commanding them, and those which they forbid, unjust, by forbidding them.' T Hobbes, *Philosophical Rudiments concerning Government and Society* (transl of *De Cive*) in W Molesworth (ed), *The English Works of Thomas Hobbes*, Vol II (London: John Bohn, 1839), 151. 'Natural Philosophy [the natural sciences] is therefore but young; but Civil Philosophy yet much younger, as being no older... than my own book *De Cive*.' T Hobbes, *Concerning Body* (transl of *De Corpore Politico*) in W Molesworth (ed), *The English Works of Thomas Hobbes*, Vol I (London: John Bohn, 1841), ix.

were small steps within the reasoning human mind, but steps with the most profound consequences for the future of humanity as a social species.

International law. Not the least of those consequences was that the pure-theory hypothesis of international law would be of a law among 'States' whose 'sovereignty' would not be compromised by that law, an hypothesis built on a contradiction, an irrationality which has flooded the rationalizing mind with confusion for two centuries and produced the pathetic chaos of theoretical writing about international law. Is international law law or isn't it? It is scarcely believable that that question remains as a supposedly significant topic of intellectual concern to this day in the ideal self-constituting of international society, as the real self-constituting of international society has struggled to control the terrible consequences of a theoretical failure in the long story of humanity's social self-constituting.

To construct the practical theory of such a misconceived international law, it was necessary to appropriate a ragbag of hypothetical concepts taken from the pure theory of society and law. The pure theory of liberal democracy had developed strongly since the end of the medieval period generating a new conceptual vocabulary, in many cases using age-old words made new within a new theoretical structure. State. Sovereignty. Government. Law. Will. Interest. Power. Independence. Equality. Custom. Consent. Agreement. Right. Duty. Liability. The generally accepted practical theory of international law borrowed these concepts, detaching them from the immense structure, of pure theory and practical theory, within which they had been given their new theoretical significance. And people began to speak of the problem of the 'relationship between international law and national law', as if it were analogous to the problem of the relationship between mind and matter or time and space. Medieval pure theory of society and law had been mixed with genetically modified concepts taken from post-medieval pure theory to produce a monstrous human world of theoretical contradictions, a world which was conceived as two worlds, a world which, in the form of practical theory, became the world in which humanity had to find a way to survive and prosper, grievously wounded by something which had been its own creation, the source of its own suffering.

4. Practical theory—potential

The potentiality of the practical theory of international law lies not in any attempt to resolve the problem of 'the relationship between international law and national law', still less to create a theory, pure or practical, of such a relationship. It lies in integrating *international law* in the theory of the universal phenomenon of *law*, at all the *phenomenal horizons* at which law may be conceptualized, and in integrating the theory, pure and practical, of *international society* in the universal phenomenon of *society*. It means an integrating of theory and *value*, since the theoretical capacity of the human mind plays a major role in actualizing the *ideal potentiality* of human society, with a view to human self-creating, self-sustaining, self-surpassing, and self-perfecting.[53]

To actualize in a new way the hypothetical potentiality of law in international society is to undertake a new effort in the multidimensional process of rational integration offered by transcendental theory, bringing into creative conjunction our observation of the phenomena of the real world of society and law at every level of human society (the real and legal self-constituting of international society) and all three levels of the theory of society and law (its ideal self-constituting). As a preliminary contribution to that process, we may attempt to list relevant current phenomena of international society and law.

(1) Currently accepted conceptions of international law (hereafter referred to as 'old international law' or OIL) contain minimal rules about its status in national law.

(2) National constitutions contain a wide variety of rules about the presence of international law (treaties and customary IL) in national law (hereafter NL). In the case of no legal system known to the present author is there a clearly determined relationship but, in many cases, it is clear that OIL is not, in principle, supreme.

(3) OIL makes use of legal institutions taken from NL (State, government, sovereignty, nationality, corporations, contract, property, and countless others) and national laws make use of institutions taken from OIL (state in the international sense, treaties, law of the sea regimes, war, etc.). But it is not clear which is submitting to which in the legal effect given to such institutions.

(4) OIL is more and more frequently designed to be *applied within* NL, either directly or after transformation through national legislation.

(5) OIL is more and more frequently addressed to *public law* aspects of NL (human rights, discrimination, torture, conditional recognition related to national constitutional standards).

(6) National legal systems are more and more the subject of external concern and the subject of external assistance in their reform. Legal services are a product in international trade. An appropriate legal system is an aspect of comparative economic advantage.

---

[53] Theoretical economists seem more ready to adopt this position. 'economic analysis has never been the product of detached intellectual curiosity about the *why* of social phenomena, but of an intense urge to reconstruct a world which gives rise to profound dissatisfaction'. F Hayek, *Economica* 13 (May 1933) 122. JM Keynes described economics as 'a science of thinking in terms of models joined to the art of choosing models which are relevant to the contemporary world'. JM Keynes, Letter to Roy Harrod, 4 July 1938, in D Moggridge (ed), *The Collected Writings of John Maynard Keynes* Vol XIV London: MacMillan, 1973) 296. Keynes urged Harrod to repel attempts 'to turn [economics] into a pseudo-natural-science'.

(7) OIL in the form of treaties and acts of intergovernmental organizations (IGO's) is more and more taking on the character of legislation, laying down detailed rules about matters traditionally dealt with by NL.

(8) The activities of IGO's are more and more taking on the character of international government and administration, that is, doing collectively what national governments and administrations traditionally do.

(9) The judicial and quasi-judicial activities of IGO's are reaching further into, and are relating more and more to, matters otherwise within national jurisdiction (eg trade regulation, investment protection, crime).

(10) National government is more and more international, in the sense that there is less and less national public decision-making (at the levels of both policy-making and the exercise of detailed legal powers) which can be conducted in isolation from international rules and institutions.

(11) Phenomena which are reminiscent of constitutional principles at the national level are apparently (albeit controversially) establishing themselves at the international level (human rights, international public-realm crimes, coercive recognition, principles of intervention, universal principles of democracy).

(12) A concept of 'world public order' seems to be emerging, as a modification of traditional structural principles (political independence, territorial integrity, non-use of force, domestic jurisdiction).

(13) A concept of 'international community' has emerged, particularly in relation to point (12) above, but seemingly wider in its implications, suggesting that those who speak in its name are claiming to speak on behalf of some sort of international 'general will'.

(14) International institutions and rules are more and more relating directly to the activities of individuals—human beings and corporations—leaving a gross uncertainty as to whether such persons are themselves participants in legal relations under OIL (or are only indirect beneficiaries).

(15) The volume of transnational non-governmental transactions—involving several national legal systems—is growing rapidly both in absolute terms and in relation to the volume of governmental transactions. Private international law is regarded as intrinsically part of NL but is itself the subject of substantial internationalization.

(16) The volume of situations in which NL takes jurisdiction over extraterritorial events and transactions is growing rapidly, and the number of cases in which OIL is imposing or permitting 'universal' jurisdiction is growing rapidly, but OIL rules of principle on the limits of national jurisdiction remain obscure and controversial.

(17) Consciousness of matters of 'common interest' to all-humanity is growing rapidly—not only material global commons and global goods (the oceans,

the environment) but also social, economic, and spiritual goods (justice and social justice, poverty, quality of life).

(18) A concept of 'international civil society' (embodied, in particular, in international non-governmental organizations) is emerging as a sort of default or embryonic form of the *international politics* which is a necessary condition for the development of effective 'general will' phenomena at the international level.

(19) The international unsociety of which OIL has acted as the law contained no pure or practical theory of *representation*. It was simply assumed that 'governments' in some obscure way 'represent' the people of the 'States' of which they claim to be the government. There is emerging a question (related to points (5) and (11) above) about the validity of that assumption.

(20) It is possible to detect an emerging sense of global 'common interest'—a necessary, but not sufficient, condition of the pure-theory hypothesis of law—as a more or less subliminal inference of existential interdependence drawn from many of the phenomena listed above, no doubt stimulated also by increasing levels of consciousness of global threats and challenges.

Such phenomena might be said to reveal three general trends—the internationalizing of the national, the nationalizing of the international, and the universalizing of value. They demonstrate the structural incoherence of the existing theory, pure and practical, of international society and its law, an incoherence which is not only irrational as an intellectual structure but also undesirable as a cause of real-world effects and events. At the same time, in negating the *structural duality* of the existing theory (two realities, two moral orders, two legal orders), they point clearly to an hypothetical potentiality which would actualize the elements of a pure theory of society outlined in above. It then becomes possible to begin to speak seriously of the emergence of something which might reasonably be called *international society*, that is, a society of all societies, a society of all-humanity. Within such a pure theory of international society, the elements of practical theory outlined above will be re-actualized in dialectical interaction with day-to-day developments in the real self-constituting of the true international society.

In negating the *structural horizontality* of inter-state old international law, it also becomes possible to begin to speak seriously of a *universal legal system* which is the legal system of all legal systems and whose primary axis is vertical. Appropriate elements of the old international law may form part of the *constitutional law* and *public law* aspects of the new international law, supplemented by newly developed constitutional institutions and by other kinds of international law of as much variety and complexity and density as those found in any advanced national legal system.[54]

---

[54] 'The nature of institutions is nothing but their coming into being [*nascimento*] at certain times and in certain guises. Whenever the time and guise are thus and so, such and not otherwise are the

Such a universal legal system would place a re-conceived international law (new international law) at the apex of a system which embraced the laws of all subordinate societies, including the State societies as subordinate societies of international society, existing by virtue of, and in accordance with, international law, which determines also the limits and relationship of their legal systems which are, as legal systems, themselves potentially universal.[55] If a society needs, in the tradition of Hobbesian pure theory, a 'common power' to act as the source of all legal power, then it is international law itself which is that ultimate power over all other powers.[56] Such a new international society and such a new international law may at last be seen, as they should always have been seen, as having an overriding purpose and an overriding ideal—to serve as effectively as possible the common interest of humanity in its self-creating, self-sustaining, self-surpassing, and self-perfecting.

institutions that come into being'. TG Bergin and MH Fish (transl), *G Vico: The New Science* (3rd edn, New York: MacMillan, 1970) 22.

[55] Private international law is re-conceived as the international law governing transnational legal phenomena and which determines the relationship between national legal systems. For further discussion of the structure of the new system, P Allott, *The Health of Nations. Society and Law beyond the State* (Cambridge: CUP, 2002) 2.44–60, ch 10.

[56] '8. This union [the coming-together of human beings to form an organized society] so made, is that which men call now-a-days a BODY POLITIC or civil society; and the Greeks call it πόλις, that is to say, a city; which may be defined as a multitude of men, united as one person by a common power, for their common peace, defence, and benefit. 9. And as this union into a city or body politic, is instituted with common power over all particular persons, or members thereof to the common good of them all; so also may thus be amongst a multitude of those members, instituted a subordinate union of certain men, for certain common actions to be done by those men for some common benefit of theirs, or of the whole city … And these subordinate bodies politic are called CORPORATIONS; and their power such over the particulars of their own society, as the whole city whereof they are members have allowed them.' From Hobbes (n 52 above), I.19, as presented in F Tönnies (ed), T Hobbes, *The Elements of Law Natural and Politics* (Cambridge: CUP, 1928) 81.

4

Deterritorialization in International Law: Moving Away from the Divide Between National and International Law

*Catherine Brölmann**

This chapter argues that we witness a move away from the divide between national and international law. The significance of the boundary between national and international law is decreasing because a separation of legal spheres, as it was the subject of intense debate in the 20th century, is based on a territorial conception of the law, while the role of territory as a parameter in international law has come to be in decline. The following briefly explores this trend and its implications for the separation between national and international law. It concludes with the proposition that alongside the territorially bound authority of the State, other normative regimes have come into existence. Although these may act out on state territory, they flow from an independent normative source and ultimately circumvent rather than 'pierce' the sovereign veil of the State.

1. A territorial divide between national and international law

The divide between national and international law is based on a territorial conception of the law. To a large extent this is a truism. States, which at least since the 18th century have been the prime organizational units, are territorially defined entities.[1] Legally this has been translated into the precept that '[e]very State enjoyed exclusive competence for developments within its territory'.[2] From the fact that

---

* Many thanks are due to the editors Janne Nijman and André Nollkaemper for their valuable comments.

[1] An historical expression of this being, eg the 'law of the *land*' (the emphasized term—in contrast to the term 'State'—notable for combining geographical and political meaning); cf, eg the Supremacy Clause of Art VI, Para 2 of the US Constitution.

[2] C Tomuschat, *Obligations for States* (1993) 241 Recueil des Cours de l'Académie de droit international 210.

international law is construed as originating in the voluntary cooperation of States,[3] that is, in a bottom-up dynamic, it follows that '[t]raditionally, international law rested on the principle of territoriality'.[4]

By consequence also the *divide* between national and international law— whether as a formal and objective separation (as 'dualists' would hold) or as an erroneous mind-set (as would be the 'monist' view)—hinges on territory. The State's territorial boundary delimitates its political and legal power, and vice versa,[5] and constitutes its border with international law.

The fundamental character of the territorial precept is readily apparent from the debate in the past decades, and from efforts to construe the unity of law or, conversely, its division in different spheres. Traditionally such efforts have revolved around the ('monist') dissolution of the state boundary or, alternatively, its ('dualist') piercing. With some simplification we can see an example of the first in Kelsen's foundational model in which national law and international law are logically connected;[6] and an example of the second in the model of Anzilotti, who like Triepel envisaged a separation between national and international law that could be bridged only by a method of *renvoi*.[7] Either way, these approaches both relate to a legal universe which recognizes territorial subdivisions of administrative authority, ie territorially bound jurisdictions.

This chapter aims for conceptual-theoretical reflection on the divide between national and international law, taking it not so much as a subject in schools of thought, but as a phenomenon in international legal life. Significantly the monist-dualist opposition is used also (and nowadays perhaps foremost) to refer to a classification of existing constitutional systems, based on the way in which these incorporate international law:

[A]lthough I have sympathy with the view of those who think the monist-dualist debate is passé, I also think it right that the difference in response to a clash of international law and domestic law in various domestic courts is substantially conditioned by whether the country concerned is monist or dualist in its approach.[8]

---

[3] As famously expressed by the 'Lotus Principle': 'International law governs relations between independent States. The rules of law binding upon States therefore emanate from their own free will as expressed in conventions or by usages generally accepted as expressing principles of law and established in order to regulate the relations between these co-existing independent communities or with a view to the achievement of common aims'. *Case of the SS 'Lotus' (France v Turkey)*, PCIJ Series A, No 10 (1927) 18. [4] Tomuschat (n 2 above) 210.

[5] See J Bartelson, *A Genealogy of Sovereignty* (Cambridge: CUP, 1995) 30, on the dual possibility of taking sovereignty as a condition for a bounded territory, and, conversely, bounded territory as a condition for sovereignty.

[6] H Kelsen, *Reine Rechtslehre; Einleitung in die rechtswissenschaftliche Problematik* (Leipzig und Wien: Deuticke, 1934); cf F Koja, *Hans Kelsen oder Die Reinheit der Rechtslehre (mit ausgewählte Texte)* (Vienna: Böhlau Verlag, 1988).

[7] D Anzilotti, *Corso di Diritto Internazionale* (Padova: CEDAM, 1955) Vol I, 58 et seq.

[8] R Higgins, *Problems and Process: International Law and How We Use It* (Oxford: Clarendon Press, 1994) 207.

Such a classification is based on the very idea of territorially bound, thus distinguishable, legal spheres, and in addition proceeds from their agreed and formalized separation.

The qualification of legal rules as 'domestic' or 'international', then, makes use of a well-tried set of criteria, including the *Normadressat* of the rule, and the subject matter it regulates.[9] But foremost the distinction between national and international law is based on the *source* of the rule, that is: a test of pedigree or set of formal criteria that gives normative force to a statement.[10] Of old this is the prime test: a norm approved in a national parliament according to a legislative procedure is domestic law; a norm agreed upon among States according to certain rules ('tacit or express consent') is international law. In contrast, the normative *scope* of a rule is not used as a criterion, which bears out the self-evidence of the territorial parameter. As national law by definition extends to national territory, it would amount to a tautological statement. The territorial scope does not determine the nature of the rule and is not a condition for a rule to be national; rather it is a consequence of its flowing from a national source of norm-setting authority.[11] The scope of 'international' rules is construed in the same way, as we see in the doctrine of international custom. Unlike treaty law, which can be construed to extend precisely to the respective territories of the states parties, the scope of custom is presumed to be 'universal', except in the rare circumstances that would give rise to 'regional custom'.[12]

Territory, as an organizing principle for political and legal authority, thus has a central role in the conceptualization of the divide between national and international law. The divide therefore is bound to be affected by the rise of other organizing principles.

2. Territory, space, and the State in an era of globalization

A central premise of this chapter, which will be elaborated upon in the next section, is that international law shows a trend towards 'deterritorialization', a term which is meant to refer specifically to *detachment of regulatory authority from a specific territory.*

At this point a preliminary note on the choice of territory as an analytical tool, and on adjacent concepts used in contemporary (legal) study, is in order. First of

---

[9] An outline of the two schools of thought (from a staunchly dualist perspective), in G Arangio-Ruiz, 'International Law and Interindividual Law', this volume, p 15.

[10] G Fitzmaurice, 'The General Principles of International Law Considered from the Standpoint of the Rule of Law' (1975-II) in 92 Recueil des Cours de l'Académie de Droit International, The development of different dualist schools, viz. of 'transformation' as opposed to 'validation' of international law in the national legal order, is left out of account here (eg A Bleckmann, *Grundprobleme und Methoden des Völkerrechts* (Freiburg: Verlag Karl Alber, 1982) 195.   [11] Cf n 2 above.

[12] Eg in the textbook by M Shaw, *International Law* (5th edn, Cambridge: CUP, 2003) 88: 'local customs are an exception to the general nature of customary law'.

all, why take *territory* as a starting point, and not the idea of *the State*? After all, the territorial basis of international law is clearly related to the fact that the state, operating on the premise of territorial sovereignty, is the prime form of political organization since the era of formation of the modern system of international law and of reinforcement, in turn, of the position of the State).

The use of 'territory' is deliberate, as it refers to a different quality than 'Statehood', and renders more precisely the point that is relevant in relation to the national-international law divide. For example the notion of non-territoriality is able to capture regimes and institutions which are state based, but which in their operation have come to be detached and operate on a different basis than territorially bound control. Statehood, on the other hand, refers to a particular form of political and administrative organization, which is not the focus of this chapter—nor is the claim, put forward at various stages since the 1950s,[13] that globalization and the rise of international regimes is leading to the demise of the nation-State. Otherwise, the prism of territory brings out best the contrast between classic international law and many of the contemporary international regimes; these are not so much 'non-statal' (in the way of a confederative structure), but rather 'non-territorial' (in the way of a regime tied to a specific functional area).

Functionality, as will appear below, is not the sole but certainly the most prominent substitute for territoriality as an organizing principle for regulatory authority. 'Functionality' is used in the broad sense, similar to the 'area of competence' or 'field of activity' mentioned by the International Court of Justice in relation to international organizations,[14] while no particular reference is intended to the 'functionalist' theory of international organization (functional institutions *should* supersede nation-States). Importantly, a functional regime is fundamentally different from an integral, political regime such as that of a State. Functionality (competence with regard to a particular function without *a priori* territorial limitation) and territoriality (competence with regard to all functions in a legal order with territorial limitation) are different parameters. Therefore States and, for example, organizations do not 'overlap' in the same way as the parts and the whole of a (con)federal structure, nor are they simply interchangeable as international legal entities.

Otherwise, using *territory* as the central notion for analysing legal developments means having considered the concept of *space*, which is fruitfully used in various disciplines. The notion of *space* in the physical-geographical sense,[15] however, is counter-intuitive in a legal context (except to describe the entirely non-spatial

---

[13] Eg J Herz, 'Rise and Demise of the Territorial States' (1957) 9 *World Politics* 473–93 and EB Haas, *Beyond the Nation-State: Functionalism and International Organization* (Stanford UP, 1964).

[14] *Legality of the Use by a State of Nuclear Weapons in Armed Conflict*, Advisory Opinion, ICJ 8 July 1996, para 19.

[15] 'An interval between two or more points or objects; a certain stretch, extent, or area of ground, surface, sky; an expanse' *Oxford English Dictionary* (2nd edn, 1989) s.v.

internet), since the aspect of formal(ized) boundness that goes with territory is lacking. In the lawyer's discourse, *territory* is politically and legally defined space.[16] Outside the positive law context of this chapter, the socio-geographic aspects of 'space' (often indicated by the term *spatiality*) are factors that influence the operation of law and law-like systems.

The notion of *spatialization* of the law, as it is used in critical social theory in particular, takes an approach essentially opposite from the one in this chapter (although it can lead to the same conclusions). Rather than proceeding from positive law it it leads thereto—law does not follow from territorially bound authority, it preceeds such territorially bound authority by *projecting* a space upon which its operations will unfold: 'One spatial tactic central to law is the construction of boundaries. Much of law concerns who is in and who is out, what is allowable in territory A versus territory B.'[17] Along these lines one can convincingly make the point, as Mayo Moran does in this volume, that a 'traditional spatialized model of law with its emphasis on the application of binding rules . . . seems to be giving way . . . '[18] and that a shift in the sources doctrine—a move away from the binary, binding-rule approach—entails a move away from the spatialised model of the law. A similar proposition is argued below on the basis of the notion of territoriality.[19]

In the same way as *deterritorialization*, an exercise in *despatialization* can aim to take the localized factor out of law and its application. Here too the notion of *space* adds to our understanding of how the law works, but from a slightly different angle. Unlike territory, however, the notion of space is not linked to power, authority, and government. *Space* is ultimately less helpful in addressing a political-legal phenomenon such as the divide between national and international law, as in itself it is not a political-legal phenomenon. This is arguably the reason why 'despatialization' in fact may end up in setting new coordinates. For example Kal Raustiala proposes a 'functional approach to constitutional powers' and argues that 'there is no a priori reason to believe that the spatial restrictions the Framers [of the U.S. Constitution] placed on the powers of the federal government cannot or should not be read functionally as well'.[20] But the 'despatialization' proposed by the author partly results in a paradox, as he essentially advocates what traditionally is termed 'extraterritorial jurisdiction'—which in effect is based on a very spatial—and territorial—conception of the law, although the State's traditional jurisdictional boundaries are transcended.[21]

---

[16] I am indebted to Janne Nijman for articulating this idea.

[17] Cited from Objectives of the Conference on Liberalism, Governance and the Geographies of Law, University of Washington, May 2007, <http://depts.washington.edu/uwch/projects_law0607.htm>, accessed on 30 January 2007.

[18] See M Moran, 'Shifting Boundaries: the Authority of International Law', this volume, 165.

[19] Section 3.2 below.

[20] K Raustiala, 'The Geography of Justice' (2005) 73 Fordham L Rev 101, 147.

[21] *Case of the SS 'Lotus' (France v Turkey)*, PCIJ Series A, No. 10 (1927) 18.

Finally, it is evident that contemporary challenges to the role of territoriality as a foundation of international law are connected to the process of globalization.[22] On a general note the change of scale in human action, relations, and communication may be taken as the most prominent factor in new developments and challenges in law. The process of globalization has brought about greater awareness of joint interests, empowerment of various stakeholders, and relations across state borders. However, 'globalization' is not the prism used in this chapter, also because the term is generally connected to a process whose prime implications are non-legal. As to its legal aspects, moreover, the term is not sufficiently precise; for one thing it could suggest that scale enlargement is leading us to a global government in the sense of a 'world State' with global political authority. But, as has been widely recognized, although 'th[e] common view posits the first level as the State level, and the second as the global level ... the reality is more complex'.[23] Indeed, globalization, in governance and other matters, seems to come about through different centres, or levels, of political organization, depending on various, functionally designed agencies. And according to many observers this is reflected in a fragmented image of 'law': 'In contrast to the constantly reiterated claims, the appearance of global regimes does not entail the integration, harmonization or, at the very least, the convergence of legal orders; rather, it transforms the internal differentiation of law.'[24]

The study of regime collisions, fragmentation and pluralism in law exists next to the endeavours in legal scholarship to identify a body of 'international constitutional law' which would establish an organic and hierarchical international legal system.[25] That quest is not at issue in this chapter, although some developments, such as when human rights would come to override other state-made rules, are relevant in either perspective. The same holds for the innovative analysis of an emerging 'global administrative law' (GAL)—rules and principles to be distilled from 'global administration', which is the part of global governance consisting of 'all rule-making and adjudications or other decisions of particular matters that are neither treaty-making nor simple dispute settlement between disputing parties'.[26]

---

[22] A broad term which is used to describe many processes; see S Marks and A Clapham, *International Human Rights Lexicon* (Oxford: OUP, 2005) 180–85, for a general description of globalization as a process of extension, intensification, acceleration, and increased impact of 'social, economic and political action across national boundaries'.

[23] S Cassese, 'Introduction: Regulation, Adjudication and Dispute Resolution Beyond the State' (2006) in *Global Administrative Law Cases and Materials*, University of Rome 'La Sapienza' (Public Law Institute) (NET) 1.

[24] A Fischer-Lescano and G Teubner, 'Regime-Collisions: The Vain Search for Legal Unity in the Fragmentation of Global Law' (2004) 25 Michigan JIL 999, 1009.

[25] Eg A Peters, 'Why Obey International Law? Global Constitutionalism Revisited' (2006) *ASIL Centennial Discussion on a Just World Under Law* available at <http://law.ubalt.edu/asil/peters.html>; See also E de Wet, 'The Value System of the International Community' (2004) 15 EJIL 97.

[26] The launch paper is B Kingsbury, N Krisch, and RB Stewart, 'The Emergence of Global Administrative Law' *IILJ Working Paper* 2004/1 (Global Administrative Law Series), 6; see also N Krisch and B Kingsbury, 'Introduction: Global Governance and Global Administrative Law in the International Legal Order' (2006) 17 EJIL 1.

The comprehensive GAL project thus tackles precisely all regulation and adjudication in the global arena that is *not* classic contractual international law, and from there logically derives the proposition that 'there is no clear line of separation between the global and the national'.[27] For its study of global 'administrative' acts, GAL can be partly opposed to international constitutional law, which searches for unity and hierarchy within the classic body of international rules and norms. Those rules and norms are also a starting point in the present chapter. Though topics of GAL study—such as regulatory activity by non-state actors—are relevant for the point it seeks to make, the present angle is a different one. From the perspective of positive international law—instrumental when looking at the distinction between national and international law—the central aspect of the new developments is not that governance goes global, but that the territorial foundation of norm-setting authority is being put in perspective.

3. The declining role of territory in international law

Work in philosophy[28] and the social sciences[29] has revealed a decline in the role of territory as an organizing principle. A correlative development is arguably found in the field of international law. Having emerged from states as the prime actors, the classic international system operates on territory as the prime nexus. In the past decades, however, there is evidence of a move away from the model of territorially bound spheres of legal authority. A central element is the shift from territorial borders to functional boundaries in the regulation of various matters in the global arena.

Sociologist Niklas Luhmann has pointed to this development in a general sense.[30] According to John Ruggie 'nonterritorial functional space is the place wherein international society is anchored';[31] and for example Saskia Sassen, from a slightly different angle, has stated that 'exclusive territoriality... is being destabilized by economic globalization and that a denationalization of national territory is

---

[27] S Cassese, 'Administrative Law Without the State? The Challenge of Global Regulation' (2005) 37 NYUJ of Int'l L & and P 663, 684.

[28] G Deleuze and F Guattari coined the term 'deterritorialization' in *Anti-Œdipus* (Paris, Minuet 1972), and refined it in *Mille Plateaux* (Paris: Minuet, 1980). In their work 'deterritorialization' encompasses both geographical and metaphorical meanings of space.

[29] See, eg J Tomlinson, *Globalization and Culture* (Chicago: University of Chicago Press, 1999), ch 4; G Canclini's and Tomlinson's notion of 'deterritorialization' is geographical (see below n 39 and accompanying text).

[30] N Luhmann, *Das Recht der Gesellschaft* (Frankfurt am Main: Suhrkamp, 1995), 571 et seq; id, *Die Gesellschaft der Gesellschaft* (Frankfurt am Main: Suhrkamp, 1997) Vol 1, 158–60; reference in A Paulus, 'From Territoriality to Functionality? Towards a Legal Methodology of Globalization' in IF Dekker and WG Werner (eds), *Governance and International Legal Theory* (Leiden/Boston: Martinus Nijhoff, 2004) 59–95; and in A Fischer-Lescano, and G Teubner, 'Regime-Collisions: The Vain Search for Legal Unity in the Fragmentation of Global Law' (2004) 25 Michigan JIL 999, 1000.

[31] JG Ruggie, 'Territoriality and Beyond: Problematizing Modernity in International Relations' (1993) 47 *International Organization* 139, 165.

now in progress, though in a highly specialized institutional and functional way'.[32] In the particular context of international law this dynamic has been addressed, for example by Teubner,[33] as an effect of globalization and a ground for regime-clash, and by Koskenniemi,[34] notably as a cause of fragmentation of international law.

How has the principle of territoriality in international law come under pressure? This is due to at least two phenomena, international and transnational. We see a decline in the role of the territorial parameter brought about by both traditional structures which have emanated from states, and by new, transboundary private structures. The latter are more squarely at odds with the terms of classic international law than international regimes. It is important, however, not to read these two phenomena as 'stages', but rather as different forms of the development of deterritorialization. Private networks are not a produced part, at least not at the formal level, of global developments via international institutions.

As to these international regimes, 'technically specialized cooperation networks' figure prominently in contemporary studies of international law.[35] These networks are normative regimes, established by a norm-setting authority that is not linked to territory, but to the issue area at stake—be it food, health, or the environment. Thus, the European Union, working together with the World Health Organization, the Food and Agriculture Organization and the World Organization for Animal Health, monitor and regulate bird flu[36] next to States, for whom animal health, food safety and economic prowess are elements of an integral political authority within a particular territory.

On the impact of these regimes on the foundations of the international law system Günther Teubner may be quoted in full:

For centuries law had followed the political logic of nation-states and was manifest in the multitude of national legal orders, each with their own territorial jurisdiction. Even international law, which viewed itself as the contract law of Nation-States, did not depart from this model. The final break with such conceptions was only signalled in the last century with the rapidly accelerating expansion of international organizations and regulatory regimes, which, in sharp contrast to their genesis within international treaties, established themselves as autonomous legal orders.[37]

---

[32] S Sassen, *Losing Control? Sovereignty in an Age of Globalization* (New York: Columbia UP, 1997) 61.

[33] Who has considerably elaborated Luhmann's thesis in relation to law; cf Fischer-Lescano and Teubner 'Regime collisions' (n 30 above).

[34] *Fragmentation Of International Law: Difficulties Arising From The Diversification And Expansion Of International Law*, Report of the Study Group of the International Law Commission finalized by M Koskenniemi (UN Doc. A/CN.4/L.682; 13 April 2006), explicit reference to the shift from territory to function, eg in para 133, n 138; see also M Koskenniemi and P Leino, 'Fragmentation of International Law. Postmodern Anxieties?' (2002) 15 Leiden Journal of International Law 553.

[35] See notably the International Law Commission Report on *Fragmentation* (n 34 above and n 45 below).

[36] <http://ec.europa.eu/food/animal/diseases/controlmeasures/avian/index_en.htm> on the 'hard' and 'soft' bindingness of various forms of standard-setting, see below section 3.2.

[37] Fischer-Lescano and Teubner 'Regime collisions' (n 24 above) 1008.

The present chapter puts transnational private networks (eg regulating the internet) together with international institutional regimes (eg the WHO monitoring health on a global scale),[38] for the reason that these phenomena are both considered vehicles for what may be described as 'deterritorialization' in international law.

The precise term is taken from the social sciences where it denotes 'detachment of social and cultural practices from specific places'.[39] As mentioned above, in this chapter 'deterritorialization' means 'detachment of regulatory authority from a specific territory'. 'Legal globalization' is often described in comprehensive terms, taking into account developments in (to use the formal terms) rule-making, adjudication, as well as enforcement.[40] It is submitted that, when proceeding from a formal-legal framework (as against the backdrop of the divide between national and international law, and the strong role of the sources doctrine in determining to which legal sphere a rule belongs), such developments have one aspect that is particularly relevant: whether or not originating in an agreement between states, these institutions and networks may come to assume *norm-setting authority* next to, or in lieu of, the state. In other words: norm-setting—to use a more flexible term than the notion of 'law-making'—authority is no longer tied to a particular territory, or: territorially bound jurisdiction.

Both types then are functional (rather than territorial) regimes, although in the case of private networks this is not their most conspicuous characteristic.[41] To say that a normative regime—a set of norms—is 'functionally defined,' is to say that it aims to regulate a certain issue area or functional area, and that its legitimacy (if not legality) is delimited by the bounds of that issue area.[42] To say that the norm-setting authority (or source of the rule) is based on function, is to say that that the 'rule-makers' derive their authority from their role in a certain issue area, not from the integral political authority of for example state legislators within a given territory.

Of course, not every non-territorial normative regime and norm-setting authority are based on function. Norm-setting authority can be derived from religion or clan-identity, or in principle from any other aspect of human life. The emphasis on *function* in various areas of scholarship, including law, results from the fact that it is the most recent and the most powerful competitor for territoriality as an organising principle for authority, legal or otherwise.

The scope of this chapter thus is fairly narrow, focused on the locus of regulatory authority. This means that the UNHCR enforcing domestic and international law by determining the status of individual refugees, is not considered as an

---

[38] As is done by Fischer-Lescano and Teubner for the purpose of analysing the phenomenon of regime collisions. On emerging private cooperation networks 'It is these regimes that give birth to "global law without the state", which is primarily responsible for the multi-dimensionality of global legal pluralism' (Fischer-Lescano and Teubner 'Regime collisions' (n 24 above) 1009.

[39] Tomlinson (n 29 above) ch 4.

[40] Cf for example the scope of the Project on Global Administrative Law (nn 23 and 26 above).

[41] This may be why Fischer-Lescano and Teubner (n 24 above) refer only to traditional international regimes explicitly as 'functional'.   [42] See (n 14 above) and accompanying text.

illustration of deterritorialization in international law. In contrast, the Appendices to the 1973 CITES Convention,[43] listing the to various degrees protected species, are. In the present context, deterritorialization thus means specifically that the locus of norm-setting authority for a given issue area, such as the market or the environment, is not, or not exclusively, in the territorial state. One consequence is that the allocation of rights and duties is to the same extent detached from the territory on which an addressee finds himself. Thus, deterritorialization breeds regimes that may address non-State actors and stakeholders, in terms of the statist paradigm, 'directly'. However, because 'directness' is a relative notion, it is to be addressed below in the context of the national law.

Developments such as these are inextricably linked to 'deterritorialization', and arguably have an element of both cause and effect. For this reason the exploratory account below briefly considers international regimes (section 3.1) and trans-national private networks (section 3.3) as vehicles of deterritorialization, but also some related developments (section 3.2): the rise of 'fuzzy normativity' next to binary normativity; and the expansion of the catalogue of actors involved, both as norm-setting authority and as normative addressee. The section on transnational networks is last, as it can—*within* the international law discourse—only be appreciated when taking these developments into account.

3.1 An international superstructure

A trend towards deterritorialization can be seen at work first of all in the 'functional' normative regimes of international life. In the 1970s Hermann Mosler employed the term 'international superstructure' to denote the layer of international institutions 'over and above' the different State systems.[44] Here the term 'international superstructure' is adopted for both normative regimes and accompanying institutional structures, and is used also to indicate that we are dealing with (originally) State-based structures and classic binding norms. Such regimes, one point of departure for the International Law Commission's study on Fragmentation,[45] are by now nothing new. The creation of the United Nations has ushered in the era of grand 'law-making' treaties and codification projects; we need only look at the UN organigram and the list of Specialized Agencies. These regimes have been subject of legal

---

[43] Cf Arts XV and XVI of the Convention. Text available at <http://www.cites.org/>.

[44] 'The international community, it is true, is still to be considered as a society of sovereign and equal States but the increasing number of organizations have come to play such an important and permanent part in international relations that they now form a kind of superstructure over and above the society of States' (H Mosler, 'The International Society as a Legal Community—Part 3: Institutionalised International Co-operation'(1974) in Recueil des Cours de l'Académie de Droit International 11, 189.

[45] 'One aspect of globalization is the emergence of technically specialized cooperation networks with a global scope: trade, environment, human rights, diplomacy, communications, medicine, crime prevention, energy production, security, indigenous cooperation and so on', *Fragmentation* (n 34 above) para 481; see also below the quote in the text accompanying n 112.

discussion from the start, and described for their 'functional' set-up and independent institutional structure in legal circles at least since the 1950s. That the rise of institutions and functional normative regimes constituted '[t]he final break'[46] with the classic set-up of international law, was perhaps less clear at the time, but in hindsight seems self-evident. As appears from the brief examples below, some of these institutional regimes, having assumed independent norm-setting authority, are a vehicle for deterritorialization in international law.

3.1.1 State addressees

The most familiar cases, which could therefore almost pass unnoticed, are those in which functionally defined, institutional regimes address regulatory action to states. Usually such regimes are an international organization of some form.[47] Conversely, not nearly all international organizations are vehicles for deterritorialization. The majority of organizations (currently around 2000 are said to exist)[48] facilitate classic inter-State activity in which the source of norm-setting authority remains with the state. However, some familiar examples of non-plenary organs possessing and exercising binding decision-making power actually go to show a shift of regulatory power to the level of the functional regime.[49]

Thus deterritorialization occurs when organizations have the power to enact norms within the normative regime of which they are an institutional component.[50] In the formal sense, this amounts to a way of international rule-making that probably transcends the contractual paradigm or the qualification 'treaty norms'. For example in the International Civil Aviation Organization 'standards' are adopted or amended by the Council by a two-thirds majority and become effective *unless* the majority of the members register their disapproval within three months. Even when the standard is duly promulgated, there is no obligation for the member States to comply: they may individually chose to 'opt out' or 'contract out' by notification to the Council. The legal effect of *failure* to notify is not clear, however, which leaves opinion divided on whether these standards are formally

---

[46] See n 37 above and accompanying text.

[47] It has been convincingly argued that conventional IGOs should not be viewed as a closed category, but rather as part of a fuzzy category to which 'treaty regimes' belong as well (cf D Simon, *L'Interpretation Judiciaire des Traités d'Organisations Internationales: Morphologie des Conventions et Fonction Jurisdictionelle* (Paris: Pedone, 1981) 488). This view has explanatory power, but is somewhat at odds with the purpose of a normative definition. A flexible approach, however, has emerged—cf eg R Churchill and G Ulfstein, 'Autonomous Institutional Arrangements in Multilateral Environmental Agreements: A Little-Noticed Phenomenon in International Law' (2000) 94 AJIL 623–59, who, on the basis of the definition proposed by HG Schermers and NM Blokker, *International Institutional Law* (The Hague: Martinus Nijhoff, 2003) §§ 29–47) qualify 'Autonomous Institutional Arrangements' such as the Ozone Secretariat to be international organizations.

[48] *Yearbook of International Organizations 2003–2004* (Munchen: Saur, 2004).

[49] See section 3.2 below on a collateral development away from 'binary normativity'.

[50] In a general sense only 'external decisions' of organizations are at issue (see Schermers and Blokker (n 49 above) § 1200 ('Internal rules are basically limited to regulating the functioning of the organization') and § 1216 ('One task of international organizations is to make rules extending beyond the mere functioning of the organization itself').

binding. But in either case, ICAO standards seem to be invariably complied with in practice. In ICAO, where the opting-out system originates, the independent norm-setting authority is particularly apparent, as the Council is not a plenary organ.[51] Comparable procedures for the enactment of 'regulatory acts' exist, eg in the WHO (where the law-making function resides in the plenary organ, however (see Arts 21 and 22)), and in several other Specialized Agencies.[52]

Several regimes sustained by a one-organ 'treaty body' show a similar practice. A degree of norm-setting authority has shifted to the institution, couched in precise and technical procedural rules. For example the 1985 Vienna Convention for the Protection of the Ozone Layer envisages a procedure for amendments in which 'adoption' in the plenary organ has the legal effect of signature subject to ratification by the states' plenipotentiaries. The procedure laid down in the 1987 Montreal Protocol on Substances which Deplete the Ozone Layer for the enactment of 'adjustments' to the original standards with regard to controlled substances takes the development one step further than in the case of the aforementioned ICAO standards: such adjustments—failing consensus adopted by a two thirds majority—are explicitly said to be binding on all parties.[53]

The most prominent example is undoubtedly the UN Security Council acting under chapter VII of the Charter, which may take decisions that are binding on all member states. In line with the inter-State orientation of the Charter, these decisions are usually directed at States (although with recent exceptions, see below).

These are familiar cases, extensively analysed for their 'supranational' aspects (from the angle of international institutional law), and for their challenge to the principle of consent (in the debate between law of treaties adherents and institutionalists, and between voluntarists and international communitarians). But they are also prototypal examples of deterritorialization in international law, in which norm-setting authority has shifted from the State level to the level of an independent functional regime. This is not prejudged by the fact that the regime as such was created by states and originally rests upon the sum of parties' territories. Nor does it make a difference in principle, only in effect, that in the examples mentioned above the norms are directed at States.

[51] Cf VD Degan, *Sources of International Law* (The Hague: Martinus Nijhoff, 1997) 6. who considers 'non-obligatory' rules' such as ICAO standards, to which, nevertheless, 'the respective states almost invariably conform themselves', as a possible newly emerging source of international law.

[52] Convention on International Civil Aviation (1944) 15 UNTS 295 (Arts 37, 54(1), 90). See Ch Alexandrowicz, *The Law-Making Functions of the Specialised Agencies of the United Nations* (Sydney: Angus and Robertson (in association with the Australian Institute of International Affairs), 1973) at 40–69 (on 'quasi-legislative acts' of Specialised Agencies); E Klein 'United Nations, Specialized Agencies' (1983) EPIL, Vol 5, 349–68; FL Kirgis, 'Specialized Law-Making Processes' in C Joyner (ed), *The United Nations and International Law* (Cambridge: CUP/ASIL, 1997) 70 et seq.

[53] Art 2(9)d of the Montreal Protocol stipulates that decisions (possibly taken by majority) are binding on all parties and enter into force six months after notification by the Secretariat. An analysis of the procedural aspects of the 1985 Ozone Convention (1513 UNTS 3) and the 1987 Montreal Protocol (1522 UNTS 3) in M Fitzmaurice, 'Modifications to the Principles of Consent in Relation to Certain Treaty Obligations' (1997) 2 Austrian Review of Int'L and European L 275, 281–83 and 291–93 (citation at 291).

3.1.2 Non-State addressees

The effect of deterritorialization is more marked, as is the relevance for the relation between national and international law,[54] when regimes with independent norm-setting authority address not only States, but also or exclusively non-State actors. In a general sense, this can be seen as a movement further away from the territorial foundation of international law.

Here the obvious example are integrational (but nonetheless functionally defined)[55] regimes such as the European Community pillar of the European Union. The 'direct effect' of Community legislation independent of the constitutional systems of the member States, established by the European Court of Justice in the 1963 *Gend en Loos* judgment,[56] means simply that (in casu) rights are conferred on individuals by European Community legislation. The requirement that such rights should be enforceable before national courts,[57] is a separate, procedural aspect of the individual's legal position. Such a separation is generally accepted, in the sense that absence of a procedural right does not prejudge the existence—though it clearly undermines the effectiveness—of a substantive right.

Other international institutions, as well, may in the exercise of their regulatory powers (or norm-setting authority) address individuals or other non-State actors. A notorious example is the Committee of the UN Security Council known as the 'Al-Qaeda and Taliban Sanctions Committee', established in 1999[58] to oversee the implementation of sanctions on Taliban-controlled Afghanistan for its support of Usama bin Laden. The committee was activated by subsequent resolutions,[59] so that the sanctions came to cover named individuals and entities associated with Al-Qaeda, Usama bin Laden and/or the Taliban wherever located. This is an exceptional development, as the UN system is emphatically state-oriented—something which was confirmed by the mechanism's flaws in procedural fairness vis-à-vis the individuals on the 'sanctions list'.[60]

---

[54] See below in section 4.

[55] Integral political authority (associated with territorial sovereignty) and function are not a priori unconnectable, but can be seen as poles of a continuum. Thus, the qualification of certain functional regimes that come to embrace a growing number of functional areas, may be open to debate. This chapter takes the view that for now, the EU and in particular its first pillar, qualify as a functional regime more than a territorial regime (namely, a confederative structure). Also along these lines Virally reasoned that the EC should be studied as a separate category from regular intergovernmental organizations (M Virally, 'La Notion de Fonction dans la Théorie de l'Organisation Internationale' in S Bastid (ed), *Mélanges offerts à Rousseau* (Paris: Pedone, 1974) 277, 288–90).

[56] And confirmed by, eg the Dutch Supreme Court only in 2004 (LJN: AR1797, Hoge Raad, 00156/04, 02-11-2004); *Gend en Loos v Nederlandse Administratie der Belastingen* judgment (Case 26/62); [1963] ECR 1; [1970] CMLR 1; note that in the Treaty establishing a Constitution for Europe (Art I-33(1)) regulations are re-named 'European laws'.

[57] *Gend en Loos v Nederlandse Administratie der Belastingen* (ibid).

[58] Resolution 1267 of 15 October 1999, para 6.

[59] Including resolutions 1333 (2000), 1390 (2002), 1455 (2003), 1526 (2004), and 1617 (2005).

[60] As appears from the Yusuf and Kadi cases decided by the European Court of First Instance, in the European sphere the normative authority of the UN as yet has been upheld, notwithstanding the

3.1.3 Human rights

As the previous category, human rights regimes are addressed to non-State actors, and they are a clear factor of deterritorialization in international law. Yet, human rights may be set apart as a somewhat exceptional case, both on a conceptual and practical level. The international regimes at issue in this chapter, as in the examples above, usually have an (even one-organ) institutional component, in which the independent norm-setting authority resides. Such authority will manifest itself by producing new norms (which, as for example in the EU context, may actually be called 'secondary' in contrast to the primary rules that established the regime) and which in a classic framework may take the form of either binding or non-binding 'recommendations' or 'resolutions'.

This is different in human rights regimes such as the one established by the 1966 Covenants, by the 1981 African Charter on Human and Peoples' Rights, the 1969 American Convention on Human Rights or the 1950 European Convention on Human Rights. Only the ICCPR committee has a semi-judicial role, but both Covenants have treaty bodies with some clear norm-setting authority to be exercised for example by giving 'general Comments'. On the other hand, the regional regimes carry an elaborate institutional structure that are the Courts, which exercise a fully fledged judicial function. Through this mechanism these courts engage in independent norm-setting, though not in the 'straightforward' way of other institutional regimes. Rather, the primary norms are elaborated and adjusted in a more diffuse process, through application and adjudication.[61]

A notable example of this is the 'living instrument' doctrine, which is a central and necessary principle of Strasbourg case law. It envisages application and interpretation of the European Convention on Human Rights 'in the light of present day conditions.'[62] In current parlance, the expression appears synonymous to 'evolutive treaty interpretation' or 'dynamic interpretation', through which a treaty 'can change its meaning in accordance with developments in State and society'.[63] From a classic legal viewpoint the living instrument approach is an uneasy notion. It is fundamentally different from an 'object and purpose' interpretation in that it is not triggered by an interpretive problem of the text, but primarily by changing social reality.[64] Such an adjustment of the norms in accordance with

---

absence of a right of individuals eg to present a request to the Security Council for review of their being listed; see Court of First Instance of the EC, *Ahmed Ali Yusuf and Al Barakaat International Foundation v Council and Commission*, T-306/01 (OJEU C 281/31 or <http://curia.europa.eu/en/content/juris/index.htm>), and *Yassin Abdullah Kadi v Council and Commission*, T-315/01 (OJEU C 281/32 or <http://curia.europa.eu/en/content/juris/index.htm>), both at 21-IX-2005.

[61] The GAL perspective (see n 26 above) likewise considers courts as regulatory entities.

[62] Cf *Tyrer v UK*, 25 April 1978, Appl nr 00005856/72, § 31; *Loizidou v Turkey* (judgment—Preliminary Objections), 23 March 1995, § 71; *Selmouni v France* (28 July 1999), para 101.

[63] Cf R Bernhardt, 'Evolutive Treaty Interpretation, especially of the European Convention on Human Rights' (1999) German Yearbook of Int'l L 11–25 at 12.

[64] Eg R Jennings and A Watts, *Oppenheim's International Law* (9th edn, Longmans, 1992) para 629.

social developments is monitored by the European Court, while the link with the 'intention' of the treaty parties moves further to the background.[65] Moreover, the doctrine of incorporation and *eo ipso* direct applicability of the substantive rights in the Convention, make that within the area covered by the treaty regime as a whole, the individual's rights are no longer based on the territorial jurisdiction under which he resorts.

Notably in the area of human rights, we can in addition see a trend to deterritorialization at a conceptual level. Here the issue is not only that norm-setting authority has effectively shifted to another level, but also that conceptually the norms become detached from their formal source, and thus become linked entirely to the addressee.

This trend in legal thought is illustrated by the question of automatic succession of human rights.[66] While not (yet) part of positive international law, there have been strong voices and doctrinal efforts to link treaty-based human rights to the individuals rather than to the States parties, and to infer 'automatic succession' even in case the successor does not wish legally to succeed to its predecessor state for that particular treaty. Such in stark contravention of the principle that treaties can only create effects for a certain territory with everything and everyone in it if the State party holds a jurisdictional title over that territory.

The issue has come up for example in relation to the transfer of Hong Kong by the United Kingdom to China. In 1976 the United Kingdom had become a party to the International Covenant on Civil and Political Rights (ICCPR), extending by declaration its regime to Hong Kong.[67] Upon cession of Hong Kong, China became the legal successor of the UK with regard to that territory, and could choose whether or not to take over for the territory of Hong Kong certain treaty obligations.[68] With regard to the ICCPR the question was complicated by the fact that China itself is not a party (it became a signatory in 1998). This rekindled discussion on automatic succession of human rights. The question remained unresolved, but in terms of the practical necessity of legal protection was settled by a joint declaration in 1994. China and the UK declared the ICCPR would be

---

[65] It is significant that in branches of international law other than human rights evolutive interpretation has not taken on. Thus in a classic inter-State setting (the use of force), the Court was reluctant to apply a dynamic interpretation: 'it does not seem to the Court that the use of nuclear weapons can be regarded as specifically prohibited on the basis of the above-mentioned provisions of the Second Hague Declaration of 1899, the Regulations annexed to the Hague Convention IV of 1907 or the 1925 Protocol' (*Legality Of The Threat Or Use Of Nuclear Weapons*, Advisory Opinion ICJ, 8 July 1996); para 13; text at <http://www.icj-cij.org/icjwww/icases/iunan/iunanframe.htm>.

[66] MT Kamminga, 'State Succession in Respect of Human Rights Treaties' (1996) 7 EJIL 469; S Joseph, 'Human Rights Committee: Recent Cases' (2002) 2 Human Rights Law Review 287; J Chan, , 'State Succession to Human Rights Treaties: Hong Kong and the International Covenant on Civil and Political Rights' (1996) 45 ICLQ 928.

[67] Declaration of territorial application available at <http://untreaty.un.org/ENGLISH/bible/englishinternetbible/partI/chapterIV/treaty6.asp>.

[68] In accordance with established doctrine; the provisions on automatic succession (Arts 33 and 34) in the 1978 Convention on State Succession in respect of Treaties—to which China is not a party—are not considered a codification of existing customary law.

applied in Hong Kong, according to the Chinese system of 'one country, two systems'.[69] However, the obligation to report ex article 40 ICCPR, an important mechanism to ensure compliance, could not be attributed to China (as it is not a party), nor to Hong Kong (as it is not independent).

In the 1996 *Genocide case* Bosnia-Herzegovina's claim that it had automatically succeeded to the former Yugoslavia as a party to the Genocide Convention at the moment of its independence was put before the International Court of Justice, but the question of automatic succession could remain unanswered.[70] Thus, in practice attempts to connect human rights to the individual rather than to territory, have not yet been overtly succesful. At the same time, as has been pointed out, 'it is striking to what extent the Human Rights Committee as well as the Commission of Human Rights, among other organs, took it for granted that the new states in the territories of former Yugoslavia and the Soviet Union would be bound by them from the moment of their emergence as independent states'.[71]

The impact of human rights' detachment from territory and territorial authority is brought out clearly by the debate on a possibly emerging human right to water.[72] The human right to water was advanced by the Committee on Economic, Social and Cultural Rights in its comment No 15,[73] and it was conspicuously absent in the Ministerial Declaration concluding the *Fourth World Water Forum* on 22 March 2006.[74] Here the idea of a deterritorialized right clashes with a highly territorialised context, as freshwater resources are traditionally brought under the legal category of 'natural resources,' and it is precisely considered to be one of the achievements of the post-colonial era that natural resources are at the disposition of the territory in which they are located.[75]

The foregoing are examples of legal deterritorialization at a conceptual level. The possible philosophical underpinnings of inalienable rights accruing to individuals, and of rights accruing to individuals rather than to fictional legal entities, exceed

[69] See <http://www.info.gov.hk/cab/topical/right4_1_1.htm>. Upon signature of the Covenant China confirmed this to ICCPR depository UN Secretary-General (n 66 above).

[70] 'Without prejudice as to whether or not the principle of "automatic succession" applies in the case of certain types of international treaties or conventions, the Court does not consider it necessary, in order to decide on its jurisdiction in this case, to make a determination on the legal issues concerning State succession in respect to treaties which have been raised by the Parties.' *Case Concerning Application of the Convention on the Prevention and Punishment of the Crime of Genocide* (*Bosnia-Herzegovina v Yugoslavia*) Preliminary Objections, ICJ, 11 July 1996, para 23).

[71] Koskenniemi and Leino, '(n 34 above) 570.

[72] SR Tully, 'The Contribution of Human Rights to Freshwater Resource Management' (2004) Yearbook of International Environmental Law, Vol 14, 101–37; S McCaffrey, 'The Human Right to Water Revisited', in E Brown Weiss, L Boisson De Chazournes, and N Bernasconi-Osterwalder (eds), *Water And International Economic Law* (Oxford: OUP, 2005) 93.

[73] CESCR, General Comment No 15: The Right to Water (Arts 11 and 12), E/C.12/2002/11, January 20, 2002.

[74] Fourth World Water Forum (4th WWF), 'Local Actions for a Global Challenge'on March 21st and 22nd, 2006 (availalable at <http://www.worldwatercouncil.org/fileadmin/ wwc/ World_Water_ Forum/WWF4/ declarations/Ministerial_Declaration_english.pdf>.)

[75] *Permanent Sovereignty Over Natural Resources*, General Assembly Resolution 1803 (XVII) of 14 December 1962.

the scope of this chapter. But these underpinnings are undoubtedly a factor in any process of 'conceptual deterritorialization'. The hypothesis that this conceptual deterritorialization is more likely to occur in relation to human rights than in relation to the broader 'technical' and less morally charged category of 'individual rights,'[76] would be an interesting one to test.

3.2 Abandoning the binary system of normativity and expanding the catalogue of actors

The above examples of 'deterritorialization' in international law are geared to norm-setting authority in a classic framework of binding law. Even when dealing with 'recommendations' of an institution, we can rely on the classic instrumentarium, as these recommendations are 'non-binding' but may 'give rise to custom'. In these examples questions of 'soft law' and 'fuzzy norms' have been purposely left aside.

In reality these forms of normativity and norm-setting action—whether or not they be termed 'law'—play an important role in international life, as is increasingly brought to the fore. For example Harold Koh sees a: 'brave new world of international law where transactional actors, sources of law, allocation of decision function and modes of regulation have all mutated into fascinating hybrid forms. International Law now comprises a complex blend of customary, positive, declarative and soft law'.[77]

The topic of non-binding norms is tackled in some excellent studies.[78] In the context of 'deterritorialization' two things are relevant in particular. The first is that without attention for the various forms and levels of normativity, it is not possible to appreciate current developments in transnational, international, and global legal relations. In order for these to be captured, the concept of 'norms' needs to include normative statements such as *Operational Standards* of the World Bank,[79] *Antarctic Recommended Measures*,[80] and the *Code of Conduct for the Protection of Children from Sexual Exploitation in Travel and Tourism*[81] next to the canonical sources of international law and binding and non-binding resolutions of organizations. Secondly, moving away from the binary system of normativity

---

[76] This new category is the result of a trend increasingly to distill individual rights from inter-State treaties outside the human rights context (cf the *LaGrand case* (*Germany v United States*), ICJ Judgment, 27 June 2001, para 78, in which an individual right to consular assistance is derived from Art 36(2) of the 1963 Vienna Convention on Consular Relations).

[77] H Koh, 'A World Transformed' (1995) 20 Yale J Int'l L, ix.

[78] For a taxonomy and analysis of the various types of non-binding norms, see C Chinkin, 'Normative Development in the International Legal System' in D Shelton (ed), *Commitment and Compliance, the Role of Non-Binding Norms in the International Legal System* (Oxford: OUP, 2000) 21.

[79] <http://wbln0018.worldbank.org/institutional/manuals/opmanual.nsf/05TOCpages /The%20World%20Bank%20Operational%20Manual?OpenDocument>.

[80] <http://www.antarctica.ac.uk/About_Antarctica/Treaty/index.html>.

[81] Private initiative for self-regulation, funded by UNICEF and supported by the World Tourism Organization (<http://www.thecode.org/>).

means moving away from the classic legal instrumentarium used by States, which is conducive to deterritorialization in international law. However, that move has in turn also been facilitated by the trend to deterritorialization. Mayo Moran indeed seems to indicate a two-way causal relationship, when she refers to the 'traditional spatialized model of law with its emphasis on the application of binding rules'.[82]

It has been proposed that 'the main problem does not lie in the international legal requirements for binding norms, but in the limitation of its law-making subjects to States'.[83] This too seems to be remedied to some extent by current developments, as another general trend is the expansion of the range of legal actors. This expansion takes place on two fronts. The range of actors with norm-setting authority extends beyond the traditional (States-only) category of norm-setting actors (the 'law-making subjects') and addressees of the norms extend beyond the classic catalogue of legal subjects ('bearers of rights and duties under international law').

Both developments can be illustrated by the 2003 *Norms on the responsibilities of transnational corporations and other business enterprises with regard to human rights.*[84] The UN Sub-Commission on the Promotion and Protection of Human Rights established a working group to gather information concerning the activities of transnational corporations. It did this by means of a widespread consultative process involving all stakeholders, governments, businesses, individuals, NGOs, trade unions, etc. and reported back to the then UN Commission Human Rights. In 2003, the norms were adopted by consensus by the Sub-Commission. Though the norms never moved past the UN Sub-Commission to reach the organs empanelled with State representatives, the Sub-Commission thus exercised norm-setting authority by 'solemnly proclaiming' the norms on social corporate responsibility, by addressing them directly to transnational corporations, and by 'urge[ing] that every effort be made so that they become generally known and respected'.[85] Indeed the norms form part of the global discourse on corporate responsibility, without entirely fitting in the framework of classic international law—in this case not because the type of norm (non-binding standards adopted by an international organization) is at odds, or the norm-setting subject is out of the ordinary, but because companies are not generally accepted as addressee of international norms.[86]

The greater variation in normativity, as well as the expansion of the group of potential norm-setting authorities and of potential *Normadressaten*, have

---

[82] See n 18 above and accompanying text.

[83] A Paulus, 'Commentary to Andreas Fischer-Lescano & Günther Teubner: The Legitimacy of International Law and the Role of the State' (2004) 25 Michigan JIL 1053.

[84] UN Doc. E/CN.4/Sub.2/2003/12/Rev.2, 26 August 2003.   [85] Ibid, 3.

[86] Thus Shaw excludes 'transnational corporations' but does mention them as potential candidates for 'acquiring' international legal personality (n 12 above, 224); contrariwise for example Dixon who on the basis of the fact that legal relations between states and corporations can be 'internationalized' concludes that such multinational enterprises have a certain degree of 'functional' legal personality (M Dixon, *Textbook on International Law* (5th edn, Oxford: OUP, 2005) 116, 117).

created room for greater inclusiveness and flexibility of normative regimes. This de-formalization of international law, rooted of course in the requirements of society,[87] at the level of political-legal structure can be characterized by deterritorialization. The partial move away from territorial, State-based law has made it possible to open up the closed category of law-making actors and the binary view on normativity, and vice versa.

3.3 Transboundary networks

Such opening-up is epitomized by another phenomenon that can count as a vehicle for the deterritorialization of international law: new normative regimes which emerge entirely outside the scope of Traditional, State-centric international law. These are patterns of constraint emerging out of a transnational private community of stakeholders. Within the framework of international law scholarship, Günther Teubner in particular has addressed these private regulatory networks.[88]

Two prime examples of transnational networks are the *lex mercatoria* and regulatory mechanism applied to the Internet. *Lex mercatoria* comprises a set of standard form contracts used throughout the world, as customary 'usage of the trade' recognized in for example Article 9 of the Vienna International Sales Convention or Section 1–103 of the American Uniform Commercial Code. For example Carbonneau sees a 'common law' of international contracts emerging.[89] Sources of law would include certain long-existing commercial practices, as well as form contracts and codifications in such documents as the Vienna Sales Convention and UNIDROIT principles. Although not every commentator is equally convinced, for example because currently less of a transnational regulatory network would exist than is claimed, or because the original law merchant was less detached from local control, than is often claimed, the international *lex mercatoria* undeniably represents a new and powerful development, both in legal practice and—in any event—in the minds of lawyers.[90]

---

[87] The Fragmentation Report's observation on functional regimes applies to the trend of such deformalization in international law as whole: there are 'spheres of life and expert cooperation that transgress national boundaries and are difficult to regulate through traditional international law. National laws seem insufficient owing to the transnational nature of the networks while international law only inadequately takes account of their specialized objectives and needs.' (n 34 above, para 481). [88] See n 38 and accompanying text.

[89] TE Carbonneau (ed), *Lex Mercatoria and Arbitration: A Discussion of the New Law Merchant* (rev edn, Yonkers-NY: Juris Publishing, 1998) and review by S Bennett (1999) 10 Am Rev Int'l Arb 159.

[90] 'The idea is that the transnational lawyers of today have their own customs, norms, and practices, and a sort of merchant law is emerging, without benefit of legislation, from their patterns of behavior.... Very likely there is less here than meets the eye' (LM Friedman, 'Erewhon: The Coming Global Legal Order' (2001) 37 Stanford JIL 347–64, at 356); cf also SE Sachs, 'From St. Ives to Cyberspace: The Modern Distortion of the Medieval "Law Merchant"' (2006) 21 American University International Law Review 685, ('Modern advocates of corporate self-regulation have drawn unlikely inspiration from the Middle Ages').

The most notable example of private regulatory action is norm-setting with regard to the Internet. The—entirely 'a-geographical'[91]—internet has triggered national, international and transnational regulatory initiatives.

When regulation of cyberspace became a point of interest, it (as an American, ie national invention) was initially addressed within the territorial model of norm-setting authority; first at the domestic law level (with intricate constructions of 'extra-territorial jurisdiction') and subsequently and increasingly at the international level.[92] Recent initiatives at the international level have not yet lead to concrete results, and in the present context are mainly of interest for the element of 'conceptual deterritorialization'.[93] The 2001 World Summit on the Information Society (WSIS) under auspices of the United Nations system appears to explore a 'non-territorial' approach. As to prospective institutional structures for internet governance, the UN Working Group on Internet Governance in 2005 proposed the establishment of a Global body such as Global Internet Council (GIC). Coupled with the proposed mechanisms for multi-stakeholder governance[94]—which involve users, companies, civil society as sources of regulatory authority—this will inevitably entail an abandonement of the territorial foundation for normative control.

Meanwhile, the true regulatory regime for the internet is an extensive grid of private, transnational networks—in casu standards bodies—which has been in place for several years creating norms and regulations in various sectors of internet management, such as ICANN, ISOC, World Wide Web Consortium, the Internet Engineering Task Force,[95] an open, all-volunteer standards organization, with no formal membership or membership requirements.

To these normative regimes, then, Teubner applies the model of 'societal constitutionalism',[96] starting from the idea that 'not every polity has a written constitution, but every polity has constitutional norms'.[97] Such a grid of *Zivilverfassungen* would not be geared to a world society but encompass various polities in functionally differentiated areas.[98] The *Zivilverfassung* thus transcends the image of a political constitution, but maintains certain principles, such as maintaining a balance between, and safeguard of, 'spontaneous public sectors (similar to the

---

[91] DG Post, 'The "Unsettled Paradox": The Internet, the State, and the Consent of the Governed' (1998) 5 Indiana Journal of Global Legal Studies 521.

[92] E Longworth, 'The Possibilities for a Legal Framework for Cyberspace' in UNESCO (ed), *Les Dimensions Internationales du Droit du Cyberespace* (Paris: Editions UNESCO, 2000) 11–87.

[93] See section 3.1.3 above.   [94] Report WGIG 2005, eg para 11.

[95] All references to be found via eg the World Wide Web Consortium page (<http://www.w3.org/>).

[96] G Teubner, 'Globale Zivilverfassungen: Alternativen zur staatszentrierten Verfassungstheorie' (2003) 63 Zeitschrift für Ausländisches öffentliches Recht und Völkerrecht 1–28; translated in G Teubner, 'Societal Constitutionalism: Alternatives to State-centred Constitutional Theory', Storrs Lectures 2003/04 Yale Law School; see also Fischer-Lescano and Teubner, 'Regime-Collisions' (n 24 above).

[97] R Ürpmann 'Internationales Verfassungsrecht' (2001) 56 Juristenzeitung quoted in Teubner, 'Zivilverfassungen . . . ', (n 96 above) 13 and Teubner, 'Societal Constitutionalism', (n 96 above) 12.

[98] Teubner, 'Zivilverfassungen' (n 96 above) 8.

fundamental rights section of the constitution) and highly formalized organized sectors (resembling the law of organization of the state, or company law)'.[99]

4. Deterritorialization and the divide between national and international law

The above has outlined international and transnational developments which have animated academic legal writing from different perspectives. The value of looking at these regulatory patterns and regimes once more, through the prism of 'territoriality', lies in their implications for the divide between national and international law.

As has been elaborated above, regimes that entail 'deterritorialization' are regimes that in practical terms constitute independent norm-setting authority next to that of the State: '[s]ystems of rule need not be territorial, . . . or, while territorially fixed, they need not be exclusive'.[100]

It is useful to recall that classic monist and dualist arguments proceed from the premise of territorially bound 'national' law, and that doctrine and theory-building on this point generally did not include sectoral regimes emanating from non-State norm-setting authority.[101] Therefore the developments addressed in this chapter are essentially located outside the classic national-international law discourse.[102].

This chapter then posits that, although we tend to conceptualize the effect of an independent sectoral regime within the territory of a state as its 'reception' in national law—whether that technically takes the form of 'incorporation' or 'transformation'[103]—a more adequate take on legal reality would be to denote it as a norm-setting authority *parallel* to that of the State, which acts out on State territory.[104] The legal boundary between national and international law therefore is not pierced or bridged, but circumvented.

The effect is not in all cases equally dramatic. As we have seen, the process of deterritorialization can involve a range of norms: from formal sources of international law to self-enforced patterns of constraint out of private or combined public-private activities. It can also involve a range of actors, both as norm-setting authority and as *Normadressat*.

---

[99] Teubner, 'Zivilverfassungen' (n 96 above) 27–28 and Teubner, 'Societal Constitutionalism' (n 96 above) 23–24.

[100] JG Ruggie, 'Territoriality and Beyond: Problematizing Modernity in International Relations' (1993) 47 International Organization 149.

[101] The main reasons arguably being that the monism-dualism debate predates the rise of institutional regimes; and that the transparent image of IGOs (and *mutatis mutandis* functional regimes in the broad sense), as predominantly 'open-structured' vehicles for State action, has persisted, and sometimes prevailed, until this day (for an extensive analysis of this point, see C Brölmann, *The Institutional Veil in Public International Law* (Oxford: Hart, 2007) chs 2–4).

[102] As is to some extent recognized also by Arangio-Ruiz and considered to be a flaw of the classic dualist model (n 9 above, this volume, 15).

[103] According to the terminology traditionally used for the two types of constitutional systems.

[104] I am indebted to Janne Nijman for articulating this idea.

Normative regimes which address states (eg the UN Security Council issuing a classic Chapter VII Resolution) are not problematic, since whether there will be normative follow-up, depends on additional action on the part of the State. In other words—a shift in normative authority can entail deterritorialization in law, but if the normative authority is addressed at States only, the *divide* between national and international law will not come into play.

This is different when the *Normadressat* is a non-State actor, such as a company or an individual, who is bound to find himself on the territory of *some* State. The private networks that regulate the architecture and use of the Internet create norms that are addressed 'directly' to individuals, that is: without the medium of the State. Naturally such norms and norm-setting authorities may clash with 'domestic law', but as they are not binding in the sense of formal international law, such a clash will not often be brought to a head—the operation of Google's search engine on computers in the territory of the Chinese Republic is one example where it did, (the agreed censure of Google the outcome!).[105]

At the other end of the spectrum are institutionalized functional regimes with independent norm-setting authority. A good example are the 'directly' effective norms of (at least first pillar) European law. By addressing the relevant non-State actors, such as individuals and corporate entities, European law norms enter national territory. However, although Community law 'enters'—or rather, disregards—the national legal sphere on its own accord, national courts have for a long time attempted to apply the classic doctrines of applied monism and dualism used for the reception of 'regular' international law. This has been visible in 'dualist' states,[106] but also in 'monist' systems. Only in 2004 for example the Netherlands Supreme Court explicitly recognized the *Gend en Loos* doctrine, proclaimed by the European Court in 1963,[107] that EU regulations are 'immediately effective' on Dutch territory, 'without additional measure'.[108]

Norms that stem from independent norm-setting authority thus do not need to be *validated* by domestic law. However, they may need to be *enforced* by the domestic system. The procedural aspect, although a separate stage, is clearly essential for the addressee of a norm—as is illustrated by cases revolving around the procedural component of international human rights, or by cases of uncontested 'supranational' regulation such as EC regulations which in practice contain instructions to states for transformation of such normative regimes. The question to what extent it

---

[105] <http://news.bbc.co.uk/1/hi/technology/4645596.stm>.

[106] On the Italian reception of Community law (which the Constitutional Court first resolved in 1984 by maintaining a complete separation between domestic and community law), eg K Oellers-Frahm, 'Das Verhältnis von Völkerrecht und Landesrecht in der italienischen Verfassung' (1974) 34 Zeitschrift für Ausländisches öffentliches Recht und Völkerrecht 330–50; G Baiocchi, 'La legge 9 marzo 1989 n. 86 sulla partecipazione dell'Italia al processo normativo comunitario e sulle procedure di esecuzione degli obblighi comunitari' in *Diritto Comunitario e degli Scambi Internazionali* (1989) 443–62; G Gaja, 'New Developments in a Continuing story: the Relationship between EEC law and Italian law'(1990) in CMLR, 83–95.   [107] n 56 above.

[108] LJN: AR1797, Hoge Raad (Supreme Court), 00156/04, 02–11-2004.

is helpful in doctrine to separate substantive and procedural rights in human rights regimes—both for the indivduals concerned and for the policy-makers and norm-setting actors that conceptualize regimes for individual legal protection—is open to further research. It is an issue that clearly becomes more urgent, as State norm-setting authority—and hence the divide between national and international law—is more often circumvented by non-territorial normative regimes.

5. Concluding remarks

This chapter has argued that the 'territorial model' of international law is challenged in different ways, and has aimed to sketch the contours of a trend towards 'deterritorialization'—that is to say, a detachment of territory. In many cases 'function' or 'issue area' has emerged as the substitute parameter. This may be found in regimes that have emanated from States, and in regimes that have emerged as private networks outside the State altogether.

The rise of both international regimes and transnational private networks, as well as the emergence of 'fuzzy normativity' and the greater range of actors involved, are part of a multi-faceted development which is currently being studied from several perspectives. In a general sense, the rise of such normative regimes is connected to the phenomenon of (to name but a few aspects) social, cultural, and economic globalization. From a legal perspective in particular, these regimes can be considered from the angle of black letter international law, in as far as concerned with intergovernmental regimes, or analysed as a factor in fragmentation, and ensuing 'regime collisions' in international law. They can be looked at for their relation with the expansion of legal actors, or for their share in the trend away from the binary division of binding non-binding rules.

This chapter has taken the prism of 'territoriality' as the notion on which classic international law turns. It has looked at different developments such as the rise of international institutions and the emerging grid of transnational networks to argue that the territorial parameter in the last decades has been steadily loosing ground—a development which we have dubbed 'deterritorialization'.

As has been outlined above, the consequence of deterritorialization for the divide between national and international law is clear and simple. When normative regimes that are based on a non-territorial source of authority and have an (*a priori*) non-territorial scope, address non-State actors it means little to say, in a way, that these actors are addressed 'directly'. These regimes do not pierce the sovereign veil of the State, they do not settle the question which law takes precedence, they do not decide whether law is all one, or on the contrary divided into different spheres. They are concurring normative regimes, that is: concurring with the State normative system. The fact that the non-State addressees of these norms almost always find themselves on the territory of *some* State—as the globe is essentially comminuted in territories—raises important questions on a procedural level, but does not prejudge the fact that the norms as such stem from a de-territorialized norm-setting authority.

The present volume deals with the divide between national law and international law. Meanwhile the view, prevailing throughout the 20th century, in which national law and international law make up the complete legal universe,[109] has been generally abandoned. But acknowledging the existence of other legal regimes (possibly amounting to 'legal orders'), does not yet say anything about their interconnectedness. This leads to a question which this chapter has not attempted to answer: are other Divides emerging? The model proposed for example by Arangio-Ruiz—in which 'inter-individual law' and 'inter-state law' are equally separated from national law and from each other[110]—would have this implication. Or has the legal universe now come to consist of so many sectoral regimes and sources of norm-setting authority, ie has become pluralist to such a degree, that strict separations are no longer possible?

According to Teubner, following Luhman, '[s]ubsequent analyses added a complementary prediction: should the law of a global society become entangled within sectoral interdependences, a wholly new form of conflicts law will emerge; an 'inter-systemic conflicts law', derived not from collisions between the distinct nations of private international law, but from collisions between distinct global social sectors.'[111]

A few concluding observations are in order. First, the approach taken in this contribution poses a potential problem of analytical stability. Transnational private networks do not fit into the system of international law. Precisely because global society encounters problems which cannot be regulated in the territorial framework, it has resorted to new methods of norm-setting. These methods are so far removed from the basic precepts of classic international law that it begs the question whether it is useful to try and consider them within the international law paradigm in the first place. In this light the title 'deterritorialization in international law' had better be changed into 'deterritorialization in global norm-setting'. But then again, the debate squarely positions itself in the international law discourse, in which new developments are set apart from established mechanisms by referring to the latter as 'classic' or 'traditional'. In this chapter the question is left open. Koskenniemi in conclusion of the ILC study on Fragmentation, holds:

This is not to say, however, that the Vienna Convention or indeed international law could not be used so as to channel and control these patterns of informal, often private interest-drawn types of regulation as well. The more complex and flexible the ways in which treaty

---

[109] cf J Barberis, 'Nouvelles questions concernant la personnalité juridique internationale' (1993) 179 Recueil des Cours de l'Académie de droit international 145, 171: 'le droit interne des états et le droit interétatique formeraient le cadre complet de l'ordre juridique universel'. It has been pointed out that the conceptual framework of an overarching 'unitary international law' is 'implicitly perpetuate[d]' by contemporary theorists such as McDougal, Falk, and Kennedy (P Trimble, 'International Law, World Order and Critical Legal Studies' (1990) 42 Stanford L Rev 811, 835).

[110] Arangio Ruiz (n 9 above), this volume, 15.

[111] Fischer-Lescano and Teubner (n 24 above) 1000.

law allows the use of framework treaties, of clusters of treaties and regimes consisting of many types of normative materials, the more such decentralized, private regulation may be grasped within the scope of international law.[112]

Second, in the relation between national and traditional international law the hierarchy, at least in the respective legal spheres, is clear. The relation between the different levels of authority involved in 'multi-level governance' is much less clear—with concomitant ambiguity regarding accountability and legitimacy.[113] An additional complication is the fact that norm-setting authority not only operates on different levels, but also on the basis of different parameters: territory (as with the State) as opposed to function (as with transnational societal links and international organizations). Especially the interaction between levels of governance based on different parameters is somewhat under-theorized. These points are related to issues of fragmentation and regime-collision, rather than to the particular question of deterritorialization, and as such lie outside the scope of this chapter. However, it is clear that they are of central importance also for further analysis along the lines of 'territoriality'.

Finally and most importantly, this chapter has indicated signs of 'deterritorialization' in international law but it has not addressed the normative aspect of this development. This is not to deny several concerns, that are readily apparent. Deterritorialization as the 'detachment of regulatory authority from a specific territory' is a political process that involves the shift of power, authority, and governance. This leads directly to questions of legitimacy of norms, and the accountability of norm-setting authority. Because of the intricacies of 'multi-level governance' mentioned above, these questions are in many cases still open.

On a general note there is no easy answer to the question whether the deterritorialization of international law, to the extent that it transcends the divide between national and international law, is a good thing. With the process of 'globalization' ongoing, the state has earned renewed credibility, while there has been some disenchantment in both scholarship and practice with international organizations. In the 1980s David Kennedy famously observed a trend towards the use of institutions for international relations,[114] but more recently, Jan Klabbers noted a 'move away from institutions', as intergovernmental organizations had lost some of their functionalist lustre—their independence now being curbed by the member States, their formalist procedures circumvented,[115] and their legitimacy questioned.[116]

---

[112] ILC Report on *Fragmentation of International Law* (n 34 above) para 490.

[113] Cf the statement in the final report on Fragmentation before the ILC: '[t]his is the background to the concern about fragmentation of international law: the rise of specialized rules and rule-systems that have no clear relationship to each other. Answers to legal questions become dependent on whom you ask, what rule-system is your focus on' (n 34 above) para 483.

[114] D Kennedy, 'The Move to Institutions' (1987) 8 Cardozo L Rev 841–988.

[115] J Klabbers, 'The Changing Image of International Organisations', in JM Coicaud and V Heiskanen (eds), *The Legitimacy of International Organizations* (United Nations University Press, 2002) 221, citation at 223.

[116] In relation to environmental regimes, see, eg D Bodansky, 'The Legitimacy of International Governance: A Coming Challenge for International Environmental Law?' (1999) 93 AJIL 596

BS Chimni had pointed out how international institutional regimes may consolidate western ideology,[117] and from a different angle Brigitte Stern turns to the State for being the 'arbitrators between market and society', 'guardians of non-mercantile values', and 'organs of solidarity'.[118]

We have been cautioned that 'the move from territoriality to functionality should not be accompanied by a move from democracy to technocracy'. To prevent this from happening, 'a minimum of public control over the private exercise of power'[119] would be required. The model of societal constitutionalism can be of valuable use for the developing *transnational* networks,[120] but it is more complex when it comes to *international* deterritorialized regimes: what does 'public control' mean in the case of functional, sectoral regimes?

The system in which strict territorial demarcation is the basis of legal authority has opened up—with consequences for the involvement of stakeholders, sources, and forms of normativity at the global stage. That normative authority to some extent has come to be detached from territory is arguably an unavoidable and in many ways positive development. Meanwhile, it is vital that in the ensuing system of sectoral interest-management ramified along mostly functional lines, norms (or 'law') do not come to be detached from their political foundation.

(concentrating especially on the democratic deficit of organizations), on theories of legitimacy ('Legitimate authority' simply means 'justified authority', and theories of legitimacy attempt to specify what factors might serve as justifications—tradition, rationality, legality, and democracy, to name a few' (601)).

[117] The author has convincingly made this point on different occasions, see, eg BS Chimni, 'Third International Institutions Today: an Imperial State in the Making' (2004) 15 EJIL 1

[118] B Stern, 'How to Regulate Globalisation' in M Byers (ed), *The Role of Law in International Politics* (Oxford: OUP, 1999) 267, 275.

[119] A Paulus, in his reply to Teubner and Fischer-Lescano (n 83 above).

[120] See Teubner, Zivilverfassungen (nn 96–98) and accompanying text.

5

The Future of International Law is Domestic (or, The European Way of Law)

Anne-Marie Slaughter and William Burke-White

International law has traditionally been just that—international. Consisting of a largely separate set of legal rules[1] and institutions, international law has long governed relationships among States. Under the traditional rules of international law, the claims of individuals could only reach the international plane when a State exercised diplomatic protection and espoused the claims of its nationals in an international forum.[2] More recently, international law has penetrated the once exclusive zone of domestic affairs to regulate the relationships between governments and their own citizens, particularly through the growing bodies of human rights law and international criminal law.[3] But even in these examples, international law has generally remained separate from and above the domestic sphere.

The classic model of international law as separate from the domestic realm fits closely with the traditional problems the international legal system sought to address, namely the facilitation of State-to-State cooperation. Whether regulating the immunities of diplomats or the rights of ships on the high seas, the traditional purposes of international law have been interstate, not intrastate.

This foundation of international law reflects the principles of Westphalian sovereignty, often seemingly made up of equal parts myth and rhetoric. In this

---

[1] Some perspectives on the monist-dualist debate assert that international legal rules exist in a unified continuum with domestic law. Monists argue that international law and domestic law are part of the same system, in which international law is hierarchically prior to domestic law. Dualists, in contrast, claim that international and domestic law are part of two distinct systems and that domestic law is generally prior to international law. JG Starke, 'Monism and Dualism in the Theory of International Law' (1936) 17 *Brit Ybk Int'l L* 66, 74–75. While both of these theories provide important linkages between international law and domestic law, for adherents of either approach the functions and institutions of international law remain largely at the international level. See ibid.

[2] *Mavromatis Palestine Concessions*, Judgment No 2, 1924, PCIJ, Series A, No 2. Yet, the decision of a state to espouse its citizen's claim is one of domestic politics—the State has no obligation to do so. International law does, however, regulate the right of the state to espouse an individual claim, limiting such rights to cases of 'close connection' usually in the form of 'real and effective nationality' between the state and the citizen. Eg *Nottebohm Case* (Lichtensein v Guatemala) ICJ Rep 1955, 4.

[3] Anne-Marie Slaughter and William Burke-White, 'An International Constitutional Moment' (2002) 42 Harvard J Int'l L 1.

conception, the State is a defined physical territory 'within which domestic polit-ical authorities are the sole arbiters of legitimate behavior'.[4] States could be part of the international legal system to the degree they chose by consenting to particular rules. Likewise, they could choose to remain apart, exerting their own sovereignty and preventing international involvement. Formally Westphalian sovereignty is the right to be left alone, to exclude, to be free from any external meddling or interference. But it is also the right to be recognized as an autonomous agent in the international system, capable of interacting with other States and entering into international agreements. With these background understandings of sovereignty, an international legal system emerged, consisting of states and limited by the prin-ciple of State consent.

Today, however, the challenges facing States and the international community alike demand very different responses and, hence, new roles for the international legal system. The processes of globalization and the emergence of new transnational threats have fundamentally changed the nature of governance and the necessary purposes of international law in the past few years. From cross-border pollution to terrorist training camps, from refugee flows to weapons proliferation, international problems have domestic roots that an interstate legal system is often powerless to address. To offer an effective response to these new challenges, the international legal system must be able to influence the domestic policies of States and harness national institutions in pursuit of global objectives.

In order to create desirable conditions in the international system, from peace to health to prosperity, international law must address the capacity and the will of domestic governments to respond to these issues at their source. The primary purpose of international law then shifts from providing independent regulation above the national state to interacting with, strengthening, and supporting domestic institutions. International law can perform this function in three prin-cipal ways: strengthening domestic institutions, backstopping them, and com-pelling them to act.

What makes this new function of international law a particular break from the past is that international law now seeks to influence political outcomes within sov-ereign States. Even in 1945 the drafters of the UN Charter still maintained the clas-sical position that international law and institutions shall not 'intervene in matters which are essentially within the domestic jurisdiction of any state'.[5] Today, how-ever, the objectives of international law and the very stability of the international system itself depend critically on domestic choices previously left to the determin-ation of national political processes—whether to enforce particular rules, establish

---

[4] Eg SD Krasner, *Sovereignty: Organized Hypocrisy* (Princeton, NJ: Princeton UP, 1999) 20 (not-ing: 'Westphalian sovereignty is violated when external actors influence or determine domestic authority structures. Domestic authority structures can be infiltrated through both coercive and vol-untary actions, through intervention and invitation . . . . The fundamental norm of Westphalian sov-ereignty is that states exist in specific territories, within which domestic political authorities are the sole arbiters of legitimate behavior.').   [5] Charter of the United Nations, at Art 2(7).

institutions, or even engage in effective governance. To ensure national governments actually function in pursuit of collective aims, international law is coming to
play a far more active role in shaping these national political choices. Taken to an
extreme, the future effectiveness of international law now turns on its ability to
influence and alter domestic politics.

These functions of international law are already well known to the members of
the European Union. Indeed, in extending membership to ten new countries over
the course of the past decade, the EU has relied on EU law as its primary tool of
reform and socialization. And even among the original member States, EU institutions continue to perform the types of backstopping, strengthening, and mandating functions described herein. Europeans themselves are coming to recognize
these uses of law; a new generation of European policy thinkers has openly proclaimed the virtues of the European way of law.

Some may, of course, argue that these new functions of international law have
no applicability outside the European context in which they were first embraced.[6]
Part of what makes these functions of international law important is that they
are now evident in contexts far more diverse than the EU. Each of the three means
through which international law is coming to influence domestic outcomes—
strengthening domestic institutions, backstopping national governance, and compelling domestic action—have now spread well beyond Europe. As we describe
below, what began as the European way of law is quickly becoming the future of
international law writ large.

While the new function of international law may be to transform domestic
politics, these processes of interaction may well have a transformative impact on
international law itself. Just as EU law has migrated from a thin set of agreements
based on the functional needs[7] of States into a far more programmatic and comprehensive legal order,[8] international law may be moving in a more programmatic
direction. International law will continue to reflect the will and practice of States.
But, to the degree it depends upon the effective functioning of national institutions,
getting those institutions to operate is quickly becoming a functional imperative

---

[6] Eg E Posner and J Yoo, 'Reply to Helfer and Slaughter' (2005) 93 California L Rev 957 (observing:
'There is no reason to think that a court that works for Europe, where political and legal institutions in
most countries are of high quality, would work for a world political community that lacks the same level
of cohesion and integration. Whatever one thinks about the EU, it is nothing like the international
community').

[7] Eg EB Haas, *The Uniting of Europe* (Stanford: Stanford University Press, 1958); EB Haas, *Beyond
the Nation-State: Functionalism and International Organization* (Stanford: Stanford University Press,
1964) 6–7 (noting that functionalists 'believe in the possibility of specifying technical and "non-
controversial" aspects of governmental conduct, and of weaving an ever-spreading web of international
institutional relationships on the basis of meeting such needs. They would concentrate on commonly
experienced needs initially, expecting the circle of the non-controversial to expand at the expense of the
political').

[8] Eg Treaty Establishing a Constitution for Europe, available at <http://europa.eu.int/constitution/
en/lstoc1_en.htm>. For a discussion, G de Burca, 'The Constitutional Challenge of New
Governance in the European Union' (2003) 28 ELR 814.

of the international legal order. Notably, we are not seeking to imbue international law with particular normative content, but rather to recognize that many international rules and indeed entire regimes are explicitly promoting effective—and preferably good—governance at the national level.

The outcome is not always so upbeat. As we emphasize in the conclusion, our vision of the principal future functions of international law assumes an intensive interaction between international law and domestic politics. But domestic politicians can manipulate international legal institutions and mandates to serve their own purposes, such as jailing political dissidents as part of complying with a Security Council resolution requiring domestic action against terrorism. More broadly, the basic positivist foundations of international law, requiring States to freely accept such interference in domestic politics, raises the possibility of manipulation and even imposition of such 'acceptance' as a result of power disparities.

Part I of this chapter identifies a new set of global threats and actual and potential responses, including the EU's uses of law to transform new members 'from the inside-out'. Part II argues that the future relevance, power, and potential of international law lie in its ability to backstop, strengthen, and compel domestic law and institutions. Part III examines the potential pitfalls and dangers of these new functions of international law. Finally, Part IV contrasts our analysis with other recent efforts to blur the boundaries between the international and domestic spheres, noting that what is distinctive about our claim is not the intermingling of two kinds of law, but rather the impact of international law on domestic politics and vice versa.

1. New threats, new responses

Rules can and often do reflect and embody aspirations for a better world. Alternatively, and equally likely, rules respond to concrete problems. The changing nature of international legal rules today responds to a new generation of worldwide problems. The most striking feature of these problems is that they arise from within States rather than from State actors themselves.

Examples abound. The terrorist attacks of September 11 were launched by a group of non-State actors operating from within the territory of Afghanistan.[9] The massive ethnic crimes in Rwanda, Congo and Sudan are, in large part, the product of rebel forces within States.[10] The most dangerous examples of nuclear proliferation can often be attributed to non-State criminal networks such as those of

---

[9] The 9/11 Commission Report (2004).

[10] Eg J Semujanga, *Origins of the Rwandan Genocide* (New York: Humanity Books Amherst, 2003); R Edgerton, *The Troubled Heart of Africa: A History of the Congo* (New York: St Martin's Press, 2002); Report of the International Commission of Inquiry on Darfur to the United Nations Secretary General, 25 January 2005, available at <http://www.un.org/News/dh/sudan/com_inq_darfur.pdf>.

AQ Kahn.[11] The 2004 Report of the Secretary General's High Level Panel on Threats, Challenges and Change identifies problems of intra-State origin such as 'poverty, infectious disease and environmental degradation ... civil war, genocide and other large scale atrocities ... nuclear, chemical and biological weapons, terrorism, and transnational organized crime' as among the core threats facing the international community today.[12]

More often than not, the origins of these threats can only be addressed directly by domestic governments that have the jurisdictional entitlements, police power, and institutional capability to act directly against them. Arresting criminals or terrorists, securing nuclear materials, and preventing pollution are within the traditional province of domestic law. The result is that the external security of many nations depends on the ability of national governments to maintain internal security sufficient to establish and enforce national law.

Where states are strong enough to combat these threats directly, international law must play a critical coordination role to ensure that governments cooperate in addressing threats before they span borders. Far too frequently, however, domestic governments lack the will or the capacity to adequately respond to these challenges. Since the early 1990s, the number of states unable to effectively govern their territories has increased. As Francis Fukuyama affirms, 'Since the end of the Cold War, weak or failing states have arguably become the single most important problem for the international order ... Weak or failing states commit human rights abuses, provoke humanitarian disasters, drive massive waves of immigration, and attack their neighbors'.[13]

Where national governments are unable or unwilling to address the origins of these threats themselves, international law may step in to help build their capacity or stiffen their will. This use of international law moves well beyond both its classical definition, as 'the rights subsisting between nations',[14] and its more modern conception, as, in part, regulating the conduct of states toward their own citizens.[15] The conception of an international legal system as a means of enabling, enhancing, and compelling the behaviour of domestic governments and actors within States is far more invasive and potentially transformative.

For many nations, ranging from the United States to Russia, from the countries of the Middle East to those of Africa, it is also far more frightening. But this is a conception of international law spreading outward from Europe. The Treaty of Westphalia, ending the bloody Thirty Years War with the principle of *cuius principio,*

---

[11] WJ Broad and DE Sanger, *Pakistani's Nuclear Black Market Seen as Offering Deepest Secrets of Bomb Building,* The New York Times, 21 March 2005, p A7.

[12] A More Secure World: Our Shared Responsibility, 2004 Report of the Secretary General's High Level Panel on Threats, Challenges and Change, UN Doc A/59/565 (2004) 23.

[13] F Fukuyma, *State Building: Governance and World Order in the Twenty First Century* (London: Profile Books, 2004) 92–93.

[14] Emmerich de Vattel described international law in the 1750s, as 'the rights subsisting between nations or states, and the obligations correspondent to those rights'. Emmerich de Vattel, *The Law of Nations* (1758) 3.   [15] Slaughter and Burke-White (n 3 above) 1.

eijus religio, has given way to the Treaty of Rome, ending a century of bloody intra-European wars with a concept of pooled sovereignty that has steadily expanded and deepened in the contemporary European Union. As the EU's legal system has evolved, the prime purpose of the European Court of Justice and even of the Commission has been less to create and impose EU law as international law than to spur national courts and regulatory agencies to embrace and enforce EU law as national law.

Moreover, as Mark Leonard writes in his provocative new book *Why Europe Will Run the 21st Century*, 'Europe's weapon is the law'.[16] He describes Europe's power in the world as 'a transformative power',[17] rooted in a strategy of democratization that is based on requiring candidate countries to 'swallow all 80,000 pages of European laws and adapt their own legislation to accommodate them', as well as then accepting continual monitoring by EU officials to ensure that they are in fact living up to their new commitments.[18] The result has been a 'rebuilding [of] these countries from the bottom up'.[19] Indeed, 'The European model is the political equivalent of the strategy of the Jesuits: if you change the country at the beginning, you have it for life.'[20]

Note the precise way that European law works in this equation. For all the 80,000 pages of regulations, the EU Council of Ministers and the EU Commission issue directives that specify ends rather than means. It is up to national legislatures and courts to decide precisely how the member State in question will fulfil a particular directive. Once those laws are passed, EU institutions—the Court and the Commission—look over national shoulders to ensure that they actually do what they commit to do. This European way of law is precisely the role that we postulate for international law generally around the world.[21]

Espen Barth Eide, a former State Secretary in the Norwegian Foreign Ministry, writes that the 'EU's "soft intervention" in the "domestic affairs" of EU member states is almost an everyday experience'.[22] This is the hallmark of EU-style 'post-Westphalian sovereignty', described so memorably by Robert Cooper, a top aide to Javier Solana, in *The Breaking of Nations*.[23] Eide and other leading European security strategists openly call for the extension of regional 'integrative projects'

---

[16] M Leonard, *Why Europe Will Run the 21st Century* (New York: Perseus Book Group, 2005) 35.

[17] Ibid, 5, quoting R Youngs, *Sharpening European Engagement* (London: The Foreign Policy Centre, 2004). [18] Ibid, 45.

[19] Ibid. [20] Ibid, 45–46.

[21] Beyond the EU system, the European Court of Human Rights has repeatedly forced European governments to change their domestic laws governing issues from prosecution of criminals to admitting homosexuals into the armed services. They are all entitled to a 'margin of discretion' in reconciling their domestic laws and practices with their treaty obligations, but the ECHR is there to ensure that the margin does not grow too wide.

[22] E Barth Eide, 'Introduction: the Role of the EU in Fostering 'Effective Multilateralism' in E Barth Eide (ed), *Effective Multilateralism: Europe, Regional Security and a Revitalized UN* (London: The Foreign Policy Centre, 2004) 1–10.

[23] R Cooper, *The Breaking of Nations: Order and Chaos in the 21st Century* (London: Atlantic Books, 2004).

based on the EU in Africa, Latin America, and Asia. The European Security Strategy (ESS), proposed by Javier Solana and passed by the European Council in December 2003,[24] fell short of openly embracing this vision, but recognized that ASEAN, MERCOSUR, and the African Union 'make an important contribution to a more orderly world'.[25]

Spreading the European way of law beyond Europe, a process that is already underway, requires a broader rethinking of the functions of international law. As in Europe, the focus of a growing number of international rules is no longer inter-state relations. It is increasingly governments' capacity and will to act in prescribed ways toward their own peoples. The result is a growing interaction between international law and domestic politics, in ways that have lasting implications for both.

2. The future functions of international law

The all-too-often inadequate domestic response to transnational threats has three separate, but related causes—a lack of domestic governance capacity, a lack of domestic will to act, and the necessity of addressing new problems that exceed the ordinary ability of States to address. International law has key leverage points to help improve the response of domestic governments on each of these dimensions. International legal rules and institutions can enhance the capacity and effectiveness of domestic institutions. If properly designed and structured they can help backstop domestic political and legal groups trying to comply with international legal obligations. Finally, they can even compel or mandate action at the national level in response to a global threat.

These alternative functions of international law effectively flip the international legal system on its head. Traditionally, international law might be seen as regulating or even compelling interstate activity. The future purpose of international law, however, becomes to reach within States, permeating domestic institutions, governance structures, and even political fora so as to enhance their effectiveness.

2.1 Strengthening domestic institutions

A primary limitation of the international system is the weakness of government institutions in so many States all over the world. Due to violence, poverty, disease,

---

[24] Javier Solana is the Secretary-General of the Council of The European Union and the European Union High Representative for the Common Foreign and Security Policy. Upon entry into force of the new EU Constitution, he is to be appointed Foreign Minister of the European Union. The European Council is the 'main decision making body of the EU' and is composed of the ministers of the member states for any particular subject area. See Council of the European Union, <http://ue.eu.int/cms3_fo/showPage.asp?id=242&lang=EN&mode=g>.

[25] *A Secure Europe in a Better World—The European Security Strategy*, 12 December 2003, available at <http://ue.eu.int/cms3_fo/showPage.ASP?id=266&lang=EN&mode=g>.

corruption, and lack of technology and training, national governments all too often lack the resources, skills, and ability to provide adequate solutions to local and transnational problems. Examples are numerous: State failure in Somalia in the early 1990s, devastation from natural catastrophes like the 2004 tsunami, civil wars such as that in Angola from 1998–2003, or the rampant corruption all too evident in Russia in the mid 1990s. A 2004 report of the Commission on Weak States and US National Security highlighted as a key national security concern the need to assist states 'whose governments are unable to do the things that their own citizens and the international community expect from them: offer protection from internal and external threats, deliver basic health services and education, and provide institutions that respond to the legitimate demands and needs of the population'.[26] Improving the capacity of government officials of all sorts—regulators, judges, and legislators—to actually govern is paramount.[27] Francis Fukuyama observes: 'For the post-September 11th period, the chief issue for global politics will not be how to cut back on stateness but how to build it up.'[28] International law has an important role to play in this process.

A critically important tool in strengthening the institutions of national governments is the formalization and inclusion of 'government networks' as mechanisms of global governance. A powerful illustration of both the new sovereignty and the new roles for international law can be found in the operation of these networks. Networks of national government officials of all kinds operate across borders to regulate individuals and corporations operating in a global economy, combat global crime, and address common problems on a global scale. As one of the co-authors has argued over the past decade, the State is not losing power so much as changing the way that it exercises its power.[29] As corporations, nongovernmental organizations (NGOs), and criminals have all begun to operate increasingly through global networks rather than nation-based hierarchies, so too have government officials. The result is an ever more dense web of government networks, allowing government officials to compensate for their decreasing territorial power by increasing their global reach.

Government networks perform a range of functions that allow them to enhance the effectiveness of domestic governance. They build trust and establish relationships among their participants that then create incentives to establish a good reputation and avoid a bad one. They exchange regular information about their own activities and develop databases of best practices, or, in the judicial case, different approaches to common legal issues. Finally, they offer technical assistance and

---

[26] JW Weinstein et al, *On The Brink, Weak States and US National Security: A Report of the Commission for Weak States and US National Security* (Centre for Global Development, Washington, 2004) 6.

[27] For a discussion of the importance of building state capacity, S Krasner (ed), *Problematic Sovereignty: Contested Rules and Political Possibilities* (New York: Columbia UP, 2001).

[28] Fukuyma (n 13 above) 120.

[29] AM Slaughter, *A New World Order* (Princeton: Princeton UP, 2004). This book synthesizes and builds on a series of articles dating back to 1994.

professional socialization to members from less developed nations—whether regulators, judges, or legislators.

Government networks are already doing a great deal to strengthen domestic governance and could still do far more. Building the basic capacity to govern in countries that often lack sufficient material and human resources to pass, implement, and apply laws effectively is itself an important and valuable consequence of government networks. Regulatory, judicial, and legislative networks all engage in capacity building directly, through training and technical assistance programs, and, indirectly, through their provision of information, coordinated policy solutions, and moral support to their members. In effect, government networks communicate to their members everywhere the message that the Zimbabwean Chief Justice understood when he was under siege: 'You are not alone'.

The best examples of transnational networks strengthening domestic governance may be in the area of regulatory export. Kal Raustiala offers a number of examples of regulatory export in the securities, environmental, and antitrust areas. According to one securities regulator he interviewed, a prime outcome of the US Securities and Exchange Commission (SEC) networking is the dissemination of 'the "regulatory gospel" of US securities law', including: 'strict insider trading rules; mandatory registration with a governmental agency of public securities issues; a mandatory disclosure system; issuer liability regarding registration statements and offering documents; broad antifraud provisions; and government oversight of brokers, dealers, exchanges, etc'.[30] In effect, US regulatory agencies offer technical assistance and training to their foreign counterparts to make their own jobs easier, in the sense that strong foreign authorities with compatible securities, environmental, and antitrust regimes will effectively extend the reach of US regulators.

The EU has enjoyed similar advantages through the International Competition Network (ICN). In fact, more countries, particularly in Eastern Europe, are copying the EU approach to competition policy, rather than the US model.[31] Although the United States originally pushed the idea of a global network of antitrust regulators under the Clinton administration, the Bush administration has proved less enthusiastic. The opening conference of the network was held in Italy in 2002 led by the head of the German competition agency. The network describes itself as:

A project-oriented, consensus-based, informal network of antitrust agencies from developed and developing countries that will address antitrust enforcement and policy issues of common interest and formulate proposals for procedural and substantive convergence through a results-oriented agenda and structure.[32]

---

[30] K Raustiala, 'Rethinking the Sovereignty Debate in International Economic Law' (2003) 6 J Int'l Econ L 841, 843.   [31] Slaughter (n 29) 175.
[32] Memorandum on the Establishment and Operation of the International Competition Network, available at <http://www.internationalcompetitionnetwork.org/mou.pdf>.

Other examples of such networks strengthening domestic capacity in the economic arena include the Basle Committee on Banking Supervision[33] and the International Organization of Securities Commissioners, which have been influential in enhancing the ability of national governments to regulate securities and maintain independent central banks.[34] The net result of these networks is twofold: first, convergence toward a set of standardized practices at the national level and, second, the creation of greater domestic regulatory capacity in participating nations.

It should not be assumed that regulatory expertise flows only from developed to developing countries. At least in the judicial arena, European and Canadian courts have learned as much from South African and Indian courts as vice versa.[35] Among regulators, local experience with a wide range of problems can count for a great deal in the exchange of best practices.

Governments can do much more to strengthen domestic governance through government networks. For example: creating a Global Justice Network of justice ministers; expanding and strengthening the International Network for Environmental Cooperation and Enforcement (INECE), composed of environmental officials; creating a Global Human Rights Network of the government officials responsible for human rights conditions; bringing networks of legislators together under the auspices of the UN and other international institutions, and expanding the inclusivity and representativeness of global financial and leadership networks (such as expanding the G-8 to the G-20). Such networks must be provided with both concrete tasks and the resources to accomplish them, largely by working together to strengthen both collective and individual governing capacity.

In addition, international law itself can both support and be supported by transgovernmental networks with the shared goal of strengthening domestic governments. Transgovernmental networks are already being used to harness the existing power of national governments in pursuit of international objectives. As the front line of authority, national government officials exercise an array of coercive and persuasive powers largely unmatched by international institutions. Operating through government networks, national governments can bring these same powers to bear on behalf of international legal obligations. They can coerce, cajole, fine, order, regulate, legislate, horse-trade, bully, or use whatever other methods that produce results within their political system. They are not subject to coercion at the transgovernmental level; on the contrary, they are likely to perceive themselves as choosing a specific course of action freely and deliberately. Yet, having decided, for whatever reasons, to adopt a particular code of best practices, to coordinate policy in a particular way, to accept the decision of a supranational tribunal, or even simply to join what seems to be an emerging international consensus on a

---

[33] D Zaring, *Informal Procedure, Hard and Soft, In International Administration* (2005) 5 Chi J Int'l L 547, 595.

[34] Ibid, 561; IOSCO, 2002 Annual Report 22 (2002), available at <http://dev.iosco.org/annual_report/PDF/IOSCO_2002.pdf>.

[35] For a discussion, Slaughter (n 29 above) 65–103.

particular issue, they can implement that decision within the limits of their own domestic power.

The international legal system could harness the power of transgovernmental networks much more effectively. For example, international law could more explicitly recognize the role of such networks and the soft regulations they often produce. Hard legal instruments could mandate or facilitate the creation of transnational networks in a range of areas of critical State weakness such as justice or human rights. Where the weakness of a particular government in a functional area poses a threat to international order, the Security Council could require state participation in such a network. The international legal system should look to government networks as an important tool in improving state capacity and should build partnerships with government networks that help integrate them into larger international legal frameworks.

Once again, the international legal system would be taking a leaf from the EU's book in this regard. Most EU law gets made and implemented through transgovernmental networks of EU officials, from ministers on down. Indeed, Mark Leonard describes the EU as 'a decentralized network that is owned by its member-states'.[36] And beyond EU members themselves, the EU has sought to extend the network model to the Middle East and North Africa through the Barcelona Process and the Euro-Mediterranean Partnership.[37]

Beyond government networks, Stephen Krasner suggests that international law and institutions can strengthen State capacity by engaging in processes of shared sovereignty with national governments. Such shared sovereignty, 'involves the creation of institutions for governing specific issue areas within a state—areas over which external and internal actors voluntarily share authority'.[38] Examples of these arrangements include the creation of special hybrid courts in Sierra Leone, East Timor and, possibly, Cambodia, involving a mix of international and domestic law and judges. Similarly, a proposed oil pipeline agreement between Chad and the World Bank would involve shared control and governance.[39] Such shared sovereignty, Krasner claims, can 'gird new political structures with more expertise, better-crafted policies, and guarantees against abuses of power' onto weak or failing states.[40]

Even within a more traditional framework, the international legal system can employ a range of mechanisms to strengthen the hand of domestic governments. Legal instruments and codes of international best practices can set standards to

---

[36] Leonard, *Why Europe Will Run the 21st Century* (New York: Perseus Book Group, 2005) 23, citing Manuel Castells, *The End of Millennium* (Oxford: Blackwell, 2000).

[37] The Euro-Mediterranean Partnership, also knows as the Barcelona Process, is 'wide framework of political, economic and social relations between the Member States of the European Union and Partners of the Southern Mediterranean' launched in Barcelona in 1995. For a discussion <http://europa.eu.int/comm/external_relations/euromed/>.

[38] SD Krasner, 'Building Democracy After Conflict: The Case for Shared Sovereignty' (2005) 16:1 Journal of Democracy 69, 76.   [39] Ibid.

[40] Ibid, 70.

give national governments benchmarks for enhancing their own capability.[41] International institutions can provide aid and assistance specifically targeted for the domestic institutions of the recipient State.

International financial institutions such as the IMF and the World Bank may have a particularly powerful role to play in building domestic capacity. Conditionality requirements give these bodies strong influence over domestic outcomes. The IMF's success in enhancing the capabilities of domestic governments is much debated.[42] The World Bank may have a better track record.[43] Part of the Bank's strategy in Africa has been to 'put countries in the driver's seat' with a 'platform of strong public capacity: capacity to formulate policies; capacity to build consensus; capacity to implement reform; and capacity to monitor results, learn lessons, and adapt accordingly'.[44] Whatever their successes and failures to date, the IMF and the World Bank have significant leverage to enhance domestic government capacity. The key issue is for them to find effective and just policies aimed at achieving this goal.

Building various mechanisms into future legal regimes as a means of promoting domestic capacity building must be an on-going priority. These mechanisms include government networks, technical assistance, benchmarks and standards, or other forms of cooperation. Abraham and Antonia Chayes have provided a model for how this can be done through 'managerial compliance'.[45] From this perspective, the task of maximizing compliance with a given set of international rules is a task more of management than enforcement, ensuring that all parties know what is expected of them, that they have the capacity to comply, and that they receive the necessary assistance.

More broadly, the success of many policies at the international level depends on political choices at the national level; for example, choices concerning the allocation of resources or the establishment of particular institutions. The effectiveness of international law may thus depend on its ability to shape political outcomes and institutional structures within States. At the same time, however, a feedback loop from domestic institutions to international institutions becomes crucial for both accountability and effectiveness. Thus the various mechanisms canvassed above to strengthen domestic government institutions must be carefully designed.

---

[41] In the field of judicial independence, the International Covenant on Civil and Political Rights (ICCPR) provides a set of such benchmarks. ICCPR, Arts 9–11. Additionally, the Rome Statute of the International Criminal Court offers further clarification and a potential legal testing ground. Rome Statute of the International Criminal Court, Art 17.

[42] For two sides of this debate, J Vreeland, *The IMF and Economic Development* (Cambridge: CUP, 2003) 160–65 (suggesting that IMF conditionality may retard domestic development); R Stone, *Lending Credibility: The International Monetary Fund and the Post-Communist Transition* (Princeton NJ: Princeton University Press, 2002) 233–34 (arguing that IMF conditionality is appropriate and beneficial).

[43] B Levy and S Kpundeh (eds), *Building State Capacity in Africa: New Approaches, Emerging Lessons* (Washington DC: WBI Development Studies, DC 2004).

[44] Ibid, cited on the World Bank Website <http://web.worldbank.org/WBSITE/EXTERNAL/WBI/0,,contentMDK:20112038~menuPK:556286~pagePK:209023~piPK:207535~theSitePK:213799,00.html>. [45] A Chayes and AH Chayes, *The New Sovereignty* (Cambridge: CUP, 1999) 4.

2.2 Backstopping domestic government

A second means through which international law can promote domestic government is by backstopping domestic institutions where they fail to act. In some ways, this idea is not new at all; it follows from a long intellectual tradition. As early as 1625, Hugo Grotius recognized that the domestic courts of various States could backstop one another. Referring to an early form of the prosecute or extradite requirement, Grotius observed: 'it is necessary that the power, in whose kingdom an offender resides, should upon the complaint of the aggrieved party, either punish him itself, or deliver him up to the discretion of that party'.[46] In other words, cooperation among the criminal justice mechanisms of States would allow them to back one another up.

Similarly, in the early 1920s, M Maurice Travers developed the concept of 'la superposition des compétences législatives concurrentes', suggesting that the layering of overlapping jurisdiction of a number of States would allow national courts to reinforce one another.[47] What is new, however, is that international institutions—rather than the national courts of third States—are making a conscious effort to backstop their national counterparts. Structural rules that explicitly seek to further this backstopping function are now embedded in the very statutes of international tribunals and institutions.

The most obvious example of international law as a backstop is the complementarity provisions of the Rome Statute of the International Criminal Court. The ICC is designed to operate only where national courts fail to act as a first line means of prosecution. Article 17 of the Rome Statute provides that the court shall determine a case is inadmissible if 'the case is being investigated or prosecuted by a State which has jurisdiction over it, unless the State is unwilling or unable genuinely to carry out the investigation or prosecution'.[48] Either in cases where a domestic institutions fail 'due to a total or substantial collapse or unavailability of its national judicial system',[49] or where a State is unwilling to prosecute 'independently or impartially', the ICC can step in and provide a second line of defence.[50] In other words, if the US were a member of the ICC and proved unable or unwilling to prosecute fully *all* those members of the military involved in the abuses at Abu Ghraib, the ICC would have jurisdiction.

Other forms of international institutional design may similarly result in a backstopping function. In various human rights courts, the requirement that individuals exhaust local remedies first may have a similar result by giving States—and particularly their domestic courts—an incentive to reach conclusions acceptable to the international institution so the international court need not intervene to

---

[46] H Grotius, *De Jure Belli ac Pacis* (1625) II c.21 sec.4.
[47] M Maurice Travers, *Le Droit Pénal International et sa Mise en Oeuvre en Temps de Paix et en Temps de Guerre* (Paris: Librairie de la Société du Recueil Sirey, 1922).
[48] Rome Statute of the International Criminal Court, Art 17(1).   [49] Ibid, Art 17(3).
[50] Ibid, Art 17(2).

review the case.[51] Similarly, the dispute resolution mechanisms of NAFTA have served as an international backstop for domestic resolution of anti-dumping cases.[52] Under NAFTA, international arbitral panels are given the authority to review domestic administrative decisions and can remand decisions back to the issuing agency with guidance on acceptable outcomes. If the agency issues an acceptable ruling, no further action is taken. But, if the panels remain unsatisfied with the agency's response, they can issue a further ruling and remand the case yet again.[53] Like the Rome Statute's complementarity regime, this remand procedure gives domestic institutions within NAFTA countries an incentive to act first and to get it right. Where they fail to do so, the international process provides a backstop.

The actual effect of such backstopping provisions in international institutional design is two-fold. First, and most obviously is to provide a second line of defense when national institutions fail. Second, and potentially more powerfully, is the ability of the international process to catalyze action at the national level. This second effect most often occurs when a domestic legal or political process exists that could be utilized should the domestic government decide to do so, but government officials, or at least some powerful group of such officials, deem that the costs of domestic action outweigh the benefits. In such cases, the existence of an international tribunal with concurrent jurisdiction can provide structural incentives that shift the cost-benefit calculation and result in the use of a domestic process that would have otherwise been neglected. As States will often prefer to adjudicate matters domestically rather than give jurisdiction to an international tribunal over which they have little or no control, they are likely to have new incentives to act locally.

The International Criminal Court already appears to be having such a catalytic effect in two of the first situations it is investigating—the Democratic Republic of Congo and the Darfur region of Sudan. In the wake of the ICC Prosecutor's 2003 announcement of an investigation in Congo, a range of efforts were initiated by certain elements within the Congolese government to reform the Congolese judiciary so as to be able to assert primacy over the ICC and undertake national

[51] Art 35 of the European Convention on Human Rights provides that 'The Court may only deal with the matter after all domestic remedies have been exhausted'. Similarly, the court can only hear cases referred by the Commission when the Commission has acknowledged a failure to reach a friendly settlement of the dispute. ECHR, Art 47.

[52] The 1988 Canadian-American Free Trade Agreement (CAFTA) and the more recent North American Free Trade Agreement both contain provisions for the creation of international panels to review the legality of administrative decisions with respect to antidumping and countervailing duty obligations. Canada-US Free Trade Agreement (1988) Chapter 19; North-American Free Trade Agreement, Art 1904, providing that 'each Party shall replace judicial review of final antidumping and countervailing duty determinations with bi-national panel review'. Though not a traditional international court or arbitration, these panels act in a judicial capacity and issue decisions binding on States parties. Certain non-traditional aspects of the panels include the fact that domestic judicial review was not completely foreclosed. J Goldstein, 'International Law and Domestic Institutions: Reconciling North-American Unfair Trade Laws' (Autumn 1996) 50 Int'l Org 541, 546.

[53] Goldstein (n 52 above) 551.

proceedings.[54] Similarly, after the Prosecutor opened an investigation in the Darfur region of Sudan, local courts, though of questionable legitimacy, were established to initiate domestic proceedings.[55] The ICC Prosecutor has himself suggested that complementarity may encourage domestic prosecutions. As he puts it, 'the absence of trials before this Court, as a consequence of the regular functioning of national institutions, would be a major success'.[56]

International legal institutions operating as a backstop need not be limited to purely international courts. Domestic adjudication may likewise enhance the willingness of the judiciaries of third states to act themselves. The recent successes of the Chilean courts in prosecuting Augusto Pinochet is, in part, due to the international community—acting largely through the Spanish judiciary—getting serious about ensuring accountability for his crimes.[57] The prosecution by Spain and the proceedings in England[58]—though they did not result in a conviction—made

[54] Reform efforts to date have included attempts to reunify the divided judiciary through nation-wide judicial conferences, establishing commissions on legislative reform, and launching a Truth and Reconciliation Commission. Personal Interview Mr Honorius Kisimba-Ngoy, Minister of Justice, Kinshasa, 29 October 2003, (interview conducted by Yuriko Kuga, Leslie Medema and Adrian Alvarez). According to the Director of the Cabinet to the Minister of Human Rights, one 'local commission [is] studying how to adapt the ICC to the DRC'. Personal Interview, Director of the Cabinet to the Minister of Human Rights, Ms Olela Okondji, Kinshasa, 29 October 2003 (interview conducted by Yuriko Kuga, Leslie Medema, and Adrian Alvarez). Similarly, 'a permanent committee within the Ministry [of Justice has been established] for reforming the domestic law' and is 'learning how to implement the ICC' crimes into domestic law. The Commission's formal name is The Commission Permanente de Réforme du Droit Congolais. Personal Interview, Director of the Cabinet to the Minister of Human Rights, Ms Olela Okondji, Kinshasa, 29 October 2003 (interview conducted by Yuriko Kuga, Leslie Medema, and Adrian Alvarez). The Congolese TRC grew out of the Inter-Congolese Dialogue and is written into the new interim constitution. Constitution De La Transition, Journal Officiel de la République Démocratique du Congo, 44 année, 5 Avril 2003, at Art 54 (noting: '*Les Institutions d'appui a la démocratie sont:... La Commission vérité et réconciliation*'). Despite the consideration of a number of draft laws, as of early 2004, an organic law for the commission has yet to be adopted Personal Interview, Dr Kuye Wadonda, President of the Truth and Reconciliation Commission, Kinshasa, DR Congo, 27 October 2003. For a more detailed discussion, see WW Burke-White, 'Complementarity in Practice: The International Criminal Court as Part of a System of Multilevel Global Governance in the Democratic Republic of Congo' (2005) 18 Leiden J Int'l L 557.

[55] *Sudan Renews Rejection to Bringing Any Sudanese Before International Criminal Court*, Sudan News Agency, 17 October 2005.

[56] Louis Moreno-Ocampo, Ceremony for the solemn undertaking of the Chief Prosecutor of the International Criminal Court, June 16, 2003, available at <http://www.icc-cpi.int/otp/otp_ceremony.html> (visited 18 October 2003). Similarly an expert paper published by the Office of the Prosecutor notes: 'The complementary regime serves as a mechanism to encourage and facilitate the compliance of States with their primary responsibility to investigate and prosecute core crimes'. Informal Expert Paper: The Principle of Complementarity in Practice, available at <http://www.icccpi.int/library/organs/otp/complementarity.pdf >.

[57] The Chilean Supreme Court has ruled that Pinochet may stand trial domestically for international crimes against Chilean citizens committed during his rule. D Sugarman, 'Will Pinochet Ever Answer to the People of Chile?', The Times (London), 14 September 2004, available at <http://www.timesonline.co.uk/article/0,,200–1257033,00.html> (Editor's note: by the time this book went to print, Pinochet had died and would no longer be prosecuted).

[58] *R v Bow Street Metropolitan Stipendiary Magistrate, ex parte Pinochet Ugarte (No 3)*[2000] 1 AC 147, 248 (HL).

clear to the Chileans that other options existed if they themselves refused to prosecute and may have bolstered the willingness of Chilean courts to hold Pinochet
accountable.

The backstopping effect of international institutions will take different forms
and often be case specific. Sometimes, the international institution will provide
maximum incentives for domestic governmental authorities to act. Other times,
the international institution may alter the balance in a domestic power struggle,
strengthening the hand of those national officials who want to act. Alternatively,
where the domestic government truly lacks the capacity to act, the international
institution could backstop domestic courts by genuinely providing another forum.
In any case, the international institution directly affects domestic government
decisions, changing the incentives for domestic action and providing a second, international, mechanism of action. In so doing, the international institution becomes a
tacit actor in domestic political processes, pressuring national governments to reach
political outcomes that would not have otherwise been available.

2.3 Compelling action by national governments

The effectiveness of international law in responding to new transnational threats
will, to an ever greater degree, require the use of national institutions. Despite the
proliferation of international courts and tribunals,[59] national governments have
retained the nearly exclusive use of their instruments of compulsive authority. In
most cases, national governments alone can use the police power, the instruments
of a national judiciary, or the military. These are the most effective tools available
to address transnational threats before they grow and spread. In many cases, backstopping and strengthening domestic institutions will be sufficient to ensure that
national governments use their power to address present and potential dangers.
At times, however, domestic governments may be unwilling to use these institutions, either due to differing perceptions of national interest, a lack of political
will, or infighting within governments themselves. In addition to backstopping
and strengthening domestic institutions, international law must find new ways to
ensure that, even in these cases, national governments do, in fact, use the tools at
their disposal to address such threats before they spread.

In some ways, using international legal rules to compel state action might be
said to fit within a classical vision of the international legal system. After all, such
rules have long sought to constrain or mandate the behaviour of States. However,
as described here, compulsion takes a very different form from traditional international legal obligations. Whereas classical international law generated obligations
on states qua states, the new compulsion function of international law seeks to compel sub-state institutions to act in particular ways. Though these obligations may

[59] Christian Tomuschat, 'International Courts and Tribunals', 1 *Encyclopedia of Public International
Law* 92–99 (Rudolph Dolzer et al. eds, 1981).

still be directed at States themselves, they specifically reference the affirmative duties of states to utilize their domestic institutions to further international objectives.

Where compulsion is necessary, binding international instruments of all kinds—from Security Council resolutions to customary law doctrines—must shift from requiring particular State behaviour vis-à-vis other States to ensuring that the domestic institutions of national governments take specific actions within their own jurisdictions. International treaties have long required national governments to enact domestic legislation of various sorts, such as the domestic criminalization of certain transnational acts.[60] International law must go still further and ensure that domestic legislation is not only passed but also used, that domestic institutions not only exist, but also work.

The use of international law to combat terrorism immediately after September 11 is a prime example of how specific obligations can be imposed on UN member states that they can fulfill only by acting at the national level and deploying domestic institutions. UN Security Council Resolution 1373, for example, requires states to 'prevent the commission of terrorist acts' and 'deny safe haven to those who finance [or] plan . . . terrorist acts'.[61] The resolution demands, among other things, domestic criminalization of the financing of terrorism, freezing of terrorist assets by national authorities, use of domestic courts to bring to justice those involved in terrorists acts, and ratification by domestic authorities of relevant anti-terrorism conventions.[62]

The White House describes Resolution 1373 as setting 'new, strict standards for all states to meet in the global war against terrorism'.[63] Likewise, the International Convention for the Suppression of the Financing of Terrorism (Financing Convention) and the International Convention for the Suppression of Terrorist Bombing (Bombing Convention) require states to take concrete domestic action. The Financing Convention obliges states to 'take appropriate measures . . . for the . . . seizure of funds used or allocated for' the financing of terrorism,[64] while the Bombing Convention requires domestic criminalization of terrorist acts and the affirmative use of national judicial institutions to bring to justice the perpetrators of terrorist acts.[65]

Resolution 1373 links both the compelling and strengthening functions of the international legal system. Beyond merely mandating domestic action, the resolution establishes a Counter-Terrorism Committee that is tasked with monitoring the implementation of the resolution and increasing the 'capability of States to

---

[60] For example, many treaties in the area of international criminal law require criminalization of certain behaviour at the national level. Eg Convention on the Suppression and Punishment of the Crime of Genocide; Convention Against Torture and Other Inhuman and Degrading Treatment.

[61] UN Security Council Resolution 1373 S/RES/1373 (2001) at 2(c) and 2(d).   [62] Ibid.

[63] The White House, National Strategy for Combating Terrorism 13 (2003), available at <http://www.whitehouse.gov/news/releases/2003/02/counter_terrorism/counter_terrorism_strategy.pdf>.

[64] International Convention for the Suppression of the Financing of Terrorism, at Art 8 (1999).

[65] International Convention for the Suppression of Terrorist Bombings, at Arts 5–7 (1998).

fight terrorism'.[66] The Committee requires regular reporting by States of steps taken to comply with Resolution 1373 and provides expert advice on issues ranging from legislative drafting to customs requirements and policing.[67] Working jointly with international, regional, and sub-regional organizations, the Committee shares 'codes, standards and best practices in their areas of competence'.[68] In addition, the Committee makes available a database of technical assistance and a team of expert advisors to assist states in compliance.[69] By April 2005, at least one report had been received from all 191 member States; the Secretary General has described State cooperation with the Committee to date as 'unprecedented and exemplary'.[70]

The Security Council's recent initiatives in the area of non-proliferation have imposed similar obligations on national governments to take affirmative domestic action. Security Council Resolution 1540, for example, requires States to adopt national legislation prohibiting the manufacture or possession of weapons of mass destruction by non-State actors and to establish export control regulations and physical protection regimes for weapons and related technologies.[71] While not going as far as the creation of the Counter-Terrorism Committee, the Security Council again recognized the importance of capacity building in ensuring domestic action and invited States to offer assistance and resources.[72] Likewise, functional international organizations such as the International Atomic Energy Agency (IAEA) have compelled States to act through their own institutions. IAEA Safeguards Agreements with nuclear States, for example, require a national system of materials controls and the use of particular accounting mechanisms.[73]

This is again the future of international law. To respond effectively to new international threats, international rules must penetrate the surface of the sovereign State, requiring governments to take specific domestic actions to meet specified targets. Sometimes simple backstopping of national institutions may be sufficient to accomplish this task. In other circumstances, assistance and the bolstering of weak State capacity may be an essential prerequisite. At yet other times, international law may have to actively compel State action. When it does so, it once again seeks to alter the political choices of national governments and to compel States to utilize their national institutions in ways they might not otherwise.

The most effective approach will often involve some combination of all three functions. Leaders and legislators should then be held accountable by both their peers and their publics for whether and how they and their governments respond.

---

[66] UN Counter-Terrorism Committee Homepage, available at <http://www.un.org/Docs/sc/committees/1373/>.

[67] UN Counter-Terrorism Committee, How Does the CTC Work With States?, available at <http://www.un.org/Docs/sc/committees/1373/work.html>.

[68] UN Counter-Terrorism Committee, Working Together to Raise State Capacity, <http://www.un.org/Docs/sc/committees/1373/capacity.html>.

[69] UN Counter-Terrorism Committee, How Can the CTC Help States? (n 67 above).

[70] Ibid.   [71] UN Security Council Resolution 1540, S/RES/1540 (2004).

[72] Ibid, 7.

[73] Eg, Agreement Between The United States of America and The International Atomic Energy Agency for the Application of Safeguards in the United States (and Protocol Thereto), 8 December 1980.

3. The dangers of using international law to shape and influence domestic politics

On one level, using international law to build the will and capacity of States to act domestically offers great opportunities to enhance the effectiveness of the international legal system. National governments will have new incentives to act. Domestic institutions will grow stronger. They can be harnessed in pursuit of international objectives. Transnational threats can be responded to more effectively and efficiently.

Yet each of the functions of the international system suggested here—backstopping, strengthening, and compelling—is a double-edged sword. Backstopping national institutions can be counterproductive to the degree States defer to an international forum as a less politically and financially costly alternative to national action.[74] Well-intentioned efforts to help, often through NGOs as well as international institutions, can end up weakening local government actors by siphoning off both funds and personnel. The process of strengthening domestic institutions, if not properly designed and implemented, can also squeeze out local domestic capacity.[75] Finally, and most dangerously, by compelling national action the international legal system may undermine local democratic processes and prevent domestic experimentation with alternate approaches.[76]

The most significant danger inherent in these new functions of international law, however, lies in the potential of national governments to co-opt the force of international law to serve their own objectives. By strengthening State capacity, international law may actually make States more effective at the very repression and abuse the interference challenge seeks to overcome. Similarly, by compelling State action, international law may give national governments new license to undertake otherwise illegal or unjust policies. Where critical values such as human rights and state security are seen to be in conflict, international legal compulsion of policies that favour one value may come at the expense of the other. This problem is particularly grave where a repressive regime is able to use compulsion at the international level as a cover or excuse to undertake its own domestic policies that may undermine legitimate opposition groups and violate citizens' rights.

---

[74] One of the co-authors has described this as a moral hazard problem. William W Burke-White, *Double-Edged Tribunals: Embracing The Domestic Political Effects of International Judicial Bodies*, working paper (2004). The most obvious example of this is the self-referral to the ICC by the government of Uganda of the situation with the Lords Resistance Army. *President of Uganda Refers Situation concerning the Lord's Resistance Army (LRA) to the ICC*, The Hague, 29 January 2004, available at <http://www.icc-cpi.int/php/index.php>. In all likelihood, the Ugandan government could have addressed this situation domestically if it did not have the option of referring the situation to the ICC.

[75] Fukuyama argues that 'The international community, including the vast numbers of NGOs that are an intimate part of it, comes so richly endowed and full of capabilities that it tends to crowd out rather than complement the extremely weak state capacities of the targeted countries'), Fukuyma (n 13 above) 103.

[76] For a discussion of the importance of such domestic experimentation, MC Dorf and CF Sabel, 'A Constitution of Democratic Experimentalism' (1998) 98 Columbia L Rev 267.

Nowhere is this danger more apparent than in the legal compulsion of counter-terrorism activity. Mary Robinson, former UN High Commissioner for Human Rights, observes: 'Repressive new laws and detention practices have been introduced in a significant number of countries, all broadly justified by the new international war on terrorism.'[77] Similarly, Kim Scheppele has documented the number of exceptions to international and domestic legal protections states have invoked under the cover of fighting terrorism.[78] Among the worst offenders, according to Human Rights First, are Tanzania, Indonesia, Russia, Pakistan, and Uzbekistan, each of which has undertaken 'draconian anti-terrorism laws' that compromise human rights and strengthen the hand of government vis-à-vis opposition groups.[79]

If these new purposes of international law are to be both effective and just, the goal must be to maximize the benefits of the backstopping, strengthening, and compelling functions while avoiding the dangers evident in the counter-terrorism case. The theoretical base of these new functions of international law is that domestic institutions can be used to further international legal objectives. Yet it is these same institutions that can become sources of abuse by national governments. The challenge, then, is to differentiate between domestic institutional structures capable of furthering the international system and those most likely to be abusive and repressive.

One way of making such distinctions is for international law to directly consider the quality of domestic institutions. States with robust, independent institutions, strong constitutional frameworks, transparent political processes, and embedded systems of checks and balances are least likely to appropriate international law for their own purposes and engage or abuse their newfound power. In these states, domestic legal protections and other institutions within the national government can prevent abuse or counter-balance the strength of other institutions. Abuses may still occur in States with good institutional frameworks. However, the assumption built into institutions like the ICC is that when abuses do occur in a well-governed State, that State's own domestic system will provide an internal correction mechanism. It is these States with independent and transparent domestic institutions that may be most receptive to the new functions of the international legal system.

The problem, of course, is that it is often the states that lack institutional independence and embedded checks and balances that are most in need of capacity building or compulsion to address threats and challenges at home, before they spread. Where international law does target such states, international rules, regimes, and institutions will have to be designed to address both the capacity and quality of domestic governance. Checks and balances will have to be embedded into the

---

[77] M Robinson, 'Shaping Globalization: The Role of Human Rights' (2003) 19 Am U Int'l L Rev 1, 12.

[78] Kim L Scheppele, 'Law in a Time of Emergency: States of Exception and the Temptations of 9/11' (2000) 6 U Pa J Const L 1001.

[79] Human Rights First, *Imbalance of Powers: How Changes to U.S. Law and Policy Since 9/11 Erode Human Rights and Civil Liberties* (2003) 76–79.

system itself, pushing not only for particular substantive outcomes but also for legitimate domestic processes to achieve those goals. Similarly, international regimes
themselves will have to balance a range of competing values—such as human rights
and national security—rather than focus on one particular goal when compelling
state action.

Finally, as is already becoming apparent, both this overall conception of international law and the specific functions described here will meet with fierce resistance from states with very strong domestic legal systems, such as the United States,
and many states with very weak legal systems but strong political rulers. European
states, as noted above, are accustomed to daily 'soft intervention'. Other states,
however, will be far less comfortable with such intervention. The US will not be
alone here, but it may well find itself with a number of unsavory bedfellows. On
the other hand, many European powers may find it more difficult than they
expect to promote an EU-inspired model of pooled sovereignty among wary former colonies.

4. International law, domestic politics

International lawyers and political scientists alike have long been fascinated with
the blurring of the boundaries between domestic and international rules and institutions. In 1956 Philip Jessup made a hegemonic move, claiming for international
lawyers not only the classic domain of international law, but also 'all law which
regulates actions or events that transcend national frontiers', which he dubbed
'transnational law'.[80] Forty-five years later, Justice Sandra Day O'Connor, a relative newcomer to the world of international law, observed: 'international law is no
longer confined in relevance to a few treaties and business agreements. Rather,
it . . . regulates actions or events that transcend national frontiers.'[81]

In political science, James Rosenau has popularized the concept of the 'domestic-foreign frontier'.[82] On this frontier, 'domestic and foreign issues converge,
intermesh, or otherwise become indistinguishable'.[83] In his conception, whereas a
boundary is an imaginary line, a frontier is 'a new and wide political space . . . continuously shifting, widening, and narrowing, erosion with respect to many issues
and reinforcement with respect to others'.[84] What Rosenau finds striking about
relations along this frontier is that individuals work out a wide range of solutions

---

[80] P Jessup, *Transnational Law* (New Haven: Yale UP, 1956) 2.
[81] Sandra Day O'Connor, 'Keynote Address' (2002) 96 ASIL PROC 348, 350.
[82] As Rosenau observes: 'we can no longer allow the domestic-foreign boundary to confound our
understanding of world affairs . . . . domestic and foreign affairs have always formed a seamless web'.
J N Rosenau, *Along the Domestic-Foreign Frontier: Exploring Governance in a Turbulent World*
(Cambridge: CUP, 1997) 4.   [83] Ibid, 5.
[84] Ibid, 4.

to various problems through a mix of domestic and international rules, rather than 'through the nation-state system'.[85]

Our proposition is actually quite different. We endorse the division between domestic and international affairs, at least conceptually. Although it is quite possible, indeed likely, that international law is expanding to include all sorts of rules and institutions that have a hybrid domestic-international character, as well as those domestic rules that reach beyond borders, we suggest that traditional public international law, meaning treaties and custom operating among nations in their mutual relations, has a distinct identity and a distinct set of functions. We are simply arguing that those functions are changing fast.

Our claim 'that the future of international law is domestic' refers not to domestic *law* but to domestic *politics*. More precisely, the future of international law lies in its ability to affect, influence, bolster, backstop, and even mandate specific actors, actions, and outcome in domestic politics. International rules and institutions will and should be designed as a set of spurs and checks on domestic political actors to ensure that they do what they should be doing anyway—eg what they have already committed to do in their domestic constitutions and laws and through their treaty and customary law obligations.

In this conception, it is perfectly fine to continue to distinguish quite concretely between an 'international' and a 'domestic' sphere, even as we recognize that the boundary between them has blurred and that they intersect and even conflict in growing ways. Indeed, it is valuable for domestic political actors—the prosecutors trying to bring a former government official to justice, the judges seeking to resist executive pressure to decide a case a particular way, the parliamentary faction trying to fight global warming—to be able to point to a mandate or a spur from a distinct and separate political space. The result will be ever more elaborate two-level games, but each game will remain on its own board, no matter how complex and dense the links between them.

What must change profoundly, however, is the legitimacy of allowing the architects of international rules and institutions to look within the domestic political sphere of all states actually and hypothetically subject to the rule or institution in question. This scrutiny cannot be done with reference to specific parties and actors in actual states, but must be based on data culled from history and across the social sciences about the likely incentives of those parties and actors in varying circumstances. The critical question must be how the content of specific rules and of the processes and procedures of institutions is likely to interact with, influence, or even change these incentives.

In short, the very concept of sovereignty itself must adapt and evolve to focus on inclusion—rather than exclusion—and to embrace—rather than reject—the influence of international rules and institutions on domestic political processes.

---

[85] Ibid, 5–6. Also M Albert and L Brock, *Debording the World of States: New Spaces in International Relations*, Working Paper 2 (Frankfurt: World Society Research Group, 1995).

This shift may well be best illustrated by the new doctrine of the responsibility to protect. The responsibility to protect first emerged from the International Commission on Intervention and State Sovereignty (ICISS), headed by former Australian Foreign Minister Gareth Evans and Special Advisor to the UN Secretary General Mohamed Sahnoun, who were in turn responding to an appeal from Kofi Annan himself.[86] In December 2001 the ICISS issued an important and influential report entitled 'The Responsibility to Protect', which essentially called for updating the UN Charter to incorporate a new understanding of sovereignty.[87]

In the Commission's conception, the core meaning of UN membership has shifted from 'the final symbol of independent sovereign statehood and thus the seal of acceptance into the community of nations',[88] to recognition of a State 'as a responsible member of the community of nations'.[89] Nations are free to choose whether or not to sign the Charter; if they do, however, they must accept the 'responsibilities of membership' flowing from their signature.[90] According to the ICISS, 'There is no transfer or dilution of State sovereignty. But there is a necessary re-characterization involved: from sovereignty as control to sovereignty as responsibility in both internal functions and external duties'.[91] Internally, a government has a responsibility to respect the dignity and basic rights of its citizens; externally, it has a responsibility to respect the sovereignty of other States.

Further, the ICISS places the responsibility to protect on both the State and on the international community as a whole. The ICISS insists that an individual state has the primary responsibility to protect the individuals within it.[92] However, where the State fails in that responsibility, a secondary responsibility falls on the international community acting through the UN. Thus, 'where a population is suffering serious harm, as a result of internal war, insurgency, repression or state failure, and the state in question is unwilling or unable to halt or avert it, the principle of non-intervention yields to the international responsibility to protect'.[93]

These shifts may seem dramatic; they are certainly bold. But in the view of a group of leading European policy thinkers asked to consider how the EU should

---

[86] In September 1999 Kofi Annan called on all UN members at the opening of the General Assembly to 'reach consensus—not only on the principle that massive and systematic violations of human rights must be checked, wherever they take place, but also on ways of deciding what action is necessary, and when, and by whom'. Kofi Annan, 'Two Concepts of Sovereignty' available at <http://www.un.org/News/ossg/sg/stories/kaecon.html>.

[87] The Responsibility to Protect, Report of the International Commission on Intervention and State Sovereignty (2001). The International Commission on Intervention and State Sovereignty (ICISS) began from the premise that 'in key respects...the mandates and capacity of international institutions have not kept pace with international needs or modern expectations'. Ibid at 1.11. More specifically, the ICISS argued that the intense debate over military protection for humanitarian purposes flowed from a 'critical gap' between the immense and unavoidable reality of mass human suffering and the existing rules and mechanisms for managing world order. At the same time, it noted a widening gap between the rules and the principles of the Charter regarding non-interference in the domestic affairs of member nations and actual state practice as it has evolved since 1945. It frames the 'responsibility to protect' as an 'emerging principle' of customary international law—not yet existing as law but already supported both by State practice and a wide variety of legal sources. Ibid at 2.24–2.27.   [88] Ibid, 2.11.

[89] Ibid, 2.14.   [90] Ibid.   [91] Ibid.   [92] Ibid, 2.29.   [93] Ibid, xi.

respond to the UN Secretary General's High Level Panel Report on Threats, Challenges, and Change, EU States should go considerably further. They should: 'Promote "the Responsibility to Protect", while also reframing the sovereignty debate to cover a principle of both *enhancing* effective and legitimate sovereignty of weak states, (through international assistance) and *conditioning* sovereignty on state behaviour'.[94]

International law and the international community itself is thus coming to have not only the right, but perhaps also the obligation to intervene in and influence what was previously the exclusive jurisdiction and political processes of national governments. By strengthening, backstopping, and compelling action at the national level, the international legal system has powerful tools at its disposal to alter domestic political outcomes.

This line of argument raises yet another (friendly, we hope) division between European and American international lawyers. Noted European (and some American) international lawyers have denounced the entire enterprise of linking international law to the systematic study of international relations as a blind for extending American power, just as we suspect some readers will interpret some of the arguments set forth here.[95]

Once again, however, it is European policy thinkers drawing on a distinctly European set of experiences who are pushing the transformative power of law. They emphasize that EU treaties are, in the end, simply international law that EU members have chosen to accept and to embed in their domestic political systems,[96] and draw corresponding conclusions about the potential power and functions of international law as a whole. We have sought to explicate those functions here. But in the end, if the future of international law is domestic, as we predict, it will be the European way of law.

---

[94] Eide (n 22 above) 9.

[95] For a number of perspectives on this point, 'Unilateralism in International Law: Its Role and Its Limits: A United States European Symposium' (2000) EJIL 10–11. Also Martin Koskenniemi, *From Apology to Utopia* (Cambridge: CUP, 1989); M Koskenniemi, S Ratner, and V Rittberger 'Comments on Chapters 1 and 2' in M Byers and G Nolte (eds), *United States Hegemony and the Foundations of International Law* (Cambridge: CUP, 2003).   [96] Leonard (n 16 above) 46.

6

Monism and Dualism: The Impact of Private Authority on the Dichotomy Between National and International Law

Christine Chinkin

1. Introduction: public and private authority

It is a truism to say that there is nothing new in private authority whereby states do not have the monopoly over people, territory, use of force, or the exercise of jurisdiction. Numerous spheres of private authority existed in the pre-Westphalian world, creating a pluralism of sub- and trans-State legal systems: inter alia religious organizations, universities, private armies, law merchants, feudal lords, private trading companies. The spheres of public and private entities merged with no clear demarcation between them, so that for example treaties were entered into by sovereigns in their own name and were thus personal rather than appertaining to the state. Harold Koh explains how '[t]he law of nations was thought to embrace private as well as public, domestic as well as transborder transactions and to encompass not simply the "law of states", but also the law between States and individuals'.[1]

Westphalia marked no immediate change. For example the US Court of Appeal has noted the fusion of international and national law that followed the mixed exercise of public and private authority that existed even in the context of the use of force ostensibly between states. In *Kadic v Karadzic* the Court observed that '[t]he liability of private persons for certain violations of customary international law and the availability of the Alien Tort Claims Act to remedy such violations was early recognized by the Executive Branch in an opinion of Attorney General Bradford in reference to acts of [private] American citizens aiding the [public] French fleet to plunder British property off the coast of Sierra Leone in 1795.'[2]

In the 19th century the distinction between international and national law became more marked in the positivist trend of the former, based upon the consent

---

[1] H Koh, 'Why Do Nations Obey International Law?' (1997) 10 Yale L J 2599, 2605.
[2] *Kadic v Karadzic* 70 F3d 232, 236 (2d Cir. 1995).

of strong, unitary sovereign States.[3] State sovereignty required a territorially and spatially, bounded national legal system—horizontally vis à vis the legal systems of other nation States and vertically with respect to any other legal order such as international law. Such a system required the assertion of a single national legal order, and the denial of the numerous forms of private authority forming non-State law. In the context of the use of force, David Kennedy notes that:

Indeed, a number of quite precise doctrines regulating the use of force simply disappeared in the nineteenth century—primarily those which authorized the mixed public and private use of force, or otherwise compromised the emerging conception of a unitary public sovereign with a monopoly over the discretionary use of force. Privateering, for example, had been a complex legal arrangement through which 'letters of marque' authorized private vessels to carry out belligerent acts. It was eliminated from the legal vocabulary by the 1856 Paris Declaration.[4]

Despite the power of the centralized State, private authorities continued to flourish and evolved different forms. What are now termed non-governmental organizations (NGOs) appeared during the 19th century.[5] As is still the case, private authority was not necessarily oppositional to the State but was involved with it in common enterprises. Thus colonial powers made private authorities integral to the public enterprise of colonization,[6] while in the Congo King Leopold II used his public status to acquire colonial territory as his private domain.[7] In the 20th century institutionalized international law began expressly to accommodate private actors, for example through allowing individuals to assert their voice against state authority through the revolutionary concept of the mandate.[8] In the interwar years private law analogies were often reverted to for the creation of international law.[9] Kennedy describes how 'Numerous European international lawyers were hard at work combing private law in a systematic search for analogies to the relations between sovereigns in international "society"—in self-conscious opposition to the late nineteenth century conviction that no such society was possible among public sovereign authorities.'[10] The United Nations Charter trusteeship

---

[3] D Kennedy, *The Dark Sides of Virtue: Reassessing International Humanitarianism* (Princeton: Princeton University Press, 2004) 240 (writing in the context of just war theories).

[4] Ibid, 245–6.

[5] There are differing opinions as to which organization can be called the first of the genre; B Seary, 'The Early History From the Congress of Vienna to the San Francisco Conference' in P Willetts (ed), *The Conscience of the World The Influence of Non-Governmental Organizations in the UN System* (Washington DC: Bookings Institution Press, 1996) 15.

[6] K Knop, *Diversity and Self-determination in International Law* (Cambridge: Cambridge UP, 2002), ch 7 shows that areas within British colonial possessions that were apparently unregulated by British public authority were deliberately left within the private sector in the knowledge that missionaries would step in and fill the regulatory gaps.

[7] A Hochschild, *King Leopold's Ghost: a Story of Greed, Terror, and Heroism in Colonial Africa* (Boston: Houghton Mifflin Books, 1999).

[8] *Admissibility of Hearings of Petitioners by the Committee on South West Africa* (Advisory Opinion) [1956] ICJ Rep 23.

[9] H Lauterpacht, *Private Law Analogies in International Law* (London: Longmans Green, 1927).

[10] D Kennedy (n 3 above) 245.

regime and Charter provision for NGO consultative status[11] with ECOSOC paved the way for the greater integration between private authority and inter-governmental institutions that had evolved by the end of the century.

In traditional analysis international law regulates inter-State behaviour while national law(s) regulate the actions of individuals and legal persons within States. The theoretical concepts of dualism and monism maintained academic validity when only states were formally recognized as having international legal personality. The dichotomy cannot withstand the recognition that it is not solely states that are subject to international law but that other actors also have international competence. It is also severely tested by the acceptance of international regulation of matters that must be given primary effect within national courts, for example human rights and environmental controls. Further, international law as the law between states, assumed a monolithic model of statehood (population, territory, government, and control[12]) that imposed uniformity onto the system. Even while it was accepted that the precise balance between national and international law depended upon national constitutional requirements,[13] there was only a limited range of choices available within a state-oriented framework. Of course the assumed uniformity between State structures was never borne out by reality, but the (re)emergence of different forms of private authority operating across State borders blows apart any such assumption.

This chapter considers some of the implications of different forms of private authority for the dichotomy between national and international law. Section 2 considers the contemporary significance of the phenomenon of private authority to an understanding of the relationship between international and national law. Section 3 seeks to identify contemporary forms of private authority and possible bases of distinction between public and private authority and section 4 explores some of the ways international and national law interact in addressing the accountability of private authorities. The chapter concludes that the relationship between national and international law may be seen as chaotic, lacking order and precision, and therefore as requiring some legal categorization in order to recapture certainty. Alternatively it may be seen as accommodating new actors and opening new spaces for diverse forms of, and arenas for, regulation.

2. Private authorities in international affairs

Given that public and private authority have long intermingled in the international legal order, what is the significance of assessing the impact of private authority on

---

[11] UN Charter, Art 71.

[12] Montevideo Convention on Rights and Duties of States 1933, Art 1; 135 LNTS 19 (1936).

[13] Eg the monist acceptance of treaties as national law thereby situating the state within the community of nations, the dualist requirement that treaties be incorporated/transformed into national law and a different constitutional status to be accorded to treaties and custom; D Feldman, 'Monism, Dualism and Constitutional Legitimacy' (1999) 20 Aust YBIL 105.

the relationship between international and national law at the beginning of the 21st century? What has changed? There are at least three possible answers to these questions. The first is simply that of scale. More forms and arrangements for private authority are recognized, in particular through the UN and other international organizations, than previously. For example, in the context of a particular form of private authority, international NGOs, 57 new NGOs were accredited to the 1968 Tehran Conference on Human Rights as opposed to 831 to the Vienna Conference twenty-five years later. An astonishing 300,000 participants attended the parallel NGO Forum at the Fourth World Conference on Women in Beijing in 1995.[14] Other forms of private authority have also proliferated and have considerable economic and political power. Such a dramatic increase in the numbers and power of trans-national non-State actors must impact upon the interaction between international and national law.

A second response is globalization. Different forms of private authority acting in a globalized world inevitably shift the accepted forms of legal ordering and require a new understanding of the interaction between international and national law. A significant impact of globalization lies in the appeal to the international that is made by the local. Instead of existing within their own territorially limited domains, private authorities operate globally (and in cyber-space), unconstrained in their transactions and activities by State boundaries. They form both single and multiple issue trans-national networks and involve themselves in matters regulated as between States by international law. Gunther has explained that the dynamic forces of globalization (trans-national expansion of the market economy, emergence of a trans-national capital market, world wide communication and information technologies and trans-national migration) 'begin[s] to change the traditional patterns of social order, in particular the common model of a sovereign national state that is based on a more or less pluralistic as well as homogenous culture'.[15] Despite these changes to social order, forms of private authority are still given legal identity primarily through national law and may be refused standing within international arenas.[16] For instance it remains the case that non-State entities are formally denied any constitutive role in the formation of international law: only States can enter into treaties and it is State practice that forms customary international

[14] A-M Clark, E Friedman, and K Hochstetler, 'The Sovereign Limits of Global Civil Society: A Comparison of NGO Participation in UN World Conferences on the Environment, Human Rights and Women' (1998) 51 World Politics 1; J Foster, *Futures Beyond Threats: The UN, Civil Society and Global Governance* (Ottawa: The North-South Institute, 2002) cited UN System and Civil Society An Inventory and Analysis of Practices, Background paper for the Secretary-General's Panel of Eminent Persons on UN Relations with Civil Society.

[15] K Gunther, 'Legal Pluralism and the Universal Code of Legality: Globalisation as a Problem of Legal Theory' available at <http://www.law.nyu.edu/clppt/program2003/readings/gunther.pdf> accessed 19 March 2007.

[16] On state resistance to NGO participation, C Chinkin, 'Human Rights and the Politics of Representation: Is there a Role for International Law?' in M Byers (ed), *The Role of Law in International Politics* (Oxford: OUP, 2000) 131, 140–42.

law.[17] Nevertheless changes in the substance and processes of international law are made in response to the demands of non-State actors acting trans-nationally that in turn reverberate within national legal systems.

A third justification for a contemporary assessment of the relationship between national and international law is the dramatic proliferation of international and regional organizations that has widened the range of institutional settings where these questions play out. These 'often functionally circumscribed—global and regional institutions overlap with the various domestic legal orders'.[18] In particular the proliferation of international courts and tribunals means that the relationship between international and municipal law is no longer a matter of the approach of a single international court (the International Court of Justice[19]) and the different constitutional responses of national courts to international norms. It now requires analysis of the relationship between multiple, sectoral, non-hierarchical international bodies and national laws and institutions. Different relationships exist between different international and national legal institutions: the former may be dependent for jurisdiction upon the exhaustion of local remedies, be complementary to national courts,[20] be superior to them,[21] or there may be recourse to fictitious devices to allow international norms to prevail within them.[22] Private authorities are storming the citadel of international courts and tribunals. Some international institutions continue to retain the traditional demarcation between the international and national by denying standing to non-State actors,[23] while others have afforded them some level of access, as parties, interveners or *amici curiae*.[24] Opening international legal institutions to a broader range of participants ensures a range of arguments across international and national law that in turn impact upon both the processes and substance of each.

In addition to international and national courts are the many international arbitral tribunals, in particular those established (and which have the potential to be established) under the nearly two thousand bilateral investment treaties (BITs)

[17] For proposals for change in this regard, I Gunning, 'Modernizing Customary International Law: the Challenge of Human Rights' (1991) 31 Virginia JIL 211.

[18] Paulus, this volume, 231.

[19] The PCIJ described the relationship: 'From the standpoint of International Law and of the Court which is its organ, municipal laws are merely facts which express the will and constitute the activities of States, in the same manner as do legal decisions or administrative measures'. *Case Concerning Certain German Interests in Polish Upper Silesia (Germany v Poland)* (Merits) PCIJ Rep Series A No 7, 19.

[20] Rome Statute of the International Criminal Court, 1998, Art 1.

[21] Statute of the International Criminal Tribunal for the Former Yugoslavia, SC Res. 827, 25 May 1993, Art 9 (2); Statute of the International Criminal Tribunal for Rwanda, SC Res. 955, 8 November 1994, Art 8 (2).

[22] P Sands, 'After Pinochet: the Proper Relationship between National and International Courts' in V Gowlland-Debbas and L Boisson de Chazournes (eds), *The International Legal System in Quest of Equity and Universality Liber Amicorum for Professor Georges Abi-Saab* (London: Kluwer Law International, 2001) 699 (discussing the Privy Council).

[23] eg the International Court of Justice; C Chinkin, *Third Parties in International Law* (Oxford: Clarendon Press, 1993) 232–37.

[24] T Treves, M Frigessi di Rattalma, A Tanzi, A Fodella, C Pitea, C Ragni (eds), *Civil Society, International Courts and Compliance Bodies* (The Hague: TMC Asser Press, 2005).

concluded between States. Recourse is had to such tribunals under a BIT dispute resolution clause, but the tribunal may have also to determine legal issues arising under contracts concluded between individual investors and the host State.

These developments all shift the discourse beyond the traditional framing of the monist-dualist question in terms of approaches of domestic courts to international law and of international courts with respect to domestic law. William Twining has argued that 'globalization and interdependence challenge "black box theories" that treat nation states or societies or legal systems as discrete, impervious entities that can be studied in isolation either internally or externally'.[25] National legal systems are not self-contained and contemporary international law is about far more than states' external relations.[26] The ongoing and fluid slipping between the international and the national requires us to look at the form, substance, process, and arenas where this occurs and to identify different institutional approaches depending upon objectives, distributional choices in allocating claims to national or international law, moral choices, ideological and political preferences, and value systems. More significant than whether theories of monism and dualism retain any usefulness is how the normative regimes of numerous private authorities intersect with each other and how national and international legal systems regulate their activities.

3. Public and private authority: the relevance of the distinction

3.1 Introduction

Assessing the impact of private authority on the relationship between national and international law requires determining what constitutes private authority. This section discusses some of the possible distinguishing criteria and the range of relationships between states and private authority, between IGOs and private authority, and between different forms of private authority. It questions why some entities seek public identity within international institutions while others prefer to remain identified as private bodies within national institutions and considers the impact of the particular institutional culture on such decisions. Finally it suggests that the bilateralism of monism/dualism must cede to the reality of pluralist legal systems.

3.2 Defining private authority

The numerous and diverse forms of non-state actors make difficult any definition of private authority. It is apparent (and has long been accepted) that it is misleading to talk about trans-national non-State actors as a homogenous grouping,[27]

---

[25] W Twining, *Globalisation and Legal Theory* (London: Butterworths, 2000) 51.   [26] Ibid.

[27] R Lipschutz, 'Reconstructing World Politics' (1999) 21 Millennium 389.

even through collective words such as international or global civil society,[28] transnational advocacy networks,[29] or global social movements.[30] Both criteria—'private' and 'authority'—suggest a range of actors without any determinative distinguishing characteristics.

The requirement of authority denotes non-State actors that exercise some degree of control or power over others. Accordingly the concept of private authority encompasses, inter alia, non-State entities exercising economic power (transnational corporations, banking institutions), military power (para-military groups, terrorist cells), social or religious power and the power of respect (family, religious organizations), the power of membership over those who wish to carry out some professional or social activity (sporting associations, unions, clubs, and professional associations), the power of shared expertise (epistemological communities such as international bankers,[31] judges, parliamentarians), and the power of moral certainty (social campaigns since at least the 18th century around such issues as slavery and the slave trade, women's suffrage, peace movements, international workers' rights, civil society movements in Eastern Europe that sculpted the political space to challenge communist regimes, and NGOs working, inter alia, on human rights, environmental issues, disarmament).

The designation 'private' in contrast to 'public' is problematic. Lord Nicholls explained in the UK House of Lords that '[t]he expression "public authority" is not defined in the [Human Rights] Act, nor is it a recognized term of art in English law, that is, an expression with a specific recognized meaning'.[32] Lord Nicholls could have said the same about 'private authority' and international law. There is a continuum of legal and factual situations that blurs any clear cut distinction between those authorities that are most evidently public and entities (and individuals)[33] within the private sector. There are variations in the derivation of authority: within the ostensibly private sector entities may derive authority from the public sector (for example through outsourcing of public functions or delegation of government power) or assume their own authority (for example through the assertion of divine authority).

There are diverse legal frameworks for the bestowal and regulation of private authority (registration, licensing, bestowal of status by national Charter, incorporation) and for regulatory control (self-regulating through internal normative systems, subject to government regulators, regulation through a mix of administrative and criminal laws). Private bodies have different relationships with the

---

[28] H Anheier, M Glasius, and M Kaldor (eds), *Global Civil Society Yearbook* (Oxford: OUP, 2001).
[29] M Keck and K Sikkink, *Activists beyond Borders* (New York: Cornell UP, 1998) 9.
[30] R Cohen and S Rai (eds), *Global Social Movements* (London: Athlone Press, 2000).
[31] A-M Slaughter, 'Governing the Global Economy through Government Networks' in M Byers (ed), *The Role of Law in International Politics* (Oxford: OUP, 2000) 177.
[32] *Parochial Church Council of the Parish of Aston Cantlow and Wilmcote with Billesley, Warwickshire v Wallbank* [2003] 3 WLR 283, para 6.
[33] G Teubner, *Global Law without a State* (Brookfield: Dartmouth, 1997) 14.

State in respect of funding (they may or may not receive government funding or be the recipients of tax benefits). The degree of internal organization also varies (legally constituted under national law with formal rules of membership and behaviour, or comprising loose networks and alliances). Private authority may be embraced as the law of the State, for example through religious institutions, or be perceived as hostile to it.

There is no one single mark of identification of private authority and the concept is contingent, fluid, and cultural. Various tests for distinguishing between public and private authority have been proposed. One suggested ground is whether the body is exercising a public or private function.[34] However this requires a shared understanding of the 'proper domain' of the State that cannot stand against the different parameters for government function that characterize different theories of the state (for example the welfare, liberal, socialist, development, market, feminist,[35] and neo-liberal State).

The International Law Commission's Articles on State Responsibility[36] might have offered an international legal distinction between State authority that gives rise to international legal responsibility for commission of a wrongful act and private authority that does not. However the Articles are neutral on any theory of the state. Article 4 designates as an act of state (public act) any conduct of an organ that 'exercises legislative, executive, judicial or any other functions, whatever position it holds in the organization of the State, and whatever its character as an organ of the central government or of a territorial unit of the State'.

But not everything that falls outside Article 4 is necessarily to be deemed the act of a private authority. Article 5 provides that the acts of other persons or entities may be attributable to the State if they are 'empowered by the law of that State to exercise elements of the governmental authority', thereby raising the question as to what constitutes elements of governmental authority. The Commentary asserts that article 5 'is intended to take account of the increasingly common phenomenon of para-statal entities . . . as well as situations where former State corporations have been privatized but retain certain public or regulatory functions'.[37] The allocation of State responsibility under international law for the actions of such entities is justified by the national law allocation to the private sector of activities deemed by international law to be public or governmental, although the Commentary recognizes that any such determination must depend upon the 'particular society, its history and traditions'.

---

[34] In *Parochial Church Council of the Parish of Aston Cantlow and Wilmcote with Billesley, Warwickshire v Wallbank* 'the possession of special powers, democratic accountability, public funding in whole or in part, an obligation to act only in the public interest, and a statutory constitution' were listed as relevant factors for the distinction: [2003] 3 WLR 283, para 7 (Lord Nicholls).

[35] C MacKinnon, *Towards a Feminist Theory of the State* (Cambridge: Harvard UP, 1989).

[36] International Law Commission Articles on Responsibility of States for Internationally Wrongful Acts 2001.

[37] J Crawford, *The International Law Commission's Articles on State Responsibility. Introduction, Text and Commentaries* (Cambridge: CUP, 2002) 100.

Of particular importance will be not just the content of the powers, but the way they are conferred on an entity, the purposes for which they are to be exercised and the extent to which the entity is accountable to government for their exercise. These are essentially questions of the application of a general standard to varied circumstances.[38]

In other words private authorities acting under national law may be required to conform with international standards when they are exercising 'public' functions. This is seen in international human rights law which continues to require compliance with what international law perceives as public functions even when the State has privatized those functions. Thus the European Court of Human Rights has held the UK liable for violations of the European Convention on Human Rights by private schools.[39] Nor can the State escape responsibility by allowing private individuals unfettered power and control over children.[40] The doctrine of due diligence asserts international regulation of private authority (including private military units[41]) that is exercised through the medium of the State in a form of dualism. The determination of whether the standard of due diligence has been attained is measured by reference to national laws with international law setting the standard against which national law is to be assessed. The concept is intended to ensure that the State retains at least notional control over the private authority but this may overstate the de facto strength of State authority and control.

Privatization has not only undercut the 'frontiers of the state' at the national level but also at the level of international governmental organizations.[42] David Kennedy has rightly noted that 'Governance has become a matter for private actors, non-governmental institutions, a matter of communication and legitimacy rather than acts of state'.[43] Again there are many examples. The Secretary-General's Global Compact initiative is a form of privatization of the UN. The UN Security Council has turned to NATO for enforcement action,[44] but NATO itself has become 'corporatized'.[45] Much of the humanitarian work of the UN High Commissioner for Refugees and the Department of Humanitarian Affairs is subcontracted to NGOs, making such ostensibly private bodies an integral and indispensable part of the UN framework. In describing what she terms a 'powershift' to private authority within the international public arena, Jessica Matthews notes that

---

[38] Ibid, 101.

[39] *Costello-Roberts v United Kingdom* (1993) 19 EHRR 112 (UK in violation of Art 3 through the use of corporal punishment within a private school).

[40] *A v United Kingdom* (100/1997/884/1096) 23 September 1998 (UK in violation of Art 3 through its failure to protect a child against beating by his stepfather).

[41] *Velasquez Rodriquez v Honduras* (1989) 28 ILM 291.

[42] P Sands, 'Turtles and Torturers: the Transformation of International Law' (2001) 33 NYUJ IL Pol 527, 541.

[43] D Kennedy, 'Introduction to an International Symposium on the International Legal Order' (2003) 16 Leiden JIL 839, 842.

[44] Eg SC Res. 1031, 15 December 1995, Part II authorizes the establishment of a multinational implementation force in cooperation with the 'organization referred to in Annex 1-A of the [Dayton] Peace Agreement', that is NATO.

[45] N Guyatt, *Another American Century The United States and the World since 9/11* (London: Zed Books, 2003) 132.

'Today NGOs deliver more official development assistance than the entire U.N. system (excluding the World Bank and the International Monetary Fund).'[46]

NGOs on the ground are 'sometimes in formal arrangement with the United Nations, but often simply assisting *ad hoc* in the distribution of aid and organization of relief efforts'.[47] This may create a dangerous gap between national and international law in that international law designates such persons as private while national legal systems fail to provide any protection. For example the Convention on the Safety of United Nations and Associated Personnel[48] is aimed at strengthening the legal protection afforded to UN and 'associated personnel' who participate in UN operations. It seeks to prevent attacks committed against such people and to punish those who commit them. However although 'United Nations operations are conducted in the common interest of the international community' (that is a public function), Article 1(b)(iii) defines 'associated personnel' narrowly as '[p]ersons deployed by a humanitarian non-governmental organization or agency under an agreement with the Secretary-General of the United Nations'. Despite the participation of non-State actors in public functions, the Convention deems them private citizens of their home State and does not accord them the same protection as is accorded to UN personnel, unless they have a contract with the UN. In this context functionalism gives way to formal legal status.

3.3 Relationships between public and private authority

Public and private authority may co-exist through complex partnerships with both states and international institutions. These may be 'partly adversarial, partly collaborative'.[49] Ignatieff gives as an example the Kimberly Process on the Certification of Rough Diamonds,[50] a process that joined public and private actors (the UN, States, and major corporations) in developing a Code of Conduct regulating the sale of 'conflict diamonds'. This is a form of international soft law that denotes internationally agreed regulatory measures in non-legally binding form that are dependant upon national systems of internal control.

NGOs now have a range of relationships with IGOs. The consultative status provided for by UN Charter, Article 71 has evolved into relationships variously described as 'honoured guests',[51] 'loose creative coalitions'[52] and, increasingly

---

[46] J Matthews, 'Powershift' (1997) 76 Foreign Affairs 50, 53.

[47] R Wedgewood, 'Legal Personality and the Role of Non-Governmental Organisations and Non-State Political Entities in the United Nations System' in R Hofmann (ed), *Non-State Actors as New Subjects of International Law* (Berlin: Duncker and Humblot, 1999) 23.

[48] GA Res. 49/59, 49 UN GAOR Supp (No 49) at 299, UN Doc. A/49/49 (1994).

[49] M Ignatieff, 'New Frontiers in Partnerships. An Interview' in S Stern and E Seligmann (eds), *The Partnership Principle New Forms of Governance in the 21st Century* (London: Archetype, 2004) 48, 52.

[50] Ibid, 52–53.

[51] E Reddy, UN Special Committee against Apartheid, cited in W Korey, *NGOs and the Universal Declaration of Human Rights* (New York: St Martin's Press, 1998) 95.

[52] K Annan, *We the Peoples: The Role of the United Nations in the 21st Century* (Millennium Report of the Secretary-General of the United Nations) para 336.

towards the end of the 20th century, as 'partnership' at the operational and conceptual levels. The UN Secretary-General has noted that '[p]artnerships with the private sector and foundations have also become extremely important to our recent successes'.[53] The legal implications of partnership between IGOs and private authorities are rarely fully explained. The relationship suggests equality, shared power and legal accountability, and common long-term goals and objectives. However little attention appears to have been given to questions of whose accountability and to whom that accountability might be owed. Can a private entity imbue itself with public authority through partnership with an IGO? Can it claim the latter's institutional immunity or standing in international arenas, or does the public body become private? Are the activities of the partnership to be judged by national or international law, or a combination of both?

Relationships between distinct forms of private authority may be confrontational, adversarial, or cooperative. Alliances may be formed between private authority and the state that are challenged by other groupings of public and private authority. Michael Ignatieff gives the example of collusion between a coercive state (Myanmar) and corporation (UNOCAL) to build an oil pipeline in the state and which led to widespread human rights abuses. The project 'blew up in its face' because of '[s]hareholder activism, NGO activism, the modern alliance between the NGOs and the press'.[54] This alliance sought 'to internationalize citizenship, to internationalize scrutiny, to make sure that corporations that are tightly bound by regulations in their domestic environment should constrain their behavior internationally'.

3.4 Arenas for the determination of public and private authority

Designation of an entity as a public or private authority may depend upon whether the determination is made in an international or a national institution. Strategic choices as to the preferred arena lead to the development of diverse normative systems and further blurring of the boundaries between national and international law.

An initial consideration is that the legal culture of the decision-making body[55] may influence whether an entity is designated as a private or public authority. Some courts—national and international—may be open to argument from other bodies while others operate as closed systems.[56] ICJ President Judge Higgins has described how some national 'judges are simply contemptuous of everything to do with international law, which they doggedly regard as unreal. Others are greatly impressed by international law, but feeling insufficiently unfamiliar with it seek at all costs to avoid making determinations upon it.'[57] Either mindset inhibits

---

[53] Ibid, para 334.   [54] M Ignatieff (n 49 above) 52.

[55] R Higgins, *Problems and Process. International Law and How We Use It* (Oxford: Clarendon Press, 1994) 206.

[56] Eg the rejection by Justice Scalia of the use of foreign law (including international human rights law) in the US Supreme Court; *Roper v Simmons*, March 1, 2005 543 US 551.

[57] R Higgins (n 55 above) 207.

developing coherent distinctions between issues of national and international law. An example was the effective conversion of a creature of international law, an intergovernmental organization, the Arab Monetary Fund, into one of national law.[58] The House of Lords held that the Statutory Instrument that allows an international organization to function under UK law in fact created the organization, a fictional device allowing the Court to avoid the legal consequences of its unwillingness to give effect to a constitutive treaty that had not been incorporated into English law. Judge Higgins continues: 'In what seems to an international lawyer as a further departure from reality, the House of Lords then determined that this international organization was actually a foreign bank [ie private authority] incorporated under the law of Abu Dhabi.'[59]

In contrast the ICJ was cautious about departing from reality when faced with a national law based private authority. In *Barcelona Traction* the Court stated:

If the Court were to decide the case in disregard of the relevant institutions of municipal law it would, without justification, invite serious difficulties. It would lose touch with reality, for there are no corresponding institutions of international law to which the Court could resort. Thus the Court has, as indicated, not only to take cognizance of municipal law but also to refer to it.[60]

Where international law doctrines depend upon national application differing perceptions of public and private function may come into play. For example, an individual's entitlement to immunity from the jurisdiction of local courts depends upon the national designation of that person as possessing sovereign or diplomatic status under international law. It may be successfully argued in a national court that a foreign public authority has lost that status through the performance of certain acts, such as commercial activities under the restrictive view of foreign State immunity, and must in consequence be treated as a private entity. Such a functional shift may also occur in criminal proceedings: General Noriega's status as head of State of Panama was disregarded when he was tried for drug-related offences under US national law.[61] In determining whether General Pinochet could be extradited to Spain, the UK House of Lords used the definition of an international crime (torture) that had been incorporated into UK law by statute.[62] It was argued before the House of Lords that a public official (the former head of State of Chile) acts in a private capacity when he instigates acts of torture, for torture cannot be a public official function.[63] The cloak of public authority was denied by function,

[58] *Arab Monetary Fund v Hashim (No 3)* [1991] 1 All ER 871.   [59] R Higgins (n 55 above) 207.

[60] *Barcelona Traction Light and Power Company Limited (Belgium v Spain)* (second phase) 1970 ICJ Rep, para 50.

[61] *US v Noriega* 746 F. Supp. 1506 (S D Fla 1990); *US v Noriega* 117 F. 3rd 1206 (11 Cir. 1997).

[62] International Convention Against Torture and other Cruel, Inhuman or Degrading Treatment or Punishment 1984, Art 1 incorporated by the Criminal Justice Act 1988, s 134.

[63] 'I believe there to be strong ground for saying that the implementation of torture as defined by the Torture Convention cannot be a state function.' *R v Bartle and the Commissioner of Police for the Metropolis and others Ex Parte Pinochet (No 3)* [1999] 2 WLR 827, para 18 (Lord Browne-Wilkinson).

despite the international human rights definition of torture that requires the instigation or acquiescence of a public official.[64]

International law is somewhat equivocal. On the one hand the ICJ has not allowed a person's formal status to be changed through allegations of his involvement in improper functions;[65] on the other hand international criminal law has removed any distinction between public and private authority with respect to jurisdiction over charges relating to war crimes, crimes against humanity, and genocide.[66]

NGOs pursue different strategies with respect to the use of national and international courts and law. They may seek recourse to international law as a universalizing phenomenon, perceiving it as transcending national laws and as an instrument through which universal standards, accountability, and implementation can be imposed upon other actors. One strategy has been to bring cases before national courts based upon international human rights standards as the 'law of nations'.[67] This is especially associated with civil litigation in the US under the Alien Tort Claims Act, 1789. Such litigation seeks to redress the unavailability and weaknesses of international fora. It also makes private bodies accountable under international law, as affirmed by the US Court of Appeal in *Kadic v Karadzic*.[68] The Court asserted that '[t]he Executive Branch has emphatically restated in this litigation its position that private persons may be found liable under the Alien Tort Act for acts of genocide, war crimes, and other violations of international humanitarian law'.

In addition to litigation in national courts based upon national standards, NGOs have sought to increase the availability of international fora through campaigns for ad hoc criminal tribunals,[69] for a permanent International Criminal Court[70] and for improved procedures under the UN human rights treaties.[71] Regulatory regimes where NGOs played an active negotiatory role typically have provisions that go further than treaties where their role was more limited, in the attempt to subject both public authorities and other forms of private authority to international law, and to enhance their own standing.[72] Through advocacy, for example in test cases,

---

[64] Convention against Torture and Other Cruel, Inhuman and Degrading Treatment, 10 December 1984, Art 1(1).

[65] *Arrest Warrant of 11 April 2000 (Democratic Republic of the Congo v Belgium)* 2002 ICJ Reports (issue and international circulation by Belgium of an arrest warrant against the Minister for Foreign Affairs of the Congo for alleged crimes against humanity violated his immunity under international law).

[66] Eg Rome Statute on the International Criminal Court 1998, Art 27; Convention on the Prevention and Punishment of the Crime of Genocide 1948, Art 4.

[67] 'The so often referred to differences between international law and national law are on the institutional, not on the legal, plane.' M Rotter, 'The International Legal Order' (2003) 16 Leiden JIL 844.

[68] 70 F.3d 232, 236 (2d Cir. 1995).

[69] The International Criminal Tribunals for Former Yugoslavia and Rwanda established by SC Res. 827, 25 May 1993 (ICTY); SC Res. 955, 8 November 1994 (ICTR).

[70] Rome Statute of the International Criminal Court 1998.

[71] Optional Protocol to the Convention on the Elimination of All Forms of Discrimination against Women, 10 December 1999.

[72] Eg the Convention for the Protection of the Marine Environment of the North-East Atlantic (Ospar Convention) 1992 Art 9 provides that the competent authorities of the States parties 'are

international law arguments are presented by NGO representatives for acceptance into national law regardless of constitutional requirements and may find favour from judges, even within a formally dualist system.[73] However such a monist approach ignores the democratic deficit of international law, which a dualist insistence upon formal incorporation seeks to protect against. Instead such NGO actions are seen (by themselves) as 'morally legitimate, in that international law provides for morally desirable standards of protection for human rights which are morally preferable to those in force under municipal law'.[74]

Other forms of private authority—trans-national corporations—seek the location that best supports their objectives, in this case enhancing profits. The trans-national operation of multinational corporations in a globalized world is not a natural phenomenon but rather a deliberate choice aimed at extending profits. Protection of corporate interests may be demanded under local law with scant regard for the inappropriateness of coercive means, or the international human rights obligations of the State. Trans-national corporations seek deregulation, freedom of action, freedom from State intervention and control in carrying out their operations and thus to insulate themselves from both international and national regulation so as to operate freely in a grey space where there is a regulatory vacuum. Nevertheless, they also seek legal protection against threats to their markets and profitability for 'globalization requires a framework of legal certainty for non-state economic actors in their international transactions and a minimum amount of effective regulation on both the international and national level'.[75] Far from seeking a clear demarcation between the competencies of international and national law they seek a space where neither is applicable—except on their own terms.

Where some form of regulation becomes politically inevitable, the preference may be for self-regulation with a blurring of legal forms (for example through the use of international soft law) and discretion as to the incidence and modalities of implementation. But this does not mean that such entities are indifferent to the international legal framework, in that they may also seek to have input into law-making to ensure it satisfies their demands. National law imbued with international law is sought both for control of private authorities and to liberate them. Where the objectives of such non-State actors are contrary to those of other non-State actors, for example NGOs, a site of contestation is set up through the struggle for dominant influence in international law-making and enforcement. In such efforts the

---

required to make available the information described in paragraph 2 of this Article to any natural or legal person'; the UN Convention on the Rights of the Child 1989, Art 45(a) and (b) provides procedural rights for 'other competent bodies' that are not contained in other UN human rights treaties.

[73] Eg *Unity Dow v A-G of Botswana* [1991] LRC (Const.) 575; [1992] LRC (Const.) 627. NGO input into and support for this test case is acknowledged in U Dow, *The Citizenship Case. A-G of Botswana v Unity Dow* (Gaborone: Lentswe La Lesedi (Pty) Ltd 1995).

[74] D Feldman, 'Monism, Dualism and Constitutional Legitimacy' (1999) 20 Aust YBIL 111.

[75] P Malanczuk, 'Discussion' in R Hofmann (ed), *Non-State Actors as New Subjects of International Law* (Berlin: Duncker and Humblot, 1999) 155.

State becomes cast not so much as an initiator or law-maker but rather as the mediator between these different forms of private authority.

Other forms of private authority that also reject intrusion and seek to remain under a double of shield of immunity from both international and national regulation are the family and religious and traditional forms of social ordering. Culture cuts across both national law (for example where custom is ring-fenced from national constitutional guarantees) and international law (for example where reservations to human rights treaties are used to prevent international supervision). It might be thought that the activities of such private bodies are minor, localized, and of little international concern. However they can encompass serious violations of human rights such as deliberate killings and legal proceedings that lack due process. *Salish* (religious) courts may take the law into their own hands, ousting both national and international law. An example is given by Amnesty International of a *Salish* court in Kaligani, which condemned a 16-year-old girl accused of having an affair with a Hindu boy to receiving 101 lashes. After the public beating, the girl died, allegedly a suicide. Amnesty International has argued that *Salish* courts are usually imposed upon local communities by people who are open to bribery and influence through the local clergy or landlords.

Community elders may also impose harsh punishments. In the case of Mukhtaran Bibi a *panchayat* (tribal council of local elders) in Pakistan ordered the rape of a young woman in response to allegations that her brother had had an affair with a higher-caste woman.[76] Ms Bibi took her case to the national courts. After an initial verdict in her favour, the decision was over-turned by a high court judge who ordered the release of the majority of the rapists only to have the original verdict reinstated by Pakistan's highest Islamic court.[77] In such scenarios the relationship between national and international law has a subordinate role to that between the forms and processes of local justice and State law.

3.5 Pluralism and the monist-dualist dichotomy

It is evident that concepts of the public and private are complex and shifting. There is no definitive determinant of public or private authority. Decisions reflect cultural and political preferences with respect to the level and quality of government intrusion. The relationship of systems of private ordering with public authority varies and different strategies are pursued according to preferences for international or national regulation and (non)intervention.

The examples of religious and traditional bodies exercising judicial authority show that private authority is not only about the exercise of power but also about the construction of normative systems. Twining argues that any 'healthy' picture

---

[76] D Walsh, 'She was Gang-raped on the Orders of Village Elders. Yesterday, Mukhtaran Bibi's Nightmare Began Again', The Guardian, 4 March 2005 available at <http://www.guardian.co.uk/international/story/0,,1430203,00.html>.   [77] The Guardian, 12 March 2005.

of the operation of legal systems must include those 'semi-autonomous social fields'—trans-national and local orderings[78]—that create normative legal orders outside the parameters of State law. The terms 'semi-autonomous social fields' captures their imprecision and porosity but 'even this is too simple for autonomy, precision (of boundaries), interdependence and even identity are all matters of degree'.[79] Such non-State orders interact *inter se*, with state legal systems and with international law and, as has been seen, sometimes with disregard for both.

Such a pluralist account of law makes redundant the monism/dualism approach to the relationship between national and international law for neither national nor international law can be seen as a single, narrowly defined system applicable within defined arenas. Paulus too has expressed the hope that 'legal recognition of the openness and pluralism of the contemporary world' will allow us to 'transcend the eternal debate between monism and dualism'.[80] Instead of seeking the boundaries of national and international law we need to examine how both operate to regulate public and private authorities. Gunther has explained that 'when there are many different public and private legislators or different kinds of private and public actors participating in different legislations in different areas and on different local, *infra*, inter—or supranational levels, then a *uniform concept of law* can no longer be maintained. Instead of it, legal theory has to deal with many different normative systems'.[81]

The diverse forms of private authority and the ensuing multiplicity of normative systems impact upon the way that we think about national and international law. The issues arise in different contexts and raise numerous questions: what is the most effective regime for the regulation and control of private authority? How can trans-national private authorities be made accountable and to whom? How can trans-national private authorities best avoid such regulation and control? What arenas are available? National or international? What doctrines of international law address these questions?

4. Responsibility of private authority under international law

4.1 Introduction

This section considers some examples of the regulation of different forms of private authority that operate at the boundaries of international and national law. It examines the responses of some national and international tribunals to the claims presented. The diversity of forms and activities of private authority, as considered above, means that these are illustrative only and do not purport to offer any

---

[78] W Twining (n 25 above) 88.   [79] Ibid, 85.   [80] See ch 9 of this volume, 2.

[81] K Gunther, 'Legal Pluralism and the Universal Code of Legality: Globalisation as a Problem of Legal Theory' available at <http://www.law.nyu.edu/clppt/program2003/readings/gunther.pdf>, (accessed 19 March 2007).

definitive account of the ways in which responsibility is allocated under international and national law.

The ILC, Articles on Responsibility of States for Internationally Wrongful Acts assume that it is the state that bears responsibility for an internationally wrongful act, and indeed Article 32 reiterates that '[t]he responsible State may not rely on the provisions of its internal law as justification for failure to comply with its obligations under this Part'. However the Articles also recognize that other entities, including private authorities, may bear international responsibility. Article 33(2) states that '[t]his Part is without prejudice to any right, arising from the international responsibility of a State, which may accrue directly to any person or entity other than a State'.

The section above discussed the choices *private* authorities make in selecting national or international institutions for raising their claims. Imposing international legal responsibility on non-State actors raises the questions of arena and choice of law from the perspectives of national and international *public* authority. Which better promote international community objectives: national or international institutions and law? On the one hand there is the lure of asserting universal jurisdiction over private authorities within national courts,[82] thereby escaping restrictive rules of territorial and personal jurisdiction and harnessing the application of international law in cases of exceptional gravity to the stronger, better organized and more effective enforcement mechanisms of domestic law. On the other hand, national courts may differ in their interpretation and application of international law or may be unwilling to accept responsibility for the enforcement of international legal standards. Certainly in the final years of the 20th century the establishment of international courts and tribunals was seen as an advance for international accountability in place of national impunity. The assertion of international jurisdiction over some forms of private authorities, such as militia members, has developed and strengthened international norms.

However the story has not been entirely positive. The assertion of international jurisdiction over private authority is not consistent and some forms, for example corporate persons, are exempt from the jurisdiction of the ICC,[83] over-turning at least the spirit of Nuremberg.[84] The principle of complementarity that is at the core of the ICC's jurisdiction[85] means that it has no priority over national courts. International, like domestic jurisdiction, can be manipulated to give effect to particular policies and demands. There is a danger that international criminal litigation may appear as a strategy towards universalizing a western-based international criminal law against individuals in non-western States, intended to impose further control upon those States (and those asserting power within them) in the name of

---

[82] Eg The Princeton Principles on Universal Jurisdiction (2001).

[83] Rome Statute of the International Criminal Court 1998, Art 25. Nor are economic crimes within the jurisdiction of the Court.

[84] *United States v Carl Krauch* (the IG Farben Case), *Trials of War Criminals before the Nuernberg Military Tribunals*, Vol VII and VIII Washington: US Government Printing Office, 1953.

[85] Rome Statute of the International Criminal Court, Articles 1 and 17.

international law, while legitimizing the actions of profit-seeking private authorities that continue their actions untouched by the apprehension of international adjudication.

4.2 Privatization of international public functions

The private corporate sector acquires public functions at the national level through privatization and the outsourcing of government functions and services. This is replicated at the international level, for example through the privatization of fundamental State obligations such as the maintenance of international peace and security and self-defence. Wedgewood has noted that private security forces appear to be a new feature on the international scene at a time when a juridical State may not command loyalty among conflicting groups and the limits of post-colonial State building have become evident.[86] It is not only unstable States that have recourse to private military companies. States that lack the resources or expertise to support the full array of military services, or seek to reduce expenditure, may also do so. In the UK it is government policy 'to outsource certain tasks that in earlier days would have been undertaken by the armed forces' as a 'cost-effective' means of obtaining military activity,[87] a trend that is likely to continue.[88]

Private military bodies may be asked to perform a range of tasks (including training and logistic support) and to serve in different capacities. One such function sought by a beleaguered government is self-defence against rebel groups in internal conflict. A State may consider that it can only achieve some form of internal stability through privatization of national security. For example in 1995, the Sierra Leone government used Executive Outcomes (EO), a South Africa-based private security company, to help end the civil war in the country.[89] EO played an active role in securing peace and stability until it was replaced by a public body—a sponsored coalition of West African troops (ECOMOG) under which war again broke out in 2000.

The priority for a privatized security company, as with any corporate concern, remains the enhancement of profit and its primary obligation must be to its shareholders. Despite the tension between private profit and public function recourse to private security does not necessarily cost a State more: the private EO operation in Sierra Leone is estimated to have cost about 4 per cent of the UN's intervention.[90]

---

[86] R Wedgewood (n 47 above) 28.

[87] *Private Military Companies: Options for Regulation* (2001–02) (House of Commons, 577), Foreword by the Secretary of State for Foreign and Commonwealth Affairs.   [88] Ibid, para 30.

[89] Executive Outcomes was also active in the Angola civil wars and is credited with securing victory for the Government, ibid, Box 1.

[90] S Fidler and T Catn, 'Colombia: Private Companies on the Frontline', Financial Times, 12 August 2003, available at <http://www.corpwatch.org/article.php?id=8028> (accessed 12 March 2005). Analysts 'have pointed out that [EO assistance] was a lower cost for a 21-month operation than the $47 million budget for a UN observer force for eight months'. *Private Military Companies: Options for Regulation* (2001–2) (House of Commons, 577) Box 2.

Nor can it be assumed that private action is more likely to lead to violations of international law, including human rights. A House of Commons consultative paper concluded: 'It is widely acknowledged that in Sierra Leone the national army was undisciplined, violent and a threat to the civilian population. The same has been said of a few in the Nigerian forces operating under ECOMOG. Nobody has suggested anything like this in Executive Outcomes' record.'[91]

In Sierra Leone the state contracted out its obligation to its citizens to maintain internal security. In other situations private contractors may enter a state at the behest of other states, through an international engagement they have undertaken, including unilateral military action and its aftermath, such as in Iraq. The use of private contractors rather than public military personnel has benefits for the service providers. States may undertake international commitments they are too stretched to fulfil, or international interventions which they wish to conceal from domestic and international scrutiny. In either case recourse to private contractors allows states to conceal their true level of involvement in military operations and allows deaths to go unnoticed. In the US there are concerns that:

private contractors are being used for military operations that are either too controversial to sell to the public or that would otherwise be subject to congressional restrictions. 'It's obviously a way to avoid scrutiny,' says Adam Isacson, of the Centre for International Policy, of the use of contractors in Colombia. 'If US military personnel were doing these jobs, US congressional committees would be asking a lot more questions about what they're doing.'[92]

4.3 National or international legal regulation?

The use of private bodies for the performance of the core international legal obligation, the maintenance of international peace and security, cuts across distinctions between international and national law. The state remains formally responsible under international law for fulfillment of its international legal obligations, including compliance with Security Council resolutions that have been adopted for the public good, and with international humanitarian law. On the one hand fragmentation of the state through allocation of public functions to private bodies undermines the State's ability to comply with these obligations. For example in 1997, the delivery of weapons to Sierra Leone by a British company, Sandline International, in apparent contravention of a UN arms embargo caused the UK government political discomfiture.[93] On the other hand privatization of state security functions 'challenges international law's traditional strictures against mercenaries' and 'private forces lack direct responsibility of a Government under the Geneva system of humanitarian law'.[94]

---

[91] *Private Military Companies: Options for Regulation* (2001–2) (House of Commons 577), para 55.
[92] S Fidler and T Catn (n 91 above).   [93] Ibid.   [94] R Wedgewood (n 47 above) 28.

Is a private body responsible under international law and what is the State's responsibility to ensure the application of international standards? What is the situation where the State lacks the capacity to assert control over private authorities? As is the case with seeking protection for private actors when engaged in public functions, the central problem is not so much the relationship between national and international law but the potential gap between the two legal systems creating a regulatory vacuum. Does (can) the international community step into the vacuum between the rule of law and public order that has been created through privatization and deregulation?[95]

The same issue—seeking effective legal regulation under either international or national law—also arises in the contexts of international administration and peacekeeping. When the Security Council uses its powers under UN Charter, chapter VII to establish an international administration (such as in Kosovo and East Timor) member States incur international obligations to act in conformity. Increasingly (and not least because of the larger number of such instances since the end of the Cold War) law and order and administrative tasks are sub-contracted to private actors. Even when international personnel are drawn from national military or civilian police forces, there is the problem of varying local standards and national regulations.[96] The problem of maintaining common international standards of behaviour is exacerbated when recruitment to international missions is sub-contracted to private agencies. For example, Dyncorp, widely used by the US as a source of personnel, advertises employment in international administrations in Iraq, Afghanistan, Timor Leste, and Liberia. Its website advertises: 'DynCorp International FZ-LLC (DIFZ) seeks law enforcement personnel to participate in an U.S. Department of State sponsored international effort to re-establish police and justice functions in post-conflict Iraq.'[97]

The lack of both a common international standard of qualification for such posts and any regulating code of conduct for those engaging in international administration, may work to the detriment of relations with local populations and has the potential to create a bad public image for the internationals. This may reverberate on the UN where no distinction is made between UN peacekeepers and other personnel. Private civilian personnel may be accorded immunity from local courts as though they were members of the military but unlike the latter are not subject to the jurisdiction of military courts of their own State. Most extensively, in Iraq the Coalition Provisional Authority renewed on 27 June 2004 (the day before the 'handover' to the Iraqi Interim Government) its Order 17 (made in

[95] D Thurer, 'The Emergence of Non-Governmental Organizations and Trans-national Enterprises in International Law and the Changing Role of the State' in R Hofmann (ed), *Non-State Actors as New Subjects of International Law* (Berlin: Duncker and Humblot, 1999) 37, 41.

[96] The UN has jurisdiction over its own civilian staff but not over military forces from member States acting on UN authorized missions. Its only recourse against military members who abuse their position is to seek their repatriation and legal proceedings against them in their own State.

[97] <http://www.lawenforcementjobs.com> (accessed 12 March 2005).

June 2003) making contractors (along with official personnel and international consultants) immune from the Iraqi legal process 'in matters relating to the terms and conditions of their contracts' and 'with respect to acts performed by them pursuant to the terms and conditions of a Contract or any sub-contract thereto'.[98] Private contractors can hide behind immunity for their actions but have the potential to disrupt relations between the State subject to international administration and the internationals. In March 2004 the killing and mutilation of the bodies of four American contractors in Fallujah led to the US Marines moving into the city and subsequent heavy casualties there.

Legal accountability for the actions of those privately contracted may rest upon the chance of the place of recruitment. The case of Kathryn Bolkovac illustrates the potential for a regulatory vacuum with respect to private authorities undertaking public tasks under international law. Kathryn Bolkovac, an American, was employed by DynCorp as a member of the international peacekeeping task force in Bosnia-Herzegovina. She informed her employers that other UN personnel were involved in trafficking and prostitution of young girls in Bosnia-Herzegovina. She was demoted and subsequently sacked. Issues of employment in UN peacekeeping missions were then raised in an action for unfair dismissal before a UK industrial tribunal (because UK employment law was the governing legal regime).[99] Ms Bolkovac succeeded in her action and DynCorp dropped its appeal. However those she accused of abusing their positions were moved to other posts and none faced disciplinary action. Continuing allegations of sexual abuse of women and children by members of UN missions show that the problem of accountability has not been resolved with respect to public officials,[100] and still less where public responsibilities have been contracted out.

Sometimes parties to litigation will have expressed clear preferences as to whether they want disputes determined in national courts or in an international arbitral tribunal and seem to have plugged the gap between international and national law by explicit contractual arrangement between the state and private authority. However when a dispute arises, the parties, or at least one party, may renege on its agreement to have recourse to a named forum and seek advantage through recourse to an alternative forum. The outcome is affected by the relationship between international and national law as understood by the particular tribunal in which the claim is adjudicated and there is no guarantee of consistency between different tribunals, as the following examples illustrate.

[98] Coalition Provisional Authority Order Number 17 (Revised) Status of the Coalition Provisional Authority, MNF-Iraq, Certain Missions and Personnel in Iraq, section 4, available at <http://www.iraqcoalition.org/regulations/20040627_CPAORD_17_Status_of_Coalition__Rev__with_Annex_A.pdf>.

[99] *Bolkovac v Dyncorp (2002) Dyncorp Last Minute U-turn In Whistleblowing Case*, Monday, 5 May 2003, Press Release, available at <http://www.scoop.co.nz/mason/stories/WO0305/S00022.htm> (accessed 19 March 2007).

[100] Prince Zeid Ra'ad Zeid Al-Hussein, *Comprehensive Review on a Strategy to Eliminate Future Sexual Exploitation and Abuse in United Nations Peacekeeping Operations*, UN Doc A/59/710 24 March 2005.

The arbitration between Sandline International and Papua New Guinea (PNG) arose out of an agreement between the PNG government and Sandline, for the latter to provide assistance to government forces in its conflict with separatists in Bougainville.[101] The agreement set out that Sandline would act 'in accord with international doctrines and in conformance with the Geneva Convention'. It also stipulated that the 'agreement shall be construed and governed in accordance with the Laws of England'. Subsequently PNG claimed the contract to be in conflict with its Constitution and void. Sandline invoked the arbitration clause. The arbitrators (Sir Edward Somers, the Right Honourable Sir Michael Kerr, and the Honourable Sir Daryl Dawson), none of whom were primarily international lawyers, held that PNG was bound to pay the amount owed to Sandline.[102] The arbitrators considered the Tribunal to be international and as such bound to apply international law, which formed part of English law (the proper law of the contract). They also held that an agreement between a State and a private authority is an international contract, not an instrument of domestic law, which means that 'one enters the realm of public international law and public policy wears a different aspect'.[103]

PNG sought leave to appeal to the Supreme Court of Queensland on the grounds, inter alia, that the arbitrators' decision amounted to an error of law in that the arbitrators had applied international law as part of the law of England and had misstated the relationship between English law and international law. In that Court, Justice Ambrose held that the Commercial Arbitration Act (Queensland) 'does not give the court jurisdiction to entertain an appeal against an award when the only error of law complained of is an error of foreign law; upon its proper construction, the term 'error of law' in section 38 refers only to an error of Queensland or Australian law.'[104]

The arbitration panel's approach revealed elements of dualism in its emphasis on the separate spheres of international and domestic law and holding that a private body enters the international sphere when it contracts with a State authority. However this dualism is blurred by the monist assertion that international law is part of English law, the law chosen by the parties to govern their contract.[105] Justice Ambrose too took a dualist, even pluralist, view in his assertion that international

---

[101] Agreement for the Provision of Military Assistance dated this 31st day of January 1997 between the Independent State of Papua New Guinea and Sandline International.

[102] *In the Matter of an International Arbitration under the UNCITRAL Rules between Sandline International Inc and the Independent State of Papua New Guinea*, 9 October 1998, 117 International Law Reports 552.   [103] Ibid, 560.

[104] *In the Matter of the Commercial Arbitration Act 1990 and In the Matter of an Application pursuant to section 38 thereof by the Independent State of PNG against Sandline International Inc.*, 30 March 1999, 117 International Law Reports 565; D Sturzaker and C Cawood, 'The Sandline Affair: Illegality and International Law' (2000) 3 International Arbitration Law Review 164.

[105] In his definition of dualism Gaja notes that within the separate and self-contained systems of municipal and international law the only existing rules are those that are part of the relevant system. However '[r]ules which are not created within the system may nevertheless be relevant for the system if they are referred to by a rule included in the system'. C Gaja, ch 2 of this volume, 2.

law differs according to the system of domestic law. Courts in different countries might construe rules of international law differently and in particular English courts would give effect to rules of English law in ways compatible with English statutory law. The arbitrators evidently sought to give effect to the contract and called upon international law principles to do so (for example the principle that internal law cannot be raised as a defence to violation of international law[106]), but were also required by its terms to apply English law. They reconciled these needs through drawing upon international and national law as each best served their objective and by collapsing boundaries between them.

A similar starting point of seeing legal instruments as appertaining to either national or international law is found in arbitrations arising out foreign investment. The private investor typically seeks the protection of international standards and rejects the national legal standards and institutions which are preferred by the home State. A clash between the two systems of law (and institutions) arises where there are separate legal documents: a BIT (an instrument of international law) between the host State and the State of the investor's nationality and a contract (an instrument of national law) between the immediate parties to the investment.

Complex issues of overlap between the two distinct bases for the parties' rights arise that are further confused by the different principles of interpretation that apply to these distinct legal instruments. For example in *Société Générale de Surveillance S.A. (SGS) v Islamic Republic of Pakistan*[107] the parties' contract provided for 'preshipment inspection' (PSI) services with respect to goods exported to Pakistan. When a dispute arose as to the adequacy of each other's performance, SGS requested arbitration under the International Centre for the Settlement of Investment Disputes (ICSID) pursuant to the BIT between Pakistan and Switzerland,[108] while Pakistan claimed that the contractual provision referring '[a]ny dispute, controversy or claim arising out of, or relating to' the PSI Agreement to arbitration in accordance with the Arbitration Act of Pakistan should prevail. Thus Pakistan presented the claims as entirely contractual, while SGS presented them as violations of international law through breach of the BIT, that is that breaches of contract were 'elevated' to breach of treaty through the operation of what is termed an 'umbrella clause'.[109] The Tribunal held that it had jurisdiction to determine SGS's allegations of violation of the BIT but no jurisdiction to determine any contractual claims which did not include any element of violation of the BIT. The Tribunal did not accord Pakistan's request to stay the BIT proceedings pending an outcome to the proceedings under the contractual agreement (national arbitration within Pakistan). The

---

[106] Vienna Convention on the Law of Treaties 1969, Art 27; International Law Commission, Articles on Responsibility of States for Internationally Wrongful Acts 2001, Art 32.

[107] Case No ARB/01/13, Decision on Objections to Jurisdiction of 6 August 2003.

[108] SGS had first commenced litigation against Pakistan in the Swiss courts, its place of domicile.

[109] The argument is that an 'umbrella clause' which 'exhorts the contracting states to respect contractual commitments with qualified investors' converts claims arising out of the performance of the contract to treaty claims. Z Douglas, 'The Hybrid Foundations of Investment Treaty Arbitration' (2003) 74 BYBIL 151, 242.

decision upholds the co-existence of rights and obligations under national law and international law arising out of the same legal transaction. The consequences of the refusal to stay proceedings have been regretted:

By refusing to accede to this request [to stay proceedings], the ICSID Tribunal in effect conceded that it is sufficient for a claimant to plead that a contractual breach simultaneously amounts to a violation of the BIT for the purposes of invoking the jurisdiction of an investment treaty tribunal and proceeding to the merits. One can readily imagine the potential for mischief produced by this result.[110]

The result identifies a sphere of international law and one of national law and requires that the two be kept distinct within separate proceedings, except where there is overlap through the same action being defined as breach of both laws. It also accepted a contract between a private authority and a State to be an instrument of national law, unlike the arbitrators in *Sandline*. However in a subsequent arbitration *Société Générale de Surveillance S.A. (SGS) v Republic of the Philippines*,[111] arising out of similar activities, SGS again commenced international arbitration under the applicable BIT while the Philippines challenged the arbitral tribunal's assertion of jurisdiction as it sought proceedings in its national courts arising out of the contractual arrangements. This time the ICSID Tribunal determined that the legal classification of the dispute was not determinative of jurisdiction and that the term 'disputes with respect to investments between a Contracting Party and an investor of the other Contracting Party' encompassed contractual claims. The Tribunal therefore rejected the assumption made in the Pakistan case 'that contractual claims by their very [national law] nature were incapable of falling within this broad definition of the *ratione materiae* competence of a treaty [international] tribunal.'[112] However the Tribunal did not accept that SGS could pick and choose which contractual provisions it wished to apply (SGS simultaneously sought performance of the contract but to avoid the exclusive contractual dispute resolution clause). The Tribunal therefore concluded that while it had jurisdiction the case was not admissible.

The recognition of the hybrid nature of investment claims is another indication of the collapse of any clear-cut dichotomy between national and international law: States and private bodies in the conclusion and performance of complex commercial transactions make strategic decisions as to their use of the substantive and procedural tools offered by each. When the transaction breaks down the ensuing litigation draws arguments from each system. The *ad hoc* nature of arbitral tribunals militates against consistency and the mindset of different adjudicators (for example as international or as private, commercial lawyers) may also influence outcomes.

---

[110] Ibid, 266 (footnote omitted).
[111] Decision of the Tribunal on Objections to Jurisdiction, Case No ARB/02/6.
[112] Ibid, 285.

International arbitration also raises the legitimacy of privatized justice. Forms of so-called alternative dispute resolution (ADR) have become immensely popular in western legal systems where those who can afford to do so may choose to opt out of the public legal system in preference for their own forms of legal ordering, for example through arbitration or such processes as 'rent-a judge'.[113] Respect for party autonomy (and time and costs pressures on the public system) support the legitimacy of such processes despite the lack of public scrutiny they entail. As has been commented: 'In its pure form . . . private ordering carries with it the possibility of the strongest disputant imposing a settlement that seems grossly unfair when measured against some external standard of justice or that infringes the rights of third parties.'[114]

In international law where there is no general compulsory system of public adjudication and parties are (generally) sovereign States, the arguments for private ordering are stronger, especially when seen as an alternative to coercive methods of dispute resolution.[115] The institutionalization of international arbitration, for example through the Permanent Court of International Arbitration, ICSID, NAFTA, and arbitrations in accordance with the UNCITRAL Model Rules are all safeguards against unregulated forms of private justice. Forum shopping by States and private authorities provides a further instance of the fluid movement between national and international law, demonstrating 'the emergence of a *lex mercatoria* or a new 'third' category of law to transcend the usual distinction between international and national law'.[116]

4.4 Private authority mimicking public authority

Private authorities have used the forms of public judicial authority to appeal to international law where national law has appeared inadequate or there is no available access to it. Peoples' Tribunals offer a form of judicial accountability outside the formalities of either national or international law and are another arena where the boundaries between the two are blurred. By observing ritualistic and formal procedures (perhaps following those of a court[117]), the participants seek to associate a (private) Peoples' Tribunal with the formal indicia of public legitimacy in order to appeal to the authority of international law to condemn national or international public authorities. Peoples' Tribunals must be decried as anarchic and

---

[113] H Astor and C Chinkin, *Dispute Resolution in Australia* (Australia: Lexis-Nexis Butterworths, 2002) 23–4, 65–67.

[114] D Greatbatch and R Dingwall, 'Selective Facilitation: Some Observations on a Strategy Used by Divorce Mediators' (1989) 23 Law and Society Review 613.

[115] The origin of the creation of the Permanent Court of International Arbitration was as an alternative to recourse to war; Hague Convention for the Pacific Settlement of International Disputes, 1899, ch II.

[116] F Kratchowil, 'The "Legalization" of World Politics?' (2003) 16 Leiden JIL 878.

[117] Eg C Chinkin, 'The Women's International Tribunal on Japanese Military Sexual Slavery' (2001) 95 AJIL 335.

lacking any legitimacy by those who deny any parallel and complementary role to private authority but they may be welcomed by those who seek means of having recourse to alternative forms of authority against recalcitrant public authorities.

Projects based on international law norms pursued by private authorities may be seen as first creating and then promoting the internalization of international law norms by public authorities,[118] forcing those authorities to make those norms part of their internal map of decision-making and thus of national law. This process assumes a movement between the international and national in contrast to the assertions of the closed systems of dualist theory without relying on the formal incorporation required by monism. It also repeats the arguable premise that imbuing the national with the international constitutes progress.

4.5 Private authority hostile to the international order

Some forms of private authority are adverse to the goals of international order or aspire to an international order based on very different values and forms of organization from those encompassed within the UN Charter. The impact of such forms of private authority on the relationship between national and international law should also be briefly considered. The most obvious example are organized networks of non-State actors, operating in accordance with privately determined policies to use violence to spread terror among civilian populations, that is terrorists.[119] Trans-national terrorist activities, requiring trans-national responses, undermine distinctions between national law and international law as public authorities move back and fore between the two legal regimes in pursuing their response. Thus a 'war against terror' denotes the international legal regime of war, while detention under national laws that deny prisoner of war (or other international law) status to those suspected of terrorist acts implies the application of national criminal or military law. Through their actions such non-State actors determine the agendas and time-tables of the international system—an anti-democratic but potent way of blurring the jurisdiction of institutions of national and international law.

At one level, the response to terrorist actions comprise an almost comforting mix of international and national law-making, for example the rapid conclusion and ratification of multilateral conventions from the late 1960s onwards (on hijacking, hostage taking, protection of vulnerable facilities and personnel). These conventions provide international law definitions for national criminal offences and broad bases of national jurisdiction along with State obligations to adopt national criminal legislation for the prosecution or extradition of alleged offenders. The anti-terrorist conventions rely upon an inter-State paradigm making offenders objects of State power and regulation. Unlike for example the Geneva Conventions, 1949,

---

[118] H Koh (n 1 above) 2599.

[119] This description does not purport to provide an international law definition of 'terrorist' or 'terrorist acts', which is as yet lacking.

common Article 3, they do not purport to impose international legal obligations upon private actors who are both non-State and anti-State. This distinction does not totally stand up however: although terrorist acts as such are not subject to the jurisdiction of the ICC, they might well constitute crimes against humanity.

Domestic courts are drawing upon national and international law in the spate of litigation arising out of terrorism, counter-terrorism, and the use of force. For example, in the case of *Al-Skeini* the UK Court of Appeal considered whether the European Convention on Human Rights applies to the actions of British forces in Iraq.[120] The applicants are the families of Iraqi civilians who had died allegedly at the hands of British forces after the end of formal military activity in March and April 2003 and during the occupation of Iraq by the Coalition Provisional Authority (CPA). In no case were the victims treated as members of the Iraqi public authorities but apparently as suspected insurgents, associates of insurgents or else were just in the same vicinity as suspected insurgents. In accordance with the UK's traditional dualist position the European Convention on Human Rights did not form part of English law until its partial incorporation by the Human Rights Act 1998. UK courts are now bound to determine the conformity of the acts of public authorities with the Convention rights, taking into account the jurisprudence of the European Court of Human Rights.[121]

In an earlier case, *Bankovic v UK* the Grand Chamber of the European Court of Human Rights had asserted that in determining the jurisdiction of the Convention it must take into account 'any relevant rules of international law'.[122] Thus UK courts must consider not only the Convention and its relationship to the Human Rights Act but also other rules of international law made applicable through Strasbourg case law with respect to UK dealings with private individuals. UK judicial decisions are informed by a wide range of international treaty law, customary law, and soft law.[123] The formal dualist position is punctured by reference to the requirements and authorities of international law in determining the extent to which public authorities are bound to secure international guarantees to private individuals.

---

[120] *R (Al Skeini and others) v Secretary of State for Defence* [2005] EWCA Civ 1609; [2006] 3 WLR 508; the case is on appeal to the House of Lords.

[121] Human Rights Act 1998, Art 2(1)(a).

[122] *Bankovic v Belgium and 16 other Contracting States* (2001), 11 Butterworths Human Rights Cases 435, para 57 (judgment of 12 December 2001).

[123] In *R v Immigration Officer at Prague Airport ex parte European Roma Rights Centre and Others* [2004] UKHL 55; [2005] 2 WLR the House of Lords referred to an extraordinary range of international instruments and documents, including: UNHCR, *Handbook on Procedures and Criteria for Determining Refugee Status*, 1992; Declaration on Territorial Asylum, 1967; American Law Institute, *Restatement of the Foreign Relations Law of the United States (Third)*; Bangkok Principles, Asian-African Legal Consultative Committee, 1966; resolutions of the Committee of Ministers of the Council of Europe; reports from the UNHCR Executive Committee; reports of the International Law Association; UN Human Rights Committee, General Comment No 31, 29 March 2004; Study for the European Council on Refugees and Exiles, 1999; reports by the Inter-American Commission for Human Rights and UN Committee on the Elimination of Racial Discrimination.

5. Conclusions

International law is about boundaries, some visible, others invisible and all constructed to achieve particular goals:[124] for example territorial boundaries, boundaries between the public and the private, between the 'insiders' and 'outsiders' of international law,[125] and the vertical boundaries between international law and national law. Boundaries allow for inclusion but also exclusion: the exclusion of the private from international legal regulation; the exclusion of outsiders from its protections and the dualist exclusion of issues of international law from national legal systems. Boundaries provide clarity, precision, and autonomy while piercing or collapsing boundaries causes anxiety, confusion, and chaos. But boundaries also impose hierarchy and certainty where none exists.

There is little certainty about the definition, scope, and effect of private authority within the international legal system other than the collapse of a simple demarcation whereby private authority is regarded as appropriately subject to national regulation and public/State authority to international regulation. Taking account of private authority undermines determining the relationship between international and national law through the binaries of monism/dualism, domestic/international, public/private, intervention/non-intervention. The illustrative examples demonstrate that a more accurate picture is of 'a random intersecting of international law with the domestic legal order'.[126] This random intersecting does not rely upon boundaries but attempts to provide functional solutions, for example where there are regulatory grey spaces between international and national law (private authorities exercising public security functions), where there are parallel regulatory regimes (between BITs and contracts) and where there are overlapping regimes (also between BITs and contracts).

This picture supports Twining's view that doctrines of monism and dualism are used to impose an artificial order upon existing legal structures. He argues that the breakdown of the binary is to be welcomed and that: 'refutation of the monistic view may be one of the most powerful strategies for building up a case for maintaining that a global jurisprudence needs to depict the phenomena of law in the modern world as to a large extent disorderly, unsystematic and serendipitous'.[127]

This might cause anxiety and a desire to impose order and predictability. But is order necessarily the goal and why is it needed? Perhaps lack of order raises concerns in international lawyers about our discipline, for example that it lacks robustness and that issues of significance might slip from our grasp.[128] But the situation need not be seen only as chaotic. It might also be argued that the international legal

---

[124] H Charlesworth and C Chinkin, *The Boundaries of International Law: A Feminist Analysis* (Manchester: Manchester University Press, 2000).

[125] G Simpson, *Great Powers and Outlaw States* (Cambridge: CUP, 2004).

[126] R Higgins (n 55 above) 209. [127] W Twining (n 25 above) 62.

[128] D Kennedy (n 43 above) 839.

system is now supplementing national law and offering alternative solutions that were not previously realized. The impact of such alternatives may be limited but nevertheless they can be drawn upon when appropriate and over time may expand their potential. This for example might be the understanding of the principle of complementarity in the ICC—that understandings drawn from international criminal jurisprudence can be used to reform national criminal laws as well as it offering an additional arena for accountability. Indeed another reason for avoiding oppositional binaries is not just that they are misleading but because they suggest clashes between the two systems, confrontation and adversarial approaches rather than cooperation and coordination. In addressing private authorities reconciliation between international and national law should be sought rather than retreat behind an artificial binary distinction between them.

Litigation—and other strategies—pursued by private authorities cross and recross the borders between the national and the international and in so doing simultaneously fragment and reinforce the structures of both systems. What we now have is '[a] new mix of private and public international law'.[129] In this new mix 'public and private actors including nation states, international organizations, multinational enterprises, non-governmental organizations, and private individuals, interact in a variety of public and private, domestic and international to make, interpret, internalize and enforce rules of trans-national law'.[130] Nor of course can this mix be static for the picture—and the role of law—is constantly changing. As Kratchowil has put it: 'We had better understand that the role of law in a globalizing world is not a simple "move" from public to private ordering, from the old notion of "sovereignty" to that of "democracy" supported by the emergence of a "world civil society", in which "forum shopping" and litigation carried out by "professionals" determine the outcomes.'[131]

---

[129] S Hobe, 'Discussion' in R Hofmann (ed), *Non-State Actors as New Subjects of International Law* (Berlin: Duncker and Humblot, 1999) 167.   [130] H Koh (n 1 above) 2599, 2627.
[131] F Kratchowil, (n 116 above).

7

Shifting Boundaries: The Authority of International Law[1]

Mayo Moran

1. Introduction

For much of the modern age, the legal imagination in common law jurisdictions has been organized by its own distinctively spatial geography.[2] Like the map of the world that served as its inspiration, the territory of the law was imagined as carved into distinct areas or jurisdictions. Conflicts of laws may be the most obvious manifestation of this conceptual landscape but it is by no means alone. As Stephen Waddams has insightfully demonstrated, even private law is pervasively thought of as 'mapped' or divided into autonomous units.[3] This is reflected in the centrality of geographically-inspired language: the distinct areas of private law are, for instance,

---

[1] This article is part of a larger project with Karen Knop on the changing nature of legal judgment, sources of law and the role of justification that attends the declining significance of the traditional binding law model. My argument here has benefited in innumerable ways from her input. I am also deeply indebted to David Dyzenhaus. On the larger project see for instance, K Knop, 'Here and There: International Law in Domestic Courts' (2000) NYU JILPol 507; K Knop, 'Reflections on Thomas Franck, Race and Nationalism, (1960): 'General Principles of Law' and Situated Generality' (2003) 35 NYU JILPol 437; M Moran' 'An Uncivil Action: The Tort of Torture and Cosmopolitan Private Law' in C Scott (ed), *Torture as Tort* (Oxford: Hart Publishing, 2001); M Moran 'Authority Influence and Persuasion: *Baker*, Charter Values and the Puzzle of Method' in D Dyzenhaus (ed), *The Unity of Public Law* (Oxford: Hart Publishing, 2004) 15; M Moran, 'Time, Place and Value' in David Dyzenhaus and Mayo Moran (eds), *Calling Power to Account: Law, Reparations and the Chinese Canadian Head Tax Case* (Toronto: University of Toronto Press, 2005); M Moran, 'Influential Authority and the Estoppel-Like Effect of International Law' in H Charlesworth and G Williams (eds) *The Fluid State* (Anandale: Federation Press, 2005); M Moran 'Inimical to Constitutional Values: Complex Migrations of Constitutional Rights' in S Choudhry (ed), *The Migration of Constitutional Ideas* (Cambridge: CUP, 2006).

[2] The argument of this chapter specifically considers the authority of international law in common law jurisdictions which are relatively dualist with respect to their approach to international treaties. Such jurisdictions are of particular theoretical significance for the argument here because they are a sharp illustration of the traditional spatialized model of the legal authority and legal judgment. Though there may well also be implications for civilian jurisdictions that are more monistic in their approach to international law, such implications merit a much more detailed separate discussion that is unfortunately beyond the scope of this paper.

[3] S Waddams, *Concepts and Categories: Dimensions of Private Law* (Cambridge: CUP, 2003).

thought of as 'bodies'—distinct and mutually exclusive. The relation between these bodies of law, domestic or extra-territorial, is thus rendered as a series of boundary disputes and the idea of 'jurisdiction' assumes a place of prominence in adjudication. The resulting picture of the decision-maker's task is 'conflicts-like' in the primacy it places on selecting and then applying the appropriate rules.[4]

The apparent quaintness of this picture, however, should not distract us from its continuing salience in contemporary debates about adjudication. In line with its conflicts-like predisposition, the understanding of legitimacy that underpins the old spatial imagination of the law remains an important force. The core judicial task, for instance, is understood as selection from among contending sets of rules. So the central problematic in adjudication is understood as revolving around *which* rules apply, rather than *how* they might apply. The question of how rules might be implicated is accordingly marginalized on this view, as the language of 'application' itself implies. This in turn illustrates how heavily the spatialized understanding relies on the distinction between binding and non-binding sources of law, invoking it not only as the criteria of correctness but as the touchstone of legitimacy. The underlying reliance on a command-style theory of adjudication also reminds us of the positivist underpinnings of this model. In this sense then, it is possible to see how ongoing disputes about adjudication are deeply indebted to this understanding which views legitimacy as constraint—adjudication is legitimate only when the discretion of decision-makers is 'bound' by rules handed down by political authorities.

As the work of Waddams suggests, this highly spatialized model of law is pervasively implicated in how we think about legal reasoning and legal theory. But in Anglo-American common law systems, it has special salience for how international treaty obligations manifest themselves in the domestic legal system. In fact, the insistence on the 'dualist' nature of these domestic legal systems with regard to such obligations is perhaps the most intact artifact of the spatialized legal imagination. This dualism means that such jurisdictions decline to give domestic effect to international treaty law until it becomes 'binding' by virtue of the incorporating acts of the domestic legislature. So, in line with traditional model's spatialized predisposition, geo-political borders particularly awaken the concern with bindingness. In part at least this is because of how the frontier of domestic law became implicated in the political ambitions of sovereignty in its all-important legal manifestation.[5] But it is also because of how a certain variant of sharply constrained domestic adjudication, certainly more imagined than real, serves as the ideal model of legitimacy in adjudication.

---

[4] I use the term 'conflict-like' reasoning to call attention in an analogical way to the emphasis on the selection of the appropriate rules as opposed to other ways of approaching the task of judgment. I explore this conflicts-like predisposition more fully and consider its relation to international law in M Moran, 'An Uncivil Action: The Tort of Torture and Cosmopolitan Private Law' in C Scott (ed), *Torture as Tort* (Oxford: Hart Publishing, 2001).

[5] HP Glenn, 'Persuasive Authority' (1987) 32 McGill LJ 26.

Yet the picture of legitimacy and decision-making at the heart of the spatialized model has never been more than at best very partial. The shifting and elusive contours of the common law are perhaps the most important illustration of this inadequacy.[6] Any model which posits that judicial reasoning must be understood in terms of the *ex ante* application of binding rules is at best inhospitable to the nature of common law reasoning. The common law's notoriously porous boundaries and the complexities of its conception of sources only compound the difficulty. No doubt it is at least in part the spatialized model's inability to give a persuasive account of a legal institution as central as the common law that is responsible for the fact that, except where 'borders' are involved, few legal commentators explicitly treat the binding rule ideal as capable of yielding much illumination. And even where borders are concerned, and thus where the spatial world view continues to exert its greatest hold over the legal imagination, the model is clearly under serious strain.

This strain is particularly apparent in those cases which involve the relationship between domestic and international law, largely because it is here that the old spatial metaphors still inspire the greatest fidelity. Even here however, the model seems increasingly unable to account for many of the ways in which courts actually use international law. The decision of the Supreme Court of Canada in *Baker*[7] can be seen as an illustration of a broader trend to conceive of the authority of international law in terms that prove very difficult to capture on the traditional binding authority model. In *Baker*, the majority held that domestic decision-makers had an obligation to exercise discretion in conformity with the core values of the ratified but unincorporated Convention on the Rights of the Child, notwithstanding its lack of domestic force. And a similar pattern can also be traced in a more dramatic set of cases where domestic courts invoke international law, regardless of its domestic bindingness, as part of the justification for refusing to give the court's imprimatur to formally valid acts that contravene the basic values of the legal order. Thus, in problems as disparate as the recognition of foreign law and the domestic enforcement of racist private agreements, the traditional spatialized model of law with its emphasis on the application of binding rules seems to be giving way to a very different understanding.

Now it may well be tempting to simply dismiss these 'unorthodox' invocations of international law as manifestations of ignorance or error, but looking to other areas of law suggests that we should not be too quick to do so. The most illuminating

---

6 I discuss these difficulties in more detail in M Moran, 'An Uncivil Action: The Tort of Torture and Cosmopolitan Private Law' in C Scott (ed), *Torture as Tort* (Oxford: Hart Publishing, 2001), drawing on work by Stephen Perry, Brian Simpson, David Dyzenhaus, and others.

7 [1999] 2 SCR 817; Madam Justice L'Heureux-Dubé, 'From Many Different Stones: A House of Justice', Notes for an Address to the International Association of Women Judges, Montreal November 10, 2001 (Manuscript on file with the author) 13, discussing persuasive authority of international law; K Knop, 'Here and There: International Law in Domestic Courts' (2000) NYU JILPol 507 arguing that it may be more illuminating to view recourse to international law in cases like *Baker* through the lens of persuasive authority than through the traditional bindingness model.

development in this regard is found in the emerging relationship between consti-tutionalized human rights and private or common law. As with international law, courts in the constitutional/private law cases separate binding force and manda-tory effect. So while constitutional rights have no force and are not binding in private or common law, they nonetheless have a special kind of effect expressed in terms of mandatory values. These cases thus serve as a doctrinally entrenched example of how *values* as well as more specific claims of entitlement and obliga-tion (rights) can exert demands on legal judgment. Like what have traditionally been termed 'binding' sources, these demands are mandatory not permissive. Yet because they take the form of *values*, like pure persuasive authority, their influence is exerted primarily at the level of deliberation and justification.

Noting the commonalities between the authority of non-binding constitutional law and the way that courts often approach the domestic effect of non-binding international law suggests that it may be too simple to dismiss these unorthodox invocations of international law. Instead, it may be that the best explanation points towards a rather different conception of authority than the one imagined by the spatialized model of law. I have suggested elsewhere that this authority can best be understood as 'influential' in form.[8] And because it turns on the mandatory influ-ence of certain legal values, it places primacy not on the selection of rules but rather on the distinctive nature of legal deliberation and justification. The legal pedigree of the rules does matter, on this view, but not in the univocal way sug-gested by the traditional model's emphasis on application. And for this reason, these gestures towards a different influential form of authority unsettle both the idea of clearly delineated 'borders' or doctrinal boundaries and the associated belief in the unique salience of binding rules.

Recognizing the operation of an influential form of authority undermines the spatialized model in large part because of how it challenges its conception of borders and boundaries. Influential authority is attentive to the mandatory or 'binding' emanations of non-binding rules across the very boundaries that the spatialized model views as tools of containment. And the nature of this influence cannot be conveniently placed on a binding rule/persuasive authority spectrum because of how influential authority undoes the traditional equation of force and effect. While the effect posited by influential authority is—like traditional bind-ing sources—mandatory, the source of the demand is not a rule but a value. And because the mandatory nature of the source is accordingly dissociated from any-thing that is recognizable as a decision-rule, the judicial task cannot be conceived as primarily a matter of selection and application. Influential authority thus shifts our attention to those moments of discretion that are marginalized by the trad-itional picture. Noting the operation of influential authority in these moments makes us aware of how legal deliberation and justification are shaped and structured.

---

[8] M Moran 'Authority Influence and Persuasion: *Baker*, Charter Values and the Puzzle of Method' in D Dyzenhaus (ed), *The Unity of Public Law* (Oxford: Hart Publishing, 2004) 15.

In this sense then, influential authority helps us to account for why these processes often manifest a distinctively legal quality that the traditional picture lacks the tools to capture. So influential authority centrally implicates justification and demands a more constructivist understanding of the role of the judge in 'creating authority'.[9] In this way, the recognition of influential authority erodes the old borders of the legal imagination and presses us to look for alternatives to its reductionist spatial metaphors.

Since the problematic of influential authority turns on how to weave together various sets of norms that operate at different levels and possess different weights, the model of judgment that it implicates is inevitably directed to rather different issues than the questions of rule selection that preoccupy the traditional model. By attending to the nature of these differences as we examine several cases dealing with domestic recourse[10] to non-binding international law and by noting the links to the constitutional/private law cases, we can begin to trace the outline of an alternative picture. Ultimately our attention may be drawn back to the relation between national boundaries and binding law. For when courts recognize the mandatory influence of international law values on the shape of domestic law they simultaneously erode both the national legal boundary protected by the domestic incorporation requirement and the associated commitment to command theory of adjudication expressed in the attachment to the unique salience of binding rules. And so at a deeper conceptual level, invoking the influential authority of non-binding international law undermines the conceptual foundations of the traditional spatialized view.

2. Domestic recourse to international law

2.1 Baker and related controversies

When the Supreme Court of Canada released its decision in *Baker* in 1999, there was considerable interest in the few short paragraphs of the majority decision that discussed the relevance of international law.[11] The case involved Ms Baker, who had lived in Canada illegally for many years and who had four children in Canada. She asked to be allowed to make an application for permanent resident status

---

[9] J Boyd White, *Acts of Hope: Creating Authority in Law and Literature* (Chicago: University of Chicago Press, 1994). Also the work of D Dyzenhaus on the role of justification including, 'The Politics of Deference: Judicial Review and Democracy' in M Taggart (ed), *The Province of Administrative Law* (Oxford: Hart Publishing, 1997) 279; D Dyzenhaus 'Law as Justification: Etienne Mureinik's Conception of Legal Culture' (1998) 14 SAJHR 11.

[10] For reasons that are probably obvious, I avoid the term 'application'.

[11] Knop (n 7 above) 507; S Toope and J Brunnée, 'A Hesitant Embrace: The Application of International Law by Canadian Courts' in D Dyzenhaus (ed), *The Unity of Public Law* (Oxford: Hart Publishing, 2004) 15, 14; G van Ert, *Using International Law in Canadian Courts* (The Hague: Kluwer Law International, 2002).

without leaving the country. The effects of a possible deportation on her children, she argued, provided sufficient 'humanitarian and compassionate reasons' to be exempted from the ordinary application requirements.[12] When the immigration officer refused this request, she sought judicial review. The two lower courts rejected her application but the Supreme Court unanimously reversed.

All members of the Supreme Court concurred that the immigration officer was biased and hence failed to reasonably exercise his discretionary power. The majority opinion, authored by Madam Justice L'Heureux-Dubé, also went on to find that any reasonable exercise of the discretionary power must, among other things, be responsive to the needs and interests of the children. Because the immigration officer's decision contained no indication that it had been made in a manner which was 'alive, attentive or sensitive' to the interests of Ms. Baker's children, it was unreasonable on that ground as well.[13] According to the majority, Canada's ratification of the Convention on the Rights of the Child (the Convention)[14] placed some imperatives on how the government's immigration powers could be exercised, notwithstanding the fact that the Convention had not been domestically incorporated. Indeed, this was the only point of disagreement in the case. The dissent by Justices Iacobucci and Cory insisted that in the absence of domestic incorporation, the Convention could have no domestic effect whatsoever.

The majority derives the imperative of attentiveness to the interests of children from a number of sources. However, the only source that specifically mandates attentiveness to the special needs of children is the Convention on the Rights of the Child. Madam Justice L'Heureux-Dubé begins her discussion of international law by describing Canada's ratification of the Convention as 'another indication of the importance of considering the interests of children'.[15] Without legislative implementation, she acknowledges, ratification alone is not sufficient to give the Convention 'direct application within Canadian law'.[16] Nevertheless, 'the values reflected in international human rights law may help inform the contextual approach to statutory interpretation'.[17] The legislature, she continues, is presumed to respect the values and principles enshrined in international law. She also refers to the 'important role of international human rights law as an aid in interpreting domestic law', particularly in the context of the Charter.[18] The conclusion is that the Convention helps 'to show the values that are central in determining' whether this decision was reasonable.[19] Similarly, she later states that the Convention and the other sources 'indicate that emphasis on the rights, interests, and needs of

---

[12] Immigration Act, RSC, 1985, c. I-2, ss 114(2).   [13] *Baker* [1999] 2 SCR 817, at 75.
[14] Convention on the Rights of the Child. Can TS 1992 No 3.
[15] Madam Justice L'Heureux-Dubé, 'From Many Different Stones: A House of Justice', Notes for an Address to the International Association of Women Judges, Montreal November 10, 2001 (manuscript on file with the author) 69.   [16] Ibid.
[17] Ibid, 70 quoting R Sullivan, *Driedger on the Construction of Statutes* (3rd edn, London: Butterworths, 1994) 330.   [18] Ibid, 70.
[19] Ibid, 71.

children and special attention to childhood are important values that should be considered' in the exercise of discretion.[20]

The result of all of this is that 'attentiveness and sensitivity to the important of the rights of children . . . is *essential*' if the decision is to be reasonable.[21] However, the interests of children will not necessarily outweigh all other interests. So while this approach gives the interests of children substantial mandatory weight in any decision, it does not amount to giving them the 'primary importance' required by Article 3(1) of the Convention.

Madam Justice L'Heureux-Dubé's justifications for invoking the Convention are compatible with a number of possibilities, some of which have been discussed in other commentary on the case.[22] But it seems clear that for the majority the fact of ratification gives the Convention a special domestic status *not* tantamount to incorporation. The *Baker* majority opinion rests on the idea that a ratified but non-binding international convention may indeed be lacking in domestic force and may yet have a mandatory domestic effect. What is mandatory on this approach however is attentiveness to the overall scheme of values and principles embodied in the Convention. As the *Baker* majority notes, this is not equivalent to enforcement of the specific rights contained in the ratified treaty. So while non-binding international law may well lack domestic force, it may simultaneously possess not just effect but mandatory domestic effect. It is just this disaggregation of force and effect that the *Baker* dissent objects to when it insists that while once implemented the Convention has full force and effect, until it is so implemented it has neither and is irrelevant.[23] And *Baker* is not alone in positing that non-binding law may well have a domestic effect that is mandatory in nature and that imposes a distinctive set of demands. Indeed a number of other cases across relatively dualist common law jurisdictions have adopted a similar approach, finding mandatory domestic effect in non-binding international law.[24]

In *Baker* and the other cases that adopt this approach, it is possible to trace a pattern of relatively consistent reasoning. Domestic courts, it seems, are increasingly willing to uncouple formal binding force and mandatory effect even in the context of international treaty law that is not domestically binding. Thus, they hold that the absence of binding domestic force, though undoubtedly important, does not preclude mandatory domestic effect. So the possibilities suggested by *Baker* and the related cases are more subtle and more complex than those inherent

---

[20] Ibid, 73.   [21] Ibid, 73 (emphasis added).

[22] K Knop (n 7 above) 507; S Toope, 'The Uses of Metaphor: International Law and the Supreme Court of Canada' [2001] CBR 534; S Toope and J Brunnée, 'A Hesitant Embrace: The Application of International Law by Canadian Courts', in D Dyzenhaus (ed), *The Unity of Public Law* (Oxford: Hart Publishing, 2004) 15; Van Ert (n 11 above) 209–29.

[23] *Baker* [1999] 2 SCR 817, 81 (per Justice Iacobucci, Cory J concurring on this point).

[24] I elaborate this argument in detail in M Moran (n 8) 15, drawing on *Minister for Immigration and Ethnic Affairs v Teoh* (1995) 128 ALR 353; *Tavita v Minister of Immigration* [1994] 2 NZLR 257; *Thomas v Baptiste* [1999] JCJ No 12 and *Ahani v Canada (Minister of Citizenship and Immigration)* [2002] OJ No 90.

in the on-off mechanism associated with traditional picture. However, before we turn to examine the nature of this effect somewhat more closely and to note other continuities with domestic law, let us briefly examine another context in which international acts, regardless of their formal domestic bindingness, are treated as giving rise to a similar kind of mandatory domestic effect.

The decision of the Judicial Committee of the Privy Council in *Thomas v Baptiste* provides another example.[25] Thomas had been convicted of murder and sentenced to death in Trinidad and Tobago. Trinidad and Tobago had ratified the American Convention on Human Rights 1969 (ACHR) and in so doing recognized both the Inter-American Commission's competence to entertain petitions from individuals and the compulsory jurisdiction of the Inter-American Court of Human Rights to give binding rulings. Following his conviction, Thomas petitioned the Commission alleging violations of his rights. The Court issued an order requiring the Government to refrain from carrying out the death sentence pending determination of the petitions. The Government was prepared to defy this order and proceed with the death sentence. On appeal, the Privy Council accepted that Thomas could not enforce the terms of the ACHR since, although it had been ratified, it had not been incorporated through domestic legislation. However, the majority insisted that the appellants were not seeking enforcement of the particular rights of the ACHR but rather the general right, implicit in the common law, not to have a pending legal process frustrated by executive action. So the ratification of the ACHR extended the meaning of the due process clause in the domestic constitution, even if only temporarily. And although the majority rejected the doctrine of legitimate expectations as too devoid of substantive content to be of assistance, it also observed that 'Executive action may give rise to a settled practice, and this in turn may found a constitutional right which cannot lawfully be withdrawn by executive action alone'.[26] Their Lordships accordingly stayed the executions pending determination of the petitions by the Commission. The dissent of Lord Goff and Lord Hobhouse insisted on the traditional position: since ratified but unincorporated treaties were not part of domestic law, in their view the rights contained therein could not affect the scope of the domestic due process guarantee.

So in the *Thomas* majority there are important conceptual links to the *Baker*-like rejection of a sharply bifurcated approach to the relationship between domestic and international law. *Thomas* also undoes the traditional equation between binding force and mandatory effect when it rejects the argument that the failure to domestically implement the ACHR rendered any decision of the Court irrelevant or without domestic effect. Instead, as in *Baker* we see the Privy Council insist that although the decision may not have direct domestic effect, it possesses a sufficiently special kind of relevance that it cannot be ignored. So here too there is an obligation of respect and though this obligation does not demand any particular conclusion,

---

[25] *Thomas v Baptiste* [1999] JCJ No 12 and *Ahani v Canada (Minister of Citizenship and Immigration)* [2002] OJ No 90.   [26] Ibid, 11.

it nonetheless imposes both constraints and positive demands on the domestic decision-making process.[27]

Another illustration of this approach to the relation between domestic and international law can be found in the English Court of Appeal decision in *Abbasi*. There, the Court considered the constraints on the prerogative power of the executive in the conduct of its diplomatic relations.[28] The case arose out of the detention of a British national by the United States in Guantanamo Bay. The claimant argued that the Foreign Office in the exercise of its prerogative powers was subject to a duty of diplomatic assistance arising out of the European Convention on Human Rights (ECHR). The Court of Appeal rejected the claim that the ECHR imposed such a duty. But in reasoning strikingly reminiscent of that found in the context of non-domestically binding treaty obligations, the Court went on to hold that the doctrine of 'legitimate expectations' nonetheless constrained the prerogative power and rendered it to that extent justiciable.

In the opinion of Lord Phillips, MR the doctrine of legitimate expectations 'provides a well-established and flexible means for giving legal effect to a settled policy or practice for the exercise of administrative discretion'.[29] The expectation could arise from an express promise or from a settled practice. So the subject is entitled to have such expectations 'properly taken into account in considering his individual case'.[30] And in outlining the nature of these expectations, Lord Phillips refers to a passage from *Teoh*—a case with important links to *Baker*[31]—that describes the ratification of a convention as a positive statement inside and outside the State. He connects this to Mr. Abbasi's claim by noting the various statements by the Foreign Office (including to the UN General Assembly) to the effect that that they would make representations on behalf of nationals abroad where there was evidence of a miscarriage of justice or of fundamental violations of that subject's human rights.[32] Traditionally, such representations are devoid of any effect or relevance in domestic law.

However, Lord Phillips queries this sharp bifurcation noting that 'it must be a "normal expectation of every citizen" that, if subjected abroad to a violation of a fundamental right, the British Government will not simply wash their hands of the matter and abandon him to his fate'.[33] Thus there is at a minimum a duty to consider making representations to the foreign government. The nature of this duty is subject to various factors, including vitally 'the nature and extent of the

---

[27] On the obligation of respect in administrative law more generally see D Dyzenhaus, 'The Politics of Deference: Judicial Review and Democracy' and D Dyzenhaus, 'Law as Justification: Etienne Mureinik's Conception of Legal Culture, (1998) 14 SAJHR 11.

[28] *R (Abbasi and another) v Secretary of State for Foreign and Commonwealth Affairs and another* [2002] EWCA Civ 159.　　　　　　　　　　　　　　　　　　　　　　[29] Ibid, 82.

[30] Ibid.

[31] On the relationship between *Baker* and *Teoh* see M Moran 'Authority Influence and Persuasion: *Baker*, Charter Values and the Puzzle of Method' in D Dyzenhaus (ed), *The Unity of Public Law* (Oxford: Hart Publishing, 2004) 15.　　　　　　　　　　　　　　[32] *Abbasi* (n 28 above) 87 and 89.

[33] Ibid, 98 quoting *R v Foreign Secretary ex parte Everett* [1989] 1 QB 811.

injustice'.[34] So when very serious injustice is claimed, it will be correspondingly difficult to justify failure to intervene. Nonetheless, 'even where there has been a gross miscarriage of justice, there may perhaps be overriding reasons of public policy' which would justify non-intervention.[35] Further, as Lord Phillips points out, none of the relevant assessments can be made unless there is some 'judgment' formed as to the gravity of the miscarriage.

There are striking parallels between the reasoning in *Abbasi* and the approaches adopted by the courts in cases like *Baker* and in *Thomas*. They all insist that the fact that a legal resource cannot be characterized as the traditional binding domestic rule does not fully answer the question of its domestic legal significance. Indeed, in these different scenarios, the courts go on to insist on a very distinctive kind of domestic effect—one that is mandatory in nature. But the fact that it is attentiveness to values that is mandatory also reflects an important difference in the nature of the associated duty. This is a duty that operates in moments of discretion and that typically attaches to the processes of deliberation and justification. So the duty in these cases does not take the form of a decision-rule that specifies a right or obligation. Instead it is a kind of mandatory attentiveness that manifests itself in the deliberative process and in the justifications given for the results of those deliberations.

For instance in *Baker* the influential authority of the Convention is manifest in the fact, although the administrative decision-maker undoubtedly has discretionary powers, in the process of exercising and justifying that discretion, the decision-maker *must* attend to and respect the values of the Convention. In this sense then, the mandatory values derived from the Convention structure and constrain the discretionary sphere of judgment, lending it distinctively legal shape. Similar dynamics are at work in *Thomas* when the Privy Council insists on respect for the additional processes agreed to when the ACHR was ratified. So although the ACHR process will not yield a decision binding in domestic law because it is not incorporated, the core values implicit in the extension of the adjudicative process beyond the domestic sphere nonetheless demand respect. Thus the Privy Council insists that a court cannot accept the view that the additional process was a mere sham or 'cruel charade'. Instead, the fact that an additional decision will be issued itself mandates restraint and respect in the ongoing domestic processes. This is not tantamount to being bound by such opinions but is rather a product of the recognition that even a non-binding opinion from a respected body makes a substantial difference to how an issue is subsequently deliberated and ultimately justified.

This idea is made express in a passage from *Briggs v Baptiste* in which the Privy Council explains its earlier related decision in *Thomas* in the following terms:

In that case there was an outstanding dispute of fact which remained to be investigated by the Commission and if necessary decided by the Court, viz. whether the defendants had had a fair trial. If the Court were to rule that the trial had not been fair and to order that the conviction be quashed, the State would be at liberty as a matter of domestic law to ignore

---

[34] Ibid, 99–100.   [35] Ibid, 100.

the order and carry out the sentence, but it is very difficult to believe that it would have done so. Trinidad and Tobago is a modern democracy which operates under the rule of law and is sensitive to its international obligations.[36]

As this suggests, what must be respected is a process which, though not binding in its outcome, nonetheless will necessarily make a difference to how the ultimate question is considered and resolved.[37] This is not to say that the domestic State will inevitably adopt the conclusions of the international body. But it does mean that such conclusions will alter the process of deliberation about what is to be done. Thus, even where the final outcome is the same, one would expect that additional and different justifications would be required to support a result that rejected the opinion of a respected deliberative body like the IACHR.[38] So although mandatory respect for the extended deliberative process does not demand a particular outcome, it does structure and constrain the sphere of discretionary decision-making in a manner that is evocative of the Convention cases. Similarly, it imposes additional demands on the process of justification.

The way that influential authority affects discretionary decision-making is particularly striking in *Abbasi* which involves the most discretionary sphere of judgment—executive prerogative. Nonetheless, the Court of Appeal insisted that there were factors that must be taken into consideration even in the exercise of such a highly discretionary decision-making power. Here as well, the influential sources of authority serve to shape and constrain this decision-making. As in the cases of influential authority discussed above, the source of the structure and constraint is found in representations that, though admittedly without binding domestic force, nonetheless give rise to certain expectations that can be enforced by individuals through a reviewing court. And here too, the relevant sources exert their demands not at the level of decision-rules but rather in the deliberative process itself. Thus, although significant latitude is inherent in the exercise of its prerogative powers, the Executive does have a duty to 'consider' making representations on behalf of its citizen abroad. And discharging this duty requires some investigation into the gravity of the miscarriage of justice. As in *Baker* and *Thomas*, though this duty does not generate specific rules, it does necessarily alter the nature of the deliberative

---

[36] *Briggs v Baptiste*, PC Appeal No 31 (1999) 15.

[37] In fact, *Briggs* serves as an illustration. In that follow-up case to *Thomas*, the Privy Council considered the significance of the Commission's opinion that although Thomas had had a fair trial, there was inappropriate post-trial delay in the context of a death penalty case. They recommended that consideration be given to either commutation of sentence or to compensation. The domestic authorities considered these possibilities but rejected them and affirmed the death penalty was thus affirmed. A majority of the Privy Council in its consideration of this concluded that since all that was required was due consideration of the Court's opinion, and since there was no indication that this was not done in good faith, the ACHR process had been respected.

[38] A similar argument regarding the First Optional Protocol under the ICCPR was made by the dissent in the Ontario Court of Appeal decision in *Ahani v Canada (Minister of Citizenship and Immigration)* [2002] OJ No 90. I discuss that case in detail in M Moran 'Authority Influence and Persuasion: *Baker*, Charter Values and the Puzzle of Method' in D Dyzenhaus (ed), *The Unity of Public Law* (Oxford: Hart Publishing, 2004) 15.

process itself. It also affects the range of justifications for failure to make representations that will be appropriate in any given case. So, the implication of *Abbasi* is that it may be open to the Executive to justify failure to make representations even in cases of 'gross miscarriages of justice'. But the effect of influential authority is apparent in the Court's insistence that this will only be possible where the justification for refusal to make representations is found in 'overriding reasons of public policy', in the language of the Court of Appeal. So here as well legal resources that are influential in form lend the exercise of discretion its distinctively legal quality.

2.2 The estoppel-like effect of international law

Thus, as we have seen, it is possible to identify a range of cases where international law, though not domestically binding, nonetheless is treated by courts as holding a kind of mandatory domestic significance that is hard to account for on the traditional picture. Before examining the larger context however, it is useful to briefly note another set of cases in which international law values also exert a mandatory effect, notwithstanding the absence of formal bindingness. In these cases, the effect is particularly dramatic for it is 'estoppel-like' in nature—that is, international law values operate to prevent a court from giving acts their claimed legal effect. Thus we find domestic courts in situations as diverse as the enforcement of private contracts and the recognition of foreign law invoking international law values as a key justification for exercising their extraordinary 'public policy' jurisdiction and refusing to give legal sanction to the relevant act. Though many cases across jurisdictions could be cited, here I will confine myself to two illustrative cases.[39]

An illustration of the estoppel-like effect of international law values in domestic public law can be found in *Re Drummond Wren*.[40] In that case, the Ontario High Court refused to enforce a racially restrictive covenant that prohibited the transfer of the subject land 'to Jews, or to persons of objectionable nationality'.[41] MacKay J invoked the principle that 'any agreement which tends to be injurious to the public or against the public good is void as being contrary to public policy'.[42] And in discussing the sources of public policy, he begins not with domestic legislation but rather with the San Francisco Charter, which Canada had signed and ratified. There is 'profound significance', MacKay J states, in that Preamble's reference to the 'dignity and worth of the human person'. He also notes that under its articles Canada pledged to respect all 'without distinction as to race, sex, language, or religion'.[43] Similarly, he points out that under the terms of the Atlantic Charter Canada subscribed to principles of freedom from fear. And even when MacKay J turns to domestic sources, it is clear that their authority is also influential not binding. Their specific provisions, Mackay J explicitly acknowledges, are inapplicable. Thus,

---

[39] I discuss this effect and the relevant case law in more detail in M Moran, 'Influential Authority and the Estoppel-Like Effect of International Law' in H Charlesworth and G Williams (eds), *The Fluid State* (Anandale: Federation Press, 2005).   [40] [1945] 4 DLR 674.
[41] Ibid, 675.   [42] Ibid, 676, quoting 7 Hals. (2nd edn) 153–54.   [43] Ibid, 677.

for instance, it is not the terms of sources like the Racial Discrimination Act that are relevant. Instead, that act figures 'as an aid in determining principles relative to public policy'.[44]

Thus here again we see international law coming to the fore, not as a source of binding decision-rules but rather as an influential resource that shapes and structures legal discretion. And the mandatory force of the values derived from these international law sources is apparent in the fact that here they prevent the court from enforcing a formally valid contract—this is the 'estoppel-like' effect of influential authority's most extreme posture. The Court's justification also reveals the power such values have, not merely to persuade but to compel. Thus, Justice Mackay describes it as a 'duty' to reject the divisive tenets of discrimination and insists that the contract 'requires' nullification on grounds of public policy. He also notes 'the wide official acceptance of international policies and declarations frowning on the type of discrimination which the covenant would seem to perpetuate'.[45] Further, he quotes an array of sources deploring racism and anti-Semitism in particular.[46] Interestingly, Mackay J also explicitly links his analysis to constitutional human rights ideals—a link which extends both to the overlapping substantive content of human rights and public policy and to the mandatory quality they share.[47] So the sphere of 'public policy', which may look unconstrained and discretionary from the perspective of the traditional picture, is in fact infused with mandatory legal values derived from a range of international and domestic sources that do not themselves generate directly applicable decision-rules. The authority of such sources, in other words, is influential not binding.

The subsequent history of *Drummond Wren* confirms its rejection of the traditional picture of legal authority in favour of some conception of the influential authority of non-binding law. *Noble v Wolf* repudiated the reasoning in *Drummond Wren* in part by disputing the idea that authority for a legal decision could be anything other than the straightforward binding authority of the traditional view. In *Noble v Wolf*, a unanimous Ontario Court of Appeal upheld a racially discriminatory covenant much like the one in *Drummond Wren*.[48] Hogg JA rejects *Drummond Wren's* reasoning precisely on the ground that the international law sources 'do not seem to have been made a part of the law of this country or of this Province by any legislative enactment of either the Dominion Parliament or the Ontario Legislature'.[49] Indeed, he insists on the 'foreignness' of international law in his reference

---

[44] Ibid, 677.   [45] Ibid, 679.   [46] Ibid, 679–81.

[47] The links between these various influential sources are also apparent in the fact that the United States Supreme Court approached a similar situation by invoking the idea that the Constitution precluded judicial enforcement of agreements that violated fundamental constitutional guarantees: *Shelley v Kraemer* 334 US 1 (1948). Further, in the companion case to *Shelley*, *Hurd v Hodge* 334 US 24 (1948), the Court held that federal courts could not enforce agreements that would be unenforceable in state courts notwithstanding the inapplicability of the Fourteenth Amendment. In his reasons, Vinson CJ stated that not only would such enforcement deny rights protected by the Civil Rights Act 1866, it would also 'be contrary to the public policy of the United States'.

[48] [1949] 4 DLR 375.   [49] Ibid, 399.

to Lord Thankerton's statement that 'there can be no justification for expanding the principles of public policy in this country by reference to the public policy of another country'.[50] And he specifically insists that this 'applies as well to the principles and obligations set forth in international covenants or charters, such as the United Nations Charter, until such time as they should be made a part of the law of the land'.[51] This rejection of *Drummond Wren* is thus to no small degree a repudiation of the idea that legal sources possess anything other than traditional binding authority and accordingly of the view that international law could have any effect in the absence of domestic force. It is thus a reassertion of the primacy of the traditional picture and its commitment to the unique salience of binding rules.

Despite repeated such attempts to reassert the traditional picture, courts faced with the prospect of giving their imprimatur to acts that seem to contravene the fundamental values of the legal order have continued to treat international law, domestically binding or not, as a resource vital to their public policy jurisdiction. This is also apparent in another set of cases, far away from the domestic corners of private law—the recognition of foreign law. Here too on rare occasions courts invoke the estoppel-like effect of mandatory values as a basis for refusing to give effect to the laws of other countries. In cases concerning the recognition of foreign law, courts are explicitly concerned, not with the validity of the foreign law (which is generally acknowledged), but rather with the extent to which they can give *effect* to the relevant law. And as courts struggle to reconcile respect for their own values with treating foreign laws with appropriate respect, we can also see the estoppel-like effect of international law values. This is because in the elaboration of the court's own fundamental values, the influence of basic norms of international law also infuses this 'limiting use' of public policy lending it a distinctively legal quality.

Differences between the law of the adjudicating court and the foreign law, far from justifying non-application by the court, actually give rise to the need for deference. As the House of Lords recently put it, 'the existence of differences is the very reason why it may be appropriate for the forum court to have recourse to the foreign law'.[52] Comity requires a kind of respect for the political choices of other sovereigns and this means that courts may well be required to give legal effect to foreign law that they view as ill-advised, even erroneous. However, the deference extended is inherently reasoned, and not automatic.[53] 'Blind adherence to foreign

---

[50] Ibid, quoting *Fender v St John-Mildmay* [1938] AC 1, 25.   [51] Ibid.

[52] *Kuwait Airways* [2002] 2 WLR 1353, 1360 (Lord Nicholls).

[53] In this sense it is possible to recognise a similar conceptual structure, also expressed in terms of deference, in the issue of judicial review of administrative action. The structure of both inquiries reflects a delicate mediation between the need to respect the integrity of some 'other' and respect for one's own fundamental values—values most authoritatively expressed in the constitution. The inherently reasoned idea of deference I draw on here is that of 'deference as respect' which has been developed by D Dyzenhaus in the administrative law context (D Dyzenhaus, 'The Politics of Deference: Judicial Review and Democracy' in M Taggart (ed), *The Province of Administrative Law* (Oxford: Hart Publishing, 1997) 279) and embraced by the Supreme Court of Canada in *Baker* [1999] 2 SCR 817.

law', the House of Lords reminds us, is not the role of the court.[54] This means that 'exceptionally and rarely, a provision of foreign law will be disregarded when it would lead to a result wholly alien to fundamental requirements of justice' as understood by the court.[55] One result of this is that a court cannot give effect to laws that profoundly violate its own core legal values. Cardozo J, for instance noted that courts will refuse to recognize foreign law where it violates a 'fundamental principle of justice'.[56] And in those rare cases in which courts have refused to give domestic effect to foreign law, it is possible to trace significant continuities with the instances of influential authority noted above. So the foreign law cases also uncouple the traditional equation of force and effect. And in this limiting use of the 'public policy' jurisdiction, international law values again play a particularly important role among the mandatory values that give public policy its distinctively juridical posture.

The important House of Lords decision in *Oppenheimer v Cattermole* ('*Oppenheimer*') serves as an illustration.[57] The case involved a German Jew who fled to England in 1939 to escape Nazi persecution. In 1948 he became a British subject and from 1953 onwards, he was paid an annual pension by the German republic. The United Kingdom taxed him on that pension and he claimed an exemption from double taxation on the ground that he had dual British and German nationality. Because he could only claim relief if he remained a German citizen, British courts had to determine the effect of an infamous 1941 decree of the Nazi government, Decree 11. Among other things, Decree 11 abrogated the citizenship of German Jews who left Germany. It also provided that the property of such persons would 'fall to the state' and that the confiscated property was to be used 'to further aims connected with the solution of the Jewish problem'.[58]

In the Court of Appeal decision in *Oppenheimer*, Buckley J emphasized the traditional positivist conception of authority. In response to the argument that English courts could not give effect to a decree that contravened international law, Buckley J held that the question of whether or not a person is a national of a country 'must be answered in light of the law of that country however inequitable, oppressive or objectionable it may be'.[59] In other words, the only law relevant to such a determination was the (then) binding law of the country of purported nationality. On this approach, English courts were obliged to recognise the 1941 decree as effective to deprive Mr Oppenheimer of his German nationality.

On appeal, however, the House of Lords rejects this traditional positivist approach to Decree 11. Thus, Lord Cross notes that while a judge should certainly be slow to refuse to give effect to the legislation of a foreign state, it is also 'part of the

---

[54] *Kuwait Airways* [2002] 2 WLR 1353, 1360, reproducing comments made by Scarman J in *In the Estate of Fuld, decd (No 3)* [1968] 675 at 698. [55] Ibid.

[56] *Loucks v Standard Oil Co of New York* 120 NE 198, 202 (1918).

[57] *Oppenheimer v Cattermole* [1973] Ch 264.   [58] [1976] AC 249 at 281 (per Lord Salmon).

[59] *Oppenheimer v Cattermole* [1973] Ch 264, 273 (per Buckley J, Orr J concurring).

public policy of this country that our courts should give effect to clearly established rules of international law'.[60] Decree 11, Lord Cross notes, visited upon German Jews a 'discriminatory withdrawal of their rights' which was then 'used as a peg upon which to hang a discriminatory confiscation of their property'.[61] The legislation thus 'takes away without compensation from a section of the citizen body singled out on racial grounds all their property' and deprives them of their citizenship.[62] He continues, 'to my mind a law of this sort constitutes so grave an infringement of human rights that the courts of this country ought to refuse to recognise it as law at all'.[63] So international law values, in this case fundamental principles of human rights, are sufficiently mandatory that they prevent the court from giving effect to a decree that would otherwise be squarely within the jurisdiction of the foreign State that promulgated it.

Here again then we see that mandatory principles of human rights drawn from international law are crucial to the content of domestic public policy. Notwithstanding the respect normally accorded to the law of a foreign sovereign, the pull of these mandatory values may actually preclude a court from giving effect to foreign law. The divergence from the traditional positivist conception of authority is apparent in the fact that, as with the examples of influential authority noted above, the concern is not with what principles of international law were binding on either the German State or the English courts at the time that the decree was enacted. Although those sources are relevant, *Oppenheimer* makes it clear that they do not exhaust legal normativity. Instead, the contours of influential authority are at work in the way that the international law values also exert demands on the adjudicating court.

Reading these cases together provides some insight into the changing nature of the relationship between domestic and international law. These 'domestic recourse' cases implicitly reject the automatic equation of force and effect. So judges in these cases often explicitly note that according to the traditional view the relevant international sources are—for a range of reasons—not domestically binding and hence lack force. But they also go on to insist that the non-binding source nonetheless possesses a mandatory effect and so demands respect. These demands manifest themselves in the deliberative process and thus necessarily affect among other things the nature of justification. We can see this effect operating to structure and constrain the discretion inherent in legal judgment across a range of cases. Noting how influential authority manifests itself in this sphere of discretionary decision-making reminds us of the impoverishment of the traditional picture which views legal decision-making as either completely fettered (when binding rules apply) or entirely unconstrained (when they do not). By contrast, paying attention to the

---

[60] [1976] AC 249, 278.   [61] Ibid, 277.   [62] Ibid, 278.

[63] Ibid, 278. See also Lord Salmon at 283, stating that courts should ask whether 'an enactment is so great an offence against human rights that it ought not to be recognized by any civilized system of law'. In the case of Decree 11, there can be no doubt, he states, that on grounds of public policy they should refuse to recognize the law.

workings of influential authority reveals the extent to which the processes of deliberation and justification that characterize much legal decision-making (including adjudication) are actually structured and constrained in distinctively legal ways that the traditional picture simply cannot capture. Unlike the spatialized understanding with its emphasis on the selection of the applicable binding rule, the picture of judgment that influential authority rests upon is complex. In part this is because its metric is weight and significance, unlike the apparent simplicity of a binary concept like bindingness. And because recognizing the influential authority of international law is such a fundamental departure from the most traditional aspect of the traditional picture, it is useful to examine a closely related but more doctrinally well-established phenomenon—the understanding of the relationship between constitutionalized human rights and private or common law.

3. Influential authority, constitutional values, and private law

The reasoning in the cases that struggle with the effect of international law that is not domestically binding is remarkably similar to that found in another 'boundary' problem—the relation of constitutional norms to traditional private and common law. In these constitutional controversies as well, the spatialized model with its reliance on the exclusive salience of binding sources offers little illumination. The result is that courts are left to develop their own vocabulary to capture what is, on the traditional view, a rather odd relation. And this has only become more noteworthy with the recent entrenchment, in several common law and mixed jurisdictions, of some form of constitutionalized human rights.

Although the question of the relation between a constitutional regime and other discrete 'bodies' of law is by no means new, recent legal developments have increased its visibility and its importance. Significant here is the growth of a distinctive form of constitutionalism characterized in part an the understanding of the constitution as composed of both distinct rights that individuals can assert against the State and a set of interconnected substantive values which manifest their effect throughout the legal system. The view of a constitution as the foundation of a mandatory system of values is certainly most clearly articulated in the German model but also runs through the family of rights-protecting documents that came into being in the aftermath of the Second World War.[64] One noteworthy feature of this system is found in its conception of the way that constitutional values 'radiate' throughout the rest of the legal system. And though the idea that the emanations of foundational legal rights may exert a distinctive kind of mandatory force did not spring into being with post-war constitutionalism, it does serve as the most doctrinally

---

[64] See for instance the discussion in Lorraine E Weinrib, 'The Supreme Court of Canada in the Age of Rights: Constitutional Democracy, the Rule of Law and Fundamental Rights Under Canada's Constitution' (2001) 80 Can Bar Rev 699; LE Weinrib, 'The Post-War Paradigm and American Exceptionalism' in S Choudhry (ed), *The Migration of Constitutional Ideas* (Cambridge: CUP, 2006).

explicit example of the phenomenon. Moreover, while the idea of the influence of mandatory values can be traced back through older cases on public policy,[65] the constitutionalized source of these 'new' mandatory values gives added strength and legitimacy to that much older idea.

Thus, it is useful to examine how courts describe the effect of constitutionalized human rights on private and common law. Rights and obligations in private common law possess their own distinctive structure.[66] And although the subject of continuing debate, the dominant approach is that constitutional human rights do not generally apply directly to private (common law) interactions between purely private parties.[67] This is the view that has generally been accepted by courts in Canada, the UK, and South Africa that have considered the relation between constitutionalized human rights norms and private or common law.[68] So for example, individuals cannot recover damages against other individuals acting in a private capacity by basing a claim on, for instance, a violation of their right to freedom of expression or their equality rights.

What we see instead is that constitutionalized human rights matter to private relations in a rather different way. They may, for instance, affect the appropriate scope of the private law causes of action. Thus, courts in Canada, the UK and South Africa have all considered the impact of the law of libel and defamation on the right to freedom of expression where the allegations of libel or defamation

---

[65] I discuss this effect in detail in M Moran, 'Influential Authority and the Estoppel-Like Effect of International Law' in H Charlesworth and G Williams (eds), *The Fluid State* (Anandale: Federation Press, 2005).

[66] For some important understandings of that structure see, for instance, E Weinrib, *The Idea of Private Law* (Cambridge, MA: HUP, 1995) and A Brudner, *The Unity of the Common Law* (Berkeley: University of California Press, 1995). On the changing relationship between public and private in face of the expansion of constituitonalized human rights in particular see P Cane, 'Accountability and the Public/Private Distinction' in N Bamforth and P Leyland (eds), *Public Law in a Multi-Layered Constitution* (Oxford: Hart Publishing, 2003) 10.

[67] On this debate generally, L Weinrib and E Weinrib, 'Constitutional Values and Private Law in Canada' in D Friedmann and D Barak-Erez (eds), *Human Rights in Private Law* (Oxford: Hart Publishing, 2001) 43; Justice Aharon Barak, 'Constitutional Human Rights and Private Law' in *Human Rights and Private Law*, ibid; M Hunt, 'The Horizontal Effect of the Human Rights Act' (n 12 above; G Phillipson, 'The Human Rights Act, "Horizontal Effect" and the Common Law: A Bang or a Whimper?' (1999) 62 MLR 824; N Bamforth, 'The Application of the Human Rights Act 1998 to Public Authorities and Private Bodies' [1999] CLJ 159; R Buxton, 'The Human Rights Act and Private Law' (2000) 116 LQR 48, HRW Wade, 'Horizons of Horizontality' (2000) 116 LQR 217; J Morgan, 'Questioning the "True Effect" of the Human Rights Act' (2002) 22 LS 259; N Bamforth, 'Understanding the Impact and Status of the Human Rights Act 1998 within English Law' NYU Hauser Global Research Papers, 2004.

[68] In Canada see for instance, *Retail, Wholesale and Department Store Union, Local 580 v Dolphin Delivery Ltd* [1986] 2 SCR 573 and *Hill v Church of Scientology of Toronto* [1995] 2 SCR 1130, 91–99. In other jurisdictions, see *De Klerk v Du Plessis* (1996) 3 SA 850 (CC); *Douglas and Zeta-Jones v Hello! Magazine* [2001] QB 967 (CA); *A v B* [2003] QB 195 (CA). There are of course some common law jurisdictions that do not follow this approach, including most prominently the Republic of Ireland where the constitution itself provides that constitutional rights may be the basis of a direct cause of action: M Hunt, 'The "Horizontal Effect" of the Human Rights Act', ibid at 427–28; AS Butler, 'Constitutional Rights in Private Litigation: A Critique and Comparative Analysis' (1993) 22 Anglo-American LR 1.

concern public figures.[69] What this demands, it seems, is that courts ensure that the private law of libel and defamation is developed in light of the overarching importance of the constitutional guarantee of freedom of expression. A similar approach is also apparent in other private and common law cases. Thus, the House of Lords ruled that the right to privacy under Article 8 of the ECHR was relevant to the law of confidence and privacy. Though the ECHR right was not directly applicable, it did give rise to a 'reasonable expectation of confidence' that expressed itself through the traditional cause of action in private common law.[70] Similarly, the right to equality may be relevant to determining the kinds of agreements a court might be called upon to enforce or the form of deference that ought to be extended to the exercise of political choices by public authorities.[71]

In cases such as these, the relevant scheme of constitutional rights does not validate or invalidate the relevant legal acts because it does not directly apply to them. In this sense, constitutional rights have no *force* in the realm of private or common law. And since the traditional view equates force and effect, this ought to mean that these rights also lack effect. But the constitutional rights/private law cases illustrate that the traditional equation between force and effect is by no means inevitable. In fact the absence of force and presence of effect is constitutive of the relationship between constitutional human rights and private common law. It is largely this feature that makes the relation such a theoretical puzzle and hence such a subject of debate. This reminds us of the attachment to the centrality of binding force and of the consequent difficulty thinking in terms that disentangle force and effect. So part of the reason the constitutional-private law relation seems so difficult to conceptualize is precisely because its core features seem difficult to render in the language of binding force.

The limited power of the traditional spatialized view to account for this relation becomes readily apparent when we look more closely at the distinctive effect of constitutional human rights on private law. This effect is not permissive but is instead mandatory or insistent. Thus it is not simply that it is open to judges to look to such rights if it seems significant or useful. As Baroness Hale noted in *Campbell*, courts not only can but *must* look to constitutionalized human rights in elaborating private common law. So the ordinary understanding of persuasive authority is not apt because rather than simply granting judges the *power* to look to them when elaborating private common law, such rights actually impose an *obligation* to do so. Unlike where authority is persuasive, failure to attend to such values could serve as a ground of appeal or of judicial review (as we saw in *Baker* and *Abbasi*, for instance).

[69] See for example *Hill v Church of Scientology of Toronto* [1995] 2 SCR 1130; *DuPlessis v De Klerk* (1996) 3 SA 850 (CC); *Douglas and Zeta-Jones v Hello! Magazine* [2001] QB 967 (CA); *A v B* [2003] QB 195 (CA). The foundational case here is of course the American Supreme Court decision in *New York Times v Sullivan*, 376 US 254 (1964).

[70] *Campbell v MGN Inc* [2004] UKHL 22, 132–33.

[71] *Canada Trust Co v Ontario Human Rights Commission* (1990) 69 DLR (4th) 321 (Ont CA), *Jane Doe v Toronto (Metropolitan) Commissioners of Police* (1989) 58 DLR. (4th) 396.

Two other features of the authority of constitutionalized human rights also echo what we noted in the above discussion of recourse to non-binding international law. Both illustrate how an influential conception of authority conjoins insistence along with the fact that it cannot be understood as a binding 'decision-rule'. If the obligations that such rights impose on private common law adjudication do not take the form of a 'rule' dictating an outcome, then how are they manifest? Influential authority's mandatory quality does distinguish it from purely persuasive authority but persuasive and influential authority also share an important feature—both operate in the relatively open-textured processes of deliberation and justification. What influential authority demands is that the influential source be respected, attended to, and considered in decision-making. So influential authority often manifests itself in the process of justification[72]—a feature it shares with persuasive authority. Unlike persuasive authority however, influential authority can demand that it be addressed and respected in a way that purely persuasive authority can not.[73]

There is one more related feature of influential authority that we should note. Where the authority of constitutionalized human rights is influential there is no argument that the relevant provisions are violated or the rights infringed. So it is not constitutional *rights* but constitutional values that necessarily influence the shape of private and common law. When constitutionalized human rights exert influential authority on the common law, what they demand is attentiveness to and respect for the core or fundamental values of that constitutional order. Commentators in the international law context have lamented recourse to 'values' in cases like *Baker* on the ground that it signals a reluctance to apply international law.[74] However, looking to the constitutional/private law relation suggests that the better explanation is found in the distinctive way legal resources may manifest themselves.

There is no doubt that legal resources often take the form of decision-rules that straightforwardly apply to a given question. But the constitutional/private law relation draws our attention to the fact that this does not exhaust the range of their possible effects. Instead, their effects may also extend well outside the force field of direct application, giving rise to mandatory values that decision-makers in the legal system *must* respect. This in turn suggests that recourse to fundamental *values* in such contexts should not be read as a weakness or limitation. In fact, by calling

---

[72] In a case like *Abbasi* where the requirement of attentiveness to the influential source rests on the Executive, demonstrating consistency with the demands of influential authority may play out differently since unlike administrative decision-makers, members of the Executive will not ordinarily issue written reasons. In such a case, a court ought to be able to explain why the Executive decision was attentive to the relevant mandatory values.

[73] For a greater elaboration of the idea and lineage of persuasive authority, HP Glenn, 'Persuasive Authority' (1987) 32 McGill LJ 26; Knop (n 7 above) 507. It is worth noting that authority is not best conceived in terms of water-tight categories, for even notionally persuasive sources may exert themselves in a fashion that approaches the insistence of influential authority and the like.

[74] Toope and Brunnée, 'A Hesitant Embrace' (n 22 above) 14; G van Ert, *Using International Law in Canadian Courts* (The Hague: Kluwer Law International, 2002).

our attention to how legal resources may possess normativity that is not limited to their undoubtedly important role as decision-rules, influential authority actually provides a more expansive account of the range of their possible effects.

But if the mandatory quality of legal resources extends well beyond their role as binding decision-rules, then the binding authority-persuasive authority dichotomy of the traditional account seems unhelpful as an explanation of legal authority. Only within a more complex understanding of legal normativity of the kind that influential authority aims at is it possible to begin to build a more nuanced account of legal normativity. In the case of constitutionalized human rights this enables us to understand how specific rights and duties in private and common law are necessarily shaped and constrained by fundamental constitutional law values. And this also brings to light the parallels with *Baker* and the other cases discussed above and in so doing helps to illuminate how international law can serve as an important source of influential authority, shaping and constraining how public power can be exercised and justified.

4. Presumptions and expectations

All of this suggests that recent treatments of international law in domestic courts that the traditional model may view as anomalous should not be dismissed too quickly. In fact, the reasoning in those cases exhibits significant continuities with other 'border disputes' about law. These similarities spring, at least in part, from the inadequacy of the traditional model and its impoverished language of bindingness. Indeed, reading the cases involving recourse to non-binding international law together with cases involving the constitutional/private law relation brings several important features to the fore.

In the international law context, it may seem odd that courts in dualist systems acknowledge that ratified but unincorporated treaties lack domestic force but then go on to find that they may nonetheless possess a certain kind of mandatory effect. This is particularly so when the effect that they insist on is not enforcement of the discrete regime but rather respect for and attentiveness to its core values. And these very features, puzzling though they may seem from the perspective of the traditional rules regarding the domestic effect of international law, actually mirror the way that courts approach another boundary problem—the relation of constitutional norms to private and common law. In that context, courts also insist on the uncoupling of force and effect in a manner reminiscent of the treatment of non-binding international law. Thus at the same time that they state that constitutional rights do not apply to private or common law, they also demand fidelity to core constitutional values in the development of private and common law. Such development, they insist, must be sensitive to the central values of the constitution notwithstanding the fact that the constitution does not apply to private or common law. Both illustrations point to the increasing inability of the traditional spatialized model of legal authority to provide insight or guidance in a legal world where the significance of many different borders is shifting and where the concept of the border itself is correspondingly less salient.

Thus, in both instances, we see at work the idea that although legal norms may certainly take the form of discrete rights-conferring rules that by no means exhausts their effect. Instead, these sets of cases illustrate how discrete rules may generate larger values or principles that play out in matters of discretion and justification that have, in important senses, always remained beyond the reach of the traditional model. Because the conflicts-like predisposition of this model treats the process of adjudication as primarily a matter of rule selection, it has had little to contribute to an understanding of how discretion might be structured and shaped (both positively and negatively) and correspondingly little to add to our understanding of the role of justification and how it ought to be evaluated. Inspired by positivism with its emphasis on the rule of recognition and the question of pedigree, the traditional model offers limited insight in the case where the problem is not which norm to select and apply but rather how to shape some requirements in light of mandatory values drawn from elsewhere, either in the domestic legal system or beyond. In such a case, the traditional model's reliance on pedigree as command is at best a very partial contribution to an account of legitimacy.

In the international law context, the traditional account has responded to difficult interpretive questions of the kind discussed above by invoking a 'presumption of conformity' with international law. At bottom however, the presumption is simply too indebted to the traditional picture and the unique salience of binding rules to be adequate as an account of what courts are doing when they have recourse to non-domestically binding international law. The presumption sits comfortably with the traditional model's rule-focused account of legitimacy because on its face enshrines a kind of defeasible conformity with the specific rights conferred by the relevant source. By invoking conformity, it confirms the traditional account's confidence in the centrality of binding rules. And by operating as a fictionalized and rebuttable presumption of intention, it depends on the positivist command-based account of legitimacy that underlies that model. But for this very reason, the failure of the presumption to provide an account of what courts are actually doing when they have recourse to non-binding international law actually tells against the traditional model more generally.

Let us first briefly examine the idea of 'conformity' at the heart of the presumption. As noted above, the notion of conformity itself presumes that the controversy in question can be resolved by simply following or conforming to the relevant rule. Yet this does not seem to capture what courts actually do with non-domestically binding international law in cases like those discussed above. Sometimes this inaptness arises because courts themselves explicitly insist that conformity with the relevant non-binding law is not actually required. *Baker* is an obvious example of this since in that case the majority explicitly states that conformity with the Convention is not required. What is instead demanded is attentiveness to its core values—essentially an obligation of respect that must be manifest in deliberations and justifications. Similarly, in *Abbasi*, it is clear that while the Executive need not act in conformity with the relevant representations, neither is it open to it to treat such representations as irrelevant. Consideration and respect again seem the operative ideas.

Moreover, in many of the cases in which courts have recourse to non-binding international law, 'conformity' seems conceptually inapt. One illustration can be found in those cases where international law yields no obligation to conform yet where courts still find that such law still imposes demands of respect on deliberation and justification. This very distinction is apparent in the Privy Council's observation in aftermath of *Thomas*. Because Trinidad and Tobago had ratified but not incorporated the ACHR, it was clear that any decision issued by ACHR bodies would not be domestically binding. But as discussed the Privy Council notes the limits of conformity or bindingness as a test for salience when it observes that while a state would formally at liberty to ignore an order that was not binding domestically, such an order would make a very significant difference to the deliberative and justificatory positions open to a State. It is for this reason that the Privy Council points out that a modern democracy which operates under the rule of law and is sensitive to its international obligations cannot simply ignore such an opinion. So while conformity is not required, taking the decision into account in some respectful way is. Noting this reminds us of the limitations of relying on an idea of conformity in many of these cases. At bottom, it is simply too indebted to the exclusive significance of binding sources to be able to capture the more diverse and more complex ways in which legal resources may figure in the processes of deliberation and justification of official actions. And because the presumption turns on conformity which is premised on domestic bindingness, it is incapable of accounting for the much more complex ideas of salience that seem at work in these cases.[75]

Further, courts often seem to have recourse to non-binding international law in situations where the deliberative and justificatory task involves weaving together complex sets of norms in order to locate the key values and principles to guide and constrain their discretion. In such cases too, the idea of 'conformity' is at best

---

[75] *Ahani v Canada (Minister of Citizenship and Immigration)* [2002] OJ No 90 is another illustration. Canada had ratified but not domestically incorporated the Optional Protocol under the ICCPR. But under the Protocol even the Committee's final views are not binding as a matter of international law. Ahani was a convention refugee who had been ordered deported for security reasons and had exhausted his domestic remedies. He petitioned the Human Rights Committee which asked Canada to stay his deportation order until it had considered the communication. When Canada refused, Ahani sought a stay of deportation pending the Committee's deliberations. The trial judge refused to issue a stay and a majority of the Ontario Court of Appeal agreed. Laskin JA stressed that to rule otherwise would have the untenable effect of converting a non-binding request in an unincorporated Protocol into a binding domestic obligation. However, Rosenberg JA issued a powerful dissent, insisting that the federal government could not frustrate the very right established through ratification. And citing *Thomas* he suggests that it would be a mistake to read the absence of an eventual binding decision as an absence of mandatory salience. Any such decision would demand that it be taken into account and would therefore make a significant difference to what the government could and could not justify.

unhelpful. The estoppel-like invocations of non-binding international law serve as an illustration. *Drummond Wren*, for instance, is reminiscent of *Baker* in its explicit rejection of the idea that the sources matter because of their rules. Indeed, given the plethora of sources invoked in that case—domestic and international, public and private—any straightforward idea of conformity would literally be unworkable. Similarly, the fact that the House of Lords in *Oppenheimer* does not even specifically cite the relevant international law norms also undermines the idea that the invocation of international law in that case can be understood in terms of a narrow, rule-dependent idea like conformity. This is confirmed by the fact that in cases like *Drummond Wren* and *Oppenheimer* any international law rules that might be deployed can hold at most analogical or interpretive significance. In *Drummond Wren* for instance, the idea of conformity cannot hope to capture the relation between the Charter of the United Nations and the enforcement of domestic contracts.

It is telling by contrast that the vocabulary of the constitutional-private law relation seems more illuminating than the language of conformity. In the constitutional-private law cases it is only too clear that conformity cannot be the operative idea for (like many of the international law cases) most constitutional rights cannot be straight-forwardly be construed to generate decision-rules in private law. Instead, echoing the recourse to international law, they are often employed in a very different way. Rather than selecting among notionally applicable rules with different content (the conflicts model), in both the constitutional and the international cases courts attempt to draw together norms and rules without regard to their formal bindingness. And far from trying to select between one and another, they read the norms together, looking for overlap. And it is these areas of overlap that are especially important in the identification of fundamental values. The task in these cases is therefore fundamentally one of construction, rather than selection. And in this constructive enterprise the notion of conformity seems to be rather beside the point.

Given the positivist predispositions of the traditional model with its emphasis on pedigree, it should not surprise us that a second important weakness of the presumption is found in its underlying commitment to a command-style account of legitimacy. It is orthodox that, as an interpretive tool, the presumption is rebuttable. Its positivistic underpinnings are apparent in the fact that, because the presumption turns on legislative intent, theoretically it is inevitably defeated by a showing of contrary intent. Yet this does not seem to accord with what actually occurs in the cases discussed above. Oddly, if the idea of conformity seemed in a sense too strong to aptly describe what courts actually do with the relevant legal resources, the focus on intention inherent in the idea of a presumption appears too weak.

The complex legacy of *Teoh*, the Australian counterpart to *Baker*, reveals the difficulty of recourse to legislative intent as an explanation. In the aftermath of *Teoh*, the legislature repeatedly attempted to assert its intent not to act in accordance with the ratified but unincorporated Convention and the courts repeatedly refused to its stated intention as dispositive.[76] Similarly, in the litigation surrounding *Thomas* the fact that Trinidad and Tobago found it was not sufficient to simply express an intent not to be bound by their international law obligations. In order to displace a mandatory domestic effect, they eventually found it necessary repudiate those obligations by withdrawing their ratification of the ACHR. This too suggests that something as weak and intention-based as an interpretive presumption cannot account for the effect that the courts in these cases invoke. Indeed, as noted above, in *Briggs* the Privy Council made it explicit that mere assertions of contrary intent would not be sufficient to displace international obligations even in the absence of domestic bindingness. These twin difficulties suggest that whatever is doing the underlying work in these cases, it is unlikely to be the presumption of conformity. At bottom, I would suggest, this is because the influential form of authority that is manifest in these cases implicates a different much more constructivist account of legal judgment than the one presumed by the traditional account.

So if the presumption seems unlikely as an explanation for the reasoning in these cases, it may be worth briefly noting the conceptual tools that the courts actu-ally invoke. What the courts seem to reach for across these very different kinds of boundary problems is something that focuses not on the legislator's perspective but rather on an objectivized citizen's point of view—the idea of reasonable or legit-imate expectations. The doctrine of legitimate expectations was discussed in the *Teoh* opinions and has been persuasively criticized in that context on a number of grounds.[77] But notwithstanding the *Teoh* controversy, subsequent cases once again reached for the doctrine of legitimate expectations. Indeed, courts have employed the idea of reasonable or legitimate expectations both in the context of fleshing out the significance of non-binding international law obligations (*Abbasi* quoting *Teoh* and other cases on this point; *Thomas* and *Briggs* using the 'more substantive' version—'settled practice') and in the context of the impact of constitutionalized rights on private law (Baroness Hale in *Campbell*). Thus, across these cases we see courts recognizing an idea of mandatory influence dissociated from binding force and reaching for the idea of legitimate expectations to provide a fuller account of why these values deserve their mandatory status.

The doctrine of legitimate expectations has had a long life in administrative law and has been the subject of much controversy in that context. Debate inside and

[76] See for instance M Allars, 'Of Cocoons and Small "c" Constitutionalism: The Principle of Legality and an Australian Perspective on *Baker*' in D Dyzenhaus (ed), *The Unity of Public Law* (Oxford: Hart Publishing, 2004) 15, ch 12.

[77] See especially the thoughtful discussion in Murray Hunt, *Using Human Rights in English Law* (Oxford: Hart Publishing, 1998). In M Moran 'Authority Influence and Persuasion: *Baker*, Charter Values and the Puzzle of Method' in D Dyzenhaus (ed), *The Unity of Public Law* (Oxford: Hart Publishing, 2004) 15, I expressed considerable sympathy with these criticisms. The controversy sur-rounding this doctrine may account for the fact that the *Baker* majority opinion allows that 'the doc-trine of legitimate expectations does not mandate a result consistent with the wording of any international instruments' (para 74). Yet as noted above, the majority goes on to immediately insist on the centrality of the values of those international instruments if administrative discretion is to be justi-fied as reasonable.

outside the courts has focused on whether the idea is simply procedural or also encompasses substantive values. Although some of the cases here undoubtedly partake of that controversy, it is profitable to step away a bit from the details of the doctrine in an effort to grasp why, across these very different categories of cases, courts invoke (and perhaps in so doing reshape) the old common law idea of legitimate expectations. Courts in these cases involving what the traditional model would view as 'boundary problems' invoke legitimate expectations in a looser more analogical way as a means of capturing a certain understanding of the relationship between State and citizen. Unlike the presumption which is distinguished by its singular focus on the State's point of view, courts in these cases seem to use legitimate expectations or some equivalent in an attempt to find a tool to integrate the citizen's understanding (the expectation) with that of the authority (the legitimacy or reasonableness of the expectation).[78] In stark contrast with the traditional model, the incorporation of multiple points of view marks an attempt at a more integrative method that contemplates multiple and complex sources of legal normativity.

And although it is beyond the scope of this paper, this may well be part of a reshaping of the idea of legitimate expectations. For as these boundary problems illustrate, the tools of the old spatialized model are increasingly unhelpful. In many of these cases, courts are faced not with a conflicts-like task of selecting and applying the rule distinguished by appropriate pedigree but rather with questions about how to approach relatively-open textured problems of judgment. Typically courts that embark on such tasks draw together complex sets of norms and principles in an effort to articulate the relationships between the legal resources that bear on the enterprise. And in such matters, the legal demands that constrain and shape the exercise of discretion can to a significant degree be understood in terms of influential authority. It is thus unsurprising that when courts face questions about how to express the demands of influential authority they invoke the idea of reasonable or legitimate expectations. As noted above, one virtue of this idea is its ability to capture a more interactive and multi-faceted understanding of the norms that structure the exercise of legal discretion.[79] Moreover, the idea of legitimacy or reasonableness is precisely the kind of 'value term' that has historically served as the means by which the common law ensured attentiveness to larger or overarching values.[80] As the courts in these cases expand on the question of when expectations demand respect on the ground of their legitimacy, they also provide some insight into how to construct a more integrative account of authority, legitimacy, and judgment.

---

[78] For a very thoughtful discussion of legitimate expectations see G Cartier, *Reconceiving Discretion: From Discretion as Power to Discretion as Dialogue* (University of Toronto, SJD thesis, 2004). I am grateful to David Dyzenhaus for drawing this work to my attention.

[79] Waddams makes a related point when he notes the complex roles of basic legal ideas like reasonable expectations and reliance, pointing out that they are often in fact 'intertwined and influential across categories', S Waddams, *Concepts and Categories: Dimensions of Private Law* (Cambridge: CUP, 2003), 16.

[80] For the use of this term, See A Barak (n 67 above) 'Constitutional Human Rights and Private Law' in D Friedmann and D Barak-Erez (eds), *Human Rights in Private Law* (Oxford: Hart Publishing, 2001).

Thus, it seems important to briefly note the kinds of background justifications that the idea of legitimate expectations draws upon. Across the very different bodies of case law examined here it is possible to identify a few key features of this idea. One very important tool is found in the emphasis on representation, promise, or holding out. Not only does this idea play an important role in the administrative law use of legitimate expectations, but it also comes to the fore when courts insist that states at a minimum cannot use the domestic incorporation requirement to make a sham of solemn promises or undertakings at the international level.

This is forcefully expressed in *Teoh* and in the companion New Zealand case *Tavita*,[81] and also plays a very important role in *Thomas* and other cases.[82] The view that representations or promises made in the international sphere may well generate demands at the domestic level even in the absence of formal bindingness is also central to *Abbasi*'s invocation of the *Teoh* principle. In *Teoh*, the court points to legitimate expectations to provide an account of why ratification is a positive statement that itself generates obligations of respect. In *Abbasi* Lord Phillips relies on this to conclude that Foreign Office policies and representations are capable of giving rise to a legitimate expectation. Thus, it must be a normal expectation of a citizen that the 'the British Government will not simply wash their hands of the matter and abandon him to his fate'.[83] In *Drummond Wren* the court also invokes a similar idea when it emphasizes the wide official acceptance of policies and declarations that deplore racial discrimination.[84] In this sense then, the idea of legitimate expectations which draws on the significance of promising or holding out seems to provide much of the underlying justification for the demands of influential authority in these cases. As the courts also note in the cases, the fact that expectations may be legitimate does not mean that they cannot be displaced. But doing so requires exactly the kind of justification that courts in these cases demand, and that the traditional model rejects as irrelevant.

The idea of legitimate or reasonable expectations also comes to the fore in judicial accounts of why constitutional human rights exert demands on the shape of private and common law. Here too, it is possible to discern an idea of undertaking or promise as the underlying account of why constitutionalized human rights exert influential authority over private and common law. Thus for instance in *Campbell* Baroness Hale draws on the idea of a reasonable expectation of confidence as a means of drawing the mandatory ECHR values into the common law cause of action. Her reasoning points to the idea that what citizens legitimately expect necessarily partakes of background constitutional values. In this sense, constitutional arrangements themselves can be understood as a set of undertakings or promises about the exercise of public power. Though more stable and systematic that the kinds of undertakings about international law discussed above, the underlying justification

---

[81] *Tavita v Minister of Immigration* [1994] 2 NZLR 257 at 266.

[82] Moran (n 8 above) 15, tracing this 'bad faith' worry through several cases involving ratified but unimplemented treaties, though without the link to legitimate expectations.

[83] *Abbasi* (n 28 above).   [84] [1945] 4 DLR 674, 679.

is the same—citizens are entitled to expect and indeed demand that public power be exercised consistently with the core values of the constitutional order.

Understanding the justification in this way also helps to explain the link to the estoppel cases. For cases like *Drummond Wren* and *Oppenheimer* draw on a like idea when they insist that courts cannot be expected to enforce acts that run contrary to the values that are fundamental to law itself. Indeed, in *De Klerk v Du Plessis* the South African Constitutional Court points to the importance of related open-textured value terms in the common law, including public policy and reasonableness, as an important means of fashioning the relationship between constitutionalized human rights and private law.[85] So the task here as well can be best understood as a constructive one of weaving together complementary norms and values in the exercise of legal judgment.

5. Conclusion

The spatialized world view that inspired the traditional model's sharp delineation of law into bodies within borders and into clearly defined external and internal borders is increasingly unable to account for much of what judges actually do. This is particularly evident when judges confront the kind of boundary problems that are endemic in legal decision-making. As we have seen, courts often respond to these inadequacies by gesturing towards a more integrative account that weaves together a complex set of complementary legal resources into some kind of understanding of legal judgment is shaped and constrained, often by influential sources of normativity. One important illustration of this is found in the way that in cases involving significant interactions across the old borders of the traditional model, courts draw on an idea of legitimate expectations as a part of an effort to generate a more interactive and constructivist account of legal normativity. So the idea of legitimate or reasonable expectations is deployed across the very boundaries that characterized the traditional model's rendering of the relationship between domestic and international, public and private law. And this in turn suggests that the reshaping of the relationship between domestic and international law is not discrete but is in fact part of a larger phenomenon—a gradual but perceptible shift away from the spatialized model that has long held the legal imagination in its grip.

---

[85] *De Klerk v Du Plessis* (1996) 3 SA 850 (CC), 110 (per Ackermann J).

8

International Law in a Process of Constitutionalization

Christian Walter

1. Introduction

Constitutionalization is a highly ambiguous term.[1] It is used in national and international contexts with various meanings. In a purely national setting it is often used in order to describe the effects of constitutional law on the interpretation of ordinary laws and has thus a comparatively clear meaning.[2] In the European Union context it is used in order to describe the 'process by which the ECJ transformed treaty into constitution'.[3] Its meaning in the international arena is much less clear. Already the idea of a 'constitution' is a matter of different points of view. The universal organizations created immediately after the Second World War, such as the ILO or the WHO, use the term 'constitution' for their constituitive documents.[4] Today, the terms 'constitution' or 'constitutionalization' are used with respect to the development of specific regimes, such as the World Trade Organisation[5] or the United Nations system of collective security.[6] In recent years they have been used more and more in order to describe a constitutional development in international

[1] C Joerges, 'Constitutionalism and Transnational Governance: Exploring a Magic Triangle' in C Joerges and others (eds), *Transnational Governance and Constitutionalism* (Oxford and Portland Oregon: Hart Publishing Ltd., 2004) 339, 373 speaks of 'a trendy concept filled up with a plethora of meanings and messages'; in a similar direction R Wahl, *Konstitutionalisierung—Leitbegriff oder Allerweltsbegriff?* (Festschrift für Winfried Brohm, Munich/Beck, 2002), 191 et seq.

[2] For Germany. Ph. Kunig, 'Verfassungsrecht und einfaches Recht—Verfassungsgerichtsbarkeit und Fachgerichtsbarkeit' (2002) 61 VVDStRL 34, 51; W Heun, Verfassungsrecht und einfaches Recht—Verfassungsgerichtsbarkeit und Fachgerichtsbarkeit (2002) 61 VVDStRL 80, 109; GF Schuppert and C Bumke, *Die Konstitutionalisierung der Rechtsordnung*, (Baden-Baden: Nomos, 2002).

[3] F Snyder, 'General Course on Constitutional Law of the European Union' (2005) Vol VI *Collected Courses of the Academy of European Law* 41, 56.

[4] Eg the ILO-Charter, 15 UNTS 35 and the WHO-Charter, Vol 14 UNTS 185.

[5] DZ Cass, 'The "Constitutionalization" of International Trade Law' (2001) 12 EJIL 39; H Schloemann and ST Ohlhoff, 'Constitutionalization and Dispute Settlement in the WTO: National Security as an Issue of Competence' (1999) 93 AJIL 424 et seq.

[6] MJ Herdegen, 'The "Constitutionalization" of the UN Security System' (1994) 27 Vanderbilt J Transnat L 135.

law.[7] Especially in German legal doctrine the terms are used in the context of qualifying the United Nations Charter as a constitution of the international community,[8] or—less focused on a specific document—as a description of fundamental values underlying international law.[9]

Despite the different usage of the term 'constitutionalization' at least one common feature can be deduced, which is the connotation of a process. In using the term 'constitutionalization' (instead of 'constitution') the idea of a static situation is rejected[10] and the term may even imply some degree of imperfection—a situation of transition from one underlying concept to another, the contours of which are not yet entirely clear.[11] There are quite different visions as to where this development may lead.[12] Some authors envision the development of a World Republic,[13] others already today see the UN Charter as a constitution for 'international society'.[14] Others argue, because of a fragmentation of international law,[15] with different

---

[7] See notably the terms 'international constitutional law' or 'international constitutionalism' used by P Allott, 'The Concept of International Law' (1999) 10 EJIL 31, 37; P Allott, 'Intergovernmental Societies and the Idea of Constitutionalism' in M Coicaud and V Heiskanen (eds), *The Legitimacy of International Organizations* (Tokyo-New York-Paris: The United Nations Univ Press, 2001) 69; PH Allott, 'The Emerging Universal Legal System, International Law' (2001) 3 FORUM du droit international 12, 16; R Uerpmann, 'Internationales Verfassungsrecht' 2001 JZ 565.

[8] B Fassbender, 'The United Nations Charter as a Constitution of the International Community' (1997–98) 36 Columbia J Transnat L 529; PM Dupuy, 'The Constitutional Dimension of the Charter of the United Nations Revisited' (1997) 1 Max Planck Ybk on United Nations Law 1; R MacDonald, 'The Charter of the United Nations in a Constitutional Perspective' (1999) 20 Australian Ybk IL (1999) 205.

[9] C Tomuschat, 'Die Internationale Gemeinschaft' (1995) 33 AVR 1; C Tomuschat, 'Obligations Arising for States Without or Against their Will' (1993-IV) 241 RdC 195, 209 et seq; B Simma, 'From Bilateralism to Community Interest in International Law' (1994-VI) 250 RdC 217 et seq; B Simma and AL Paulus, 'The "International Community": Facing the Challenge of Globalization' (1998) 9 EJIL 266; PH Sands, 'Unilateralism, Values, and International Law' (2000) 11 EJIL 291, 300; AL Paulus, *Die Internationale Gemeinschaft im Völkerrecht—Eine Untersuchung zur Entwicklung des Völkerrechts im Zeitalter der Globalisierung* (München: Beck, 2001); B Faßbender, 'Der Schutz der Menschenrechte als zentraler Inhalt des völkerrechtlichen Gemeinwohls' 2003 EuGRZ 1.

[10] C Möllers, 'Transnational Governance without a Public Law?' in C Joerges and others (eds), *Transnational Governance and Constitutionalism* (Oxford and Portland, Oregon/Hart, 2004) 329, 334 et seq; TH Cottier and M Hertig, 'The Prospects of 21st Century Constitutionalism' (2003) 7 Max Planck Ybk on UN L 261, 283 and 296 et seq; A Fischer-Lescano, 'Globalverfassung: Verfassung der Weltgesellschaft' (2002) 88 ARSP 349, 351; M Kotzur, 'Weltrecht ohne Weltstaat—die Nationale (Verfassungs-) Gerichtsbarkeit als Motor Völkerrechtlicher Konstitutionalisierungsprozesse?' 2002 DÖV 195 at 200 et seq.

[11] AM Slaughter, 'Judicial Globalization' (2000) 40 Virginia JIL 1103, 1104 uses the term 'messy' with respect to informal coordination between Courts across the borders of different legal orders.

[12] A von Bogdandy, 'Demokratie, Globalisierung, Zukunft des Völkerrechts—eine Bestandsaufnahme' (2003) 63 ZaöRV 853.

[13] O Höffe, *Demokratie im Zeitalter der Globalisierung* (München, Beck, 1999) 295 and 296 et seq; in a similar direction R Falk and A Strauss, 'On the Creation of a Global Peoples Assembly: Legitimacy and the Power of Public Sovereignty' (2000) 36 Stanford JIL 191.   [14] See the references in n 8.

[15] M Koskenniemi and P Leino, 'Fragmentation of International Law—Postmodern Anxieties' (2002) 15 Leiden JIL 553. The ILC created a special 'Study Group on Fragmentation of International Law', GAOR, 55th Session, Supplement No 10 (A/55/10), para 729; see also the latest Report of the study group UN Doc A/CN.4/L.702 of 18 July 2006 entitled 'Difficulties Arising from the Diversification and Expansion of International Law'.

shades of detail, for the network structure of a polycentric society.[16] In these conceptions hierarchies are replaced either by 'mutual observation between network nodes' and a 'sequence of decisions within a variety of observational positions... which never leads to one final collective decision on substantive norms'[17] or by a collision law between conflicting legal orders which has yet to be developed.[18]

What are the consequences of these conceptions for the divide between national and international law? This divide is of no importance for the idea of a world republic. In that concept, law would be monopolized inside the world republic, the divide between inside and outside would cease to exist. For the proponents of a polycentric society the divide between different regimes and between different internal environments of the legal system is of more importance than the divide between national and international. Therefore they focus on this question.[19] The following discussion is based on an approach which lies somewhere in between the positions just described. The basic analytical observation is a shift from actor-centrism to subject-matter-orientation in the general structure of international law. The argument is developed by comparing the notion of 'constitution' in national law and in the current debate in international law. In the first section of this chapter it will be argued that simply transferring the notion of 'constitution' from the national context to the level of international law is insufficient to meet the current challenges.[20] Hence, the idea of creating a 'world republic' should be abandoned for the time being. The reason for this is *not* that the concepts of 'constitution' and 'state' are inextricably linked with each other.[21] On the contrary, it is quite possible to separate State and constitution and to transfer the notion of constitution into non-State contexts.[22] The point is, that the concept of constitution changes its meaning when it is transferred and this change of meaning is reinforced by the current structural changes of the international system: the disaggregation of the state on the one hand,[23] and the process of sectoralization which international

---

[16] A Fischer-Lescano and G Teubner, 'Regime-Collisions: The Vain Search for Legal Unity in the Fragmentation of Global Law' (2004) 25 Michigan JIL 999; AM Slaughter, *A New World Order* (Oxford: Princeton UP, 2004) speaks of a 'network of networks' (135 et seq.); N Walker, 'The Idea of Constitutional Pluralism' (2002) 65 The Modern Law Rev 317; G Anders, 'Lawyers and Anthropologists, A Legal Pluralist Approach to Global Governance', in IF Dekker and WG Werner (eds), *Governance and International Legal Theory*, (Leiden: Boston, Nijhoff, 2004) 37; TH Vesting, 'Die Staatsrechtslehre und die Veränderung ihres Gegenstandes: Konsequenzen von Europäisierung und Internationalisierung' (2004) 63 VVDStRL 41.

[17] Fischer-Lescano and Teubner (n 16 above) 999, 1018 and 1039 et seq.

[18] TH Vesting, 'Die Staatsrechtslehre und die Veränderung ihres Gegenstandes: Konsequenzen von Europäisierung und Internationalisierung' (2004) 63 VVDStRL 41, 66.

[19] Fischer-Lescano and Teubner (n 16 above) 999, 1014 et seq.

[20] G Teubner, 'Globale Zivilverfassungen' (2003) 63 ZaöRV 1, 3.

[21] A theoretical approach which is based on that assumption may be found in J Isensee, 'Staat und Verfassung' in J Isensee and P Kirchhof (eds), *Handbuch des Staatsrechts der Bundesrepublik Deutschland* (Heidelberg/Müller, 2004) 3 Aufl. §15, para 1 et seq.

[22] Walker, 'The Idea of Constitutional Pluralism' (n 16 above) 320.

[23] Among the various contributions in that regard, J Habermas, 'Beyond the Nation-State? On some Consequences of Economic Globalization' in EO Eriksen and JE Fossum (eds), *Democracy in the European Union—Integration through Deliberation?* (London: Routledge, 2000) 29; AM Slaughter,

law is undergoing on the other,[24] make it very unlikely that—in the foreseeable future—we will have '*an* international constitution' for '*the* international community'. Instead, we are confronted with an order consisting of 'partial constitutions' (on the international level as well as in the national context; since the emergence of a system of 'international governance' also reduces the national constitutions to partial constitutions[25]) and of 'constitutional elements' which may be found in various contexts. But viewed as a whole, the emerging order lacks an overall constitution. The sectoralization of international law necessesarily implies a move from actor-centrism to subject-matter-orientation.

The second part of this chapter develops a critical point of view towards two alternative concepts. The first concerns the description of 'international governance' from the perspective of a network structure, the second concerns models of legal pluralism.[26] These concepts seem acceptable as an analytical description of the current developments and problems. But on a normative level one may doubt whether it is possible to speak of a process of constitutionalization of the international system or even of an 'international constitutional law'[27] without at least some degree of hierarchy. In this respect, the terms 'constitution' and 'constitutionalization' necessarily remain linked to the background of national constitutional law from whence they have been borrowed.[28] This argument will be set out a little bit more in detail in the second part of the chapter.

What are, then, possible answers concerning the divide between national and international? In the third and main part, I suggest a re-conceptualization of international law by departing from its traditional actor-centrism.[29] My proposition is to build on the general shift from actor-centrism to subject-matter-orientation, which can be currently witnessed in international law in general, also with respect to the legal bases upon which the whole construction of international law rests. I suggest a departure from the strong focus which the current construction of international law places on the notion of '*international* legal personality' as a specific

---

A New World Order (Oxford: Princeton UP, 2004) 12 et seq; O Schachter, 'The Decline of the Nation-State and its Implications for International Law' (1997/98) 36 Columbia J Transnat L 7; C Schreuer, 'The Waning of the Sovereign State—Towards a New Paradigm for International Law?' (1993) 4 EJIL 447, 453; P Saladin, *Wozu noch Staaten? Zu den Funktionen des Modernen Demokratischen Rechtsstaats in einer Zunehmend Überstaatlichen Welt* (Bern: Stämpfli, 1995) 19 et seq.

[24] The term sectoralization is preferred here because it does not go along with the negative connoatation which is connected with the term 'fragmentation', for the latter see the references in n 15 above.

[25] P Häberle, 'Das Grundgesetz als Teilverfassung im Kontext der EU/EG—eine Problemskizze' in *Festschrift für Hartmut Schiedermair* (Heidelberg: Müller, 2001) 81 et seq.   [26] See n 16 above.

[27] See the references in n 7.

[28] AL Paulus, 'Commentary to Andreas Fischer-Lescano and Gunther Teubner, 'The Legitimacy of International Law and the Role of the State' (2004) 25 Michigan JIL 1047, 1056 et seq; R Wahl, *Konstitutionalisierung—Leitbegriff oder Allerweltsbegriff?* (Festschrift für Winfried Brohm München: Beck, 2002) 206.

[29] F Schorkopf and C Walter, 'Elements of Constitutionalization: Multilevel Structures of Human Rights Protection in General International and WTO-Law' (2003) 4 German LJ 1359, 1361 et seq, available at <http://www.germanlawjournal.com/article.php?id=348>.

kind of legal personality which is restricted to a limited number of actors (States, international organizations, etc.). This traditional construction basically reflects the actor-centrism of the current system. An alternative would be to simply ask whether a specific legal issue is governed by international law. In other words the decisive question is whether or not a 'public international law relationship' (Völkerrechtsverhältnis) does exist. The advantage of this proposition is seen in the possibility to take up some of the concerns voiced by *Gunther Teubner* and others. Most importantly, this proposition is able to deal with the changing role of the individual in international law in a conceptual manner.[30] At the same time, the concept remains open to traditional hierarchies created by public law in general and especially by national constitutional law—and thus takes into account an important criticism which may be voiced against *Teubner's* 'societal constitutionalism'.

The concept of 'public international law relationship' has immediate consequences for the relationship between national and international law, since it generally leads to the direct applicability of international legal norms within the context of domestic law. This attributes an important role to the national judiciary. I discuss the practical consequences of such an enhanced role for the judiciary and defend the proposition against the potential criticism that it is nothing more than a different point of departure in a circular reasoning.

The final parts sketch a model in which processes of constitutionalization on different levels may be analyzed and taken into account in order to develop an inclusive international law. Here, it is argued that 'constitutionalization of international law' has to be seen as a deliberative process in which new forms of hierarchies are gradually being developed.

2. Disaggregating constitutional law: partial constitutions and constitutional elements

Why do I argue against the qualification of the United Nations Charter as a constitution for the 'international community'? It is true that the Charter includes many features which are similar to those which we find in national constitutions. It stems from a 'constitutional moment', it sets up a system of governance, creates a hierarchy of norms and defines its members.[31] One may even find some more elements of a constitution. However, there are also several difficulties.[32] One is that of the members. There can be no doubt that the Charter is the constitutive document of a community of States.[33] In that sense it forms part of the traditional

---

[30] B Grzeszick, 'Rechte des Einzelnen im Völkerrecht' (2005) 43 AVR 312; O Dörr, 'Privatisierung des Völkerrechts' (2005) JZ, 905.

[31] These are the criteria mentioned by Fassbender (n 8 above) 529, 573 et seq.

[32] AL Paulus, 'From Territoriality to Functionality? Towards a Legal Methodology of Globalization' in IF Dekker and WG Werner (eds), *Governance and International Legal Theory* (Leiden-Boston, 2004) 59, 63 et seq.   [33] Arts 3 and 4 of the UN Charter.

fabric of international law as a law between States. If the Charter is seen as 'Constitution of the International Community' it becomes necessary to determine who the members of the international community are. Is it still a 'community of states' as it was formulated in Article 53 of the Vienna Convention on the Law of Treaties in the late 1960s? By now, the notion of 'international community' seems to have moved beyond that of a community of States.[34] In its commentary on the 2001 Draft Articles on State Responsibility the International Law Commission defines the 'international community as a whole'[35] as the 'totality of other subjects' to which a State owes an obligation[36] and it includes among those subjects by definition all other States[37] but also implicitly non-State actors.[38] This leads to the conclusion that, if the Charter is to be the constitution of the international community, then the provisions concerning membership in the Charter do not adequately reflect the current state of international law.

A related aspect is that the Charter does not contain a catalogue of individual rights. It mentions the issue of human rights in several provisions, however only in a very general manner and with respect to their promotion in the national setting of the member states.[39] While one may convincingly argue that the Council is bound by fundamental human rights,[40] the difference to national constitutional systems in that respect remains nevertheless quite obvious. The lacuna in the Charter was recently strongly underlined when the Security Council, for the first time, adopted measures which produced effects on the rights of individuals in the member States.[41] Thus, with respect to human rights protection, the term 'Charter' evokes associations with other fundamental documents setting out the rights of peoples, nations, and individuals, which the UN Charter does not live up to.[42]

The most important difference with respect to national constitutions lies in the structure of the object which is to be constituted. In national constitutional law this object has several characteristics, the most important of which is that the State purports to exercise public power within territorial limits but without restrictions as to possible subject matters of regulation.[43] Relying on the notion of internal

[34] The Draft Articles on State Responsibility Adopted by the International Law Commission in 2001 speak of the 'international community as a whole' without mentioning states as constituent elements, see Arts 25(1)(b); 33(1); 42(b); and 48(1)(b).
[35] This is also the term used by the ICJ in *Barcelona Traction, Light and Power Company, Limited, Second Phase* [1970] ICJ Rep 4, para 33.
[36] Commentaries to the draft articles on Responsibility of States for internationally wrongful acts adopted by the International Law Commission at its fifty-third session (2001) 72, available at <http://www.un.org/law/ilc/texts/State_responsibility/responsibilityfra.htm> accessed 8 March 2005.
[37] Ibid, 322.   [38] Ibid, 234.
[39] R Wolfrum, 'Commentary on Art. 1, para. 9, and commentary on Art. 56, para 4' in B Simma (ed), *The Charter of the United Nations. A Commentary* (2nd edn, Oxford: Oxford University Press, 2002).
[40] E de Wet and A Nollkaemper, 'Review of Security Council Decisions by National Courts' (2002) 45 German Ybk IL 166, 171 et seq.
[41] SC Res. 1333 of 19 December 2000 required the freezing of financial resources of individuals and organizations associated with Osama bin Laden and the Al-Qaeda.
[42] Paulus, 'From Territoriality to Functionality?' (n 32 above) 59, 63 et seq.
[43] C Walter, 'Constitutionalizing (Inter)national Governance—Possibilities for and Limits to the Development of an International Constitutional Law' (2001) 44 German Ybk IL 170, 192.

sovereignty, in the traditional concept the nation State may take up any given subject matter and adopt a regulation for it.[44] Furthermore, it 'facilitated the political activation of its citizens. It was the national community that generated a new kind of connection between persons who had been strangers to one another.'[45] In sum, the nation State and its constitution in the traditional concept provided a 'homology of territory, community and political capacity',[46] and thus achieved a bundling of constitutional functions in one political unit by a single legal document.[47]

International human rights regulations have created some restrictions as to the forms of regulation, but in principle this idea has remained unchanged. There is one regional exception to this model, which is the European Community. In those areas where the Community has been given exclusive competence, eg the Common Commercial Policy, the member States have lost their own competence and—even in the absence of Community legislation—may not regulate these areas.[48] This indicates a sectoral division of competencies between different actors according to certain subject matters (such as environment, transport, consumer protections, etc.) which was unknown to the traditional system. It is crucially important to take into account this sectoralization of competencies in order to correctly analyse the current changes in the relationship between international law and national (constitutional) law, because it not only holds true for the development within the European Community, but also with respect to international governance in general. We witness the emergence of a sectorally organized international order: International Criminal Law, International Trade Law, International Environmental Law, etc. Each of these sectorally confined regimes develops rules which not only address States as subjects of international law, but in which the individual is granted specific rights or made subject to certain obligations. These regimes are becoming more and more institutionalized. Often they even set up organs for dispute settlement, again sectorally limited, a development which has nourished the debate on 'fragmentation' of international law.[49]

---

[44] H Mosler, *The International Society as a Legal Community* (Alphen aan den Rijn/Sijthoff: Noordhoff, 1980) 16: 'It has become common to speak of international organisations as constitutions. They have indeed essential features of a constitution. *Their object is, however, restricted compared with the traditional meaning of a constitution as the supreme law capable of regulating everything and binding everybody within its territorial jurisdiction.*' (emphasis added).

[45] J Habermas, 'The European Nation State—its Achievements and its Limitations' in *Rechtstheorie* (Beiheft, 1997) 109, 112.

[46] Walker, 'The Idea of Constitutional Pluralism' (n 16 above) 320.

[47] Walter (n 43 above) 170, 192.

[48] P Craig and G De Burca, *EU Law: Text, Cases and Materials*, 3rd edn, (Oxford: OUP, 2003) 129.

[49] Notably the *Swordfish-Case* between the European Community and Chile has contributed to that debate; in the WTO the case is dealt with as DS 193. The case is, however, on hold since March 2001, see the information available at <http://www.wto.org/english/tratop_e/dispu_e/cases_e/ds193_e .htm>. The parallel ITLOS-Proceedings have also been put on hold see M Orellana, 'The EU and Chile Suspend the Swordfish Case Proceedings at the WTO and the International Tribunal of the Law of the Sea', ASIL Insight Nr 60, 2001, available at <http://www.asil.org/insights/insigh60.htm>; for the ensuring debate on multiple international dispute settlement mechanisms see J Neumann, 'Die materielle und prozessuale Koordination völkerrechtlicher Ordnungen—Die Problematik paralleler Streitbeilegungsverfahren am Beispiel des Schwertfisch-Falls' (2001) 61 ZaöRV 529; JI Charney,

This highlights the important difference between the concept of 'constitution' in the context of the State and the current developments: while the State exercised competencies which were territorially limited but potentially unlimited in respect of the subject matters to be regulated, the new international legal order has brought about actors which are functionally limited but which may have the possibility for global or almost global regulation with only few territorial restrictions, depending on the range of membership.

It is the sectoralization or functional differentiation which leads to the conclusion that conceiving the United Nations Charter as a constitution of the international community does not solve the current problems. The idea of the Charter being the constitution of the international community does not sufficiently take into account the sectoral differentiation of the international system. The model of the Charter as a constitution of the international community does not give answers as to how the international order should react to sectoral differentiation. It suggests a hierarchy of norms only with respect to the relationship between the Charter and other norms of national or international law. But it does not take into account that the Charter is in itself sectorally limited.

Does this mean that there is nothing to the debate on an 'international constitutional law'? Of course not. The point is rather that the model of the Charter as a constitution of the international community takes too much of its orientation from traditional structures.[50] It is necessary to take a closer look at the functions of constitutional law and to abandon the idea of *a* (!) constitution. The international community is and has been developing several partial constitutions and the international order has assumed functions which correspond to those which were— and of course still are—assumed by national constitutional law. International law today supplements and in part replaces national constitutions. But it does not have *a* constitution.[51] Along with the disaggregating nation State, the notion of constitution disaggregates into constitutional functions and partial constitutions. This implies that already today (and even more in the future) there is more than one public law regime which applies to the same persons and the same subject matter.

3. Advantages and disadvantages of the network-model

The developments just described have led several observers to conceptualize the current system of governance as a network in which elements of national and

'Is International Law Threatened by Multiple International Tribunals?' (1998) 271 Recueil des Cours 101; T Buergenthal, 'Proliferation of International Courts and Tribunals: Is it Good or is it Bad?' (2001) 14 Leiden JIL 267; K Oellers-Frahm 'Multiplication of International Courts and Tribunals and Conflicting Jurisdictions—Problems and Solutions' (2001) 5 Max Plack Ybk on UN Law 67.

[50] To that extent the propositions developed here follow the criticism voiced by G Teubner, 'Societal Constitutionalism: Alternatives to State-Centered Constitutional Theory?' in C Joerges and others (eds), *Transnational Governance and Constitutionalism* (Oxford and Portland Oregon: Hart Publishing Ltd., 2004) 3, 7.   [51] Walter (n 43 above) 170, 173.

international law, of public and private law, are connected without hierarchy.[52] This model has the important advantage that it can plausibly describe what is currently happening in practice. Even where the States are in principle free to participate in a given treaty mechanism, and thus the notion of sovereignty could be kept alive at least on a theoretical level, it has to be admitted that in practice many situations do not leave much choice; the price for staying away simply being to high.[53] The network model may accommodate such political constraints more easily than the traditional distinctions.

3.1 Inclusion of private actors and informal mechanisms

The idea of a network may also quite easily include private actors and consider their factual influence on the international system. The role of private actors, especially NGOs and multinational companies, has puzzled international lawyers for several years.[54] However in the networks conception they are simply another knot in the fabric. Important examples include ICANN as the 'ruler of the Internet'[55] or multinational corporations.[56] The network model, therefore, has the advantage of flexibility, precisely because it does not require hierarchies. The network structure may also accommodate a development towards informal mechanisms of transnational corporations, which has been described and analysed in recent years. A prominent example is the informal cooperation of the national Central Banks through the Basle Committee.[57]

---

[52] See the references in n 26.

[53] In this context one may refer to the 1989 Basel Convention on the Control of Transboundary Movements of Hazardous Wastes and their Disposal (ILM 28 (1989), 657). This Convention prohibits the export of *any* waste to states that are not parties to it (Art 4, section 5 of the Convention: 'A Party shall not permit hazardous wastes or other wastes to be exported to a non-Party or to be imported from a non-Party).' Thus, the economic consequences with respect to the export of waste in general are used as an incentive to encourage participation in this Convention. The mechanism is very simple: the more states become parties to the Convention, the stronger the economic pressure to participate in the Convention becomes as the number of possible trade partners for non-members diminishes. The Convention regulates the procedures for exporting hazardous wastes in detail and has even pre-framed the details of a corresponding EU-regulation.

[54] Various contributions in R Hofmann (ed), *Non-State Actors as New Subjects of International Law* (Berlin: Duncker & Humblot, 1999); S Hobe, 'Global Challenges to Statehood: The Increasing Importance of Non-Governmental Organizations' (1998) 5 Indiana J Global Legal Stud 191; S Hobe, 'Der Rechtsstatus der Nichtregierungsorganisationen nach Geltendem Völkerrecht' (1999) 37 AVR 152; K Nowrot, 'Legal Consequences of Globalization: The Status of Non-Governmental Organizations under International Law' (1999) 6 Indiana J Global Legal Stud 579; W Hummer, 'Internationale Nichtstaatliche Organisationen im Zeitalter der Globalisierung—Abgrenzung, Handlungsbefugnissle, Rechtsnatur' (2000) 39 BDGVR 45.

[55] On the history of ICANN and its antecedents, J Weinberg, 'ICANN and the Problem of Legitimacy' (2000) 50 Duke LJ 187, 192.

[56] For instance PT Muchlinski, 'Human Rights and Multinationals: Is there a Problem?' (2001) 77 International Affairs 31.

[57] For this and further examples, AM Slaughter, 'Governing the Global Economy through Government Networks' in M Byers (ed), *The Role of Law in International Politics. Essays in International Relations and International Law* (2000) 177, 181 et seq.

3.2 Informal constitutionalization through the judiciary

The most important development with respect to the constitutionalization of international law which may easily be explained in the network model is, however, informal cooperation of national and international courts. The matter has been addressed with respect to the meetings of the European constitutional Courts and more generally concerning the comparative consideration of foreign decisions in similar cases.[58] It has received further momentum in recent years when the US Supreme Court started to take up a comparative approach in some of its decisions on politically important issues such as the criminalization of sodomy[59] and the death penalty.[60] When confronted with the question of the constitutionality of the death penalty for mentally ill persons, Justice Stevens wrote for the majority in what may become a famous footnote 21, that 'within the world community, the imposition of the death penalty for crimes committed by mentally retarded offenders is overwhelmingly disapproved'.[61] This reference to 'the world community' provoked disagreement of the Chief Justice, who failed to see 'how the views of other countries regarding the punishment of their citizens provide any support for the Court's ultimate determination'.[62] An even stronger disagreement was voiced by Justice Scalia in the sodomy case:

Constitutional entitlements do not spring into existence because some States choose to lessen or eliminate criminal sanctions on certain behavior. Much less do they spring into existence, as the Court seems to believe, because *foreign nations* decriminalize conduct. The Court's discussion of these foreign views (ignoring, of course, the many countries that have retained criminal prohibitions on sodomy) is therefore meaningless dicta. Dangerous dicta, however, since this Court . . . should not impose foreign moods, fads, or fashions on Americans. (Foster v. Florida, 537 U. S. 990, n. (2002) (Thomas, J., concurring in denial of certiorari).[63]

The current disagreement among the Justices in the US Supreme Court[64] is illustrative of the possibilities for a convergence of standards through comparative law as an informal tool in the hand of the judiciary. It is informal in the sense that no rules exist which could guide the choice of the material to which reference is made and it is also informal because not even the comparative approach as such is mandatory. However, it is undeniable that there is a growing tendency among high national courts and international tribunals, especially those which deal with the protection of human rights, to follow such a comparative approach if they consider it appropriate in a given case.[65] The network model may view the courts as knots in the fabric and thus describe this development adequately.

---

[58] Slaughter (n 11 above) 1103.   [59] *Lawrence and Garner v Texas* 539 US (2003).

[60] *Atkins v Virginia* 536 US 304 (2002).

[61] *Lawrence and Garner v Texas* 539 US (2003), n 21 of the majority opinion.

[62] Ibid, the Chief Justice, dissenting.

[63] Ibid, Justice Scalia dissenting at 14, available at <http://supct.law.cornell.edu/supct/html/02-102.ZS.html>.   [64] It continued in March 2005 in *Roper v Simmons* 543 U.S. (2005).

[65] Slaughter (n 11 above) 1103, 1117; GL Neuman, 'The Uses of International Law in Constitutional Interpretation' (2004) 98 AJIL 82; C Walter, 'Dezentrale Konstitutionalisierung durch Nationale und

3.3 Lack of normalcy and hierarchy as deficit of the network model and pluralist conceptions of international law: the continuing role for the State

However, the network model has at least one important disadvantage: it cannot provide for hierarchies which are necessary if certain functions which have been fulfilled by national constitutional law under the old structure are kept.[66] How do we ensure that under a new system of international governance democratic structures are implemented?[67] How do we ensure that the exercise of the now diverse public power is made subject to human rights constraints? The difficulties already mentioned which have arisen in the context of the lists of terrorist organizations, illustrate this problem perfectly well. Member States are put into the position of either meeting their international obligations (and freeze funds of persons who maintain that they have been put on the list without proper cause and without legal remedies) or they install their own mechanism of control and possibly breach their international obligations if that is the required outcome of the procedure.

The problem is genuinely constitutional: it concerns the protection of the individual against the exercise of public power. In that sense it differs from purely private legal relationships which some of the network models include. It thus illustrates that merely accepting the network structure and its absence of hierarchies is not enough—at least not from a public law perspective which is guided by the functions fulfilled by national constitutions in the traditional context. Since we will not have a coherent and dogmatically consistent constitutional structure for the network as such, it is all the more important to ensure that the basic functions of national constitutional law continue to be fulfilled under the new structure. Of course, the problem could be solved if we had an 'international constitutional law' which sets the necessary standards and demands mechanisms of judicial control.

Internationale Gerichte: Überlegungen zur Rechtsvergleichung als Methode im öffentlichen Recht' in J Oebbecke (ed), *Nichtnormative Steuerung in Dezentralen Systemen* (Neuhardenberg: Franz Steiner Verlag Stuttgart, 2005).

[66] Similar criticism in Paulus (n 28 above) 1047, 1056 et seq and C Möllers, 'Transnational Governance without a Public Law?' in C Joerges and others (eds), *Transnational Governance and Constitutionalism* (Oxford and Portland Oregon: Hart Publishing Ltd. 2004) 329, 334 et seq.

[67] The problem has been raised many times. See the overview on different approaches given in A von Bogdandy, 'Demokratie, Globalisierung, Zukunft des Völkerrechts—eine Bestandsaufnahme' (2003) 63 ZaöRV 853; also S Marks, 'Democracy and International Governance' in J M Coicaud and V Heiskanen (eds), *The Legitimacy of International Organizations* (Tokyo-New York-Paris The United Nations University Press, 2001) 47; R Falk and A Strauss 'On the Creation of a Global Peoples Assembly: Legitimacy and the Power of Public Sovereignty' (2000) 63 Stanford JIL 191; JA Frowein, 'Constitutionalism in the Face of the Changing Nation State', in C Starck (ed), *Constitutionalism, Universalism and Democracy—a Comparative Analysis* (Baden-Baden: Nomos, 1999) 53, 69; EW Böckenförde, *Die Zukunft politischer Autonomie—Demokratie und Staatlichkeit im Zeichen von Globalisierung, Europäisierung und Individualisierung* in EW Böckenförde, *Staat, Nation, Europa Studien zur Staatslehre, Verfassungstheorie und Rechtsphilosophie* (Frankfurt: Suhrkamp, 1999) 103 et seq; E Stein, 'International Integration and Democracy: No Love at First Sight' (2001) 95 AJIL 489.

However, where is this universally applicable international law? And do we really have common standards that can be applied in such situations?

These questions point to a continuing and important function of the State under the new structures. The public power exercised by the organs of the State is necessary in order to vest an international organization with the exercise of public power—and it is necessary in order to establish the necessary limitations of that power. The jurisprudence of both the European Court of Human Rights and the German Federal Constitutional Court may be interpreted in the sense of establishing a duty of the member States (or the German Government) to assure application and control of basic human rights standards when they create international organizations and vest them with the exercise of public power ('Schutzpflicht').[68] In a sense these developments reverse the distribution of roles between international law and the state with respect to human rights protection. In the development of human rights law since 1945, States appear as a threat for human rights and are thus made subject to international human rights obligations. When security action moves from the internal sphere of States to the level of international institutions, human rights concerns follow. Where the international institutions in question do not provide for mechanisms of control, States and their organs (ie national courts) reappear as guardians against possible violations of human rights from the international sphere.

At the same time, these questions raise doubts as to whether one should include *purely* private norm systems into the debate on 'constitutionalization', even when the norms set and enforced in these systems are of high general importance. A closer look reveals that these systems operate in the shadow of a public law framework.[69] The internet, which is the most prominent example of this type, is not a subject which is intrinsically private and immune from public law regulation. It is intrinsically international, but that fact does not in itself exclude a public law regulation through an international agency set up by an international treaty concluded by governments. To give a concrete example, a framework convention setting up certain norms concerning the internet and imposing certain duties on ICANN and other private entities would qualify differently from the existing relationship between ICANN and other private persons. Depending on what the convention entitles ICANN to do, it may also influence the qualification of the relationship between ICANN and its clients.

---

[68] For details, Walter (n 43 above) 170, 196 et seq; for a similar line of argument with respect to the control of Security Council Resolutions by national courts de Wet and Nollkaemper (n 40 above) 166, 188 et seq.

[69] HH Trute 'The Impact of Global Networks on Political Institutions and Democracy' in C Engel and KH Keller (eds), *Governance of Global Networks in the Light of Differing Local Values* (Baden-Baden, 2000) 131, 148; C Möllers, 'Transnational Governance without a Public Law?' in C Joerges and others (eds), *Transnational Governance and Constitutionalism* (Oxford and Portland Oregon: Hart Publishing Ltd., 2004) 329, 332; cf J von Bernstorff, 'The Structural Limitations of Network Governance, ICANN as a Case in Point', in C Joerges and others (eds), *Transnational Governance and Constitutionalism* (Oxford and Portland Oregon: Hart Publishing Ltd., 2004) 257, 277 et seq.

4. From actor-orientation to subject matter-orientation: The 'public international law relationship' ('Völkerrechtsverhältnis') as a substitute for international legal personality

4.1 Actor-orientation and subject matter-orientation

Classic international law is an actor-centered law. Any given text-book on international law will invariably deal extensively with the subjects of international law. It will describe states as the main subjects of international law, then move on to international organizations, treat the problems which go along with de facto regimes and, after having described the traditional but untypical subjects like the Holy See and the Sovereign Military and Hospitaller Order of St John of Jerusalem of Rhodes and of Malta, it will—more or less cautiously—deal with the individual and with transnational corporations.

And yet, at a second look, the acceptance of the individual as a subject of international law, at least in some areas, puts into question the notion of international legal personality as a central pillar of the system. Depending on the specific issue in question, if it is correct that it is possible that the individual may claim rights which are rooted in international law (or may be subject to duties which stem from international law), then it is difficult to see why we still put so much emphasis on the notion of subjects of international law.[70] The strong focus on subjects of international law under the traditional doctrine relates closely to a concept of international law which is based on a limited number of actors. Under the traditional system it was possible to look at the actors and determine whether or not their relationship was governed by public international law. The difficulty of determining the applicable law now is a reflection of the complexity faced under a new doctrine. Today, we may have private individuals and still be confronted with a situation which is governed by public international law.

An interesting practical example is a treaty concerning the turning over of certain parts of an airbase in Frankfurt by the United States Airforces to the Frankfurt Airport Company. The treaty was concluded in 1999 between a variety of very different actors: the Federal Republic of Germany (represented by the Ministry of Finance), the Government of the United States of America (represented by the US Air Forces in Europe), the Frankfurt Airport Ltd (a private company under German Company Law, represented by its President), the State (Bundesland) of Hessen (represented by its Ministry of Finance), and the State (Bundesland) of Rheinland-Pfalz (also represented by its Ministry of Finance).[71] An uninformed

---

[70] J Delbrück, 'Structural Changes in the International System and its Legal Order: International Law in an Era of Globalization' (2001) 1 SZIER 24: 'the *numerus clausus* of subjects of international law is no longer valid'.   [71] GVBl. Rheinland-Pfalz Nr 8 of 27 June 2003, 81.

observer from the outside, who just sees the actors and not the applicable law, could not tell whether to apply international law or not. A look at the actors alone does not answer the question anymore. Why, then, should international lawyers continue to focus so strongly on the actors?

There is an alternative to the actor-centered concept. A look into the national legal systems reveals that there we are perfectly capable of distinguishing capacities for certain action from the legal personality as such. There can be no doubt that each individual is endowed with legal personality, while not being able to perform certain acts. As individuals we usually cannot legislate, we cannot adopt administrative acts, etc. However, these limitations do not depend on our legal personality. Whether or not a person can act in a specific manner depends on the applicable norms which allow or prohibit a certain action, not on his or her legal personality. The same idea could be transferred to international law. One would then have to ask which norms govern a specific behaviour. The question would not be 'who acts?', but rather whether the action in question is governed by public international law or not. The focus consequently shifts from the international legal personality to what could be called a 'public international law relationship'. The current focus on states as sovereign actors would be replaced by a concept which rests on 'subjects of law' as such.[72]

If the observation is correct that the reason for the primordial relevance of the notion of subjects of international law is the actor-centered structure of traditional international law, and if it is equally correct that the traditional actor-centered order is currently being, if not replaced, then supplemented and in part modified by a subject-oriented structure,[73] then it may help as a first step to give up the notion of international legal personality as the cornerstone of public international law and replace it with the notion of a 'public international law relationship'. This would break down the 'big question' of the relationship between international law and municipal law in general to the much smaller issue of the relationship between the two legal orders in a given legal situation and it could allow for different answers according to the subject matter and the actors concerned. It would most probably change little as to the outcome of specific legal disputes, but it would contribute to a re-conceptualization of international law which takes into account current developments.

4.2 Consequences for the divide between national and international law

A concept of international law which puts less emphasis on the role of international legal personality necessarily reduces the importance of the divide between

---

[72] Eg K Dicke, 'Erscheinungsformen und Wirkungen von Globalisierung in Struktur und Recht des Internationalen Systems auf universeller und regionaler Ebene sowie gegenläufige Renationalisierungstendenzen' (2000) 39 BDGVR 13, 34 et seq and 37, who speaks of a 'global law of mankind'.
[73] JB Auby, *La Globalisation, le Droit et l'État* (Paris: Montchrestien, 2003) 115, 117 who speaks in that context of a change in the nature of international law itself.

national and international law. It implies that international law may apply directly and without transformation to individuals. The creation of this consequence is precisely the motive for its introduction. It is not necessary, however, to enter the difficult waters of the theories of monism and dualism in order to present the most important consequences of the concept.[74] The concept is certainly incompatible with strict dualist positions, since it implies that international law may directly grant rights to individuals or impose duties upon them. But the concept never-theless requires that an international legal norm be applicable to the situation in question and it thus fits all other shades of dualist and monist positions.

While it is true that the decision on the applicability of international law is still largely defined by national constitutional law, the concept of a 'public international law relationship' proposed here would have as one major consequence that it precludes arguments which deny direct applicability to international legal norms *simply because of their international character*. The concept thus necessarily pierces the veil of national sovereignty which is much more present under the current conceptions which are based on international legal personality. The concept of the 'public international law relationship' implies that—if a 'public international law relationship' has been determined to exist in a given case—the international law in question is directly applicable.

This proposed concept has consequences on the separation of powers between the different branches of government. Assessing whether or not a 'public inter-national law relationship' exists and what precise meaning it has, falls within the sole responsibility of the judiciary.[75] Just as in the national context, courts have the possibility and the duty to interpret the applicable norms, even if the concepts used may be broad or vague at times. And just as in the national context the broad-ness and vagueness need not prevent courts from applying the international norms considered directly applicable under the doctrine proposed here. It has been rightly stressed that the traditional doctrine of direct applicability, which requires the norms in question to be sufficiently precise,[76] 'reflects an outdated distinction of rule-making on the one hand, and application of rules on the other'.[77] This distinction was of course much more present in continental European civil law than under the Anglo-American tradition.[78] But even in civil law traditions courts are more

---

[74] For a comparative overview of the practice in several states, H Keller, 'Rechtsvergleichende Aspecte zur Monismus-Dualismus-Diskussion', 1999 SZIER 225; also the arguments in favour of a dualist con-cept presented in the comprehensive study by G Arangio-Ruiz, 'Dualism Revisited—International Law and Interindividual Law' (2003) 86 Rivista di Diritto Internazionale 909; also C Amrhein-Hofmann, *Monismus und Dualismus in den Völkerrechtslehren* (Berlin: Duncker & Humblot, 2003).

[75] T Cottier, 'A Theory of Direct Effect in Global Law' in *European Integration and International Co-ordination, Studies in Transnational Economic Law in Honour of Claus-Dieter Ehlermann* (The Hague-London-New York: Kluwer Law International, 2002) 99, 116.

[76] I Brownlie, *Principles of Public International Law* (6th edn, Oxford: Oxford University Press, 2003) 538.   [77] T Cottier (n 75 above) 99, 118.

[78] For instance the description of law and the task of the judge given by Oliver Wendell Holmes: 'I have tried to see the law as an organic whole. I have also tried to see it as a reaction between tradition on the one side and the changing desires and needs of a community on the other. I have studied tradition

and more viewed as part of a continuous law-generating process.[79] The concept of 'public international law relationship' thus places the national courts and the centre of the intersection between national and international law. It is up to them to decide on whether and when to apply international norms in disputes involving individuals.

4.3 Direct applicability, supremacy, and constitutional functions

In order to avoid misunderstandings the distinction between the notions of direct applicability and supremacy must be stressed. Accepting that international law is directly applicable to individuals does not automatically entail that it takes supremacy over national constitutional law. A look at European Community Law underlines the distinction. The European Court of Justice developed these notions in two decisions[80] and there is no logical necessity to grant directly applicable international norms automatic supremacy over national constitutional law.[81]

If international law is in principle rendered directly applicable under the conditions just described, it becomes all the more important to assure that in its application essential standards of human rights are protected. This implies that the question of supremacy must expressly be left to the autonomy of national constitutional law. This implies that—in principle—international law, which is directly applied, remains subject to constitutional guarantees just as any other national law. One may think of some modifications a long the lines of the 'as long as' doctrine which the German Federal Constitutional Court developed in the context of EC law.[82] In that sense one may say that 'as long as' the law of the international regime in question does not provide for an adequate system of human rights protection against decisions which affect individual rights, the protection of these rights has

in order that I might understand how it came to be what it is, and to estimate its worth with regard to our present needs; am my references to the Year Books often have had a sceptical end. I have considered the present tendencies and desires of society and have tried to realize that its different portions want different things, and that my business was to express not my personal wish, but the resultant, as nearly as I could guess, of the pressure of the past and the conflicting wills of the present'. OW Holmes, 'Twenty Years in Retrospect' in R Posner (ed), *The Essential Holmes, Selections From Letters, Speeches, Judicial Opinions and Other Writings of Oliver Wendell Holmes, Jr.*, (Chicago-London: University of Chicago Press, 1992) 151.

[79] The German Federal Constitutional Court has put this into the following words: '*Der Richter war in Europa niemals "la bouche qui prononce les paroles de la loi"; das römische Recht, das englische common law, das Gemeine Recht waren weithin richterliche Rechtsschöpfungen ebenso wie in jüngerer Zeit etwa in Frankreich die Herausbildung allgemeiner Rechtsgrundsätze des Verwaltungsrechts durch den Staatsrat oder in Deutschland das allgemeine Verwaltungsrecht, weite Teile des Arbeitsrechts oder die Sicherungsrechte im privatrechtlichen Geschäftsverkehr*' BVerfGE 75 223 (243).

[80] *Van Gend & Loos*, ECJ Reports 1963, 1 (direct applicability) and *Costa/Enel*, ECJ Reports 1964, 1141 (supremacy).

[81] KH Ladeur, 'Globalization and Public Governance—A Contradiction?' in KH Ladeur (ed), *Public Governance in the Age of Globalization* (Aldershot-Burlington, Ashgate, 2004) 1, 14. who rightly only refers to the V*an Gend & Loos* Case in the context of 'piercing the veil of sovereignty'.

[82] BVerfGE 37, 271 (285); 73, 339 (387) and BVerfGE 89, 155 (175).

to remain on the level of national institutions (ie the national courts).[83] In fact, the European Court of Human Rights only recently took up this idea, when it developed its own standard of control with respect to European Community Law in the *Bosphorus* case.[84] In that sense the divide between national and international law is still alive.

4.4 International legal personality and the 'public international law relationship'—are they merely two sides of the same coin?

One may be tempted to ask whether the proposition of a public international law relationship really implies a fundamental change in the construction of international law. It might be argued that, after all, international legal personality is determined by the attribution of rights or duties by international law,[85] which, in essence, is exactly what the public international law relationship describes. From this perspective, the advantage of the proposal seems rather limited.

While the general observation of the close relationship between the two concepts of course cannot be denied, their conceptual difference nevertheless merits being highlighted. The most obvious and most important difference is that the exclusivity which currently is attributed to subjects of international law is reduced. It becomes normal, even natural, that subjects other than states can be considered subjects of international law. If the first part of the twentieth century was basically concerned with the gradual acceptance of international organizations as subjects of international law,[86] the second half of the century was characterized by the gradual movement of the individual and international organizations into the position of a subject of international law. These two important developments in international law are more accurately reflected in the concept of public international law relationship than in the traditional structure of international law. In that sense, the concept of public international law relationship is not merely a different starting point in a circular argument, but rather a different perspective on the same problem. The problem, of course, remains essentially the same, since determining the existence of a public international law relationship implies asking questions quite similar to the ones that were asked when an actor had to be qualified as a subject of international law. However, I do not argue that my proposal solves the problem. The point is that the public international law relationship provides for the better analytical perspective. Its main advantage is that it can accurately reflect the growing importance of non-State international actors in international law. Furthermore,

---

[83] The German Federal Constitutional Court has in fact already extended this jurisprudence beyond the context of EC law, BVerfG NJW 2001, 2705; for criticism C Walter, 'Grundrechtsschutz gegen Hoheitsakte internationaler Organisationen' 2004 AÖR 39 et seq.

[84] *Bosphorus*, ECHR, Appl.Nr. 45036/98 of 30 June 2005; available at <http://cmiskp.echr.coe.int/tkp197/search.asp?skin=hudoc-en>.

[85] J Klabbers, 'The concept of legal personality' (2005) 11 Jus Gentium 35, 39.

[86] H Mosler, 'Subjects of International Law' in R Bernhardt (ed), *Encyclopedia of Public International Law*, Vol III (Amsterdam: Elsevier, 1997) 710, 711.

the previously described direct applicability of international law in the domestic legal order[87] is a significant practical consequence which is generated by the change of perspective suggested here.

5. Tentative conclusions: elements for the constitutionalization of international law

In this final part of the chapter, three currently important elements of the process of constitutionalization will be addressed: hierarchy and the structure of international law, legitimacy and the role of the State, and finally the issue of inclusiveness.

5.1 Regimes, hierarchy, human rights, and the State

The problem of coordination is inherent in the development of a sectoralized international law. How do the different regimes relate to each other? If trade and environment require different action and we have different respective dispute settlement mechanisms, forum shopping and a different outcome of the dispute according the forum addressed cannot be completely excluded. The problem is reduced to some extent because there are no objections if each system decides different aspects of the same dispute according to its own norms and its own logic. Hence, the same States may bring the same dispute concerning fisheries to the dispute settlement mechanisms provided for under the Law of the Sea Convention as far as the law of the sea is concerned, while simultaneously or consecutively turning to WTO dispute settlement as far as international trade law is of relevance. Beyond this easy case, eg in areas where different mechanisms apply the same norms of general international law, one may rely on the method of mutual observation and analysis proposed by Fischer-Lescano and Teubner.[88] Those who see a real danger of fragmentation may find some consolation in Judge Simma's observation that the members of international tribunals and courts are, above all others, 'constantly and painstakingly aware of the necessity to preserve the coherence of international law'.[89]

The issue of human rights protection must be distinguished from this effort of regime coordination. In the international relations terminology—from where the helpful idea and terminology of regimes has come into international law—human rights protection is also sometimes labelled as a regime of its own.[90] From the perspective of the functions of constitutional law, however, human rights protection

---

[87] See above 3.2.

[88] Fischer-Lescano and Teubner (n 16 above) 999.

[89] B Simma, 'Fragmentation in a Positive Light' (2004) 25 Michigan JIL 845, 846.

[90] SD Krasner, 'Sovereignty, Regimes and Human Rights' in V Rittberger (ed), *Regime Theory and International Relations* (Oxford: Clarendon Press, 1993) 139.

is a cross-cutting issue. Human rights have to be respected irrespective of the regime concerned, and for these structural reasons, their protection does not qualify as a regime which can be seen parallel to the other regimes. At least in the long run, it will be necessary to have a hierarchical solution for the human rights issue. International human rights offer a nucleus for the development of such a hierarchical solution. But neither procedural mechanisms nor substantive standards have been reached in order to completely shift the issue of human rights protection from the national level. For the time being hierarchies may be created within each of the regimes in question.[91] It may even be argued that States are under a positive obligation to strive for the establishment of such regime-specific mechanisms of protection.[92] In the absence of such regime-specific human rights protection, it is up to national courts to ensure an adequate level of protection by—if necessary—not applying the international decision in question.[93] This development sheds an interesting light on changes in the role of the formerly sovereign State: the perspective of constitutional functions highlights its new role as a transmitter of international obligations from human rights treaties into institutionalized international regimes.

5.2 Collisions of different rationalities and the role of the State

The emerging sectoralized international order also requires a reconsideration of traditional frontlines between constitutionalists and international lawyers. A major problem of sectoralization on the international level is that we lack an institution which could balance competing interests across the regimes. Each regime tends to follow its own logic. One of the tasks fulfilled by parliament in the political system of the nation State is to provide for such balanced decisions, taking into account competing interests to the extent possible. However, parliaments are only included in the process of negotiations at a rather late stage.

The practical problems of such a development can be illustrated by a look at the interpretation and application of the so-called Aarhus Convention on access to information on environmental issues.[94] The Convention is of particular interest in the context of internationalization and globalization because it sets out detailed procedural requirements to which national administrative law has to be adapted.[95]

---

[91] For an illustration of the position of the European Court of Human Rights on the matter, *Waite and Kennedy v Germany* (Appl No 26083/94), available at <http://hudoc.echr.coe.int>.

[92] Walter (n 43 above) 170, 197 et seq.

[93] See nn 82 and 83 above and the corresponding text.

[94] Convention on Access to Information, Public Participation in Decision-making and Access to Justice in Environmental Matters, Doc. ECE/CEP/43; available at <http://www.unece.org/env/pp/treatytext.htm> (accessed 15 March 2005); for details of the negotiation history, M Zschiesche, 'Die Aarhus-Konvention—mehr Bürgerbeteiligung durch umweltrechtliche Standards?' (2001) 12 ZUR 177; P Jeder, 'Neue Entwicklungen im Umweltrecht vor dem Hintergrund der Aarhus-Konvention' 2002 Jahrbuch des Umwelt- und Technikrechts 145, 147.

[95] On the participatory concept of the convention, M Prieur, 'La Convention d'Aarhus, Instrument Universel de la Démocratie Environnementale' 1999 Revue juridique de l'environnement (Numéro special) 9 et seq, 11 et seq.

Furthermore, it goes beyond the inter-State structure of traditional environmental law because it expressly grants rights to individuals and environmental NGO's.[96] In granting specific procedural rights to NGOs dealing with environmental law the Convention follows a concept of 'participatory democracy'.[97] It has therefore been rightly seen as part of the 'constitutionalization of international law'.[98] Finally, it will not only be binding on States but also on the EU and is thus one of those international conventions which affect the community and its member States likewise.[99]

The Aarhus Convention grants certain groups and individuals access to information which is relevant for the protection of the environment. In addition, it provides for procedures of public interest litigation which members of the public in general (and not only the public concerned) may start. Such public interest litigation is something which is still foreign to traditional German administrative law, which is focused on rights of the individual and their infringement. In recent years, this general rule has already been modified to some extent, but in principle it is still applicable.

German legislation has in recent years tried to develop rules for assuring speedy administrative procedures.[100] Such general rules include for instance the requirement for a non governmental organisation which aims at environmental protection to participate in the administrative procedure if it wants later to be able to start public interest litigation. The reason behind this rule is to avoid purely obstructive strategies. A rule of similar scope is that no public interest litigation is admitted when—even in the case of a successful action—a renewed administrative procedure would lead to the same result. This means that the right of participation for environmental interest groups in administrative procedures is seen as a means to a specific end (a balanced administrative decision) but not an end in itself. A time-consuming and senseless repetition of procedures in case of purely formal mistakes should thus be avoided. On the occasion of its signature the German Government accordingly made the following declaration:

The text of the Convention raises a number of difficult questions regarding its practical implementation in the German legal system which it was not possible to finally resolve during the period provided for the signing of the Convention. These questions require careful consideration, including a consideration of the legislative consequences, before the Convention becomes binding under international law.

---

[96] A Epiney and M Scheyli, *Die Aarhus-Konvention—Rechtliche Tragweite und Implikationen für das Schweizerische Recht* (Freiburg: Switzerland, 2000) 23.

[97] C Calliess, 'Die Umweltrechtliche Verbandsklage nach der Novellierung des Bundesnaturschutzgesetzes—Tendenzen zu einer "Privatisierung des Gemeinwohls" im Verwaltungsrecht?' (2003) NJW 97, 100; *Th v Danwitz*, Aarhus-Konvention: Umweltinformation, Öffentlichkeitsbeteiligung, Zugang zu den Gerichten' 2004 NVwZ 272, 274.　　　　[98] Epiney and Scheyli (n 96 above) 94.

[99] COM (2003) 625 of 24 October 2003.

[100] Notably the so-called '*Genehmigungsbeschleunigungsgesetz*' (Act on the Accelaration of Administrative Authorizations) of 12 September 1996, BGBl. 1996 I S. 1354.

The Federal Republic of Germany assumes that implementing the Convention through German administrative enforcement will not lead to developments which counteract efforts towards deregulation and speeding up procedures.[101]

The problem of the Aarhus Convention is that it does not mention in concrete terms the relationship between such general procedural rules and the rules concerning rights of participation and of court action enshrined in the Convention. What has recently happened in German doctrine of environmental law is that arguments have been presented by which the application of such general rules of procedural law is blocked by the rules laid down in the Aarhus Convention.[102] It is argued that the express aim of the Aarhus Convention to enhance environmental protection by giving special rights of participation to environmental interest groups would be jeopardized if such procedural rules were applicable in cases which fall into the scope of application of the Convention. These arguments follow exclusively the rationality of environmental protection and remain within the sectoral logic of the regime from which they stem. However, they do not take into account other public interest considerations, such as speedy administrative procedures.

This example illustrates the fact that the rationality of the Aarhus Convention, which in this case follows the sectoral logic of environmental protection, may collide with the different rationality of national procedural law. We tend to view this as a collision between national and international law and apply the principles which exist in order to solve such collisions. The situation may even result in a conflict between international lawyers who perceive themselves as more open to international developments and national administrative lawyers who are reproached with having a narrow national view of the matter.

However, this is only one perception of the problem, and a limited one at that. A closer look reveals that the issue is not so much one of the coordination between national and international law, as one of different rationalities of the different regimes. One could imagine a multilateral treaty aimed at the mutual promotion of private investments and in which the parties commit themselves to speeding up their internal administrative procedures. Such a treaty could include provisions which, in the interest of promoting private investment, require the abolition of procedures which are an aim in themselves. It could also require the repetition of procedures, the outcome of which is already clear. This would again be a treaty which follows the logic of a specific regime, only a different regime and a different logic. This—still purely theoretical—example illustrates that we are dealing not so much with a conflict between national and international law but rather with a conflict of different rationalities of different national and/or international regimes.

The problem which arises with international solutions such as the Aarhus Convention, is that these treaties are negotiated mainly by those who work in the specific area covered and who follow the logic of the corresponding regime. This is

---

101 Available at <http://www.unece.org/env/pp/ctreaty.htm> (accessed 15 March 2005).
102 A Schink, 'Die Aarhus-Konvention und das Deutsche Umweltrecht' (2003) 1 EurUP 27, 35.

illustrated by the German Declaration on the occasion of its signature which high-lights that there were doubts as to the proper balancing of competing interests. Such balancing, which is the task of national parliaments in the traditional setting, is much more difficult to maintain under the new structures. If such balancing is not performed during the negotiations, it is difficult to included it at later stages, because these are mainly concerned with the implementation of the treaty obligations. If the analysis is correct of a partial blindness of each regime for concerns which lie outside its main focus, a twofold conclusion has to be drawn. First, it is of course possible to remain aware of that danger and to try to include such considerations to the extent possible already at the stage of negotiations. But second, apart from that, it may also become necessary to allow for a flexible application of the sectorally developed inter-national law in order to give member States of such conventions the necessary lee-way to accommodate competing interests. The Aarhus Convention allows for such flexible solutions if its provisions are interpreted accordingly.[103]

This conclusion contrasts to some extent with the traditional frontlines between internationalists and national constitutionalists. The predominant view of inter-nationalists concerning the relationship between national constitutional law and international law is that international law should generally prevail, and constitu-tionalists from the national perspective tend to criticize the dangers of an 'inter-nationalization' of national law. The examples of the Aarhus Convention and the theoretical investment treaty show where the respective positions merge: the analysis of the development in international law requires a new role of public law and the State. The perspectives of both the international lawyer and the constitutional lawyer are necessary in order to draw attention to that phenomenon.

5.3 Constitutionalization, fragmentation, and inclusiveness

The project of developing an international constitutional law goes beyond the technicalities of human rights protection or the coordination of different rational-ities stemming from different sectoralized regimes:

If one sticks to the principles of equality and autonomy of states, which today find their foundation in the right of self-determination of peoples, there is no alternative to a further constitutionalization in order to assure the necessary restructuring of international law. This requires a strong new impetus, similar to the one of 1945. It may only come from those peoples which have given themselves constitutions based on the principle of rule of law and which acknowledge the rule of law also in international relations—being aware of the fact that at the beginning of the 21st century only an international policy and international institutions based on considerations of the 'common good' can assure a common future of humankind.[104]

---

[103] Eg S Stec and others, 'The Aarhus-Convention: An Implementation Guide', 130, available at <http://www.unece.org/env/pp/acig.pdf> (accessed 15 March 2005).

[104] B Faßbender, 'Der Schutz der Menschenrechte als zentraler Inhalt des völkerrechtlichen Gemeinwohls', 2003 EuGRZ 1, 16—translation by the author.

In this quotation the common good ('Gemeinwohl') is mentioned as an aim by which the development of the future structures of international law should be guided. The idea resembles what in German constitutional theory is known as 'Integrationsfunktion' (integration function) of constitutional law.[105] On an abstract level, one could hardly agree more with the idea. In that view, international law serves as a means of integrating the international community. However, at a second glance, one may ask whether it is wise to burden the common future with (not only politically but also legally defined) requirements of 'common good' and 'rule of law'. Living currently through divergent perspectives of these notions on both sides of the Atlantic we should reassure ourselves whether we really agree on the same content when these notions are invoked in different areas of the world. And even more importantly, does such a project properly take into account possible North-South divergences over the future role and structure of international law?[106] Martti Koskenniemi's presentation at the Founding Conference of the European Society for International Law in Florence has highlighted that it is possible to read such a project as hegemonic in itself—a hegemony of European legal culture as opposed to American legal culture, and most probably also as opposed to the legal culture and political interests of many other countries.[107] Even if one does not agree with propositions that constitutionalism requires an underlying revolutionary myth,[108] one can see that the project described by Fassbender is too ambitious. What is required, therefore, is a less ambitious and thus, hopefully, more inclusive approach.

Here again, the development of sectorally limited regimes offers possibilities. An important advantage is that functionally limited cooperation presents a chance to develop common positions in some areas while maintaining differences in others. It remains below the ambitious project of defining a 'common interest' of the 'international community' as such. Like-minded States may cooperate in areas where they share common interests and convictions, while keeping their distance in other fields.

6. Future prospects for the 'constitutionalization of international law'

What does all this mean for the constitutionalization of international law? It certainly underlines its character as an open-ended process, it highlights the imperfections

---

[105] It is associated with R Smend, *Verfassung und Verfassungsrecht* (München: Duncker & Humblot, 1928).

[106] B Chimni, 'International Institutions Today: An Imperial Global State in the Making' (2004) 15 EJIL 1.

[107] M Koskenniemi, 'International Law in Europe: Between Tradition and Renewal', <http://www.valt.helsinki.fi/blogs/eci/Florence.pdf> (accessed 15 March 2005), 5 et seq.

[108] U Haltern, 'Internationales Verfassungsrecht? Anmerkungen zu einer kopernikanischen Wende' (2003) 128 AöR 511, 532 et seq and 554.

of this process, but it also points to possible advantages. At least two possible areas for further 'constitutionalization' may be mentioned. The first area concerns the developments within the various regimes. Such regimes exist both on the regional and the universal level and they differ according to the interests of a specific region. Processes of constitutionalization will be ongoing within each of these regimes. Depending on their respective subject matters, these regimes may contribute to a feeling of belonging together and sharing certain values. The intensity of such processes will certainly also depend on the number of participating States and their cultural and political homogeneity. Any type of institutionalized international cooperation has the potential for such constitutional developments. One may, for instance, refer to the development of NATO, where, in spite of all current difficulties and in spite of its sectoral limitation to issues of regional security, NATO's extension towards the East shows inclusiveness towards new members, the participation of which would never have been thought possible only a few years ago.

The second consequence concerns processes of constitutionalization of international governance as such. It is possible to predict that over time we will witness within sectorally limited regimes certain common features. They may be very general at the beginning, but they may move to more specific legal consequences in future development. The oft-mentioned notions of *ius cogens* and *erga omnes obligations* only refer to very general principles, the most concrete probably being the crime of genocide (and even there the assessment of certain developments may vary according to the different social, cultural and legal backgrounds of the States). But the other principles which are usually referred to as consisting of obligations *erga omnes* or *ius cogens* are far too general to ever be applied in a concrete case without raising any legal dispute. Understood in that sense, a constitutionalization of international law is not a hegemonic but a deliberative project. It offers different grades of inclusion and requires a continuous discourse within and in between the various regimes.

Under these conditions, regimes may be viewed as laboratories from which generally applicable principles of international law emerge. Current developments are a fascinating re-structuring of international law in general.[109] The predominant focus on actors is more and more supplemented by an increasing interest in subject matter oriented regimes. The tentative answers which we currently have for this challenge are necessarily vague. Many issues of hierarchy will remain open for quite some time, and in that sense we will have to put up with hybrid structures. In the mean time, international lawyers have an open field for analysis of the developments in each of the different regimes concerned and of international governance in general. These analyses must aim at filtering common constitutional characteristics from developments within each of the sectorally limited regimes (as a process of their internal constitutionalization), and—now truly labelled as a

---

[109] P Zumbansen, 'Die vergangene Zukunft des Völkerrechts' (2001) 34 KJ 46.

process of constitutionalization of international law—the development of universal constitutional elements in those areas, where issues common to all regimes are addressed.

However, nowhere will we find a constitution in the traditional sense. Nowhere exists *the* constitution of *the* international community. There simply is no continuity for the bundling of constitutional functions which was once provided for in the nation State and by its constitution. Just as with any other good-bye to seemingly easy structures of the past, this causes some mourning. But there is consolation. Each of the developments mentioned, those within the regimes concerned and those across regime borders, serves as a small contribution to the constitutionalization of international law, a process which presents an exciting intellectual challenge for years to come.

9

The Emergence of the International Community and the Divide Between International and Domestic Law

Andreas L Paulus

1. Introduction

Recent developments, from September 11 to the war in Iraq, have pushed the idea of an international community based on common values and international law further away than ever. The counter-image of international community, the 'clash of civilizations',[1] appears much nearer to reality. It is however precisely the multiplicity of religious and ethical approaches to the world that make the agreement on a minimum of common values so important. It is one of the main tasks of international law to provide rules of coexistence and, increasingly, to find avenues to solutions to global problems not in spite, but because of the global pluralism of value and belief systems.

Analyzing the international community requires more than the development of abstract concepts, however. It demands for the analysis of the impact of the concept on legal, social, and political practice, including an analysis of its effects on the persons at the receiving end, so to speak. Which purposes does the term serve? Is the invocation of the 'international community' a move to hide one's own lust for power behind a smokescreen of high-mindedness—in other words, 'kitsch'?[2] Or does it serve the useful purpose of pointing to a claim of authority rooted not

---

[1] S Huntington, *The Clash of Civilizations and the Remaking of World Order* (New York: Simon & Schuster, 1996).

[2] M Koskenniemi has used the word 'kitsch' for general concepts of international law such as *jus cogens* and obligations *erga omnes*, M Koskenniemi 'International Law in Europe: Between Tradition and Renewal' (2005) 16 EJIL 113, 121–23. His critics (see O Gerstenberg, 'What International Law Should (Not) Become. A Comment on Koskenniemi' (2005) 16 EJIL 125; PM Dupuy, 'Some Reflections on Contemporary International Law and the Appeal to Universal Values: A Response to Martti Koskenniemi' (2005) 16 EJIL 131) have generally failed to see that Koskenniemi distinguishes between uses of these concepts as 'kitsch' and, following Milan Kundera, the possibility of averting this danger by recognizing it, ibid, 123.

in a domestic source, but in some internationally agreed basic values of global import? Obviously, to answer these questions in any comprehensive way in 25, or even 250, pages is impossible.[3] In line with the purpose of this volume, we approach them from the perspective of domestic courts faced with the interpretation and application of laws and values of the 'international community' in their jurisprudence.

Traditionally, the relationship between international and domestic law was conceptualized either as inter-relationship of two distinct legal orders (dualism) or as the offspring of one universal legal order (monism). However, as we shall see, the radical opposition between monism and dualism fails to grasp the (post)modern plurality of legal orders at the international level and the complicated inter-connectedness between 'the international' and 'the domestic'. Neither radical integration of all legal orders (monism) nor radical separation between international and national legal orders will do. In line with these developments, the practice of domestic courts—courts that may be suspected of a national rather than international bias—demonstrates that the stalwarts of the domestic legal order will neither ignore international standards nor accept them as unassailable.

Some caveats are in order, however. In such a short article, it is impossible to analyse all or even a great many of domestic legal regimes. The mix of continental and common law as well as of 'monist' and so-called 'dualist' legal orders may justify our choice of three States: Germany, a civil law country with a tradition of constitutional adjudication oscillating between monism and dualism, the United Kingdom, an Anglo-Saxon country known for its dualism regarding international treaties, and the United States, not only the only superpower, but also a traditionally monist country in which the very possibility of citing foreign sources has however become subject to a vigorous and sometimes abusive debate.[4]

First, however, the term 'international community' itself merits some attention. We will look at three different understandings of the international community, institutionalist, (neo)liberal, and postmodernist. It will turn out that different models of international community come nevertheless to comparable results as to the relationship between the international and the domestic legal community. We will then proceed to conceptualize the emerging pluralism regarding the relationship between the international and domestic legal orders. Finally, the impact of

---

[3] For pre-September 11-analysis, eg G Abi-Saab, 'Whither the International Community?' (1998) 9 EJIL 248–65; RJ Dupuy, *La communauté internationale entre le mythe et l'histoire* (Paris: Economica, 1986); AL Paulus, *Die internationale Gemeinschaft im Völkerrecht* (München: CH Beck, 2001); B Simma and AL Paulus, 'The International Community: Facing the Challenge of Globalization' (1998) 9 EJIL 266–77; Tomuschat 'International Law: Ensuring the Survival of Mankind on the Eve of a New Century' (1999) 281 RdC 72–90; after September 11, see PM Dupuy, 'L'unité de l'ordre juridique international. Cours général de droit international public (2000)' (2002) 297 RdC 207, 245–68; E Kwakwa, 'The International Community, international law, and the United States: three in one, two against one, or one and the same?' in M Byers and G Nolte (eds), *United States Hegemony and the Foundations of International Law* (Cambridge: CUP, 2003) 25–56; A Paulus, 'The Influence of the United States on the concept of the "International Community"' ibid 57–90; as well as the comments by Martti Koskenniemi, Steven Ratner, and Volker Rittberger, ibid, 91–114; P Allott, *Eunomia: New Order for a New World* (2nd edn, Oxford and New York: OUP, 2001); AM Slaughter, *A New World Order* (Princeton and Oxford: Princeton UP, 2004).   [4] See n 85 below and accompanying text.

international and foreign judgments and legal opinions on domestic jurisprudence in the United States, the United Kingdom, and Germany will provide some recent evidence for the integration of the 'international legal community'.

In the conclusion, we intend to show that domestic courts do not regard the 'international community' as a repository of moral values or laws superior to their own. International law, as the law of the international community, will be regarded as formal authority only in the instance domestic law renders it binding for the court in question. Domestic law, not international law continues to determine the breadth of the influence of international law in the domestic legal order. International community values may however inform the understanding of principles and values enshrined in domestic law. In this respect, the 'international community' is not regarded as a higher authority, but as one of several influences that weigh on the decision of an actual case, and often not the controlling one. But the impact of international judicial pronouncements on the interpretation of domestic law testifies to a fertilization of domestic law by the concept of international community.

2. The 'international community' and the role of domestic courts

Before we can look at the influence of conceptions of the international community on domestic case law, we have to define our understanding of the term. Every concept of international law is based on an understanding of the social structure international law applies to. Accordingly, every theory of international law involves, explicitly or implicitly, a concept of international community or society. At the same time, those 'background understandings' are mostly not of an exclusively legal character. Thus, international law does not require the acceptance of one, or any, of the following conceptualizations. And yet, conceptions of 'international community' shed light on the respective roles of the international and the domestic legal spheres. This article will single out three strands of responses to these questions—institutionalist-communitarian, (neo-)liberal, and postmodernist. It will also show, however, that the three points of view are coming to remarkably similar responses regarding the role of international law in the domestic legal order.

Concepts of international law and order do not exist somewhere in a vaccuum. Rather, they are related to perceptions of political and legal events. Both the terrorist attacks on the United States of September 11, 2001, and the war waged against Iraq led by the United States, a war that was, according to most accounts, contrary to international law,[5] challenge traditional concepts of an international community based on 'sovereign equality' of States, as Article 2, paragraph 1, of the Charter of the United Nations has it. September 11 puts into question the conceptualization

---

[5] For the present author's view, A Paulus, 'The War Against Iraq and the Future of International Law: Hegemony or Pluralism?' (2004) 25 Michigan JIL 691, 695–713; L Fisler Damrosch, Bernard H Oxman (eds), 'Agora: Future Implications of the Iraq Conflict' (2003) 97 AJIL 553.

of the international community as a 'community of States' with little, if any, direct participation of individuals in global governance. If the main security threat does not emanate from States but from terrorist groups of individuals, States appear to have lost some of their monopoly on the use of force. If the remaining superpower feels free to ignore the most basic rules of international law regarding the prohibition on the use of force, but demands strict adherence from other States, sovereign equality cannot be taken for granted, not even as a normative ideal.

Do September 11 and Iraq uncover permanent flaws in the idea of an international community based on a global political 'overlapping consensus'[6] and the rule of law, or do they merely reflect the broadening of globalization from the economic to the political realm? International law can serve both as a constraint on power—for instance prohibiting the use of force—and as a translation of power into concrete orders and prohibitions. If the international community threatened the 'right to survival' of societies by rendering the State incapable of countering new threats from non-governmental actors such as Al-Qaeda by legal means, States might choose to protect themselves now as they see fit and look for international justification later. In addition, domestic courts may question the legitimacy of a legal order that emanates from the consensus of States independently of their democratic legitimacy. If, on the other hand, the so-called 'global war on terror'[7] resulted in an international law embodying the writ of a superpower rather than the sovereign equality of States, the international adherence to international law would suffer. However, the United States does not seem to lay out a coherent vision of a hegemonic international order.[8] Let us have a look at some conceptualizations of the international community to see whether and how they accommodate the situation after 'September 11' and 'Iraq'. We will thus use recent developments as a kind of 'hard case' for different conceptualizations of the international community.

2.1 Institutionalist theory and globalization

Many international lawyers base the development of a true international community or society on a societal consciousness encompassing the whole of humanity.[9] Discourse ethics and democracy theory emphasized the need to embed global

---

[6] On the term 'overlapping consensus', J Rawls, *Political Liberalism* (New York: Columbia UP, 1993) 147 et seq. For its application to the global realm, eg TM Franck, *Fairness of International Law and Institutions* (Oxford: Clarendon Press, 1995) 14; BR Roth *Governmental Illegitimacy in International Law* (Oxford: Clarendon Press, 1999) 6.

[7] 'Global War on Terror' is the label attached by the Bush Jr administration to the struggle against Al-Quaeda and other terrorist groups. Attempts by the Pentagon to relabel the term to 'global struggle against violent extremism', G Packer, 'Name Calling', The New Yorker (8 August 2005) available at <http://www.newyorker.com>, visited 8 August 2005) appear to have failed to convince the US President, see RW Stevenson, 'President Makes It Clear: Phrase is "War on Terror" ', New York Times (4 August 2005) 12.

[8] Cf DF Vagts, 'Hegemonic International Law' (2001) 95 AJIL 843. Also JE Alvarez, 'Hegemonic International Law Revisited' (2003) 95 AJIL 873; Nico Krisch, 'International Law in Times of Hegemony' (2005) 16 EJIL 369.

[9] Eg P Allott, *Eunomia: New Order for a New World* (2nd edn, Oxford and New York: OUP, 2001); RJ Dupuy (n 3 above).

democracy into institutional designs.[10] Wolfgang Friedmann established the distinction between the 'classical' law of coexistence and the 'modern' law of cooperation.[11] Taking up that distinction, some contemporary scholars, especially in the German constitutional tradition, developed concepts of a much more dense, and much more institutionalized, international community. In that view, international law moves— or should move—'from bilateralism to community interest' (Bruno Simma),[12] is about to establish 'world interior politics' (Jost Delbrück),[13] or shall ensure 'the survival of mankind on the eve of a new century' (Christian Tomuschat).[14] Instances of this 'new order' in contemporary international law can be seen, eg in *jus cogens*, obligations *erga omnes*, in the concept of the common heritage of mankind,[15] in the alleged 'constitutionalization' of the UN Security System[16] and of the WTO trade system[17] and, of course, in the establishment of the International Criminal Court.[18] Those who believe in a parallelism between legal norms and institutions— what Georges Abi-Saab has called the 'law or fundamental hypothesis of "legal physics"'[19]—now demand the strengthening of global institutions to implement laws for the regulation of globalization.

However, institutionalism faces increasing difficulty with the current political mood after September 11 and Iraq. The terrorist attacks on the United States have confirmed the critical attitude of the United States towards European institutionalism. The US Government, at the time by-and-large supported by the American public, concluded that America needed to protect itself, and would not depend on the support of others.[20] Indeed, in the widely cited book by Robert Kagan,[21]

---

[10] J Habermas, *Die Einbeziehung des Anderen* (Frankfurt am Main: Suhrkamp, 1996) 133, 672; D Held, *Democracy and the Global Order* (Stanford: Stanford UP, 1995).

[11] W Friedmann, *The Changing Structure of International Law* (London: Stevens & Sons, 1964); also WC Jenks, *A Common Law of Mankind* (London: Stevens & Sons, 1958); D Mitrany, *A Working Peace System* (Chicago: Quadrangle, 1966).

[12] B Simma, 'From Bilateralism to Community Interest in International Law' (1994-VI) 250 RdC 217.

[13] J Delbrück, 'Globalization of Law, Politics, and Markets—Implications for Domestic Law—A European Perspective' (1993/4) 1 Indiana J of Global Legal Studies 9.

[14] Tomuschat (n 3 above) 1   [15] Dupuy (n 3 above) 159–68.

[16] B Fassbender, *UN Security Council Reform and the Right to Veto: A Constitutional Perspective* (The Hague: Kluwer, 1998) 114; J Abr Frowein, 'Reactions by Not Directly Affected States to Breaches of Public International Law' (1994-IV) 248 RdC 345, 355–6; Simma (n 12 above) 258–62, para 25–26 (but see—considerably more skeptical—id. 'Comments on Global Governance, the United Nations, and the Place of Law' [1998] 9 Finnish YbIL 61, 65); C Tomuschat, 'Obligations Arising for States without or against Their Will' (1993-VI) 241 RdC 195, 216–40.

[17] EU Petersmann, 'How to Reform the UN System? Constitutionalism, International Law, and International Organizations' (1997) 10 Leiden JIL 421.

[18] Rome Statute of the International Criminal Court, July 17, 1998, 2187 *UNTS* 90, (1998) 37 ILM 999. The Preamble speaks several times of the 'most serious crimes of concern to the international community as a whole'.   [19] Abi-Saab (n 3 above) 248, 256.

[20] George W Bush, State of the Union Address, January 8, 2003, 39 Weekly Compilation of Presidential Documents (January 28, 2003), 109, p 116, available at <http://www.whitehouse.gov> (accessed 6 November 2003): 'Yet the course of this nation does not depend on the decisions of others'.

[21] R Kagan, *Of Paradise and Power* (New York: Knopf, 2003); R Kagan 'Power and Weakness' (2002) 113 Policy Review 3.

European institutionalism is presented as a system for good times only. In the European paradise, slow and bureaucratic institutions may be useful, but the world writ large is a dangerous place, in which an America untied by international institutions needs to provide order—in the best interests of the world in general, and Europe in particular.

Of course, since the Iraq adventure seems to have turned into a quagmire, such self-assuredness appears increasingly unwarranted. In a postscript to his book, Kagan admits that the exercise of power needs legitimacy to be successful, and that international institutions in general, and Europe in particular, can provide it.[22] However, he charges Europe with not fulfilling that role properly when it withholds legitimacy from American unilateral actions that the United States deems necessary for the maintenance of international peace and security. Thus, the display of military power needs to be grounded in legitimacy to provide for order. However, what power can legitimacy have if it has no other option than to approve the use of force? Nevertheless, there seems to be agreement that international institutions may indeed serve a useful legitimizing function even for the single superpower.

Thus, the aftermath of September 11 has not lead to a diminishing of the role of international institutions, and has not stopped the institutionalization of international or rather global relations. Indeed, one could make the point that the role of the Security Council has been enhanced rather than diminished: its lack of approval made the attack on Iraq even more risky, and the result so far certainly does not invite repetition. Both the United States and the United Kingdom brought forward legal arguments that presented their action as an implementation of, rather than derogation from, existing Security Council mandates.[23] Indeed, although they did not receive backing from the Security Council for the attack itself, the United States and the United Kingdom returned to the Council to legitimize the occupation and the establishment of a new democratic order in Iraq.[24]

In areas beyond security, from trade to health and human rights, it is even more difficult to question the idea of an unstoppable march of globalization towards the construction of global institutions. The German sociologist Niklas Luhmann has first described this development as a move from territoriality to functionality,[25]

---

[22] R Kagan, 'America's Crisis of Legitimacy' (2004) 83:2 Foreign Affairs 65.

[23] Letter dated 20 March 2003 from the Permanent Representative of the United States of America to the United Nations Addressed to the President of the Security Council, UN Doc. S/2003/351 (2003); letter dated 20 March 2003 from the Permanent Representative of the United Kingdom of Great Britain and Northern Ireland to the United Nations Addressed to the President of the Security Council, UN Doc. S/2003/350 (2003). Also Lord Goldsmith, 'Iraq: Legality of Armed Force', 646 Parl. Deb., House of Lords (5th Ser.) (2003) WA2-WA3; William H Taft IV and TF Buchwald, 'Preemption, Iraq, and International Law' (2003) 97 AJIL 557.

[24] SC Res. 1511, UN SCOR, 58th Sess, 4844th mtg., at 3, UN Doc. SC/RES/1511 (2003); SC Res. 1483, UN GAOR, 58th Sess, UN Doc. S/RES/1483 (2003). Finally, it was the UN who legitimized the end of the formal occupation, SC Res. 1546, 8 June 2004, UN Doc. S/RES/1546 (2004), para 2 and passim.

[25] N Luhmann, *Das Recht der Gesellschaft* (Frankfurt am Main: Suhrkamp, 1995) 571 et seq; N Luhmann, 1 *Die Gesellschaft der Gesellschaft* (Frankfurt am Main: Suhrkamp, 1997) 158–60.

from a world of sovereign territorial States to a world of functional institutions. The main characteristic of international institutionalism consists in the multiplicity of institutions in the international realm without an overarching hierarchy.[26] Thus, international institutionalism will not end in a world State, but will have to deal with pluralism and multiplicity of institutional designs, from governmental to non-governmental actors.

The role of the State in these areas is hotly disputed: for some, the legitimacy of these regimes does not so much derive from the authority of the States members, but from the efficient fulfilment of the function in question.[27] Such justification recalls Hans-Peter Ipsen's functional legitimation of the European Communities.[28] This attempt proved insufficient, however, in the course of the further development of the European Economic Community to the European Union.[29] Some suggest the development of global democracy on the same lines—a peoples' chamber of the UN General Assembly might constitute a beginning.[30] Others, such as Jürgen Habermas, have insisted on the nation State as the primary place of democratic legitimation, control, and accountability.[31] Further means of legitimation seem necessary, in particular for the more informal exercise of power by international bodies not subject to State control.

Courts and tribunals, both international and domestic, play a central role in adjudicating competing claims of legitimacy. In a hierarchical version of the institutionalist model, we would expect domestic courts to accept international decisions as authoritative, at least in the case of quasi-constitutional rules and principles, as

[26] For a more detailed analysis, A Fischer-Lescano and G Teubner, 'Regime-Collisions: The Vain Search for Legal Unity in the Fragmentation of Global Law' (2004) 25 Michigan JIL 999, 1004–17; AL Paulus, 'From Territoriality to Functionality? Towards a Legal Methodology of Globalization' in IF Dekker and WG Werner (eds), *Governance and International Legal Theory* (Leiden/Boston: Nijhoff, 2004) 59, 62–74. The disagreements between Teubner/Fischer-Lescano and the present author relate to the question of whether international law provides for a minimum of value-glue between different legal régimes, AL Paulus, 'The Legitimacy of International Law and the Role of the State', (2004) 25 Michigan JIL 1047–58; and Teubner's and Fischer-Lescano's reply, 'Consensus as a Fiction of Global Law' (2004) 25 Michigan JIL 999, 1059–73.

[27] Cf A Fischer-Lescano and G Teubner, 'Regime-Collisions: The Vain Search for Legal Unity in the Fragmentation of Global Law' (2004) 25 Michigan JIL 999, 1015–17, who regard collisions of different regimes as collisions between the diverse rationalities within global society. Their cure lies in a constitutionalization of the particular rather than in the search for a representation of the general, see id 'Consensus as a Fiction of Global Law' (2004) 25 Michigan JIL 999, 1072–73.

[28] HP Ipsen, *Europäisches Gemeinschaftsrecht* (Tübingen: Mohr, 1972) 196, The European Communities as 'Zweckverbände funktioneller Integration' (my translation: 'purposive association of functional integration').

[29] Eg E Stein, 'Lawyers, Judges and the Making of a Transnational Constitution' (1981) 75 AJIL 1. For criticism of the use of the term constitution, D Grimm, 'Der Vertrag' F.A.Z., Nr 109, 12 May 2005, 6; for further reflections, C Möllers, 'Verfassunggebende Gewalt—Verfassung—Konstitutionalisierung', in Armin von Bogdandy (ed), *Europäisches Verfassungsrecht* (Berlin: Springer, 2003) 1–57; JHH Weiler, *The Constitution of Europe* (Cambridge: CUP, 1999) 221–34. Also the Treaty Establishing a Constitution for Europe, available at <http://www.europa.eu.int/constitution/en/lstoc1_en.htm>, accessed 17 May 2005. However, in the substantive sense, the EU has its 'constitution' in the existing treaties.

[30] T Franck, *Fairness of International Law and Institutions* (Oxford: Clarendon, 1995) 483.

[31] J Habermas, *Die Einbeziehung des Anderen* (Frankfurt am Main: Suhrkamp, 1996) 225, 672.

expressed, for example, in the concept of *jus cogens*.[32] In the functional model, they are less likely to follow international rulings as a matter of hierarchy, but will accept the need for international regulation and accord high value to international decisions and rules as the means of regulating international relations. But a domestic court adhering to a functional model of international community will insist on the need to fit the rules and principles from the international realm into its own system. It may tie international regulation to considerations of subsidiarity. In other words, courts will be hesitant to admit international intervention in matters that can sufficiently be dealt with by the domestic legal order alone. This is even more valid for political organs implementing international rulings, as evident in the case of the WTO.[33]

2.2 Neoliberalism and September 11

The inter-State model of international community, in which individual human beings acquire rights and duties only via their national States, appears to be in trouble when not only goods and services, but also individuals are increasingly moving internationally, and where their ideas cross borders via the Internet or other means of global communication. A liberal concept of international community draws the consequences of these developments by focusing on individual rights and duties. Liberals and neoliberals demand a reconstruction of international law on an inter-individual basis. Informal 'government networks' may become effective regulators, balanced by a minimum of effective domestic control.

Whereas more moderate representatives of liberal ethics, such as John Rawls,[34] justified classical international law as allowing for multiple, diverse societies, more radical philosophers challenge the almost exclusive focus of Rawls's earlier work on national societies and demand the establishment of a 'world social order' fulfilling the promises of human rights at the international level.[35] The international

---

[32] Art 53 of the Vienna Convention on the Law of Treaties, 23 May 1969, 1155 UNTS 331. Indeed, at least one international tribunal has claimed such allegiance, eg *Furundžija*, (1999) 38 ILM 349–50, para 155. For a domestic pronouncement in this regard, *Pinochet III* [1999] 2 WLR 841 E/F (Browne-Wilkinson). For an evaluation of the role of *jus cogens*, A Paulus, 'Jus cogens Between Hegemony and Fragmentation: An Attempt at a Re-appraisal', (2005) 74 Nordic JIL 297.

[33] Eg the reaction of the Bush administration to *United States—Definitive Safeguard Measures on Imports of Certain Steel Products*, Report of the Appellate Body, Nov. 10, 2003, WT/DS248/AB/R, WT/DS249/AB/R, WT/DS251/AB/R, WT/DS252/AB/R, WT/DS253/AB/R, WT/DS254/AB/R, WT/DS258/AB/R, WT/DS259/AB/R, available at <http://www.wto.org/english/tratop_e/dispu_e/dispu_status_e.htm> (accessed 1 March 2004); Steel Proclamation, Dec. 4, 2003 and President's Statement on Steel, Dec. 4, 2003, both available at <http://www.whitehouse.gov> (accessed 23 May 2005).

[34] John Rawls, *A Theory of Justice* (Cambridge/Mass: Harvard UP, 1971) 377 et seq; John Rawls, 'The Law of Peoples' in S Shute and S Hurley (eds), *On Human Rights: The Oxford Amnesty Lectures* (New York: Basic Books, 1993) 41; John Rawls, *The Law of Peoples with The Idea of Public Reason Revisited* (Cambridge, Mass and London: Harvard UP, 1999) 3–128.

[35] CR Beitz, *Political Theory and International Relations* (Princeton: Princeton UP, 1979) 8–9, 128; TW Pogge, *Realizing Rawls* (Ithaca and London: Cornell UP, 1989) 244 et seq; but see Rawls (n 34 above) 242 et seq; FR Tesón, 'The Kantian Theory of International Law' (1992) 92 Columbia LR 53, 84, 97.

community is not based on formal legitimacy alone, but also incorporates material fairness, with 'shared moral imperatives and values'.[36] The institutional expression of liberal values is less important than the protection of individual rights by whomever contributes to this task. In a liberal community of individuals, the justification of State sovereignty is removed when the State fails to protect the rights of its citizens. In the case of some writers, this position translates into a justification of unilateral intervention for the protection of human rights—from Kosovo to Iraq.[37]

As the US 2002 National Security Strategy demonstrates,[38] September 11 has bolstered the views of those who share both the belief in the superiority of 'Western' values and the disdain for strong international institutions beyond the (democratic) nation State. Control of the superpower seems less important than the confidence in its values and ability to act for the common good—or, rather, for the safeguard of individual rights of people everywhere. Islamic fundamentalists have literally declared war against liberal democracy, and the only recipe against these enemies of liberty is accepting the challenge. Mechanisms of negotiation, accommodation, and consensus seem inapt to counter the threat. 'Either you are with us, or you are with the terrorists.'[39] As the Iraq war shows, this odd combination of liberalism with Schmittian concepts of friend and foe may become a self-fulfilling prophecy.

Different liberal approaches will also have competing ideas regarding the role of courts and tribunals. Anne-Marie Slaughter has concluded that the State as unitary actor has largely become an abstraction far from reality. Rather, the liberal State is 'disaggregated' into its component parts, in particular in the three branches of government, legislative, executive, judicial.[40] Accordingly, these branches of government are becoming separate, if not independent, actors at the international level, building 'transgovernmental' networks with their counterparts from other

---

[36] Rawls (n 34 above) 10–11.

[37] F Tesón, *Humanitarian Intervention: An Inquiry into Law and Morality* (2nd edn, New York: Transnational, 1997) 98: 'Because protection of human rights is the justification of having states in the first place, only governments that represent the people (in the sense of having their consent and respecting their rights) are entitled to the protection afforded by international law'. The moderate liberals who dominate international institutions regard such intervention as a collective duty rather than individual prerogative, G Evans and others, *The Responsibility to Protect. Report of the International Commission on Intervention and State Sovereignty* (IDRC, 2001) available at <http://www.iciss.ca/report-en.asp> (visited 23 May 2005); High-level Panel on Threats, Challenges and Change, A more secure world: our shared responsibility, UN Doc. A/59/565, 2 Dec. 2004, paras 183–209 available at <http://www.un.org/secureworld> (accessed 23 May 2005).

[38] The National Security Strategy of the United States of America (Sept. 2002) available at <http://www.whitehouse.gov/nsc/nss.pdf> (accessed 23 May 2005).

[39] George W Bush, 'Address to the Nation by the President of the United States', 147 *Congressional Record* H5737, 5859, 5861 (daily edn. 20 Sept. 2001).

[40] Slaughter (n 3 above) 131–65 and *passim*; AM Slaughter 'International Law in a World of Liberal States' (1995) 6 European JIL 503. For a criticism from a 'sovereignist' standpoint, K Anderson, 'Squaring the Circle? Reconciling Sovereignty and Global Governance Through Global Government Networks' (2005) 118 Harvard L Rev 1955; from a more institutionalist standpoint, P Alston, 'The Myopia of the Handmaidens. International Lawyers and Globalization' (1997) 8 EJIL 435.

liberal States. 'Transjudicial networks' of judges and lawyers[41] play an increasing role in the self-awareness of courts and tribunals all over the world:

What these judges share above all is the recognition of one another as participants in a common judicial enterprise. They see each other not only as servants and representatives of a particular government or polity, but also as fellow members of a profession that transcends national borders. . . . The system these judges are creating is better described as a community of courts than as a centralized hierarchy.[42]

Of course, this community also includes 'legitimate differences'. Nevertheless, lawyers from liberal States are considered to have as much, if not more, in common with each other than with their domestic counterparts in the other branches of government.

For the anti-institutionalist, neo-liberal variety, a liberal and democratic sovereign State does not need to accept precedents made within a global community that does not provide for the adequate protection of human rights and does not fulfil even the most basic criteria of democratic legitimacy. For others, international adjudication will be persuasive, but only as long as it conforms to substantive liberal and democratic values. It is thus telling that many liberals emphasize (democratic) legitimacy over international legality.[43] Networks of domestic institutions are preferable to global courts and tribunals with the authority to issue decisions binding for both liberal and non-liberal States. Hence Slaughter's emphasis on community over hierarchy. Nevertheless, the liberal view of the international community does not lead to incompatible solutions regarding the role of domestic courts versus the international legal order: as long as the latter provides for liberal values, liberals will embrace the use of reasoning from other than domestic sources, be they foreign or international. If (neo-)liberalism endorses the loss of State exclusivity and stresses the universality of human rights, it will not stop at State borders. Courts and tribunals from liberal States are regarded as part of a transnational community of judges, and should openly and transparently engage in dialogue.

2.3 The postmodern critique of international community

In a *postmodern* understanding, community is not possible without exclusion and suppression of 'the other'. And indeed, the exclusion of others is as much the part of a community concept as their inclusion.[44] Thus, 'community' may be used as an ideological construct for the maintenance of structures of power, excluding

---

[41] Slaughter (n 3 above) 53–103, AM Slaughter, 'A Global Community of Courts' (2003) 44 Harvard ILJ 191.   [42] Slaughter (n 3 above) 68.

[43] Eg AM Slaughter, 'Good Reasons for Going Around the U.N.' New York Times, 18 March 2003, p A33. For a more radical version of this argument Tesón (n 37 above) Slaughter has since come to the conclusion that her conditions for legitimacy have not been met, AM Slaughter, 'The Use of Force in Iraq: Illegal and Illegitimate' (2004) ASIL Proceedings of the 98th Annual Meeting 262–63.

[44] Cf UN Secretary-General KA Annan, 'Fighting Terrorism on a Global Front' New York Times, 21 September 2001, 35.

the 'other', the marginal, the different. Postmodernists criticize both the social-democratic enthusiasm for new international bureaucracies and the neoliberal reliance on liberal values.

The liberal concept of community is rejected because it does not take account of the multiplicity of ethical approaches and marginalizes those opposed to the dominant liberal model.[45] In the last resort, liberal models of the international community stabilize—voluntarily or involuntarily—American hegemony. The reliance on the market hides the political nature of this choice and ultimately strives in vain to protect neoliberalism from critique. The postmodern critique of institutionalism is no less acerbic than the neoliberal one: the vision of communitarian unity[46] shares the vice of the ideal of a liberal community: it excludes and marginalizes the outsider. In addition, an international institutionalism cannot cure the lack of legitimacy of its universalism. In the eyes of some postmodernists, international community is thus nothing but a 'reification'[47] of a theoretical construct for ideological purposes.[48] In the words of David Kennedy, 'international law [is] not as a set of rules or institutions, but... a group of professional disciplines in which people pursue projects in various quite different institutional, political, and national settings'.[49]

The reactions to September 11 not only by the Bush administration, but also in Europe have demonstrated how the language of community may be (ab)used for curtailing civil liberties. The language of 'either you are with us or with the terrorists'[50] shows the utility of 'community' for exclusion of critique. Nevertheless, the ideological (ab)use of international law in general, and the community concept in particular, should not obscure the need for finding a more than subjective basis for grounding an international legal order which appears under increasing strain, even existential threat. Maybe this is indeed the time for the defence of an international legal community of some sort, based on imperfect, but consensual legal rules as the expression of, in Martti Koskenniemi's apt term, a 'culture of formalism'.[51] In this vein, the true test for the 'emergence' of an international community does not consist in the justificatory value of the community concept, but in the inclusiveness of its results.

More liberal mainstreamers—institutionalists and neoliberals alike—point to the postmodernist lack of a normative vision as either resulting in an unfettered

[45] D Kennedy, 'The Disciplines of International Law and Policy' (2000) 12 Leiden JIL 9, 123.

[46] Cf M Koskenniemi, 'Repetition as Reform: Georges Abi-Saab Cours Général de droit international public' (1998) 9 EJIL 405, 411: '[I]t is time to let go of the myth of a progressive history that moves from institutional fragmentation to unity'.

[47] For the meaning of this term, A Carty, 'Critical International Law: Recent Trends in the Theory of International Law' (1991) 2 EJIL 66, 67.

[48] Kennedy (n 45 above) 9, 83–4. Also Koskenniemi (n 2 above) 113, who speaks of 'kitsch' in this regard.   [49] D Kennedy (n 45 above) 9, 83.

[50] See n 39 above and accompanying text.

[51] M Koskenniemi, *The Gentle Civilizer of Nations: The Rise and Fall of International Law 1870–1960* (Cambridge: CUP, 2003) 494 et seq.

political realism,[52] or in a complete lack of defence against the fundamentalist challenge.[53] If any normative international legal project is rejected, there is indeed no yardstick to evaluate international behaviour of States, or terrorists, or anybody else. But such critique needs to differentiate between legitimate ideology critique and an extreme moral relativism—which most postmodernists reject.

Postmodernists will not be opposed to the use of international 'communitarian' concepts in the domestic legal order by courts, but they will not accept the invocation of a 'global consensus' as a substitute for arguing about the merits of particular value-choices or as a justification for power and violence. They may also point to the multiplicity of international actors and the options open to courts in this regard. If the use of international law in a domestic context brings domestic society to recognize the rights of the outsider rather than rejecting him or her as alien, the emergence of an international community may be useful.

Indeed, the use of international sources can both be a means to escape domestic parochialism, but also entail a weakening of domestic protections for groups and individuals. International law may help to uphold civil liberties against their curtailment by domestic anti-terrorism laws, but it can also contribute to implementing the will of the permanent members of the Security Council in violation of domestic rights of individuals. The problem with a focus on the outcomes—and here postmodernism fares no better than other Realisms—is that it does not itself provide a normative yardstick indicating how to evaluate competing claims of authority.

2.4 Conclusion

As it turns out, none of the 'community' models presented here requires a hierarchical relationship between 'community values' and domestic law. Rather, if applied to current circumstances, these models emphasize the choice inherent in the 'implementation' of international rules and principles by another, domestic legal system. The institutionalist urge of hierarchy will be tempered by the multiplicity and contradictory character of international institutional designs; the (neo)liberal scepticism towards self-serving bureaucracies will emphasize common liberal values, but question a vertical relationship between international and domestic courts and tribunals; and the postmodernist critique will urge the domestic courts to resist the temptation to blindly follow international precedents instead of making a conscious choice. As different and, at times, contradictory designs of international community are today, the introduction of a Kelsenian hierarchy between international and domestic legal communities is unlikely to be on the top of any of these agendas. Nor should it be so.

---

[52] Cf J Habermas, *Der philosophische Diskurs der Moderne* (Frankfurt: Suhrkamp, 1985) 11–12 and *passim*. Similarly C Brown, *International Relations Theory: New Normative Approaches* (New York: Columbia UP, 1992) 218, 237. For a more extensive treatment, A Paulus, 'International Law After Postmodernity' (2001) 14 Leiden JIL 727.

[53] Eg T Franck, 'Epistemology at a Time of Perplexity' (2002) 13 EJIL 1025.

3. Unity and pluralism of the international legal community

We will now turn to the conceptualization of the relationship between the international and the domestic legal community. Our treatment of the different conceptions of community has shown that we should be wary of any suggestion that international law and domestic law could simply merge into one hierarchical system. As we shall see, the opposite is the case: a turn from the strict separation of two relatively closed systems of law—'international' and 'domestic'—is giving way to a much more pluralistic conception. In this part, we will discuss the general relationship between the international and the domestic order, before we look at its repercussions in some domestic legal systems.

As Giorgio Gaja describes the situation in his contribution to this volume,[54] traditional legal discourse only knew of two incompatible positions regarding the relationship between the international and domestic legal orders: either they were part of one single legal order, be it national or international ('monism'),[55] or the international and domestic legal orders were entirely distinct ('dualism').[56] To accommodate reality, both theories had to modify their extreme positions, however: either the international legal order left a lot of room for individual States to disregard international legal constraints, or domestic law had to accommodate the specificity of international law, and thus needed constantly to defer certain decisions to the 'other' legal order. Neither a complete integration nor a complete separation of the international and the domestic legal spheres would do justice to the diverse ways in which international norms enter domestic law, but also are limited by it. Dualism starts from the proposition that one could regard the domestic or international legal system as absolutely closed, as self-contained regimes in the strictest meaning of the term. Similarly, monism is also based on the vision of a single, global, and closed international legal order. Such closeness, however, seems to be more and more illusory.

Maybe it is possible, however, to transcend the debate between monism and dualism by a recognition of the pluralism and diversity of legal systems. This recognition also extends to different legal régimes within international law itself. The question of openness or closeness of a legal system cannot, in practice, be decided in a clear-cut fashion. Most domestic constitutions regulate in one way or the other the application of international law in the domestic realm. Regardless of whether it takes a 'monist' or 'dualist' approach to the relationship of the domestic and international legal orders, the domestic legal order needs to regulate the application of

---

[54] Ch 2 of this volume.

[55] For an impassioned plea, H Kelsen, *Introduction to the Problems of Legal Theory* (Reine Rechtslehre, 1934), B Litschewski Paulson and SL Paulson (transl), (Oxford: Clarendon, 1992) 111–25; H Kelsen, *Reine Rechtslehre* (2nd edn, Wien Leipzig: Franz Deuticke, 1960) 328–45; *Pure Theory of Law* (transl) (California: Univ of Cal Press, 1967) 328–47.

[56] For a recent exposition of dualism, Gaetano Arangio-Ruiz, 'Dualism Revisited, International Law and Interindividual Law' (2003) 86 Rivista di diritto internazionale 909–99, with further references, in particular at 909 (n 1); see also ch 1 in this volume.

international law in its domestic legal order, and it needs to define the relationship between domestic and international norms. As the German legal order shows, a domestic legal system may also differentiate between treaties, on the one hand, and customary law and general principles, on the other.[57] British law also regards international law as part of the law of the land as far as common law is concerned, but requires a transformation and implementation of international treaties into domestic law by an Act of Parliament.[58] From that angle, monism and dualism become a matter of degree of the integration of international law into a domestic order, not of kind.

As Giorgio Gaja has further observed,[59] a division between international and domestic law regarding the addressees of the respective norms is becoming increasingly difficult. The rule that international law does not directly address itself to individuals always allowed for exceptions. Rules of international law requiring direct effect in domestic law exist not only in European law. However, the difference used to be that, in the case of international rules, domestic law could insist on the need of a specific domestic act of transformation, whereas, according to the doctrines of supremacy and direct effect enshrined in Community law,[60] European Community norms have to be incorporated in a generalized way 'once and for all'.

But it is increasingly doubtful that this difference is still as absolute as it used to be. In the *LaGrand case*, the International Court of Justice directly addressed an order to an individual State organ rather than to the State as such. Although the final decision of the Court emphasized the discretion of the United States as to the means by which it achieves a reconsideration of its domestic Court decisions impaired by a violation of the 1963 Vienna Convention on Consular Relations,[61] the ICJ had no doubt whatsoever that its order on provisional measures was not only addressed to the United States as a State, but also to the Governor of Arizona.[62]

---

[57] Treaties are incorporated into German law by parliamentary consent to ratification or accession (Art 59, *Grundgesetz für die Bundesrepublik Deutschland* [Basic Law for the Federal Republic of Germany], 23 May 1949, Federal Gazette 1949 I, p. 1, last amended 26 July 2002, Federal Gazette 2002 I, p. 2863). For the incorporation of general rules, Art 25: '*Die allgemeinen Regeln des Völkerrechts sind Bestandteil des Bundesrechts. Sie gehen den Gesetzen vor und erzeugen Rechte und Pflichten unmittelbar für die Bewohner des Bundesgebiets*'. (The general rules of international law shall be an integral part of federal law. They shall take precedence over the laws and directly create rights and duties for the inhabitants of the federal territory.)

[58] For international customary law as 'part of the law of the land' in England and Wales, Blackstone, *Commentaries on the Laws of England* IV (1769) Ch V 20. For the incorporation of treaties, eg I Brownlie, *Principles of Public International Law* (6th edn, Oxford: OUP, 2003) 41–42.

[59] Ch 2 of this volume.

[60] *Van Gend & Loos*, Case 26/62 [1963] ECR 1 (direct effect); *Costa v ENEL*, Case 6/64 [1964] ECR 585 (supremacy).

[61] Vienna Convention on Consular Relations of April 24, 1963, 596 UNTS 261; *LaGrand (Germany v United States of America)*, 2001 ICJ Rep 466 para 125: 'The choice of means must be left to the United States'. The impact of this phrase on US domestic law was further spelt out in *Avena and other Mexican Nationals (Mexico v United States of America)*, 2004 ICJ Rep 12 para 138–41, 153(9).

[62] *LaGrand (Germany v United States of America)*, Provisional Measures, Order of 3 March 1999, 1999 ICJ Rep 16 para 28: 'whereas the Governor of Arizona is under the obligation to act in conformity with the international undertakings of the United States'.

The decisive element seems to lie in the individual rights contained in Article 36, paragraph 1 of the Vienna Convention[63] and the effectiveness required by Article 36, paragraph 2 of the Vienna Convention for their domestic implementation. Thus, individual rights seem to lift the 'corporate veil' of State sovereignty from the standpoint of international law, just as international criminal law renders certain individual conduct directly punishable at the international level. By granting individuals rights and obligations on the international plane, international law thus pierces the veil of 'juridical personality' of the State.

It does not change the international requirements as such that international law leaves it to the State to choose between implementing its international obligations by providing for their direct effect in the domestic legal order or by transforming them into domestic law by special national legislation. Accordingly, the *Blaškić* decision of the ICTY does not argue that international law could never regulate the behaviour of national organs or individuals, but that international law usually leaves it to the discretion of States to determine the organ responsible for the implementation of international law[64]—a statement that fully accords with the *LaGrand* and *Avena* jurisprudence of the International Court of Justice.[65]

Even where international legal rules do not enjoy direct effect, their impact on domestic law may be profound, though. One example is the Counter-Terrorism Committee established by SC Res. 1373 in the aftermath of the terrorist attacks on the United States of September 11, 2001.[66] All States are required to block funds of the organisations or businesses designated as terrorists by the Committee—with no international legal control over this determination whatsoever. Due to a lack of information on the grounds of such Security Council determination, the control of these lists by domestic courts appears difficult, if not impossible. Nevertheless, they seem to be the only legal means of control of these designations by the Security Council. Thus, the lack of direct effect of Security Council determinations in the domestic legal order may not result in a loss of effectiveness.

Similar considerations apply to *jus cogens*. Some international tribunals have deduced far-reaching consequences from *jus cogens* norms regardless of the lack of consensus concerning both their content and effects. Thus, in *Furundžija*, an

---

[63] On the character of Art 36, para 1 of the 1963 Vienna Convention on Consular Relations as individual right, see *LaGrand (Germany v United States of America), Provisional Measures, Order of 3 March 1999*, 1999 ICJ Rep16 para 77. It seems of no significant impact in this context that the court did not rule on the character of Art 36 para 1 as a *human* right (ibid, para 78).

[64] International Criminal Tribunal for the Former Yugoslavia, Appeals Chamber, *Prosecutor v Blaskic*, Judgment on the Request of the Republic of Croatia for Review of the Decision of Trial Chamber II of 18 July 1997, Oct. 29, 1997, 110 I.L.R. 607, 688, at 712, para 43. Also ibid, 713–15, paras 46–48 where the Appeals Chamber emphasizes that it may issue orders to individuals in their private capacity.

[65] *Avena and other Mexican Nationals (Mexico v United States of America)*, 2004 ICJ Rep 12; *LaGrand (Germany v United States of America), Provisional Measures, Order of 3 March 1999*, 1999 ICJ Rep 16.

[66] UN Security Council Res. 1373, Sept. 28, 2001. On the problem in general, E de Wet and A Nollkaemper, *Review of the Security Council by Member States* (Antwerp: Intersentia, 2003).

ICTY Trial Chamber has deduced universal jurisdiction of States from the *jus cogens* character of the prohibition on torture, and has—more relevant in our context— denied not only treaties, but also domestic laws contrary to *jus cogens* 'international recognition'—whatever that implies in practice.[67] Nevertheless, the stark legal condemnation which attaches to violations of *jus cogens* indeed requires international law not to allow States to disregard these prohibitions in their domestic legal order. A strict substantive separation of international and domestic law as postulated by traditional dualism seems thus more and more implausible. There increasingly exists, in Giorgio Gaja's terms,[68] a 'continuity between international society and municipal societies' and this cannot but affect the respective legal orders, too.

On the other hand, this does not imply a return to a Kelsenian monism.[69] The vision of a hierachical unity of international and domestic laws is more threatening than reassuring, in particular at a juncture where the temptations of superpower hegemony appear stronger than ever. In addition, our postmodern skepticism towards grand foundational schemes does not allow for one-size-fits-all solutions. We are faced with a profoundly pluralist international order, in which several— often functionally circumscribed—global and regional institutions overlap with the various domestic legal orders. In the words of David Leebron, '[w]e inhabit a world of "multi-multilateralism"—numerous multilateral regimes with sometimes overlapping, indeed sometimes conflicting, mandates'.[70]

Most international instruments, such as the United Nations Convention on the Law of the Sea (UNCLOS), the Statute of the International Criminal Court,

---

[67] ICTY, Trial Chamber, *Prosecutor v Furundžija*, Dec. 10, 1998, (1999) 38 ILM 349–50, paras 155, 156. The Swiss constitution has recently excluded derogations of *jus cogens* from amendments, Bundesverfassung der Schweizerischen Eidgenossenschaft [Constitution of the Swiss Confederation] of 18 April 1999, Arts 139 (new), para 2, 193, para 4, and 194, para 2, AS 99, 2556, as of 11 May 2004, available at <http://www.admin.ch/ch/d/sr/101> [German], <http://www.oefre.unibe.ch/law/icl/ sz00000_.html> (unofficial English translation) accessed 1 March 2005. The German Constitutional Court has also discussed the question of whether *jus cogens* can void a contrary bilateral treaty, *Lastenausgleichsabgabe [Burden Compensation Levy]*, 7 April 1965, 18 BVerfGE, 441, at 448–49, or whether it creates a duty of non-recognition for acts of expropriation, *Expropriations in Eastern Germany*, BVerfG, 2 BvR 955/00, 26 October 2004, paras 97, 116–23 available at <http://www.bverfg. de/entscheidungen/rs20041026_2bvr095500.html>. The British House of Lords has referred to *jus cogens* to justify the exercise of universal jurisdiction, *Pinochet III* [1999] 2 WLR 841 E/F (Browne-Wilkinson). In the US, some courts have used *jus cogens* as an argument for the binding character of international rules in the domestic legal order, eg *Doe I v Unocal Corp* 395 F3d9 932, at 948 (9th Cir., 18 September 2002), *vacated & reh'g en banc granted* by 395 F3d 978 (9th Cir., 14 February 2003); the matter was settled out of court after *Sosa v Alvarez-Machain* 124 SCt 2739 (29 June 2004). Others have refused to invalidate immunity in cases of alleged violations of *jus cogens* norms by individuals, eg *Ye v Zemin* 383 F.3d 620, 626, 627 (7th Cir. 2004); *Princz v Federal Republic of Germany* 26 F3d 1166, 1173 (DC Cir 1994); *Siderman de Blake v Republic of Argentina* 965 F2d 699, 718–19 (9th Cir 1992). Famously, both the ICJ and the ECHR have similarly upheld claims of immunity in such cases, eg *Arrest Warrant of 11 April 2000 (Democratic Republic of the Congo v Belgium)*, 14 February 2002, (2002) 41 *ILM* 536 at 551, para 59; *Al-Adsani v United Kingdom*, Application no 35763/97, Judgment, 21 Nov. 2001, ECHR Reports 2001-XI, p 79, at 101–103, paras 61–66. But see the Joint Dissenting Opinion, ibid 111, 112. For a more detailed discussion see Paulus (n 32 above) 297, ch 3 and 4.   [68] See ch 2 in this volume.

[69] See n 55 above and accompanying text.

[70] DW Leebron, 'Linkages' (2002) AJIL 96 5, 17. See also n 25 above and accompanying text.

or, to a certain extent, WTO/GATT, contain their own rules which determine their relationship to general international law. They do not integrate general international law as part and parcel of their own schemes. For instance, Article 311 of the UN Convention on the Law of the Sea only refers to other conventional instruments but not to customary international law,[71] and the Rome Statute of the International Criminal Court gives precedence to its own rules over those of general international law.[72] Often, the relationship of these special regimes to international law—or their 'self-contained' character—is hotly disputed, for instance in the case of WTO dispute settlement.[73] Some of these disputes may be solved by reference to general rules of treaty interpretation, as incorporated by Article 3, paragraph 2 of the Dispute Settlement Understanding.[74] But here, we are faced with the same problem as in the incorporation clauses of domestic constitutions: do they integrate their treaty regime as part and parcel of international law or do they incorporate general international law into their own legal system? Attempts at a hierarchization of the institutions competent for the application of these norms, in particular in the United Nations and the International Court of Justice, or 'super-norms', as in the case of *jus cogens*, were only of limited effect.[75]

This profound pluralism of the international legal order is further accentuated by regional institutions, in particular in Europe. With its particularly demanding characteristics of supremacy and direct effect in the domestic legal orders, European Community law often serves as an intermediary between international and domestic

---

[71] United Nations Convention on the Law of the Sea, 30 Apr. 1982, 1833 UNTS 3, Art 311.

[72] Art 21 of the Rome Statute of the International Criminal Court, July 1998, 2187 UNTS 3, reads: 'The Court shall apply: (a) In the first place, this Statute, Elements of Crimes and its Rules of Procedure and Evidence; (b) In the second place, where appropriate, applicable treaties and the principles and rules of international law.' Note that the hierarchy employed here gives precedence to the rules of the Court, not to general international law.

[73] Arts 3.2 and 7 of the Understanding on Rules and Procedures Governing the Settlement of Disputes [hereafter referred to as hereinafter DSU], Marrakesh Agreement Establishing the World Trade Organization, 15 Apr. 1994, Annex 2, 1869 UNTS 401. Also Art 20 of the General Agreement on Tariffs and Trade (GATT 1994), Marrakesh Agreement Establishing the World Trade Organization, 15 April 1994, Annex 1a, 1867 UNTS, pp 4, 190, (1994) 33 ILM 1154 (amending and renewing the General Agreement on Tariffs and Trade (GATT 1947), 30 Oct. 1947, 55 UNTS, p 187, amended 278 UNTS 168; 572 UNTS 320), dealing with exceptions to the obligations under the GATT for the sake of (unilateral) domestic measures for the protection of other values than trade. On the discussion concerning the relevance of general international law to trade law, on the one hand, J Pauwelyn, 'The Role of Public International Law in the WTO: How Far Can We Go' (2001) 95 AJIL 535, 541–50; on the other JP Trachtman, 'Institutional Linkage: Transcending 'Trade and...'' (2002) 96 AJIL 77, 88 (n 28). Art 3.2 does not rule out the exercise of judicial restraint and deference to other regimes, especially in areas of overlap see, eg HL Schoemann and S Ohlhoff, ' "Constitutionalization" and Dispute Settlement in the WTO: National Security as an Issue of Competence' (1999) 93 AJIL 424, 424–5, n 2.

[74] The relevant phrase of Art 3, para 2 DSU reads: 'The Members recognize that [the WTO dispute settlement system] serves . . . to clarify the existing provisions of [the WTO] agreements in accordance with customary rules of interpretation of public international law.'

[75] For further analysis, AL Paulus, 'From Territoriality to Functionality? Towards a Legal Methodology of Globalization' in IF Dekker and WG Werner (eds), *Governance and International Legal Theory* (Leiden/Boston: Nijhoff, 2004) 59, 62–74.

law, for instance in the case of the demands of the Counter-Terrorism Committee established by the Security Council.[76] However, the European Community legal order itself has to solve the problem of its own relationship to international law, too. Thus, sometimes, the European legal order seems to belong to international law—in particular when domestic constitutions incorporate it by way of clauses intended for international law—at other times, in particular vis-à-vis international institutions, the EU fulfils the role of a State. Domestic law has difficulty to simply incorporate 'international law' because this presupposes a decision on which part of international law is directly applicable in the domestic legal order—and, more and more frequently, on the decision of value conflicts not only between international and national law, but also within the more and more diverse body of international norms and rules.

Thus, a monist concept of the international legal order can simply not grasp the complexities of the relationship of all those different legal orders with different rules of incorporation of other systems, including the corpus of general international law. On another occasion, I have argued that the pluralism of the contemporary legal world requires a profound change of the legal methodology, leading away from attempts of hierarchization towards a culture of dialogue and accommodation.[77] The traditional dualism, on the other hand, with its insistence on completeness and closeness of legal systems, is also incapable of understanding this seamless web of legal systems, functional, regional, domestic, with concomitant differentiated rules of incorporation and recognition of other systems of norms. This is also valid for the rules 'transforming' international rules into domestic ones, ranging from European law via self-executing international rules towards general principles and classical norms addressed to the State as a whole. Many of these systems being partial and functional in character, it would not make sense for them to regard these other systems simply as 'facts'.[78] Rather, in the words of Neil MacCormick: '[T]he most appropriate analysis of the relations of legal systems is pluralistic rather than monistic, and interactive rather than hierarchical'.[79] This is not only valid as to the relationship between European and domestic law, but also applies to the relationship of domestic and international law.

Thus, in the age of globalization, the dualist insistence on separateness and closedness of legal orders is doomed to fail just as much as the monist attempts of

---

[76] For details regarding the implementation of these resolutions, see the contributions in E de Wet and A Nollkaemper, *Review of the Security Council by Member States* (Antwerp: Intersentia, 2003).

[77] For a plea for such a relationship with regard to European Union law, P Kirchhof, 'The Balance of Powers between National and European Institutions' (1999) 5 European LJ 225; N MacCormick, *Questioning Sovereignty* (Oxford: OUP, 1999) 117–21. While these authors disagree on the precise scope of the supremacy of European Union law, this is a separate matter.

[78] But see the jurisprudence of the Permanent Court of International Justice, *Certain German Interests in Upper Silesia*, PCIJ Rep Series A No 17, 19. For a critical review of these and other PCIJ and ICJ pronouncements on domestic law, I Brownlie, *Principles of Public International Law* (6th edn, Oxford: OUP, 2003) 38–40. See also ch 2 in this volume.

[79] N MacCormick, *Questioning Sovereignty* (Oxford: OUP, 1999) 171.

harmonization and hierarchization. In a post-foundational era, we have no choice but to recognize the pluralism of values, norms, and institutions, and the concomitant pluralism of legal orders, which render the classical dichotomy between 'domestic' and 'international' norms increasingly futile, but do not allow either for the monist pretension of unity.

4. International community and the domestic realm: domestic courts and the impact of international on domestic law

For domestic courts, the pluralism of legal orders implies that the general characterization of the relationship between 'international' and 'national' law as 'monist' or 'dualist' will often not be very helpful. Other mechanisms, such as the principle of 'consistent interpretation' of domestic law in accordance with international law,[80] are complicating the relationship between international and domestic law even further. It is hardly surprising, then, that domestic courts will decide matters of incorporation of international community norms and values in a highly circumspect and relative, eg pluralist, fashion rather than relying on the age-old conceptualizations of monism and dualism. On the other hand, the integration of many Western States into the global institutions and the global economy, as well as their universalist traditions rooted in Western philosophy from Locke to Kant, will both pull them into some kind of value-based community beyond their borders.

The domestic jurisprudence shall help us to determine the impact of 'international community concepts' on the interpretation of domestic law and to thereby gauge some insights into the development of an international legal community of courts and tribunals. As indicated in the Introduction, we will look to the practice of domestic courts in three 'Western' countries, namely Germany, the United Kingdom, and the United States. Of course, this choice of examples is quite arbitrary. Nevertheless, the Western bias may be justified because it is there where independent courts play a determinant role in the implementation of legal rules for the authoritative settlement of conflicts in society. Recent judgments of African and Latin American courts and the Israeli Supreme Court also refer extensively both to international and foreign case law.[81] In our selection of recent cases, Germany may represent countries in the civil law tradition, whereas the United States is a

---

[80] G Betlem and A Nollkaemper, 'Giving Effect to Public International Law and European Community Law before Domestic Courts: A Comparative Analysis of Consistent Interpretation' (2003) 14 EJIL 569; for recent US case law, AL Paulus, 'From Neglect to Defiance. The United States and International Adjudication' (2004) 15 EJIL 783, 804.

[81] For a recent example of an African Court fulfilling the same function in a human rights-related matter, eg Constitutional Court of South Africa, *Kaunda v The President of South Africa*, 4 August 2004 (2005) 44 ILM 173 which cites extensively foreign sources, eg the lead opinion by Chaskalson, Chief Justice, paras 71–76; J O'Regan, ibid 210 (212) para 222: '[O]ur Constitution recognises and asserts that, after decades of isolation, South Africa is now a member of the community of nations, and a bearer of obligations and responsibilities in terms of international law'; also Supreme Court of

monist and the United Kingdom, as far as treaties are concerned,[82] a dualist country. Germany and Britain are part of the system of the European Convention on Human Rights, the United States is not.

An important distinction has to be kept in mind, however: we have to distinguish between (1) the role of international law in the domestic legal order and (2) the question of whether domestic courts may look to judgments of foreign courts when they decide issues of domestic law. The first question asks whether the domestic court will keep its domestic legal order strictly separate from the international legal order, as dualism would require, or whether it integrates international into domestic law in a 'monist' fashion. The question of the use of foreign judgments in jurisprudence, on the contrary, regards the engagement of the courts in the transjudicial dialogue with their brethren in the rest of the world. The treatment of both questions, however, may be regarded as a yardstick for the integration of the respective domestic legal order in the international legal community which goes beyond international law in the stricter sense of the term.

4.1 The US Supreme Court and the 'international community'

We shall first turn to the practice of the United States as the practice of the most powerful State. If the domestic courts of the single superpower pay regard to what they perceive as the voice of the international community, there would be at least some indication that international community goes beyond academic discussions on the high ground of intellectual self-reference, but has real world implications in the domestic legal order.

4.1.1 The relevance of the international community to the interpretation of the US Constitution

The US Constitution itself is positive towards the influence of international law proper in the US legal system. According to Article VI, clause 2 of the Constitution, 'all Treaties made, or which shall be made, under the Authority of the United States, shall be the supreme Law of the Land; and the Judges in every State shall be bound thereby, any Thing in the Constitution or Laws of any State to the Contrary notwithstanding'. Historically, the implementation of the peace treaties with

Argentina, *Julio Héctor Simon*, 14 June 2005, available at <http://www.clarin.com/diario/2005/06/14/um/fallopuntofinal.doc> (accessed 15 September 2005) (decision declaring Argentina's Amnesty Laws unconstitutional with reference to Inter-American Court of Human Rights jurisprudence and international law); Israeli Supreme Court, *Fence Surrounding Alfei Menashe*, HCJ 7957/04, 15 September 2005, English press communiqué available at <http://elyon1.court.gov.il/heb/dover/html/hodaot_hanhalat.htm#msg4862> (accessed 15 September 2005) (ICJ Advisory Opinion authority for international law, but not for its application to incomplete facts); for a broader overview, C McCrudden, 'A Common Law of Human Rights?: Transnational Judicial Conversations on Constitutional Rights' (2000) 20 OJLS 499.   [82] See n 58 above and accompanying text.

Britain was one of the reasons for drafting the constitution in the first place.[83] As to customary law, until recently, its place within the domestic legal order was hotly debated, some younger authors being of the opinion that customary international law was left to the states rather than the union.[84] Before we deal with the recent resolution of this issue by the Supreme Court, we will first turn to the question of whether foreign judgments and other non-binding legal opinions beyond the domestic sphere are a legitimate part of modern constitutional jurisprudence.

The use of international and foreign law sources by the US Supreme Court has become very controversial recently. Conservative Republicans, in particular, regard the citation of foreign law sources as an imposition by the Court on the US electorate and as a violation of the separation of powers.[85] For example, the former chairman of the Judiciary Committee of the House of Representatives, James Sensenbrenner, is particularly upset with 'courts citing foreign sources of authority in their rulings'.[86] According to Sensenbrenner,

America's sovereignty and the integrity of our legal process are threatened by a jurisprudence predicated upon laws and judicial decisions alien to our Constitution and foreign to our system of self-government. . . . Inappropriate judicial adherence to foreign laws and tribunals threatens American sovereignty, unsettles the separation of powers, presidential and Senate treaty-making authority, and undermines the legitimacy of the judicial process.

As evidence, Sensenbrenner cites the Supreme Court decision in *Roper v Simmons*,[87] invalidating the death penalty for juveniles, that is, persons under 18 at the time of the commission of the crime. According to Sensenbrenner, the majority opinion in

---

[83] *The Records of the Federal Convention of 1787* at 19 (M Farrand, ed, 1911) (quoting Edmund Randolph) 316–17 (quoting James Madison); *The Federalist*, Nos 3, 4 (John Jay), 42 (John Madison). Frederick W Marks III, *Independence on Trial: Foreign Affairs and the* (1986), 4–5, 151, 177–78. Also CA Bradley and JL Goldsmith, 'The Abiding Relevance of Federalism to U.S. Foreign Relations' (1998) 92 AJIL 675, 677.

[84] In favour of the 'modern position' regarding customary international law as federal law, *Restatement (Third) of Foreign Relations Law of the United States* § 432(2) (American Law Inst. 1987), at § 111; L Henkin, *Foreign Affairs and the US Constitution* (2nd edn, Oxford: Clarendon Press, 1996) 233–35; L Henkin, 'International Law as Law in the United States' (1984) 82 Michigan L Rev 1555; PC Jessup, 'The Doctrine of Erie Railroad v. Tompkins Applied to International Law' (1939) 33 AJIL 740, 743. Cf CA Bradley and JL Goldsmith, 'Customary International Law as Federal Common Law: A Critique of the Modern Position' (1997) 110 Harv L Rev 815. (Against them H Hongju Koh, 'Is International Law Really State Law?' (1998) 111 Harv L Rev 1824; GL Neuman, 'Human Rights on the Eve of the Next Century: Sense and Nonsense About Customary International Law: A Response to Professors Bradley and Goldsmith' (1997) 66 Fordham L Rev 371, 371–83.) The 'modern position' has now apparently been accepted by the Supreme Court, *Sosa v Alvarez-Machain* 124 S Ct (2004) 2739, 2764–65, but see 2772–73 (Scalia J concurring).

[85] JJ Holland, 'DeLay Criticizes Supreme Court Justice', Washington Post, 20 April 2005; C Hulse, 'DeLay Outlines Strategy Against Federal Judges', New York Times, 20 April 2005, A 20. Also F Rich, 'A High-Tech Lynching in Prime Time', New York Times, 25 April 2005, Sect. 4. Also H Res. 97, 109th Cong 'Reaffirmation of American Independence Resolution' introduced on February 15 2005, available at <http://www.house.gov> (accessed 23 May 2005) and the parallel draft Senate Res. 92, available at <http://www.senate.gov> (accessed 23 May 2005).

[86] Representative F James Sensenbrenner Jr, 'Zale Lecture in Public Policy', Stanford University, 9 May 2005, available at <http://judiciary.house.gov/media/pdfs/stanfordjudgesspeechpressversion505. pdf> (accessed 14 May 2005).   [87] 543 US 551, 125 SCt 1183 (2005).

this decision 'lacks coherent and intellectual honesty' because it cited the UN Convention on the Rights of the Child[88] which the US Senate did not ratify precisely because it prohibits the 'juvenile death penalty'. Sensenbrenner likens this citation to the colonial rule of King George against whom the American Revolution once rose:

The authority of American government rests solely and irrevocably upon the consent of the governed. The American people have not consented to rule by foreign powers or tribunals, and have never authorized our courts to rely upon foreign judgments and pronouncements when interpreting either American statutory or constitutional provisions.

Sensenbrenner's criticism goes right to the heart of the relationship between the domestic judiciary and the international community. He rejects any domestic reliance on foreign pronouncements—at least as long the latter have not been endorsed by the legislature.

However, the question remains of whether the US constitution really excludes the mere citation of foreign legal pronouncements. One of the moderate conservative voices on the Court, retired Justice Sandra Day O'Connor, recently argued that 'conclusions reached by other countries and by the international community should at times constitute persuasive authority in American courts'.[89] O'Connor deplored the lack of a 'robust ... transnational jurisprudence' of US Courts. Of course, she did not argue that such authorities can somehow bind the Supreme Court to accept an otherwise unavailable construction, but may further the understanding of one's own legal order.

The debate dates back to the late 1980s, when the Court grappled with the consequences of the continuing use of the death penalty, in particular regarding the execution of mentally retarded persons and juveniles. In 1988, the Court decided that the Eighth Amendment banning 'cruel and unusual punishment' prevented the execution of juveniles under 16 at the time of the commission of the crime.[90] The plurality opinion in this case also referred to the standards of the 'international community'. One year later, however, Justice O'Connor switched sides.[91] In a footnote, the new plurality now argued 'that it is American conceptions of decency that are dispositive, rejecting the contention ... that the sentencing practices of other countries are relevant'.[92]

---

[88] 20 November 1989, 1577 UNTS 3, ratified by or acceded to by all States with the exception of the US and the dysfunctional State of Somalia.

[89] Justice Sandra Day O'Connor, 'Keynote Address', ASIL Proceedings of the 96th Annual Meeting, 13–16 March 2000, 348, 350. Similarly id. 'Remarks' Southern Center for International Studies, Atlanta, Oct. 28, 2003, available at <http://www.southerncenter.org/OConnor_transcript.pdf> (accessed 23 May 2005).

[90] *Thompson v Oklahoma* 487 US 815 (1988). For a brief presentation of this history, *State ex rel Simmons v Roper* 112 SW3d 397, 401–03 (Mo 2003), *cert. granted.* 124 SCt 1171 (2004). Also H Hongju Koh, 'International Law as Part of Our Law' (2004) 98 AJIL 43, 46 et seq; but see RP Alford, 'Misusing International Sources to Interpret the Constitution' (2004) 98 AJIL 57, 58–59.

[91] *Stanford v Kentucky* 492 US 361 (1989).

[92] Ibid 369 (n 1). But see 389 (Brennan J dissenting).

This debate has now again come to the forefront—Justices Antonin Scalia and Stephen Breyer recently publicly debated each other about the question.[93] In *Atkins* and *Lawrence*, the Supreme Court has explicitly taken account of the opinion of both foreign and regional courts and tribunals. In *Atkins*, the Court, if only in a footnote, considered the overwhelming disapproval of the world community of the execution of mentally retarded persons as evidence for the outlawing of that practice as 'cruel and unusual'.[94] In *Lawrence*,[95] the Supreme Court cited European Court of Human Rights case law for the proposition that homosexual conduct in private is none of the State's business. The Supreme Court of one State, Missouri, declared the death penalty for juveniles unconstitutional, noting 'that the views of the international community have consistently grown in opposition to the death penalty for juveniles'. Just as later the Supreme Court, the state court referred to the UN Convention on the Rights of the Child, though it is still not ratified by the US, and statistics by Amnesty International that showed that only the US, Iran and the Democratic Republic of the Congo still executed juveniles.[96]

Finally, on 1 March 2005, a majority of the Supreme Court declared the juvenile death penalty unconstitutional. The opinion by the moderate Anthony Kennedy includes a whole chapter on the rejection of the juvenile death penalty by the international community: 'Our determination that the death penalty is disproportionate punishment for offenders under 18 finds confirmation in the stark reality that the United States is the only country in the world that continues to give official sanction to the juvenile death penalty.'[97]

The majority confirms the observation in the previous plurality opinion in *Thompson v Oklahoma* that '[w]e have previously recognized the relevance of the views of the international community in determining whether a punishment is cruel and unusual'.[98] The Court qualifies the relevance of international opinion, however, by insisting that '[t]his reality does not become controlling, for the task of interpreting the Eighth Amendment remains our responsibility'.[99] The dissenting justice Sandra Day O'Connor took issue with the Court's proportionality analysis

---

[93] A Scalia and S Breyer, 'Constitutional Relevance of Foreign Court Decisions' American University, Jan. 13, 2005, Transcript available at <http://www.wcl.american.edu/secle/founders/2005/050113.cfm> (accessed 23 May 2005).

[94] *Atkins* v *Virginia* 536 US 304, 316 n 21; 122 SCt 2242, 2249 (2002) (referring to the disapproval of the world community of the execution of the mentally retarded); *Lawrence* v *Texas* 123 SCt 2473 (2003), at 2481, 2483; but see *Atkins* 536 US at 321, 325; 122 SCt at 2252, 2254 (Rehnquist CJ, dissenting) and 536 US at 337 (Scalia J, dissenting) ('Equally irrelevant are the practices of the 'world community,' whose notions of justice are (thankfully) not always those of our people'). Similarly *Lawrence* 123 S Ct at 2488, 2495 (Scalia J, dissenting).

[95] *Lawrence v Texas* 123 SCt 2473 (2003) 2481, 2483.

[96] *State ex rel Simmons v Roper* 112 SW3d 397, 401–403 (Mo.banc 2003); *cert. granted.* 124 SCt 1171 (2004) 411.   [97] *Roper v Simmons* 543 US 551 [2005] 575.

[98] Ibid, 1198–99 citing *Thompson v Oklahoma* 487 US 815, 831 n 31, 108 SCt 2687, 2696 n 31, which refers in turn to *Trop v Dulles* 356 US 86, 102, and n 35, 78 SCt 590, 598, and n 35, 2 LEd 630 (1958); *Coker v Georgia* 433 US 596, n 10; 97 SCt 2868, n 10; *Enmund v Florida* 458 US 796–97, n 22, 102 SCt, 3376–77 n 22.   [99] *Roper v Simmons* 543 US 551, 575.

and believed that, absent a national consensus, international opinion could not play a confirmatory role.[100] But she emphasized that:

this Nation's evolving understanding of human dignity certainly is neither wholly isolated from, nor inherently at odds with, the values prevailing in other countries. On the contrary, we should not be surprised to find congruence between domestic and international values, especially where the international community has reached clear agreement—expressed in international law or in the domestic laws of individual countries—that a particular form of punishment is inconsistent with fundamental human rights. At least, the existence of an international consensus of this nature can serve to confirm the reasonableness of a consonant and genuine American consensus.[101]

As of March 2007, this opinion may be taken to express the view of five out of nine Supreme Court justices.[102] International legal opinion may confirm, but cannot substitute, domestic consensus. The United States considers itself a part of the international community, but reserves for itself—as any other State will—the right to dissent from it. A domestic court will first and foremost look at its own constituency for determining its values. But it may—in a time of globalization, increasingly so—recognize that the United States and its people are part of a wider international community of laws and values, even when interpreting domestic law.

In each case, the opposition from the conservative members of the Court was ferocious: in *Atkins*, the late Chief Justice Rehnquist devoted a large part of his dissenting opinion to the rejection of the citation of foreign sources for interpreting the constitution.[103] In a similar vein, Justice Scalia opined that '[e]qually irrelevant [as public opinion polls] are the practices of the "world community", whose notions of justice are (thankfully) not always those of our people'.[104] The last sentence is indicative of more than a mere legalistic rejection of international views. Justice Scalia regards the 'world community' not necessarily as a place of

[100] Ibid, 1215 (O'Connor J, dissenting).

[101] Ibid, 1215–16. Citations omitted. For the relevance of foreign and international law, O'Connor cites to the following cases: *Atkins* 536 US 317 n 21; 122 SCt 2242; *Thompson* 487 US 830–31 and n 31; 108 SCt 2687 (plurality opinion); *Enmund* 458 US 796–97, n 22; 102 SCt 3368; *Coker* 433 US at 596 n 10; 97 SCt 2861 (plurality opinion); *Trop* 356 US 102–03; 78 SCt 590 (plurality opinion).

[102] In his confirmation hearing before the US Senate, CJ Rehnquist's successor, CJ Roberts, has expressed considerable doubts regarding the citation of foreign judgments by the US Supreme Court. See Second Day of Hearings on the Nomination of Judge Roberts, 13 Sept. 2005, Trancript, available at <http://www.nytimes.com/2005/09/13/politics/politicsspecial1/13text-roberts.html?pagewanted=all> (accessed 14 September 2005): 'If we're relying on a decision from a German judge about what our Constitution means, no president accountable to the people appointed that judge and no Senate accountable to the people confirmed that judge. And yet he's playing a role in shaping the law that binds the people in this country. I think that's a concern that has to be addressed. The other part of it that would concern me is that, relying on foreign precedent doesn't confine judges. It doesn't limit their discretion the way relying on domestic precedent does. Domestic precedent can confine and shape the discretion of the judges. Foreign law, you can find anything you want. If you don't find it in the decisions of France or Italy, it's in the decisions of Somalia or Japan or Indonesia or wherever.' Roberts did not speak of a merely persuasive use of foreign judgments, though.

[103] *Atkins* 536 US 321, 325; 122 SCt 2252, 2254 (Rehnquist CJ dissenting).

[104] *Atkins* 536 US 337 (Scalia J dissenting).

high-minded principles, but also as a danger zone for the established local habits and mores. Scalia rejects 'the basic premise of the Court's argument—that American law should conform to the laws of the rest of the world'.[105] Nevertheless, it needs to be emphasized that even Justice Scalia is not opposed to the use of foreign sources as such: in the interest of 'uniform treaty interpretation', or when a statute implements international law, he will look at the practice of other States—sometimes even more so than his brethren.[106] Thus, the purview of the debate may be much smaller than one may expect.

As unremarkable as this may appear from a continental European viewpoint— after all, the Supreme Court did not interpret the US Constitution *contra constitutionem* or against its explicit wording—the conscious provocation by the majority of the Court of the conservative opposition is a remarkable statement as to the integration of the United States into the international legal community. Indeed, the core of the difference between the opponents of the use of foreign sources and the majority of the Court may lie in whether one regards the role of judges in the United States as basically comparable to those of other liberal democracies or whether one emphasizes the uniqueness of the US tradition—and its emphasis on the exclusive prerogative of American legislatures of defining US values and laws.[107]

4.1.2 *International law and US laws—recent Supreme Court decisions*

Other recent decisions of the Supreme Court bear out this trend. In *Sosa v Alvarez-Machain*,[108] the Court resolved, almost en passant, the debate regarding the status of customary international law within the US legal order.[109] The name Alvarez-Machain stands for one of the most controversial, and internationally most criticized, Supreme Court decisions virtually ignoring treaty interpretation according to object and purpose as well as customary international law on foreign abductions.[110] After it had turned out that Mr. Alvarez-Machain was innocent,[111] he sued for damages, inter alia under the 1789 Alien Tort Statute giving US courts jurisdiction 'of all causes where an alien sues for a tort only in violation of the law of nations or a treaty of the United States'.[112] We need not bother here with the rather peculiar details of the use of this statute for human rights litigation before United States

---

[105] *Roper v Simmons* 543 US 551, 624 (Scalia J dissenting).

[106] Eg *Olympic Airways v Husain* 124 SCt 1221, 1232 (2004) (Scalia J dissenting). For a more complete rendition of his views, Scalia, 'Keynote Address: Foreign Legal Authority in the Federal Courts' (2004) 98 ASIL Proceedings 505. Of course, Scalia also uses English materials from the drafting history of the constitution, ibid 506.

[107] Breyer in A Scalia and S Breyer, 'Constitutional Relevance of Foreign Court Decisions' American University, January 13, 2005, Transcript available at <http://www.wcl.american.edu/secle/founders/2005/050113.cfm> (accessed 23 May 2005), 11, 19, 23–24.

[108] *Sosa v Alvarez-Machain* 124 SCt 2739 (2004).

[109] Ibid, 2764–65. For further references, see n 84 above.

[110] *US v Alvarez-Machain* 504 US 655 (1992).

[111] *Sosa v Alvarez-Machain*, 124 SCt 2739 (2004).

[112] Act of September 24, 1789, ch. 20, §9*(b)*, 1 Stat. 79.

courts.[113] Suffice it to say that although Sosa's claim was ultimately rejected, the Court continues to provide possibilities to sue for violations of international law.

The depth of the disagreement within the Supreme Court is palpable in its dealing with human rights. For the conservative dissenters, Justice Scalia argued that '[t]he notion that a law of nations, redefined to mean the consensus of states on *any* subject, can be used by a private citizen to control a sovereign's treatment of its own citizens within its own territory is a 20th-century invention of internationalist law professors and human-rights advocates'.[114] For Scalia, the progress of international law from the regulation of inter-State conduct to providing for individual human rights is a threat to US sovereignty and democracy.[115]

One may certainly agree with Justice Scalia that the *Filartiga*-line of cases owes something to 'internationalist law professors and human-rights advocates'. But it does not necessarily follow international law. Rather, it stands for another American 'Sonderweg': whereas the rest of the world tries to implement human rights by multilateral monitoring of States as well as criminal prosecution of individuals, the United States provides for civil suits against perpetrators. To European ears, the obsession with a 1789 Statute sounds as strange as the suggestion that international law could provide the very 'cause of action' missing in the Alien Tort Statute, or that international law may provide for punitive damages. The point here is that the United States strives to implement international human rights in its own way. But it is remarkable that the majority of the Court adopts a modern understanding of international law that embodies human rights, up to the point where domestic courts may enforce them by granting damages for extraterritorial violations of international human rights norms.

The US Supreme Court attitude towards international law does not aspire to a world legal federalism, to transferring to the world a government by laws rather than (mostly) men.[116] In the words of Arthur Weisburd, the Court 'does not see itself in the first instance as but one court in a supra-national judicial system, but rather as the Supreme Court of the United States'.[117]

After the change in its composition in the years 2005–06, the Supreme Court seems even less likely to accept international decisions as authoritative interpretation

---

[113]　*Filartiga v Pena-Irala* 630 F2d 876 (2nd Cir, 1980).

[114]　*Sosa v Alvarez-Machain*, 124 SCt 2739 (2004), 2775–76 (Scalia J dissenting).

[115]　Cf J Rubenfeld, 'The Two World Orders' (2003) 27 Wilson Quarterly 22; K Anderson, 'Squaring the Circle? Reconciling Sovereignty and Global Governance Through Global Government Networks' (2005) 118 Harv L Rev 1955, 1287–88. Cf, AM Slaughter, 'A Dangerous Myth', 95 Prospect (February 2004), available at <http://www.prospect-magazine.co.uk> (accessed 23 May 2005); Slaughter, Rubenfeld and Zakaria, 'Debate: Is International Law a Threat to Democracy?' Council on Foreign Relations February 2004, available at <http://www.cfr.org> (accessed 23 May 2005).

[116]　In that vein, B Simma, 'International Adjudication and US Policy—Past, Present, and Future' in: Norman Dorsen and Prosser Gifford (eds), *Democracy and the Rule of Law* (Washington: CQ Press, 2001) 39, 56.

[117]　AM Weisburd, 'International Courts and American Courts' (2000) 21 Michigan JIL 877, 939. Weisburd is generally hostile to an increasing role of international jurisprudence before US courts.

of US obligations. In the *Sanchez-Llamas* case, a majority of the Roberts court decided that decisions of the International Court of Justice are not binding for the interpretation of international treaties in US law, even if the US has consented to their exercise of jurisdiction.[118] While the majority of the US Supreme Court lectured the ICJ as to the impact of an adversarial system on raising claims, however, it did not deny that it had to give effect to the substantive standards of the treaty, however in its own rather than the international court's interpretation. Rather, it demanded the prerogative of treaty interpretation for itself. But the very next day, a different majority of the Court—only Justice Kennedy belonged in both cases to the majority—, in the *Hamdan* case, cited the ICJ indirectly as authority for the interpretation of international law, just as much as the three dissenters had done in *Sanchez-Llamas*.[119] Thus, the authority of international courts within the US legal order remains subject to debate. However, its relevance in the broadest sense of the term seems not to be disputed.

It follows from the recent treatment of international legal issues by the US Supreme Court that the Court regards international law, at least as far as it is self-executing, as part of US law. However, the Supreme Court, and, as it seems after *Avena* and *Medellin*, also the Executive Branch, will differentiate between international norms accepted by the United States, and those which the United States did not endorse; and it will also distinguish between the substantive norms incorporated into US law and international legal determinations of their contents. Thus, the Supreme Court seems to regard its role as one of critical reception of international principles into the American legal system, if and to the extent they do not contradict the constitution. However cautious and circumspect this approach may appear, it remains remarkable that the majority of the Supreme Court sticks to it in spite of considerable opposition, both on the bench and in the legislature.

4.2 International human rights norms in Europe

European attitudes towards international community values and their adjudication by international as well as domestic courts are certainly not as sceptical as American

---

[118] *Sanchez-Llamas v Oregon*, 126 SCt 2669 (2006) 2682–2686. The majority was 5–3, Justice Ginsburg not taking sides with regard to the effects to be given to violations of the right to consular information, ibid, 126 SCt 2688 (Ginsburg J, concurring). However, the US government has asked State courts to implement the ICJ judgment in the *Avena* case with regard to the defendants in question, see US President George W Bush: Memorandum for the US Attorney General Regarding Compliance with the ICJ's *Avena* decision (2005) 44 ILM 950; even before this memorandum, the state of Oklahoma complied, see *Torres v Oklahoma*, Case No PCD-04-442 (Oklcr 13 May 2004); Gov Henry Grants Clemency to Death Row Inmate Torres, 13 May 2004, available at <http://www.govenor.state.ok.us> (accessed 23 May 2004). On the position of German courts on the matter, see note 120 et seq below and accompanying text.

[119] See *Hamdan v Rumsfeld*, 126 S.Ct. 2749, 2796 Fn 61, citing to the ICJ and the international Criminal Tribunal for the former Yugoslavia. See also *Sanchez-Llamas*, 126 SCt 2690, 2690–2701 (Breyer J, dissenting), with further references as to the role of ICJ case law in US Courts.

ones. But such a general observation may hide more than it reveals. As examples, we will look at the attitude of German courts regarding the implementation of the Vienna Convention on Consular Relations—the very matter for which Germany initiated the *LaGrand* proceedings against the United States before the International Court of Justice—and at the one instance where Europe may have some claim to a model of implementation of human rights, namely the system of the European Convention on Human Rights. Recent action in two jurisdictions, the United Kingdom and Germany, show that the attitudes of European courts toward international legal pronouncements in general and the European human rights system in particular are not that different from the majority of the US Supreme Court.

4.2.1 Germany: Towards a 'cooperative relationship' between domestic and international courts and tribunals

Under the prevailing interpretation of Article 59 of the German constitution, the Grundgesetz,[120] duly ratified treaties are part of German law enjoying the status of federal statutes, just as under Article VI clause 2 of the United States Constitution. In two recent cases, the German Constitutional Court has clarified the role it accords to decisions of international courts and tribunals in the domestic legal order. In the *Görgülü* case regarding a father's access to his son against the will of foster parents, the Court has time and again demanded that regional courts follow, as a rule, decisions of the European Court of Human Rights. In cases involving the right to consular information under the Vienna Convention on Consular Relations, a chamber of the Court has transferred the *Görgülü* precedent to decisions of the International Court of Justice, and regarded them as normative guidelines even when technically not binding.[121]

In the first of the three decisions regarding the father's right of access,[122] the Federal Constitutional Court emphasized that only the 'violation of fundamental principles of the constitution' may justify the violation of international law.[123] As to the effect of judgments of international courts and tribunals, the highest German court added that: '[s]ince the European Convention on Human Rights—*as interpreted by the ECHR*—has the status of a formal federal statute, it shares the primacy of statute law and must therefore be complied with by the judiciary'.[124]

As to the relationship of the interpretation of the Convention by the European Court of Human Rights and the interpretation of German law, the Constitutional Court decided:

As long as applicable methodological standards leave scope for interpretation and weighing of interests, German courts must give precedence to interpretation in accordance with

---

[120] Eg decisions of the Constitutional Court, 74 BVerfGE 358 at 370; 82 BVerfGE 106, 120.

[121] BVerfG, 2 BvR 2115/01 of 19 September 2006, <http://www.bverfg.de/entscheidungen/rk20060919_2bvr211501.html> (accessed 18 March 2007).

[122] 111 BVerfGE 307 (2004, in German). The following citations are to the English translation provided by the Court, available at BVerfG, 2 BvR 1481/04 of 14 October 2004, <http://www.bverfg.de/entscheidungen/rs20041014_2bvr148104e.html> (visited 23 May 2005).   [123] Ibid, para 35.

[124] Ibid, para 53, emphasis added.

the Convention. The situation is different only if observing the decision of the ECHR . . . clearly violates statute law to the contrary or German constitutional provisions, in particular also the fundamental rights of third parties. 'Take into account' means taking notice of the Convention provision as interpreted by the ECHR and applying it to the case, provided the application does not violate prior-ranking law, in particular constitutional law.[125]

Thus, there is no primacy of international law and decisions of international courts over constitutional law, but the deference due to the rulings of the ECHR is considerable. In particular, the German Constitutional Court does not only regard the Convention itself, but also its interpretation by the European Court of Human Rights as authoritative.

What emerges from the decision is that German courts are usually bound by the interpretation of the European Convention by the European Court of Human Rights. Only in a case in which such decision may violate the German constitution itself, the situation is more ambiguous, because the Constitution according to its own terms is superior in rank to the Convention. Even in the case at hand, where there was an arguable case of contradictory constitutional interpretations between the German court and the European Court of Human Rights, the Constitutional Court sent the case back to the lower court, and when this court did not comply, issued three further rulings putting the judgment of the European Court of Human Rights into effect.[126]

In a 2006 Chamber decision, the Federal Constitutional Court has transferred the reasoning of the *Görgülü* decisions to the relationship between the International Court of Justice and the Federal Constitutional Court.[127] Accordingly, the principle of 'friendliness to international law' enshrined in the German constitution, as well as the obligation of the judiciary to respect 'law and justice' (Gesetz and Recht) pursuant to Article 20 para. 3 of the German Basic Law, require domestic courts to 'take into account' decisions of the International Court of Justice when binding on Germany pursuant to their constituent treaty.[128] In line with the *Görgülü* decisions, however, 'taking into account' means 'taking notice of the Convention provision as interpreted by [the international court] and applying it to the case, provided the application does not violate prior-ranking law, in particular constitutional law'.[129] But even when ICJ decisions are not technically binding, the decision accords them a 'function as normative guideline' ('normative

---

[125] Ibid, para 62.
[126] BVerfG decision of 28 December 2004, 1 BvR 2790/04; decision of 5 April 2005, 1 BvR 1664/04; decision of 10 June 2005, 1 BvR 2790/04; available at <http://www.bverfg.de>.
[127] BVerfG, 2 BvR 2115/01 of 19 September 2006 note 121 above. For a comparison of this decision with the one of the Supreme Court in *Sanchez-Llamas* note 118 above, see J Gogolin, 'Avena and Sanchez-Llamas Come to Germany—The German Constitutional *German Law Journal Courts* Upholds Rights under the Vienna Convention on Consular Relations', (2007) 8 261.
[128] BVerfG, 2 BvR 2115/01 of 19 September 2006, para 58.
[129] See n 131 above and accompanying text.

Leitfunktion') in the German legal order.[130] Due to the failure of the Federal Supreme Court to properly consider the ICJ decisions, the Chamber of the constitutional court quashed two of the three decisions in question and referred them back to the Federal Supreme Court.

Thus, the German Constitutional Court does not recognize any inherent hierarchical authority of international courts in their interpretation of international rules, but will usually regard its relationship with international courts, just as much as with the European Court of Justice, as 'cooperative'.[131] It will thus integrate international legal pronouncements into German domestic law not as a matter of hierarchy, but as a matter of deference to the international community. Nevertheless, the general practice is one of deference and indeed implementation.

4.2.2 Human rights in the United Kingdom: towards direct effect

In the United Kingdom, a clear trend is emerging towards a direct effect of most human rights in the domestic legal order—a development even more remarkable because it conflicts with the traditional supremacy of parliament. The British drafters have developed a host of ingenious instruments to square the circle and combine parliamentary supremacy with direct effect of international human rights jurisprudence.

The United Kingdom has a reputation as a classical dualist country, in which Parliament needs to implement all international agreements before they can have direct effect within the domestic legal order. However, at the latest since the British accession to the European Communities in 1973, this statement is fraught with qualifications. First of all, in the Common Law tradition, customary international law is considered part of the law of the land.[132] Since the ratification of a treaty is an act of the Crown, an act of parliament needs to introduce treaties into the domestic legal order. In practice, the executive branch will only ratify treaties which are or at least will be implemented by parliament, however[133] In the case of European law, in the absence of a parliamentary act revoking the accession to the

---

130 BVerfG, 2 BvR 2115/01 of 19 September 2006, para 62.

131 This was famously the description of the relationship in the Maastricht decision on European integration, BVerfGE 89, 155, 175 ('Kooperationsverhältnis'—cooperative relationship between ECJ and BVerfG regarding the protection of human rights). See *British Railways Board v Pickin* [1974] AC 765.

132 See the references above (n 58) as well as R Jennings and A Watts, *Oppenheim's International Law* vol 1 (9th edn, London & New York: Longman, 1992) 56–58 with further references. Characteristically, English courts do not feel bound by precedent on the meaning of international law because of the further development of international law, eg Court of Appeal, *Trendtex v Central Bank of Nigeria* [1977] All ER 881, per Lord Denning, MR; House of Lords, *Io Congreso del Partido* [1983] AC 244 (accepting the restrictive theory of State immunity against former HL precedent without much discussion on this issue). More cautious: I Brownlie, *Principles of Public International Law* (6th edn, Oxford: OUP, 2003) 42–44, with further references.

133 R Jennings and A Watts, *Oppenheim's International Law* vol 1 (9th edn London & New York: Longman, 1992) 61 (the so-called 'Ponsonby Rule' at n 31).

European Union, European law will enjoy both direct effect and supremacy over British law.[134]

Since the adoption of the Human Rights Act in 1998,[135] the impact of European human rights has almost reached the amount of deference to the European Union. According to the Act, 'so far as it is possible to do so, primary legislation and subordinate legislation must be read and given effect in a way which is compatible with the Convention rights'.[136] If such interpretation is impossible, however, the respective court is limited to making a formal 'declaration of incompatibility'.[137] Such a declaration 'does not affect the validity, continuing operation or enforcement of the provision in respect of which it is given'.[138] Thus, it appears that the status of the European Convention on Human Rights in British law is quite modest. However, it is the practical effects in case of such a declaration we should look at.

A recent case displays a remarkable impact indeed:[139] In *A v Secretary of State*,[140] the Appellate Committee of the House of Lords, the highest British court, considered the British Anti-terrorism, Crime and Security Act 2001[141] and concluded on 16 December 2004 that the arrest of foreign terror suspects only violated the prohibition of discrimination and the right to freedom contained in the European Convention on Human Rights. The Law Lords did not display any reluctance to cite international and foreign sources in interpreting the Act, from the Supreme Court of Canada[142] to the UN Commission of Human Rights[143] and the—obviously non-governmental—International Law Association,[144] let alone the citation, mandated by the Human Rights Act, of the European Court of Human Rights whose judgments permeate the opinions of all of the Law Lords.

However, because of section 4 of the Human Rights Act 1998,[145] the judgment on the Anti-terrorism Act resulted in a so-called declaration of incompatibility only, ie the House of Lords declared the detention contrary to the European

---

[134] European Communities Act 1972, Chapter 68, available at <http://www.opsi.gov.uk/acts/acts1972/19720068.htm> (accessed 16 May 2005). Also s 3 (1) on the authoritative nature of the pronouncements of the European Court of Justice.

[135] Human Rights Act 1998, Chapter 42, available at <http://www.hmso.gov.uk/acts/acts1998/19980042.htm> (accessed 16 May 2005). [136] s 3(1).

[137] s 4(2). This procedure also applies to secondary legislation, when primary legislation prevents its overruling. [138] s 4(6)(a).

[139] As to the number of declarations of incompatibility and their impact, opinions may differ, eg M Verbeet, *Die Stellung der Judikative im englischen Verfassungsgefüge nach dem Human Rights Act 1998* (Stuttgart: Boorberg, 2004) 62 and n 188.

[140] UK House of Lords, *A and Others v Secretary of State for the Home Department* [2004] UKHL 56, [2004] QB 329–486, [2005] 1 WLR 414, available at <http://www.publications.parliament.uk/pa/ld200405/ldjudgmt/jd041216/a&oth-1.htm> (accessed 16 May 2005).

[141] Anti-terrorism, Crime and Security Act 2001, Chapter 24, available at <http://www.opsi.gov.uk/acts/acts2001/20010024.htm> (accessed 16 May 2005).

[142] Eg the lead opinion by Lord Bingham of Cornhill, paras 30, 39, and the lone dissent by Lord Walker of Gestingthorpe para 214. [143] Lord Bingham ibid, para 61.

[144] ibid, para 63. [145] See n 137 above and accompanying text.

Convention.[146] The detention powers under sections 21–23 of the Anti-Terrorism legislation were due to lapse on 10 November 2006,[147] but they were subject to regular prolongation by both Houses of Parliament,[148] coming up regularly in March 2005. Parliament could have confirmed the law, exercising its prerogative to overrule the Appellate Committee of the House of Lords. But parliament did not do so. Rather, it approved the Detention of Terrorism Act 2005[149] that does not discriminate between foreign and domestic terrorism suspect, and provides for house arrest and similar limitations of personal liberty for terrorism suspects. After a modification of the original government proposal, a judge must approve the house arrest, but for other measures, no such approval is needed.[150] In addition, the standard of evidence is reduced.

The reaction of parliament to the court's declaration of incompatibility of the British anti-terror measures against foreigners with the European Convention testifies to the relevance of the human rights review by the House of Lords, a review which extensively uses international sources to restrict security measures by the government.

4.3 Conclusion: The relationship between the international community and domestic society in domestic case law

The examples have not only shown the differences of attitude towards the use of international and foreign law precedent before domestic courts, but also interesting commonalities: all courts have referred extensively to foreign judgments and/or international decisions, even when they were not technically binding on them. In spite of the opposition of conservative Justices, the US Supreme Court has even used an international legal consensus on the question of the execution of juveniles as additional material for its conclusions about the meaning of decency in the 6th Amendment baring 'cruel and unusual punishment'. But none of the courts concerned has used international and foreign sources *tel quel*, so to speak, but as sources from alien origin that need some integration in their own domestic system. The US justices did not only disagree on the use of foreign sources, but also on the application of domestic precedent. The British Law Lords did not question the limitations of their role in leaving the implementing decision on the

---

[146] UK House of Lords, *A and Others v Secretary of State for the Home Department* [2004] UKHL 56, [2004] QB 329–486, [2005] 1 WLR 414, para 73 (Lord Bingham).

[147] Anti-terrorism, Crime and Security Act 2001, available at <http://www.opsi.gov.uk/acts/acts2001/20010024.htm> (accessed 16 May 2005), s 29 (7); O Sands 'British Detention of Terrorism Act 2005' ASIL Insights, Apr. 27, 2005, available at <http://www.asil.org/insights> (accessed 16 May 2005).   [148] s 29, sub-ss 2 and 3.

[149] Prevention of Terrorism Act 2005, Chapter 2, available at <http://www.opsi.gov.uk/acts/acts2005/20050002.htm> (accessed 16 May 2005).

[150] The highly critical 9th report of session 2004–05 of the Joint Committee on Human Rights of House of Lords and House of Commons is available at <http://news.bbc.co.uk/nol/shared/bsp/hi/pdfs/25_02_05_prevention_terrorism_report.pdf> (accessed 16 May 2005).

compatibility of UK anti-terrorism legislation with the European Convention on Human Rights to Parliament. Finally, even the German Constitutional Court found limitations of the application of European Human Rights Law in the German constitution and in the structure of German law. All these courts see their role firmly anchored in their national legal order, but regard looking to foreign and international sources as a necessary element of judicial decision-making.

5. Conclusion: towards a pluralist international community

The results we have arrived at demonstrate that the appeal of the vision of an 'international community', based on more than co-existence or an hegemonic project, is still existent, even in the highest court of the single superpower, as visible both in the use of foreign judgments and authority as well as in an increasing reliance on international law, including international human rights law, within the domestic legal order. In the words of Justice O'Connor: 'International law . . . will be a factor or a force in gaining a greater consensus among all nations concerning basic principles of relations with nations that, as of now, are withholding their agreement on some aspects. It can be, and is, a help in our search for a more peaceful world.'[151]

Is this kitsch, as Martti Koskenniemi has called recently the reliance on abstract feel-good concepts that are not translated into real action?[152] Maybe, when the deference to standards of international community is not born out in practice. But in the cases analysed here, we have seen that it matters whether domestic courts regard their task as strictly limited to their own constituents or as, if only occasionally, involving the views and interpretations of a larger, indeed world-wide audience. Of course, there are also pitfalls of this practice. International views may well be contradictory, or go against settled domestic rights. In other words, the use of international sources may actually limit and not extend individual rights.[153] However, if used for gaining insight, not for disposing of a case, non-binding international sources may actually be helpful. Indeed, a judge who has taken international decisions into account should rather be allowed to be candid about what he did rather than apply its insights in the closet, so to speak. It is all the more remarkable that five of the nine US Justices felt compelled to include considerations of foreign law in their rationales for deciding cases—even if foreign law alone can never be dispositive of a case.

Thus, whether the international community exists largely depends on whether States, international lawyers, and the public opinion, take judicial views from abroad

---

[151] Justice Sandra Day O'Connor, 'Keynote Address', ASIL Proceedings of the 96th Annual Meeting, 13–16 March, 2000, 348, 352.   [152] Koskenniemi (n 2 above) 113.

[153] P Alford, 'Misusing International Sources to Interpret the Constitution' (2004) 98 AJIL 57, 64–67.

into account. The 'international community' is not tangible. To cite a former US President in a completely different context: its 'being' 'depends on what the meaning of the word "is" is'.[154] Rather, one should regard it as a certain procedure how to arrive at fair decisions: not to limit oneself to parochial pronouncements of one's own legal system, but to also look for guidance elsewhere, to insights from foreign and international sources, and to regard one's own opinions also as addressed to a wider community. The international community will thus not be a foreign enforcer of decisions against the will of States, but give an indication of global legal opinion. In the age of globalization, domestic decisions affect a broader community and are themselves part of a larger context than the nation State. In this vein, domestic courts are playing an indispensable role as interpreters and 'translators' of international standards and principles into action.

Certainly, this is far away from a supranational understanding of international law similar to EU law. Direct effect of international law will remain the exception rather than becoming the rule. The 'recognition' of international law by many domestic orders will rather follow the spirit of the 1776 US Declaration of Independence showing a 'decent respect to the opinions of [hu]mankind'—a community which reaches beyond States to individuals and their non-State associations that requires respect and consideration, but—if not required by international law—no strict adherence.[155] Domestic courts play an indispensable role at the gatekeepers of domestic law, deciding—more so than in European law[156]—on what rules and decisions will ultimately cross the bridge from foreign or international law into domestic law.[157]

Such a result is compatible with each of our community models. For an institutionalist, it entails, however, a less hierarchical, pluralist understanding of community. There may be common values as expressed, in particular, in *jus cogens* norms,[158] and some international norms are incorporated into domestic law either because they are deemed directly applicable or because of an act of transformation into domestic law. However, the profound pluralism of the contemporary international community prevents the emergence of a Kelsenian, monist structure. A (neo)liberal understanding of community correctly identifies the addressee of the decisions in question, namely the individual. But it may underestimate law's enmeshment into

---

[154] KW Starr, Office of the Independent Counsel, Transcript of President William Clinton's Videotape Testimony to the Grand Jury (17 August 1998).

[155] Cf *Medellín v Dretke*, 544 US 660. 125 SCt 1622.

[156] For the considerable empowering of lower local courts by European law, JHH Weiler, *The Constitution of Europe* (Cambridge: CUP, 1999) 188–218.

[157] The image is taken from former German constitutional Court judge—and critic of supremacy of European law—P Kirchhof, 'Der deutsche Staat im Prozeß der Europäischen Integration' in 7 *Handbuch des Staatsrechts* (Müller: Heidelberg, 1992) § 183, marginal note 65. Also U di Fabio, *Das Recht offener Staaten* (München: Beck, 1998).

[158] See nn 32 and 67 above (n 32) and (n 67) and accompanying texts.

a particular social fabric or national community that may prevent the application of one solution to all. Indeed, postmodernists are right to insist on the contested nature of all values, local or global, and on the open, and at times compromissory or even complicit nature of each and every legal decision. On the other hand, the legal community beyond borders may indeed provide for more guidance to local authorities and courts than a strong postmodern relativism would be ready to accept.

The international community appears thus not as a superior system encompassing all other, lesser, domestic ones. Rather, it is a shortcut for the direct and indirect dealings of State authorities, non-State organizations and businesses, as well as individual citizens beyond State boundaries, and indeed a common endeavour to tackle contemporary problems for which the State alone is incapable of acting. Rather than embodying command and obeisance, the relationship between the international community and the nation State will remain a relationship of mutual accommodation and learning.

10

The Globalization of State Constitutions

Anne Peters

1. Introduction

'No one really knows precisely what globalization is, but nearly everyone thinks that it has some effects on domestic constitutional orders', an eminent US-American constitutional scholar stated not so long ago.[1] A European voice in the same vein:

The process of globalisation has created powerful legal and economic dilemmas. It promotes economic competition between the different policy choices of different political communities and, in that process, it limits the freedom of choice of those political communities. This embodies a challenge to the paradigms of constitutionalism, including the State's monopoly of constitutionalism, the autonomy of national political communities and the traditional forms of participation and representation.[2]

In this chapter, I undertake to analyse the effects of globalization on State constitutions, to categorize them and to promote compensatory constitutionalism on the global plane as an adequate response to the current and presumably continuing process of globalization of State constitutions.

The chapter begins with the hypothesis that national (State) constitutions have to adapt to globalization and in fact are already reacting. Firstly the two contested concepts involved, namely 'globalization' (Part 2), and 'constitution' (Part 3) will be discussed. Part 4 deals with the globalization of constitutional form. In particular, the question of hierarchy between international law and State constitutions seems unresolved. It is suggested that consistent interpretation and a readiness to ascribe less importance to the formal origin of norms could overcome hierarchical thinking and would improve global constitutional governance. Part 5 describes

---

[1] Mark Tushnet, *The New Constitutional Order* (Princeton and Oxford: Princeton UP, 2003) 142.
[2] Miguel Poares Maduro, 'The Constitutional Challenge of Globalization? Protecting Common Values', contribution to 'European identity now and in the future: Europe tomorrow: shared fate or common political future?' Final colloquy—Strasbourg, 18–19 April 2002, <http://www.coe.int/T/E/Com/Files/Themes/Identity/Col3_DiscMaduro.ASP>, (accessed 4 March 2007). See also Christian Joerges and others (eds), *Transnational Governance and Constitutionalism* (Oxford and Portland Oregon: Hart Publishing, 2004).

the globalization of core constitutional principles. It shows how global governance affects and even undermines basic principles such as the rule of law, democracy, social security, and territorial organization. In Part 6, I analyse how State constitutions are further adapted to globalization in substance, both by way of amendments and through dynamic interpretation. Part 7 summarizes the findings and concludes with the suggestion that constitutionalist thinking could be extended, with due caution, to world order.

This chapter suffers from a Western European bias to the extent that my examples from national constitutions are not based on a systematic and methodologically reflected study of the world's State constitutions and the relevant constitutional case law. The examples do not therefore 'prove' my hypotheses, but serve as an illustration and might stimulate further empirical research.[3]

2. Globalization

I use the term globalization to refer to the ongoing process of economic, political, cultural, and military intertwinement and the mutual interdependence of nations, enterprizes, and people that goes with it.[4] *Economic globalization*, constituting the core of globalization, was triggered by the soaring progress of communications and information technology, the demise of the socialist block's planned economies and the ensuing liberalization of world trade. The production factors of capital and labour were thereby rendered mobile or available beyond State borders. As a consequence, transboundary economic transactions and foreign investments have dramatically increased. Furthermore, economic production has been integrated to form a network of industry, banking and finance brokers. Although the quantitative

---

[3] The English translations of the constitutional provisions mentioned in the following text, unless indicated otherwise, are taken from 'International constitutional law, English', <http://www.verfassungen.de>. For an online resource on international law in domestic courts see <http://ildc.oxfordlawreports.com/public/login>.

[4] This process is the result of individual and collective action, which has in part been made possible by new technologies and other changing conditions. It often reacts to real or imagined 'necessities', has inadverted side-effects, and is accompanied by a changed perception. The historical process is not linear, does not cover the entire globe, and is accompanied by simultaneous de-globalizing processes. For a description and explanation of the phenomenon of globalization see Ian Clark, *Globalization and Fragmentation: International Relations in the Twentieth Century* (Oxford: OUP, 1997) (with a focus on globalization and fragmentation in the 20th century); Ulrich Beck (ed), *Was ist Globalisierung?* (Frankfurt A.M.: Suhrkamp, 1999); Thomas L Friedman, *The Lexus and the Olive Tree: Understanding Globalization* (New York: Farrar Straus Giroux, 1999); Tomas Larsson, *The Race to the Top: The Real Story of Globalization* (Washington DC: Cato Institute, 2001); Maria Rosa Ferrarese, *Le istituzioni della globalizzazione* (Bologna: Il Mulino, 2000); Jan Aart Scholte, *Globalization: A Critical Introduction* (Basingstoke: Palgrave Houndmils, 2000) (critical perspective); Jörg Dürrschmidt, *Globalisierung* (transcript: Bielefeld, 2002) (social sciences); Rüdiger Safranski, *Wieviel Globalisierung erträgt der Mensch?* (München: Carl Hanser, 2003) (philosophical). See for a good historical account Jürgen Osterhammel and Niels P Petersson, *Geschichte der Globalisierung: Dimensionen, Prozesse, Epochen* (München: Beck, 2003); Data in Le Monde diplomatique (ed), *Atlas der Globalisierung* (Berlin: taz, 2003).

assessment of globalization is difficult,[5] and although Africa remains a blind spot on the map of globalization, it is relatively undisputed that since the 1980s the above-mentioned factors have generated a novel quality of economic interdependence.

Globalization also has numerous noneconomic faces. On the one hand, a '*global-ization of problems*' is occurring, or is perceived as such. Globalization here refers both to the causes and consequences of problems, which must be tackled on a polit-ical level. Sustainable problem-solving in the field of environmental protection, vehicular traffic, migration, and terrorism can no longer be focused on the level of the nation State alone.

The corollary of the transboundary problems is the *globalization of individual action*. Thanks to improved and cheap means of transnational communication and travel, individuals can pursue joint projects much more easily than before. For technical reasons, nations States are less able to prevent individual contacts and communications through new media. The consequence of this 'condensation of time and space'[6] is a quantitative increase and a qualitative strengthening of non-State actors in international politics.

In addition to, and overlapping with, the above, *cultural globalization* is also taking place. Through mass media, consumer goods, and travel, cultures are con-verging. Although the US-American culture is dominant, it is transformed locally by creative appropriation. The 'clashes of civilizations' which occur simultan-eously, do not rule out convergence and hybridization.

In reaction to and in parallel with these manifestations of globalization, struc-tures of *global governance* are emerging.[7] Governance, in contrast to government, denotes the activity not only of State institutions, but also that of private entities; economy, Non Governmental Organizations (NGOs) or hybrid private-public institutions which pursue objectives in the common interest.[8] One aspect of global governance includes those parts of law which are already globalized. *Legal globalization* is characterized by the diversification of law-making processes and law implementation mechanisms and an intensification of the participation of nonstate actors.[9] One particular aspect of legal globalization is the globalization

---

[5] On empirical measurements of 'globalization' by means of specific indicators, Harald Germann and others, 'Messung der Globalisierung: ein Paradoxon' in Ulrich Steger (ed), *Facetten der Globalisierung: Ökonomische, soziale und politische Aspekte* (Berlin: Springer, 1999).

[6] Osterhammel and Petersson (n 4 above) 12.

[7] Figuratively speaking, global governance is a network rather than a hierarchy, encompasses pub-lic and private law instruments and takes place on the national, international, transnational, and supranational levels. See Commission on Global Governance, *Our Global Neighbourhood: The Report of the Commission on Global Governance* (Oxford: OUP, 1995); see also Ulrich Brand and others, *Global Governance* (Münster: Westfälisches Dampfboot, 2000); Karsten Nowrot, 'Global Governance and International Law' in Christian Tietje and others (eds), *Beiträge zum Transnationalen Wirt-schaftsrecht 33* (Halle-Wittenberg: Institut für Wirtschaftsrecht, Martin-Luther-Universität, 2004).

[8] James N Rosenau, 'Governance, Order, and Change in World Politics' in James N Rosenau and Ernst-Otto Czempiel (eds), *Governance Without Government* (Cambridge: CUP, 1992) 7.

[9] Nowrot (n 7 above) 6–12. Also Klaus F Röhl and Stefan Magen, 'Die Rolle des Rechts im Prozeß der Globalisierung' (1996) 17 Zeitschrift für Rechtssoziologie 1–57.

of constitutional law. I prefer the term 'globalization' over 'denationalization'[10] or 'internationalization'[11] of constitutional law to highlight that the process which will be analysed in detail in this chapter is not only a consequence, but also an element and a motor of the broader phenomenon of globalization. Due to increased reference to international law, orientation at international precepts, the incorporation of international standards into domestic constitutions, and constitutional reforms responding to new international instruments, institutions, and procedures, State constitutions are visibly changing. On the other hand, constitutional actors, notably courts, attempt to resist global encroachment of core constitutional principles. This resistance however, cannot prevent global governance from partially undermining domestic constitutional principles. Thereby, State constitutions are invisibly and in a rather negative way 'globalized'. Both the formal, or structural, and the substantial globalization of constitutions will be explored in this chapter.

Contemporary *criticism* of globalization concentrates on economic globalization. As far as the globalization of constitutions is concerned, this criticism is still important because it refers in particular to the erosion of the social State. This will be discussed later (part 5.3).

3. State constitutions

3.1 Formal properties

State constitutions are normally said to have typical formal characteristics. One is that they are codified in one document. '*La Constitution, à l'origine, est d'abord un acte écrit*'.[12] The 'writtenness' is an essential element of the modern, North American and European Continental notion of constitution. The quest for a constitutional *charter* was the primary objective of the constitutionalist movement in America, not least in reaction to the English Constitution, which the American colonists deemed arbitrary and unjust. The English Constitution consisted and still consists, of various charters, bills, judicial pronouncements, and constitutional conventions. It is therefore in part an 'unwritten' constitution.

The second traditional formal property of constitutional law is that it supersedes ordinary law. The technical device to secure a constitution's superiority is a special amending procedure which shields the constitution from modification

---

[10] Gràinne de Búrca and Oliver Gerstenberg, 'The Denationalization of Constitutional Law' (2006) 47 Harv ILJ 243–62, 252.

[11] Brun-Otto Bryde, 'Konstitutionalisierung des Völkerrechts und Internationalisierung des Verfassungsrechts' (2003) 42 Der Staat 61–75.

[12] Dominique Rousseau, 'Une résurrection: La notion de Constitution' (1990) 106 Revue du droit public et de la science politique en France et l'étranger 5.

through ordinary legislation. Again, the Constitution of the United Kingdom is an exception, because the parliament of the United Kingdom has, by virtue of parliamentary sovereignty, the power to make and amend laws of a constitutional quality in the ordinary legislative procedure. The UK Constitution is therefore a 'flexible' as opposed to a 'rigid' constitution in terms of the distinction established by James Bryce.[13] Also the Constitution of the German Empire (1871–1918) was a 'flexible' constitution.[14]

The third formal feature of codified constitutions is that they are made by a *pouvoir constituant* in a kind of constitutional big bang. The most influential theorists of the *pouvoir constituant*, the French revolutionist Abbé Sieyès[15] and the German jurist Carl Schmitt[16] formulated their conceptions with a view to the political revolutions of their time, which brought new constitutions abruptly into being, accompanied by upheaval, chaos, and violence (1789 in France, 1918 in Germany). Again, England is the exception, because its constitutional law evolved continuously over the centuries. It is also widely acknowledged that constitutions are living instruments[17] which are more or less silently modified and transformed through judicial and political practice.[18]

3.2 Substantive components of (legitimate) State constitutions

The substantive components of constitutions are contested among lawyers. The broadest notion of a constitution refers to the bulk of laws *organizing and institutionalizing a polity*. The narrower, functional notion of a constitution relates to rules and principles *fulfilling typical constitutional functions*. In regard to the latter,

---

[13] According to James Bryce, flexible constitutions 'proceed from the same authorities which make the ordinary laws; and they are promulgated or repealed in the same way as ordinary laws'. In a polity with a flexible constitution, 'all laws (excluding of course by-laws, municipal regulations, and so forth) are of the same rank and exert the same force. There is, moreover, only one legislative authority competent to pass laws in all cases and for all purposes.' In contrast, 'the distinctive mark of these Rigid Constitutions is their superiority to ordinary statutes. They are not the work of the ordinary legislature, and therefore cannot be changed by it.' James Bryce, 'Essay III: Flexible and Rigid Constitutions' in James Bryce, *Studies in History and Jurisprudence* Vol I (New York: OUP, 1901, reprint 1980) 150–51 and 217–18.

[14] Georg Meyer and Gerhard Anschütz, *Lehrbuch des Deutschen Staatsrechts* (Berlin: Duncker & Humblot, 1919) 743–44.

[15] Abbé Sieyès, *Qu'est-ce qu'est le tiers état?* (Genève: Librairie Droz, 1979, orig 1789) 119.

[16] Carl Schmitt, *Verfassungslehre* (München: Duncker & Humblot, 1928) 75–76.

[17] A constitutional act calls 'into life a being the development of which could not have been foreseen completely by the most gifted of its begetters.' Justice O Wendell Holmes in *Missouri v Holland* 252 US 416, 433 (1919).

[18] The most important German theorists holding this view are Rudolf Smend, 'Verfassung und Verfassungsrecht' in Rudolf Smend, *Staatsrechtliche Abhandlungen* (3rd edn, Berlin: Duncker & Humblot, 1994) 192–93; Peter Häberle, 'Verfassungsinterpretation und Verfassunggebung' in Peter Häberle, *Verfassung als öffentlicher Prozess: Materialien zu einer Verfassungstheorie der offenen Gesellschaft* (Berlin: Duncker & Humblot, 1978) 182–224; Friedrich Müller, *Fragment (über) verfassunggebende Gewalt des Volkes* (Berlin: Duncker & Humblot, 1995, manuscript of 1967/68) 15, 22, 34.

the traditional constitutional functions are to constitute a political entity as a legal entity, to organize it, to limit political power, to offer political and moral guidelines, to justify governance, and finally, to contribute to integration.[19]

The third and narrowest notion, which I would like to call a *legitimist notion* of a constitution, is the one underlying the constitutionalism of the 18th and 19th centuries. It was enunciated most famously in Article 16 of the French Declaration of the Rights of Man and Citizens of 26 August 1789: '*Toute societé dans laquelle la garantie des droits n'est pas assurée, ni la séparation des pouvoirs déterminée, n'a point de constitution*'. Human rights and separation of powers are the necessary contents of a constitution. From this perspective, 'constitution' is a value-laden concept.

For the purposes of this chapter, it is irrelevant whether the content (which has expanded since 1789) is considered as an integral part of the concept of constitution (the legitimist notion of a constitution) or whether the incorporation of certain basic principles is a virtue which a constitution (as a neutral concept) may possess or not possess and which makes that constitution more legitimate. In any case, contemporary State constitutions need a minimum content in order to be considered legitimate: they must satisfy requirements of the rule of law and democracy; they must gear the State towards guaranteeing human rights, human security, and welfare; and they must organize the State territory efficiently, eventually by means of decentralization, devolution, or federalism. State constitutions which are more or less deficient in some or all of these respects are more or less illegitimate according to nascent global standards of legitimacy.[20]

4. The globalization of constitutional form

4.1 Modification of the concept of constitution

The *concept* of constitution is affected by globalization. More precisely, it has been broadened by the juridification of international, non-State regimes. Although the State constitution remains the most important type of constitution in a normative sense, it is no longer the only 'true' (political, normative, more-than-organizational) constitution. The foundational documents of polities beyond the State, for example the founding treaties of the European Union (EU), are widely considered to be 'true' constitutions as well.

4.2 Defeat of the claim to totality

Globalization has also modified the State constitutions' claim to totality. The State constitution is no longer (if it ever was) a total constitution. It has become

---

[19] See Anne Peters, *Elemente einer Theorie der Verfassung Europas* (Berlin: Duncker & Humblot, 2001) 76 et seq.

[20] See below on global constitutional convergence within broad margins (part 6.2)

increasingly obvious that the State constitution cannot regulate the totality of political power. The State constitution has therefore been downgraded to a *partial constitution* which forms part of a compound constitutional system together with nonstate constitutional law. The various partial constitutional orders involved complement each other to some extent. Arguably, therefore, the wealth of international guarantees might allow State constitutions to be slimmed down. If global regulation with regard to global problems functions successfully, national regulation is no longer needed or may even be counterproductive.[21]

4.3 Expansion of the territorial scope of State constitutions

The intensification of extra-territorial governmental or quasi-governmental police activity (or activity in the grey zone between military and police), including coercion and potential physical abuse, might call for an expansion of the territorial scope of the relevant human rights guarantees which form the core of constitutional law, independently of their formal locus of codification (in a national or an international instrument). The question of an eventual extraterritorial application of laws is of course not limited to constitutional law, but is becoming particularly relevant due to the increase in potentially abusive State action. Recent cases have included the military attacks by armed forces of NATO member States in Serbia,[22] the detention of hundreds of persons who were apprehended by the US army in Afghanistan and other places in the US-military base Guantánamo Bay,[23] extraterritorial abductions by the police, drug enforcement officers and the like,[24] the possible location of secret prisons of the US-American secret service in Europe and other regions of the world, the interrogation of prisoners in Iraq by personnel of US security firms, and the activities of Israeli armed forces in Palestinian territories.

---

[21] Consequently, it would make sense to take ordinary political decisions either in the ordinary legislative process within nation States, or to tackle them in international treaties, but not to eternalize them in State constitutions. Thomas Cottier and Daniel Wüger, 'Auswirkungen der Globalisierung auf das Verfassungsrecht: Eine Diskussionsgrundlage' in Beat Sitter-Liver (ed), *Herausgeforderte Verfassung: Die Schweiz im globalen Konzert* (Freiburg: Universitätsverlag, 1999) 257, 262.

[22] ECHR, *Bankovic v 17 member states*, decision on inadmissibility of 12 December 2001, (2001) 22 HRLJ 453, refusing to apply the ECHR outside the territory of the member States. See also ECHR, *Case of Saddam Hussein*, decision on admissibility of 15 March 2006, http://www.echr.coe.int/eng/press/2006/March/HUSSEIN%20ADMISSIBILITY%20DECISION.htm (accessed 22 January 2007). Saddam Hussein asserted that the Court had jurisdiction because the respondent States were occupying powers in Iraq, because he was under their direct authority and control or because they were responsible for the acts of their agents abroad. However, the Court did not find 'any jurisdictional link between the applicant and the respondent States'.

[23] See US Supreme Court, *Rasul et al v Bush* 542 US 466 (2004), admitting statutory *habeas corpus* review for the detainees in Guantánamo Bay; *Hamdan v Rumsfeld* 126 S Ct 2749 (2006) of 29 June 2006, on the detainees' right to a fair trial before a regularly constituted court.

[24] See US Supreme Court, *Sosa v Alvarez Machain*, 542 US 692 (2004) on the very limited jurisdiction of US-American federal district courts based on the Alien Torts Claims Act of 1789 (USC Title 28, § 1350: 'The district courts shall have original jurisdiction of any civil action by an alien for a tort only, committed in violation of the law of nations or a treaty of the United States').

In the first place of course, the activities of entities with executive functions beyond a State's borders (police, military, security forces or the respective private contractors, technical assistance personnel, private NGOs) are governed by the laws of the State in which the activities occur, including the constitutional guarantees. But often the constitutional guarantees of those States fall short of international minimum guarantees and/or are not properly enforced by local authorities. In such situations, both an alternative forum and alternative substantial standards to evaluate the extraterritorial conduct of State or quasi-State actors must be sought. In the absence of competent international bodies, jurisdiction is incumbent most naturally on the controlling authorities (supervisory bodies, courts) of the sender State. They might apply either the (constitutional) law of the actors' state of origin to extra-territorial actors[25] or even international constitutional guarantees. Both approaches raise the problem of extra-territoriality. The question is whether the fundamental guarantees of the State constitution or the relevant international guarantees (eg the ECHR or the ICCPR) by which a sender State is bound, are applicable outside the State's territory viz. outside the 'treaty territory'.[26] These two issues are probably linked. Maybe the applicability of a domestic guarantee could obliterate the application of an international guarantee or vice versa. Recent cases have demonstrated that national and international constitutional guarantees have become, in functional terms, interchangeable and raise similar structural problems.

4.4 Erosion of the hierarchy between national constitutional law and international law

The central formal feature of the State constitution, namely its *superiority* over other law, is called into question by new international provisions which relate to constitutional matters. Public international law claims itself to be superior to domestic law, including State constitutional law. However, most national constitutions do not yield to that claim of precedence.

4.4.1 The claim to superiority by international law

Although the question of hierarchy between international law and domestic law has been extensively debated for more than 100 years, the specific relationship between international treaties (as the most relevant legal source) and domestic *constitutional* law has been neglected.[27]

---

[25] Cf, eg The American Law Institute, Restatement (Third) of Foreign Relations Law, Vol 2, § 721, 'Applicability of Constitutional Safeguards' at 230: 'The provisions of the United States Constitution safeguarding individual rights . . . generally limit governmental authority whether it is exercised in the United States or abroad.'

[26] See ICJ, *Advisory Opinion, Legal Consequences of the Construction of a Wall in the Occupied Palestinian Territory* (2004), <http://www.icj-cij.org/icjwww/idocket/imwp/imwpframe.htm>, paras 107–111, on the applicability of the ICCPR outside the national territory.

[27] Scholarly contributions under the heading 'international law and constitutional law' mostly deal with questions such as the constitutional provisions on the position of international law in the

The position of many international adjudicatory bodies is that international law takes precedence over *all* national law, including State constitutions. This has occasionally been stated explicitly in the rulings of international courts and tribunals. In the *Montijo* Award, the arbitrator stated that 'a treaty is superior to the constitution, which latter must give way. The legislation of the republic must be adapted to the treaty, not the treaty to the laws.'[28] The Permanent Court of International Justice (PCIJ) found that 'a state cannot adduce as against another state its own *Constitution* with a view to evading obligations incumbent upon it under international law or treaties in force'.[29] The ECJ asserted the priority of EC law over the member States' constitutions: '[T]he law, stemming from the Treaty, an independent source of law, cannot because of its very nature be overridden by rules of national law,...Therefore the validity of a Community measure or its effect within a member state cannot be affected by allegations that it runs counter to either fundamental rights as formulated *by the constitution of that state or the principles of a national constitutional structure.*'[30] And in a recent decision on UN sanctions against individuals, the Tribunal of the European Community explicitly denied the prevalence of EU member State constitutions over resolutions of the Security Council. It held that 'the applicants' arguments based,...on the necessity of transposing Security Council resolutions into the domestic law of the Member States, *in accordance with the constitutional provisions* and fundamental principles of that law, must be *rejected*'.[31]

Occasionally however, international documents have granted deference to national constitutional law. For instance, Article IV of the Biological Weapons Convention[32] and Article VII of the Chemical Weapons Convention[33] oblige the

---

internal legal order *in general*, constitutional provisions on treaty-making powers, or constitutional bans on war. See the references in nn 36, 98, and 207 below.

[28] Case of the '*Montijo*': Agreement between the United States and Colombia of August 17, 1874, award of 26 July 1875, in John Bassett Moore, *History and Digest of International Arbitrations to which the United States has been a Party*, Vol 2 (Government Printing Office, Washington 1898) 1421, 1440.

[29] PCIJ, *Treatment of Polish Nationals and other Persons of Polish Origin or Speech in the Danzig Territory*, Series A/B, No 44 (1932), 24 (emphasis added).

[30] ECJ, Case 11/70 *Internationale Handelsgesellschaft v Einfuhr- und Vorratsstelle für Getreide- und Futtermittel* [1970] ECR 1125, para 3, emphasis added.

[31] Case T-306/01 *Yusuf and Al Barakaat v Council and Commission*, ECR 2005, II-3533 paras 258 and 202.

[32] Convention on the Prohibition of the Development, Production and Stockpiling of Bacteriological (Biological) and Toxin Weapons and on their Destruction, 10 April 1972 (Vol 1015, No 14860, p 163), Art IV: 'Each state Party to this Convention shall, *in accordance with its constitutional processes*, take any necessary measures to prohibit and prevent the development, production, stockpiling, acquisition or retention of the agents, toxins, weapons, equipment and means of delivery specified in Article I of the Convention, within the territory of such state, under its jurisdiction or under its control anywhere' (emphasis added).

[33] Chemical Weapons Convention (Convention on the Prohibition of the Development, Production, Stockpiling and Use of Chemical Weapons and on their Destruction), 3 September 1992, UNTS Vol 1974, No 33757, p 45, Art VII on national implementation measures: '1. Each state Party shall, *in accordance with its constitutional processes*, adopt the necessary measures to implement its obligations under this Convention' (emphasis added).

State parties to prohibit the relevant weapons only 'in accordance with [their] constitutional processes'.

4.4.2 *State constitutions obedience or resistance to international law*

The claim that international law trumps State constitutions has never been fully accepted by the responsible actors in the national constitutional orders. This is true even for the domestic (constitutional) courts of the member States in the EU vis-à-vis EC law. Generally speaking, the states do not grant international (or European) law priority over their national constitutions.

That said, it must be admitted that this assertion can only in part rely on the text of State constitutions, because constitutional provisions which clarify the hierarchy between international law and the domestic *constitution* are quite rare. Not unsurprisingly, the issue seems to be tackled almost exclusively in young, mostly post-transition State constitutions, which have been created in an era already marked by globalization. But even with regard to these modern constitutions Judge Vereshtin has noted 'a clear tendency towards "*de jure* recognition" of the primacy of international law by new constitutions... but not [a placement of international law] above the constitution itself'.[34]

Consider firstly the *rare cases of State constitutions which defer to international law.* Both the Constitution of Belgium (1994)[35] and the Constitution of the Netherlands (1983)[36] grant international law precedence over national constitutional law, although in neither case is this entirely clear.

Numerous state constitutions explicitly recognize the priority of international human rights treaties, but not of other treaties (eg the Czech Republic and Slovakia),

[34] Vladlen S Vereshchetin, 'New Constitutions and the Old Problem of the Relationship Between International Law and National Law' (1996) 7 EJIL 29–41, 29 and 37.

[35] There is no explicit constitutional provision to this effect. In a 1971 case, the Belgian Supreme Court held: 'When the conflict is one between a rule of domestic law and a rule of international law having direct effect within the domestic legal order, the rule established by the treaty must prevail; its pre-eminence follows from the very nature of international treaty law'. (Cour de Cassation (1ière chambre), *Etat Belge v Fromagerie Franco-Suisse Le Ski* ('Le ski'), judgment of 27 May 1971, (1971) 7 revue trimestrielle de droit européen 494–501; Engl. translation in (1972) 9 CMLR 229, 230). More recently, the Court confirmed explicitly that the ECHR has priority over the Belgian Constitution (Belgian Cour de Cassation, Dutch Section, 2nd Chamber, *Vlaamse Concentratie*, Decision of 9 November 2004, para 14.1: '*que la Convention de sauvegarde des droits de l'homme et des libertés fondamentales prime la Constitution*'), <http://www.juridat.be>. Annotation by Eva Brems, 'Belgium: The Vlaams Blok Political Party convicted indirectly of racism' (2006) 4 I Con 702, 710.

[36] The Constitution of the Netherlands of 17 February 1983 prescribes in Art 91(3) 'Any provisions of a treaty that conflict with the Constitution or which lead to conflicts with it may be approved by the Houses of the states General only if at least two-thirds of the votes cast are in favour.' Although Article 94 explicitly grants precedence to international treaties only over statutes ('Statutory regulations in force within the Kingdom shall not be applicable if such application is in conflict with provisions of treaties that are binding on all persons or of resolutions by international institutions.'), Art 94 should properly be understood in the sense that the Dutch Constitution defers to international treaties. The opinion of Dutch scholars seems to be divided: see Antonio Cassese, 'Modern Constitutions and International Law' (1985-II) 192 RdC 331–475, 409–411, with further references to Dutch literature.

or explicitly rank only international *jus cogens* above the State constitution (eg Switzerland). These special cases of potential supra-constitutional international norms will be discussed below (section 4.4.4).

Some State constitutions grant (some) international instruments a status *equal* to the State constitution. This appears to be the case for Austria and Italy. In Austria, any international treaty provision which might give rise to constitutional problems is declared, either in the act of its publication or otherwise, to effect a revision of the Austrian Constitution. These provisions therefore enjoy a constitutional status. This practice has led to the existence of numerous provisions of a constitutional character in various treaties, but which are not mentioned in the Austrian constitutional document itself.[37] In Italy too, international law may have a constitutional rank, depending on the formal status of the concrete domestic law which has endorsed the international treaty in question (*legge di esecuzione*).[38] Moreover, the Italian Constitution contains a novel provision on State and regional legislative power, clearly spelling out that European and international law limit governmental powers.[39] This idea of limitation may imply a constitutional status of international law.

In those constitutional systems where international law and domestic constitutional law have a formally equal rank, the resolution of potential conflicts is entirely left to the constitutional actors. Overall, even in the abovementioned more or less 'globalist' constitutional orders, the question of hierarchy between international law and the State constitution is pervaded by doubts and uncertainties.

An atypical case is the United Kingdom, where no formal constitution with precedence over statutory law exists. Rather, the idea of parliamentary supremacy constitutes the core constitutional principle. Against this background, it is constitutionally significant that EC law prevails over parliamentary Acts.[40] On the other hand, the courts exercise their power to disregard Acts of Parliament which are contrary to EC law only very cautiously.[41]

[37] Georg Ress and Christoph Schreuer, 'Wechselwirkungen zwischen Völkerrecht und Verfassung bei der Auslegung völkerrechtlicher Verträge' (1982) 23 Berichte der Deutschen Gesellschaft für Völkerrecht 61, 85; Hanspeter Neuhold and others (eds), *Österreichisches Handbuch des Völkerrechts*, Vol 1 (2nd edn, Wien: Manz, 2004), para 589. Cf Art 50(3) of the Austrian *Bundesverfassungsgesetz* of 10 November 1920 (7 December 1929), implying that international treaties may revise the State constitution: 'should constitutional law be modified or completed by the treaty . . . such treaties or such provisions as are contained in the treaty shall be explictly specified as "modifiying the constitution"'. (English translation available at <http://www.bka.gv.at/DesktopDefault.aspx?TabID=4780> (accessed 23 March 2006)).

[38] The Italian example demonstrates that even a dualistic scheme of incorporating international treaties into the domestic order by means of a transformative domestic act does not compel lawyers to grant an international treaty (in *gestalt* of the domestic act) a sub-constitutional status.

[39] See Art 117 of the Italian Constitution as amended on 18 October 2001: '(1) Legislative power belongs to the State and the regions in accordance with the constitution and *within the limits set by European Union law and international obligation*' (emphasis added).

[40] House of Lords, *Factortame Ltd v Secretary of State for Transport* ('Factortame II'), [1991] AC 603, repr. in Andrew Oppenheimer (ed), *The Relationship between European Community Law and National Law, The Cases* (Cambridge: CUP, 1994) 882.

[41] Eg *R v Secretary of State for Employment ex parte the Equal Opportunities Commission* [1994] 2 WLR 409–428.

The more common posture of State constitutions towards international law is not deferent. Examples of State constitutions which explicitly claim the *superiority of State constitutional law over international law* (or parts of it) are the Constitution of Belarus (1994),[42] the Constitution of Georgia (1995),[43] and the South African Constitution (1996).[44] Some State constitutions clearly grant international law priority over ordinary statutes, but not over the domestic constitution itself (see eg the Greek Constitution (1975),[45] the Constitution of Estonia (1992)[46] and the Constitution of Poland (1997)).[47] In a landmark decision of 2006, the Lithuanian Constitutional Court ruled that the State of Lithuania's Constitution (which is silent on this question of hierarchy) is superior to international treaties.[48] Finally,

[42] Constitution of Belarus of 1 March 1994, Art 128(2): 'Other enforceable enactments of state bodies and public associations, international treaty, or other obligations that are deemed by the Constitutional Court to be *contrary to the Constitution*, the laws or instruments of international law ratified by the Republic of Belarus shall be deemed *invalid* as a whole or in a particular part thereof from a time determined by the Constitutional Court' (emphasis added).

[43] Constitution of Georgia of 24 August 1995, Art 6(2): 'The legislation of Georgia corresponds with universally recognized norms and principles of international law. International treaties or agreements concluded with and by Georgia, *if they do not contradict the Constitution of Georgia*, take precedence over domestic normative acts' (emphasis added). Available in English at <http://members.tripod.com/ggdavid/georgia/const1.htm>.

[44] Constitution of South Africa of 8 May 1996, s 232 on customary international law: 'Customary international law is law in the Republic *unless it is inconsistent with the Constitution* or an Act of Parliament' (emphasis added).

[45] Art 28 of the Greek Constitution of 11 June 1975: '(1) The generally recognized rules of international law and the international conventions after their ratification by law and their having been put into effect in accordance with their respective terms, shall constitute an integral part of Greek law and *override any law provision to the contrary*. The application of the rules of international law and international conventions in the case of aliens shall always be effected on condition of reciprocity' (emphasis added). What is here translated as 'law provisions' includes only secondary laws, not the Greek Constitution.

[46] Art 123 of the Estonian Constitution of 28 June 1992: '(1) The Republic of Estonia shall not conclude foreign treaties which are in conflict with the Constitution. (2) If Estonian laws or other acts are in conflict with foreign treaties ratified by the Parliament, the articles of the foreign treaty shall be applied.'

[47] Art 91 of the Polish Constitution of 2 April 1997: '(1) After promulgation thereof in the Journal of Laws of the Republic of Poland (Dziennik Ustaw), a ratified international agreement shall constitute part of the domestic legal order and shall be applied directly, unless its application depends on the enactment of a statute. (2) An international agreement ratified upon prior consent granted by statute shall have *precedence over statutes* if such an agreement cannot be reconciled with the provisions of such statutes. (3) If an agreement, ratified by the Republic of Poland, establishing an international organization so provides, the laws established by it shall be applied directly and have *precedence in the event of a conflict of laws*' (emphasis added).

[48] Constitutional Court of Lithuania, Case No 17/02-24/02-06/03-22/04 on the limitation of the rights of ownership in areas of particular value and in forest land, ruling of 14 March 2006, para 9.4. 'Thus, the Constitution consolidates not only the principle that in cases when national legal acts establish the legal regulation which competes with that established in an international treaty, then the international treaty is to be applied, but also, in regard of European Union law, establishes expressis verbis the collision rule, which consolidates the priority of application of European Union legal acts in the cases where the provisions of the European Union arising from the founding Treaties of the European Union compete with the legal regulation established in Lithuanian national legal acts (regardless of what their legal power is), *save the Constitution itself*' (emphasis added). English translation available at <http://www.lrkt.lt/Documents1_e.html>.

the Russian Constitution of 1993 is important in political terms. Article 79 holds: 'The Russian Federation may participate in inter-state associations and delegate some of its powers to them in accordance with international agreements *if this does not restrict human or civil rights and liberties or contravene the fundamentals of the constitutional system of the Russian Federation.*'[49] A 2003 decision of the Russian Supreme Court confirmed that international law has priority over the laws of the Russian Federation, but not over the Russian Constitution, except maybe for the generally recognized principles of international law, 'deviation from which is impermissible'.[50]

In earlier epochs, constitution-makers have seldom reflected on the hierarchical position of the State constitution vis-à-vis international law. The ranking of older State constitutions has mostly been defined in constitutional case law. Under Article 6 of the American Constitution in the second clause: 'all Treaties made ... under the Authority of the United States, shall be the supreme Law of the Land'.[51] Treaty provisions operating as law of the US are granted authority equal to that of Acts of Congress, and in the case of conflict, the act most recently passed prevails.[52] Within this scheme, it is formally consistent that all conventional norms have effects in the national legal order only within constitutional limits.[53] The

---

[49] Russian Constitution of 12 December 1993 (emphasis added).

[50] Supreme Court of the Russian Federation (plenum), decision No 5 of 10 October 2003 on the application by ordinary courts of the universally recognised principles and norms of international law and the international treaties of the Russian Federation, (2004) 25 HRLJ 108–11, paras 1 and 8.

[51] This formula derives from Blackstone's commentaries on the laws of England, stating that 'the law of nations ... is here adopted in its full extent by the common law, and is held to be a part of the law of the land'. William Blackstone, *Commentaries on the Laws of England*, Vol 4 (13th edn, London: Cadell & Davies, 1809) 67. No internal executive act is needed to give effect to the international norm within the municipal order. For the reception of international law in the US American domestic order most instructively, Jordan J Paust, *International Law as Law of the United States* (2nd edn, Durham: Carolina Academic Press, Durham, 2003).

[52] *Head Money Cases* 112 US 580, 599 (1884); *Whitney v Robertson* 124 US 190, 194 (1887); *Chae Chan Ping v US* 130 US 581, 599 (1889). See also Restatement (Third) of Foreign Relations Law (1986), § 115(2). To the extent of conflict, a subsequent self-executing treaty provision prevails over a statute. Vice versa, an Act of Congress can—in the internal order—supersede an earlier provision of an international agreement. See Senator Jesse Helms, US Senate Committee on Foreign Relations, Address before the UN Security Council, 20 January 2000: 'Under our system, when international treaties are ratified they simply become US law. As such, they carry no greater or lesser weight than any other domestic US law. Treaty obligations can be superseded by a simple act of Congress.... Thus, when the United States joins a treaty organization, it holds no legal authority over us'. <http://usinfo.state.gov/regional/af/unmonth/t0012005.htm> (accessed 17 March 2006). Disregard by US authorities for an earlier international treaty of course does not relieve the US of its international obligation (Restatement (Third) of Foreign Relations Law (1986), § 115(1) (a) and (b)). To avoid violation of international law, statutes must therefore be interpreted in the light of the pre-existing international agreement so as not to conflict with the latter: *Murray v Schooner Charming Betsy* 6 US (2 Cranch) 64, 118 (1804). This principle of interpretation derives from the general assumption that Congress does not intend to repudiate an international obligation by nullifying an international agreement as domestic law.

[53] Paust (n 51 above) 99, with numerous references to the Supreme Court practice in n 1, 123. See also Louis Henkin, *Foreign Affairs and the United States Constitution* (2nd edn, Oxford: Clarendon Press, 1996) 187: 'Treaties, surely, are also subject to the Bill of Rights'.

American Supreme Court justifies the supremacy of the constitution over international treaties with the language of the constitution's treaty clause (Article VI), the history of its adoption, the objections of the framers and the entire constitutional history.[54] The government routinely subjects international treaties to conflicting constitutional provisions.[55]

In *France*, the Constitution grants duly ratified and published treaties priority over statutes under the condition of reciprocity (Article 55, French Constitution).[56] Interestingly enough, this provision remained a dead letter, with the French courts largely ignoring international law until the 1980s. French courts began to recognize the priority of international treaties over French statutes only after the ratification of the ECHR in 1974 and the acceptance of the individual complaint mechanism in 1981. When the risk became real of the judgment of an international court being issued against France, due to the possibility of an individual filing a complaint to the European Court of Human Rights, the French courts started to apply the Convention frequently. The purpose was to avoid negative Strasbourg rulings.[57] The French Constitutional Council (*Conseil Constitutionnel*) is competent to decide whether international treaties are compatible with the French Constitution. Ratification of an international treaty that is in conflict with the Constitution can take place only after an eventual constitutional revision (Article 54, French Constitution).[58]

This scheme implies that the French Constitution ranks above treaty law. It is therefore consistent that the Administrative Court (*Conseil d'Etat*) held that

---

[54] *Reid v Covert* 354 US 1, 16–7 (1957): 'no agreement with a foreign nation can confer power on Congress, or any other branch of Government, which is free from the restraints of the Constitution... The prohibitions of the Constitution were designed to apply to all branches of the National Government and they cannot be nullified by the Executive or the Executive and the Senate combined.'

[55] See the US reservation to the Genocide Convention of 1948 in *Multilateral Treaties as Deposited with the Secretary-General—Status as at 31 December 2002*, Vol 1, part I, Ch IV, at 124: 'nothing in this Convention requires or authorizes legislation or other action, by the United States of America prohibited by the Constitution of the United States as interpreted by the United States'. Objections against this reservation were lodged by Denmark, Estonia, Finland, Norway, Ireland, Mexico, Netherlands and Sweden on the grounds that no State party may invoke the provisions of its internal law as justification for failure to perform a treaty (Ibid, 125 et seq.). Such objections led the US to formulate an identical statement in special notes intended to be less visible than a 'reservation'. See also the UN Convention against Torture of 1984: Note No 11, Communication of the United States of America the Secretary-General requesting that a notification should be made to all ratifying parties. <http://untreaty.un.org/ENGLISH/bible/englishinternetbible/partI/chapterIV/treaty14.asp> (accessed 17 March 2006).

[56] Article 55 of the French Constitution of 4 October 1958: 'Duly ratified or approved treaties or agreements shall, upon their publication, override laws, subject, for each agreement or treaty, to its application by the other party.'

[57] Constance Grewe, 'Die Grundrechte und ihre richterliche Kontrolle in Frankreich' (2002) 29 EuGRZ 209, 212.

[58] Article 54 of the French Constitution (introduced in 1992): 'If, upon the demand of the President of the Republic, the Prime Minister or the President of one or other Assembly or sixty deputies or sixty senators, the Constitutional Council has ruled that an international agreement contains a clause contrary to the Constitution, the ratification or approval of this agreement shall not be authorized until the Constitution has been revised.'

'*la suprématie ainsi conférée aux engagements internationaux ne s'applique pas, dans l'ordre interne, aux dispositions de nature constitutionnelle*'.[59] This position was more or less explicitly confirmed by the *Conseil Constitutionnel* in its recent ruling on the European Constitutional Treaty: '*[L]orsque des engagements souscrits à cette fin contiennent une clause contraire à la Constitution, remettent en cause les droits et libertés constitutionnellement garantis ou portent atteinte aux conditions essentielles d' exercice de la souveraineté nationale, l'autorisation de les ratifier appelle une révision constitutionnelle*'.[60] Consequently, international treaties must be interpreted in conformity with fundamental principles recognized by the French Republic which form part of French constitutional law.[61]

In the same vein, the Austrian Constitutional Court refused to re-interpret the Austrian Constitution so as to comply with the broad reading of Article 6 ECHR by the European Court of Human Rights and explicitly disrespected the Court's case law on the notion of 'civil rights'.[62] Finally, the German Constitutional Court affirmed in its *Görgülü*-ruling that the Fundamental Law 'does not waive the sovereignty contained in the last instance in the German Constitution'.[63]

Not infrequently, reservations to international treaties seek to give effect to the adhering State's national constitution in deviation from the treaty provisions.[64] It

---

[59] Judgment of 30 October 1998, *Sarran* (1998), Revue fr. de droit admin. 1081–1090 (1999) 126 J.D.I. 745, 748); also in Marceau Long and others, *Les grands arrêts de la jurisprudence administrative* (15th edn, Paris: Dalloz, 2005), No 106. See in the same sense the French Superior Court (*Cour de Cassation*), *Pauline Fraisse*, decision No 450 of 2 June 2000.

[60] *Conseil Constitutionnnel of France*, decision No 505 DC of 19 November 2004 (Traité établissant une Constitution pour L'Europe), (2004) JORF 19885, para 7. Also *Conseil Constitutionnel of France*, No 92–308 DC of 9 April 1992 on the Treaty of Maastricht (Traité de Maastricht): An international treaty may not impinge '*aux conditions essentielles d'exercise de la souveraineté nationale*'.

[61] French *Conseil d'Etat*, *Moussa Koné*, judgment of 3 July 1996 on the interpretation of a bilateral extradition treaty.

[62] Austrian Constitutional Court (*Verfassungsgerichtshof*), judgment of 14 October 1987, *Miltner*, part 4g, Verfassungsgerichtshof Sammlung (VfSlg. 11500/1987).

[63] Constitutional Court (Bundesverfassungsgericht/BVerfG), order of 14 October 2004—*Görgülü* (2004) 57 NJW, 3407 (2004) 59 JZ 1171, para 35; English translation available at <http://www.bverfg.de>. For the superiority of the German Fundamental Law over international law in scholarship see Ress, in Ress and Schreuer (n 37 above) 47. See more recently in the same sense Christian Hillgruber, 'Zwingendes Völkerrecht—Dispositives Verfassungsrecht: Verkehrte juristische Welt?', *Jahrbuch des öffentlichen Rechts der Gegenwart NF* 54 (2006), 517, 91–93.

[64] One example is the numerous reservations to the Convention on the Elimination of all Forms of Discrimination against Women (CEDAW) of 18 December 1979, UNTS Vol 1249, No 20378, p 13. The Maldives declared: 'The Republic of Maldives does not see itself bound by any provisions of the convention which obliges to change its constitution and laws in any manner.' Lesotho, Malaysia, und Pakistan subject the entire CEDAW to their constitutions. Turkey, Tunisia, and other states have made reservations to the effect that domestic law prevails in specific instances. See also the Declaration of Tunisia on the Convention on the Rights of the Child: 'The Government of the Republic of Tunisia declares that it shall not, in implementation of this Convention, adopt any legislative or statutory decision that conflicts with the Tunisian Constitution.' See the following Reservations and Declarations on the ICESCR by Pakistan: 'While the Government of Islamic Republic of Pakistan accepts the provisions embodied in the International Covenant on Economic, Social and Cultural Rights, it will implement the said provisions in a progressive manner, in keeping with the existing economic conditions and the development plans of the country. The provisions of the Covenant shall, however, be *subject to the provisions of the Constitution* of the Islamic Republic of Pakistan' (emphasis added). Bangladesh on

can hardly be concluded from this practice *e contrario* that without such reservations, States generally consider international treaties to supersede their national constitution. On the contrary, this practice should be interpreted as making explicit the States' persistent concern for the safeguarding of domestic constitutional precepts.

4.4.3 National courts' control of infringements of the State constitution by international (or European) acts

National (constitutional) courts have begun to react to the increased powers of international institutions and to the increased quantity and quality of international norms. First, as pointed out above, some courts have confirmed the supremacy of their state constitution as a whole, or of core constitutional principles, over international law. Second and probably more importantly, some national (constitutional) courts claim the final word on potential infringements of the State constitution by acts of international institutions.

Decisions of this statist type have been rendered, for instance, in Spain,[65] Denmark[66] and Ireland,[67] where the national courts rejected the priority of EC law over the State constitution and/or claimed jurisdiction over EC acts. The German Constitutional Court, which, because of the Maastricht decision of 1993 mentioned

Arts 2 and 3 of the ICESCR: 'The Government of the People' Republic of Bangladesh will implement articles 2 and 3 in so far as they relate to equality between man and woman, *in accordance with the relevant provisions of its Constitution* and in particular, in respect to certain aspects of economic rights viz. law of inheritance' (emphasis added). Statement by China made upon ratification of the ICESCR: 'The application of Article 8.1(a) of the Covenant to the People's Republic of China shall be *consistent with the relevant provisions of the Constitution* of the People's Republic of China, Trade Union Law of the People's Republic of China and Labor Law of the People's Republic of China' (emphasis added). Most of these declarations and reservations have met objections by a number of Western European States.

[65] The Spanish Constitutional Court, in judgment 64/91 of 22 March 1991, *Asepesco*, implies that the national authorities are bound by the Spanish Constitution when implementing EC law. The Constitutional Court claimed jurisdiction: 'Furthermore, it is also evident that where a constitutional complaint action is brought against an act of the public authorities, taken for the implementation of a provision of Community law, alleging the violation of a fundamental right, such an action falls within the jurisdiction of the Constitutional Court' (English translation in Andrew Oppenheimer (ed), *The Relationship between European Community Law and National Law, The Cases* (Cambridge: CUP, 1994) 705, 706).

[66] Danish High Court, Maastricht Judgment of 6 April 1998, para 9.6: 'Therefore Danish Courts may consider an Act of the Community inapplicable in Denmark, if the extraordinary situation should arise that it could be established with the necessary certainty that an Act by the Community, which has been confirmed by the European Court, builds on an application of the Treaty which lies beyond the transfer of sovereignty effected by the accession treaty' (German translation in (1999) 26 EuGRZ 49; English translation by the author). [1998] Ugeskrift for Retsvaesen (UfR), H 800; English annotation by Sten Harck and Henrik Palmer Olsen, 'Decision Concerning the Maastricht Treaty' (1999) 93 AJIL 209–214.

[67] Irish Supreme Court, judgment of 19 December 1989, *Society for the Protection of Unborn Children Ireland v Grogan* [1990] ILRM 350, 361 (separate opinion Walsh J): '[I]t cannot be one of the objectives of the European Communities that a member state should be obliged to permit activities which are clearly designed to set at nought the constitutional guarantees for the protection within the State of a fundamental human right'.

above,[68] has become notorious for its claim to have the ultimate word in matters of European integration, is probably not the most statist court in Europe. In its so-called *Bananas* order of 2000, the Court clarified that it does not claim jurisdiction in each individual case of an alleged violation of German fundamental rights by EU Acts, but only in the event of a general failure of fundamental rights protection by the ECJ.[69] Should the exceptional situation arise in which the German Federal Constitutional Court will exercise its jurisdiction, it will not require European institutions to observe the full 'German' fundamental rights standard, but only a minimum standard.

Arguably, this posture is not entirely unsound. It probably constitutes an 'emergency brake' and thereby one condition for the opening-up of States' constitutions towards the international sphere.[70] Overall, the message of the national judiciaries is mixed, and national (constitutional) courts sometimes appear somewhat schizophrenic. For instance, the above-mentioned *Görgülü*-order of the German Federal Constitutional Court on the one hand emphasized the sovereignty of the German Constitution, and construed the relationship between international law and domestic law in a strictly dualist fashion.[71] Most importantly, it downgraded the ECHR, which it did not acknowledge as a strict prescript for the German authorities, but merely as a text to be 'taken into account' within the limits of German Constitutional principles.[72] On the other hand, the Court assumed in the *Görgülü*-order the existence of 'a gradually developing international community of democratic states under the rule of law'.[73] The Court confirmed that the German Basic Law must be interpreted in the light of the Convention and, most importantly, opened the way for constitutional complaints relating to a disregard of judgments of the European Court of Human Rights by German authorities. If a German court does not 'take into account' a Strasburg ruling (which means either to comply with it or to justify why the national court did not comply), complainants can instigate a constitutional complaint (*Verfassungsbeschwerde*) before the German Federal Constitutional Court. Such complaints must formally rely on the infringement of the principle of the rule of law (Art 20, clause 3, German Constitution) and of those domestic fundamental rights which correspond to the Convention guarantee at issue.[74]

This section has demonstrated that competing claims to superiority are raised by the international and the domestic constitutional actors. For a long time, the

---

[68] BVerfGE 89, 155 (1992).

[69] BVerfG order of 7 June 2000, *Banana Market* (2000) 53 Neue Juristische Wochenschrift (NJW) 3124.

[70] Cf Cottier and Wüger (n 21 above) 263–64. The authors argue that international norms which disregard fundamental rights and suffer from democratic deficiencies should be unenforceable in the domestic legal order. They deem such a 'constitutional right to resistance' necessary for the States to be able to accept as a general matter the supremacy and an eventual direct applicability of international law.

[71] *Görgülü*, BVerfG, (2004) 57 NJW 3407, (2004) 59 JZ 1171, paras 34–35. Official English translation available at <http://www.bverfg.de>. [72] Ibid, paras 47–50.

[73] Ibid, para 36. [74] Ibid, para 63.

irreconcilability between the international actor's claim to superiority and States' attitudes to the contrary remained a theoretical issue. This was because international law was, until recently, both more technical and more vague than today. Therefore, no prominent concrete *constitutional conflicts* arose. Only in the last decade has the intensification of global governance increased the potential for conflicts between international law and domestic constitutional law.

4.4.4 Special and superior international norms?

To complete the picture, it must be mentioned that the hierarchical position of some international norms vis-à-vis State constitutions is special. The first special case is the law of the European Community. Many member states of the EU consider EC law to be somewhat 'stronger' than general international law and are probably more ready to accept its precedence over domestic constitutional law. However, as pointed out above, these attitudes are far from consistent. Not infrequently, both national constitutional provisions and the language of national courts relate to European and general law indiscriminately. The special position of EC law vis-à-vis national constitutional law will not be discussed further here.

The second extraordinary case is that of *international human rights treaties*, in particular the ECHR. The constitutions of several post-transition countries (Romania (1991),[75] Slovakia (1992),[76] and the Czech Republic (1992)[77]) explicitly grant international treaties on human rights precedence over domestic 'law'. The respective constitutional wording allows for a reading which includes precedence over the domestic constitution. However, this conclusion has to my knowledge not been drawn in the case law. Due to its paramount importance and substance, the ECHR is itself a kind of 'constitutional instrument'.[78] As a consequence, the status of the ECHR as domestic constitutional or even supra-constitutional law has been discussed for some time by European scholars.[79] However, the practice of the member States has not followed scholarly proposals. For instance, in the already mentioned *Görgülü*-decision, the German Constitutional Court repeated that the Convention

---

[75] Art 20 of the Constitution of Romania of 8 December 1991: '(1) Constitutional provisions concerning the citizens' rights and liberties shall be interpreted and enforced in conformity with the Universal Declaration of Human Rights, with the covenants and other treaties Romania is a party to. (2) Where inconsistencies exist between the covenants and treaties on fundamental human rights Romania is a party to and internal laws, the international regulations shall take precedence.'

[76] Art 11 of the Slovak Constitution of 1 September 1992: 'International treaties on human rights and basic liberties that were ratified by the Slovak Republic and promulgated in a manner determined by law take precedence over its own laws, provided that they secure a greater extent of constitutional rights and liberties.'

[77] Art 10 of the Constitution of the Czech Republic of 16 December 1992: 'Ratified and promulgated international accords on human rights and fundamental freedoms, to which the Czech Republic has committed itself, are immediately binding and are superior to law.'

[78] ECHR, *Loizidou v Turkey* (preliminary objections), Series A 310 (1995), para 75.

[79] See for the German debate Thomas Giegerich, 'Wirkung und Rang der EMRK' in Rainer Grote and Thilo Marauhn (eds), *EMRK/GG: Konkordanzkommentar* (Tübingen: Mohr Siebeck, 2006), Chapter 2.

enjoys only the rank of a federal Act, and can be applied only within the confines of the German Basic Law.[80]

In most other member States too, the ECHR ranges in the hierarchy of norms below the State constitutions, either between the constitutions and statutes, or on the same footing as a domestic statute.[81] In some member States, namely Austria[82] and Italy,[83] globalist lawyers and courts seems to accord the ECHR the same domestic status as constitutional law, although this is probably not uncontroversial. In the Netherlands and in Belgium, the Convention has a supra-constitutional status.[84]

One distinct case is the Constitution of Bosnia and Herzegovina, because that constitution was adopted as part of the international Peace Accord of Dayton of 1995,[85] and because the State is still more or less under international administration. Article II, section 2 of the Bosnian Constitution provides that '[t]he rights and freedoms set forth in the European Convention for the Protection of Human Rights and Fundamental Freedoms and its Protocols shall apply directly in Bosnia and Herzegovina. *These shall have priority over all other law.*'[86] It is disputed whether the phrase 'other' law implies that the ECHR does *not* have priority over the Bosnian Constitution itself.

Another special case to consider is that of peremptory norms of international law. *Jus cogens* is in some States accepted as superior even to the State constitution.[87] The Swiss Constitution makes this explicit in its text.[88] Although outright

---

[80] *Görgülü*, BVerfG (2004) 57 NJW, 3407; (2004) 59 JZ 1171, paras 30 and 35.

[81] See the country reports in Robert Blackburn and Jörg Polakiewicz (eds), *Fundamental Rights in Europe: The European Convention on Human Rights and its Member States, 1950–2000* (Oxford: OUP, 2001); Helen Keller and Alec Sweet Stone (eds), *The Reception of the ECHR in Europe* (2008 forthcoming).

[82] Art II, para 7 of the *Bundesverfassungsgesetz, mit dem Bestimmungen des Bundesverfassungsgesetzes in der Fassung von 1929 über Staatsverträge abgeändert und ergänzt werden*, of 4 March 1964, Austrian BGBl. 59/1964.

[83] For the view that the ECHR enjoys a special *'forza di resistencia'* which precludes constitutional review of its provisions, see Guiseppe de Vergottini, *Diritto costituzionale* (4th edn, Milano: CEDAM, 2004) 38–39. On the diverging views in Italian scholarship on the position of the Convention in Italian law see Enzo Meriggiola, 'Italy' in Blackburn and Polakiewicz (n 81) 475, 480.

[84] For the Netherlands, see Leo F Zwaak, 'The Netherlands' in Blackburn and Polakiewicz (n 81) 595, 599. For Belgium, see Belgian Cour de Cassation, Dutch Section, 2nd Chamber, *Vlaamse Concentratie*, Decision of 9 November 2004.

[85] The constitution is Annex 4 to the General Framework Agreement for Peace in Bosnia and Herzegovina of 14 December 1995, (1996) 35 ILM 75, 118). On the absorption of the international elements into the Constitution of Bosnia and Herzegovina, see the landmark decision of the Constitutional Court of 2000 concerning a law enacted by the High Representative for Bosnia and Herzegovina, Constitutional Court of Bosnia and Herzegovina, case No 9/000, decision of 3 November 2000, para 9: The High Representative derives his powers from the 1995 Dayton Agreement and its annex. However, the Constitutional Court held that the High Representative was acting as an 'institution of Bosnia and Herzegovina' (rather than as an international official), and that his acts could be reviewed accordingly.   [86] Emphasis added.

[87] See, eg cautiously Paust (n 51 above) 115 and 117.   [88] Art 139(2) and 194(2) BV.

clashes between *jus cogens* and domestic constitutional norms are not very likely, divergences as regards the scope of entrenched prohibitions might arise. For instance, the principle of *non refoulement*, which has arguably gained the status of a peremptory norm, might be interpreted differently by state authorities and by international institutions. Some States used to limit the application of the principle to those who have already entered State territory, while notably the United Nations High Commissioner for Refugees favours a broader interpretation and applies *non refoulement* to the moment at which asylum seekers present themselves for entry into the State.[89] In such a case of divergence, it matters whether the international or the domestic 'version' of the *jus cogens* principle applies.

Recently, conflict arose with regard to the *jus cogens* prohibition of torture. The question is whether exceptional circumstances, eg the 'ticking bomb-situation' in the course of the war on terror, exceptionally allow torture. To recognize the priority of the international precept here would mean that the stricter interpretation given to the prohibition on torture by international bodies must prevail (at least when they have the authority to issue binding decisions), even if domestic actors might favour a more lenient application of that prohibition.[90]

However, to conclude the discussion of hierarchy, it must be noted that a State's judicial practice in applying or not applying international treaty provisions directly is as important as, if not more important than, any abstract hierarchy between national law and domestic (constitutional) law.[91] The supremacy of international law is real only if a municipal court can review a domestic act for its compatibility with international law. This hinges in part on the criteria of direct effect. If no judicial review is available, any constitutional clause granting superiority of international law over the national constitution is basically a dead letter.

5. The globalization of core constitutional principles

Globalization and global governance affect and sometimes undermine basic constitutional principles. In this section, I discuss the globalization of four traditional

---

[89] Guy S Goodwin-Gill, *The Refugee in International Law* (2nd edn, Oxford: Clarendon, 1998) 121–24 and 168, n 234 with further references.

[90] For an 'autonomous' and quite lenient interpretation of the peremptory prohibition on torture: Office of the Assistant Attorney General, *Memorandum for Alberto R. Gonzales, Counsel to the President* of 1 August 2002, re Standards of Conduct for Interrogation under 18 USC §§ 2340–2340A (implementing the UN Torture Convention in US American law), available at <http://www.washingtonpost. com/wpsrv/nation/documents/dojinterrogationmemo20020801.pdf> (accessed 23 March 2006). But see Office of the Assistant Attorney General, *Memorandum for James B. Comey, Deputy Attorney General* of 30 December 2004, which supersedes the August 2002 memorandum in its entirety and modifies the analysis of the legal standards in important respects, <http://www.usdoj.gov/olc/dagmemo. pdf> (accessed 3 April 2006).

[91] Cf Helen Keller, *Rezeption des Völkerrechts* (Berlin: Springer, 2003) 15: The granting of direct effect in a concrete case is a good indicator for the friendliness of a legal order towards international law. See ibid for legal and political reasons for granting or denial of direct effect.

constitutional principles: rule of law, democracy, social security, and the organization of territory. These principles may have 'Western' historical origins, but are meanwhile widely—even if in part only nominally—acknowledged as necessary ingredients of a good State constitution.[92] Their acceptance does not necessarily reflect a global mono-culture. The principles correspond to human value judgments worldwide, can be justified by various cultural and philosophical traditions, and are broad enough to accommodate a diversity of constitutional practices.[93]

5.1 Globalization of the rule of law

5.1.1 The traditional idea

The primary constitutional principle is the *rule of law/Rechtsstaatlichkeit/état de droit*. The German notion of *Rechtsstaat* (received in France as *état de droit*), and the Anglo-Saxon rule of law are traceable back to Aristotle's formula of the government of laws, not of men.[94] The foundational treaties of both the Council of Europe and the European Union state that the rule of law is acknowledged by all the member States and therefore forms the basis of both organizations.[95] The government of the United States has emphatically been termed 'a government of laws, not of men'.[96]

The idea of a rule of law is inherently vague. Its substance and contours have evolved over time. Depending on the constitutional tradition, the outlook of the time, and scholarly preferences, quite different aspects have been highlighted in academia.[97] The following elements (both formal and substantive) are frequently cited as constituting the rule of law: the requirement that government in all its action is bound by the law; the transparency of government action; the separation of powers or checks and balances; equality; due process/minimal guarantees of

[92] See in this sense Bruce Ackerman, 'The Rise of World Constitutionalism' (1997) 83 Virginia L Rev 771–97; Peter Häberle, 'Verfassungsentwicklungen in Osteuropa—aus der Sicht der Rechtsphilosophie und der Verfassungslehre' (1992) 117 Archiv des öffentlichen Rechts 169, 170 on the '*Weltstunde des Verfassungsstaates*'.

[93] In contrast to the view espoused here, critical legal scholars either deny that State constitutions are indeed converging or opine that global constitutional convergence is the result of the imposition of particular ('Western') values and a particular view on constitutions and amounts to 'neocolonialism'. See, eg Susan Marks, 'The End of History? Reflections on Some International Legal Theses' (1997) 3 EJIL 449–77.

[94] Aristotle (approx 350 BC), *Politik* in Franz F Schwarz (ed and transl) (Stuttgart: Reclam, 1989) Book III, 16, 1287a.

[95] The Preamble of the Statute of the Council of Europe of 5 May 1949 proclaims the 'rule of law'. According to Art 6, s 1 of the Treaty on the EU, the European Union is founded inter alia on the 'rule of law', which is 'common to the member states'.

[96] US Supreme Court, *Marbury v Madison* 5 US (1 Cranch) 137, at 163 (1803).

[97] Constance Grewe and Hélène Ruiz Fabri, *Droits constitutionnels européens* (Paris: PUF, 1995) 22–32; Rainer Grote, 'Rule of Law/Rechtsstaat and "Etat de droit"' in Christian Starck (ed), *Constitutionalism, Universalism, and Democracy—A Comparative Analysis* (Baden-Baden: Nomos, 1999) 269–306; with a focus on the British tradition Hilaire Barnett, *Constitutional and Administrative Law* (5th edn, London: Cavendish Publishing, 2004) 69–95.

fairness/fundamental rights protection; and finally judicial review of governmental action. Globalization and global governance affect all of these elements.

5.1.2 Positive effects of globalization

It has been noted that 'it is increasingly deemed appropriate by more recently created states to incorporate the essence of the international law of human rights into their domestic legal systems, in order to ensure their conformity to global standards'.[98] The direct or indirect adoption of international standards in national constitutions is *improving the human rights record* in many states at least nominally. This has happened most prominently in the post-socialist countries and in South Africa.[99] But the flow-back is not limited to weak States or States in transition. For example, the new Swiss Constitution of 1999 more or less copied the rights of the ECHR into its constitutional fundamental rights catalogue. In the United Kingdom, the adoption of the Human Rights Act of 1998[100] made the ECHR applicable by British courts and thereby 'brought rights home'.[101] Even if the primary intention of the incorporation of the ECHR was to reduce the unusually high number of Strasburg negative sentences in relation to the UK and to intercept international control, the effect has been to improve the protection of individual rights, be it only because the claimant gains an additional judicial level.

Second, free trade strengthens the *classical liberal rights*, notably property, entrepreneurial freedom, and free movement. This strengthens the rule of law, because, although the concept of 'rule of law'/'*Rechtsstaat*'/'*Etat de droit*' has historically evolved distinctly of fundamental rights protection, its ultimate purpose has always been to impose effective limits on the exercise of public authority in order to safeguard the rights and liberties of the citizens.[102] Some liberal authors opine that the effective enjoyment of economic rights naturally incites citizens to claim political freedom as well.[103] However, the experience of the last 20 years has not confirmed the expectation that the granting of economic rights gradually destroys tyrannical regimes.[104]

---

[98] Thomas M Franck and Arun K Thiruvengadam, 'International Law and Constitution-Making' (2003) 2 Chinese Journal of International Law 467–518, 517. 'If there is one substantive area where most states have shown great willingness to be open to principles of international law, it has been the area of human rights' (at 518).

[99] For a case-study of how external forces of legal globalization, brought into play via internal constitutional mechanisms, have contributed to the founding and carving out of municipal human rights law in South Africa, see ch 11 of this book.

[100] Chapter 42; also in Halsbury's Statutes of England and Wales, 5th edn, Vol 7 (2004) 674–798; <http://www.hmso.gov.uk/acts/acts1998/80042--d.htm> (accessed 16 January 2006).

[101] Government of the UK, *White Paper: Rights Brought Home, The Human Rights Bill* (presented to Parliament by the Secretary of State for the Home Department by Command of her Majesty October 1997).

[102] Grote, in Starck (n 97 above) 304; Grewe and Ruiz Fabri, (n 97 above) 30.

[103] Milton Friedman, *Capitalism and Freedom* (Chicago: Chicago UP, 1962) 10 arguing that capitalism is a necessary, albeit not sufficient condition of political freedom.

[104] For recent empirical studies on the relationship between political and economic freedom see Eberhard Scholing and Vincenz Timmermann, 'Der Zusammenhang zwischen politischer und

Third, global governance spreads and divides political power among different levels of action and among different actors. It can therefore be considered a '*vertical*' *separation of powers*. The checks and balances which might result are an asset in terms of the rule of law.

Finally, the new means of obtaining and sharing information and communication and the media, which form an important basis and element of globalization, create *global publicity*. Tyrannical regimes are being exposed to the critical view of the global public. Situations of lawlessness quickly become public and can be denounced by civil society activists who act globally.

5.1.3 Negative effects of globalization

Globalization and global governance affect the rule of law not only in positive, but also in negative ways. First, global governance leads to *deficiencies in legal protection*. Acts of international organizations are normally not challengeable in (national or international) courts and tribunals. In search of redress against acts of international actors, individuals cannot, as a rule, act by themselves in international fora. Instead, they depend on diplomatic protection provided by their State of origin. However, individuals are generally not entitled to such protection and it is often not granted due to political considerations. In national fora, affected individuals can only challenge the domestic implementing acts. However, courts tend to refuse to scrutinize these acts because they are pre-determined by international precepts. One area in which shocking deficiencies in judicial protection have been unveiled is where sanctions are imposed by the UN Security Council against individuals, such as the freezing of assets or bans on travelling. These sanctions must be implemented by UN member States, but judicial protection is basically unavailable either on the national or the international level.[105]

Legal clarity and transparency tend to suffer in the process of legal globalization. The enmeshments on the supra-State level render political and legal processes increasingly complex. Decision-makers and responsible actors are frequently not clearly identifiable.

Another tendency which may be detrimental to the rule of law is the 'softening' of the law in the course of globalization. Both in the international and the European

---

ökonomischer Freiheit: Eine empirische Untersuchung' (2000) 136 Schweizerische Zeitschrift für Volkswirtschaft und Statistik 1–23; Bruce Bueno Mesquita and George W Downs, 'Development and Democracy' (2005) 84 Foreign Affairs 77–86, concluding: 'As events now suggest, the link between economic development and what is generally called liberal democracy is actually quite weak and may even be getting weaker.'

105 For a limited review (for violation of *jus cogens* only) of Security Council Resolutions sanctioning individuals see European Court of First Instance, Cases T-306/01 *Yusuf and Al Barakaat v Council and Commission*, ECR 2005, II-3533 and T-315/01 *Yassin Abdullah Kadi v Council and Commission*, ECR, II-3649. In both cases appeals to the ECJ were pending in January 2007 (Cases C-415/05 P and C-402/05 P). See also Case T-253/02 *Ayadi v Council of the EU* and case T-49/04 *Hassan*, both judgments of the Court of First Instance of 12 July 2006; *Mujahedin-e Khalq Organisation v Council and Commission* (T-228/02), judgment of 12 December 2006.

realm, soft regulation is proliferating.[106] Soft law is situated in a grey zone between law and politics. Because it is not legally binding as such and not justiciable, the widespread use of soft law risks undermining the normative power of the law and thereby the rule of law as well.

A further element of the rule of law that may be compromised by globalization is *legal oversight* which guarantees respect for the law in the course of the implementation of public tasks.[107] The administrative control of legality is modified by globalization, because the new actors entrusted with functions in the public interest (international organizations, NGOs, transnational corporations) do not form part of the State bureaucracy and can be subjected to control at best indirectly. However, the outsourcing of public tasks is to a certain extent irreconcilable with the maintenance of complete governmental control. The loss of control can only be compensated by an *ex post facto* control of legality by courts. So the deficiencies relating to the rule of law are probably the price which must be paid for efficiency gains.

5.1.4 Reactions of domestic constitutional actors

In order to adapt the functioning of the rule of law to conditions of global governance and globalization and to counteract the emerging rule of law-deficiencies, various strategies are open to constitutional actors.

a) Judicial review of foreign affairs

One option might be the intensification of the so far rather lenient judicial review by national courts in matters of foreign policy. Traditionally, domestic courts (including constitutional courts) have exercised self-restraint in this field. Governmental measures linked to foreign affairs have been routinely treated as 'political questions' or as '*actes de gouvernement*' and are rarely subjected to judicial review.[108] However, the nonavailability of judicial protection in domestic fora appears less appropriate in the era of globalization in which domestic and international affairs are no longer clearly distinguishable and flow into each other. This phenomenon has aptly been termed 'global home affairs' ('*Welt-Innenpolitik*' by Carl Friedrich Freiherr von Weizsäcker)[109] or 'global domestic law' ('*Weltinnenrecht*' by Jost

---

[106] Dinah Shelton (ed), *Committment and Compliance: The Role of Non-Binding Norms in the International Legal System* (Oxford: OUP, 2003); Linda Senden, *Soft Law in European Community Law* (Oxford: OUP, 2004).

[107] Legal supervision is sided by political and financial oversights which actually belong to the democratic context.

[108] In Switzerland, Art 83 lit. a) of the *Bundesgerichtsgesetz* precludes judicial action against administrative acts concerning the foreign security of the country, neutrality, diplomatic protection, and all other foreign affairs. According to older case law, this provision '*stellt aber einen eigentlichen Vorbehalt zugunsten der politischen Gewalt dar. Regierungsakte wie andere wesentlich politische Entscheide der Verwaltung auf diesem Gebiete sollen der Prüfung durch das Verwaltungsgericht entzogen bleiben*', BGE 96 I 733 (1970).

[109] Carl Friedrich Freiherr von Weizsäcker, *Bedingungen des Friedens* (Vandenhoeck und Ruprecht: Göttingen 1964) 8 and 13.

Delbrück[110]). Scholars have therefore called for the abandonment of judicial self-restraint in matters of foreign policy.[111] Indeed, some case law pointing in that direction is emerging.[112]

One of the most affected constitutional systems is that of the United Kingdom. The British Constitution is currently in a process of 'juridification' or 'judicialisation',[113] which appears to have been largely induced by European integration and globalization. For instance, the use of the English doctrine of the act of State as a barrier to judicial review 'is diminishing since at least in Europe, the barriers between international and national law are being eroded. The claim that "acts of foreign policy" affecting individuals should be beyond judicial scrutiny is unlikely to be welcomed today.'[114] A prominent example of the intensification of judicial review is the *Abbasi* case (2003), in which the English Court of Appeal departed from the traditional position that the exercise of diplomatic protection is a matter beyond the jurisdiction of courts.[115] In that case, the court accepted a complaint by a British detainee in Guantánamo Bay who was dissatisfied with the measures of protection offered by the British Government and who sought judicial review to compel representations about the illegality of his detention. Although the court rejected the claim that a general duty to exercise specific protective measures existed, it assumed that legitimate expectations could arise in that context. Thereby, it acknowledged that applications such as Abbasi's did fall within the jurisdiction of the courts. Whether the trend of intensification of judicial review will continue remains to be seen.

b) Respect for human rights by global or transnational actors

We have seen that global governance empowers nonstate actors that act globally, such as international and supranational organizations, nongovernmental organizations, and transnational corporations. The increase of their activities and powers bears the risk of curtailing individual liberty. However, the new global and transnational actors are not directly bound by national or international human rights instruments.

---

[110] Klaus Dicke and others (eds), *Weltinnenrecht, Liber amicorum Jost Delbrück* (Berlin: Duncker & Humblot, 2005).

[111] Cottier and Wüger (n 21 above) 265–66. See also Thomas Cottier and Maya Hertig, 'The Prospects of 21st Century Constitutionalism' (2003) 7 Max Planck UNYB 261, 326–27, demanding more coherent standards of judicial review on the basis of a uniform criterion of justiciability both on the international and on the national plane.

[112] For a discussion on the shrinking terrain of French 'actes de government' in the context of foreign affairs, see René Chapus, *Droit administratif general*, Vol 1 (14th edn, Paris: Montchrestien, 2000) 938.

[113] The anticipated creation of a Supreme Court is a mere symptom or consequence of that tendency. Gernot Sydow, 'Der geplante Supreme Court für das Vereinigte Königreich im Spiegel der britischen Verfassungsreform' (2004) 64 ZaöRV 66–67.

[114] Anthony Bradley and Keith D Ewing, *Constitutional and Administrative Law* (13th edn, Harlow: Pearson Education, 2003) 316.

[115] UK Supreme Court of Judicature, Court of Appeal, Civil Division, *Abbasi v Secretary of State for Foreign and Commonwealth Affairs* (2003) 42 ILM 355.

One strategy for upholding a high standard of human rights protection despite the globalization of governance is to *focus on the States themselves* which have transferred powers to international institutions and organizations. With a view to the ECHR, the European Court of Human Rights held that member States are obliged to secure Convention rights even after a transfer of competences, eg to the European Community. Member States' responsibility therefore continues even after such transfer.[116] From that perspective, States are in principle (under certain conditions) liable for serious infringements of human rights by international organizations of which they are members. However, the more autonomous the international institutions are from the member States (independent organs, majority votes), the less appropriate the attribution of their acts to member States appears.

A more promising remedy against the undermining of fundamental rights protection through global governance might be the extension of human rights obligations to global and transnational actors. This concerns both public entities, namely international organizations, and private entities, namely transnational enterprises. The more intense the activity of international organizations becomes, the more plausible the claim that they must respect human rights. Not surprisingly, the EC/EU was the first organization to be confronted with this problem.

In this context, a possible constitutional strategy is to oblige international organizations to respect the *'national' fundamental rights* as codified in the national constitutions of the member States. This would allow constitutional review of an international organization's acts by the courts of its member States. Notably, with regard to the EC/EU, the claim of the German Constitutional Court to control the compatibility of EC/EU Acts with 'German' fundamental rights has given rise to intense academic debate and has provoked a conflict between the courts involved.[117] The highly undesirable consequence of that construction is that, depending on the member States concerned, differing standards apply to the activity of an organization. This runs counter to ideals of fairness and equal protection and hampers international integration.

The alternative strategy for safeguarding human rights in the era of global governance is to oblige international actors to comply with *international* human rights standards. The EU meanwhile possesses its own Charter of Fundamental Rights[118] (a soft-law document) which binds the institutions of the Union and the member States when they are implementing EU law.[119]

---

[116] ECHR, *Matthews v UK* [1999] ECHR I-251, para 32.

[117] See the German Constitutional Court: BVerfGE 89, 155, *Maastricht* (1992); BVerfG order of 7 June 2000, *Banana Market* ((2000) 53 Neue Juristische Wochenschrift (NJW) 3124); BVerfG judgment of 18 July 2005, *European Arrest Warrant* ((2005) 58 NJW). See also BVerfG order of 4 April 2001 on 'German' fundamental rights protection against acts of the European patent office ((2001) 54 NJW 2705).

[118] Charter of Fundamental Rights of the EU of 7 December 2000 (OJ 2000 C 364, 1).

[119] Ibid, Art 51.

The law is far less advanced with regard to the UN. UN-peacekeeping and peace-enforcement activity has raised the question of whether UN military personnel is bound by the international humanitarian conventions ratified only by states.[120] Since 1990, sanctions imposed by the Security Council (ranging from economic deprivation to the freezing of assets and travel bans) have provoked the question of whether the Security Council is bound to observe international human rights guarantees, notably social rights and procedural guarantees such as the right to a hearing, the presumption of innocence and the right to judicial review.[121]

Not only international organizations, but also transnational enterprises have by and large acquired the power to impede the fundamental rights of workers and other individuals, either directly or indirectly through collaboration with tyrannical regimes. In consequence, the human rights obligations and responsibilities of transnational enterprises are intensely discussed,[122] and soft regulation to that effect is being elaborated.[123]

Overall, it seems as if the instruments, mechanisms and procedures of domestic constitutional law alone are not sufficient to make up for deficiencies in the rule of law created by global governance. A remedial strategy must be comprehensive and must cover the various levels of the emerging multi-level system of constitutional governance. The resolution of the UN General Assembly on the 2005 World Summit Outcome recognizing the need for universal adherence to and implementation of the '*rule of law at both the national and international level*'[124] therefore makes perfect sense.

---

[120] See Nigel D White and Dirk Klaasen (eds), *The UN, Human Rights and Post-Conflict Situations* (Manchester: Manchester UP, 2005).

[121] See Marc Bossuyt, *The Adverse Consequences of Economic Sanctions on the Enjoyment of Human Rights. Working Paper for the Commission on Human Rights*, UN Doc. E/CN.4/Sub.2/2000/33 of 21 June 2000; August Reinisch, 'Developing Human Rights and Humanitarian Law Accountability of the Security Council for the Implementation of Economic Sanctions' (2001) 95 AJIL 851–71; Erika De Wet, 'Human Rights Limitations to Economic Enforcement Measures Under Article 41 of the United Nations Charter and the Iraqi Sanctions Regime' (2001) 14 LJIL 277–300; Elias Davidsson, 'Legal Boundaries to UN Sanctions' (2003) 7 The International Journal of Human Rights 1–50.

[122] David Weissbrodt and Muria Kruger, 'Norms of the Responsibilities of Transnational Corporations and Other Business Enterprises with Regard to Human Rights' (2003) 97 AJIL 901–922; Anne Peters, 'Sind transnationale Unternehmen verpflichtet, (internationale) Menschenrechte zu respektieren und zu fördern?' in Peter Kirchschläger and others (eds), *Menschenrechte und Wirtschaft im Spannungsfeld zwischen State und Nonstate Actors* (Bern: Stämpfli, 2006) 127–35.

[123] See the OECD Guidelines for Multinational Enterprises of 27 June 2000, DAFFE/IME/WPG (2000)15/FINAL; the Tripartite Declaration of Principles concerning Multinational Enterprises and Social Policy of 17 November 2000, (2002) 41 ILM 186 et seq; the Johannesburg Plan of Implementation, revised version of 23 September 2002 (Doc A/CONF.199/20), para 49; the Norms of the Responsibilities of Transnational Corporations and Other Business Enterprises of the UN Sub-Commission on the Promotion and Protection of Human Rights, UN Doc. E/CN.4/Sub.2/2003//12/Rev.2 (2003) of 13 August 2003; Report of the United Nations High Commissioner on Human Rights on the Responsibilities of Transnational Corporations and Related Business Enterprises with regard to Human Rights, contained in a Report of Sub-Commission on the Promotion and Protection of Human Rights, UN Doc. E/CN.4/2005/91 of 15 February 2005; European Commission Decision 2004/116. [124] UN Doc. A/RES/60/1 of 24 October 2005, para 134 (emphasis added).

5.2 Globalization of democracy

5.2.1 *The problem*

The second basic constitutional principle is democracy. This principle is extremely broad and loaded with various, even competing meanings. It has undergone important changes throughout its history and has been criticized as meaningless because of its vagueness. Despite all the debates on the details, the Gettysburg formula put forward by Abraham Lincoln probably still finds wide approval. According to Lincoln, democracy is 'government by the people, of the people, and for the people'.[125] Put differently, democratic government requires that citizens are allowed to give their *input*, that they have some sense of responsibility towards the polity and their co-citizens, and that political processes produce *outputs* in the interests of the citizens.

All of these elements appear to be affected by globalization and interlocking trends.[126] However, the relationships between democratization and globalization are complex. On the one hand, an international obligation to organize national government in a democratic fashion appears to be emerging. Numerous international legal provisions (both universal and regional in scope) and important soft law documents grant individuals the right to participate in the conduct of their states' public affairs and the right to vote in national elections,[127] or generally call on states to establish democratic governments.[128] This issue is beyond the scope of this chapter.[129]

---

[125] Abraham Lincoln, 'Gettysburg address' of 19 November 1863, Library of Congress Exhibition, <http://www.loc.gov/exhibits/gadd/gadrft.html>. For comprehensive introductions into the subject see Boris DeWiel, *Democracy: A History of Ideas* (Vancouver: UBC Press, 2001); Albert Weale, *Democracy* (Basingstoke: McMillan, 1999); Sanford Lakoff, *Democracy: History, Theory, Practice* (Boulder: Westview Press, 1996); Giovanni Sartori, *Democratic Theory* (Westport: Greenwood Press, 1973, orig. 1962).

[126] Numerous other developments, such as the technocratization of politics or the bypassing of traditional democratic intermediaries by individual networking made possible by communication mediums, are closely linked to the phenomenon of globalization.

[127] Art 21 Universal Declaration of Human Rights, Art 25 ICCPR, Art 23(1) ACHR, Art 13(1) Banjul-Charter.

[128] See Arts 2(b), 9 OAS-Charter (last amended on 10 June 1993); Preamble of the Statute of the Council of Europe of 5 May 1949; Preamble of the NATO-Treaty of 4 April 1949; CSCE-Charter of Paris for a New Europe of 21 November 1993; UN Commission on Human Rights, Res. 1999/57 of 27 April 1999 'Promotion of the right to democracy'; OAS Interamerican Democratic Charter of 11 September 2001 (text in (2001) 41 ILM 1289); Implementation of the United Nations Millennium Declaration, UN Doc. A/57/270 of 31 July 2002, Part V.: 'Human rights, democracy and good governance', paras 82 et seq; Resolution of the UN General Assembly on the 2005 World Summit Outcome, UN Doc. A/RES/60/1 of 24 October 2005, paras 135–36: 'We reaffirm that democracy is a universal value based on the freely expressed will of the people to determine their own political, economic, social and cultural systems and their full participation in all aspects of their lives. We also reaffirm that while democracies share common features, there is no single model of democracy, *that it does not belong to any country or region*, and reaffirm the necessity of due respect for sovereignty and the right of self-determination. We renew our commitment to support democracy by strengthening countries' capacity to implement the principles and practices of democracy' (emphasis added).

[129] Gregory Fox and Brad Roth (eds), *Democratic Governance and International Law* (Cambridge: CUP, 2000); Steven Wheatley, 'Democracy in International Law: A European Perspective' (2002) 51 ICLQ 225–47.

On the other hand, domestic democracy, which was designed as a form of government within the closed nation State, is being modified (or, depending on the observer's outlook, undermined, eroded, or merely transformed) by internationalization and globalization. The concern of this chapter is limited to the second issue, the transformation of domestic democracy by globalization.[130]

5.2.2 Positive effects of globalization

Globalization may have a positive impact on the functioning of national democracies.[131] First, new techniques of communication allow for global publicity. The consequence is that *pressure by public opinion* can be exercised transnationally. Undemocratic political élites are now finding it harder than before to defend their powers and privileges.

Second, free trade supports democracy under the liberal premise that it *contributes to wealth gains* of all market participants. Individuals need a minimum of material security to afford to act as citizens and to engage in democratic structures.[132] However, the current reality is that the free trade regime is implemented selectively, is accompanied by painful transition symptoms, and does not appear to be reducing the massive worldwide wealth gap.

A third democracy-supporting effect of the regime of the World Trade Organization (WTO) in particular is its potential function as '*representation reinforcement*',[133] which is however both empirically and normatively contested. In the eyes

---

[130] Paul G Cerny, 'Globalization and Erosion of Democracy' (1999) 36 European Journal of Political Research 1–26 with the thesis that democracy is impossible in a globalized world; Ian Shapiro and Casiano Hacker-Cordón (eds), *Democracy's Edges* (Cambridge: CUP, 1999) with contributions inter alia by Altvater, Dahl and Held; Klaus Dieter Wolf, *Die neue Staatsraison—Zwischenstaatliche Kooperation als Demokratieproblem in der Weltgesellschaft* (Baden-Baden: Nomos, 2000) with models of democratization beyond the nation state at 177 et seq; Scholte (n 4 above) 261–82; Hauke Brunkhorst, *Solidarität* (Frankfurt a.M.: Suhrkamp, 2002); Molly Beutz, 'Functional Democracy: Responding to Failures of Accountability' (2003) 44 Harv ILJ 387–431; Armin von Bogdandy, 'Demokratie, Globalisierung, Zukunft des Völkerrechts—eine Bestandsaufnahme' (2003) 63 ZaöRV 853–77; Juliane Kokott, 'Souveräne Gleichheit und Demokratie im Völkerrecht' (2004) 64 ZaöRV 525–32; Joseph HH Weiler, 'The Geology of International Law—Governance, Democracy and Legitimacy' (2004) 64 ZaöRV 547–62. See for the democratic deficiencies of governance by international organizations the intensive discussion on the EU (eg Marcel Kaufmann, *Europäische Integration und Demokratieprinzip* (Baden-Baden: Nomos, 1997); Peters, *Elemente einer Theorie* (n 19 above) 626–760; Andreas Tiedtke, *Demokratie in der Europäischen Union* (Berlin: Duncker & Humblot, 2005)). See Eric Stein, 'International Integration and Democracy: No Love at First Sight' (2001) 95 AJIL 489–534, on democracy-legitimacy deficits in the WHO, WTO, NAFTA and EU. For a critique of globalization focusing on democratic deficiencies see Elmar Altvater and Birgit Mahnkopf, *Grenzen der Globalisierung: Ökonomie, Ökologie und Politik in der Weltgesellschaft* (6th edn, Münster: Westfälisches Dampfboot, 2004) 478–516.

[131] Will Kymlicka, 'Citizenship in an Era of Globalization: Commentary on Held' in Ian Shapiro and Casiano Hacker-Cordón (eds), *Democracy's Edges* (Cambridge: CUP, 1999) 112–125; Von Bogdandy, 'Demokratie' (n 130 above) 863–64; Jagdish Bhagwati, *In Defense of Globalization* (New York: OUP, 2004) 93–105.

[132] On empirical links between wealth and democracy classically see Seymour Martin Lipset, 'Some Social Requisites of Democracy: Economic Development and Political Legitimacy' (1959) 53 The American Political Science Review 69–105; Bhagwati (n 131 above) 93–96.

[133] John Hart Ely, *Democracy and Distrust* (Cambridge: Harvard UP, 1980).

of adherents, WTO commitments function as a corrective to the domestic political process in which interest-seeking lobbies and protectionist groups are able to rouse undue attention for their group interests.[134] This distortion is neutralized by the externalized commitment of member states to free trade. Thereby membership of the WTO helps a State to realize the political and legislative processes in the economic domain in a fairer manner. National trade politics become more respectful of popular preferences, and the 'protectionist bias' in domestic economic policy is corrected by going above the level of the State.[135] This benefits at least in part the diffuse, unorganized and therefore weaker segments of the citizenry, such as consumers or tax-payers.[136] Overall, the result is probably an improvement of the representativeness of the democratic process.

5.2.3 Negative effects of globalization

Globalization undermines the operation of national democracy in various ways. First, the *reduced capacity of nation States to tackle and solve political problems* poses a democratic problem. As a result of the transboundary character of many pressing issues (and due to financial constraints and information deficiencies), States have been forced to delegate public tasks to non-State, supra-State and international actors. In terms of democracy, this general loss of effectiveness reduces self-determination, or the democratic output. Here we face a kind of indirect decline of democracy.[137]

Second, in the age of global interdependencies, state activities have become further-reaching and more extraterritorial. This means that *political decisions produce externalities* by affecting people across State borders. The classic example is the utilization of nuclear power. The installation of a nuclear weapon system, the construction of a nuclear power plant and the performance of nuclear tests may crucially affect persons residing in neighbouring States. Other decisions such as tax reductions or the raising of environmental standards give rise to similar transnational effects. The democratic difficulty lies in the fact that the affected individuals have not elected the decision-makers and can in no way control them.

---

[134] This explanation of protectionism draws on the interest group theory of Mancur Olson, *Die Logik des kollektiven Handelns* (Tübingen: Mohr Siebeck, 2004/1968). For a description, critique, and empirical confirmation of the theory see Elmar Rieger and Stephan Leibfried, *Limits to Globalization* (Cambridge: Polity Press, 2003) 61–62. However, this assertion is highly contested on empirical grounds. Cf Peter J Katzenstein, *Small States in World Markets. Industrial Policy in Europe* (Ithaca/London: Cornell UP, 1985); Peter J Katzenstein, 'Small States and Small States Revisited' (2003) 8 New Political Economy 9–30.

[135] Ernst Ulrich Petersmann, 'The Transformation of the World Trading System' (2004) 6 EJIL 161, 178–82; Peter Tobias Stoll, 'Freihandel und Verfassung. Einzelstaatliche Gewährleistungen und die konstitutionelle Funktion der Welthandelsordnung' (1997) 57 ZaöRV 113–14; Kal Raustiala, 'Rethinking the Sovereignty Debate in International Economic Law' (2003) 6 JIEL 841, 863–65.

[136] However, consumers in states with a high standard of protection (relating, eg to genetically engineered food, ecologically safe production of goods, etc.) are also oriented towards protectionism.

[137] Michael J Sandel, *Democracy's Discontent: America in Search of a Public Philosophy* (Cambridge, Mass: Belknap Press of Harvard UP, 1996) 202.

A further structural change to democracy results from the increased influence of experts ('*technocracy*').[138] Because of the complexity and the technicalities of events which must be regulated, supervized, or merely taken into account by governments, their political options are reduced. Elected politicians may still take decisions, but technical experts define the options. The traditional role of politicians and political parties is thereby partly taken over by unelected experts. Democratic rule in a traditional sense can no longer be sustained under these conditions.

Third, parliamentarism is undermined[139] by *new means of individual communication and obtaining information* (email and the Internet). The internet offers citizens new possibilities of 'voice' (eg spontaneous protest and boycotts organized via mailing lists) and 'exit' (eg tax evasion), and thereby new possibilities for persuading the governing élite to respond to their demands. Citizens are less dependent on mediation and intervention by parliament.

Fourth, deals are negotiated between government institutions (eg between regions in neighbouring States), between government and civil society actors, or between political parties ('*negotiated democracy*').[140] The negotiating State affects democratic structures in various respects. As far as non-State decision-makers are involved, they are not politically and constitutionally responsible at all. On the government side, the engagements are undertaken by the executive. The predominance of the executive branch implies less democracy, because governments are not always directly elected as parliaments are. When the executive actors agree to reject regulation, the national parliament is bypassed entirely. When a deal is incorporated into formal law, the role of parliament is more or less an acclamatory one. Pessimist observers might view this process as an undermining of democracy. A more optimist assessment is that parliamentary democracies are being transformed in the direction of deliberative negotiation democracy.[141]

A fifth aspect is the *internationalization of majoritarian law-making*. The international institutions are so far away from the citizens that the idea of a democratic mandate or entrustment via the member States' governments is rather fictitious. General and binding rules drawn up by international institutions cause democratic problems if they are brought in by majority vote, such as (under limited conditions) in the Council of Ministers of the EU. A member State, whose representatives have been overruled, has not consented to that particular decision. It is of little relevance that democratic States base the transfer of sovereign power to international or supranational organizations on a decision taken by the national legislator. The member States' approval of the founding treaty of the international

---

[138] Gottfried Rickert, *Technokratie und Demokratie* (Frankfurt a.M.: Peter Lang, 1991); Frank Fischer, *Technocracy and the Politics of Expertise* (Newbury Park, Cal.: Sage Publications, 1990).

[139] But see for a more optimisitic account of parliamentarism Armin von Bogdandy, 'Parlamentarismus in Europa: eine Verfalls- oder Erfolgsgeschichte?' (2005) 130 Archiv des öffentlichen Rechts 445–64.   [140] Arthur Benz, *Kooperative Verwaltung* (Baden-Baden: Nomos, 1994).

[141] Cf Klaus Armingeon, 'The Effects of Negotiation Democracy. A Comparative Analysis' (2002) 41 European Journal of Political Research 81–105.

organization concerned may lie in the distant past and be too general a blanket-permission to constitute a meaningful approval of concrete decisions taken within the organization, especially if that organization has evolved and expanded dynamically.

Obviously, the democratic ideal does not allow a self-induced complete release of control over international organizations by States, because this would destroy the democratic right to self-determination of future generations.[142] However, the right to recall in the form of the right to withdraw from international organizations, is in most cases illusory, because complex interdependence counsels against ever exercising it. This option is therefore no real democratic safeguard.

Nonstate entities, such as transnational NGOs and transnational enterprises which increasingly act as co-law-makers, do not enjoy any democratic mandate. On the other hand, such entities, especially NGOs, provide information, participate in the public discourse and create and constitute a democratic public. However, it is doubtful whether such informal deliberation, in which the influence of interest groups is uneven, can substitute constitutional, formal democratic procedures.

Sixth, a consequence of globalization is the growing *intransparency and nonpublicity* of regulation, adjudication, and enforcement at all levels of governance. To give but one example, important food standards are set by the Codex Alimentarius Commission,[143] which is a sub-entity of the Food and Agriculture Organization of the United Nations (FAO) and the World Health Organization (WHO), by way of simple majority decision taken in secret vote and behind closed doors.[144] Such intransparent law making affects not only the rule of law, but also the democratic principle: only if governance is public, can civil society, which is an important democratic actor, especially in a framework of deliberative democracy, cushion functional deficiencies of parliaments.

5.2.4 Reactions of domestic constitutional actors

The democratic deficiencies resulting from globalization call for remedial action. We will take a very selective look at the most relevant legal procedure in this context, namely the conclusion of international treaties. Other strategies aimed at improving deliberation, representation, and democratic oversight will not be further discussed here, as they raise numerous and not genuinely legal questions.

Because in a democratic state all law must have a democratic basis, international (treaty) law is acceptable as a part of the domestic legal order only if it is democratically justified. Therefore, democratic constitutions traditionally provide for some kind of parliamentary participation in the conclusion of international treaties. Parliaments may be involved before the international act of ratification, such as in

---

[142] Cf Karl Popper, *Die offene Gesellschaft und ihre Feinde* (Tübingen: Mohr UTB, 1945/1980) 173.

[143] Members of the Commission are representatives of the member States of FAO and WHO; NGOs have observer status <http://www.codexalimentarius.net> (accessed 16 January 2006).

[144] Meinhard Hilf and Stefan Oeter, *WTO-Recht* (Baden-Baden: Nomos, 2004) 369.

Switzerland. There, the Federal Assembly must empower the Government (the Federal Council) to ratify international treaties (Art 166, s 2 of the Swiss Constitution (BV)). In many constitutional systems (notably the more 'dualist' ones), parliamentary approval functions as the decisive constitutional act which incorporates the international treaty into the domestic order. This is the case in the United Kingdom and in Germany.[145]

However, the more important international regulation becomes in terms of quantity and quality, the less convincing the traditional predominant role of the national executives becomes in the process of negotiating and adopting international treaties. The executive branch in most democratic States is not directly elected by the people. Under conditions of global governance, a proper democratic foundation of international treaties appears to require *extended parliamentary participation* in the negotiation and conclusion of a treaty.[146]

It therefore makes sense that the pending British Constitutional reform bill seeks to endorse the British parliament's authority for treaty-making and for deciding on the State's participation in armed conflict.[147] Notably the power to declare war has been, until now, a royal prerogative which eclipsed parliamentary participation. The new reform bill will erase this prerogative. In Germany too, the procedure for parliamentary approval of military activity abroad has recently been enshrined in a formal federal law.[148]

In the same vein, those constitutional systems which comprise elements of direct democracy, such as Switzerland or France, would be well advised to broaden the possibilities for direct participation of the citizens with regard to global governance. This has become increasingly important as national parliaments have been, as we have seen, generally weakened by a variety of factors more or less linked to globalization. In Switzerland, the citizens' referendum with regard to international treaties has recently been revised. The range of international treaties subject to a popular vote on request of a certain number of citizens has been expanded.[149] In addition, the 'package referendum' has been created. If an international treaty requires implementation by national laws or even by constitutional amendment, parliament can combine the necessary parliamentary approval of the treaty with an act of approval to the implementing legislation.[150] The consequence is that an optional or even compulsory popular referendum on an international treaty relates

---

[145] For Germany see Art 59, s 2 of the Basic Law (*Grundgesetz, GG*).

[146] Joanna Harrington, 'Scrutiny and Approval: The Role for Westminster-style Parliaments in Treaty-Making' (2006) 55 International and Comparative Law Quarterly 121–60, concluding that 'in the increasing interdependence of our globalized world' parliaments should be integrated into the process *prior* to the conclusion of a treaty (158–59).

[147] The Constitutional Reform (Prerogative Powers and Civil Service etc), Bill Sched 1 (parliamentary authority for treaties and war etc.), as brought from the House of Lords on 25 July 2006.

[148] *Gesetz über die parlamentarische Beteiligung bei der Entscheidung über den Einsatz bewaffneter Streitkräfte im Ausland* of 18 March 2005, BGBl. I 2005, 775.

[149] Art 141(2)(d) BV, in force since 1 August 2003.

[150] Art 141(a) BV, in force since 1 August 2003.

to the entire package (treaty plus implementing legislation). The purpose of the package referendum is to improve the predictability of Swiss foreign politics and to avoid contradictory decisions such as when the approval of a treaty is followed by a defeat of the implementing legislation in a referendum.[151]

As we have seen with regard to the rule of law, it looks as if the hollowing out of domestic democracy can hardly be counteracted by reforms on the national level alone. Notably, the strengthening of the rights of domestic parliaments in governmental decision-making in foreign affairs is necessary, but not sufficient to safeguard democracy. This insight leads to the quest for a compensatory *democratization of global governance*: 'Democracy within a nation-state requires democracy within a network of intersecting international forces and relations. This is the meaning of democratization today.'[152] This highly complex issue will not be dealt with in this chapter. Suffice it to say that reform proposals to that end are discussed within the two most important global institutions, namely the UN[153] and the WTO.[154] Also, the most integrated regional organization, the EC/EU is being democratized slowly but steadily.

Notably, the *transparency* of global and European governance has been improved. The Resolution of the UN General Assembly on the 2005 World Summit Outcome asks for more transparency of the work of all bodies of the UN.[155] However, the valuable suggestion that the permanent members of the UN Security Council be obliged to give reasons for a veto has so far not been implemented.[156] On the other hand, the WTO dispute settlement procedure has been opened to the public.[157]

---

[151] Message of the federal government (*Botschaft des Bundesrates zur Volksrechtereform*), Bundesblatt (BBl) 2001, 6080, 6092.

[152] This was the quest formulated 15 years ago by a pioneering scholar. David Held, 'Democracy, the Nation-state and the Global System' in David Held (ed), *Political Theory Today* (Cambridge: Polity Press, 1991) 232.

[153] *We the Peoples: Civil Society, the United Nations and Global Governance: Report of the Panel of Eminent Persons on United Nations—Civil Society Relations* (June 2004), UN Doc. A/58/817, <http://www.un-ngls.org/UNreform.htm> (accessed 16 January 2006).

[154] Robert Housman, 'Democratizing International Trade Decision-Making' (1994) 27 Cornell International Law Journal 699–747; Markus Krajewski, 'Democratic Legitimacy and Constitutional Perspectives of WTO Law' (2001) 35 Journal of World Trade 167–86; Erika Mann, 'Parliamentary Dimensions in the WTO—More than Just a Vision?' (2004) 7 JIEL 659–65; James Bacchus, 'A Few Thoughts on Legitimacy, Democracy and the WTO' (2004) 7 JIEL 667–73.

[155] UN Doc. A/RES/60/1 of 24 October 2005, Chapter V on 'Strengthening the United Nations', paras 153, 154, 160 and 161.

[156] Draft General Assembly Resolution, circulated by Costa Rica, Jordan, Liechtenstein, Singapore and Switzerland of 17 March 2006, UN Doc A/60/L.49, 'Improving the Working Methods of the Security Council', para. 13: 'A permanent member using its veto should explain the reason for doing so at the time the relevant resolution is rejected in the Council and a copy of the explanation should be circulated as a Security Council document to all members of the organization.' The proposed GA Resolution was not adopted. Although the Note of the President of the Security Council of 19 July 2006, UN Doc S/2006/507, touched upon several issues contained in the draft, it did not endorse the idea of making the veto more transparent.

[157] In September 2005, the first public panel proceeding took place. See WTO: 2005 News Items of 12 September 2005. <http://www.wto.org> (accessed 16 January 2006).

Likewise, legislation of the Council of Ministers of the EU has been public since 2002.[158]

5.3 Globalization of solidarity and welfare

5.3.1 Globalization as a threat to the welfare State

The third basic constitutional principle is *solidarity* or *welfare*. Social elements are, to varying degrees, a stable element of European constitutionalism.[159] The core tasks of a social State are the creation of an acceptable social balance among individuals, the guarantee of social security, the creation and preservation of social peace, and the increase and spread of the wealth among citizens and inhabitants.

It is often asserted that the required potential for solidarity for distributional politics exists only within individual nations. From that perspective, a social polity is per definition national. In this chapter we therefore concentrate on social elements beyond actual redistribution policies. Globalization and European harmonization affect these social elements and are frequently regarded as a threat to social achievements.[160]

Rieger and Leibfried have convincingly demonstrated that the social State and free trade as the core of economic globalization are not in opposition to one another. Trade policy and social policy are functionally equivalent to the extent that both strive to secure an income for workers that is independent of fluctuations which are subject to market conditions.[161] Social policy and a liberal foreign trade policy are complementary means to increase wealth.[162]

---

[158] Public deliberations under Arts 7–8 of the rules of procedure of the Council, decision of the Council 2002/682/EG, Euratom of 22 July 2002 (OJ 2002 L 230/7); publication of the results of votes according to Art 207(3), sentence 3 TEC and Art 9 of the Rules.

[159] Chapter IV, 'Solidarity' of the European Charter on Fundamental Rights of 7 December 2000 (OJ C 364/1); for the Council of Europe the European Social Charter of 1961 (ETS No 35; revised in 1996, ETS No 163). For an explicit provision in a State constitution see Art 20(1) of the German Basic Law on the 'social State'. On welfare States in Europe in a comparative perspective see Rainer Hofmann and others (eds), *Armut und Verfassung: Sozialstaatlichkeit im europäischen Vergleich* (Wien: Verlag Österreich, 1998); in a political science perspective Gösta Esping-Andersen, 'After the Golden Age? Welfare State Dilemmas in a Global Economy' and 'Conclusions' in Gösta Esping-Andersen (ed), *Welfare States in Transition. National Adaptations in Global Economies* (London: Sage, 1996) 1–31, 256–67; on the historical evolution of the welfare State in North America and Europe the contributions in Peter Flora and Arnold J Heidenheimer (eds), *The Development of Welfare States in Europe and America* (New Brunswick, NJ: Transaction Books, 1981) 17–121.

[160] Eyal Benvenisti and Georg Nolte (eds), *The Welfare State, Globalization, and International Law* (Berlin: Springer, 2003); Rieger and Leibfried (n 134 above); Scholte (n 4 above) 218–60. On how EU law forces member States to reorganize their welfare States see Gareth Davies, 'The Process and Side-Effects of Harmonisation of European Welfare States' (Jean Monnet Working Paper MWP No 02/06). Davies concludes that the harmonization of welfare services is potentially further reaching than often realized, and difficult to reverse, and that this has probably greater implications for national identity and social structure than for welfare itself.   [161] Rieger and Leibfried (n 134 above) 66.

[162] Ibid, 133.

However, the critics of globalization address first and foremost the social consequences.[163] Economic globalization and the selective enforcement of free trade by
the rich states that close up their own markets, especially against trade in textiles
and agricultural products, is said to broaden the welfare gap between the rich and
poor countries.[164] It is also argued that transnational enterprises enrich themselves unduly, for example by exploitation of cheap labour or child labour.

In fact, the mobility of capital holders has resulted in States competing to have
production facilities sited on their territory. It is plausible to assume that governmental wooing of national and foreign investors incites States to lower taxes
(thus reducing the means which could finance, among other things, social projects) and labour standards which render production more costly. Against this
background, critics of globalization assert that it has led to a reduction of governmental social spending, salaries, and safety standards in the rich countries (a
phenomenon known as the 'race to the bottom').[165] Empirical investigations do
not entirely confirm these assertions but do show that antagonistic tendencies
also exist. Globalization apparently has both negative and positive consequences
for the social State, but the effects are complex and it is difficult to establish
causalities.[166]

5.3.2 Reactions of domestic constitutional actors

In this ambivalent situation, diverse and even contrary political and legal action is
taken by the States, and various conflicting claims are made in different academic
and political quarters. Electors demand the mitigation of the adverse effects of globalization. As a consequence, and somewhat paradoxically, the political incentive
to maintain or even increase the level of social spending is growing, although the

---

[163] The theoretical and political background of the globalization critique ranges from anti-capitalism,
anti-imperialism, anti-colonialism, anti-Americanism to the environmentalist camp or communi-
tarism. Eg, Hans-Peter Martin and Harald Schumann, *Die Globalisierungsfalle: Der Angriff auf
Demokratie und Wohlstand* (Reinbeck bei Hamburg: Rowohl, 1996) on globalization as an 'attack on
democracy and wealth'; John Gray, *False Dawn: The Delusions of Global Capitalism* (London: Granta
Books, 1998); Oxfam, *Rigged Rules and Double Standards: Trade, Globalization and the Fight Against
Poverty* <http://www.maketradefair.com/assets/english/report_english.pdf> (accessed 16 January 2006);
Altvater and Mannkopf (n 130 above). On the *positive* effects of globalization in social, economic and
political respects the special counsellor of the UN on globalization of 2001, Bhagwati (n 131 above).

[164] Oxfam, *Rigged Rules and Double Standards: Trade, Globalization and the Fight Against Poverty*
<http://www.maketradefair.com/assets/english/report_english.pdf> (accessed 16 January 2006).

[165] Eg Ramesh Mishra, *Globalization and the Welfare State* (London: Edward Elgar, 1999). But see
Tomas Larsson, *The Race to the Top: The Real Story of Globalization* (Washington DC: Cato Institute,
2001).

[166] For a nuanced explanation of the antagonist phenomena of welfare retrenchment and the
expansion of welfare spending, Alexander Hicks and Christopher Zorn, 'Economic Globalization, the
Macro Economy, and Reversals of Welfare: Expansion in Affluent Democracies, 1978–94' (2005) 59
International Organization 631–62. See also Bhagwati (n 131 above) 67, 71–72, 98–102, and 122–34
refuting the assertions of an increase of the global welfare gap, the increase of child labour, the lowering
of labour protection standards and the salaries due to globalization.

capacity of States to maintain that spending is reduced by globalization.[167] So, depending on their strength, the relevant constitutional actors of the welfare State (including governments, political parties, and unions) can neutralize the pressures of globalization by political action.[168] This institutional factor has prevented a significant dismantling of the social State by globalization (at least in coordinated market economies).[169] In fact, the tax yield of the OECD[170] States has not declined in the last 30 years, but rather has risen and burdens mainly the middle income groups ('race to the middle').[171]

Moreover, union activism seeking to protect the domestic labour force from the removal of their jobs to workers at competing cheaper sites of production in other nations might indeed contribute to a rise in salaries and labour standards. The emergence of welfare States outside Europe would moderate the pressure of globalization.[172]

Constitutional lawyers have claimed that the transitional difficulties attributable to globalization should be mitigated by the introduction of actionable social rights in state constitutions.[173] However, given the mobility of production factors, it seems obvious that social standards can no longer be fully guaranteed through national (constitutional) provisions. It therefore seems logical to augment the international labour and social standards and to extend their regional scope in order to prevent salary and social dumping and to level the playing field for transnational enterprises.[174] On the other hand, the competitive advantage of the poorer countries is taken away by precisely such levelling, which might thereby hamper potential economic progress. We may conclude that despite serious pressure towards globalization, the European social State has so far been surprisingly resistant,[175] but that its continued functioning can in the long run not be upheld without serious modifications.

---

[167] Linda Weiss, 'Is the State Being "Transformed" by Globalisation?' in Linda Weiss (ed), *States in the Global Economy. Bringing Democratic Institutions Back in* (Cambridge: CUP, 2003) 15; Bhagwati (n 131 above) 99.

[168] Duane Swank, 'Withering Welfare? Globalisation, Political Economic Institutions, and Contemporary Welfare States' in Weiss, *States in the Global Economy* (n 167 above) 58; Rieger and Leibfried (n 134 above) 51.

[169] Swank in Weiss (n 168 above) and Esping-Andersen (n 159 above) esp. 5–6, 16, who both explain the resistance mainly by the existence of institutions and their defence of vested privileges.

[170] Organisation for Economic Cooperation and Development.

[171] Linda Weiss, 'Introduction' in Weiss, *States in the Global Economy* (n 167 above) 294–95 with further references.

[172] Stein Kuhnle, 'European Welfare Lessons of the 1990s' in Stein Kuhnle (ed), *The Survival of the European Welfare State* (London: Routledge, 2000) 236.

[173] Cottier and Wüger (n 21 above) 258.

[174] See the quest for a 'global social policy' by Mishra (n 165 above) 111–32.

[175] Esping-Andersen (n 159 above) 265: '[T]he welfare state is the child of politics and so, also will be its future. It is, indeed, when we bring in the political dimension that we are most inclined to conclude that the welfare state is here to stay'. Optimistic assessment also by Kuhnle (n 172 above).

5.4 Globalization of the territorial organization

5.4.1 Constitutional convergence and revival of federalism

The final substantive principle of state constitutions touched by globalization is the organization of territory. Constitutional lawyers use to classify nation States into 'unitary' and 'federal' States. In reality however, 'federal' and 'unitary' are not precise definitions, but rather convenient points on a political spectrum ranging from loose associations of countries for particular purposes to one-government States.[176]

The process of globalization has specifically challenged the *centralized* nation State:[177] Important European unitary States such as the United Kingdom and France have recently been moving along the spectrum of unitary to federal by devolution (in the UK substantially since 1998) and '*décentralisation*' (important progress by revision of the French Constitution in 2005). So here, as with regard to other constitutional principles, we witness some transnational convergence.

The emergence of global and European governance has revitalized the debate on the meaning and functions of federalism as a form of political and geographical order both within and, crucially, even *beyond* State confines.[178] The underlying issue of this 'revival of federalism'[179] is that under conditions of globalization, the traditional nation State has turned out to be too small to deal with certain problems which are genuinely global (eg climate change, infectious diseases, migration, and terrorism) and which require an international response. On the other hand, the nation State appears too large to handle many other issues which call for local solutions, to satisfy the psychological needs of individuals for collective affiliation, and to provide a sense of belonging which is threatened by the globalization and standardization of cultures and by the extinction of traditions. We will now look more closely at federal arrangements affected by globalization.

5.4.2 Features of federalist polities subject to globalization

It is generally acknowledged that a federal polity is characterized by two structural features: First, competencies in certain issue-areas, such as policing or culture, are

---

[176] John Alder, *Constitutional and Administrative Law* (5th edn, London: Palgave, Macmillan, 2005) 102.

[177] Sergio Fabbrini, 'The Puzzle of the Compound Republic. The US, EU and the Implications for Federalization' in Sergio Fabbrini (ed), *Nation, Federalism, and Democracy* (Bologna: Editrice ompositri, 2001) 55, 57.

[178] Jost Delbrück, 'Transnational Federalism: Problems and Prospects of Allocating Public Authority Beyond the State' (2004) 11 Indiana Journal of Global Legal Studies 31–55; Tanja Börzel, Föderative Staaten in einer entgrenzten Welt: Regionaler Standortwettbewerb oder gemeinsames Regieren jenseits des Nationalstaates?' in Arthur Benz/Gerhard Lehmbruch (eds), *Föderalismus: Analysen in entwicklungsgeschichtlicher und vergleichender Perspektive*, 42 Politische Vierteljahresschrift Sonderheft (32/2001), 363–88 on the 'revitalization' of territorial politics, partly in form of governance beyond the nation State (at 382).   [179] Tushnet, *The New Constitutional Order* (n 1 above) 142.

conferred upon sub-entities (eg States, provinces, *Kantone, Länder*), so that those sub-units can, within these reserved spheres, exercise their powers and take decisions in an autonomous fashion. Second, the sub-entities are granted constitutional rights to participate in decision-making on the superior level of government (eg through a second parliamentary chamber and/or through special procedures for the approval of federal laws). Both features of federalist political organization are potentially influenced by regional and global integration (see notably the discussion on the autonomy of sub-units below, section 5.4.3).

Other traditional aspects of federalism (and the concept as such) are also touched upon and affected by globalization and Europeanization. This begins with the traditional categorical distinction between the (constitution-based, national, dense) federation and the (treaty-based, international, loose) confederation. The creation of hybrid transnational polities, notably the EU, has arguably overcome that dichotomy. A related classic theme of federalism is the seat of sovereignty within federalist States. The theoretical debate has been invigorated by new thinking on the modification of sovereignty in the course of European and global integration. New and not-so-new concepts such as 'pooled', 'fused', or 'divided' sovereignty have repercussions on the understanding of sovereignty in a federal State.

Another question is whether global governance has so far affected the federalist institutions and arrangements, such as the voting-procedures in two-chamber parliaments. Empirical analyses suggest that most federations have adapted to the pressures of global and regional integration change without major transformations to their institutions.[180]

Finally, globalization might modify political identities in federal societies. As citizens of federations already enjoy the dual citizenship of the federation and the sub-units, one might expect the development of transnational identities. This does indeed seem to be the case in Europe, where EU-citizenship matters (without however repressing the national and regional identities). With regard to other regions, however, empirical research shows that transnational identities are 'weak to non-existent' between federations and their global and regional partners.[181] Overall, global and regional integration do not seem to foster new transnational identities.

5.4.3 Centralizing and decentralizing effects of globalization

Globalization risks *upsetting the distribution of competencies* among the federal government and the sub-units.[182] In this regard, however, two antagonistic trends are

---

[180] Harvey Lazar and others, 'Divergent Trajectories: The Impact of Global and Regional Integration on Federal Systems' in Lazar and others (eds), *The Impact of Global and Regional Integration on Federal Systems: A Comparative Analysis* (Montreal: McGill's UP, Montreal 2003) 1–2 and 11–18.

[181] Ibid, 1–2 and 18–22, quote at 18.

[182] In Cottier and Wüger (n 21 above) 266–67, the authors ask whether the rigid separation of competencies of federation and sub units still makes sense under the conditions of internationalization. They assume that in the future many issues will be regulated jointly by both levels of government under international precepts.

visible. On the one hand, global integration may, somewhat paradoxically, *empower constituent sub-units*.[183] Even 'localities have become veritable partners in the emerging global legal order, where states still hold sway but where nonstate actors become increasingly influential'.[184]

Generally speaking, globalization facilitates increased regional cooperation (agreements between federal sub units), and also cooperation across State boundaries.[185] As a consequence, constituent units may find that the internationalization of their constitutional responsibilities provides a de facto basis whereby they enter the world of international diplomacy. Sub-units may thereby effectively encroach on what had previously been a national government's monopoly or near-monopoly in the realm of international relations.[186] Further 'downward pulls' may be exercised notably by economic integration. International regulatory and fiscal competition might call for more decentralization within nation states to make them more efficient.[187] Improved access to global markets and trade across national boundaries due to the global trade regime and international economic integration reduces the dependence of States, provinces, and *Länder* on federation-wide domestic markets. In consequence, smaller governing units gain economic autonomy in relation to their federal government and become more viable in economic terms.[188]

Finally, social pressure unleashed by globalization increases the demand for social legitimacy. Opportunities for political participation of citizens on the regional level may be one means to satisfy these demands.[189] This suggests that the political powers of sub-units could be strengthened as a remedy against a possible delegitimization induced by globalization.[190]

On the other hand, global and European integration *undermines the competencies of sub-units* and therefore also their autonomy. This 'upward pull' of globalization seems inevitable because international affairs in all federal systems, including treaty-making powers, are more or less exclusively conferred to the federal actors. Global governance means cooperation within international organizations, treaties,

---

[183] 'The general point . . . is that governing units smaller than nations can take on larger roles even as the nation's power evaporates. One might say, however, that the American states might be gaining more and more power over less and less important subjects'. Tushnet, *The New Constitutional Order* (n 1 above) 142.

[184] Yishai Blank, 'Localism in the New Global Order' (2006) 47 Harvard ILJ 263–81, 281.

[185] For example, the regional and cohesion politics of the EU since the 1990s provide money for concrete projects of regional cooperation. Markus Kotzur, *Grenznachbarschaftliche Zusammenarbeit in Europa* (Berlin: Duncker & Humblot, 2004).   [186] Lazar and others, (n 180 above) 4.

[187] Cf Alfed C Aman, 'Globalization and Federalism: Governance at the Domestic Level' in Aseem Prakash and Jeffrey A Hart (eds), *Coping with Globalization* (London: Routledge, 2000) 94–114.   [188] Lazar and others (n 180 above) 4.

[189] Thomas Fleiner, 'Kantone und Globalisierung' in Thomas Cottier and Alexandra Caplazi (eds), *Die Kantone im Integrationsprozess* (Bern: Stämpfli, 2000) 56–57.

[190] Cf Egypt Human Development Report 2004: Choosing Dezentralization for Good Governance. Institute of National Planning, Egypt, in technical cooperation with the UNDP. <http://www.undp.org.eg/publications/HDP-2004-E%20.pdf> (accessed on 22 January 2007).

and other global regimes. This affects classes of issues which were previously, from a purely internal perspective, wholly or mainly within the purview of the sub-entities.[191] A case in point is EUROPOL police cooperation. The consequence is that, through the avenue of treaty powers, the sub-entities' autonomous powers are undermined by the transfer of powers to the international level. In order to avoid this seemingly inevitable erosion of State powers, it has occasionally been proposed that the central government's treaty powers be interpreted as merely collateral in the sense that they may not be an independent source of national authority. Under such a construction, the federal agents would be allowed to conclude international treaties only on the basis of some other constitutional competence. This reading would however render obsolete the very constitutional provisions which confer the power to conduct foreign affairs to the federation and it has therefore remained a purely academic suggestion.

Particular problems in this context are created by non self-executing treaties which require further implementation by domestic laws. If the federal government enters into international engagements in a subject area in which the sub-entities are normally competent, the question arises which level of government may enact the necessary implementing legislation and whether federal government may direct or compel the sub-entities to legislate. This problem has led treaty makers to add 'federalist' understandings or even reservations to international agreements.[192] The alternative, for some federal States, is to abstain from participation in international regimes which might cause implementation difficulties due to internal federalism.[193]

An example of centralizing effects produced by an international agreement was provided in recent litigation arising from the Vienna Convention on Consular Relations. This treaty obliges the Contracting Parties to allow foreign detainees to contact a consular officer of their home State and also requires that detainees are informed about their rights. In some federal States, according to the federalist distribution of competencies, these international obligations can be fulfilled only

---

[191] Lazar and others (n 180 above) 4.

[192] Eg the US Senate Resolution of Advice and Consent to Ratification of the International Covenant on Civil and Political Rights of 2 April 1992, declaring '[t]hat the United States understands that this Covenant shall be implemented by the Federal Government to the extent that it exercises legislative and judicial jurisdiction over the matters covered therein, and otherwise by the state and local governments; to the extent that state and local governments exercise jurisdiction over such matters, the Federal Government shall take measures appropriate to the Federal system to the end that the competent authorities of the state or local governments may take appropriate measures for the fulfillment of the Covenant'. 102 Cong Rec, S4781 at S483, III (5), available at <http://thomas.loc.gov/>. Switzerland deposited the following reservation to the ICCPR, concerning the guarantee of secret ballot in Art 25, para (b): 'The present provision shall be applied without prejudice to the cantonal and communal laws, which provide for or permit elections within assemblies to be held by a means other than secret ballot.'

[193] Mark Tushnet considers 'it unlikely that the United States will enter into treaties or international agreements raising serious federalism questions'. Tushnet, *The New Constitutional Order* (n 1 above) 164.

by sub-State police officials. This situation caused a problem in the *Breard* and *LaGrand* cases concerning a Paraguayan viz. two German death row candidates incarcerated in Virginia and Arizona, respectively. Under Article 27 of the Vienna Convention on the Law of Treaties, a State party may not invoke the provisions of its internal law as justification for its failure to perform a treaty.[194] Unsurprisingly, the International Court of Justice (ICJ) did not accept any federalist 'excuse' for the United States' nonfulfilment of the various obligations at issue in the cases.[195] Most importantly, the ICJ ordered the US national government 'to take all measures at its disposal' to ensure the suspension of the execution of the convicts, although the decision about the execution fell in the exclusive competence of the states Virginia and Arizona. Thereby, an international court at least indirectly interfered with the federalist balance within a nation State.

The diagnosis of the erosion of the first federalist feature, ie the competency reserves of the constituent units, has motivated the quest to strengthen the participation of sub-entities in decision-making on the federal level (and thereby indirectly on the international plane), or even directly in the international realm. The idea behind this is that improved participation might compensate for the loss of autonomy and shared rule might make up for the loss of self-rule.[196] Such direct or indirect participation of the sub-units in international governance may be realized by means of special committees,[197] liaison offices, observers, better and swifter information transfer, by granting a right to the relevant sub-entities to be informed and/or heard,[198] by early warning mechanisms, or even enhanced powers of the second chamber of parliament. Both Switzerland and Germany have enacted legislation to this effect.[199]

---

[194] However, the federal distribution of competencies is normally fixed in the State constitution itself. Given the fact that most domestic constitutions claim superiority over 'ordinary' international law, it might be argued that Art 27 VCLT does not relate to domestic constitutional precepts, such as federalism, which might bar the fulfilment of an international obligation.

[195] ICJ, *Case Concerning the Vienna Convention on Consular Relations—Request for Provisional Measures (Paraguay v the USA)*, ICJ Reports (1998) 248 ('*Breard*-case'); ICJ, *LaGrand Case (Germany v USA)*, ICJ Reports (2001) 466, paras 67, 95, 115.

[196] Martin Meißner, *Die Bundesländer und die Europäischen Gemeinschaften: Eine Garantie des Bundesstaatsprinzips unter Berücksichtigung der Kompetenzkompensation und der Regelung des Art. 23 GG n.F.* (Baden-Baden: Nomos, 1996); Doris König, *Die Übertragung von Hoheitsrechten im Rahmen des europäischen Integrationsprozesses* (Berlin: Duncker & Humblot, 2000) 523 et seq.

[197] Arts 263–65 TEC on the Committee of the Regions.

[198] Eg the new Swiss law on the *Vernehmlassungsverfahren*, which regulates a particular phase of the legislative procedure in which all segments of civil society can submit their views on a federal bill. In order to give the cantons a say in the shaping of foreign policy, a formalized hearing is compulsory with regard to international treaties which affect 'essential interests of the cantons'. Art 3(1)(c) of the *Bundesgesetz über das Vernehmlassungsverfahren* of 18 March 2005 (SR 172.061).

[199] Switzerland, *Bundesgesetz über die Mitwirkung der Kantone an der Aussenpolitik des Bundes* of 22 December 1999 (SR 138.1) and Art. 3 *Vernehmlassungsverfahren* of 18 March 2005 (SR 172.061). For Germany see the revised Art. 23 GG (adopted in 1992) and the *Gesetz über die Zusammenarbeit von Bund und Ländern in Angelegenheiten der Europäischen Union* of 12 March

This shift from self-rule to shared rule might preserve federalism, albeit in a different form. It is however, doubtful whether the new type of 'participatory federalism' can really compensate for the loss of autonomy for constituent units.[200]

However, comparative analysis of the impact of global and regional integration on federal systems has demonstrated that the overall loss of autonomy of sub-units in different federal States is not as great as the complaints of the German *Länder* vis-à-vis European integration might suggest.[201] The impact of global and regional integration on federal systems is *not unidirectional*. Rather, case studies show that similar change pressures produce divergent outcomes in different federations. Put differently, globalization supports greater centralization in some federations, but enhanced decentralization in others. The common external effects are obviously mediated by the uniqueness of each political entity's set-up and context. In no case has global and regional integration reversed the pre-existing centralization or decentralization processes within a federation.[202]

To conclude, federal states, notably Germany, appear to experience an 'hourglass process' with the powers of the central government simultaneously shifting 'up' (eg to Brussels), *and* 'down', to the *Länder* or provinces.[203] Nevertheless, federal systems have proved to be astonishingly stable notwithstanding the change pressures exerted by the processes of globalization. This stability may be explained by adherence to tradition, path dependency, or by the mutual neutralization of the diverse and antagonist 'upwards' and 'downwards' effects of global integration.[204] Lazar, Telford, and Watts summarize: '[T]o date, at least, the federal systems of governance we have examined have had the flexibility to adapt to international change pressures without undermining the federal bargains that are fundamental to their stability'.[205]

6. The techniques of constitutional adaptation

In this part, I analyse *how* State constitutions adapt to globalization.[206] The constitutional text can be adapted by formal constitutional amendment or informal

1993, BGBl. 1993 I, 313. Christian Schede, *Der Bundesrat und die Europäische Union: Die Beteiligung des Bundesrates nach dem neuen Artikel 23 des Grundgesetzes* (Frankfurt a.M.: Peter Lang, 1994); Michael Paul, *Die Mitwirkung der Bundesländer an der Rechtsetzung der Europäischen Gemeinschaften de lege lata und de lege ferenda* (Frankfurt a.M.: Peter Lang, 1996). Stefan Mayer, *Regionale Europapolitik: Die österreichischen Bundesländer und die europäische Integration* (Wien: Wilhem Braunmüller, 2002).

[200] Note that the 2006 reform of German federalism pursues the inverse strategy of reducing the participation of the German *Länder* in the *Bundesrat* (whose blocking potential had proved to obstruct federal politics) and enlarging the sphere of autonomy of the *Länder*.

[201] On the German griefs, Juliane Kokott, 'Federal States in Federal Europe: The German Länder and Problems of European Integration' (1997) 3 European Public Law 607–34; Rüdiger Gerst, *Föderalismus in Deutschland und Europa: Was bleibt den deutschen Ländern?* (Bamberg: Leibniz-Verlag, 2000).

[202] Harvey Lazar and others (n 180 above) 1–2.

[203] Ibid, 23–24.   [204] Ibid, 7.   [205] Ibid, 2.

[206] A special issue is the adaptation of domestic constitutional law to EU law. National constitutional or supreme courts ruling on the relationship of the State constitution to EU law often make

novel interpretation (the latter process is known as '*Verfassungswandel*', in German constitutional theory).

6.1 Increased reference to international law and international institutions in State constitutions

State constitutions have traditionally included references to foreign affairs and to international law.[207] Classic examples are constitutional clauses on the powers of state organs in foreign affairs, especially with regard to the conclusion of international treaties.[208] However, in recent decades, domestic constitutional provisions relating to international law and international institutions have been significantly refined.[209]

State constitutions nowadays provide for the binding force of international law within the domestic sphere and sometimes explicitly and sweepingly recognize the primacy of international law over domestic law[210]—although primacy over the domestic *constitution* is frequently not accepted, as we have seen (Part 4.4).

Reference is made in many State constitutions to international organizations, especially to the United Nations.[211] State constitutions also contain clauses on the State's accession to international organizations.[212] In the constitutions of EU member States, provision is made for the transfer of sovereign powers to the EU or

general statements on the relation between international law (in general) and the domestic constitution. Such decisions are therefore also mentioned. Specific problems relating solely to the relationship between national constitutional law and EC/EU law are beyond the scope of this paper. On that question see Peters, *Elemente einer Theorie* (n 19 above) 310–24.

[207] Eg Cassese (n 36 above) 475; Sadok Belaid, 'Droit international et droit constitutionnel: Les développements récents' in Rafaa Ben Achour and Slim Laghmani (eds), *Droit international et droits internes: Développements récents* (Paris: Pedone, 1998) 47–79; Franck and Thiruvengadam (n 98 above) 467–518.

[208] Eg Art 2 §2 US Constitution of 17 September 1787; Art 59 German Basic Law of 23 May 1949.

[209] With a view to post-communist Eastern European constitutions, Vereshtin (n 34 above) 29–41.

[210] Art 15(4) of the Russian Constitution of 12 December 1993: 'The commonly recognized principles and norms of the international law and the international treaties of the Russian Federation are a component part of its legal system. If an international treaty of the Russian Federation stipulates other rules than those stipulated by the law, the rules of the international treaty apply.' For similar supremacy clauses in new constitutions of the East (eg in Estonia, Armenia, Kazakhstan, Tadzhikistan, Turkmenistan, Belarus) Vereshtin (n 34 above) 34.

[211] Art 28 of the Algerian Constitution of 19 November 1976, as amended on 28 November 1996: 'Algeria works for the reinforcement of international cooperation and to the development of friendly relations among states, on equal basis, mutual interest and non interference in the internal affairs. It endorses the principles and objectives of the United Nations Charter.'

[212] Random examples: s 20 of the Danish Constitution of 5 June 1953 on the delegation of powers: '(1) Powers vested in the authorities of the Realm under this Constitution Act may, to such extent as shall be provided by Statute, be delegated to international authorities set up by mutual agreement with other states for the promotion of international rules of law and co-operation.' (See for an important Danish Supreme Court judgment interpreting s 20 with a view to the Treaty of Maastricht above n 66).

the pooling of sovereignty within the EU.[213] Most recently, clauses regarding the International Criminal Court (ICC), concerning jurisdiction or surrender to the ICC have been introduced.[214]

Frequently, special clauses enshrine international human rights,[215] give them priority over domestic law[216] or guarantee access to international control mechanisms.[217] These constitutional provisions have not instantaneously led to a satisfactory human rights record in many countries. However, good law which corresponds to international standards is a minimum condition for improvements according to many international actors and voices in civil society.

Numerous factors account for the proliferation of constitutional references to international law. First, the collapse of the socialist bloc a decade ago necessitated the elaboration of entirely new constitutions for former communist countries turning to a liberal rule of law and market economy. In a way that is typical of polities with a totalitarian past; the transformed states are ready (or are urged) to pledge fidelity to international law.[218] Second, regional integration within the EU has progressed and requires constitutional amendments by the member States. In addition, new international institutions with far-reaching powers, such as the ICC, have been created.

Finally, the international community, or at least its most powerful members, have been supervising regime changes and have induced, accompanied, steered, or

Art 24 of the German Basic Law: [International organizations]: '(1) The Federation may by a law transfer sovereign powers to international organizations. (1a) Insofar as the Länder are competent to exercise state powers and to perform state functions, they may, with the consent of the Federal Government, transfer sovereign powers to transfrontier institutions in neighboring regions. (2) With a view to maintaining peace, the Federation may enter into a system of mutual collective security; in doing so it shall consent to such limitations upon its sovereign powers as will bring about and secure a lasting peace in Europe and among the nations of the world. (3) For the settlement of disputes between states, the Federation shall accede to agreements providing for general, comprehensive, and compulsory international arbitration' (accessible via <http://www.bundesregierung.de/en/The-Federal-Government>). Art 136 of the Constitution of Lithuania of 25 October 1992 runs: 'The Republic of Lithuania shall participate in international organizations provided that they do not contradict the interests and independence of the state.'

[213] See references below in text accompanying nn 236 and 237.

[214] Art 53–2 French Constitution (constitutional revision of 8 July 1999); Art 16(2), second sentence, German Basic Law (constitutional revision of 29 November 2000).

[215] Art 17(1) of the Russian Constitution of 12 December 1993 holds: 'The basic rights and liberties in conformity with the commonly recognized principles and norms of the international law are recognized and guaranteed in the Russian Federation and under this Constitution.'

[216] Art 20 of the Constitution of Romania of 8 December 1991; Art 11 of the Slovak Constitution of 1 September 1992; Art 10 of the Constitution of the Czech Republic of 16 December 1992. See above, Part 4.4.4, nn 75–77 for the text of those provisions.

[217] Art 46 of the Russian Constitution of 12 December 1993 holds: '(3) In conformity with the international treaties of the Russian Federation, everyone has the right to turn to interstate organs concerned with the protection of human rights and liberties when all the means of legal protection available within the state have been exhausted.'

[218] Vereshchetin (n 34 above) 29–41, 30 with references to Art 28 of the Greek Constitution (1975); Art 8 of the Portuguese Constitution (1976); Art 96 of the Spanish Constitution (1978), all of them marking the new beginning after the defeat of dictatorship.

even installed new state constitutions,[219] such as the constitutions of Cambodia (1993), Bosnia and Herzegovina (1995),[220] South Africa (1996), East Timor (2002), Afghanistan (2004), Iraq (interim constitution of 2004) or Sri Lanka (ongoing), and Kosovo (ongoing). Daniel Thürer has recently described these processes as 'cosmopolitan constitutional development', and demonstrated how intensely international law conditioned, steered, and modelled those constitutional processes. The resulting state constitutions resemble each other strongly. They are 'chipped off the same block', based on the modern canon of fundamental rights, rule of law, democracy, and separation of powers.[221]

6.2 International law as a stimulus for constitutional reform and horizontal and vertical constitutional convergence

The formal hierarchy between international law and domestic constitutions appears less relevant because of the increasing permeability and convergence of State constitutions. Traditionally, national constitutional principles have been exported to the international level. For example, the national principle of democracy was transferred to the international level where it was transformed and developed further into an international law principle of self-determination.[222] Nowadays, international standards relating to human rights protection, good governance, or even democracy, are frequently incorporated into national constitutions. This has correctly been called an '*intrusion massive des normes et standards externes dans les droits publics internes*'.[223]

Because the origins of those standards frequently lie in domestic constitutional law, the integration of international standards into domestic constitutional law is to some extent the 're-import' of a product which has been modified (sometimes diluted) and which has become more or less universalized in a global discourse. For example, human rights were conceived as legal entitlements 200 years ago on the national level. That conception was transferred to the international level after the Second World War.[224] Today, the idea of legal protection of human rights

---

[219] Typology by Daniel Thürer, 'Kosmopolitische Verfassungsentwicklungen', in Daniel Thürer, *Kosmopolitisches Staatsrecht Vol. 1* (Zürich: Schulthess, 2005) 3–39.

[220] Edin Sarcevic, 'Der völkerrechtliche Vertrag als "Gestaltungsinstrument" der Verfassungsgebung: Das Daytoner Verfassungsexperiment mit Präzedenzwirkung?' (2001) 39 Archiv des Völkerrechts 297–339.   [221] Thürer (n 219 above) 25 (translation by the author).

[222] The link between democracy and the self-determination of a people is manifest eg in the Resolution of the UN General Assembly on the 2005 World Summit Outcome, UN Doc. A/RES/60/1 of 24 October 2005, para 135: 'We reaffirm that democracy is a universal value based on the freely expressed will of the people to determine their own political, economic, social and cultural systems.'

[223] Jean-Bernard Auby, 'Globalisation et droit public' (2002) 14 European Review of Public Law 1219–47, 1232.

[224] Robert Badinter, 'La mondialisation de la protection juridique des droits fondamentaux' in Rémy Cabrillac and others (eds), *Libertés et droits fondamentaux* (11th edn, Paris: Dalloz, 2005) 119–37.

flows back into the constitutional orders of those states which have otherwise not satisfied human rights standards.

This reception of international standards leads to a *'vertical' convergence* of constitutional and international law: in other words a globalization of State constitutions and a constitutionalization of international (or global) law.[225] Simultaneously, a *'horizontal' approximation* of State constitutions takes place. This approximation is promoted by constitutional case law: '[t]he last two decades have seen an unprecedented evolution in international and transnational judicial dialogue, especially around human rights issues'.[226] Quite correctly, scholars have diagnosed a 'heightened convergence in the law in distinct areas, perhaps the most robust being transnational human rights law'.[227] In academia, *constitutional comparison*, a previously remote discipline in which few were interested, has gained popularity. Only under the influence of European integration and globalization has scholarship at large begun to acknowledge its practical usefulness.[228] Increasingly, international (and foreign constitutional) law is becoming an argument in the national constitutional discourse.[229] Anne-Marie Slaughter has called this 'constitutional cross-fertilization'.[230]

An example for cross-fertilization outside the human rights area is the transnational career of the idea of legitimate expectations, which was imported into French administrative law from German law. An even more prominent case in point is the principle of proportionality. Proportionality had been elucidated as a constitutional principle notably in Germany. The German approach arguably influenced the case law of both the European Court of Justice and the European Court of Human Rights. The rulings of those courts have paved the way for the

---

[225] Bryde (n 11 above).

[226] Cherie Booth and Max du Plessis, 'Home Alone? The US Supreme Court and International and Transnational Judicial Learning' (2005) European Human Rights L Rev 127–47, 141.

[227] Ruti Teitel, 'Comparative Constitutional Law in a Global Age' (2004) 117 Harv L Rev 2570, 2593. On legal harmonization in the field of human rights Laurent Scheeck, 'The Relation between the European Courts and Integration through Human Rights' (2005) 65 ZaöRV 837–85; Jörg Paul Müller, 'Koordination des Grundrechtsschutzes in Europa—Einleitungsreferat' (2005) 124 Zeitschrift für Schweizerisches Recht 9–30.

[228] Grewe and Ruiz Fabri (n 97 above) 22–32; Mark Tushnet, 'The Possibilities of Comparative Constitutional Law' (1999) 108 Yale LJ 1225–1305; Norman Dorsen and others, *Comparative Constitutionalism: Cases and Materials* (American Case Book Series, St Paul, Minn., 2003); Guiseppe de Vergottini, *Diritto costituzionale comparato* (6th edn, Padua: Cedam, 2004); Bernd Wieser, *Vergleichendes Verfassungsrecht* (Wien: Springer Verlag, 2005).

[229] Vicki C Jackson, 'Constitutional Comparisons: Convergence, Resistance, Engagement', (2005) 119 Harv L Rev 109–28; Christian Walter, 'Dezentrale Konstitutionalisierung durch nationale und internationale Gerichte: Überlegungen zur Rechtsvergleichung als Methode im öffentlichen Recht' in Janbernd Oebekke (ed), *Nicht-normative Steuerung in dezentralen Systemen* (Stuttgart: Franz Steiner, 2005) 205–30.

[230] Anne Marie Slaughter, 'Judicial Globalization' (2000) 40 Virginia Journal of International Law 1103–19, P IV (1116–19); Anne Marie Slaughter, *A New World Order* (Princeton: Princeton UP, 2004). In earlier scholarship Sujit Choudhry, 'Globalization in Search of Justification: Toward a Theory of Comparative Constitutional Interpretation' (1999) 74 Indiana LJ 819–92.

acceptance of the principle of proportionality in the domestic constitutional order of the United Kingdom. British courts came to accept proportionality as a ground of judicial review which is stricter than the traditional British tests.[231]

In the epoch of globalization, States have strong political motives to amend and reform their state constitutions in order to become a member of certain international organizations.[232] Increasingly, international actors use norms of international law as a point of reference from which to evaluate a national constitution. Pertinent examples are the international prescriptions (hard and soft) on democracy, including free and regular elections. They are used by international institutions, including the United Nations, as guidelines for the reform of State constitutions.[233] The most intense and far-reaching pressure or stimulation of domestic constitutional reform has been exercised by the Council of Europe, the EU, and NATO. The States of Eastern and Central Europe had to undertake serious constitutional reforms in order to be admitted as members to the Council of Europe.[234] Empirical studies have demonstrated that the 'international socialization' of that region took place due to the the EU and NATO accession conditionalities. These conditionalities require States to implement liberal human rights and democracy norms. This in fact formed a necessary condition of sustained compliance with those norms. However, long-term effectiveness has so far only been secured in regimes which were already at least on the path to liberalism before accession (eg in the Czech Republic, Estonia, Hungary, Latvia, Lithuania, Poland, and Slovenia), but not in antiliberal regimes (such as Belarus, Ukraine, Serbia, or Russia).[235]

---

[231] Cf Alder (n 176 above) 383–86.

[232] Didier Maus, 'The Influence of Contemporary International Law on the Exercise of Constituent Power' in Antero Jyränki (ed), *National Constitutions in the Era of Integration* (The Hague: Kluwer, 1999) 50.

[233] Cf the activities of the UN Democracy Fund, established on 4 July 2005, <http://www-unfoundation.org>.

[234] The Parliamentary Assembly monitors member states and supervises the national constitutional reforms needed to comply with membership requirements. See, eg, Parliamentary Assembly, *Respect des obligations et des engagements de l'Armenie*, Res. 1532 (2007). On the increasing demands that the Council of Europe, in particular its Parliamentary Assembly brought to bear on new post-communist constitutions, Heinrich Klebes and Despina Chatzivassiliou, 'Problèmes d'ordre constitutionnel dans le processus d'adhésion d'Etats de l'Europe centrale et orientale au Conseil de l'Europe' (1996) 8 Revue universelle des droits de l'homme 269–86; Jean-François Flauss, 'Les conditions d'admission des pays d'Europe centrale et orientale au sein du Conseil de l'Europe' (1994) 5 EJIL 401–22, concluding that the function of admission was 'surtout de contribuer à l'extension d'une certaine légitimité constitutionelle, et même d'un certain modèle constitutionnel' (at 421). A well-known problem in this context is that the requirements were applied somewhat selectively by the Council of Europe.

[235] Frank Schimmelfennig, 'Strategic Calculation and International Socialisation: Membership Initiatives, Party Constellations, and Sustained Compliance in Central and Eastern Europe', (2005) 59 International Organization 827–60. See also Anneli Albi, *EU Enlargement and the Constitutions of Central and Eastern Europe* (Cambridge: Cambridge UP, 2005).

The Treaty of Maastricht of 1992, which founded the EU and which substantially reformed the European Community, triggered constitutional revisions in most of the then twelve member States, including the powerful members France and Germany. For instance, a new Article 23 on the European Union was introduced into the German Basic Law.[236] The French constitution was enriched by a new Title XV.[237]

Finally, the United Kingdom's current and very important constitutional evolution has to a significant extent, albeit not exclusively, been induced by European integration and global governance.[238] For instance, recent litigation concerning the European Communities Act of 1972 (by which the UK had acceded the EC) led courts to acknowledge a hierarchy of parliamentary Acts. Thereby, European integration has contributed to a crucial structural change, namely the establishment of an embryonic constitution enjoying supremacy over ordinary laws.[239] Moreover, the 2005 establishment of an institutionally independent Supreme Court for the United Kingdom appears to have been triggered by concerns about complying with Art 6 ECHR.[240] Finally, the Human Rights Act 1998[241] which has incorporated the ECHR into the law of the UK, has profoundly changed the state's constitution. English and Scottish justices have described this transformation in strong words. According to Lord Steyn, the Human Rights Act has created a 'new legal landscape' and 'is now part of what is otherwise an unwritten

---

[236] Art 23 German Basic Law (constitutional revision of 21 December 1992).

[237] Title XV of the French Constitution (constitutional revision of 25 June 1992). This title has been subject to further amendments. For instance, a new Art 88–2 was inserted to allow for the European Arrest Warrant (loi constitutionnelle no 2003–267 of 25 March 2003).

[238] Anthony King names and explains twelve changes of constitutional significance, among them 'Europe' and the Human Rights Act 1998; Anthony King, *Does the United Kingdom still have a Constitution?* (London: Sweet & Maxwell, 2001) 53–76: '[T]he truth is that the United Kingdom's constitution changed more between 1970 and 2000, especially between 1997 and 2000, than during any comparable period since the middle of the 18th century'. Martin Loughlin, *Sword and Scales, An Examination of the Relationship Between Law and Politics* (Oxford: Hart, 2000) 4: 'But many recent developments—including participation in the European project,... the passage of the Human Rights Act 1998 ... suggest that we are now taking steps to transform our "political constitution" into a constitution which rests on a foundation of law.'

[239] House of Lords, *Thoburn v Sunderland City Council* [2003] QB 151 at 186–87, paras 62–64 *per* Laws LJ: 'We should recognise a hierarchy of Acts of Parliament: as it were "ordinary" statutes and "constitutional" statutes.... Ordinary statutes may be impliedly repealed. Constitutional statutes may not.... A constitutional statute can only be repealed, or amended in a way which significantly affects it provisions toughing fundamental rights or otherwise the relation between citizens and state, by unambiguous words on the face of the later statute. This development ... gives us most of the benefits of a written constitution, in which fundamental rights are accorded special respect. But it preserves the sovereignty of the legislature and the flexibility of our uncodified constitution.' According to Lord Laws, statutes with such 'constitutional' rank are notably the Magna Charta 1998, the Bill of Rights 1689, the European Communities Act 1972, the Human Rights Act 1998, the Scotland Act 1998, and the Government of Wales Act 1998.

[240] Gernot Sydow, 'Der geplante Supreme Court für das Vereinigte Königreich im Spiegel der britischen Verfassungsreform' (2004) 64 ZaöRV 66–67 92, with further references.

[241] Chapter 42; also in *Halsbury's Statutes of England and Wales*, 5th edn, Vol 7 (2004) 674–798; <http://www.hmso.gov.uk/acts/acts1998/80042--d.htm> (accessed 16 January 2006).

constitution'.[242] Lord Slynn of Hadley stressed that the 1998 Act requires 'that long or well entrenched ideas may have to be put aside, sacred calves culled'.[243] Lord Reed diagnosed 'a very important shift in thinking about the constitution. It is fundamental to that shift that human rights are no longer dependent solely on conventions, ... the Convention guarantees the protection of rights through legal processes, rather than political processes.'[244] This transformation from a political constitution to a law-based constitution has led a commentator to conclude: 'The traditional British constitution ... is dead. *Requiescat in pace.*'[245]

6.3 Interpretation of State constitutions in conformity with international law

Clashes between domestic constitutional law and international law can be reduced to a minimum through *consistent interpretation* of State constitutions. Indeed, the well-established practice of interpreting domestic statutes in conformity with international or European law[246] in the era of globalization has been extended to the interpretation of domestic constitutional law. This means that national constitutions are more and more often interpreted in the light of international law.

For example, the Portuguese constitution of 1976, [247] the Spanish constitution of 1978,[248] the Romanian constitution of 1991,[249] and the South African constitution of 1996[250] explicitly require that the state constitution must be interpreted in conformity with international human rights law. Notably the South African

---

[242] Lord Steyn, 'The New Legal Landscape' (2000) 5 European Human Rights Law Review 549–54, 550.   [243] House of Lords, *R v Lambert* [2001] All ER 577, 581, para 6.
[244] Appeal Court, High Court of Judiciary (Scotland), *Starrs v Ruxton* (2000) JC 208 (Lord Reed).
[245] King (n 238 above) 81.
[246] Interpretation of domestic law in conformity with EC law is required by the Marleasing principle, ECJ, Case C-106/89, *Marleasing v La Comercial Internacional de Aliméntation*, [1990] ECR I-4135, paras 8–9. On the principle of consistent interpretation, Gerrit Betlem and André Nollkaemper, 'Giving Effect to Public International Law and European Community Law before Domestic Courts: A Comparative Analysis of the Practice of Consistent Interpretation' (2003) 14 EJIL 569–89.
[247] Art 16(2) of the Portuguese Constitution of 2 April 1976: 'The provisions of the Constitution and laws relating to fundamental rights are to be read and interpreted in harmony with the Universal Declaration of Human Rights.'
[248] Art 10(2) of the Spanish Constitution of 29 December 1978: 'The norms relative to basic rights and liberties which are recognized by the Constitution shall be interpreted in conformity with the Universal Declaration of Human Rights and the international treaties and agreements on those matters ratified by Spain.'
[249] Art 20(1) of the Romanian Constitution of 8 December 1991. See n 75 for the text of that provision.
[250] Constitution of South Africa of 8 May 1996: s 233 (Application of international law): 'When interpreting any legislation, every court must prefer any reasonable interpretation of the legislation that is *consistent with international law* over any alternative interpretation that is inconsistent with international law'. Section 39 on Interpretation of Bill of Rights: '(1) When interpreting the Bill of Rights, a court, tribunal or forum (a) must promote the values that underlie an open and democratic society based on human dignity, equality and freedom; (b) *must consider international law*; and (c) *may consider foreign law*' (emphasis added).

constitutional court has become famous for its 'universalist interpretation'[251] of constitutional rights, in a series of judgments relating mostly to criminal processes.

The Supreme Court of Canada also relies quite heavily on constitutional comparison and on international law in constitutional cases.[252] In a case concerning deportation to a country in which there is the risk of torture, the Court interpreted the Canadian Charter of Rights and Freedoms as follows: '[T]he principles... of the Charter cannot be considered in isolation from the international norms which they reflect. A complete understanding of the Act and the Charter requires consideration of the international perspective.'[253] However, the Supreme Court explicitly rejected any binding force of international law over the Canadian Constitution: '[I]n seeking the meaning of the Canadian Constitution, the courts may be informed by international law. Our concern is not with Canada's international obligations qua obligations; rather, our concern is with the principles of fundamental justice. *We look to international law as evidence of these principles and not as controlling itself*.'[254]

Less frequently, German[255] and Swiss[256] courts have interpreted the State constitution under due consideration for international law, most often in the light of the ECHR.

---

[251] Choudhry (n 230 above) 841–65; see also Lourens du Plessis, ch 11 of this book, both with further references to and analysis of the South African constitutional case law.

[252] Eg Supreme Court of Canada, *Baker v Canada* [1999] 2 SCR 817; *USA v Burns* [2001] 1 SCR 283, paras 79–92. On the Canadian approach in scholarship, Karen Knop, 'Here and There: International Law in Domestic Courts' (2000) 32 NYU Journal of International Law & Politics 501–35, concluding that 'the caselaw displays only a muddled enthusiasm for international law that has led to confusion and uncertainty about its exact value in Canadian courts', 515.

[253] Supreme Court of Canada, *Suresh v Canada (Minister of Citizenship and Immigration)*, judgment of 11 January 2002, (2002) 41 ILM 945, para 59

[254] Ibid, para 60 (emphasis added). In the end, the Court concluded 'that the better view is that international law rejects deportation to torture, even where national security interests are at stake. This is the norm which best informs the content of the principles of fundamental justice under s. 7 of the Charter' (para 75).

[255] On the interpretation of the German Constitution in conformity with the ECHR: BVerfGE 74, 358, 370 (1987); BVerfGE 82, 106, 120 (1990); BVerfG, *Görgülü* (2004) 57 NJW 3407, (2004) 59 JZ 1171, para 32. But note that the German Federal Administrative Court (inversely) interpreted the Geneva Convention on Refugees 'within the framework of the value order of the Basic Law' (BVerwGE 49, 44, 47–48 (1975), translation by the author). Other cases vaguely suggest the supremacy of international law over the Basic Law: BVerfGE *Rudolf Hess*, 55, 349 at 368 (1980), stated that in an extreme case, the erroneous interpretation of international law, eg the UN Charter, by a German authority could violate an individual's constitutional right to be protected from arbitrary state action. In the *Teso*-order, BVerfGE 77, 137, 155 (1987), the German Constitutional court had to apply the constitutional provisions relating to the German nationality. In this context, it had to pronounce itself on the status of the Federal Republic of Germany as a subject of public international law, also in relation to the then existing Democratic Republic of Germany. The court here referred to customary international law principles on state identity and state succession. It can be argued that the Constitutional Court interpreted the German Basic Law in the light of customary international law. However, the case was quite specific and does not lend itself to generalization.

[256] BGE 102 Ia 279, 284 E. 2(b) and (c) (1976)—*Minellli* on the interpretation of *constitutional* rights of prisoners in the light of the ECHR, including ECHR judgments and relevant soft law: '*Die Haftbedingungen der Gefangenen sind daher in erster Linie an den Grundrechten der Bundesverfassung zu messen. Bei deren Konkretisierung sind jedoch die Garantien der Konvention und die Rechtsprechung*

Furthermore, the English Human Rights Act (1998) requires domestic courts to interpret domestic legislation (which includes provisions with constitutional substance) in conformity with the ECHR and to take into account the case law of the Human Rights Court.[257] In a landmark decision, the British House of Lords declared illegal the infinite detention of foreigners suspected of terrorism without charge or trial. The Law Lords drew on decisions of the European Court of Human Rights, on the UN Human Rights Covenant, as interpreted by the Committee's General Comments, and on various other international instruments. The judgment also referred to opinions of the Supreme Court of Canada and the United States, and other US courts.[258] Observers rightly characterized this ruling as 'a strong example of the increasing interdependence of domestic and international law'.[259]

Even the United States' Supreme Court has recently come up with a new approach which at least marks a step in the direction of interpreting the US-constitution consistently with international law. While US scholars have long argued that international treaties should be used as guidelines for the interpretation of the US Constitution,[260] the Supreme Court had been very reluctant to refer to foreign and international sources and case law. One explanation is the traditional US American concern for the countermajoritarian difficulty of constitutional review. From this perspective, reliance on foreign or international preferences fails to

---

der Europäischen Kommission und des Europäischen Gerichtshofes für Menschenrechte zu berücksichtigen. Am 19. Januar 1973 beschloss das Ministerkomitee des Europarates die Resolution (73) 5 betreffend Mindestgrundsätze für die Behandlung der Gefangenen.... Die Mindestgrundsätze enthalten keine die Mitgliedstaaten des Europarates völkerrechtlich bindende Vorschriften. Ihre Nichtbeachtung kann daher auch nicht mit staatsrechtlicher Beschwerde gerügt werden. Da sie—wie die Europäische Menschenrecht-skonvention—ihre Grundlage in der gemeinsamen Rechtsüberzeugung der Mitgliedstaaten des Europarates finden, sind die bei der Konkretisierung der Grundrechtsgewährleistungen der Bundesverfassung gleichwohl zu berücksichtigen. Wo den Mindestgrundsätzen der Charakter eigentlicher Grundrechtsverbürgungen zukommt, wird sich das Bundesgericht zu ihnen nicht leichthin in Gegensatz stellen'. See also René Rhinow, *Grundzüge des Schweizerischen Verfassungsrechts* (Basel: Helbig & Lichtenhahn, 2003) para 3218; Daniel Thürer, 'Verfassungsrecht und Völkerrecht' in René Rhinow and others (eds), *Verfassungsrecht der Schweiz* (Zürich: Schulthess, 2001) 179, 191.

[257] Human Rights Act 1998, s 3(1): 'So far as it is possible to do so, primary legislation and subordinate legislation must be read and given effect in a way which is compatible with the Convention rights.' This provision has been called the 'heart of the Act' (Alder (n 175 above) 433). Also s 2(1): 'A court or tribunal determining a question which has arisen in connection with a Convention right must take into account any judgment, decision, declaration or advisory opinion of the European Court of Human Rights.'

[258] House of Lords, *Anti-Terrorism Crime and Security Act (2001)*, judgment of 16 December 2004, [2004] UKHL 56, opinion Lord Bingham of Cornhill.

[259] Lizette Alvarez, 'British Court says Detention Violate Rights', New York Times, 17 December 2004, p A1. Also Ruth Bader Ginsburg, 'A Decent Respect to the Opinions of Humankind: The Value of a Comparative Perspective in Constitutional Adjudication' (2005) 99 Proceedings ASIL 351–59, 355.

[260] In particular Jordan Paust pointed out: 'Thus, although a treaty could not prevail in the case of an unavoidable clash with constitutional norms, a treaty can be incorporated indirectly in aid of interpreting constitutional precepts, and, of course, in aid of reinterpreting those precepts. In this sense, the domestic status of a treaty norm can be enhanced by incorporation into the Constitution, however indirectly' Paust (n 51 above) 134 and 101.

consider the preferences of the American people.[261] But in 2003, the Court began to cite foreign and international case law and has admitted it to be materially relevant for the Court's majority's analysis.[262] In a 2005 five-to-four-decision the Supreme Court departed from precedent and declared the death penalty for juvenile offenders a 'cruel and unusual punishment' in terms of the 8th Amendment to the US Constitution. The Court here referred to the 'opinion of the world community' as supportive, but not decisive in its conclusions.[263] This novel trend ranks among the 'most hotly disputed questions at the United States Supreme Court',[264] has been sharply criticized by individual justices, and has attracted international attention.[265] The fact that the Supreme Court's majority is willing to stir up controversy shows that it now takes international law more seriously than before.

Through the practice of consistent interpretation, international law exercises an *indirect effect* on national constitutional law. The practice of voluntary acceptance of the guiding authority of international law over constitutional law contributes to constitutional harmonization. This is not an end in itself, but appears useful, not least for adapting old constitutions to contemporary social problems.[266]

---

[261] *Roper v Simmons*, US Supreme Court of 1 March 2005, 543 US (2005), J Scalia, dissenting: 'Though the views of our own citizens are essentially irrelevant to the Court's decision today, the views of other countries and the so-called international community take center stage.... I do not believe that approval by other nations and peoples should buttress our commitment to American principles any more than (what should logically follow) disapproval by "other nations and peoples" should weaken that commitment.'

[262] See already *Atkins v Virginia* 536 US 304 (2002) on the death penalty for mentally ill offenders, where the Court cited an *amicus curiae* brief of the EU in a footnote. The breakthrough was *Lawrence v Texas* 123 SCt 2472, 2483 (2003) on homosexual conduct ('sodomy'), citing case law of the ECHR in order to bolster departure from Supreme Court precedent. Also *Grutter v Bollinger* 539 US 309, 342 (2003), concurring opinion Justice Ginsburg, with reference to the international Convention on the Elimination of all Forms of Racism.

[263] *Roper v Simmons* US Supreme Court of 1 March 2005, 543 US (2005), opinion of the Court delivered by J Kennedy: 'The opinion of the world community, while not controlling our outcome, does provide respected and significant confirmation for our own conclusions.'

[264] Norman Dorsen, 'The Relevance of Foreign Legal Materials in U.S. Constitutional Cases: A Conversation Between Justice Antonin Scalia and Justice Stephen Breyer, Introduction' (2005) 3 I Con 519.

[265] On this issue in US American scholarship, AJIL Agora 'The United States Constitution and International Law' (2004) 98 AJIL 42–108 (contributions by Harold Hongju Koh, Roger P Alford, Michael D Ramsey, Gerald L Neumann, T Alexander Aleinikoff); Mark Tushnet, 'Transnational/ Domestic Constitutional Law' (2004) 37 Loyola of Los Angeles Law Review 239–69; Ruth Bader Ginsburg, 'A Decent Respect to the Opinions of Humankind: The Value of a Comparative Perspective in Constitutional Adjudication' (2005) 99 Proceedings ASIL 351–59. For European views: Andrea Bianchi, 'International Law in US Courts: The Myth of Lohengrin Revisited' (2004) 15 EJIL 751–81; Cherie Booth and Max du Plessis, 'Home Alone? The US Supreme Court and International and Transnational Judicial Learning' (2005) European Human Rights L Rev 127–47; Helen Keller and Daniela Thurnherr, *Taking International Law Seriously: A European Perspective on the U.S. Attitude Towards International Law* (Bern: Staempfli, 2005).

[266] 'It is profoundly necessary in an era of increasing interdependence among nations to rediscover and identify trends in judicial decision-making which serve to limit federal power. Recognition of such trends can help minimize conflicts between U.S. law and international law and thereby facilitate more harmonious international relations', Jordan J Paust, *International Law as Law of the United States* (2nd edn, Durham: Carolina Academic Press, 2003) 99.

6.4 Application of international law as de facto constitutional review

An interesting consequence of the increased application of international norms, notably of human rights provisions, by national courts is the emergence of a new type of de facto constitutional review, even in countries which do not otherwise provide for constitutional review. In some states, such as Switzerland, the Netherlands, and France, courts have begun to admit individual complaints which claim that a provision of an international treaty has been violated by the government. These courts have invalidated or discarded national (legislative, executive, judicial) acts due to their incompatibility with international law.

The Swiss federal constitution explicitly compels the Swiss Federal Tribunal to apply federal statutes, even if a statute turns out to be unconstitutional.[267] However, in a landmark decision in 1999, the Federal Tribunal held that a federal statute which runs counter to prescriptions of the ECHR must be set aside.[268] Because the Convention rights are largely identical to the constitutional fundamental rights, the Federal Tribunal in fact set aside a federal law on constitutional grounds without being empowered by the Swiss constitution to do so. This judicial strategy was criticized in the national discourse on the grounds that it introduced the constitutional review of federal statutes through the backdoor, especially in light of the fact that this had been expressly rejected in the course of a recent constitutional reform of the Swiss judicial system.

In France, the *Conseil Constitutionnel* is not competent to determine whether French laws are compatible with international (or European Community) law. However, the French superior courts have taken over this task and have begun to review whether municipal law is in conformity with international treaties.[269] The Administrative Court (*Conseil d' Etat*) has realised that review of the conformity of municipal law with international human rights treaties amounts to a de facto constitutional control.[270]

In the Netherlands, Article 120 of the Constitution prohibits the courts from considering constitutional challenges to an act of parliament.[271] However, the

---

[267] Art 191 BV.   [268] BGE 125 II 417 (1999)—*PKK*.

[269] Cour de Cassation of 23 May 1975, *Administration des douanes v Société 'Cafés Jacques Vabre'* (1975) 11 Revue trimestrielle de droit européen 336; Conseil d' Etat, judgment of 20 October 1989, No 108243, *Nicolo*, english translation in Andrew Oppenheimer (ed), *The Relationship between European Community Law and National Law, The Cases* (Cambridge: CUP, 1994) 225; German translation in (1990) 17 EuGRZ 99.

[270] Opinion of the *commissaire du gouvernement* C Bergeal of 5 December 1997 before the *Conseil d'Etat* in the case *Mme Lambert* (1998) Actualité Juridique—droit administratif (AJDA), 149 at 152. In this case, the compatibility of a law with Art 6 ECHR was at issue. The Commissioner of the government stated: '*Nous ne pensons pas, en effet, que les exigences de l'article 6 soient différentes de celles qui résultent déjà du préambule de la Constitution . . . Et il nous paraît particulièrement souhaitable, lorsque, comme en l'espèce, la disposition législative litigieuse n'a pas été soumise au contrôle du Conseil constitutionnel . . . que vous assuriez par la voie de l'exception de l'inconventionnalité, sur le fondement de l'article 6 § 1, le même contrôle que celui que le Conseil constitutionnel aurait exercé.*'

[271] Art 120, Dutch Constitution: '*De rechter treedt niet in de beoordeling van de grondwettigheid van wetten en verdragen*' ('The judge does not examine the constitutionality of statutes and [international] treaties').

courts do review acts of parliament against self-executing provisions in international instruments. This has resulted in fundamental rights treaties such as the ECHR taking the stage in Dutch jurisprudence, arguably at the expense of the fundamental rights in the Constitution.[272]

The Danish Supreme Court in its *Tvind*-judgment of 1999 exercised constitutional control for the first time and declared a parliamentary statute unconstitutional.[273] Although the Supreme Court did not mention international law, the availment of this power was probably inspired by foreign and international models.[274]

7. Conclusions

The following conclusions are primarily descriptive. From the above it can be said that State constitutions are globalized in form and substance.

7.1 Globalization of constitutional form

With regard to the form and concept of the State constitution, we have seen that globalization and global governance are undermining the national constitutions' claims of uniqueness, totality, and supremacy.

Both international and national constitutional guarantees are confronted with the rise of extra-territorial State action in times of globalization. This phenomenon calls for the *extra-territorial application* of both State constitutional law and international constitution-like guarantees.

In respect of the traditional constitutional characteristic of being the *supreme law*, the picture is chequered. State (constitutional) courts assume both globalist and statist postures. On the one hand, constitutional and international actors cooperate, and constitutional and international norms complement each other. On the other hand, we note tensions and contradictions between State constitutional law and international law. In order to mitigate these tensions, new modes of prevention and solution of conflicts between international law and State constitutional law need to be designed.[275]

---

272 Jaap de Visser, 'Constitutional Law: The Netherlands' (2004) 15 European Review of Public Law (ERPL/REDP) 829–30.

273 Judgment of 19 February 1999, (1999) UfR 481; extracts in German translation in (2000) 60 ZaöRV 884.

274 The Supreme Court's President Niels Pontoppidan referred to the ECHR and to the ECJ. Fredrik Thoms, 'Das Tvind-Urteil des dänischen Obersten Gerichtshofs' (2000) 60 ZaöRV 858 (882).

275 Cottier and Wüger (n 21 above) 270 suggest introducing an international consultation procedure in the style of the Swiss *Vernehmlassungsverfahren*, as it is already foreseen in Art 2.9 TBT-Agreement with regard to national technical regulations. See Art 2.9: 'Whenever a relevant international standard does not exist or the technical content of a proposed technical regulation is not in accordance with the technical content of relevant international standards, and if the technical regulation may have a significant effect on trade of other members, members shall: 2.9.1 publish a notice in a publication at an early appropriate stage, in such a manner as to enable interested parties in other members to become

There are some important findings regarding *the formal hierarchy between international law and domestic constitutions*. This hierarchy matters less in times of globalization[276] for three main reasons. First, States have strong political motives to amend and reform their State constitutions in order to gain membership in various global or regional regimes. Second, the idea of a hierarchy of norms is put into perspective by vertical and horizontal constitutional harmonization. Third, the existing practice of interpreting state constitutions in conformity with international law is irreconcilable with a strict hierarchy between constitutional law and international law as a whole. On the one hand, the national courts still operate on the assumption that state constitutions are superior to international law, while on the other hand the same courts interpret those State constitutions in the light of international law (most often in conformity with the ECHR).

This observation leads to suggest prescriptively that less attention should be paid to the formal sources of law, and more to the substance of the rules in question.[277] The ranking of the norms at stake should be assessed in a more subtle manner, according to their substantial weight and significance.

Such a nonformalist, substance-oriented perspective implies that on the one hand certain less significant provisions in state constitutions would have to give way to important international norms. Inversely, *fundamental rights guarantees should prevail over less important norms (independent of their locus and type of codification)*. The approach suggested here is an academic proposition, but finds an empirical basis in the emerging national constitutional practice of treating international human rights treaties differently from ordinary international law, either by granting them precedence over State constitutions, or by using them, more than any other category of international law, as guidelines for the interpretation of State constitutions.[278]

Admittedly, this new approach does not offer strict guidance, because it is debatable which norms are 'important' in terms of substance, and because it does not resolve clashes between a 'domestic' human right on the one side and an 'international' human right on the other. However, the fundamental idea is that what counts is the substance, not the formal category of conflicting norms.

---

acquainted with it, that they propose to introduce a particular technical regulation; . . . 2.9.4 Without discrimination, allow reasonable time for other members to make comments in writing, discuss these comments upon request, and take these written comments and the results of these discussions into account.' (Agreement on Technical Barriers to Trade of 15 April 1994, [1994] OJ L 336/86).

[276] Cottier and Wüger (n 21 above) 263, suggesting that the relationship between international law and domestic law is not based on hierarchy, but rather is a 'communicative' relationship. Also Thomas Vesting, 'Die Staatsrechtslehre und die Veränderung ihres Gegenstandes: Konsequenzen von Europäisierung und Internationalisierung' (2004) 63 Veröffentlichungen der Vereinigung der Deutschen Staatsrechtslehrer 41, 66: *In der neuen Ordnung des Rechtspluralismus würde es aber keinen pauschalen Anwendungsvorrang der einen Rechtsordnung mehr vor der anderen geben'*.

[277] Cf De Búrca and Gerstenberg (n 10 above) 252. The authors conceive of international human rights law and international adjudication as a 'practice of justification'. Under this view, 'the relationship between human rights and constitutional rights can be understood as one of mutual backup and multi-layered justification'.   [278] See above, parts 4.4 and 6.3.

Such a flexible approach appears to correspond better with the current state of global legal integration than does the idea of a strict hierarchy, particularly in human rights matters. From this perspective, international law and State constitutions find themselves in a fluent state of *interaction* and *reciprocal influence*.[279]

7.2 Globalization of constitutional principles

In respect of constitutional principles, globalization facilitates, but also renders more difficult the fulfilment of traditional constitutional precepts. A *positive* consequence of global governance is the significant horizontal and vertical convergence of constitutional institutions and values. State constitutions are permeated by international law, notably by international human rights guarantees (via formal amendments and judge-made *Verfassungswandel*). This development is laudable, because it 'offers an alternative conception of legitimacy, grounded in core human rights and aimed at reinforcing the nascent global order'.[280]

Conversly, a rather *problematic* consequence of moving the locus of decision-making to the supra-state level is that the operation of constitutional principles is to some extent undermined. Probably some novel mechanisms will need to be devised in order to prevent the rule of law, democracy, social elements, and federalism from becoming dysfunctional and empty.

In functional terms, international and national constitutional guarantees have become to some extent interchangeable. For instance, international law standards may substitute unenforceable constitutional standards and empower national courts ('de facto constitutional control').

To conclude the descriptive analysis, I wish to stress that the current evolution of national legal orders in all their details is not a story of continuous harmonization and convergence. We are in fact witnessing a 'cohabitation between legal unity . . . and differentiation', a 'contrast between a universal legal patrimony, which reinforces the legal unity of the world, and the extreme variety of local legal systems.[281] The globalization of the law allows and should continue to allow the diversity of national legal regimes, but only on the basis of some common core (constitutional) principles.

7.3 Compensatory constitutionalism on the global plane?

On the basis of these findings, I make one prescriptive claim. I suggest that the globalization of constitutions as described above constitutes an important argument in favour of exploring further the idea of 'global (or international) constitutionalism'. Global constitutionalism means '[t]he extension of constitutionalist

---

[279] Cf Ress and Schreuer (n 37 above) 7–56 and 57–91.   [280] Teitel (n 226 above) 2593.
[281] Sabino Cassese, 'The Globalization of Law', (2005) 37 New York University Journal of International law & Politics, 973, esp. at 986–88. Cassese emphasizes the 'tension between increasing unity and increasing differentiations' and even diagnoses a widening gap over time.

thinking to world order',[282] without, however, over-stretching the scope or exaggerating the significance and the universality of constitutional principles. The picture of globalized State constitutions painted here leads to the conclusion that classical constitutional principles (rule of law, democracy, welfare elements, federalism) can no longer be implemented on the national constitutional level alone. If political and legal actors wish to preserve constitutionalism in the era of globalization, they should build a global constitutional law in which the globalization-induced deficiencies of State constitutions are compensated by complementary international constitutional law. But that is another story.[283]

---

[282] Richard Falk, 'The Pathways of Global Constitutionalism' in Richard Falk and others (eds), *The Foundations of World Peace* (Albany, NY: State University of New York Press, 1993) 13, 14.

[283] Anne Peters, 'Compensatory Constitutionalism: The Function and Potential of Fundamental International Norms and Structures' (2006) 19 Leiden Journal of International Law 579–610.

11

International Law and the Evolution of (domestic) Human-Rights Law in Post-1994 South Africa

Lourens du Plessis

1. Setting the scene

Everyone shall enjoy all *universally accepted* fundamental rights, freedoms and civil liberties, which shall be provided for and protected by entrenched and justiciable provisions in the Constitution (emphasis added).

The founding parents of 'the new South Africa', at a crucial point in the birth process of their scion, couched their aspirations and expectations in XXXIV Constitutional Principles (CPs) that formed part of a transitional (or interim) Constitution.[1] This Constitution, in its turn, prescribed the way forward for the adoption of a 'final Constitution',[2] and the CPs marked out this way to a significant extent. The words quoted above, coming from CP II,[3] express the heartfelt need of a long-time pariah for 'universal acceptance' and its aspiration to be(-come) a well thought-of inhabitant of the global village.[4]

Pre-dating the arrival of full democracy in South Africa by a hundred years, a court in an independent (Boer) republic that became a British colony in 1900 and one of the provinces of the Union of South Africa in 1910,[5] declared that the municipal law of the (then) republic

must be interpreted in such a way as not to conflict with the principles of international law . . . '[T]he state which disclaims the authority of international law places herself outside

---

[1] Constitution of the Republic of South Africa, Act 200 of 1993, Sched 4.

[2] The constitution-making process will be elaborated on in section 3.1.

[3] This CP concludes with the following phrase: 'which shall be drafted after having given due consideration to inter alia the fundamental rights contained in Chapter 3 of this Constitution'.

[4] Which eventually saw the light as the Constitution of the Republic of South Africa, 1996 entering into force on 4 February 1997.

[5] I refer here to the South African Republic (*Zuid-Afrikaanse Republiek*) that eventually became the province of Transvaal in the Union of South Africa in 1910.

the circle of civilized nations.' It is only by a strict adherence to these recognized principles that our young state can hope to acquire and maintain the respect of all civilized communities, and so preserve its own national independence.[6]

This *dictum* is indicative not only of a positive attitude towards international law, but also of a resolve to play a constructive role in international affairs. By and large South Africa, during the first half of the twentieth century, did play such a role as, for instance, a faithful member of the League of Nations, entrusted with a mandate to administer South West Africa (nowadays Namibia), and as a founder member of the United Nations.[7] Since the mid-1940s South Africa, in spite of its protestations that apartheid was 'a domestic affair', came under increasing scrutiny and eventually vigorous attack because of its racial policies. Quite unintended (and unwillingly) South Africa then became a major contributor to developing a post-World War II international law—in a 'negative' sense, that is, as the 'target' of an increasing body of treaty and customary law designed to promote human rights and racial equality and to facilitate the process of decolonization: 'While apartheid undermined and discredited the law of South Africa, it succeeded, perversely, in injecting notions of racial equality, self-determination and respect for human rights into an international legal order that in 1945 had few developed rules on these subjects.'[8]

Since the early 1990s South Africans' resolve to negotiate both a peaceful and a decided farewell to apartheid, was evident from, amongst others, an openness to 'influences from outside' and, in particular, an exceedingly positive attitude towards international law as a formative and informative force in the legal order of a new South Africa. In the case of the minority white South African government and the judiciary this was a drastically changed attitude. Previously there had, for instance, been a handful of loner lawyers (and the odd academic) who tried to persuade South African courts (and other law enforcement agencies) to invoke enlightened precepts and standards of international human rights protection in dealing with specific cases.[9]

Sadly these endeavours were mostly to no avail. Since the early 1990s and especially since 27 April 1994—the date on which South Africa's first fully democratic (transitional) Constitution took effect—external and internal forces have favoured and indeed compelled unprecedented confidence in international law. Shedding its status as pariah, South Africa was drawn into the mainstream of the post World War II globalization of the law, especially constitutional law, manifesting itself in an ever increasing integration of international and domestic law and a

---

[6] *CC Maynard et alii v The Field Cornet of Pretoria* (1894) (1) SAR 214 223

[7] See J Dugard, *International Law: A South African Perspective* (2nd edn, Cape Town: Kenwyn Juta & Co, 2000) 19–20.   [8] Dugard (n 7 above) 21.

[9] Cf, eg *S v Tuhadeleni and Others* (1969) (1) SA 153 (A); *Sobukwe v Minister of Justice* (1972) (1) SA 693 (A); *Nduli v Minister of Justice* (1978) (1) SA 893 (A); *Nkondo v Minister of Police* (1980) (2) SA 894 (O); *S v Adams; S v Werner* (1981) (1) SA 187 (A); *Tutu v Minister of Internal Affairs* (1982) (4) SA 571 (T) and *S v Ebrahim* (1991) (2) SA 553 (A).

ready reliance on legal comparison.[10] Mechanisms triggering and facilitating these forces of globalisation were built into South Africa's new constitutional order. This chapter is a case study of how, over the last twelve years or so, external forces of legal globalization, brought into play via internal constitutional mechanisms, have contributed to the founding and carving out of municipal human rights law in South Africa almost from scratch. It started off with two constitutional texts—the transitional (1993) and the final (1996) Constitutions[11]—both inspired by and providing for reliance on international (human rights) law.[12] The study commences with a brief overview of the international law dimensions of especially the 1996 constitutional text. Judicial precedent is a most significant source of law in South Africa. Case law in which aspects of the interaction between international and domestic human rights law have been considered and governing precepts developed, will thus also have to be looked at. I shall discuss a handful of cases which, from my (inevitably subjective) perspective, constitute defining moments in the judiciary's reliance on international law to construe and shape domestic human rights law, trying to identify some trends in the courts' approach to and use of international law in the human rights arena.

It might as well be stated right from the outset that the picture emerging from this case study will be one of a decided (national) friendliness towards international law in post-1994 South Africa. However—and this is my hypothesis—international law friendliness does not automatically translate into optimal reliance on or use of international law in specific cases. To put it differently: it cannot be taken for granted that a domestic jurisdiction's openness to and positive disposition towards international (human rights) law will necessarily result in the strongest possible or most profitable reliance on or implementation of international law by adjudicative bodies and other law-enforcing agencies in that jurisdiction.

I am not aware of an accepted 'instrument of measurement' that can precisely express or specify the 'strength' of a State's (and its organs'—notably also its courts') abidance by, reliance on or implementation of international law. As a human rights constitutionalist, specializing in constitutional and statutory interpretation, I am furthermore not wont to the analytical aids of international law, such as the *monism-dualism* or the *hard law-soft law* distinctions.[13] When considering the degree of

---

[10] See in general for observations on this openness towards the international community and its effects on the approach to international law: N Botha, 'The Coming of Age of Public International Law in South Africa' (1992/1993) 18 SAYIL 36; G Erasmus, 'The Incorporation of Trade Agreements and Rules of Origin: The Extent of Constitutional Guidance' (2003) 28 SAYIL 157–58, and J Ford 'International and Comparative Influence on the Rights Jurisprudence of South Africa's Constitutional Court' in M du Plessis and S Pete (eds), *Constitutional Democracy in South Africa 1994–2004: Essays in Honour of the Howard College School of Law* (Durban: Butterworths, 2004) 33–51, 35.

[11] Cf n 1 and n 4.

[12] And for generous reliance on legal comparison—but this is not the topic under discussion in the present study.

[13] Dugard (n 7 above) 124–27. From recent literature it seems that these conventional distinctions have at any rate become increasingly contentious cf, eg W Scholtz, 'A Few Thoughts on s 231 of the South African Constitution, Act 108 of 1996' (2004) 29 SAYIL 202, 204–05. Readers of this volume

reliance on or implementation of international law, I shall thus content myself with a straightforward, descriptive distinction between invoking international law as a *prescriptive* authority, on the one hand, and seeking its guidance as *persuasive* force, on the other. As prescriptive authority international law asserts itself with the same intensity as any form of municipal law ('as it stands'), while persuasive international law instruments and texts are most often summoned as aids to the contextualization and construction of (municipal and international) prescriptive law. The distinction between prescriptive and persuasive international law is by no means watertight and it is therefore a descriptive aid of some (but limited) assistance.

In the discussion that follows reference will sometimes also be made to 'non-binding international law'. This is a 'South Africanism', and something of a misnomer, because *non*-binding international *law* does not really exist. However, as will be pointed out in the course of the discussion, the South African Constitutional Court has come to afford international law *binding on South Africa* (in terms of sections 231–233 of the Constitution) and international law *not binding* on South Africa (in this manner) similar weight as aids—and often even prescriptive guides—to constitutional interpretation. It is this latter category of international law that will be referred to as 'non-binding international law' for short.

2. International law and the text of the (1996) Constitution

2.1 Couching fundamental rights in the Bill of Rights

The Bill of Rights in South Africa's Constitution is, to a large extent, an encyclopaedia of international human rights law gleaned from multifarious international declarations, covenants, and conventions. The text of the Chapter on Fundamental Rights in the transitional (1993) Constitution[14] was already strongly inspired by the International Bill of Human Rights—that is, the Universal Declaration of Human Rights of 1948 (UDHR), the International Covenant on Economic, Social and Cultural Rights of 1966 (ICESCR) and the International Covenant on Civil and Political Rights of 1966 (ICCPR)—as well as by the European Convention on Human Rights and Fundamental Freedoms of 1950 (ECHR).[15] The Technical Committee drafting the Bill of Rights[16] in South Africa's final Constitution, was at pains to justify the inclusion of the vast majority of rights in the Bill—and in

---

will be struck by the fact that many trends and tendencies discussed in this chapter with reference to the South African context, accord with trends and tendencies discussed by Anne Peters in the chapter *The Globalisation of State Constitutions* (ch 10).

[14] Transitional Constitution 1993, ch 3.

[15] L du Plessis and H Corder, *Understanding South Africa's Transitional Bill of Rights* (Cape Town: Kenwyn Juta & Co, 1994) 47, 120–21.

[16] Constitutional Assembly Theme Committee 4 *Draft Bill of Rights* Undated, ch 2.

some instances also formulations they proposed—with reference to the enshrinement of those rights in international documents and instruments (and, it must be added, the constitutions of other municipal jurisdictions too).[17] In addition to the documents and instruments referred to above, the Technical Committee also frequently and freely drew on the American Convention on Human Rights of 1969 (ACHR), the African Charter on Human and Peoples' Rights of 1981 ('the Banjul Charter'), the International Covenant on the Elimination of all Forms of Racial Discrimination of 1966 (ICEFRD), the Convention on the Elimination of all forms of Discrimination against Women of 1979 (CEDAW) and the Convention on the Rights of the Child of 1989 (CRC).

A comprehensive study of where, how and to which extent provisions originating from international human-rights documents and instruments feature in South Africa's Bill of Rights (and in other sections of the Constitution—especially those articulating and proclaiming foundational constitutional values[18]) will call for a chapter in its own right. For the time being an aphoristic pin-pointing of some features of the South African Bill of Rights as a municipal law-text[19] drawing on prescriptive and persuasive international law instruments, will have to suffice.

The Bill of Rights mostly enshrines generally accepted fundamental human rights in a manner that echoes, both in substance and style, guarantees of those rights in classical human rights documents, including the all-timers constituting the International Bill of Human Rights. The precise terms in which these fundamental rights are couched in provisions of the South African Bill of Rights deviate to some extent from the *ipsissima verba* of their counterparts in international documents and instruments, but in most instances these deviances are but phraseological and stylistic aberrations that can be explained by the South African drafters' conscious and consistent efforts to plain language the text so as 'to ensure the clarity and accessibility of the Bill of Rights'.[20]

In some instances the wording or style of sections in the South African Bill of Rights, for no apparent reason, deviates from that of fairly standardized formulations in international documents and instruments. In section 12(1) of the Constitution, for instance, the 'right to *freedom* and security of the person' (emphasis added) is entrenched. International documents and instruments mentioning this right speak of *liberty* and security of the person.[21] The outcome of constitutional negotiations in South Africa was to a large extent determined by ideological tension between egalitarianism (or an equality-centred approach) and libertarianism

---

[17] Cf, eg Constitutional Assembly Theme Committee 4 *Draft Bill of Rights* Undated.

[18] For instance Constitution of South Africa of 8 May 1996, s 1.

[19] It could of course also be added that the Bill of Rights is an abstract, prescriptive law-text with ultimate authority, but for present purposes reference to these qualities of the Bill of Rights is not indispensable.

[20] Constitutional Assembly Theme Committee 4 *Draft Bill of Rights* Undated 'Overview of Method of Work'.   [21] Eg the UDHR, Art 3, the ICCPR, Art 9(1) and the Banjul Charter, Art 6.

(or a liberty-centred approach).[22] Though 'freedom' and 'liberty' are synonyms, the South African constitutional negotiators, as a concession to the equality-centred approach, probably thought that 'freedom' is not quite such a strong term as 'liberty' and that the use of the former might preclude a construction of section 12(1) allowing for the recognition of a general freedom right (instead of a right to freedom *of the person* only).[23] The guarantee of freedom of conscience, religion, thought, belief, and opinion in section 15(1) of the South African Constitution is phrased in general terms, and in that sense it is rather comprehensive. On the other hand, the broad terms in which the right to freedom of religion is guaranteed could also be seen to be rather lean (or minimalistic) compared to the phraseology in leading international documents and instruments. These latter texts typically also state that the right to religious freedom may be exercised individually or in community with others, and that it includes the right to manifest one's religion openly as well as the right not to have a religion.[24] There is no apparent reason for the leaner formulation of the right to religious freedom in the South African Bill of Rights. What can be said, though, is that there seems to be a preference in domestic Bills of Rights, especially those of relatively recent origin, for guaranteeing the right to religious freedom in similarly lean terms.[25]

In at least one instance a right included in the transitional Constitution was not included in the final Constitution apparently because this right 'does not appear in any international human rights instruments and finds little support in foreign Constitutions'.[26] The right in question was the right freely to engage in economic activity which was guaranteed in Section 26 of the transitional Constitution.

In a few rare—but in terms of their domestic effect not insignificant—instances rights not widely (and of necessity) recognized in international documents and instruments, have been entrenched in the South African Bill of Rights, namely the right of access to information[27] and rights to just administrative action.[28] Liberally minded participants in the constitution-making process, perceiving of excesses in South Africa's apartheid past mainly as resulting from an inability to contain executive arbitrariness, strongly insisted on the inclusion of these (by international standards rather atypical) rights in the Bill of Rights.

---

[22] Du Plessis and Corder (n 15 above) 23–35.

[23] In *Ferreira v Levin NO* (1996) (4) BCLR (1)*; Vryenhoek v Powell NO* (1996) (1) SA 984 (CC) a majority of the Constitutional Court, with reference to a similarly phrased provision in the transitional Bill of Rights (s 11) indeed held that the word 'freedom' and the phrase 'of the person' are not to be read disjunctively and that a general right to freedom was therefore not what had been entrenched in the predecessor to s 12(1).

[24] Eg the UDHR, Art 18; the ICCPR, Art 18 and the Declaration on the Elimination of all Forms of Intolerance and of Discrimination based on Religion or Belief Art 1 read with Art 6; cf also LM du Plessis, 'Grondwetlike Beskerming vir Godsdiensregte as Groepsregte in Suid-Afrika' (2002) 43 Nederduits-Gereformeerd Teologiese Tydskrif 214–15.

[25] For examples, cf Du Plessis, 'Grondwetlike Beskerming' (n 24 above) 214, 215.

[26] Constitutional Assembly Theme Committee 4 *Draft Bill of Rights* Undated 106.

[27] Constitution of South Africa 1996, s 32; and cf Constitutional Assembly Theme Committee 4 *Draft Bill of Rights* Undated 196–201.   [28] Ibid, s 33; and cf ibid, 202–08.

In other instances reliance on international law facilitated, to an appreciable extent, the resolution of controversies resulting from constitution-making parties' decidedly dissimilar stands on some issues. How to verbalize the need for (and in what terms to authorize) affirmative action in the South African Constitution was, for instance, pretty controversial—and not unexpectedly so. Section 9(2) of the Constitution, the compromise eventually agreed on, echoes, to a considerable extent, Article 1(4) of ICEFRD and Article 4 of CEDAW:[29] 'Equality includes the full and equal enjoyment of all rights and freedoms. To promote the achievement of equality, legislative and other measures designed to protect or advance persons, or categories of persons, disadvantaged by unfair discrimination may be taken.' Far from being disdainful of cultural and linguistic ('minority') rights, an appreciable number of South Africa's constitution-makers nevertheless feared that (especially white and Afrikaner) minorities privileged under apartheid, might pin their hopes on gratuitous reliance on linguistic and cultural rights (based on ethnic affiliation) to prolong a skewed distribution of privilege in certain areas—education in particular.[30] Some Afrikaner interest groups indeed strongly contended for significant protection of (their) 'group rights'. With Article 27 of the ICCPR as its template,[31] section 31 of the South African Constitution seeks to negotiate both the aspirations of traditionally disadvantaged groups and the fears of advantaged minorities. Section 30 entrenches everyone's right to use the language and to participate in the cultural life of their choice. Section 31(1) then goes on to state that persons belonging to a cultural, religious or linguistic community *may not be denied* the right, with other members of that community:

(a) to enjoy their culture, practise their religion and use their language; and
(b) to form, join and maintain cultural, religious and linguistic associations and other organs of civil society.

Section 31(2) is at pains to stipulate that section 31(1) rights may not be exercised in a manner inconsistent with any provision of the Bill of Rights. Section 29(2), (also) with cautionary reservations (derived from, amongst others, examples in international law[32]), caters for the provision of education in the language of someone's choice:

Everyone has the right to receive education in the official language or languages of their choice in public educational institutions where that education is reasonably practicable. In order to ensure the effective access to, and implementation of, this right, the state must consider all reasonable educational alternatives, including single medium institutions, taking into account –

   (a) equity;
   (b) practicability; and
   (c) the need to redress the results of past racially discriminatory laws and practices.

---

[29] Cf also Constitutional Assembly Theme Committee 4 *Draft Bill of Rights* Undated 7.

[30] L du Plessis, 'Legal and Constitutional Means designed to Facilitate the Integration of Diverse Cultures in South Africa: A Provisional Assessment' (2002) 13 Stellenbosch Law Review 370–72.

[31] Constitutional Assembly Theme Committee 4 *Draft Bill of Rights* Undated 191.

[32] Ibid, 169.

The interpretation of the predecessor to section 29(2)[33] in the light of international law standards came to the fore in a constitutional case that will be discussed below.[34]

The inclusion of socio-economic entitlements to basic necessities of life in a Bill of Rights is controversial given the widespread belief that a wholesale guarantee of *rights* to even the most basic necessities of life is economically unsustainable. Constitution-makers in South Africa found themselves on the horns of a dilemma, knowing that something had to be said in the Bill of Rights about socio-economic entitlements, but lacking phraseology to dispel the fears of economic unsustainability. Drawing on international instruments and, in particular, Article 2 of the ICESCR, the Constitutional Assembly eventually agreed on a formula whereby 'rights to have access to' certain basic necessities of life are proclaimed and 'the state' is enjoined to 'take reasonable legislative and other measures, within its available resources, to achieve the progressive realisation' of these rights. Rights to have access to adequate housing (section 26), health care, food, water, and social security (section 27) are guaranteed in this manner.

Arguably the most divisive controversy among the constitution-makers was whether or not to entrench property rights in the Bill of Rights. Though it is not uncommon for international documents and instruments to recognize that property rights are worthy of protection, the South African constitution-makers did not seek and therefore did not get much help from that quarter.[35] This goes to show that an 'internal' dispute can become too politicized even for the 'external' helping hand of international law to assist its resolution.

The inclusion in a nation's supreme constitution of provisions derived from international documents and instruments is, subject to caveats about the interpretation of the international law so included,[36] a most (and probably *the most*) powerful method of incorporating international (human-rights) law in the municipal law of that nation. Such an inclusion, in South Africa's case, followed not from an actual or perceived compliance with any legal duty but, quite unceremoniously (though not less powerfully), from the mindset of the constitution-makers reflecting, on the one hand, a resolve to come forward with an internationally respectable constitution (and Bill of Rights) and, on the other, adequate confidence in international human rights law (in its various manifestations) to warrant the enactment of some of its provisions, in abstract format, in the nation's supreme, prescriptive law.

2.2 Provision for reliance on and implementation of international law

The Constitution provides for reliance on and the implementation of international law, first, in a legally technical way, laying down 'black-letter law' to deal with the

---

[33] To wit transitional Constitution 1993, s 32(b) and (c)   [34] See section 3.3.

[35] Constitutional Assembly Theme Committee 4 *Draft Bill of Rights* Undated 126–37.

[36] See section 2.2.2.

recognition, status, and force of international law vis-à-vis municipal law. This is how constitutions can normally be expected to deal with international law. Second, the interpretation clause in the Bill of Rights[37]—and section 39(1)(b) in particular—enjoins adjudicators interpreting the Bill of Rights *to consider* international law thus allowing (without necessarily prescribing) reliance on international law. These two modes of reliance on and implementation of international law will next be considered seriatim.[38]

2.2.1 'Black-letter' constitutional law

Section 231 of the Constitution, dealing with international agreements, asserts that the 'negotiating and signing of all international agreements' is the responsibility of the national executive.[39] 'An international agreement binds the Republic only after it has been approved by resolution in both the National Assembly and the National Council of Provinces'.[40] However, '[a]n international agreement of a technical, administrative or executive nature, or an agreement which does not require either ratification or accession, entered into by the national executive, binds the Republic without approval by the National Assembly and the National Council of Provinces, but must be tabled in the Assembly and the Council within a reasonable time'.[41] An international agreement can become domestic law 'when it is enacted into law by national legislation; but a self-executing provision of an agreement that has been approved by Parliament is law in the Republic unless it is inconsistent with the Constitution or an Act of Parliament'.[42] South Africa is still bound by international agreements which were binding on it when the 1996 Constitution took effect.[43]

Customary international law is recognised as 'law in the Republic unless it is inconsistent with the Constitution or an Act of Parliament'.[44] Section 233 is a constitutionalization—and by that very token not a mere restatement (see below)—of a long-standing, common-law presumption of statutory interpretation.[45] The section requires 'every court' interpreting legislation to 'prefer any reasonable interpretation ... consistent with international law over any alternative interpretation that is inconsistent with international law'. Erasmus correctly points out that section 233, unlike the conventional presumption, is of effect even where there is no ambiguity in the legislation to be construed—all that is needed for the section to kick in, is the existence of international law on the topic or issue under consideration.[46]

Sections 231–33, as supreme law demonstrating a curious blend of monistic and dualistic elements, provide a prescriptive, normative framework within which international law, in its turn, can acquire prescriptive, normative effect. International law

---

[37] Constitution 1996, s 39   [38] In sections 2.2.1 and 2.2.2 below respectively.
[39] Constitution 1996, s 231(1).   [40] Ibid, s 231(2).   [41] Ibid, s 231(3).
[42] Ibid, s 231(4).   [43] Ibid, s 231(5).   [44] Ibid, s 232.
[45] L du Plessis, *Re-Interpretation of Statutes* (Durban: Butterworths, 2002) 173.
[46] Erasmus, 'The Incorporation of Trade Agreements' (n 10 above) 157.

that does not fall within this framework does not have such prescriptive effect[47]—at least not formally. The South African experience has shown that, wide-ranging enthusiasm for the incorporation of international human rights law in domestic law notwithstanding, numerous practical obstacles, mainly in the executive sphere of government, inhibit endeavours to include international law-texts in this framework.[48] The question, for instance, often is whether there are mechanisms in place to ensure South Africa's compliance with treaty or convention obligations, especially the obligation to report to the relevant international monitoring agencies at regular intervals. The capacity to comply with international obligations cannot be taken for granted in a state that had, for a long time, isolated itself from the international community, no matter how strong the subsequent resolve of that state to become a respectable member of that community again. Against this background section 39(1)(b) of the Constitution, that will be discussed next, gains in significance.

2.2.2 *Considering international law in Bill of Rights interpretation in terms of the Interpretation Clause (section 39(1)(b))*

Section 39(1)(b) has so far engendered the bulk of constitutional jurisprudence on the interaction of international and domestic law. To put this provision in perspective, the first two subsections of section 39 (the 'interpretation clause' in the Bill of Rights) are quoted in full:

(1) When interpreting the Bill of Rights, a court, tribunal or forum—
    (a) must promote the values that underlie an open and democratic society based on human dignity, equality and freedom;
    (b) must consider international law; and
    (c) may consider foreign law.
(2) When interpreting any legislation, and when developing the common law or customary law, every court, tribunal or forum must promote the spirit, purport and objects of the Bill of Rights.

Section 39(1)(b) directs, in prescriptive language, the attention of 'a court, tribunal or forum' to international law (they '*must*'), but in the same breath the manner of reliance on international law is not prescribed: the language of the provision (they 'must *consider*') is sufficiently broad to (i) prompt consideration of international law-texts to determine whether they constitute binding law in terms of the provisions of sections 231–33 of the Constitution, (ii) to justify recourse to international law-texts on the strength (merely) of their persuasive force, or (iii) to sustain a conclusion that international law considered is not applicable. Section 39(1)(b) is actually unnecessary for purpose (i): a court must at any rate be alert to law that (possibly) binds it.

---

[47] Except perhaps that the 'international law' referred to in s 233 might include non-binding (and therefore non-prescriptive) international law.

[48] An insightful case study in this regard is ME Olivier, 'South Africa and International Human Rights Agreements: Procedure, Policy and Practice (Part 1)' (2003) 2 Tydskrif vir die Suid-Afrikaanse Reg 310.

Seeing that so much in the Bill of Rights derives from sources of international law, section 39(1)(b) creates the curious situation where constitutional provisions with their origins in international law, are required to be construed considering international law! Recognized procedures for and aids to the construction of international law—for instance, Articles 31–33 of the Vienna Convention on the Law of Treaties—may be relied on to determine what 'international law' in a given situation and/or with reference to a specific issue is. This does not, however, mean that the Constitution and Bill of Rights themselves have to be interpreted as if they were sources of international law: they are to be construed in accordance with recognised procedures and strategies for the interpretation of enacted (domestic) law, duly honouring the Constitution's status as supreme law.[49] In the South African context a constitutional provision derived from an international law source could thus be construed to have a meaning different to its accepted meaning in international law. It is, as a matter of fact, conceivable that *considering* (which also means 'weighing the merits of'[50]) international law, may indeed induce such a construction of a human rights provision in the domestic Bill of Rights.

3. Defining case law moments in the evolution of South Africa's human rights jurisprudence informed by international law

A handful of defining constitutional precedents have mapped the routes that ought (and ought not) to be followed through the landscape of international law in order to reach desired destinations in the territory of domestic human rights law. First among these—not chronologically, but as the (Constitutional Court's own) highest regarded authority on the 'correct interpretation' of the Constitution—is the *First Certification* judgment.[51] This judgment will be discussed first, followed by six other judgments—some of them predating the *Certification* judgment—in chronological order.

3.1 *Certification of the Constitution of the Republic of South Africa, 1996, In re ex parte Chairperson of the Constitutional Assembly*[52] (1995)

The founding parents of the new constitutional order in South Africa referred to at the beginning of this chapter were, at the time when the Constitutional Principles

---

[49] Cf, however, the South African Constitutional Court's (contrary) view on the status of the Vienna Convention on the Law of Treaties in constitutional interpretation in section 3.2 below.

[50] *The Shorter Oxford English Dictionary on CD-ROM* (5th edn, Version 2.0, Oxford: OUP, 2002).

[51] *Certification of the Constitution of the Republic of South Africa* (1996), *In re Ex parte Chairperson of the Constitutional Assembly* (1996) (10) BCLR 1253 (1996 (4) SA 744) ((CC)). See para 43 of the judgment for the reasons why the Constitutional Court holds its own judgment in such high esteem.

[52] (1996) (10) BCLR 1253 (1996 (4) SA 744) (CC).

(CPs) were formulated, the representatives of twenty six political interest groups who negotiated and agreed on a text for an interim or transitional constitution (IC)[53] providing for, amongst others, the election of a Constitutional Assembly (CA) and for procedures to put a final constitution in place. The XXXIV CPs were included in Schedule 4 to the transitional Constitution as general, founding directives with which a final constitution was required to comply, and the Constitutional Court was entrusted with the mammoth responsibility to certify compliance of the new constitutional text (NT) with the XXXIV CPs—hence the two *Certification* judgments.[54] CP II was quoted as opening lines to this chapter.

In the *First Certification* judgment a unanimous Constitutional Court observed that It is no coincidence that the drafters of the CPs 'having in CP I established the principle that the state they contemplated would be a democracy, immediately proceeded to describe one of its key attributes in CP II'.[55] The court then continued:

In CP II they . . . stipulated that the NT must provide for a bill of rights, constitutionally safeguarded and enforceable by the Courts.

The method the drafters of the CPs adopted to give content to the Bill of Rights was to refer to 'all universally accepted fundamental rights, freedoms and civil liberties'. There are two components to this: 'fundamental rights, freedoms and civil liberties' and 'universally accepted'[56]

The court understood the latter component to entail the following[57]:

Although a strict literal interpretation should not be given to 'universal', for that may result in giving little content to CP II, it nevertheless establishes a strict test. It is clear that the drafters intended that only those rights that have gained a wide measure of international acceptance as fundamental human rights must necessarily be included in the NT. Beyond that prescription, the CA enjoys a discretion. That this is the case is apparent too from the instruction given in the closing clause of CP II which requires the CA to give 'due consideration to inter alia the fundamental rights contained in chap 3' of the IC. The CA was clearly not obliged to duplicate those rights, nor to match them. They merely had to be duly considered.

---

[53] Transitional Constitution 1993. Actually, by the time the CPs were agreed on, six of the initial twenty six interest groups had withdrawn from the process.

[54] s 71(1) of the IC required the NT to comply with the XXXIV CPs in Sched 4 and s 71(2) charged the Constitutional Court with the responsibility to certify such compliance for the NT to become of force and effect. This was a rather unusual responsibility to entrust to an unelected, judicial body. On 8 May 1996 the Constitutional Assembly adopted a NT which, according to the Constitutional Court in its *First Certification* judgment on 6 September 1996, failed to comply with the CPs in a number of respects. The court accordingly declined to certify it. The Constitutional Assembly reconvened and on 11 October 1996 passed with the requisite majority an amended text of the new constitution (the AT) which addressed the grounds for non-certification set out in the *First Certification* judgment. The Constitutional Court, in a *Second Certification* judgment, certified the AT on 4 December 1996 and on 10 December the then President on the Republic of South Africa, Nelson Mandela, signed the AT into law taking effect on 4 February 1997. The Constitution resulting from this process, largely fits Anne Peters's description of state constitutions in para III of her chapter on *The Globalization of State Constitutions*.

[55] *Certification of the Constitution of the Republic of South Africa* (n 52 above) para 48.

[56] Ibid, para 49.   [57] Ibid, para 51.

The 'universally accepted fundamental rights, freedoms and civil liberties' required by the CP is a narrower group of rights than that entrenched by the IC . . . To the extent that the IC afforded rights which went beyond the 'universally accepted' norm, the CA was entitled to reduce them to that measure. By like token, the CA was entitled to formulate rights more generously than would be required by the 'universally accepted' norm, or even to establish new rights.

The Constitutional Court read CP II strictly/literally in order to arrive at a minimalist understanding of it: 'universally accepted' is a minimum standard beyond which the South African constitution-makers were free to go (and had indeed gone) by, for instance, entrenching a right to just administrative action and a right of access to information.[58] But the court remained silent on what the criteria for that minimum standard were and on how far the CA's discretion to include rights beyond that minimum standard went. Would it, for instance, have been admissible to include a right to carry firearms in the Bill of Rights? And was the fact that a right to free economic activity is not widely recognized in the international arena sufficient reason to exclude it from the Bill of Rights?[59]

Actually the *First Certification* judgment does not provide very useful guidance on recourse to international law in the development of a South African human-rights jurisprudence, and it bears out the hypothesis[60] that a domestic judiciary's positive (or 'friendly') attitude towards international law as a source informing the construction and development of municipal human rights law, does not necessarily translate into optimal reliance on or use of international law. Perhaps the Constitutional Court thought that it was unnecessary to use the certification of the Constitution as an occasion to say more about the role and status of international law in domestic jurisprudence since it had elaborated on the topic before (as will next be shown).

3.2 *S v Makwanyane and Another*[61] (1995)

Mkwanyane, the Constitutional Court's inaugural judgment (so to speak),[62] is a benchmark in several respects. The Constitutional Court was called upon to test the constitutional validity of a statutory provision[63] authorizing the imposition of the death penalty for murder. The main line of attack on the impugned legislation was that the death penalty is cruel, inhuman and degrading punishment and that statutory authorization to impose it contradicted a constitutional guarantee against such punishment.[64] The issue involved, impelled the Constitutional Court to feel

---

[58] Cf section 2.1.   [59] Cf section 2.1.   [60] See s 1.

[61] (1995) (6) BCLR 665 (1995 (3) SA 391) (1995 (2) SACR 1) (CC).

[62] Francois Venter 'The Politics of Constitutional Adjudication' (2005) 65 Zeitschrift für ausländisches öffentliches Recht und Völkerrecht 143.

[63] Criminal Procedure Act 51 of 1977, s 277(1)(a).

[64] Embodied in s 11(2) of the transitional Constitution 1993 and s 12 (1)(c) of the Constitution of 1996, s 12(1)(e)

the international community's pulse on standards of punishment. This provided the court with a golden opportunity to reflect on the interaction of domestic and international law, pursuant to the constitutional injunction to have regard to international law when interpreting the Bill of Rights.[65]

So contentious an issue was capital punishment during constitutional negotiations, that the negotiators eventually had to break the deadlock by opting for a 'Solomonic solution'[66]: the death penalty was not mentioned in the (transitional) Constitution at all, leaving it to the (still to be established) Constitutional Court to settle this controversy.[67] Chaskalson P in his judgment in the *Makwanyane* case[68] thus thought it necessary to take the genesis of the constitutional text into account, but to justify this *modus operandi*, he was left with a South African common law on statutory interpretation prone to pit itself against—but not wholly excluding—reliance on preparatory material to construe enacted law.[69] Chaskalson P then got beyond the conventional common law restraints by arguing that reliance on *travaux préparatoires* is appropriate in constitutional interpretation, because it is accepted in other 'countries in which the Constitution is . . . supreme law'—and he gave examples.[70] 'The European Court of Human Rights and the United Nations Committee on Human Rights', he then continued, (also) 'all allow their deliberations to be informed by *travaux préparatoires*'.[71] He cited Article 32 of the Vienna Convention on the Law of Treaties 1969 as authority for the contention that *travaux préparatoires* may thus be relied on—also in constitutional interpretation. The Vienna 'Convention on Conventions' is 'international law' as contemplated in section 35(1) of the transitional (and section 39(1)(b) of the 1996) Constitution (see below), but Articles 31–33 of the Convention is international law applicable (only or, at least, primarily) to the interpretation of *international* documents and instruments ('treaties') *and not to* the interpretation of a domestic Constitution.[72] However, since the Constitutional Court, as South Africa's highest court in constitutional matters, has held (albeit probably *per errorem*) that the 'Convention on Conventions' may be relied on to guide the interpretation of

---

[65] In *Makwanyane* the Constitutional Court still worked with the predecessor to the present s 39(1)(b) of the Constitution, to wit s 35(1) of the IC which enjoined a court of law interpreting the Bill of Rights to 'have regard to public international law'. In s 39(1)(b) of the present (1996) Constitution a 'court, tribunal or forum' is required to *consider* international law.

[66] *Makwanyane* (n 61 above) paras 22 and 25.

[67] It is of course also not referred to in the final Constitution either, but the reason for this 'silence' is that *Makwanyane* is taken to be the authority that has excluded the possibility of capital punishment once and for all.

[68] The judges were unanimous in their finding that capital punishment was unconstitutional, but each one of them handed down a separate judgment. The Chaskalson judgment set the tone and dealt most fully with all the issues canvassed by the parties before the court. Most of the other judgments elaborated on matters that were not so fully dealt with in the Chaskalson judgment.

[69] *Makwanyane* (n 61 above) para 14; cf also Du Plessis, *Re-Interpretation* (n 45 above) 268–69.

[70] Ibid, para 16.   [71] Ibid, para 16.

[72] Cf, eg the reasoning supporting this conclusion in section 2.2.2.

South Africa's Constitution and Bill of Rights, this has become part of the law (of interpretation) as it stands, providing a telling example of how an entirely persuasive international law-text can, through judicial law-making, be turned into prescriptive domestic law.

Chaskalson P thought that in the specific circumstances of the *Makwanyane* case 'international and foreign authorities [were] of value because they analyse arguments for and against the death sentence and show how Courts of other jurisdictions have dealt with this vexed issue. For that reason alone they require... attention.'[73] He added that the said authorities may also have to be considered because of their relevance to section 35(1) of the transitional Constitution,[74] the somewhat differently worded predecessor to section 39(1)(b) of the 1996 Constitution.[75]

Chaskalson P then proceeded with an overview of relevant international law authorities and especially foreign case law, which he concluded with the following directive observations[76]:

In dealing with comparative law we must bear in mind that we are required to construe the South African Constitution, and not an international instrument or the constitution of some foreign country, and that this has to be done with due regard to our legal system, our history and circumstances, and the structure and language of our own Constitution. We can derive assistance from public international law and foreign case law, but we are in no way bound to follow it.[77]

This dictum, on the one hand, confirms a point that was previously emphasized: the South African Constitution and Bill of Rights are to be construed in accordance with recognized procedures and strategies for the interpretation of enacted (domestic) law and not as if they were sources of international law. This means that, in the South African context, a constitutional provision derived from an international-law source could be construed to have a meaning different to its accepted meaning in international law.[78] On the other hand there is a baffling flaw in Chaskalson P's dictum: not only does it treat international law and foreign case law in the same breath, but it also suggests that they are the same type of normative authority—an oft-repeated misconception in later cases. In the judgment of the Constitutional Court, in *Sanderson v Attorney-General, Eastern Cape*,[79] Kriegler J, for instance, had the following to say about the effect of section 35(1) of the transitional and section 39(1)(b) and (c) of the 1996 Constitution: 'In this context I wish to repeat a warning I have expressed in the past. Comparative research is generally valuable and is all the more so when dealing with problems new to our

---

[73] *Makwanyane* (n 61 above) para 34.   [74] Ibid, para 34.

[75] s 39(1)(b) differs from the s 35(1) only in one respect that could be material: the latter enjoined and authorised adjudicators 'to have regard to' public international law and foreign case law respectively while the former uses the verb 'consider'—cf n 65 and section 2.2.2 above.

[76] Based on *dicta* of Kentridge J in *S v Zuma and Others* 1995 (4) BCLR 401 (1995 (2) SA 642) (CC) with regard to foreign case law in particular.   [77] *S v Makwanyane* (n 61 above) para 39.

[78] Cf section 2.2.2.   [79] 1997 (12) BCLR 1675 (1998 (2) SA 38) (CC), para 26.

jurisprudence but well developed in mature constitutional democracies. Both the interim and the final Constitutions, moreover, indicate that comparative research is either mandatory or advisable.'

Botha and Olivier quite correctly observe that this *dictum* (in the context in which it occurs) in point of fact suggests that '(public) international law' mentioned in sections 35(1) and 39(1)(b) is synonymous to foreign case law mentioned (also) in section 35(1) of the transitional and section 39(1)(c) of the 1996 Constitution— which actually means that any possible effects of sections 231 and 232[80] of the (1996) Constitution, successors to section 231 of the transitional Constitution, are entirely overlooked.[81]

Chaskalson P in *Makwanyane* observed that section 231 of the transitional Constitution 'sets the requirements' for customary international law and the ratification and accession to international agreements 'to be binding [law] within South Africa'.[82] The purpose of his observation is to introduce the more significant finding that

[i]n the context of s 35(1), public international law would include non-binding as well as binding law. They may both be used under the section as tools of interpretation. International agreements and customary international law accordingly provide a framework within which Chapter 3 can be evaluated and understood, and for that purpose, decisions of tribunals dealing with comparable instruments, such as the United Nations Committee on Human Rights, the Inter-American Commission on Human Rights, the Inter-American Court of Human Rights, the European Commission on Human Rights, and the European Court of Human Rights, and in appropriate cases, reports of specialised agencies such as the International Labour Organisation, may provide guidance as to the correct interpretation of particular provisions of Chapter 3 [the Bill of Rights].[83]

Chaskalson P cites John Dugard[84] as authority for this finding, but Botha and Olivier[85] quite convincingly contend that what Dugard had in mind probably were the (less than 'free for all') 'traditional sources of international law' recognized in Article 38(1) of the Statute of the International Court of Justice. Dugard apparently confirmed this position in a subsequent article.[86] Chaskalson P thus misinterpreted the source on which he relied and once more laid down binding (that is, *prescriptive*) case law *per errorem*, as it were. This piece of judge-made law has in

---

[80] Cf section 2.2.1.

[81] In *Fraser v Children's Court, Pretoria North, and Others* (1997) (6) BCLR (1997 (2) SA 261) (CC) para 30 Mahomed DP anticipates a discussion of the legal position of unmarried fathers 'in certain foreign jurisdictions' and then includes under this heading reference to a judgment of the European Court of Human Rights.   [82] *Makwanyane* (n 61 above) para 35.

[83] *Makwanyane* (n 61 above) para 35.

[84] J Dugard, 'International Human Rights' in D van Wyk, J Dugard, B de Villiers and D Davis (eds), *Rights and Constitutionalism: The New South African Legal Order* (Cape Town: Kenwyn Juta & Co Ltd, 1994) 171.

[85] N Botha and M Olivier, 'Ten Years of International Law in the South African Courts' (2004) 29 SAYIL 42–46.

[86] J Dugard, 'International Law and the "final" Constitution' (1995) 11 SAJHR 2 241.

the meantime turned out to be of considerable consequence in the evolution of South Africa's domestic human rights law drawing on sources of international law in a decidedly direct and monistic manner.[87]

Chaskalson P's discussion of international and foreign comparative law commenced with observations indicative of an ever increasing abolition of or, at least, a decidedly decreasing reliance on capital punishment worldwide.[88] His announcement that '[c]apital punishment is not prohibited by public international law'[89] therefore comes as a bit of an anticlimax. And yet this is not *cadit quaestio*—the absence of a downright prohibition of capital punishment in international law is but 'a factor that has to be taken into account in deciding whether it is cruel, inhuman or degrading punishment' within the meaning of section 11(2) of the transitional Constitution.[90] Chaskalson P made much of differences between the text of South Africa's transitional Constitution and international and foreign documents and instruments which leave room for the death penalty, stressing the fact that section 9 of the transitional Constitution guaranteed the right to life without any qualification.[91] In concluding 'that the death sentence by definition is cruel and degrading punishment' Chaskalson P relied on at least one international authority, to wit the United Nations Committee on Human Rights.[92]

3.3 *Ex parte Gauteng Legislature: In re Dispute Concerning the Constitutionality of Certain Provisions of the Gauteng School Education Bill of 1995*[93] (1996)

On the petition of various members of the Gauteng Provincial Legislature the Speaker requested the Constitutional Court to resolve a dispute that arose concerning the constitutionality of certain provisions of a bill dealing with the provision and control of education in public schools. Among the provisions targeted by the petitioners was clause 19(1) of the bill, prohibiting the use of language competence testing as a requirement for admission to a public school. Section 32(b) of the transitional Constitution guaranteed everyone's right to instruction in the language of his or her choice where this is reasonably practicable, and section 32(c) the right to establish, where practicable, educational institutions based on a common culture, language or religion, provided that there shall be no discrimination on the ground of race.[94] According to the Petitioners, mainly representing the interests of (white) Afrikaans speakers, Clause 19(1) fell foul of these guarantees since it undermined the ability of schools to cater for education in a specific language.[95]

---

[87] Cf also Z Motala and C Ramaphosa, *Constitutional Law: An Analysis and Cases* (OUP, Oxford 2002) 37.   [88] *Makwanyane* (n 61 above) para 33.
[89] Ibid, para 36.   [90] Ibid.   [91] Ibid, paras 36–39.   [92] Ibid, para 90.
[93] 1996 (4) BCLR 537 (1996 (3) SA 165) (CC).
[94] s 32(a) guaranteed a right to basic education and to equal access to educational institutions. The successor to s 32 is s 29 of the 1996 Constitution—see section 2.1.
[95] The petitioners' other challenges are not dealt with, since the judgment of Sachs J that actually dealt with international law issues, dealt mainly with the question of language.

Sachs J prefaced his minority judgment in this case by voicing a preparedness to give effect to international human rights law on minority protection 'even if straining against the text' of section 32 of the transitional Constitution.[96] He agreed with the majority[97] of the court that a straightforward reading of section 32 ran counter to the contentions of the petitioners, but found it necessary nonetheless to consider the possibility that reliance on international law principles with regard to minority rights, might lead to a different result.[98] Such an inquiry requires locating the issue in its broad domestic historical and constitutional context[99] and in doing so Sachs J made four assumptions in favour of the Petitioners which he then contextualized—and (counter-) 'balanced', as it were—with three significant considerations highlighted by the Constitution.[100]

His next step was to consider section 32's compliance with six universally accepted principles, gleaned from international law sources on the protection of minorities,[101] situating the said principles in the domestic context. These principles, engaged with varying degrees of relevance and intensity, were (i) the *right to existence*[102]; (ii) *non-discrimination*[103]; (iii) *equal rights*[104]; (iv) *the right to develop autonomously within civil society*[105]; (v) *affirmative action*[106], and (vi) *positive support from the State*.[107] Sachs J eventually agreed with the interpretation placed on section 32(c) in the majority judgment and concluded (in addition) that international law on the subject reinforced the conclusion of the majority. This minority judgment is a good illustration of—as opposed to just an argumentation about— the dynamics of a duly contextualized interaction between international and municipal human rights law on a topical issue.

3.4 *Azanian Peoples Organisation (AZAPO) and Others v President of the Republic of South Africa and Others*[108] (1996)

The text of South Africa's transitional Constitution concluded with a most unusual 'postamble'[109] entitled 'National Unity and Reconciliation' and 'for all purposes . . . deemed to form part of the substance of' the Constitution.[110] The postamble emphasised the need for national reconciliation and a healing of the divisions of the past, and required amnesty to be granted 'in respect of acts, omissions and offences associated with political objectives and committed in the course of the conflicts of the past'. It furthermore instructed Parliament to determine a cut-off date and procedures to apply for such amnesty. The Promotion of National Unity and Reconciliation Act[111] was subsequently enacted. The act stipulated conditions—and laid down the procedures to apply—for amnesty. A Truth and Reconciliation

---

[96] *Gauteng* (n 93 above) para 44.   [97] Ibid, para 1–37.   [98] Ibid, para 44.
[99] Ibid, para 45.   [100] Ibid, para 50.   [101] *Gauteng* (n 93 above), paras 55–68.
[102] Ibid, para 70.   [103] Ibid, para 71.   [104] Ibid, para 72–74.
[105] Ibid, para 75–81.   [106] Ibid, para 82–83.   [107] Ibid, para 83–89.
[108] 1996 (8) BCLR 1015 (1996 (4) SA 672) (CC).   [109] As opposed to a *preamble*.
[110] Cf s 232(4) of the transitional Constitution 1993.
[111] Promotion of National Unity and Reconciliation Act 34 of 1995.

Commission (TRC) was called into existence[112] the Amnesty Committee of which was authorized to grant the perpetrators of the acts, omissions, and offences aforesaid immunity from both criminal prosecution and civil liability, provided that they fully disclosed all the relevant facts relating to acts associated with a political objective. Section 20(7) was the provision confirming that such immunity would be consequent upon a successful application for amnesty.

AZAPO challenged the constitutionality of section 20(7) alleging that it breached every person's right (guaranteed in section 22 of the transitional Constitution) 'to have justiciable disputes settled by a court of law or... another independent and impartial forum'. Mahomed DP handed down the Constitutional Court's majority judgment,[113] steadily considering the constitutional merits and demerits of the amnesty process. Of present interest is chiefly the section of the judgment dealing with AZAPO's contention that a State is required by international law, and a series of Geneva Conventions in particular, to prosecute those responsible for gross human rights violations (such as wilful killing, torture, or inhuman treatment and wilfully causing great suffering or serious injury to body or health) and that section 20(7) of the act thus breached international law.[114] In terms of the said Conventions: 'The High Contracting Parties undertake to enact any legislation necessary to provide effective penal sanctions for persons committing, or ordering to be committed, any of the grave breaches.'

The court verbalized its approach to reliance on international law in the present instance as follows:[115]

The issue which falls to be determined in this Court is whether section 20(7) of the Act is inconsistent with the Constitution. If it is, the enquiry as to whether or not international law prescribes a different duty is irrelevant to that determination. International law and the contents of international treaties to which South Africa might or might not be a party at any particular time are, in my view, relevant only in the interpretation of the Constitution itself, on the grounds that the lawmakers of the Constitution should not lightly be presumed to authorise any law which might constitute a breach of the obligations of the State in terms of international law. International conventions and treaties do not become part of the municipal law of our country, enforceable at the instance of private individuals in our courts, until and unless they are incorporated into the municipal law by legislative enactment.

According to Mahomed DP this last contention derived from section 231 of the transitional Constitution, the constitutional 'black-letter law' on the recognition, status and force of international law preceding sections 231 and 232 of the 1996 Constitution.[116] An evidently literal(-ist) reading of section 231 of the transitional

---

[112] Cf s 3.   [113] Didcott J handed down a separate concurring judgment.
[114] *AZAPO* (n 108) para 25.   [115] Ibid para 26.
[116] See section 2.2.1; cf also section 3.2, s 231 of the transitional Constitution provided as follows:
  '(1) All rights and obligations under international agreements which immediately before the commencement of this Constitution were vested in or binding on the Republic within the meaning of the previous Constitution, shall be vested in or binding on the Republic under this Constitution, unless provided otherwise by an Act of Parliament.

Constitution brought the court to the conclusion 'that when Parliament agrees to the ratification of or accession to an international agreement such agreement becomes part of the law of the country only if Parliament expressly so provides and the agreement is not inconsistent with the Constitution'.[117] An Act of Parliament can furthermore, so the court thought, 'override any contrary rights or obligations under international agreements entered into before the commencement of the Constitution'.[118] Section 35(1) of the transitional Constitution—the predecessor to Section 39(1)(b) of the 1996 Constitution[119]—is, in the court's view, also perfectly consistent with the foregoing conclusions. 'The court is directed *only* to 'have regard' to public international law if it is applicable to the protection of the rights entrenched in the chapter'[120] (emphasis added).

Specific rules of international law embodied in the Geneva Conventions would, according to Mahomed DP, be irrelevant if the impugned section 20(7) had indeed been authorised by the Constitution, but the Conventions on which the Applicants relied in any event did not assist their case. First, it was doubtful, on technical grounds pertaining to the nature of the conflict in South Africa, whether these Conventions applied.[121] Second, international law attaches dissimilar consequences to severe acts of violence carried out in the course of a war between States, and such acts committed, within the territory of a sovereign State, pursuant to a conflict between the forces of that state and dissident forces operating under responsible command. Under the Geneva Conventions a contracting state is under no obligation to prosecute perpetrators in the latter category, even for 'grave breaches' of human rights. This is so because upon cessation of the conflict, erstwhile adversaries most often have to face the prospect of living and working with each other, and it is then best left to the state concerned to decide what measures will be most conducive to national reconciliation and reconstruction.[122] So far the court's findings.

The Constitutional Court's judgment in *AZAPO* was handed down on 25 July 1996—one year, one month and nineteen days after the *Makwanyane* judgment of 6 June 1995. Save for the absence of Kentridge AJ in *AZAPO*, the panels of concurring judges in *AZAPO* and *Makwanyane* respectively were identical. This piece of empirical evidence highlights the bizarreness of the switch in the court's view on the implementation of international law: the magnanimous monism of *Makwanyane* made way for a determinate dualism in *AZAPO*. International law scholars have pointed out that the fixation of the court in *AZAPO* with the Geneva

(2) Parliament shall, subject to this Constitution, be competent to agree to the ratification of or accession to an international agreement negotiated and signed in terms of section 82 (1) (*i*).

(3) Where Parliament agrees to the ratification of or accession to an international agreement under subsection (2), such international agreement shall be binding on the Republic and shall form part of the law of the Republic, provided Parliament expressly so provides and such agreement is not inconsistent with this Constitution.

(4) The rules of customary international law binding on the Republic, shall, unless inconsistent with this Constitution or an Act of Parliament, form part of the law of the Republic.'

---

[117] *AZAPO* (n 108 above) para 27.   [118] Ibid, para 27.   [119] See section 3.2.
[120] *AZAPO* (n 108 above) para 27.   [121] Ibid, para 29.   [122] Ibid, para 30–31.

Conventions as sources of international law on amnesty, was ill-conceived, since cogent authority in other sources of international law point to a sustained obligation of States always to prosecute the perpetrators of grave breaches of human rights, irrespective of the nature of the conflict in the course of which such breaches occurred.[123] The court's understanding that, in terms of the Geneva Conventions, acts of violence in a war between States and in a conflict between a State and its dissident citizens (may) attract dissimilar consequences, has also been questioned.[124]

A final assessment of the two foregoing points of criticism (which, I must add, seems to be rather valid) is best left to international law experts. The critical observations that now follow are directed at the Constitutional Court's interpretive strategy in *AZAPO*.

A dictum of Chaskalson P in *Makwanyane* in which he stated that international agreements and customary international law provide a framework within which the Bill of Rights in the transitional Constitution could be evaluated and understood, was previously quoted.[125] Mokgoro J, in a somewhat more categorical vein, voiced a similar sentiment, stating that the transitional Constitution: 'requires courts to proceed to public international law and foreign case law for guidance in constitutional interpretation, thereby promoting the ideal and internationally accepted values in the cultivation of a human rights jurisprudence for South Africa'.[126]

Very little became of this strategy in *AZAPO*, the only case in which the Constitutional Court considered the (transitional) Constitution's 'black-letter law' on the recognition, status, and force of international law. In *Makwanyane* Chaskalson P referred to section 231 of the transitional Constitution to introduce his significant findings on the generous use of international law sources to assist the construction of provisions of the Bill of Rights in that Constitution.[127] In *AZAPO* a literal interpretation of section 231 (and section 231(1) in particular) was invoked to rein in the effects of international law—and bear in mind that section 231 was to a large extent but a transitional arrangement lacking the sophistication of sections 231–33 of the 1996 Constitution. Ziyad Motala, for instance, describes section 231(1) of the transitional Constitution as 'a claw-back clause allowing parliament to change treaty obligations and customary international law rules with respect to international agreements'.[128]

Section 35(1) of the transitional Constitution, the court found, was perfectly consistent with section 231 of that Constitution because '[t]he court is directed only to "have regard" to public international law if it is applicable to the protection of the rights entrenched in' the Bill of Rights.[129] One of the startling implications of this finding is that section 231 of the transitional Constitution had to be invoked

---

[123] Z Motala, 'The Constitutional Court's Approach to International Law and its Method of Interpretation in the *"Amnesty Decision": Intellectual Honesty or Political Expediency?* (1996) 21 South African Yearbook of International Law 31, 38–40 and 48–52.   [124] Ibid, 29, 31 and 53–57.
[125] *S v Makwanyane* (n 61 above) para 35; cf section 3.2.   [126] Ibid, para 304.
[127] Ibid, para 35; cf section 3.2.
[128] Motala, 'The Constitutional Court's Approach' (n 123 above) 29, 35.
[129] *AZAPO* (n 108 above) para 27.

to determine what may qualify as (binding) international law to which the court had to have regard in terms of section 35(1). Sections 231 and 35(1) provided for two different ways of invoking international law for two different purposes, namely, in the first instance, to determine what binding international law is and, in the second instance, to aid the interpretation of a domestic Bill of Rights.[130] This Chaskalson P rightly saw—hence his conclusion that the section 35(1) reference to international law covered non-binding international law too. However, this finding was no invitation to rely on international law in an arbitrary ('free for all') manner: there was (and under the 1996 Constitution still is) an obligation to 'have regard to' (the present version reads 'to consider') international law. The prescriptive authority of the Constitution was/is thus invoked peremptorily, to direct attention to international law in its broad signification, and then to consider its application. What the *AZAPO* findings amounted to was that section 231 had to be invoked to determine to what international law a court was bound, and section 35(1) would then serve as justification for reliance on such binding international law to construe provisions of the Bill of Rights. That is absurd. A court, tribunal, or forum or any other law-enforcing agency must at any rate be alert to law that (possibly) binds it and must 'obey' such law if it is found to be binding. There is no need for a special provision to remind any such organ that it should have regard to (or should consider) such binding law: it is its duty to do so.[131] Section 35(1) of the transitional Constitution could thus not have had (and section 39(1)(b) of the 1996 Constitution does not have) any function other than prompting regard to (or consideration of) international law not binding in terms of section 231 of the transitional (or sections 231–33 of the 1996) Constitution.

3.5 *Government of the RSA and Others v Grootboom and Others* (2000)[132]

In *Grootboom* the Respondents, 510 children and 390 adults, had been evicted from their informal homes situated on private land earmarked for formal low-cost housing. They applied to the Cape High Court for an order requiring the government to provide them with adequate basic shelter or housing until they obtained permanent accommodation. The High Court, concentrating mainly on the children's right to basic shelter, ordered the Appellants, all of them organs of State responsible for the provision of housing, to provide the Respondents with shelter. The Appellants appealed first to the Supreme Court of Appeal and finally to the Constitutional Court.

The Constitutional Court focused on the construction of section 26 of the (1996) Constitution guaranteeing everyone's right to adequate housing[133] and enjoining the state to take reasonable legislative and other measures within its available resources to achieve the realisation of this right.[134] Reflecting on the justiciability

---

[130] Constitution of 1996, ss 231–33 and s 39(1)(b) presently fulfil the same two functions.
[131] Cf section 2.2.1.   [132] 2000 (11) BCLR 1169 (2001 (1) SA 46) (CC).
[133] Constitution 1996, s 26(1).   [134] Ibid, s 26(2); cf also section 2.1.

and enforceability of socioeconomic rights (and the right of access to housing in particular) as well as the nature and extent of positive obligations on the state attendant upon constitutional guarantees of such rights, the Constitutional Court per Yacoob J considered, amongst others, sources of international law. He quoted the dictum of Chaskalson P in *Makwanyane* in which he stated that international agreements and customary international law provide a framework within which the Bill of Rights in the transitional Constitution could be evaluated and understood,[135] but then added a significant qualification[136]: 'The relevant international law can be a guide to interpretation but the weight to be attached to any particular principle or rule of international law will vary. However, where the relevant principle of international law binds South Africa, it may be directly applicable'.

The court thus honoured—and, bearing in mind the judgment in *AZAPO*,[137] indeed restored—the distinction between international law binding on South Africa and other sources of international law that must, in addition to binding law, be considered in the interpretation of the Bill of Rights. The court concentrated its inquiry mainly on Articles 11.1 and 2.1 of the ICESCR and pointed out differences of interpretive significance between the formulation of these provisions of the Covenant and section 26 of the South African Constitution.[138] However, the court accepted a submission of the *amici* in the case that the relevant general comments issued by the United Nations Committee on Economic, Social and Cultural Rights regarding the interpretation of the ICESCR 'constitute a significant guide to the interpretation of section 26'.[139] The purpose of the Committee, consisting of 18 independent experts, is to assist the United Nations Economic and Social Council to carry out its responsibilities relating to the implementation of the ICESCR. The court allowed itself to be guided by the Committee's general comments in order to determine what the notion of 'a minimum core' of socioeconomic rights entails. By doing this, the court further developed the *Makwanyane* standard on recourse to non-binding international law, authorising reliance on a text very much suggested by common sense, but not necessarily prescriptive as *international law*. There is a possibility, though, that the Committee's general comments may be of relevance for South Africa because they constitute an instance of international-law interpretation of international human rights, but the court did not consider this possibility.

3.6 *Mohamed and Another v President of the RSA and Others*[140] (2001) and *Kaunda and Others v President of the RSA and Others (2)*[141] (2004)

The erstwhile pariah of international human rights law has become one of its staunchest protectors in the international arena—this is the message of the *Mohamed*

---

[135] *Makwanyane* (n 61 above) para 35; cf section 3.2. [136] *Grootboom* (n 132 above) para 26.
[137] See section 3.4. [138] Ibid, para 28. [139] Ibid, para 29.
[140] (2001) (7) BCLR 685 (2001 (3) SA 893) (CC). [141] (2004) (10) BCLR 1009 (CC).

judgment. The role of protector in the international arena is finite, though, and especially the judiciary must watch its step, lest it disturbs the delicate balance of power
back home—this is the message of *Kaunda*.

In *Mohamed* the Constitutional Court had the opportunity to revisit the death
penalty, albeit in a seemingly roundabout way. Mohamed, a foreign national, was
arrested by South African immigration authorities as an illegal immigrant and
handed over to United States agents for removal to the United States of America
where the prosecuting authority was waiting to arraign him on capital charges related
to his alleged involvement in the bombing in 1998 of the United States Embassy
in Dar es Salaam. The South African immigration authorities acted in breach of
procedures laid down in the Aliens Control Act[142] to procure this 'handing over'
that professed to be a deportation.

A unanimous Constitutional Court held that what had taken place was actually
an extradition in disguise which was also unlawful in the absence of an undertaking by the United States government that Mohamed would not be executed if
convicted. Such a handing over infringed the arrested person's constitutional rights
to life, to dignity and not to be subjected to cruel, inhuman, or degrading punishment. In the circumstances the South African government was actually charged
with *an obligation* to seek an assurance from the receiving State that the death penalty
will not be imposed. The court described its finding in *Makwanyane*[143] 'that capital punishment is inconsistent with the values and provisions of the interim Constitution' as the cornerstone of the argument that the South African authorities
were under the obligation aforesaid.[144] It furthermore reiterated its principal findings in *Makwanyane* adding 'that the international community shares this Court's
view of the death sentence, even in the context of international tribunals with
jurisdiction over the most egregious offences, including genocide'.[145] The court
described its finding that Mohamed had been deported unlawfully[146] as 'a serious
finding':

South Africa is a young democracy still finding its way to full compliance with the values
and ideals enshrined in the Constitution. It is therefore important that the State lead by
example... [W]e saw in the past what happens when the State bends the law to its own
ends and now, in the new era of constitutionality, we may be tempted to use questionable
measures in the war against crime. The lesson becomes particularly important when dealing with those who aim to destroy the system of government through law by means of
organised violence. The legitimacy of the constitutional order is undermined rather than
reinforced when the State acts unlawfully.[147]

In considering appropriate relief the court thought that it is desirable that its views be
appropriately conveyed to the trial court in the United States[148] and, furthermore,

---

[142] Aliens Control Act, Act 96 of 1991.   [143] See section 3.2.
[144] *Mohamed* (n 140 above) para 38.   [145] Ibid, para. 39.
[146] The court also dismissed the respondents' contention that Mohamed had agreed to the handing over, thus rendering their action lawful.   [147] *Mohamed* (n 140 above) para 68.
[148] Ibid, para 70.

that it would not be 'a breach of the separation of state power as between the executive and the judiciary' to order 'the relevant organs of State in South Africa to do whatever may be within their power to remedy the wrong here done to Mohamed by their actions, or to ameliorate at best the consequential prejudice caused to him'.[149] The court accordingly declared Mohamed's handing over to the United States unlawful and authorized and directed the Director of the Constitutional Court 'to cause the full text of this judgement to be drawn to the attention of and to be delivered to' the administrative head of the relevant trial court in the United States.[150] Mohamed was eventually convicted in the United States, but not sentenced to death. It is of course not a foregone conclusion that the proceedings in South Africa's Constitutional Court and their aftermath in any way co-determined this outcome.

In sum then, *Mohamed* is a precedent of 'international significance' not so much because the Constitutional Court dealt decisively with issues of international law, but because it used the opportunity to state how it conceived of South Africa's reputation and standing in the international arena, and what it was prepared to do to enhance both.

In the *Kaunda* case 69 Applicants, arrested and detained in Zimbabwe and then charged with various offences, sought the South African government's intervention on their behalf to secure their release or extradition to South Africa and to protect them against assault and detention in atrocious conditions while still in Zimbabwe. They also sought an order directing the South African government to help prevent their extradition by the Zimbabwean government to Equatorial Guinea where they could be tried for an alleged plot to overthrow the government of that country and thus be exposed to the risk of a death penalty. The Applicants submitted that the South African government had a duty to intervene and protect their rights to life, dignity, freedom, and security of the person (including the right not to be treated or punished in a cruel, inhuman or degrading way) and also the right to a fair trial enshrined in the Constitution. South African security agencies allegedly passed intelligence information to the Zimbabwean government which resulted in the Applicants' arrest and detention and, according to the Applicants, this exacerbating factor underlined the South African government's duty to respect, protect, promote and fulfil their rights in the Bill of Rights. In the Pretoria High Court Ngoepe JP dismissed the application and the Applicants appealed directly to the Constitutional Court.

Citing section 232 of the Constitution—thereby to signal its reliance on customary international law—a majority of the Constitutional Court per Chaskalson CJ held that '[t]raditionally, international law has acknowledged that States have the right to protect their nationals beyond their borders but are under no obligation to do so'.[151] The court attached considerable weight to the opinion of a Special Rapporteur of the International Law Commission on the meaning of 'diplomatic

---

[149] Ibid, para 71.   [150] Ibid, para 73.   [151] *Kaunda* (n 141 above) para 23.

protection'[152] concluding that under current (customary) international law diplomatic protection is not recognized and cannot be enforced as a human right. Diplomatic protection remained the prerogative of the State to be exercised at its discretion.[153]

Turning to the law as it stands in South Africa the court availed itself of an interpretive aid seldom brought into play by South African courts, to wit section 233 of the Constitution,[154] which prescribes preference for 'any reasonable interpretation of the legislation that is consistent with international law over any alternative interpretation that is inconsistent with international law'. Chaskalson CJ did not hesitate to conclude that section 233 'must apply equally to the provisions of the Bill of Rights and the Constitution as a whole'.[155] Disappointingly though he set section 233 on par with section 39(1)(b) of the Constitution and thereby failed to recognize that these two *different* provisions could only have been meant to cater for dissimilar eventualities.[156] He continued to point out that there is a paucity of references to a right to diplomatic protection in international law (also in sources where one would expect references to such a right to occur). It would not have been out of place for the South African Constitution to entrench such a right, but given its absence in international law and taking into account the section 233 requirement that the Constitution must as far as possible be construed in conformity with international law, such a right then had to be spelt out in the Constitution expressly before it could be enforced.[157]

The court furthermore held that the Constitution has no application beyond South Africa's physical borders. Foreigners are indeed entitled to respect, protection and promotion of their rights, but they lose this benefit once they leave the country.[158] After an examination of international law on the extraterritorial application of domestic (human rights) law, the court concluded that nationals are as a general rule in the same position as foreigners who had left the country:[159] 'There may be special circumstances where the laws of a State are applicable to nationals beyond the State's borders, but only if the application of the law does not interfere with the sovereignty of other States.'[160]

South African nationals facing adverse state action in a foreign country are entitled nevertheless to request the South African government to help protect them against acts which might violate accepted norms of international human rights law, and the government is obliged to consider such requests and deal with them in an appropriate manner. The (administrative) action of the government in these matters is justiciable and, in particular, subject to constitutional control.[161]

The court distinguished the *Mohamed* and *Kaunda* cases on the basis that Mohamed had been arrested in South Africa and then sent to the United States by South African government officials without first securing assurance that Mohamed

---

[152] Ibid, para 25–28.   [153] Ibid, para 29.   [154] See section 2.2.1.
[155] *Kaunda* (n 141 above) para 33.   [156] See sections 2.2.2 and 3. 4.
[157] *Kaunda* (n 141 above) para 34.   [158] Ibid, para 36.   [159] Ibid, paras 38–44.
[160] Ibid, para 44.   [161] Ibid, para 44.

would not be executed, while the *Kaunda* applicants were all arrested outside South Africa where they found themselves of their own volition. In *Mohamed* the organs of State involved moreover acted unlawfully[162] while South African officials' passing on of intelligence about the alleged intentions and the whereabouts of the applicants to Zimbabwean authorities, was quite lawful and in indeed consistent with healthy (inter-)State practice.[163]

That certain issues—including the nature and exact scope of a government's duty to protect its citizens in a foreign country against violations of their rights under international law—are not as clear-cut as a superficial reading of the majority judgment in *Kaunda* might intimate, is demonstrated by the fact that the court was divided on the preferred outcome of the case. A minority, consisting of O'Regan and Mokgoro JJ, for instance, thought that a wake-up call for the executive in the form of a declaratory order (and not the full mandamus the Applicants had asked for) would not have been inappropriate in the present case.

4. In conclusion

Are there any generalizable trends in the interaction of South African domestic and international human rights law that can be held out as exemplary? Looking at the case law—and this study has focused just on the jurisprudence of the Constitutional Court—one trend seems to be that variables and imponderables, mainly on the local scene, impede a credible detection of readily extrapolatable trends. However, enough emerged from this study to substantiate the initial hypothesis that international law friendliness in a domestic jurisdiction does not automatically translate into optimal reliance on or use of international law in, for example, constitutional adjudication.[164] The South African courts' openness to and positive disposition towards international (human-rights) law has thus not always translated into the strongest possible or most profitable reliance on, and optimally skilful implementation of, international law. This is not necessarily attributable to a peculiarly South African form of parochialism or chauvinism (Anne Peters,[165] as matter of fact, notes a general reluctance among responsible actors in national constitutional orders to accept that international law trumps state constitutions), but rather to (i) deficiencies in the capacity of South African courts and other organs of state to deal with international law and (ii) (in some specific instances) to the preponderance of domestic political pressure(s). These two factors, impacting adversely on dealings with international law, will now briefly be looked at seriatim wherafter, in final conclusion, (iii) an assessment of possible damage will be made and workable remedial action will be considered.

---

[162] Ibid, para 47.   [163] *Kaunda* (n 141 above) paras 51–53.   [164] See section 1.
[165] See Peters, this volume para. V(2)(c). Peters also points out that the South African Constitutional Court has become famous for its 'universalist interpretation'—see para V(4).

4.1 Deficient capacity

Deficiencies in their capacity to deal with international law is most evident from South African courts' tendency to shy away from 'black-letter' international law as well as ('black-letter') constitutional law dealing with the recognition, status, and force of international law vis-à-vis municipal law and embodied as supreme law in sections 231–33 of the Constitution. Section 233 of the Constitution, which provides for a rather helpful and effective procedure in statutory interpretation,[166] has, for instance, since the commencement of the Constitution on 4 February 1997, only been referred to twice in constitutional jurisprudence: once (almost in passing) by Sachs J in the case of *S v Baloyi*[167] to justify his preferred interpretation of an act and once by Chaskalson CJ in the *Kaunda* case.[168] Bear in mind that for the interpretation of all enacted law other than the Bill of Rights (Chapter 2 of the Constitution) section 39(1)(b) of the Constitution, that requires consideration of international law,[169] is strictly speaking not applicable, and sections 231–33 are the appropriate provisions to put international law on stage in construing this 'other law'. That the paucity of reliance on section 233 has to do with an inadequate knowledge and awareness of international law, was painfully illustrated (as recently as 2003) in *AM Moola Group Ltd and Others v Commissioner, South African Revenue Service and Others*,[170] a case in which a South African court at the highest level, to wit the Supreme Court of Appeal, dealing with an issue of international trade law, completely overlooked section 233 as applicable, binding (or prescriptive—as opposed to persuasive) law in that particular case.[171] For a court to overlook a binding provision of the supreme Constitution, is indeed a serious blunder!

Deficient capacity in dealing with international law has also resulted in South African courts choosing overwhelmingly the section 39(1)(b) (in preference to the sections 231–33) route when they appeal to international law for interpretive purposes. And then, almost invariably and without doubt erroneously, they conflate international law and foreign (case) law.[172] This blunder deprecates 'international law as its stands in South Africa'. International law is very much comparable to South African case law with regard to the manner in which it obtains. In the context of *stare decisis* case law can either be binding or non-binding in a particular instance. When it is binding it is prescriptive (law); when it is non-binding it has persuasive force.[173] Likewise international law can be binding (on South African organs of state and on citizens) as prescriptive law by virtue of sections 231 and 232 of the Constitution or it can be 'non-binding' in this formal sense, but still

---

[166] See section 2.2.1; see also below.
[167] 2000 (1) BCLR 86(2000 (2) SA 245) (CC) para 13.   [168] See section 3.6.
[169] See section 2.2.2.   [170] 2003 (6) SA 244 (SCA).
[171] The case has been discussed by Erasmus, 'The Incorporation of Trade Agreements' (n 46 above) 157.
[172] The latter *may*, in terms of s 39(1)(c) of the Constitution, be considered in the interpretation of the Bill of Rights.
[173] L du Plessis, *An Introduction to Law* (3rd edn, Cape Town: Kenwyn Juta & Co, 1999) 240–46.

have persuasive force. Foreign law, however, can only have persuasive force either as envisaged in section 39(1)(c) (when the Bill of Rights is construed) or else because it has come to a judicial decision-maker's attention through legal comparison. 'Law as its stands in South Africa' can, however, not implicate *foreign* law. What international and foreign law have in common is that in interpretive endeavours they draw attention to a bigger world beyond the physical and mental borders of the own country—and international law does so more compellingly (or prescriptively) than foreign law does.

4.2 Political pressure

The *AZAPO* case[174] stands as an example of how domestic politics can put a court's dealings with international law under pressure, and the illustrative value of the example increases when one compares (and reflects on the marked differences between) the *AZAPO* and *Makwanyane* judgments in this regard. *AZAPO* has been described as a 'political' (and politicised) judgment thereby to account for the Constitutional Court's unsatisfactory treatment of international law in that case.[175] But this is an oversimplification. Degree-wise *Makwanyane*[176] surely was at least as 'political' as *AZAPO* was, for the Constitutional Court was expected to perform a function (and, in fact, to cast a die) that politicians were (due to insurmountable differences among themselves) not up to—and the court obliged wholeheartedly while, at the same time, it seized the opportunity to articulate its stand on key issues involved in constitutional interpretation and adjudication, including appropriate reliance on international law. Human rights adjudication involving constitutional review is at any rate always political, for as Heinz Klug reminds us[177]:

Particular histories and contexts—both *international* and local—play a significant part in setting the stage upon which judicial review is introduced. While its ability to build legitimacy through its formal judicial role is a source of strength, the comparative institutional weakness of the judicial branch . . . requires the judiciary to be circumspect in its exercise of authority over the more resourced and powerful arms of government. In asserting its constitutional powers the judiciary constantly recognizes its ultimate reliance on both the executive and legislative branches to enforce its holdings on the one hand and to protect its independence on the other[178] (emphasis added).

Makwanyane ended up as a judicial tour de force—a 'bold assertion of constitutional rights and powers'.[179] This came about because the Constitutional Court was the 'politically authorised' Solomon expected to resolve a controversy of significant political proportions. What followed was a trailblazing and directional judgment,

---

[174] Cf section 3.4.
[175] This is the gist of an article by Z Motala 'The Constitutional Court's Approach' (n 123 above) 29–59; cf also Botha and Olivier, 'Ten Years' (n 85 above) 51.   [176] Cf section 3.2.
[177] H Klug, 'Introducing the Devil: An Institutional Analysis of the Power of Constitutional Review' (1997) 13 SAJHR 85 189.   [178] Ibid, 185, 189.
[179] Ibid, 185, 194.

the outcome of which will, up to this day, probably not receive majority support in a popular referendum! And international law was one of the vital forces in occasioning this outcome.

AZAPO, because it dealt with the constitutional tenability of amnesty, touched a very raw political nerve. Amnesty was central to the politically negotiated truth and reconciliation process in South Africa, holding the key to a 'new' democracy memorialising the past without allowing it to eclipse the future. Had the court in *AZAPO* struck down the impugned section 20(7) of the Promotion of National Unity and Reconciliation Act, the truth and reconciliation process would have been jeopardized. International law stood (or was perceived to stand) in the way of the politically most feasible judgment in the circumstances (which would have been one leaving section 20(7) intact). Striking down section 20(7) would have had consequences sufficiently far-reaching to compromise the court's 'right to decide' vis-à-vis political decision-makers (who were expected to honour a political deal struck during constitutional negotiations). Unfortunately *AZAPO* ended up being an ineptly crafted judgment, especially on international law issues. In order to contain the effects of international law in the particular circumstances as much as possible, the court had resort to an overly literal and formalistic reading of the constitutional provisions designed to cater for the recognition and implementation of international law. The court's consideration of possibly applicable international law was moreover fragmentary and incomplete. In short, judicial performance in the *AZAPO* case showed that political pressure can exacerbate deficiencies in a court's capacity duly to engage with international law.

In *Kaunda*[180] the Constitutional Court was once again beset with political dilemmas—which this time also involved relations with a neighbouring State—and once more the weaknesses in the majority judgment in this case can probably be traced back to the court's political predicament. But a court's reliance on international law when seized with a (domestic) political controversy, can also yield instructive consequences—especially if the controversy in question has international law relevance too. Sachs J's minority judgment in the *Gauteng Schools* case,[181] which considered the implications of self-determination for minority groups in a crucial area, is a telling example of how political controversy can also prompt a carefully crafted (and instructive) judgment. The *Mohamed* case again, illustrates that adjudication with appreciable international directedness, can provide a domestic court with a platform to convey—'for the world to know'—what it intends doing to maintain constitutional democracy in its jurisdictional sphere and in a manner that would earn it the respect and cooperation of its peers.

4.3 Assessment

The conclusions so far, will probably give pause to international law scholars favourably impressed by a general disposition of international law friendliness in

---

[180] Cf section 3.6.   [181] Cf section 3.3.

South Africa since 1994, but at the same time, when looking more closely, concerned about the many holes in the approach of adjudicative bodies and other law-enforcing agencies to the implementation of international law. From this perspective optimal reliance on or use of international law is (unfortunately) not too often achieved. There are instances where more decided, more complete and more nuanced guidance on the (most desirable) interaction between international and national law could have been given. This is certainly true of the *Certification* judgement,[182] and not wholly inapplicable to even a judgement as monumental as *Makwanyane*.

Assessing the South African scene through the eyes of a human rights constitutionalist, fascinated by the continuous creation and recreation of 'new law' in the field over the last ten years, I am rather optimistic, though—and even impressed. International law has, in most remarkable ways, become part of the exceedingly dynamic and complex making and adaptation of (constitutional) human rights law in South Africa. Section 39(1)(b) of the Constitution makes for a suppleness congruent with (and essential because of) the dynamism of this process. Fears about adverse consequences of the *AZAPO* judgment for international law have in the meantime been allayed. On the manner of implementation of international law there has been overwhelming preference for *Makwanyane* to *AZAPO*, and in *Grootboom* the Constitutional Court significantly qualified its approach in *Makwanyane*,[183] thereby eliciting the following hopeful observation from Botha and Olivier:[184]

Yacoob's dictum offers a ray of hope for a turnabout in the neglect international law has suffered at the hands of the Constitutional Court since the Makwanyane case. Not only does Yacoob J acknowledge the varying weight to be attached to different sources of non-binding law, but he also recognises that the value of international law is not in all cases limited to an interpretive aid. Sources of international law binding on South Africa do form an integral part of South African law, and must be applied as such.

Actually the *Grootboom* case presented the Constitutional Court with another '*Makwanyane* moment' which required it to state, in unequivocal terms, its position on the adjudication of socioeconomic rights, but without compromising its 'right/authority to decide' vis-à-vis the executive. *Makwanyane* moments have mostly produced constructive reliance on and engagement with international law while the *AZAPO* type of cases have mostly brought about a fragmentary and formalistic use of international law and the constitutional provisions kick-starting it. This contrast has shown in more instances where South African courts engaged with international law, for instance (as intimated before), in *Mohamed* (in the first category) compared with *Kaunda* (in the second category).

To concretize human rights law is to participate in the dynamic and complex process of writing the bigger narrative of human rights in South Africa. It cannot

---

[182] Cf 3.1.   [183] See 3.5.
[184] Botha and Olivier, 'Ten Years' (n 85 above) 66.

be a grand or master narrative, planned in advance (and in detail), and with an ever consistent storyline. There are too many aberrations, inconsistencies, and imponderables involved. It is therefore also impossible to gauge with any reliable precision the specific 'contribution' of international law to this big narrative. If this study has as much as indicated *approximately* how dynamic a force international law has become in the evolution of South African human-rights law since 1994—a dearth of international-law skills and capacity in the field among South African jurists notwithstanding—then it might just have qualified to count as a new perspective on the divide (and interaction) between international and national law in an erstwhile pariah state.

12

Beyond the Divide

Janne Nijman and André Nollkaemper

The chapters in this book present a complex and at times confusing picture. On the one hand, the fundamental dualistic proposition (that is: the formal separation between the domestic and the international legal order)[1] remains a powerful characterization of positive law. Its key proposition is still largely valid: the validity of a rule of international law in the domestic legal order continues to be contingent on an authorizing rule of domestic law and vice versa. Dualism also remains powerful as a normative perspective. It emphasizes the separate identity and autonomy of domestic political communities over an undefined international community whose role in law-making and law-enforcement continues to suffer from problems of legitimacy[2] and which is challenged by what some would term the instrumentalization by a hegemon.[3]

On the other hand, dualism has only limited power to describe, explain, and predict the multiple interactions between the international legal order and domestic legal spheres that characterizes our age. It is true that, as Arangio-Ruiz points out, such interactions were always recognized in dualist theory, without affecting the fundamental distinction between international and domestic law.[4] One may question, however, whether these interactions have not become so manifold as to have undermined the self-contained nature of international and domestic legal systems. International legal scholarship cannot disregard the many formal and informal channels of communication between international and domestic societies. Even if these would not invalidate the basic rule that international law has no automatic validity in the domestic legal order, they circumvent it and render it much less

---

[1] Arangio-Ruiz, this volume 20; Gaja, this volume 52–53.

[2] See on legitimacy: Walter, this volume, 195–98; Brölmann, this volume, 108; D Bodansky, 'The Legitimacy of International Governance: a Coming Challenge for International Environmental Law' (1999) 93 AJIL 596; M Kumm, 'The Legitimacy of International Law: a Constitutionalist Framework of Analysis' (2004) 15 EJIL 907.

[3] See Paulus, this volume, 219. See for an excellent critique of the instrumentalization of and withdrawal from international law by hegemons, N Krisch, 'International Law in Times of Hegemony: Unequal Power and the Shaping of the International Legal Order'(2005) 16 EJIL 369,371. See also on the relationship of hegemony and international law, eg DF Vagts, 'Hegemonic International Law' (2001) 95 AJIL 843 and JE Alvarez, 'Hegemonic International Law Revisited' (2003) 95 AJIL 873.

[4] Arangio-Ruiz, this volume, 18–19.

relevant. It is in this respect that the divide between international and domestic law is eroding.

However, it is far from clear what model would replace dualism as the previously dominant concept of the (dis-)connection between international and domestic law. The chapters in this book provide different, partly overlapping and partly competing, perspectives on possible alternatives. By way of conclusion, in this chapter we will integrate the dominant lines of argument of the different chapters and suggest some directions in which the law and legal reasoning seem to be developing.

We start by identifying three trends that several chapters in this book have highlighted: the emergence of common values, the dispersion of authority and deformalization (s 1–3). We then discuss three fundamental questions that are raised by these developments and that determine our perspectives on the future development of the interaction between the international and the domestic sphere: the nature and limits of the concept of law itself (s 4), the role of normative argument (s 5), and the consequences thereof for the position of the domestic judge (s 6). In s 7, we present some tentative final conclusions.

1. Common values

Our first proposition is that the recognition of hierarchically higher universal values, highlighted in several chapters in this book, may fundamentally undermine the divide between international and domestic law. Though this argument is often made by reference to 'common' or 'universal' values, this in itself may not be enough to sustain the proposition. The mere fact that certain values are common to many or all States need not in itself have any effect on the divide between international and domestic law as, after all, much of international law consists of or reflects common values. The more precise proposition is that the fact that the international legal order recognizes that some common values possess a higher degree of normativity has an impact on the divide between international and domestic law.

The idea that 'higher norms' have a special relationship to domestic law has gained some support. Many states have ensured in their constitutional laws the supremacy of human rights standards—a position they do not grant to other international standards.[5] Some domestic courts have recognized that the normal barriers that exist between the domestic and the international legal order might give way when confronted with an international norm of a special value. This is one explanation of what happened in cases like *Baker*.[6] Moran's concept of influential authority builds on the mandatory influence of certain legal values, thus placing primacy on the distinctive nature of legal deliberation and justification.[7] This suggests that, while the supremacy of international law in itself is without effect in domestic legal

---

[5] Peters, this volume, 295; Du Plessis, this volume, 318.
[6] [1999] 2 SCR 817; see Moran, this volume, 167.   [7] Moran, this volume, 166.

orders, that may well be different for the supremacy of certain universal values. The domestically rather powerless notion of supremacy of international law would be replaced by a notion of supremacy of universal values that would be able to pierce the divide between the domestic and the international sphere.

This proposition raises two questions. The first question is why certain international norms would be treated, as far as its reception into domestic law is concerned, differently from the way a normal norm of international law is treated. The second question is what the scope of this development is—does it only apply to rules of *jus cogens* or does this concern a broader category?

As to the first question, the fact that some rules of international law may impinge on domestic law in a different manner to other rules of international law need not be immediately compelling. Traditionally, the rules of international law that govern the relationship between international and domestic law do not normally distinguish between different shades of normativity. A State has to comply with all rules of international law that are binding on it and has to make the adjustments in its domestic legal order that allow that State to comply with international law— without regard to a hierarchical differentiation. Indeed, the argument that there would be a special position for hierarchically higher rules might easily lead one to the *a contrario* argument that States would not similarly be obliged with 'normal rules' of international law.[8]

Part of the answer to the question of why some norms would impact differently on domestic legal orders is that the acceptance of universal common values into the national legal orders is driven by the compelling force of their normative (moral) force and authority. The same normative power which explains that the international legal order treats certain rules differently (in particular *jus cogens*, but arguably also a wider category of human rights norms),[9] would also explain why common values transcend the divide between the international and the domestic legal order. Another side of this coin is that, in particular, when it concerns universal values, domestic courts may seem themselves to be addressing a world-wide community. The values of the international community are an indication of a global legal opinion that at the same time infiltrates domestic legal orders and is sustained by the opinions of domestic actors.[10]

An alternative answer is that the recognition of common values would undermine the basis of the divide, that is: the dominance of national societies that each had formed their own distinct legal order, protected against outside influence from the international sphere. With the recognition of the existence of an international

---

[8] E de Wet, 'The Prohibition of Torture as an International Norm of Jus Cogens and its Implications for National and Customary Law' (2004) 15 EJIL 100.

[9] See, eg B Simma, 'International Human Rights and General International Law: a Comparative Analysis' (1995) *Collected Courses of the Academy of European Law* 153. See generally on hierarchy JHH Weiler and Andreas L Paulus, The Structure of Change in International Law or Is There a Hierarchy of Norms in International Law' (1997) 8 EJIL 545 and M Koskenniemi, 'Hierarchy in International Law: A Sketch' (1997) 8 EJIL 566.   [10] Paulus, this volume, 250.

community, of which all domestic communities are part, the basis of that claim to autonomy would fade away. Those norms that protect the interests of the international community as a whole would automatically protect the interests of domestic societies. This argument would thus rest not (only) on hierarchy as such, but also on the related proposition that for hierarchically higher norms, consent of states with the validity of the norm as well as its incorporation in domestic law can be presumed. This is in line with Paulus' observation that the international community is not a foreign enforcer of decisions against the will of States, but gives an indication of global legal opinion: 'In the age of globalization, domestic decisions affect a broader community and are themselves part of a larger context than the nation State. In this vein, domestic courts are playing an indispensable role as interpreters and "translators" of international standards and principles into action.'[11]

The second question is what would be the scope of the impact of hierarchically higher norms on domestic law. Some of the practice and literature seems to confine the potential impact of hierarchy on the divide between international and domestic law to the narrowest category of hierarchy: *jus cogens*.[12] However, there is also practice that resorts to a broader group of universal values, in particular human rights law, which certainly cannot entirely be qualified as *jus cogens*. When domestic courts resort to 'common values' even if not strictly part of its domestic legal system,[13] this does not seem to be confined to the category of *jus cogens*. Obviously, the broader the category, the more fundamental its attack on the dualist premise.

Recognition of the fact that hierarchically higher values lead to a fundamental change in the relationship between international law and domestic law can in a certain sense be understood as a recurrence of the monist tradition in international law. This hierarchy differs, however, from the traditional monist-dualist discussion on the superiority of either national or international law. The 'hierarchization' is one of substance, or content, not one of formality. Rather than discerning one single system of law as stemming from eg one hypothetical (hence formal, Kelsenian) basic norm, the system finds some sort of substantive common source in a basis of universal values. As formulated by Du Plessis, domestic systems follow 'the pulse of the international community'.[14] This may remind one of Lauterpacht who in a way attempted to combine Kelsen's formal conception of law as a hierarchical universal system of norms with 'the tree of justice'[15] and its natural law roots.[16] The

---

[11] Ibid, 249. See also, J Allard and A Garapon, *Les Juges dans la Mondialisation: la Nouvelle Révolution du Droit* (Paris: Le Seuil, 2005).

[12] De Wet (n 9 above). See also WN Ferdinandusse, *Direct Application of International Law in National Courts* (The Hague: TMC Asser Press, 2006) 163–71.

[13] Du Plessis, this volume, 312.   [14] Du Plessis, this volume, 321–22.

[15] H Lauterpacht, 'Kelsen's Pure Science of Law' in E Lauterpacht (ed), *International Law, the Collected Papers of Hersch Lauterpacht* (1970–1978) Vol. 2, 428.

[16] Lauterpacht noted on the superiority of fundamental human rights to positive law that these are 'rights superior to the law of the Sovereign State' recognition of which 'signif[ies] the recognition of a higher, fundamental law not only on the part of States but also, through international law, on the part of the organised international community itself'. For Lauterpacht, natural law rules are 'the

careful and perhaps hesitant opening to or inclusion of the natural law concept is due to the necessity of being able to come up with an answer in case of a conflict of rules or norms. In case of such a conflict, for (the monist) Lauterpacht 'respect of the sanctity of human personality' would indicate ultimately the right answer. Natural law as a 'higher' law has *persuasive* but potent *authority* of reason and principle derived from the necessary coexistence of a plurality of States'.[17]

It is true that an alternative reading is possible, in which hierarchy is 'simply' based on the recognition by States and other relevant actors that some norms are more important than others, and that such norms should have a greater effect in domestic law—without a necessary agreement on the source (natural law or otherwise) of such graduation. However, it is hard to identify in international legal practice an express basis for such graduation, let alone for any consequences that would have for domestic law. In any case, at a more fundamental level such developments will still be driven by some form of acceptance that there exists a hierarchy of values.

Such (transnational/global) judicial consciousness of a hierarchy of values as part of the law is in line with the initial post-WWII renaissance of natural law thinking that has challenged more classic legal positivism and that has shaped a discourse (from the 1960s and 1970s) which in many ways has moved beyond the 'hard' positivism—natural law dichotomy.[18] Thanks to (particularly) HLA Hart and the debate he generated, contemporary legal positivism continues to uphold the separation of morality and law, yet has come to recognize there may be valid legal norms which are not positive law rules yet which meet the 'rule of recognition' nonetheless. In other words, in less strict versions of positivism the formal pedigree may be supplemented with substantive (moral) conditions (provided that such condition is part of the 'rule of recognition'). Moral reasoning—as to what the law is in a given case or due to 'open' legal norms—has thus become part of positive law itself. In this modern, more moderate, version of legal positivism, the administration of justice is based on more than legal rules in a narrow sense. In Hart's words: 'the rule of recognition may incorporate as criteria of legal validity conformity with moral principles or substantive values'.[19]

---

foundation of [the] ultimate validity' of positive international law. Being 'an expression of moral claims' natural law is 'a standard of [positive law's] approximation of justice'. H Lauterpacht, *International Law and Human Rights* (London: Stevens & Sons Limited, 1950) 70–72.

[17] H Lauterpacht, 'The Grotian Tradition of International Law' (1946) 23 BYIL 1–53 also published in E Lauterpacht (ed), *International Law, the Collected Papers of Hersch Lauterpacht* (1970–78) Vol 2, 329, emphasis added.

[18] See for the importance of basic values of human dignity and of a free society, eg MS McDougal, HD Lasswell and WM Reisman, 'The World Constitutive Process of Authoritative Decision' *in* MS McDougal and WM Reisman, *International Law Essays. A Supplement to International Law in Contemporary Perspective* (New York: Foundation Press, 1981) 191. See, for the circumvention of the divide between national and international law, MS McDougal, 'The Impact of International Law upon National Law: A Policy-oriented Perspective' (1958) in McDougal et al, *Studies in World Public Order* (New Haven: Yale UP, 1960), at 171.

[19] HLA Hart, *The Concept of Law*, with Postscript edited by PA Bulloch and J Raz (2nd edn, New York: OUP, 1994) 250. Moreover, the positivist Hart agreed to a 'core of indisputable truth in the

While Hart ultimately held on to the separation of morality and law—and thus, 'law as rules'—Ronald Dworkin repudiated the separation of law and moral values and accepted moral reasoning as part of legal reasoning. His approach to 'principles as law' and 'law as interpretation' renounced a formal rule of recognition,[20] which specifies for the judiciary what is law (rules)—and can be validly applied as such—and what is 'merely' morality, hence, lacking validity. Morality—impossible to separate from law or the administration of law—will contribute to 'taking rights seriously'.[21] In other words, not only the rules of law but also its principles (which capture the values of individual rights) have to be taken seriously—being inherent part of the law—and to be respected fully when a judge interprets the law ('law as integrity').[22] As rights ('a matter of political morality'[23]) represent moral values, the primacy of rights—'rights as trumps'[24]—boils down to a hierarchy of norms.

Read against this general background of developments in modern legal theory, this alternative basis for monism—assuming a hierarchy of values as a basis for piercing the international-domestic law divide—may explain that, depending on the case, either international law may trump domestic law or vice versa. The relationship is not pre-determined by a formal legal relationship, but is determined by the substantive weight of the norm. In case a domestic court is confronted with contradictory norms, it needs to take into account the moral quality of the norms in order to decide which one is superior. In other words, it is not by definition that international law trumps national law or the other way around. It depends on the circumstances of the case and the moral quality of the norm and not merely on its formal source. This is highly relevant for '*Solange*' type of cases in domestic courts. Hierarchy arises because of the normative or moral superiority, it is not formalized in structure or permanent, but seems to depend on the case at issue.[25]

This line of value-based reasoning helps explain why so much of the modern, in particular continental, literature pertaining to the relationship between international and domestic law speaks the language of constitutional law: it speaks about

doctrines of natural law'. Ibid, 146. Or, to use his famous phrase 'the minimum content of natural law', without it—it should be admitted—social life is not possible and a community does not exist. However, such recognition is not the same as bringing down the separation between law and morality or grounding the former on the latter, it merely agrees to man's social condition.

[20] R Dworkin, *Taking Rights Seriously* (Cambridge: Harvard UP, 1977) 39 et seq.

[21] R Dworkin, *Taking Rights Seriously* (n 21 above) 22: 'when lawyers reason or dispute about legal rights and obligations, particularly in those hard cases when our problems with these concepts seem most acute, they make use of standards that do not function as rules, but operate differently as principles, policies, and other sorts of standards'. A policy is goal-oriented and belongs to the realm of the collective, a principle is a standard which has to be 'observed . . . because it is a requirement of justice or fairness or some other dimension of morality'.

[22] The administration of the law is here indeed administration of justice, the judge is involved in the interpretation of law in which he includes the moral and political principles and values of the law. See, eg R Dworkin, *Law's Empire* (1986) 238–39. He has moreover to exercise judgment such as to provide 'the *best* constructive interpretation of the community's legal practice'. Ibid, 225, emphasis added.

[23] Dworkin, *Taking Rights Seriously* (n 21 above) 90.

[24] Dworkin, *Taking Rights Seriously* (n 21 above) xi and xv.

[25] Walter, this volume, 11.

the role of fundamental values (whether domestic or international) that curtail the exercise of public power.[26] In this volume, Anne Peters notes that this leads to 'globalization of constitutional law'.[27] The recognition of fundamental international values and their infiltration into domestic law fits in a dominant pattern in modern international constitutional legal scholarship in which the objective to bring all power under the rule of law and to strive for a fairer more just world order does not only require a strengthening of *international* institutions and organizations as the panacea for the realization of international law,[28] but also of *national* institutions and organizations in their role of realizing international law. This is not only an efficient road to go,[29] it seems also to find its basis in the more principled idea that it is not the formal source (national or international law) or the (formal) national or international legal order which determines the hierarchy or superiority but the extent to which the norm reflects/represents the universal value. In the international (constitutional) order unity is secured by one (natural law or otherwise) source of core universal values. The international community is based on an internationally shared value system which generates international legal norms to be realized in both national and international courts. The international community is conceived of as a multi-level polity underpinned by common ground, ie a core value system.

The approach of the Global Administrative Law project appears in some ways to be based on the assumption that global administrative law lacks a constitutional foundation.[30] Yet, one need not see the constitutional and administrative law project as mutually exclusive. In part, the different perceptions of global order are not so much objective descriptions of a legal reality, as expressions of understandings by observers of the prevailing dynamics.[31] In any case they are rather extreme sketches of such dynamics and in reality may easily mix.

Indeed, we emphasize, with most of the authors in this book who have addressed this perspective, that the recognition of universal, hierarchically superior values is only part of the picture and that it is challenged by multiple competing perspectives. Questions of fragmentation,[32] political challenges to the infiltration of international law,[33] the continued separation of domestic political communities,[34] and more generally pluralism[35] mean that the scope of the proposition is limited to certain

[26] Walter, this volume, ch 8; Paulus, this volume, ch 9; Peters, this volume, ch 10.
[27] Peters, this volume, 254.   [28] Paulus, this volume, 220.
[29] Slaughter and Burke-White, this volume, 128.
[30] Sabino Cassese, 'Administrative law without the state? The Challenge of Global Regulation' (2005) 37 NYUJ of Int'l L & P 687–88. See for a critique of the quest for principles for a global administrative law and a plea against constitutionalism and in favour of a global administrative law based on pluralism (principles of diversity and subsidiarity) rather than on universal values, C Harlow, 'Global Administrative Law: the Quest for Principles and Values' (2006) 17 EJIL 187.
[31] Compare B Kingsbury, N Krisch and R Stewart, 'The Emergence of Global Administrative Law' (2005) 68 Law and Contemporary Problems 43.
[32] Walter, this volume, 212; Paulus this volume, 222.
[33] Du Plessis, this volume, 337.   [34] Arango-Ruiz, this volume, 51.
[35] Paulus, this volume, 248, see further *infra* 359.

situations and conditions[36] and needs to be complemented by alternative perspectives. Moreover, much of the theoretical work in this direction is based on undue reliance on a relatively narrow sample of (western) empirical material that needs to be balanced by a more global perspective which undoubtedly would provide much evidence for competing perspectives.[37]

2. Dispersion of authority

Our second proposition is that the dispersion of authority away from the centralized nation state circumvents the divide between international and domestic law. Processes of globalization, the increased cross-border movements of services, goods and capital, mobility, and communication all contribute to a new legal reality in which the state, which has traditionally guarded the door between the international and the domestic sphere, has lost its controlling power. Legal authority has shifted away from the State in both vertical and horizontal directions. Many States respond to internationalization and globalization by the 'pooling or sharing of sovereign functions'.[38] They allow international bodies to oversee and sometimes even implement and enforce domestic legislation. At the same time, authority has moved away from the state in horizontal directions. In such diverse areas as economic transactions, individual rights, and individual crimes, private persons are more and more drawn into an internationalized order, no longer shielded by, and invisible within, the State.[39]

The boundaries between international and national law become much less relevant when considering the more informal arrangements between private persons, corporations etc. This does not necessarily mean that these new actors have become part of 'the' international legal order (if such a unified international legal order could still be found), or that we have now seen a collapse between the international and national domain. This is not a matter of penetration of the sovereignty shield, but, as noted by Catherine Brölmann, of circumventing the divide.[40]

Private actors may have formed their own private international order that has little to do with national law, international law or any 'relationship' between them.[41] For instance, multinational corporations escape the national legal order, but are hardly integrated in the international legal order. There is room in between, or room outside these orders. The changing position of private parties may signal that the distinction between a national and an international domain may be too

---

[36] Compare Gaja, this volume, 62.

[37] The ILDC project seeks to balance some of the empirical bias in much of the theoretical work.

[38] M Ignatieff 'State Failure and Nation-building' in JL Holzgrefe, RO Keohane (eds), *Humanitarian Intervention* (Cambridge: CUP, 2003) 311–13.   [39] Chinkin, this volume, ch 6.

[40] Brölmann, this volume, 106.

[41] G Teubner, 'Globale Zivilverfassussungen: Alternativen zur Staatszentrierten Verfassungstheorie' (2003) 63 Zeitschrift für ausländisches öffentliches Recht und Völkerrecht 1.

simple and that we have to recognize more pluralistic perspectives, for which neither monism nor dualism provide helpful theoretical or conceptual tools. One of the challenges that globalization poses to legal theory is precisely the emergence of 'non-State' legal orders, and the resulting need for a conceptual framework which enables our discipline to accommodate different legal cultures. [42]

The divide is a metaphor whose symbolic property and communicative power has been formidable. It is part of classic international law language and imagery. The debate on monism and dualism picked up as part of the *Rechtsstaat* and *Etat de Droit* debate during the Interbellum when the influence of constitutional law scholars (such as Kelsen, Scelle, and Verdross) on international law was significant. The modern view of the State as an organ of the international community and—in Kelsen's words—as 'a subsystem, directly under international law'[43] challenged the more classic dogmas of state, sovereignty, and international law on which dualism was based as well as the orthodox monist idea of international law as '*äussere Staatsrecht*'.[44]

Today, the situation has changed considerably. The defining position of the State is undermined from the inside and from the outside. From the inside, disaggregation of the state alters the communication between international law and domestic law.[45] Disaggregation does not mean, as sometimes is erroneously thought, that the State is about to disappear. Far from it. But the phenomenon does reflect that State organs often do play a more visible and at times autonomous role vis-à-vis international law. The defining position of the State is also undermined from the outside, in the sense that there are legal and non-legal regimes emerging outside the traditional (inter-)State structures, which seek to regulate acts of private actors that largely have become immune from the power of States and of international law.

As sovereignty has declined in importance, global decision-making functions are now executed by a complex rugby scrum of nation-states, intergovernmental organizations, regional compacts, nongovernmental organizations, and informal regimes and networks. The system has become 'neomonistic', with new channels opening for the inter-penetration of international and domestic law through judicial decision, legislation, and executive action. New forms of dispute resolution, executive action, administrative decision-making and enforcement, and legislation have emerged as part of a transnational legal process that influences national conduct, transforms national interests, and helps constitute and reconstitute national

---

[42] W Twining, *Globalisation and Legal Theory* (London: Butterworths, 2000) 51.

[43] B Litchewski, SL Paulson (transl), and H Kelsen, *Introduction to the Problems of Legal Theory: A Translation of the First Edition of 'Reine Rechtslere' or Pure Theory of Law* (Oxford: Clarendon Press, 1992) 122. To Kelsen, the State *was* the domestic legal order, *not* the entity that creates this order ie *State as Law*.

[44] 'Das *äussere Staatsrecht* geht von dem Verhältnisse selbständige Staaten aus … beruht … auf unterschiedenen souveränen Willen'; GWF Hegel, *Georg Wilhelm Friedrich Hegel's Grundlinien der Philosophie des Rechts: mit Hegels eigenhändige Randbemerkungen in seinem Handexemplar der Rechtsphilosophie*, J Hoffmeister (ed) (Hamburg: Meier, 1967) para 330.

[45] Slaughter and Burke-White, this volume, 116.

identities.[46] In this new legal reality, which Koh terms *transnational legal process*—we see a 'process whereby an international law rule is interpreted through the interaction of transnational actors in a variety of law-declaring fora, then internalized into a nation's domestic legal system'.[47] The project on Global Administrative Law, which examines accountability processes of administrative action in a global administrative space, is similarly unhindered by the classical dichotomy between national polities and the inter-State sphere.[48] In the same line, it is now increasingly common to refer to domestic law and domestic institutions as instruments of international governance.[49] Krisch speculates about the 'replacement of international law by domestic law' as a form or instrument of international regulation and dominance[50] if the phenomenon of the imposition of domestic legal rules, which 'mirror international rules',[51] on other jurisdictions (eg unilateral conditions for market access and aid or anti-terrorism measures) further increase. All of this does much to circumvent and undermine the controlling power of the divide between international and domestic law.

Rather than the State as one pillar separated from yet in relation with international law, the disaggregated State has many points of attribution, many channels through which international norms continue or discontinue into the national order, and, moreover, is supplemented by such channels that operate wholly outside the state structure. Both the monist and dualist model suggest a general (dis) continuity with the position/function of the legislature as a pivotal, linch-pin in the case of monism and more of a national gatekeeper from the dualist perspective. With the phenomenon of the global governmental networks such a general description of the relationship between international and national law is obsolete. No longer can we talk of *The* Divide; it rather becomes a more fluid set of continuities and discontinuities between international and national law.

In the hierarchy of law, all legal norms are nicely connected from source to addressee. It is clear where a norm draws authority from and to whom it is ultimately addressed. The unity of the legal order 'consists in the chain that emerges as one traces the creation of norms, and thus their validity back to other norms, whose own creation is determined in turn by still other norms'. Ultimately, this leads 'to the basic norm . . . and thus to the ultimate basis of validity, which establishes the unity of this chain of creation'.[52] In the new situation, it seems that this *chain of*

---

[46] Ibid.

[47] HH Koh, 'The 1998 Frankel Lecture: Bringing International Law Home' (1998) 35 Houst L Rev 625.   [48] Kingsbury et al (n 32 above) 25.

[49] CA Whytock, 'Domestic Courts and Global Governance' (11 August, 2006). Available at SSRN: <http://ssrn.com/abstract=923907>.

[50] Krisch (n 3 above) 400 et seq. Ibid, for the repercussions for international law of the extension of principles of domestic law and politics to the global level.

[51] Ibid, 403. Also interesting in this respect is the Arafat Accountability Act, which Senator McDonnell introduced to the US Senate to hold the PLO, the Palestinian Authority, and Yasser Arafat personally accountable for failing their Oslo Accords promises towards peace. Bill S. 2194 107th US Congress (2001–2002) never passed.   [52] Kelsen (n 44 above) 64.

creation has been broken and that new and different chains have emerged. The *basic norm* is no longer the sole 'common source' which secures the unity in the plurality of all norms. Or can one convincingly argue that this still is the common source but that now other non-State based systems also spring from the promise to keep one's word, captured by the old adagium *pacta sunt servanda*?[53] Could one say that the basic norm now delegates (if not expressly, then by inaction) law-making authority not solely to governments, but that new actors are delegated authority—or rather, new actors are authorised to use their power effectively and create norms? The *chain of creation* has multiplied and now non-State and non-national forms of authority emerge. These can be effective and legitimate, but without the traditional State coercive element that for many was the defining element of law. While Kelsen conceptually unified public and private law,[54] today outside public international law new systems emerge. Rather then unification, we see the emergence of relatively autonomous non-State regimes.

All this may prima facie seem to limit the controlling power of (international) constitutional law that after all historically has been tied to the State. However, as noted in this volume by Walter, there is no inevitable reason why this would necessarily be so.[55] One of the challenges for the scholars examining these developments from the perspective of (international) constitutional law, whether internationalized domestic constitutional law or constitutionalized international law, is to examine whether its conceptual power can extend to other sources of authority.

3. Deformalization

The third development in modern international law that impinges upon the relationship between international law and domestic law is the process of de-formalization. Several contributions to this volume have noted the shortcomings of a positivist account of international law as inadequate in describing the many, formal and informal, faces of international law authority. Today, we find new concepts to describe

---

[53] See for the basic norm in international law, ibid, 107 et seq. The early Kelsen adhered to *pacta sunt servanda* as the basis of the universal legal order. However, in the second revised edition of *The Pure Theory of Law* (1960) he distanced himself from his earlier position. H Kelsen, *The Pure Theory of Law* (2nd revised edn, 1960) 216. See for his most firm utterance on *pacta sunt servanda* as the basis of international law, H Kelsen, *Das Problem der Souveränität und die Theorie des Völkerrechts, Beitrag zu Einer Reinen Rechtslehre* (Tubingen: Mohr, 1920) 217, 262, and 284.

[54] Kelsen (n 44 above), at 94: 'It will seem not at all so paradoxical, then, that from the universalistic standpoint of the Pure Theory of Law, always focused on the whole of the legal system *qua* so-called will of the state, both the private law transaction and the authoritative directive are perceived as acts of the state, that is, as material facts of law creation that are imputable to the unity of the legal system. The Pure Theory of Law thereby relativizes the opposition between private and public law, transforming it into an intra-systemic opposition, from the absolute, extra-systemic opposition of traditional legal theory, that is, from the difference between law and non-law, between law and State. And the Pure Theory proves itself as a science by breaking down the ideology, too, that is linked with absolutizing the opposition between private and public law'.   [55] Walter, this volume, 214.

extra-positivist pools of international law authority. We find, for instance, extra-positivist sources of authority such as 'persuasive authority', 'influential authority', or 'procedural authority of the international community' rooted in the idea of common values.[56]

The idea of being obliged to comply with international law is not the same as international law's inherent normative pull which causes States to take international law into account. The forces of the normative pull are not limited to the legal form. Also non-binding international law can be absorbed by the national order because of its normative pull influencing domestic legal practices. Moran's concept of *influential authority* builds on the mandatory influence of certain legal values thus placing primacy on the distinctive nature of legal deliberation and justification, rather than on binding authority.[57]

On the basis of the chapters in this book, we can distinguish several forms of deformalization. One is that the normal formal channels of communication between international legal obligations and the domestic legal order are circumvented. Koh argues in this context that a powerful model of compliance with international law is the 'interaction, interpretation, and internalization of international norms into domestic legal structures'.[58] This has little to do with technical modes of incorporation and transformation. Indeed the divide is transcended and circumvented in ways different to our traditional legislative incorporating mechanism. An illuminating example of the transcendence of the divide bypassing the issue of bindingness and simply adopting the values contained in (non-binding) international law as normative and directive for domestic policy and laws, is the initiative of the Mayor of Seattle to give (local) effect to norms contained in the Kyoto protocol—an instrument that the United States has failed to ratify.[59]

Another form of deformalization is the deformalization of international law itself. Domestic organs increasingly apply and give effect to international norms that are not binding as a matter of international law or, in the alternative, that are not binding on the State. From the perspective of domestic organs, the distinction between norms that are binding and that are not binding may become less relevant.[60] One somewhat perverse effect of this development is that it may lead to an equation of foreign law and international law and devalue the status of international law.[61]

---

[56] See Moran, this volume, 166. Compare Justice O'Conner in her keynote address 'Although international law and the law of other nations are rarely binding upon our decisions in U.S. courts, conclusions reached by other countries and by the international community should at times constitute *persuasive authority* in American courts. This is sometimes called "transjudicialism"'. Proceedings of ASIL Annual Meeting 2002 (Washington DC) 350, emphasis added.

[57] Moran, this volume, 166.   [58] Koh (n 48 above).

[59] The US Mayors Climate Protection Agreement is an initiative of the Mayor of Seattle to advance the Kyoto Protocol objectives at a local, city level where the US Federal Government declines. See <http://www.seattle.gov/mayor/climate/>.   [60] Du Plessis, this volume.

[61] Du Plessis this volume, 321–25; K Knop, 'Here and There: International Law in Domestic Courts' (2000) 32 NY J of Int'l L and Pol 501.

The deformalization of law may have significant consequences for the ways in which international norms are given effect in domestic legal order. One such consequence is the empowerment of the domestic judges vis-à-vis the legislature which fails in incorporating international norms into the national legal order. The extra-positive international law normativity which the judiciary invokes in the cases of *Baker* may be seen as a manifestation of the resilience of the *Trias Politica*—the self-correcting capacity of the State. We conceive of this phenomenon as 'the re-alignment of the State'. The domestic judiciary finds ways—empowered by the compelling normative force of international norms and values—to go where the legislature has not dared to tread.[62] Being equipped with international law as a source guiding interpretation of the law in hard cases, the judiciary is empowered to give direction in controversial social and political issues. While Anne-Marie Slaughter can argue that the State's powers disaggregate as they conjoined transnationally in global governmental networks,[63] one thus can posit as a possible counter-development that by responding to the normative pull of international law, the judiciary ensures that the State complies with international law and thus re-aligns its (sub)position within the international legal order. Is this the 'neo-monist' self-regulation of the State as subsystem of international law?

The deformalization of international law as a current development redirects us to a meta-juridical level of analysis: who or what validates non-positive law sources of international law? What may grant (democratic) legitimacy to international law which is not only non-binding but by lacking the consent of States also lacks the (hypothetical) authority coming from the governed represented by their governments. After all, consent remains the main legitimacy-conferring power.[64] Are there other ways of international representation of the governed and thus other kinds of authority? How do we assess the legitimacy of private authority?[65]

Part of the answer is found in the fact that deformalization is a parallel development to the emergence of common values. International law does not (only) find its authority in binding rules and principles, ie in conformity with the positivist model but is in a way more substantive since it is grounded on international norms as keepers of universal common *values* rather than as binding rules of positive international law. In this role, (binding or non-binding) international norms have authority because of the values they represent and even if they are not binding they may be directive in the interpretation of national law on the same issues. However, this clearly is only part of the answer and cannot account for all fundamental problems of legitimacy caused by the emergence of private authority.

---

[62] On a similar note, J Allard and A Garapon (n 13 above) who observe in order to understand the globalisation of law (*mondialisation du droit*) '[i]l faut … s'intéresser aux acteurs eux-mêmes et singulièrement aux juges'. Ibid, at 6.   [63] Slaugher and Burke-White, this volume, 117.   [64] Bodanksky (n 2 above).   [65] Chinkin, this volume, 158.

4. (Limits to) the expansion of international law

The above three developments (the normative power of fundamental values, the dispersion of authority to actors, and the process of deformalization) all push the limits of the legal domain. They may alter the communication between international society and domestic societies. But are we still operating within the field of international law? Or have they altered the identity of international law?

Two answers present themselves. A positivist reading would be that while there are obviously multiple forms of communication between the international and the domestic domain that circumvent the formal legal principles of validation, and while such forms are of obvious interest to international lawyers, they do not in themselves constitute or change law.[66] There is merit in this position. But an inevitable consequence is that we then should recognize that the domain of (international law) is only a small element (that perhaps has become less relevant over time) in a complex normative interaction between international and domestic spheres which includes many forms of normativity other then legal rules. It is a position that recognizes the modesty of the international legal project.

A different reading is possible if one adopts a notion of law that is not only source-based but is also based on authority and effectiveness.[67] It is often said that international law can only live in a 'balance of power' situation. As Reisman has already observed, the validity of international law is not only a purely formal validity of positive law, it also depends on its efficacy, ie actual behaviour of the addressees has to correspond to the law in order for law to be valid.[68]

From this starting point several interferences can be made. One is that domestic organs, in particular courts, are able to draw certain norms into the legal system, thereby granting them validity. If extra-positivist sources of international law are drawn on by domestic courts, it is hard to maintain that this process operates outside the law. They draw on substantive authority and grant international law effectiveness, thereby making and shaping the law. Allard and Garapon observe: 'Longtemps cantonnés à l'interprétation rigoreuse de droit, les juges sont peut-être aujourd'hui les agents les plus actifs de sa mondialisation et, partant, les ingénieurs de sa transformation'.[69]

A more far reaching interference would be that norms operating outside the international legal order could in this way obtain validity. One might argue that if public international law is ineffective in a certain area and new legal regimes emerge

---

[66] P Weil, 'Towards Relative Normativity in International Law?' (1983) 77 AJIL 413.

[67] WM Reisman, 'A Hard Look at Soft Law' (1988) 82 Proceedings of the American Society of International Law 373. Comparable approaches can be found in D Shelton (ed), *Commitment and Compliance, The Role of Non-Binding Norms in the International Legal System* (Oxford: OUP, 2000) 449–51; KW Abbott, RO Keohane, A Moravcsik, AM Slaughter, and D Snidal, 'The Concept of Legalization' (2000) 54 International Organization 401.   [68] Reisman (n 68 above).

[69] J Allard and A Garapon (n 12 above) 6.

which actors do comply with, that would grant them (legal) validity. Such effective regimes emerging outside public international law may be said to find their ultimate source of legal validity in the meta-positivist norm of *pacta sunt servanda*—the (moral) obligation to keep one's promise. It empowers the actors of these newly emerging regimes to regulate their conduct by the rules they create—the new 'chains of creation'. This then also would be a basis for global legal pluralism .

Whether one opts for the perspective of narrow positivism, recognizing the legal relevance, but not international legal validity, of non-State regimes or for a broader perspective including power and effectiveness as validity-granting variables will be a choice dependent on one's assumptions on the nature and function of international law. The question may be asked whether for most practical purposes (notably: the regulation of matters of common interest), the result will not be virtually similar. Nonetheless, it directs us back to the most fundamental questions of law (and legal theory).

Thomas Franck has observed that 'international law has entered its postontological era'.[70] With the current debate on domestic application of international law—if, when, and how?—we have returned to what seems one of the eternal questions of our discipline about the bindingness of international law. But what used to be a question about the ontology of international law becomes, in the context of today, a question about its substantive normative authority. As Karen Knop pointed out convincingly the relevance of international law 'is not based on bindingness' alone. With her challenge to the 'on/off switches for the domestic application of international law' she offered an alternative approach 'where the authority of international law is persuasive rather than binding'.[71] This book provides additional support for the erosion of the binary normativity of international law is further evaluated and its erosion equally evaluated.

5. Return to the normative debate

In the final analysis the construction of the relationship between the international and the domestic legal order is largely a normative question. Though international lawyers rightly often exercise restraint and do not move into pure activism to promote certain values or moral objectives, the international lawyer also cannot shy away from normative questions. That also holds for the study of the relationship between national and international law. Scholarship that aims to develop international law theory on the relationship between national and international law cannot do without a normative take or dimension. It is, after all, inherent in the structure of the theories on the relationship since the origins of the monism-dualism debate.

---

[70] TM Franck, *Fairness in International Law and Institutions* (Oxford: OUP, 1995) 6.
[71] K Knop, 'Here and There: International Law in Domestic Courts' (2000) 32 New York U. J. Int'l L. & Pol. 501, 520, 515 and 535.

The history of the monism-dualism debate demonstrates that disinterested and detached scholarship is rare. Taken as archetypes, the dualist perspective upholds the principles of State sovereignty and domestic jurisdiction. The message is that national law is supreme, sovereign on moral choices, international normativity does not trump (neither democratically nor authoritarian produced) national law unless parliament says so. In contrast, monism tends to assume the (moral) supremacy of international law rather than of the State. Often, the monist perspective means to carve space for the individual within the international community. Through human rights law, democracy entered the debate. Initially, monism was presented as the true defender of democratic and *Rechtsstaat* values as it conceives of the State as under the rule of law or identical to the legal order.

At the end of his analysis and the unfolding of his *Reine Rechtslehre*, Hans Kelsen pointed out that the choice between supremacy of State and international norms ultimately concerns a non-legal, ethico-political, and value-loaded choice.[72] Kelsen did not shy away from this choice. In his view, dualism incorporates a tendency to favour autocracy rather than democracy and ultimately reduces international law to mere morality.[73]

The normative choice has not become much easier since the days of Kelsen. It is true that the moral standards of public international law have become a source of inspiration and aspiration of (national) legal development. The supremacy of international law has given direction to the development of national law, in particular, in human rights issues. The aspirational dimension and the premise of its moral supremacy remain central to (a monist outlook on) international law and influences much of the thinking in this book.

However, the guiding function of international law is no longer self-evident. In the current state of international law, with the numerous assaults on its relevance on the one hand and on its legitimacy on the other, international law may no longer be able to appeal to moral supremacy. Considering the faltered state international law is in since 9/11, the normative attraction of dualism has increased: when international norms seem to be violated or misinterpreted more easily and international normative standards are tainted, the state order has to uphold (national) values and norms. There is also another ethico-political consideration, as from a democratic perspective dualism offers a larger degree of popular representation.

Though much of the parameters of the debate have changed since the original monism-dualism debate, there is remarkable continuity in the fundamentally normative nature of the debate and the competing values that are at stake.

[72] See Kelsen (n 44 above) 45–46, 111–25. See JE Nijman, *The Concept of International Legal Personality: An Inquiry into the History and Theory of International Law* (The Hague: TMC Asser Press, 2004) 149–92

[73] Kelsen (1926) 276–77, 288: '[L]a construction dualiste... aboutit à faire de ce qu'on appelle le droit international tout simplement une sorte de morale ou de droit naturel, et non pas un droit véritable, au sens plein du mot, au sens ou l'on qualifie le droit interne de «droit positif.» Seul le droit interne pourrait alors définir ce qui est droit et ce qui ne l'est pas.... Dans ces conditions, la construction dualiste implique la négation de la nature juridique du «droit international.» See also, Kelsen (n 44 above) at 107 et seq.

6. Consequences for the position of the domestic judge

The dominant role of normative considerations in choosing and mediating between the extremes of monism and dualism manifests itself pre-eminently before the domestic judge. On the one hand, some domestic judges seem to value what they perceive as the morally advanced character of international law when they have recourse to international law. The evolution of the national-international law relationship contributes to the empowerment of the domestic judiciary.[74] On the other hand, domestic courts have to protect fundamental values of the rule of law against international law. The role of the national judge is then in the *dialogue* between the international and national legal order.

This perspective shifts our focus away from the divide to a more normatively-laden role of the judiciary that straddles the boundaries between the international and the domestic legal order. This is not too dissimilar from the judge's role to exercise judgment in Dworkin's theory of adjudication—*Law as integrity*[75]—and from his conception of 'law as principles'. Positivism is traditionally considered to be attractive to the judiciary for the lucidity of the judges task: apply the law rather than to find or create the law. In the positivist outlook, the judge is predicable and reliable and mostly abstains from value judgments. In Dworkin's view, however, judges—and jurists in general—do not tell what the law is without deploying values in making their judgments; they exercise judgment by interpreting the law—including the law's values and principles in their constructive interpretive act in order to find the *best* law and judgment for the people concerned and society at large, that is, what contributes to a just and fair society.[76]

Judgments based on value-judgments rather than on the applicable positive legal rules alone have to be justified. It is the judiciary's duty to pursue legal reasoning in a objectifying way—structured, predictable, transparent, and taking account of law's moral commitments and the values concerned. Hard cases exemplify that law is never beyond dispute, there is always an element of what the law *should* be (in these cases). Where moral commitments and value choices come into play in the margins or 'at the outskirts' of the legal system, judges will seek a way to object-ify their choice. It is here where international law plays a guiding and support-ing role. After all, legal questions are questions of value which are answered through law, ie the legal system of rules and principles. Where moral or value choices are necessary and judges search for a source to legitimize the value judgment to be

[74] As illustrated by du Plessis, this volume, 319; Walter, this volume, 212; Slaughter and Burke-White, this volume, 125.

[75] Eg Dworkin (n 23 above) 225 et seq. 'Law as integrity, then, requires a judge to test his interpretation of any part of the great network of political structures and dcisions of his community by asking whether it could form part of a coherent theory justifying the network as a whole, ibid 245. See also Dworkin, 'Hard Cases' in *Taking Rights Seriously* (n 21 above) 81 et seq.

[76] Dworkin (n 23 above) 225: 'According to law as integrity, propositions of law are true if they figure in or follow from the principles of justice, fairness, and procedural due process that provide the best constructive interpretation of the community's legal practice.'

made, domestic judges can draw on international law as a source of moral commitment.

Much of this line of reasoning has relevance to the reception of international law in domestic courts. The chapters by Moran, Paulus, and Du Plessis demonstrate how judges resort to international law norms to justify their value judgments. The judiciary uses international law as a recognized source of common values and high moral standard to advance national law and justice. Better than the formalism of legal positivism, Dworkin's perspective on law and the judiciary fits the findings in several chapters in this book on the role of the domestic judge and his application of international law.

In this process of deformalization, in which international law is used by domestic judges, sometimes no matter what its formal status is, the divide simply becomes less relevant—being a formal (theoretical) construction. Values objectified as such in international law are indispensable for adjudication. International law serves the domestic judge in reasoning his way out of the national legal box and enables him to serve the citizens by being a defender of justice and as interpreter as well as critic of value judgments.

Through this directive function, the dialectic nature/discursive identity of international law is manifest. In practice, international law here is a source of morality: as objectified, positive morality. International law as principles and common values may be conceived of as to express the moral commitments of the international community as well as the national communities. This is not a negation of international law or of its *legal* role in national orders—like it was in the 19th century—rather we observe an additional role next to its formal or direct binding force. In this respect, Du Plessis' study of the South African situation is a case in point. It attests to the use of international law in this guiding role by domestic judges.[77] Du Plessis observes that 'international law *not binding* (on South Africa) (in this manner) similar weight as aids—and often even prescriptive guides—to constitutional interpretation'.[78] This guiding role of international law standards for domestic judges was facilitated by domestic constitutional mechanisms.[79] The SA Constitution is also a case in point with regard to the influence of globalization on domestic law: universal common values were included in the national constitution in order to be *internationally* re-accepted as 'civilized'.[80] Although this case study gives a mixed picture in some ways, it also affirms much of the more theoretical finds in the other contributions to this volume. Du Plessis concludes that 'International law has, in most remarkable ways, become part of the exceedingly dynamic and complex making and adaptation of (constitutional) human-rights law in South Africa'.[81] This fits well with the observation by Slaughter and Burke-White that it is this trait of international law as container of common values that

---

[77] Du Plessis, this volume 311.   [78] Du Plessis, this volume, 312.   [79] Ibid.
[80] Du Plessis, this volume, 310.   [81] Ibid, 339.

will make its future *domestic* in another way—ie its force will be in national political debates, outside and inside parliament. International law then becomes a normative force in the national political context.[82] As Dworkin observed: 'Law's empire is defined by attitude, not territory or power or process.'[83] International law's empire is currently (largely) defined by the constructive attitude of domestic judges.

7. Final remarks

Phillip Allott pointed out that the divide is a phenomenon that exists mainly in our minds. If indeed it is a problem of theoretical perception, it needs to be resolved by a project of integration at that level.[84] The contributions to this book show that there are powerful perspectives that allow us to transcend the divide and think more of a fluid set of continuities and discontinuities between international and national law.

The existence of common fundamental values, the quest for new (sources of) authority and the deformalization of law, all contribute to the transcending or circumventing of the divide between national and international law. In order to give effect to international law in the domestic order, the authorizing mechanism used to lie in the hands of the national legislature. Several chapters in this book have demonstrated that to an increasing extent, the domestic judiciary and executive organs have become alternative authorizing mechanism. While it is very well possible to cling to a dualist position separating international from domestic validity and legality, the explanatory and normative power of such a model has been reduced to a minimum.

And yet, the contributions to this book have also highlighted the counter-perspective of a continued dominance of State and its legal order. The proposition that the process of globalization has caused a crisis of the nation-State (popular during the 1990s) is less convincing today particularly since security threats have increased the demands of strong States.[85] The re-affirmation of sovereignty and the national protection of domestic values contributes to a confirmation of a sharp demarcation between the international and national legal order. The situation is rather similar in the relation between the authority of international law and private authority, operating largely outside State structures.

The resulting situation is, for want of a better conceptualization, best described as a situation of global legal pluralism. This global legal pluralism is not the same as the legal pluralism that often was used as synonymous to dualism.[86] Rather, it

---

[82] Slaughter and Burke-White, this volume, 130.   [83] Dworkin (n 23 above) 413.
[84] Allott, this volume, 64.
[85] B Stern, 'How to Regulate Globalisation' in M Byers (ed), *The Role of Law in International Politics* (Oxford: OUP, 1999) 275–96.   [86] Gaja, this volume, 53.

refers to diverse State and non-State and mixed legal regimes created by a diversity of communities. Moreover, this book has provided much support for the view that this global legal pluralism, and related fragmentation, is embedded in a community of principles. It is such principles—which translate or capture values— that allow co-existence and cooperation between multiple legal systems, within States as well as private law regimes beyond the State. This conception of pluralism within a community of principles, at the same time piercing, transcending, and circumventing the divide between international and domestic law without bringing it to an end, offers an attractive basis for claims of political legitimacy in an international community of independent States and other actors, who will continue to disagree about political morality and wisdom.[87]

[87] Cf Dworkin, *Law's Empire* (n 23 above) 411.

Index

domestic judiciary (*cont.*):
  norms 354, 357–8
  Peoples' Tribunals 158–9
  precedent 243
  pluralism 234–5, 247–9
  positivism 354, 357–8
  principles, law as 357
  public international law relationships
    178–9, 205–6
  reception of international law 105
  regulation 119
  religion 148–9
  rule of law 357
  rule of recognition 346
  South Africa 180–1, 190, 300–1, 309,
    311–12, 319–40
  treaties and conventions 165, 243–5
  United Kingdom 21, 171–2, 177–8, 180–1,
    186, 234, 245–7, 302
  United States 165, 200, 234–43, 247–8,
    302–3
  values 165, 342–3, 357–8
  Vienna Convention on Consular Relations
    243–4
domestic/foreign frontier 130–1
domestic law *see* **national law**
Du Plessis, Laurens 344, 358, 359
dualism/monism debate 2–3, 6–8, 15–17,
  32–3, 161–2
  authority 57, 139, 160
  common values 344, 346
  complementarity 17
  conflicts of law 53
  decentralization 37, 51
  definition of dualism 52–4, 57–9, 62
  democracy, crisis of 6–7, 9, 10
  direct applicability of international law 59,
    206
  domestic judiciary 20, 105, 139, 147,
    234–5
  European Convention on Human Rights
    160
  federalism 9, 29
  globalization 10–12, 233–4, 359
  hierarchy 344–5
  individuals 6–10, 18–19, 32, 206
  integration 228–9
  Interbellum crisis of international law 6–7,
    8, 15
  interindividual law 18, 46–9
  internalization of international law norms
    159
  international organizations, accounting for
    39–43
  international courts and tribunals 19–20,
    22, 155–6
  inter-state law 10, 48–9, 60

  inter-state relations 19–20, 49
  juristic persons 18–19
  legal personality 136
  legitimacy 341, 356
  national law transformed into international
    law 59–60
  neomonism 349, 353
  norms 16–17, 355–6
  phenomena, definition and systemization of
    legal 22, 39–43, 49
  pluralism 17, 36, 48, 53, 148–9, 228–9,
    231, 233–4, 249, 359
  positivism 8, 341
  primacy 16, 19–20
  private authority 139, 160
  public international law and national law,
    relationship between 6–10, 16, 20,
    31–5, 39, 54, 217, 341–2
  relationships and *milieux*, distinctions
    between 31–2, 33, 39
  rule of law 356
  self-contained systems of international and
    national law 53–4, 57–9, 62
  South Africa 317–18
  state
    concept of the 22–31, 33–4
    mysticism 7–8
    power, restrictions on 9
    practice 20–1
    sovereignty 7, 8, 10
  subject matters 31–2
  supranational organizations, accounting for
    39–43
  supremacy 206–7, 356
  territoriality 85, 104
  treaties and conventions 164, 184
  United Kingdom 245–6
  universal legal system 47
  values 9, 344, 346
  voluntarism 7, 57–8
Dworkin, Ronald 346, 357–8, 359
Dyncorp 153–4

effectiveness, principle of 39
**email and Internet, parliamentarism
  undermined by** 281
environmental protection 119, 209–12, 280
erga omnes **obligations** 214, 220
estoppel 174–9, 186
ethnic crimes 113
Europe *see also* **European Community/Union**
  constitutions, globalization of 259–65
  domestic judiciary 242–7
  Europeanization 289
  harmonization 285
  human rights norms 242–7
  institutionalism 220–1

Ingram Content Group UK Ltd.
Milton Keynes UK
UKHW020428160323
418662UK00003B/147